D0154290

C. 1

Race, Radicalism, Religion, and Restriction

Immigration in the Pacific Northwest, 1890–1924

Kristofer Allerfeldt

Jeremy Black, Advisory Editor

PRAEGER

Westport, Connecticut
London

Library of Congress Cataloging-in-Publication Data

Allerfeldt, Kristofer, 1959–

Race, radicalism, religion, and restriction : immigration in the Pacific Northwest, 1890–1924 / Kristofer Allerfeldt.

p. cm.

Includes bibliographical references and index.

ISBN 0–275–97854–0 (alk. paper)

1. Oregon—Emigration and immigration—History. 2. Washington (State)—Emigration and immigration—History. 3. Nativism. 4. United States—Emigration and immigration—Government policy—History. I. Black, Jeremy. II. Title.

JV7070.A45 2003

325.795'09'041—dc21 2002073466

British Library Cataloguing in Publication Data is available.

Library of Congress Catalog Card Number: 2002073466
ISBN: 0–275–97854–0

First published in 2003

Praeger Publishers, 88 Post Road West, Westport, CT 06881
An imprint of Greenwood Publishing Group, Inc.
www.praeger.com

Printed in the United States of America

The paper used in this book complies with the Permanent Paper Standard issued by the National Information Standards Organization (Z39.48–1984).

10 9 8 7 6 5 4 3 2 1

Copyright Acknowledgments

The author and publisher gratefully acknowledge permission to use the following:

From the Oregon Historical Society: Titus, Ben, "Former Klan Member" (unpublished manuscript), pp. 12–13, Ku Klux Klan Records (Mss 22); Chamberlain, George E. Letter to G. H. Thomas, June 20, 1904, George Early Chamberlain Papers (Mss 1025); MacColl, E. Kimbark, "Eight Unique Contributions to Oregon Public Life" (Typescript of Lecture to Oregon Jewish Museum, July 23, 1992), E. Kimbark MacColl Papers (Mss 2440–1); Toth, Alex, "American Catholicism and Immigration" (unpublished manuscript) (Mss 2400).

From the University of Oregon Libraries, William C. Smith Papers, Series A & B on microfilm: "Interview with AR ('Dog Face') Johnson, Mill Superintendant [sic.]," Ernest Dolge, Inc. Tacoma, Washington, p. 4, reel 3; "Interview with Williamson, Federal Narcotics Agent," reel 4; "Eatonville Lumber Co., Interview with Mr. Galbraith Jnr.," reel 4; "Interview with Mrs. Tiro Shinowara, A Teacher in a Japanese Language School, Seattle," reel 2.

From the University of Oregon Libraries, Ben W. Olcott Papers, Collection AX 81: Seit Back, attorney, Portland, to Olcott, April 30, 1916, Scrapbooks, Vol. 1, p. 58.

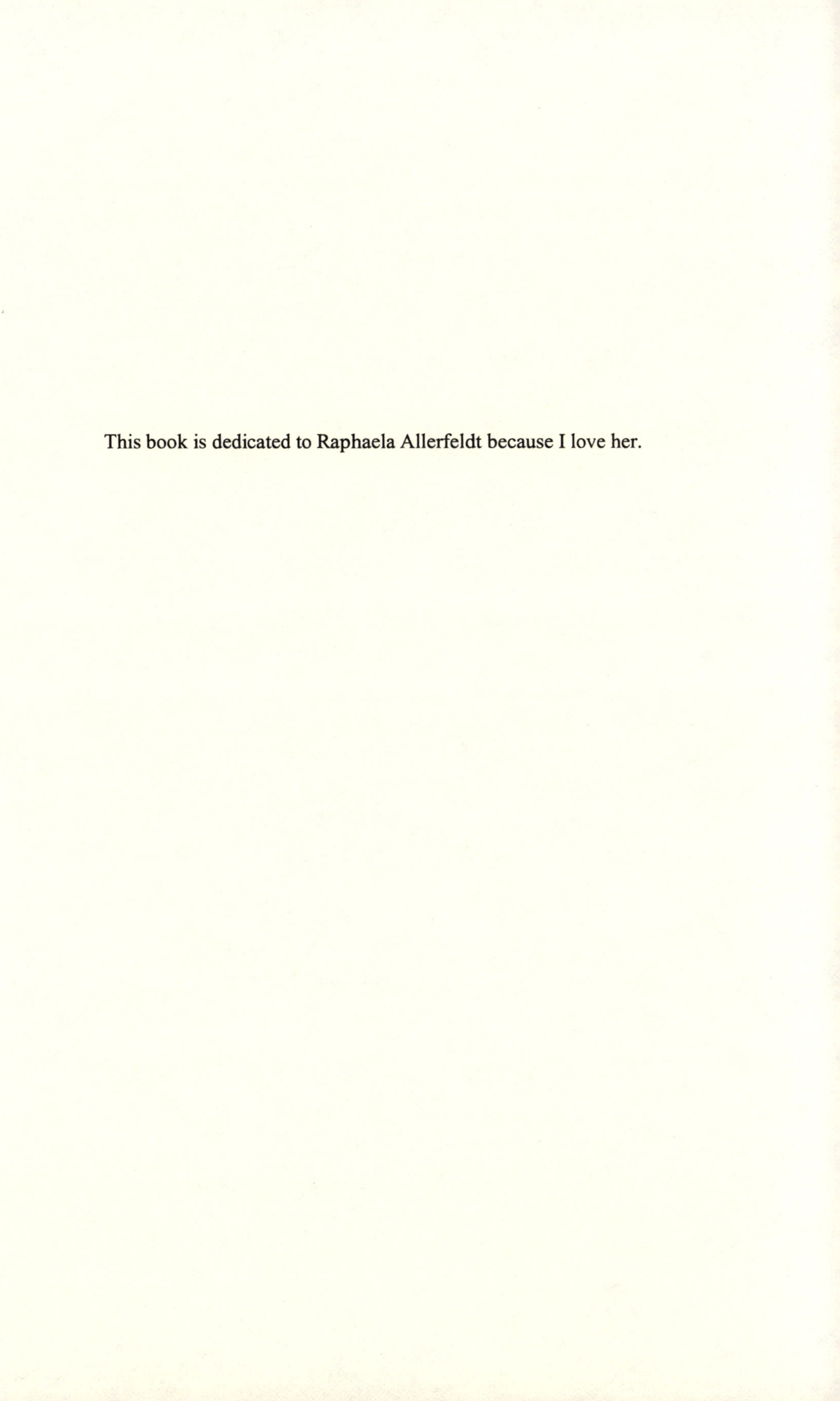

This book is dedicated to Raphaela Allerfeldt because I love her.

CONTENTS

AKNOWLEDGMENTS

There are too many people to thank for their help and support, and I know I will leave some out. My apologies to them.

All my family must come first. My wife Raphaela and my girls Matilda and Frederika deserve the most thanks. They allowed me to indulge my passion for history and even re-organized and re-decorated my study! Close to them must come Brad Yamamoto—the most hospitable and amiable of all men and a true friend and my brother Carl who made me feel it was always possible.

Professor Jeremy Black's friendship and interest in my work has always been the greatest help and there is no doubt I would never have got this far had it not been for his belief in my ability. The completion of this project owes much to the encouragement and gentle and patient guidance of Dr. Joseph Smith. It was his and Mel Dadswell's invaluable advice that made me rethink many aspects and concentrate my efforts on the themes that emerged.

I fell in love with the Pacific Northwest and was amazed by how helpful and friendly people were, particularly the staff in the archives and libraries I visited and I enjoyed my research immeasurably, largely because of them. I would like to thank the staff of the Jewish Historical Society of Oregon; Multnomah public library; the libraries at Portland State, Gonzaga University, Washington State and the University of Oregon; the Polson Museum; the Archives of the Arch-Diocese of Seattle; the Catholic Sentinel and the Timberlands Libraries at Olympia and Hoquiam. In particular I would like to thank David Horowitz at Portland, Linda Long at Eugene and John Larson and John C. (Solidarity Forever!) Hughes at Hoquiam.

There are some people that I encountered on my research who will always remain firm friends, chief amongst these must be Bob and Ann (Kate) Kingston and Hilary Richrod. Also Norman Dizon and Jay Windisch could not have been more helpful and I hope one day I will be able to return all the favours they did for me. I cannot wait to be in the Northwest again, I miss it.

I would also like to thank Katie Chase, my Project Editor at Praeger, for her patience with my punctuation and my inability to follow instructions.

1

WHY THE NORTHWEST?

Examinations of American immigration frequently center on a relatively short period around the turn of the twentieth century. The emergence, and shortly afterwards, dominance of new sources of immigrants define the start of this period-immigrants from the Mediterranean, the Balkans, Eastern Europe and the Middle East. The close of the period is determined by the second of two congressional acts that essentially fixed the limits of American immigration for the best part of the next four decades. Images of this immigration tend to center on dramatic pictures of hopeful men, women and children crowded with their pathetically limited belongings on the decks of steamships, frequently with the Statue of Liberty, or some other American landmark, forming a backdrop. There are photographs of bewildered people being examined and interviewed by immigration officials in the bleakly functional halls of Ellis Island; pictures of poorly dressed people trading from barrows on the streets in the slum "colonies" of New York or Boston, or women working in factories amid banks of textile looms, men standing by rows of hanging, slaughtered animals or families sitting, cramped, in squalid tenement rooms. Closer examination of contemporary material reveals articles condemning the threat of poverty, crime, corruption, dirt and disease seen as being imported along with these immigrants. There are cartoons which illustrate the immigrants' clannishness, backwardness and general undesirability. Scholarly works were published that scientifically detailed the physical, mental and philosophical differences between the "old" immigrants and the "new". Scrutiny of the legislation of the period shows growing numbers of immigrant groups being excluded–from prostitutes, the obviously diseased and anarchists, to those unable to demonstrate the means to independently support themselves or those imported as contract labor. The one common feature of most of these sources is their seeming concentration on the East and Middle West of America.

The majority of the studies devoted to the immigration of this period reflect this East Coast bias. Bearing in mind the vastly greater numbers of immigrants entering through East Coast ports, this is hardly surprising. When studies of the era's nativism have mentioned the West Coast, it is almost exclusively in the context of anti-Asian pressures, or briefly while discussing the re-emergence of the Ku Klux Klan in the 1920s and the impact of the Industrial Workers of the World (the IWW; also called Wobblies) on attitudes toward immigration. These anti-Oriental works tend to concentrate on studies of the California sandlot movement which had, with the 1882 Chinese Exclusion Act, already achieved many of its aims prior to the start of the period in question.[1] There may be brief allusions to the Alien Land Laws—again largely in a California context. Even those studies devoted to Japanese exclusion tend to deal with the anti-Japanese movements in Oregon and Washington State as satellites in the orbit of a California tendency. [2] Similarly, the region's importance is downplayed with the Red Scare and the Klan being treated as manifestations of national post-war hostility to immigration in general.[3] The picture seems to be one of the region's hostility to immigrants as following national, or Californian trends in nativism.[4]

For the sake of this study, the Pacific Northwest is defined as the two states, Oregon and Washington. Such a geographical limitation presents some problems. For example, it does not include, as other historical works have, the state of Idaho or the Canadian province of British Columbia,[5] although adjoining regions may be mentioned as the borders were notoriously fluid at this point. However, such a division does provide some interesting insights. Perhaps foremost among these is the impact of the lapse between gaining statehood—Oregon became a state in 1859, Washington 30 years later.[6] This provides a surprisingly stark contrast in the nature of immigration and the responses to that influx. However, having defined the geographic area, it is also important to place the region in a national context, for it is not the aim of this study to dispute the impact of national or regional feeling on the area's restrictionists, or to promote the Northwest as the origin of nativist sentiment. It does attempt to demonstrate that there were features of the immigration debate that were influenced by elements peculiar, if not unique, to the area. It seeks to demonstrate that the Northwest has been neglected as an area of study and that such a study could have an impact on the perspective of studies of contemporary nativist feeling. By analyzing the hostility to immigrants in an area where large-scale immigration was a relatively *new* phenomenon, the contemporary distinctions between "new" and "old" immigration would appear to have less validity, exposing what could be seen as the underlying causes of nativism. The two states form an area where "boosters" who platted cities and sparked land and lumber booms gave way to some of the nation's most xenophobic local political organizations and committed restrictionists in Congress, all within a period of less than 30 years. At the very least, such a study could be of value by highlighting the hostility of "recent" immigrants to the prospective, or actual, arrival of other immigrants—either of the same or different "groups".

Although any such study will meet with familiar difficulties of methodology, not least the reliability of statistics or the difficulties of evaluating the motives behind them, a more or less traditional[7]—if sometimes artificially constraining—structure will be used. It would seem germane to begin by assessing the statistical importance and the motivation of immigration in the two states. Investigation of the foreign-born population of the area can be used to form a point of reference for the opposition to immigration, with relation both to other areas and other times. Crucial questions will emerge from such an examination. How real was the "wave" of immigration in the two States during the period? Was it significantly different in its composition and how did it compare with other regions of America? How different was the ethnic mix at the start compared with the end of the period? Who was restriction intended to exclude and who was actually excluded? Lurking behind these questions is the now hackneyed motif of the frontier—be it Frederick Jackson Turner's safety valve, or the modern scholar's wage-earning variety.

If the Northwest thought of itself as a frontier, or even a wilderness, then this perception must be considered, as it can be held to be one of a tangle of elements that formed the basis for exclusion or inclusion in the area's societies. Was it that as the frontier was "tamed", the population felt themselves more a part of the Union, and inherited "national" prejudices, even on occasion with the additional zeal of the convert? Alternatively, was it that as the wilderness disappeared the population hankered for a less complex life, wishing to exclude those who brought these complexities with them? Underlying these issues are questions of conservation, ownership of property, nationalism and regionalism in an era of national and global demographic, technological, economic and political change—changes which led to a polarization of political opinion that was to play an essential role in the attitudes of the population in general, and "nativists" in particular, towards immigration. The Northwest felt these changes, often particularly violently. Examination of these tensions will form the basis for two further chapters. The radical immigrants and the strains they produced will form one chapter. Another will be an inquiry into the religious pressures for exclusion. These investigations will frequently overlap with each other and the final chapter—the all-pervading contemporary issue of immigration exclusion and race.

Almost coincidentally each one of these sections will largely deal with a single group. The religious part will deal almost exclusively with Roman Catholics and the radical segment will concentrate largely on the IWW. In the racial chapter the issue will largely be an examination of the pressures to exclude the Japanese. This is not because these were the only groups that were seen to represent a threat, but they were the most significant during the period of this study. They were frequently the most important in terms of their numbers, the controversy they generated, the support or opposition they attracted and the legislation they inspired–both locally and federally. Other seemingly significant groups will be barely be dealt with. For example, in 1924 Oregon's Klan prevented what was considered a radically inclined Russian Christian sect—the Doukhobors—leaving Canada and settling in the Willamette Valley.[8] It was estimated that there could have been as many as 10,000 of these "fanatics", but nevertheless they were of little significance to the overall pattern of restriction. Nativists rallied against them only once; their immigration did not represent an ongoing threat.

Similarly, although there was pressure to prevent the use of black labor as strike-breakers and there were efforts to introduce segregation—as well as frequent anti-black violence—this group will be excluded from the study. The black population was almost totally native-born, not immigrant, and thus they fall beyond the remit of this study.[9] Other groups will be largely ignored because their exclusion had already been achieved—as with the Chinese—or their status was ambivalent, as with the Filipinos. Other groups persecuted in other regions escape attention because of their negligible impact—such as Mexicans. Yet other nationalities/races are dismissed from the study because of an inability, or lack of desire, of many nativists to distinguish them from others—as was the case with the Koreans who were generally thought to be Japanese, or at least rarely distinguished from and more often than not treated as the same as the Japanese. Perhaps the best way of explaining these inclusions and exclusions is to examine the scale of the various immigrations into the region.

IMMIGRATION IN THE NORTHWEST

In 1842, 112 people in 18 wagons left Independence, Missouri, for the Oregon Territory. In the following year 1,000 pioneers left in 120 wagons.[10] From the early 1840s the populations of the two territories/states grew rapidly, as Table 1.1 demonstrates.

Table 1.1: Population of Oregon and Washington, 1840-1890[11]

Date	Approximate population of Oregon (Territory/State)	Approximate population of Washington (Territory/State)
1840	7,000	N/A
1850	12,000	1,000
1860	52,000	12,000
1870	91,000	24,000
1880	175,000	75,000
1890	314,000	357,000

Much was done to encourage the expansion of the region. The Organic Law of Oregon 1843-44 and the federal Oregon Donation Land Law of September 1850 had validated claims to plots of 640 acres per settling family and a further

320 acres to be made available after the initial claim. This represented double the national norm and acted as a huge spur to immigration.[12] The Northwest held a special allure throughout the second half of the nineteenth century. The area of trapping and timber, of "fur and fir", gave way in the 1840s to the promise of rich, unexploited agricultural potential in a temperate region—"Oregon fever". The fertile Willamette, Umpqua and Rogue River valleys attracted increasing numbers, braving disease, privation and hostility on the increasingly renowned Oregon Trail.

Significantly, the 1844 Act in Relation to [Oregon] Land Claims limited these hopeful farmers to white citizens, when it laid out that "no person shall hold a claim under the provision of the act except free males, over the age of eighteen, who would be entitled to vote if of lawful age."[13] The vast bulk of early immigrants arrived from the western regions of the Union and was American-born, as one historian has put it—"The Far West was formed out of a rib taken from the side of Middle America."[14] In 1850 an estimated 23 percent were originally residents of Arkansas, Missouri and Iowa. A further 22 percent arrived from Ohio, Indiana, Illinois, Michigan and Wisconsin, with only 19 percent coming from the most densely populated states of Atlantic and Gulf regions of the eastern seaboard in which some three quarters of Americans resided.[15] Of the total 13,000 territorial residents in 1850, a little over 6 percent of those identified were foreign-born.[16] By comparison, in the Minnesota Territory the foreign-born made up over 30 percent of the population in 1850. Oregon's 6 percent was nearly half the national average of just over 11 percent.[17]

Initially, the composition of Oregon's small foreign-born population complied with the national pattern for the period. Their birthplaces tended to be predominantly Northern European, the countries that dominated American immigration during the period. As Table 1.2 indicates[18] the influence was largely British, or Canadian, Irish and German.[19] This predominantly Nordic composition was to be of increasing importance throughout the period. Not only was the region able to point to a pioneer heritage that conformed with the increasingly dominant ideals of Nordic supremacists, but also the high proportion of Irish, Canadian and Germans served to inspire fears of attempts by Catholics to dominate the region.

The Northwest attracted increasing numbers of hopeful immigrants as reports became more and more widespread, claiming negligible efforts bringing huge rewards in the region's lumber and agricultural enterprises. By the 1860s the majority of the aboriginal tribes had been quieted—either by war as with the Cayuse, Yakima, Spokane and later (1877) the Nez Percé, disease or treaty as with the Coeur d'Alenes, Flatheads and Blackfeet. Little seemed to stand in the way of the rapid exploitation of the huge resources of the region. The area possessed a seemingly endless supply of huge Douglas firs or Western red cedar—trees which could yield as much high-quality timber in a single butt as entire stands of yellow pine or other traditional American varieties of tree. Rivers could provide easy transportation, power and access. It was claimed that many diseases of both livestock and crops were virtually unknown; yields of crops and animal produce normally exceeded other regions; rainfall was reliable; winters were mild and yet land was still available.[20] Added to these attractions, gold was discovered, first in Colville in the 1850s and later in the Fraser Valley and the Cascades.

Table 1.2: Population and Percentage Foreign-born in Oregon, 1850

Country of Birth	Population of Oregon Territory in 1850	Percentage of Foreign-born Oregon population in 1850
Britain	322	24
Ireland	196	15
France	45	3.4
"Germany"	156	12
Scandinavia	17	1.3
Canada	293	22
Others	273	22.3

These lures increasingly attracted the foreign-born. Arguably, in some cases this was because the foreign-born immigrant was more susceptible to the often-inflated claims of the land boosters and speculators. As late as 1902, some publications continued to assure the potential immigrant that this was the pioneers' paradise:

> The climate is mild in winter and never excessively warm in summer. There is no question about the productiveness of the soil. In no part of the world is a man paid so well for the amount of work done, and the more the soil is cultivated, the better it produces and yet we have no weeds to contend with that our Eastern friends do.[21]

That the European-born seemed to respond more readily to such claims can be interpreted to some extent as the result of foreign-born innocence, or gullibility, and immigrant optimism. It can also be seen as the benefit of the immigrants' rootlessness. Often, having fewer ties—social or economic—and frequently more ambition than many of the native-born, the foreign-born were as a consequence more mobile. Of course these facts did not escape the boosters and the foreign-born were consistently targeted directly with considerable success. Between 1850 and 1890, the foreign-born population increased—not only in relation to the percentage of American-born residents in the Union but also as a proportion of Oregon's population. Also, where the national figure remained relatively constant, at an average of around 14 percent, Oregon's figures increased decade on decade. The national decline in the foreign-born as a percentage of the Union's total population in the 1870s represented the period of Oregon's greatest increase. As can be seen in Table 1.3, as immigration picked up pace in the Northwest, foreign-born immigrants felt "Oregon Fever" to a greater degree than native-born.[22] There were more practical reasons for changes in the pattern of the region's immigrant population. A large proportion of those who emigrated to the region –often native-born or, if foreign-born, largely "Nordic"—arrived in order to escape the bitter winters, the arid summers and the general ferocity of the climate of the mid-western states. For example, in 1882, three parties of Volga-German relocated to the Northwest, driven out of Kansas by locusts, storms and tornadoes.[23] Reluctant to return East—which would have been tantamount to admitting defeat—or to abandon their agricultural dream, they continued West.

Table 1.3: Immigration to the United States and Oregon, 1850-90

Year	Foreign-born in the United States	Approximate % foreign-born among the United States population	Foreign-born in Oregon	% of foreign-born in Oregon population in relation to Territorial/State population
1850	2,244,602	11	710	5.9
1860	4,138,697	14	5,123	9.8
1870	5,567,229	14	11,600	12.8
1880	6,679,943	13	30,563	17.5
1890	9,249,560	15	57,317	18.3

By contrast, many of the Northwest's foreign-born settlers originally came from areas which had similar climates—Britain, Ireland or, again, most markedly, Scandinavia. Between 1890 and 1910 some 150,000 Scandinavians settled in the Northwest and by the end of the period they made up some 20 percent of the region's foreign-born.[24] They often had more knowledge and experience of the types of agriculture, forestry and increasingly, horticulture which were beginning to dominate the area. These differed significantly from the forms imposed by harsher Middle West or more humid Southern climates of which the majority of native-born immigrants had experience. This was the case both in crops grown and harvested and, consequently, methods of cultivation. Too cool for corn or tobacco, the area began to be dominated by the production of wheat, forage crops, livestock, beans, pulses, potatoes, apples, peaches and pears as well as the harvesting of the ubiquitous coniferous timber. Added to this—as with Norwegians in the fjords of Puget Sound—many of these Northern European settlers found the region's topography to be familiar, reminiscent of their European homelands. The result was that, much in the same way as their native-born contemporaries and predecessors, a great deal of the promotion of the region came from kith and kin already settled in the area. Relatives wrote frequently of the opportunities of the area and often sent funds to their family members on the East Coast or in Europe. These were settlers who were drawn by the same features, and frequently sought the same objectives, as the resident populations. The pull of community was great and assimilation was relatively easy.

It was not merely "pull factors" which drew the foreign-born immigrants. The effects of general European population growth coupled with a collapse of the agricultural economy in the Continent's industrialized states proved devastating to rural Europe. Between 1870 and 1910, Britain and Germany experienced some 60 percent increase in their populations and yet agricultural prices, and consequently profits, dropped. In the 1870s Britain's land and wheat prices halved. In the same period in Scandinavia the population grew by nearly 40 percent.[25] Sweden, which removed tariffs in 1865, reeled from the effects of crop failures throughout the 1860s that produced widespread famine, added to which the shift from wooden to iron ships crippled the country's timber industry which traditionally shored up the nation's agricultural income.[26] Some 3.5 million people left Europe for the Americas in the 1870s. Over 1.5 million alone left Britain. More than 0.5 million left Germany and nearly a quarter of a million left Scandinavia.[27] Often rural, they fled the results of enclosure or economic downturn. This was frequently and ironically deepened, if not caused, by the importing of increasing quantities of cheap "New World" produce—livestock as well as meat and cereals.[28]

Although many of these immigrants sought to escape the effects of technological improvements in agriculture and the cheap imports encouraged by the prevalent free trade gospel, it was these same developments, which enabled them to leave. This was the dawn of a period when the benefits of ever cheaper, more secure, faster trans-oceanic trade, and its corollary, relatively unregulated human transport, made emigration to escape the privations and poverty of rural Europe a real possibility for an ever larger part of this swelling population. Even in these early days of regularized trans-Atlantic steam travel, the figures are impressive. By 1873, 173 steamships operating for 17 companies operated between Europe and New York alone.[29]

The technology that enabled this revolution in oceanic travel also had similar impact on land. Steam brought the immigrant across the ocean and steam transported the immigrant across the American continent. In 1882 it was estimated 2 billion people worldwide used the developing rail networks throughout Europe, its colonies and the New World.[30] This new technology had far-reaching effects on American immigration. The impact on German migration of the 1880s is informative. Rail transport not only had catastrophic consequences for Germany's rural population by turning Germany from a net food producer into a net food importer as a result of cheap Russian grain imports, it also provided easy, reliable and efficient transport to ports via which emigrants could embark for the Americas. German trans-Atlantic migration almost doubled in the 1880s. During the decade over 1.33 million Germans migrated to the Americas. Similarly, Scandinavian and Irish migration nearly tripled and British emigration had jumped by the end of the decade to over 2.25 million.[31] The United States was the main recipient of these immigrants. In 1882

0.25 million Germans, nearly 200,000 British and Irish and over a 100,000 Scandinavians arrived in America.

Once in America, a rail system, which had been almost doubling decade on decade since the 1860s, could transport them away from the East Coast's over-populated cities to the Northwest in a fraction of the time, without the danger, discomfort and expense of the Oregon Trail.[32] The populations of the Northwestern states reflected this convenience. Oregon grew some 80 percent in the 1880s, Idaho, by comparison, grew by approximately 160 percent, but, most spectacularly, the Washington Territory grew by almost 400 percent.[33] These figures demonstrate not only Washington's rapid overtaking of Oregon as the main destination for immigrants to the Northwest, but a closer analysis of the situation suggests crucial changes in the nature of this immigration.

In the 1870s Oregon was still primarily attracting rural migrants who hoped to continue to lead a life based around the ownership of land. In the 1880s Washington was increasingly attracting laborers to work in the growing lumber processing, salmon fishing and packing and associated industries of Puget Sound and the Pacific Coast; the mines and smelters of the Inland Empire; railway and city construction as well as in the expanding horticultural and agricultural enterprises.[34] The effects of this industrialization were marked. There were changes in the racial composition of the workers in these industrial regions as Southern European and Japanese labor contractors targeted impoverished regions of their home countries for cheap, plentiful, compliant emigrant workers. Although this demand for manpower was to be found in parts of Oregon, and equally, many of those attracted to Washington also sought land, it was the scale of the Washington Territory's commercial and industrial expansion that lay behind this growing appetite for immigrant labor. In the decade to 1890, the nascent State of Washington's industrial output had grown from representing under a third of the value of its southern neighbor's, to exceeding it, as Table 1.4 would indicate.[35]

Further, it is telling that in 1890, Washington's marginally larger population produced only two-thirds of Oregon's agricultural products. In the decade to 1900, Oregonians engaged in "manufacturies" declined from one in eight to less than one in ten.[36] Washington represented a new Northwest and this new Northwest was increasingly evolving into an urban environment. As with the rest of continental America, in the Northwest the proportion of the population living in settlements of over 2,500 grew with the new century. In Oregon, the percentage of these urbanites increased from nearly 28 in 1890 to almost 50 in 1920; in Washington this same percentage expanded from 36 to 54. What is more telling is that over the same period the proportion of the population living in the region's five main cities doubled. In 1890, a little under 150,000, nearly 18 percent of the region's total population, lived in the five main cities of the region—Portland, Seattle, Tacoma, Walla Walla and Spokane. By 1920 there were just below 800,000, or around 37 percent. The population increase of the area's two main cities would also seem to substantiate this change in the occupational emphasis of the region as shown in Table 1.5.[37]

Arguably, even those occupations that would often have been considered rural seemed to be adopting industrial methods in the scale of their enterprises and working conditions. The region's lumber industry grew from the small pioneer enterprises into huge highly capitalized, mechanized and impersonal industries. The seemingly unlimited potential of the Northwest's fisheries and horticultural ventures allowed for the financing and development of equally sophisticated expensive canneries, large scale packing houses and refrigerated rail carriages. The placer miner was replaced by the large-scale hydraulic miner. The size of these enterprises may not have compared with Eastern textile mills or Mid-Western steel plants, but they were nonetheless, far removed from the self-sufficient, freedom-loving, bucolic, individualistic enterprises mythologized in the ideal of Paul Bunyan's forested West.

Table 1.4: Value of Industrial and Agricultural Products in Oregon and Washington, 1880-1890

	1880	1890	Percentage increase
Total Population			
Oregon	174,768	313,767	80
Washington	75,116	349,390	380
Value of industrial Products $			
Oregon	10,900,000	41,400,000	280
Washington	3,300,000	41,800,000	1100
Value of Agricultural Products $			
Oregon	13,200,000	22,600,000	65
Washington	4,200,000	14,000,000	230

Table 1.5: Portland and Seattle Population, 1860-1910

Census	Portland	Seattle
1860	2,874	302
1870	8,293	1,107
1880	17,577	3,533
1890	46,385	42,837
1900	90,426	80,671
1910	207,214	237,194

Many in the region accepted these changes. Some welcomed them, putting the effort that had previously gone into promoting the sale of agricultural land into the promotion of urban developments. Perhaps the most striking example of this was the advertising of Tacoma in the early 1880s as the "London on the Pacific", by the flamboyant balloonist George F. Train, who, it was claimed, circumnavigated the world in less than Jules Verne's obligatory 80 days. Train's exploits contributed to Tacoma's " staggering under a boom of the boomiest [Becoming an unsophisticated town where] the rude boarded pavements of the main streets rumbled under the heels of furious men all actively engaged in hunting drinks and eligible corner lots."[38] The city was expanding at a legendary rate in the 1880s, inspiring a popular song "Watch Tacoma Grow". By 1890, Tacoma had exploded from a village of a little over 1,000 residents to a modern city of over 36,000. This fabled "City of Destiny" was selling goods valued at over $5 million a year, launching new ships, servicing a fleet of over 130 vessels and communicating on over a half of Washington State's 940 telephones.[39]

Foreign-born immigrants accounted for a considerable proportion of this urban growth—and not only in Tacoma. Since the early days of settlement, the Northwest's foreign-born had settled disproportionately in urban areas.[40] In Portland the percentage of foreign-born settling in the municipal area jumped from some 5 percent in 1850 to nearly 45 percent in 1910, the period of the city's greatest expansion. At the turn of the twentieth century, the Rose City was second only to San Francisco in terms of foreign-born population in cities west of the Rockies. This phenomenon was even more apparent as Seattle's population soared in the decade to 1910. In 1870, Seattle had 279 foreign-born residents, by 1910 it had over 67,000.[41] As America pulled away from the slump of the mid-1890s, the surging extractive industries of the region made this boom situation similar for Spokane, Tacoma and Vancouver (Washington) as well as many other minor cities.

At the opening of the period of this study, the farmer was no longer the typical immigrant. As the era of free land came to a close, many of those arriving still sought to settle land. By 1900, some 30,026 claims had been registered under the Homestead and Desert Law Acts on 4,302,689 acres of Washington State land.[42] Yet, increasingly the allocations proved too small to be viable on the marginal, dry, forested and elevated land that remained, and many prospective farmers found themselves drawn into the burgeoning "Wage Earners Frontier" in order to gain the necessary resources to realize that aim.[43] This widely asserted transformation in the objectives of immigrants was borne out by other changes. The methods of attracting immigrants also became more commercial with financial, industrial, real estate and railroad agencies targeting them as sources of revenue, labor and investment.

Some of these efforts were organized along local lines by Chambers of Commerce and Boards of Trade.[44] Some were more grandiose, inspired by visions of populating massive, prosperous new cities. Again the example of Tacoma is particularly relevant. The city was seen as having almost unlimited potential because "the sum total of Tacoma's resources...are vastly superior to those of Chicago...it is only a question of time when a greater city than Chicago or New York will flourish on the more salubrious shores of Puget Sound."[45] The region retained its boosters even as the Progressive mainstream in the nation as a whole stepped up its warnings of the dire consequences of "unlimited" immigration. The region suffered from a clash of interests. Throughout the

Progressive Era the politicians the region elected to sit in the U.S. Congress supported immigration restriction, to a man. For example, all Oregon and Washington's senators and congressmen voted in favor of the 1912 and 1916 Literacy Bills and against the presidential vetoes which followed.[46] Nevertheless, many of the local politicians still sought increased immigration to settle the embryonic towns, provide labor and consume produce.

Rather than taking the Progressive stance and seeking to alleviate immigrant poverty, improve immigrant housing or advocate immigrant relocation or immigration restriction, Oregon's Immigration Commission promoted the state to potential immigrants. With a significant annual budget—rising from $25,000 at its foundation in 1911 to $50,000 by 1914—the commission published and mailed some 250,000 pamphlets detailing agricultural information in English, German, Norwegian and Swedish to potential settler-farmers.[47] Even after the massive Dillingham report had unequivocally demonstrated to its Progressive sponsors that continued mass immigration would damage American democracy, society and, of course, the American economy, the primary purpose of Oregon's Immigration Commission remained to attract the right immigrants, rather than to limit immigration. Similarly, in Washington the sole attempt by Olympia to investigate immigration was a 1914 conference on the "Immigration Problem".

Again, the report this body produced was hardly in line with what is usually seen as the national mood of Progressive reformers. The conference was largely dedicated to discussion of methods for reducing the price of agricultural land, settling the large tracts of exhausted forestry lands and advertising for increased immigration to the state.[48] A contrast of Oregon and California investigations into immigration is illustrative. In 1913, California's Progressive Governor Hiram Johnson established an Immigration Commission. This body approached immigration from a traditionally Progressive angle, it was almost exclusively concerned with the dangers of increased immigration—the ubquitous tidal wave of undesirable European immigration—that loomed especially large with the imminent opening of the Panama Canal.[49] In August 1913, Johnson warned Immigration Commissioner, Simon S. Lubin, that: "If immigration [from the Panama]...Canal is permitted to congest our cities...ultimately the conditions of awful poverty presented by our Eastern Cities will be reproduced in our centers of population in California. All of us wish to avoid this danger."[50] On the other hand, as late as December 1914, the Oregon Immigration Commission's only comment on this influx was to state a wish to attract retiring "canal employees who might be leaving the service soon [because] These employees have usually been getting good salaries and have substantial savings."[51]

This promotion of, and touting for, immigration became more important as the Northern and Western European nations industrialized and colonized and the traditional sources of immigration began to die away. German emigration to America dropped to under 40,000 per annum in the 1890s and by 1912 it was less than 20,000. Between 1901 and 1912 America changed from being the choice of over 60 percent of British and Irish emigrants, to making up the destination of only 25 percent. In their efforts to fill their steamships and trains; to sell land, building plots or populate regions; and to provide labor for the nation's emerging large scale manufacturing industries, new sources of immigration were targeted. Such targeting was aided by the expulsive effects of early industrialization and, in some regions, persecution combined with new freedom to emigrate which in themselves caused an increase in Southern and Eastern European immigration. Italian immigration in America grew from around 12,000 per annum in 1880 to 300,000 in 1914. In the same period, the Austro-Hungarian immigration grew from some 17,000 to over 300,000.[52] Similar expansions took place throughout the period in Polish, Russian, Greek and other nationals' immigration to America.[53] As Table 1.6 demonstrates, nationally, the numbers of these "new" immigrants overtook those of the old "Nordic" immigrants in the 1890s and from thence continued to rise.[54]

Table 1.6: Percentage of Old and New Immigration Entering the United States 1860-1920

Decade	Percentage of "Old" Immigration entering The United States	Percentage of "New" Immigration entering The United States
1860-70	98.4	1.6
1870-80	91.6	8.4
1880-90	80.2	19.8
1890-1900	48.4	51.6
1900-10	23.3	76.7
1910-20	22.8	77.2

This was not the case throughout the Northwest. The attractions that drew in increasing numbers of the "new" immigrants to the burgeoning cities of the Eastern seaboard did not apply to the Northwest. The region lacked the communications, ethnic diversity and existing national communities. The Northwest was rarely the first destination of those arriving in America from Europe. Much of the hostility to the period's European immigration stemmed from the perception that these in-comers arrived in the Eastern ports—in Boston or New York—and, unlike their precursors, they remained stubbornly in the squalid confines of the colonies they and their countrymen formed. They did not seek to move West. Nevertheless, the main cities of the region did attract foreign-born communities, but overwhelmingly from the "old" sources of immigration. In the Northwest's major cities the "old" sources of European immigrants still remained dominant even as the numbers of European immigrants increased as Tables 1.7 and 1.8 demonstrate.[55]

Portland was not New York, Seattle was not Boston. Although the numbers of immigrants arriving in Oregon increased in the last decade of the nineteenth century and the first decade of the twentieth, the proportion of "old" to "new" immigrants remained relatively constant or declined. For example, there were some 2,600 Russians among Oregon's total 30,500 foreign-born in 1880, by 1910 they comprised 5,300 out of 113,000. This equates to Russian-born residents making up some 8.5 percent of Oregon's foreign-born population in 1880 as opposed to 4.5 percent in 1910. Even in the region's urban areas—those which would be thought to attract disproportionate numbers of the "new" immigration—restrictionists would be hard pressed to find evidence of a deluge. For example, although Portland's foreign-born population declined marginally between 1910 and 1920, the proportion of "new" immigrants declined more sharply. Added to this, during the same decade the "old", Nordic, sources increased in both relative and real terms. For Oregon the issues of "Race Suicide" which were driving much of Eastern restrictionism can hardly be seen as a real threat in terms of swelling immigrant numbers.

Table 1.7: The Old Immigration in the Major Cities of the Northwest, 1900-1930

CITY (Total Foreign-born population)	Canada	Scandinavia	UK	Germany	Ireland
Portland					
1900 (25,876)	2209	2975	2804	4469	1741
1910 (50,312)	5211	8723	5363	7490	2262
1920 (49,778)	6458	9340	6104	6028	2915
1930 (50,228)	8451	9248	6820	5283	1053
Spokane					
1900 (7,833)	1821	1938	1508	1326	540
1910 (21,820)	4350	5786	2898	2755	1021
1920 (17,096)	3845	4590	2517	1992	717
1930 (16,493)	3853	4333	2197	1908	478
Tacoma					
1900 (11,032)	1651	3429	1743	1424	714
1910 (22,498)	2883	7731	2572	2545	916
1920 (n/a)	N/A	N/A	N/A	N/A	N/A
1930 (20,492)	3155	6810	2751	1520	396
Seattle					
1900 (22,003)	3,786	4,662	3,329	2,735	1,576
1910 (67,456)	10,717	17,749	8,553	6,176	3,177
1920 (80,976)	13,887	21,600	11,675	4,827	3,455
1930 (78,342)	15,745	21,366	12,169	4,608	2,008

The results for like comparisons made by contrasting Seattle's population in 1910 with that of 1920 demonstrate that Seattle, unlike Portland, attracted increasing numbers of the New immigration. For example, in 1910 Italians made up a little over 0.1 percent of Seattle's foreign-born population. In 1920 they made up almost 4 percent. Moreover, between 1890 and 1910 while Portland's population quadrupled, the percentage of foreign-born to total population declined by almost 15 percent, whereas in Seattle the total population grew by a slightly larger figure while its foreign-born population rose by over 10 percent.[56] These figures are lower than would be expected, given that Washington State's total population, grew from some 350,000 to slightly under one and half million in the two decades after 1890—a rise of a little over 400 percent. Most of the growth came from the internal migration of the American-born. The figures for Washington's foreign-born actually declined relative to the native-born population—from some 26 percent in 1890 to around 17 percent in 1910—and this decline continued throughout the period. By way of comparison the figures for the same ratio in New York State show an increase from around the same percentage in 1890, to some 30 percent in 1910. In Illinois, the figures remained relatively constant dropping from 22 to 21 percent. The national percentage dipped slightly from 14.8 to 14.5 percent in the same period.[57]

Table 1.8: The New Immigration in the Major Cities of the Northwest, 1900-1930

CITY (Total Foreign-born population)	Italy	Poland	Russia	Austria Hungary
Portland				
1900 (25,876)	631	193	984	367
1910 (50,312)	2557	N/A	4892	3132
1920 (49,778)	2847	1537	3837	2118
1930 (50,228)	2988	1333	4472	1023
Spokane				
1900 (7,833)	135	14	140	158
1910 (21,820)	1545	N/A	879	838
1920 (17,096)	922	154	508	377
1930 (16,493)	980	184	436	279
Tacoma				
1900 (11,032)	187	34	72	372
1910 (22,498)	1202	N/A	988	1523
1920 (n/a)	N/A	N/A	N/A	N/A
1930 (20,492)	1186	380	779	281
Seattle				
1900 (22,003)	362	78	309	377
1910 (67,456)	720	N/A	3877	2370
1920 (80,976)	3094	881	3349	1762
1930 (78,342)	3457	975	2640	1049

To the bulk of the Northwest's residents, particularly in rural areas, the problems immigration brought in its wake were troubles that, other than in their Japanese guise, could still be avoided. This meant that ambitious politicians could become restrictionists and manipulate the threat that immigration represented. They had a variety of audiences to whom they could play a variety of messages. To a general audience it could be the threat to the region's education, morals, health or prosperity. To the mill owner the message could be based on radical Europeans threatening regional stability and his profitability. To the farmer it could be the Japanese threatening his markets. To the lumber worker it could be the Greek, Italian, Chinese or Japanese laborer undercutting his wages. It was simple for the Klan, American Protective Association (APA) or American Federation of Labor (AFL) nativist to exaggerate the threat posed by any group of immigrants, for throughout the period the national press kept up a constant barrage of immigration horror stories which warned of a unstoppable flood of diseased, immoral, ill-educated paupers threatening to invade America. It was perhaps all the more effective as the local population had little personal knowledge of these groups. Even when these groups entered the region they were frequently diffused into smaller groups than those disembarking on the Eastern seaboard. They were often more a novelty than a threat. Nonetheless, a Bolshevik or Jew is much more threatening in the abstract than the flesh, especially when he has already been demonized in the public imagination.

FROM "PIONEER" TO "IMMIGRANT"

If the emergence of opposition to immigration in the Northwest cannot realistically be seen as a result of a quantitative change throughout the period, as on the East Coast, then the explanation must lie in changes in the perception of immigration throughout the period. An obvious point of departure for analysis of this change is the examination of the resident's image of the area and how this related to the immigrant. As has been already noted, the early immigration to the Oregon Territory was to a great extent homogeneous, if not by nationality, at least by intent. Residents of the region had always been suspicious of in-comers. The Hudson's Bay Company had sought to protect its investment by reducing American encroachments into "its" territory. In the 1830s and early 1840s, the company had deliberately, efficiently and effectively exterminated the valuable fur species, especially beaver, in the Snake and Willamette valleys in order to create a "fur desert" in the region, a buffer zone, to discourage the westward advance of American trappers.[58]

Even the earliest attempts to encourage immigration contained provisos to protect existing residents. The initial, July 1843, Organic Law favored those who were already resident in the region. It allowed a mere 20 days for new arrivals to stake and register their claims. By contrast, those who had already staked claims by the time the legislation came into force had an entire year in which to register. Even when this was altered to two months for all claimants, property improvement and residence requirements continued to favor those already resident.[59] Some limitations on immigration were less deliberate. In the most desirable areas speculators had cashed in on the high demand for fertile land with consequent subdivisions of properties and an escalation of land prices. Before statehood, the region's first newspaper, the *Oregon Spectator*, warned prospective immigrants that they would most likely "find the same disposition for speculation in land claims that you may have found at an earlier period in some of the new territory of the Mississippi valley...[and also to] beware of town speculators."[60] At other times it was more or less violent claim jumping, squatting or trespassing. In such cases, local communities invariably favored existing residents over recent arrivals, frequently regardless of the legitimacy of the disputed claims.

Nevertheless, initially such incidents were rare. It has been argued that the very process of the Oregon Trail led to the formation of a strong sense of kinship.[61] Privations endured on the five to six months of hard overland travel, the planning, shared expectations and disciplines necessary for such an undertaking and the risks inherent formed a bond between immigrants. Added to this the sheer time, cost and other difficulties faced by European immigrants in order to be in a position to undertake the trek—for example, the knowledge of, and arrival at, a "Western" point of departure and acceptance by other travelers—presumed a certain "inclusiveness" among these immigrants. Many of these foreign-born had already settled in Mid-Western areas, had been accepted by, or formed, communities with whom they traveled and with whom they re-located. Once they had arrived in the Northwest they were frequently financially, if not physically, exhausted. They were reliant on residents for employment and hospitality. The harshness and simplicity of pioneer life bred a strong sense of community. In general, the early foreign-born immigrants were given the opportunity to prove themselves as neighbors, employees and friends regardless of their place of origin. They were not condemned as the corrupt, urban, alien, impoverished, disease-ridden immigrants who were later assumed to congregate in the growing slums of the East Coast—these were people fired by the same motives as their American-born counterparts, they were pioneers.

To some extent this commonality evaporated with the advent of rail travel. Not only were the communal bonds of the trail removed by the ease of the outward journey, return was equally simple:

> When, about fifteen years ago, the great Slav invasion began, the American frontier was remote, shrunken, and forbidding. The newcomers were not in quest of cheap land, with independence, so much as of paying jobs from which they might hoard "big money" and return well off to their homes.[62]

If the settling of Oregon was the result of the covered wagon, with all that went with that, the settling of Washington was the result of the railroad. An illustration of this is the expansion of Washington's three main cities in the late 1880s and early 1890s. The population of Seattle, which from 1893 became James J. Hill's Great Northern Railway's Pacific terminus, grew by 1,000 percent, overtaking Walla Walla—which the trans-continental railways bypassed—as Washington's most populous city. Tacoma, from 1873—Henry Villard's Northern Pacific terminus—grew by some 3,000 percent and Spokane, the rail hub of the Inland Empire, by 6,000 percent. Portland, in spite of its reluctance to lose its regional supremacy, continued to rely on the source of its early growth—the confluence of the Willamette and Columbia rivers. The city displayed some ambivalence to the railroads and arguably this contributed to her comparatively sluggish expansion in the period—"Portland people were the toll takers at the gate. In time they became conservative, took fewer risks and [merely] relied on the position of their tollgate."[63] The result was the "Rose City" metropolitan area grew by a mere 164 percent.[64] It could be held that Oregon represented nineteenth-century expansion, while Washington represented the twentieth-century variety. The one inspired by "Manifest Destiny", individualism and the search for rural Eden, the other the result of extractive capitalism, the corporate entity and financial security. One was Turner's redemptive "winning [of] a wilderness"[65], the other the more prosaic "Wage Earner's Frontier". The railroad became the symbol of this wage earners' frontier.

Whilst providing the means to ship produce and import supplies, the railroad also had some undesirable effects. To the conservative, it embodied the total opposite of the human-scale, self-reliant, but inclusive, rural, frontier ethos. Highly capitalized, technologically advanced and impersonal, it threatened to break down the traditional pioneer values of the region. The railroads sought mass immigration in order to sell the millions of acres of land gained under federal land grants, to provide passengers and cheap labor, to build, maintain and run the lines themselves. They promoted immigration. In 1883 the Northern Pacific Railroad had 831 promotional agents in Britain alone, with a more than 100 others in continental Europe, largely in Germany and Scandinavia. By 1888 the Northern Pacific advertised in over 3,000 newspapers and had distributed some 650,000 brochures. The land sales figures of the Northern Pacific reflected this investment—climbing from 389,000 acres in 1896 to 1 million by 1899, to 2 million in 1901.[66] Population density in Oregon had doubled in the two decades to 1910. In Washington it tripled, as Table 1.9 shows.[67] Initially this was greeted with enthusiasm by many local institutions. Local and town councils, many local papers, Chambers of Commerce, the Grange and other farmers' institutions joined in promoting the "unlimited resources [of the region, which] are capable of giving support to an unlimited population."[68]

Table 1.9: Population Density in Oregon and Washington, 1890-1920

Year of Census	Population density in Oregon per square mile	Population density in Washington per square mile
1890	3.3	5.3
1900	4.3	7.8
1910	7	17.1
1920	8.2	20.3

By the early 1900s it was becoming apparent that these resources were not unlimited, at least in Oregon. Over-grazing in some of the Eastern areas of the state led to the creation of "cold deserts". By 1901, federal surveyors found South Eastern Oregon "very unpromising [in] appearance...altogether too closely pastured", with this over-grazing dangerously reducing "the protection of the surface soil from the erosive action of water." [69] Attempts to irrigate some of these areas were unsuccessful—as with the 1914 Tumalo reservoir project. The much-vaunted techniques of "scientific dry farming" which had successfully transformed wheat production in the Walla Walla area, often proved to be expensive failures such as in the Bend, Prineville and Burns area of Oregon.[70] Even in the well-watered and fertile areas, as the old aboriginal practice of burning died out, weed encroachment became a serious problem in pastures and arable crops.[71] In many cases the homesteaders, who had been encouraged by the railroads and other boosters, simply abandoned their land and returned East or moved to the cities and posed a new and increasingly serious welfare burden to the State.[72]

By 1911, the high costs and arduous labor of clearing the stumps of felled areas coupled with the creation of 2.5 million acres of forest reserve in Washington alone meant that agricultural land reached up to $500 an acre in some fertile regions of the state. Prices in many areas doubled in the first decade of the Twentieth century, the norm for such land had risen to between $100 and $200 per acre.[73] Speculation bloated land values. When W.T. Clark started to build the Wenatchee Canal in Eastern Washington in 1902 land in the region jumped from $25 an acre to $400.[74] Irrigation pushed the costs of land-ownership still higher. It was estimated that to establish a viable orchard in the Yakima valley required a minimum investment of $1,890 to purchase and plant the land and build a homestead. To pay the irrigation fees, which ran at between $50 to $60 an acre, would amount to at least another $2,000.[75]

Even logged-off land was commanding prices which, when the area necessary for a viable business, labor and time out of production were considered, made it prohibitively expensive for many immigrants. Whereas boosters declared logged-off debris—brash wood, stumps and timber—to be an asset, which could be sold at up to $200 an acre, the reality was expense and labor. Huge stumps, tangled roots and weeds and pioneer species trees meant that reclamation was often more expensive than the purchase of agricultural land already in production. During the first decades of the twentieth century, the costs of clearing logged off lands were estimated at some 400 man-hours, 34 horse-hours and $40 worth of dynamite for a single acre by traditional methods. Mechanized stump pullers could speed up the process to nearly an acre a day, but a trained crew would cost upwards of $300 a day. Further, neither of these estimates included draining, tilling, seeding, fencing or fertilizing. Few were willing to undertake such work during which they would see no return. Between 1901 and 1917 in Island County, Washington, the average farm increased by only half an acre of cutover land a year.[76] It was hardly surprising that by the middle of the decade some commentators who had previously boasted of the unlimited space and resources of the area accepted Turner's thesis and saw the era of free land as closed.[77]

The immigrant of the twentieth century could not be the pioneer of the nineteenth, that heroic stalwart of American legend. The Northwest had adopted this mythology and imbued the region's initial American settlers with a status superior even to that of the already beatified Western pioneer :

> The Oregon emigrant was not a gold seeker like those who flocked to California in 1849; he was not driven into exile like the Mormons who colonized Utah; he was not primarily a hunter nor a trapper; he was a restless American of vigorous body and mind, who was ready to risk the dangers and privations of a long overland journey to reach a country that would satisfy his desire to mind his own business in his own way and allay his discontent with the land of his birth....This type of American is extinct because there are no longer any lands in America for this type of American pioneer to conquer....The railroads that web the country were the death of the old type of hardy, daring men who marched the country from the Missouri to the Columbia.[78]

Even if he had the super-human qualities of his American "ancestors", in large measure the foreign-born found himself excluded from land-ownership by the escalating costs. Many of the foreign-born who did enter agriculture in the region were "second-stage" immigrants who moved from other areas of the Union. This was particularly true of Scandinavian immigrants, many of whom moved from the Dakotas, Minnesota and Wisconsin to Washington in the first decade of the twentieth century.[79] Others were Japanese, encouraged by their associations, who encountered a range of hostile responses and were eventually excluded from land-ownership.

The bulk of those arriving on the East Coast did not have the means to purchase land, a fact that even the ever-optimistic railroad immigration agents realized:

> If you had an influx of this foreign immigration, like it comes over Ellis Island for a few months, you wouldn't have a place to take care of them, nor could you provide labor for them. They have no money to buy land with....We found that every foreigner who comes through Ellis Island has in his possession just enough to get along with...there were mighty few who had $15.[80]

This did little to quiet the dread in some quarters of the impoverished "hordes" of European and Asian immigration, especially as escalating land prices seemed to be rapidly removing the safety valve of reclaimable land. The Populist, and later Progressive, Oregon Democrat, Sylvester Pennoyer voiced an extreme example of this feeling. In his vision, the expense of land would create a small number of large scale landowners—land Trusts"—that would force the small "yeoman" farmers off their land, import cheap labor from Asia and Europe and, in collusion with the "railroad trusts", set up a new form of feudalism.[81] To some extent these fears were fed throughout the period by national organizations associated with nativism.

In reality, census figures indicate that in the first decade of the twentieth century, although some large farming concerns evolved, the general drift was not towards an increase in the number of "corporate" farms, rather there was a steady upward trend in owner-occupation. Certainly, the numbers of those employed in farming doubled in the first decade of the twentieth century in Washington and increased by 75 percent in Oregon. However, the proportion of farms of over 1,000 acres remained more or less constant at nearly 4 percent in Oregon and around 3 percent in Washington. The number of owner-occupiers rose from 74 percent of all farmers to 83 percent in Washington and from 69 percent to 82 percent in Oregon.[82] Nevertheless, the fear of the influence of commercialization was real. Populism, the Grange movement and APAism, as well as their later incarnations all contained elements of rural restrictionism. Policies motivated by the conviction that immigration represented the sinister machinations of external powers working against the interests of the individual farmer, miner, lumberman or fisherman—those were the occupations which represented the original pioneer spirit of the region.

Industrialization, even in the extractive industries of the Northwest, seemed to be rapidly removing individual freedom.[83] The region's fisheries developed more costly but effective methods of harvesting, canning, processing and distributing the produce of the rich fishing grounds of the coastal and inland waters, which both lowered the prices and necessitated greater co-operation, labor and capital. In agriculture the farmer was increasingly tied to the railroads, the elevator companies and the international markets, as well as the banks, to market his produce and finance his business. In mining the sole placer miner was forced to give way to the more efficient, sophisticated and productive hydraulic mining enterprises that demanded higher financial input, increased labor and larger stakes which were often beyond the individuals' resources. Escalating prices for virgin forest, particularly in the wake of the turn-of-the-century lumber speculation boom triggered by Weyerhaeuser's massive 1900 purchase, largely removed the option of individual pioneer-forestry. Also plant costs rose as the lumber industry developed efficient, but highly capital-intensive methods of over-coming the growing distances from cheap riverine lumber movement as the areas' waterfront forests became increasingly logged off. Methods of lumber milling became more mechanized, productive and expensive—and thus ever more dominated by those who could afford such economies of scale and ride out the ferocious economic cycles of boom and bust which came to dominate the industry.

To some, the immigrants represented unfairly cheap labor. To others they represented an unwelcome reminder of how fragile the veneer of civilization in the area really was, how late their collective incorporation into the Union was. Often it re-enforced to individuals how recent their personal integration into the community was. The existing resident population of rural areas had evolved institutions that reflected their "American" self-perception—schools, churches and business and social organizations. Institutions, from the Grange to the Chamber of Commerce, which while operating on a local level also served to tie them into greater, national bodies. Although often isolated—"island communities"—this isolation frequently tended to re-enforce rather than break the bonds of "American-ness", especially in an era of growing mass communications.

Support for exclusion of certain immigrants could demonstrate the need of even recent immigrant residents to be perceived as American in order to be accepted in these insular communities, particularly in the post-1917 period of "one hundred percent American" and anti-radical fervor. It was the very isolated frontier nature of these communities which first created, and then exaggerated, the need for conformity to this common, "American", bond. Zealous in conservation of their communities, this zeal was re-enforced by the novelty and, thus perceived fragility of the community, as real or imaginary immigrants threatened to alter its composition. American and, more important, "Western" by nature, these communities frequently saw direct action, in the tradition of the frontiersman, as the most expedient course. In its most extreme form, this was apparent in the local authorities' tacit approval of the violence meted out to "alien" Wobblies at Everett in 1916 and Centralia in 1919.[84]

As has been demonstrated, the "new" immigration of the period was largely urban; nevertheless, this lack of foreign-born rural immigrants frequently increased the vehemence of pressure for measures against those who did arrive. Lack of real experience of massive foreign-born immigration laid these rural communities open to exaggerated threats of the dangers alien immigrants posed—a fact religiously motivated nativists and the Klan used to considerable advantage. Also, unsurprisingly, in areas of high immigration, where the immigrant vote was, or had the potential to become, a political consideration, restrictionism was frequently greeted with ambivalence, or actively resisted.[85] For example, from 1912 to 1932 the isolated coastal lumber region of Grays Harbor returned to Congress the mono-maniacal restrictionist, Albert Johnson, who declared his crusade to be motivated by the imminent threat to the region posed by a "horde" of Japanese immigrants. His mission continued to receive local support although this Japanese "horde" never amounted to more than a hundred settlers in the area.[86] Seattle, by contrast, had a considerable and growing immigrant community—the largest of which was, significantly, Japanese—and yet produced no such restrictionist of national importance.

This is not to suggest that the influence of the frontier on immigration restriction was unique to these smaller, rural communities. Portland's much-vaunted pride in its heritage led to the rapid creation of a social elite, particularly those worthies listed in the *Portland "400" Directory*.[87] This elite felt itself all the more exclusive for competing with the brash commercialism of Washington and California and with the arriviste nature of Seattle, Tacoma or Spokane. If not able, as many were, to pride themselves on their ancient New England roots, the cultural achievements and venerable heritage of both the city and the settlements in the Willamette Valley gave Portland's elite, and many less elevated Oregonians, a feeling of superiority over their neighbors. They were the pioneer settlers' descendants. They resented the immigrant wageworkers flooding into the area on similar grounds to their Eastern patrician counterparts, bluebloods such as Madison Grant, Captain John B.Trevor or Henry Cabot Lodge. The image of the frontier merely re-enforced this resentment by acting as a constant reminder that they lived in, in the words of Jesse Applegate, "a land but just emerging from a state of barbarism."[88]

NOTES

[1] See Robert Edward Wynne, *Reaction to the Chinese in the Pacific Northwest and British Columbia 1850-1910* (New York, 1978).
[2] For example, probably the leading text on Japanese exclusion—Roger Daniels, *The Politics of Prejudice; The Anti-Japanese Movement in California and the Struggle for Japanese Exclusion* (Berkeley, 1977)—sets out to study nothing but the Californian movement and refers to the Pacific Northwest only obliquely. The same is largely true of his later, more general works. Although Yuji Ichioka's *The Issei: The World of the First Generation Japanese Immigrants, 1885-1924* (New York, 1988) gives some emphasis to Northwestern pressures, in general it tends to concentrate on California's overwhelming preponderance of Japanese and the consequently better-documented California restriction movement. Of the works studied which concentrate on the Northwest, the two most significant are Linda Tamura, *The Hood River Issei: An Oral History of Japanese Settlers in Oregon's Hood River Valley* (Urbana, 1993) and Marjorie R. Stearns, *The History of the Japanese People in Oregon* (unpublished PhD Thesis, University of Oregon, Eugene, 1937). The former is a study of a specific community and largely mentions the effects rather than the political causes of restriction. The latter studies only the smaller Oregon population, ignoring the second largest Japanese population in America at the time—the Seattle community. This study aims to study the reaction of both States, and if anything tends to concentrate on Washington.
[3] This is certainly true of John Higham's expansive and defining *Strangers in the Land: Patterns of American Nativism, 1860-1925* (New Brunswick, 1955) which sees a progressive movement towards restriction as a result of a conjunction of racial theory, religious prejudice and fear of revolution in the 1920s largely brought about by the reverberations of the First World War.

Although it is difficult to argue with this assessment, Higham's emphasis is almost entirely based around the Eastern and Mid-Western regions.

[4] Maldwyn Jones, *American Immigration* (rev.ed. Chicago, 1992), sees the 1911 Dillingham Report with its statistical condemnation of the Southern and Eastern Europeans as the starting point for the restrictionist movement in earnest. Again such an approach concentrates on this Eastern/Middle Western bias radiating to the Western areas in general and the Northwest in particular.

[5] Authors have divided the area in a variety of ways. For example Carlos A. Schwantes, *The Pacific Northwest: An Interpretive History* (Lincoln, Nebraska, 1989) defines its area as Washington, Oregon and Idaho. Schwantes' editorial collaboration with G. Thomas Edward, *Experiences in a Promised Land: Essays in Pacific Northwest History* (Seattle, 1986) defines the region as Washington and Oregon. His *Radical Heritage: Labor, Socialism and Reform in Washington and British Columbia 1885-1917* (Moscow, Idaho, 1979) ignores the labor movement in Oregon. Essentially all such divisions are artificial and largely draw on the sources available to the historian and the scope and time-scale of the subject matter.

[6] The opposite approach is taken by William L. Lang, *Centennial West: Essays on the Northern Tier States* (Seattle, 1991) who sees Washington, Idaho, Montana, Wyoming and North and South Dakota as a geo-political region—for they all joined the Union in 1889-90.

[7] Most studies of nativism draw on the format laid out in John Higham's classic, *Strangers in the Land*, op.cit.

[8] For details see the *Oregonian* November 3, 1983.

[9] See Elizabeth McLagan, *A Peculiar Paradise: A History of Blacks in Oregon 1788-1940* (Portland, 1980), and Quintard Taylor, *In Search of the Racial Frontier: African Americans in the Making of the American West* (New York, 1998) and *The Forging of a Black Community: Seattle's Central District from 1870 Through the Civil Rights Era* (Seattle, 1994).

[10] See James W. Scott et al., *Historical Atlas of Washington* (Norman, Oklahoma, 1988) p.29.

[11] Figures for 1840 taken from Alex Toth, *American Catholicism and Immigration* (Unpublished paper, MSS 2400, held at the Oregon Historical Society, 1973) p.1 The remaining figures have been taken, and extrapolated, from analysis of United States (decennial) Census data cited at Inter-university Consortium for Political and Social Research, *Historical, Demographic, Economic, and Social Data: The United States, 1790-1970* [Computer file]. (Ann Arbor, no date).

[12] See William A. Bowen, *The Willamette Valley: Settlement on the Oregon Frontier* (Seattle, 1978) pp.69-70 on Organic law and the spread of property rights.

[13] See "An Act in Relation to Land Claims" of June 25, 1844, section 5 cited in Bowen, op.cit. p.70.

[14] James Henry Taylor, *The Restriction of European Immigration, 1890-1924* (PhD Thesis, Berkeley, 1933) p.203.
[15] Figures taken from United States Census, 1850 cited in Gordon B. Dodds, *The American Northwest: A History of Oregon and Washington* (Arlington Heights, Illinois, 1986) p.70.
[16] Figures taken from Bowen, op.cit. p.25.
[17] See Superintendent of the Census (1853), *Seventh Census of the United States* (Washington, D.C., 1853) p.xxxvii.
[18] Figures extrapolated from ibid., table XV, and p.xxxvii.
[19] "Others" include Asians, Southern and Central Americans, Russians and some 143 (11 percent) whose origins were unknown.
[20] For examples of the boosters claims see The Oregon State Immigration Commission, *The State of Oregon: Its Resources and Opportunities* (Salem, 1914) pp.21-42.
[21] A letter from F.A. Hopkins of Sherman, Washington published in the Great Northern's boosting magazine the *Northwest Magazine* volume 20:2 (February, 1902) 4.
[22] Figures taken and extrapolated from Bowen, op.cit.p.25, Paul G. Merriam, "The Other Portland": A Statistical Note on Foreign-Born, 1860-1910" *Oregon Historical Quarterly* 80 (1979) 258-268; the Inter-university Consortium for Political and Social Research, op.cit. and Superintendent of the Census (1853), op.cit. p.xxxvii.
[23] See Richard D. Scheuerman, "From Wagon Trails to Iron Rails: Russian German Immigration to the Pacific Northwest" *Journal of the American Society of Germans from Russia* 2:2 (Fall, 1979) 40.
[24] Figures taken from Janet E. Rasmussen, *New Land, New Lives: Scandinavian Immigrants to the Pacific Northwest* (Seattle, 1993) p.7.
[25] Figures taken from Walter Nugent, *Crossings: The Great Trans-Atlantic Migrations, 1870-1914* (Bloomington, Indiana, 1995) p.17.
[26] See Eric Hobsbawm, *The Age of Empire 1875-1914* (London, 1988) pp.35-37.
[27] Figures taken from National Bureau of Economic Research figures in Walter F Wilcox (ed.), *International Migration,* vol. I (New York, 1929) pp.230-231.
[28] By 1900 the United States was exporting nearly over 210,000 live cattle and sheep to Europe along with huge tonnages of meat enabled by the advent of refrigeration holds from 1875. See David Budlong Tyler, *Steam Conquers the Atlantic* (New York, 1939) pp.363-364.
[29] See ibid. p.359
[30] M. Mulhall, *Dictionary of Statistics* (London, 1892) p.573, cited in Hobsbawm, op.cit., p.27.
[31] Figures taken from Wilcox, op.cit. pp.230-231.
[32] A statistical analysis of railroad building in the Americas is available in B.R.Mitchell, *International Historical Statistics: The Americas and Australasia* (Detroit, 1983) pp.656-658. A recent analysis of the effect of the continental railroad on American demographics is available in Donald William Meinig, *The*

Shaping of America: A Geographical Perspective on 500 Years of History. Volume 3: Transcontinental America 1850-1915 (New Haven, Connecticut, 1998) pp.4-30.

[33] Figures taken, and extrapolated, from analysis of United States (decennial) Census data cited at Inter-university Consortium for Political and Social Research, op.cit.

[34] See Charles M.Gates, "A Historical Sketch of the Economic Development of Washington since Statehood" *Pacific Northwest Quarterly* 39 (July, 1948) 214-232

[35] Figures taken from Lancaster Pollard, "The Pacific Northwest: A Regional Study" *Oregon Historical Quarterly* 52 (December, 1951) 220.

[36] Figures taken from Earl Pomeroy, *The Pacific Slope: A History of California, Oregon, Washington, Idaho, Utah and Nevada* (New York, 1965) p.116.

[37] Figures taken and extrapolated from Schwantes (1989) op.cit. p.192, and United States (decennial) Census data cited at Inter-university Consortium for Political and Social Research, op.cit.

[38] Rudyard Kipling, *From Sea to Sea and other Sketches: Letters of Travel* vol.II (rev.ed. London, 1924) p.46.

[39] See Murray Morgan, *Puget's Sound: A Narrative of Early Tacoma and the Southern Sound* (Seattle, 1979) pp.253-274.

[40] See Bowen, op.cit. p.95.

[41] Figures taken from United States (decennial) Census data cited at Inter-university Consortium for Political and Social Research, op.cit; Norbert MacDonald, "Population Growth and Change in Seattle and Vancouver, 1880-1960" *Pacific Historical Review* 39 (1970) 297-321 and Merriam, op.cit. 258-268

[42] Figures extrapolated from Scott op.cit.p.26.

[43] For an analysis of the capitalization of the Northwest see William G. Robbins, *Colony and Empire: The Capitalist Transformation of the American West* (Lawrence, Kansas, 1994) pp.121-142.

[44] See Arthur J. Brown, "The Promotion of Emigration to Washington 1854-1909" *Pacific Northwest Quarterly* 36 (January, 1945) 3-17.

[45] A Tacoma booster's pamphlet cited in Lawrence H. Larsen, *The Urban West at the End of the Frontier* (Lawrence, Kansas, 1978) p.5.

[46] See the *Congressional Record* volumes 48, p.5023; 49, pp.864, 3318 & 3429; 51, p.291; 52, pp.3077-3078; 53, p.5194 and 59, p.316.

[47] See Leslie W. Koepplin, *A Relationship of Reform: Immigrants and Progressives in the Far West* (New York, 1990) pp.108-109

[48] Washington State Bureau of Statistics and Immigration, *Official Report of the State Immigration Conference Held March 27 and 28, 1914* (Olympia, 1914).

[49] See Samuel E. Wood, *The California State Commission of Immigration and Housing* (PhD Thesis, Berkeley, 1942).

[50] Hiram Johnson to Simon S. Lubin, August 20th, 1913 cited in Koepplin, op.cit. p.115.

[51] Oregon State Immigration Commission and Development League, *Biennial Report [1913-1914]* (Portland, 1914) p.18.
[52] Figures taken from Jones, op.cit. pp.168-73.
[53] For details of the nations which composed the "New" immigration see Immigration Commission (Dillingham), *Immigration Commission, Emigration Conditions* vol.4 (Washington, D.C., 1911) p.21.
[54] Table compiled from figures in Roy L. Garis, *Immigration Restriction: A Study of the Opposition to and Regulation of Immigration into the United States* (New York, 1927) pp.205-207.
[55] Figures for 1890 are available from the Department of the Interior, *Compendium, 11th Census, 1890 Part I. Population* (Washington, D.C., 1892) pp.570 &578. Unlike later years this does not detail the place of nativity of immigrants, merely city totals, so these figures are not used. For the 1900 figures, The United States Census Office, *Abstract of the Twelfth Census of the United States, 1900* (Washington, DC, 1902) pp.105 & 106-108. The 1910 figures are taken from the Department of Commerce and Labor, Bureau of the Census, *Thirteenth Census of the United States Taken in the Year 1910, Abstract of the Census* (Washington, D.C., 1913) p.213. The 1920 figures are from the Department of Commerce, Bureau of Census, *Abstract of the Fourteenth Census of the United States, 1920* (Washington, D.C., 1923) pp.314-319. The 1930 figures are taken from the Department of Commerce, Bureau of Census, *Abstract of the Fifteenth Census of the United States* (Washington, D.C., 1933) pp.136-137.
[56] Figures extrapolated from United States (decennial) Census data cited at Inter-university Consortium for Political and Social Research, op.cit; Merriam, op.cit, 263, 267-268 and MacDonald, op.cit. 308 &310
[57] Figures extrapolated from United States (decennial) Census data cited at Inter-university Consortium for Political and Social Research, op.cit.
[58] See William G.Robins, *Landscapes of Promise: The Oregon Story, 1800-1940* (Seattle, 1997) p.56
[59] See Matthew P. Deady (ed.), *The Organic and Other General Laws of Oregon, 1843-1872* (Salem, 1874) pp.63-64 and 77-78.
[60] *Oregon Spectator* September 30, 1847.
[61] A concise analysis among the huge, if rarely scholarly, literature on the Oregon Trail is available in Dodds, op.cit. pp.64-75.
[62] Edward Alsworth Ross, *The Old World in the New; The Significance of Past and Present Immigration to the American People* (New York, 1914) pp.124-125.
[63] "A member of an old Portland family" cited in Leslie Scott, "Early Portland Contrasts" *Oregon Historical Quarterly* 32:4 (December, 1931) 313
[64] Figures taken from Thomas and Schwantes op.cit. pp.81-82.
[65] Frederick Jackson Turner, *The Frontier in American History* (New York, 1958) p.2.

[66] See C. Seigfried Mickelson, *Promotional Activities of the Northern Pacific's Land and Immigration Departments* (Master's Thesis, University of Minnesota, 1940) p.192, John Arthur Brown, *The Means of Promoting Immigration to the Northwest and Washington to 1910* (Unpublished Master's Thesis, University of Washington, 1942) and James B. Hedges, "Promotion of Immigration to the Pacific Northwest by the Railroads" *Mississippi Valley History Review* 15 (September, 1928) 183-203.

[67] Figures taken from United States (decennial) Census data cited at Inter-university Consortium for Political and Social Research, op.cit.

[68] *Oregonian* January 28, 1890

[69] David Griffiths, *Forage Conditions on the Northern Border of the Great Basin* US Dept of Agriculture, Bureau of Plant Industry, Bulletin no. 15 (1902) 28, 55 cited in Robbins, op.cit. pp.164-165.

[70] See Geoffrey L. Buckley, "Desertification of the Camp Creek Drainage in Central Oregon" *Yearbook of the Association of Pacific Coast Geographers* 55 (1993) 116-117 (cited in Robbins, op.cit. p.168) and for an authoritative account of the trials involved in the growth of a ranching empire (the John Sparks ranches) see James A. Young and B. Abbot Sparks *Cattle in the Cold Desert* (Logan, Utah, 1985).

[71] See Robert T. Boyd, "Strategies of Indian Burning in the Willamette Valley" *Canadian Journal of Anthropology* 5 (Fall 1986) 70.

[72] See Barbara Allen, *Homesteading the High Desert* (Logan, Utah, 1987) and eyewitness Isaiah Bowman, "The Pioneer Fringe" *American Geographic Society Special Publication no. 13.* (New York, 1931)

[73] For details of land values in Washington State see Washington State Bureau of Statistics and Immigration, *Official Report of the State Immigration Conference* (Olympia, 1914) pp.45-48. For details of forestry conservation in Washington see Lawrence Rakestraw, *A History of Forest Conservation in the Pacific Northwest, 1891-1913* (Doctoral Thesis, University of Washington, 1955) pp.125-153.

[74] Figures taken from John Fahey, *The Inland Empire: Unfolding Years, 1879-1929* (Seattle, 1986) p.97.

[75] Figures extrapolated from George M. Allen, *Irrigated Lands of Washington State* (Olympia, 1910) p.49.

[76] Figures taken from Richard White, *Land Use, Environment and Social Change: The Shaping of Island County, Washington* (rev.ed. Seattle, 1992) p.128.

[77] For example see the *Oregonian* August 25, 1906.

[78] The *Tacoma Ledger* November 29, 1892.

[79] See United States Senate, *Senate Document 747: Reports of the Immigration Commission. Abstracts of Reports.* 61st Congress, 3rd session pp.548 & 651.

[80] E.C. Leedy, general immigration agent of the Great Northern railroad, to the Washington State Immigration Conference, Olympia, March 27, 1914 cited in Washington State Bureau of Statistics and Immigration, op.cit., p.26.

[81] As the Democrat governor of Oregon put it—"Today the great producing and laboring classes of our state are being ground down between the upper and nether millstones of corporate power and cheap servile labor...it will only be a few years before the Willamette valley will be the home only of rich capitalists and [their] Chinese serfs." Sylvester Pennoyer, Oregon Governor 1886-1890, cited in Thomas and Schwantes, op.cit. p.191.

[82] Figures extrapolated from Schwantes (1989) op.cit. p.253 and United States (decennial) Census data cited at Inter-university Consortium for Political and Social Research, op.cit. For the growth of an agri-business see Alexander Campbell McGregor, *Counting Sheep: From open Range to Agribusiness on the Columbia Plateau* (Seattle, 1982).

[83] See Schwantes (1989) op.cit. pp.250-265.

[84] See Norman Clark, "Everett, 1916, and Beyond" *Pacific Northwest Quarterly* 57 (April, 1966).

[85] For examples of the political influence of the immigrant vote see Henry Beardsell Leonard, *The Open Gates; The Protest Against the Movement to Restrict European Immigration, 1896-1924* (PhD Thesis Northwestern University, Illinois, 1967).

[86] See Albert Johnson in an autobiographical series "Some Reminiscences" in the *Washingtonian* July 17, 1934.

[87] See Paul G. Merriam, " Urban elite in the Far West: Portland, Oregon, 1870-1890" *Arizona and the West* 18 (1976) 41-52.

[88] Jesse Applegate, "Umpqua Agriculture, 1851" *Oregon Historical Quarterly* 32 (June, 1931) 140.

2

RELIGION AS A MOTIVATION FOR IMMIGRATION EXCLUSION

> The Pope has given the command to make America Catholic. The first step is in electing one of the American Cardinals to the papacy; the removal of St Peter's to Washington; Cardinal Gibbons to be [made] president, and every non-Catholic to be driven out of the Army and Navy.[1]

From the Pilgrim Fathers to the Progressive era and beyond, religion informed America's image of itself, its mythology and aspirations, its political, economic and social systems. It was apparent in the enshrined principle of the separation of church and state, in the public education system and in that principle of "Manifest Destiny"—and its corollary, racial theory—which was used so frequently to justify Westward expansion. By the late nineteenth century, religion had evolved for the Western nativist into a Protestant, personal, self-reliant, non-hierarchical, but fundamentally progressive basis of American identity. The most frequently quoted historian of American expansion claimed that the West as a whole continued the Protestant, activist tradition, preaching "a new gospel, for the Western radical became convinced that he must sacrifice his ideal of individualism and free competition in order to maintain his ideal of democracy…[that of] the people themselves shaping their own affairs."[2]

American Protestantism represented nationalist and patriotic principles as well as continuity—a means of justifying both territorial expansion and social inclusion. The territories that Westward movement incorporated into the Union were not Protestant. These were regions which had been populated by aboriginal animists, as in the Dakotas, or Hispanic Catholics as in California or New

Mexico. As one commentator has succinctly put it, in their continental expansion the "Americans" "routed not only the Indians but also the Jesuits and Conquistadors".[3] Protestantism became a mark of the "American" social order, just as Catholicism had been the indication of their Spanish or French predecessors. It was redolent with related secular principles, iconography and mythology. By the turn of the twentieth century, Western Protestantism was becoming a fundamentally nostalgic Protestantism. It was an American Protestantism, a frontier Protestantism, with the white clapboard church and the little red schoolhouse—symbols of idyllic, more often than not rural, community and safety. It formed an "American" identity, a bond and a heritage—especially in times of growing challenges to religious certainty; times seemingly tolerant of morality in decay, increasing violence and, by the 1920s, times of declining church attendance.[4] By the end of the period, American society increasingly reflected the ongoing trends of secularization intellectually, with the challenges of biology and instinct, of Darwin and Freud in particular. This trend was also apparent in America's leisure, with the massive growth of alternative pursuits such as motoring and large-scale spectator sports. Nevertheless, in spite of these challenges, or arguably because of them, it is often held that Protestantism retained its importance in American nativist thought.[5]

Put simply, there were two elements to the Northwest's Protestant-based nativism. One is based on the protection and nurturing of a bright, optimistic, utopian vision of the region. The other is dedicated to the defense against enemies outlined in a dark concept of the territory as beleaguered by forces hostile to American Protestantism. Missionaries, reformers and other idealistic settlers saw the region as unsullied, a blank canvas. This was a region in which there was no status quo to retain. Nevertheless, these settlers frequently drew on potent historical precedents. To them American democracy was underpinned by this elemental, nebulous, but vibrantly American, Puritan Protestantism and the redemptive qualities of the frontier. In many ways they saw these two as inseparable, the one informing the other. Simple, unadorned frontier life reflected in simple, unadorned religion.

This was particularly true of the Northwest—the "farthest frontier". In the last region to lose its frontier isolation and individualism, this ruggedness was tempered by the influence of missionaries from the earliest days of settlement. There remained an ideal that such settlers should form the basis of the region's immigrants. All the incomers should be fired by this same redemptive dream, this same missionary zeal. While these visionaries "rode their circuits" they must have been supremely aware of the precarious nature of Protestantism in the region. To the north was Canada, with its large Catholic population and the all-too-recent legacy of its invasive imperial Hudson's Bay Company which had seemed to be firmly in the Catholics' pockets.[6] To the south lay California with its huge reservoir of Mexican Catholics. Much of the local population was made up of an undesirable mix of heathen aborigine, heretical Catholic or Godless mountain man. A great deal of the region's religious friction stems from this early siege mentality. From Josiah Strong and Lyman Beecher's dire warnings for the West, through the American Protective Association's religious-political paranoia to the Klan's exclusive, pseudo-religious fraternity, the Protestant mood is frequently aggressively defensive.

With the issue of religion, the constitutional prohibition on religious discrimination meant that nativists had to be especially circumspect, which makes disentangling the already complex elements increasingly difficult. Added to this the Christian ethos advocated fraternity and charity, which in the racially divided, harsh conditions of the pioneering days even the most convinced of the Calvinist elect could not ignore. Therefore, in order to gain effective levels of support, those advocating religious discrimination had to insinuate a religious element into other motives for immigrant exclusion. Religion was linked with race, national security and cultural identity. To some nativists, in spite of the Constitutional prohibition, religion was nationality. While those in favor of limiting non-Protestant immigration, or conversely maintaining free immigration, often felt they could appeal to their communities safe in the knowledge that they had a supposedly common belief system, self-interest could frequently interpose. Even in the relatively autonomous, insular and homogeneous Protestant communities of the Northwest, traditional belief in self-reliance and individuality competed with regional and local interests. Would the Baptist minister's message of anti-Catholic immigration restriction have equal appeal to both the lumber worker and mill-owner? Were religious bodies universally in favor of free immigration for all their co-religionists?

It has to be accepted that any examination of the motivation behind religious anti-immigrant discrimination is going to have elements which owe little, if anything, to the religion of those immigrants. Elements where religion forms little more than a convenient figleaf to disguise a variety of fears and motivations—ranging from, most important, personal ambition to a dread of modernity informed by fanciful wishes to return simpler past. For example, to what extent was anti-Semitism a religious phenomenon stemming from deicide or was it more dependent on racial and economic issues? Similarly, to what degree was anti-Asian sentiment, based on perceptions of the "fatalistic" Asian religions' seemingly "un-American" acceptance of poverty, disease and death? Was anti-Catholicism genuinely driven by political or theological sentiments? Should such an inquiry include or exclude the pressures against Marxists and other atheists? Given such considerations there are still methods of evaluating the importance of religion to the Northwest's nativist canon. Perhaps the best starting point is an examination of the scale of non-Protestant immigration, both nationally and regionally, during the period.

NON-PROTESTANT IMMIGRATION, 1890-1920

America was by far the most popular destination for emigrants in the last quarter of the nineteenth century. Between 1871 and 1911 the United States received over 20 million immigrants. By way of comparison Canada received just under two million in the same period, Brazil and Argentina a little over 6 million and Australia and New Zealand 2.5 million.[7] The vast bulk of this immigration took place in the final decade of the nineteenth century and the first decade of the twentieth. In the period 1830 to 1880 an average of 250,000 immigrants entered the United States per year. By 1890 this annual total had reached 400,000. In 1905 the annual figure had reached 1 million. Between 1900 and 1910 nearly 9 million immigrants were recorded entering the country. The source of these immigrants had also changed from being overwhelmingly British, Irish, German and Scandinavian to being composed of a mixture of predominantly Slavic, Central European, Mediterranean and, largely on the West Coast, Asian peoples. Not only had the geographic emphasis shifted, so had the religious. No longer were the bulk of immigrants Protestant, they were now in the minority. By 1896, the total number of Jews, Catholics, Russian and Greek Orthodox, Hindus, Buddhists and Muslims overtook the sum of Protestant arrivals and this trend continued throughout the period of this study.[8] Between 1845 and 1900 an estimated 4 million, largely Catholic, Irish entered the United States. Over half of these arrived in the period 1865 to 1900. Between 1865 and 1900, an estimated 700,000 German Catholics entered America. To these figures can be added 1.9 million Italians from 1888 to 1910 and the largely Catholic Polish population had reached 1.14 million by 1920. [9]

Although Catholic growth was the most spectacular and, by and large, the most targeted by Northwestern nativists, even these figures remained small as a percentage of the total population. By 1916 the Catholic Church in the continental United States boasted between 16.5 million and 18 million adherents—the total United States population, according to the decennial census, in 1920 was around 106 million. Catholics, therefore, made up a little over 16 percent of the total United States population. This, nevertheless, represented the largest single religious denomination in the country. The figure for American Catholics jumped to over 28 million, if American protectorates were included. Some idea of the scale of American Catholicism is apparent in the fact that in the same year the continental American Catholic Church claimed 19,572 priests, 10,058 churches and 85 seminaries training over 6,000 students.[10] By way of comparison, in 1922, the Jewish population of America was estimated at somewhere between 2.5 to 3 million.[11] Alarming as these figures may have been to nativists, it was Catholic expansion and the seemingly endless potential for this to increase that excited most nativist attention. For example the *Catholic Directory* for 1922 cited an annual increase in America's Catholic population of some 68 percent more than the increase of the previous year.[12] This was partly the result of immigration, and partly the result of conversion.[13]

The figures for the Northwest were equally troubling for nativists. Various prophets had warned that Rome would concentrate on the emerging West. In 1885 Josiah Strong warned of this threat: "As the West is to dominate the nation, she [Rome] intends to dominate the West. In the United States a little more than one-eighth [by 1916 it was closer to one-fifth] of the population is Catholic; in the territories taken together, more than one-third."[14] By 1909,

Catholicism dominated the church going population in sixteen states and territories—half of those were in the West.[15] Although not one of these states, Washington, the state with the greatest per capita of foreign-born residents in the period within the Union, displayed a considerable growth in its Catholic population. Between 1900 and 1910 the Catholic population of both Washington and Oregon more than doubled. The consequent growth in the region's clergy, institutions, property and religiously educated students reflected this massive expansion, as Table 2.1 illustrates.[16]

Table 2.1: Expansion of the Catholic Church in Oregon and Washington, 1890-1930.

	State	1890	1900	1910	1920	1930
Catholic population	Oregon	17,000	34,000	42,000	60,000	64,000
	Washington	40,000	42,000	90,000	106,000	120,000
Priests	Oregon	43	67	90	155	187
	Washington	39	83	133	222	296
Churches And Chapels	Oregon	60	82	113	131	191
	Washington	64	160	239	237?	216
Academies	Oregon	13	14	15	16	17
	Washington	3	20	24	18	18
Baptisms	Oregon	770	1000			1879
	Washington	n/a	n/a		4,298	3790
Children in Catholic Schools	Oregon	2,040	2,021	4,500	7,100	8,147
	Washington	n/a	2,600	n/a	(includes academies) 7,773	11,790
Parochial schools	Oregon	9	23	36	40	N/a
	Washington	n/a	17	32	46	60

Other non-Protestant religions expanded equally fast, although the Catholic Church continued to far outweigh the other main non-Protestant religions in numerical terms throughout the region as Table 2.2 demonstrates.[17]

The figures for the Northwest were even more striking at a local level. Taking the Catholic Churches, the example of Saint Mary's Parish at Mount Angel, in Oregon, although exceptional in terms of expansion, illustrates the trend. Between 1880 and 1920 the congregation expanded from 9 to 450 families. In 1910, when Father Dominic Waedenschwyler took over as parish priest at Saint Mary's, he had around 1,200 parishioners, by his retirement in 1929 he left some 2,000 to his successor.[18] As the period progressed and ethnic diversity in the area grew, the "new" Southern and Eastern European immigrant parishes grew especially fast. The Slovak parish of Saint Joseph in Tacoma grew from some 554 parishioners in 1919, when its records started, to 900 by 1924. Tacoma's Polish Catholic parish, Saint Stanislaus, later Saints Peter and Paul, saw its congregation expand from 112 in 1909 to 212 in 1924 and the city had an Italian parish, Saint Rita's, with some 3,000 members in 1924.[19]

Table 2.2: The Growth of the Leading non-Protestant Religions in Oregon and Washington, 1890-1926

	"Roman Catholic"	"Jewish Congregations"	"Eastern (Russian, Greek, Serbian and Romanian) Orthodox Churches"
Oregon 1890	35,566	1,165	N/A
Washington 1890	24,527	880	N/A
Oregon 1906	41,549	414 (Heads of families only)	311
Washington 1906	88,213	150 (Heads of families only)	574
Oregon 1916	49,728	1,135	3500
Washington 1916	97,418	2,950	2,065
Oregon 1926	55,574	13,050	486 (not all parishes reported)
Washington 1926	121,249	12,000	2,145

THE HISTORICAL CONTEXT

The size and organizational strength of the Catholic Church in America throughout the period begs the question as to why it was not accepted as an "American" phenomenon, just as, for instance, the Lutheran or Methodist churches had become. There were no widespread pleas for the restriction of Lutheran, or even Russian or Greek Orthodox, immigration on ostensible religious grounds as there were demands for the limitation of Jewish and Catholic immigration. In both cases there was a traditional animosity brought from Europe. In the Northwest there was a long tradition of anti-Catholicism. Roman Catholicism was well established in the Oregon Territory before the Oregon Trail opened up to bring in the bulk of early American settlers. The Catholic Church had established a mission in Oregon near Fort Vancouver in 1838, when two priests arrived at the request of French Canadian former Hudson's Bay Company trappers. A Methodist ministry had served the Fort and its environs since 1836. The two missions co-existed un-easily, serving their congregations and competing in ministering to, and the consequent conversion of, the aboriginal population. Even under the harsh conditions of the frontier, traditional doctrinal and political/ecclesiastical prejudices nourished the mutual suspicion between the two missions.

This underlying hostility dramatically surfaced on November 31, 1847. After having heard of a disturbance while baptizing nearby infant Cayuse Indian measles victims, Father John Baptist Brouillet arrived at the Waiilatpu American Board Mission. He found the missionary, Dr. Marcus Whitman, his wife Narcissa and eight others massacred by local Cayuse Indians. Having buried the victims, Brouillet set out to inform the nearby Reverend Henry Harmon Spalding of the massacre and warn him of the personal danger he faced. Brouillet was captured and held hostage by the Cayuse after having been followed by them to his meeting with Spalding. Although, according to his own account,[20] Brouillet successfully pleaded for Spalding's freedom and remained a hostage of the Cayuse, witnessing further atrocities for over a month, the Protestant minister swiftly accused the Catholic Church of complicity in the massacre:

> There is universal suspicion, strengthened by every day's silence, fastening down upon Catholicism through the part of some of its adherents [who] are said to have acted directly or indirectly on the bloody Tragedy. It is said that Catholics took part in the murders and in the distribution of the plundered goods....It is said that they actually placed the seal of their bloody approbation upon the bloody dead, by baptising the children [the measles victims] of the murderers.[21]

This account of the massacre entered local popular mythology. By the efforts of Spalding and his descendants in particular, Whitman became a symbol of Oregon's Protestant pioneer past. He also became a rallying figure for anti-Catholic nativists, a martyr to the greed and duplicity of the Catholic Church. The incident not only generated considerable overt anti-Catholic feeling in print—the controversy over the veracity of Spalding's claims raged into, and beyond, the period of this study—but it also demonstrated that the roots of later anti-Catholic sentiment were present even in the pre-statehood days of Oregon.[22]

This prejudice was informed by both local and national components. The arrival of the Catholic ministry in the Oregon Territory followed the publication in the East of two of the most influential anti-Catholic texts of nineteenth-century America. The New England Calvinist, revivalist and evangelist, Lyman Beecher's *A Plea For the West* (Cincinnati, 1835) laid out a program for the limitation of Catholic immigration—particularly to the then "frontier" of the Mississippi Valley and beyond. Along with Benedict Fenwick and Samuel F.B. Morse, of code fame, Beecher portrayed a struggle for souls which owed much to the contemporary perception of the Founding Fathers. American values needed to be upheld in a clash between democratic, egalitarian Protestantism, as he held existed in the United States, and the hierarchical, autocratic Vatican. In his account, the threat was not inherent in the United States but stemmed more from the fact that the Catholic Church was surrounding the Union in Spanish and French America and that these powers would launch a two-pronged attack on the as yet embryonic Protestantism of the West. Meanwhile, Jesuits and nuns were attempting to win over youngsters in Protestant areas—as with the Ursuline convent in Charlestown, Massachusetts[23]—throughout the country "undermining their Protestant education—until they become either skeptics or devotees, or at least the friends and apologists and auxiliaries of Catholics."[24]

These fears had parallels in the Oregon Territory. The aboriginal population was regarded as childlike, if often wayward and willful. During the bitter Cayuse War (1848-50) that followed the Whitman Massacre, the Jesuit Father Joset of Yakima demanded a repeal of the law prohibiting the distribution of firearms to the Indian population. Although Joset, justifiably, claimed the firearms were to be used for hunting and protection against marauding Blackfeet, when the arms arrived they were intercepted amid accusations of Catholic support of the "rebel" Cayuse and their proposals to use the Indians as tools of Catholic domination. A bill was proposed in the Oregon legislature for the expulsion of all Catholic clergy in the territory which was rejected by a two to one vote.[25] Nevertheless, this incident serves to illustrate the deep-rooted mistrust of both Catholic intentions and loyalty that was to become the linchpin of later objections to Papal authority. It also gives a point of origin for the persistent myth in the Northwest of Catholic arms-caches, such as the claim that St. Patrick's Church in Butte, Montana, housed "One thousand stands of arms ready to be used at a moments notice in shooting down APAs when the Pope should give the word."[26]

Beecher outlined a future in which the Catholic Church sought not only to foster these resident allies, but also proposed to bolster their numbers by shipping hordes of reactionary, impoverished Catholics to the New World.[27] Once in America this rabble would gain citizenship and vote according to their 'Vienna-Vatican' masters and re-create their union of church and state in the Mississippi Valley. This was given additional weight by fears of the seeming collapse of European Catholic monarchies—in France, with the enforced abdication of Charles X, and in the Austrian Empire, with Kossuth's persistence sapping Hapsburg security with the re-emergence of the polyglot Empire's perennial nationalities problem. Beecher argued that with the imminent demise of Europe's two great Catholic monarchies, the Vatican's policy would simply be to relocate to the New World. As anti-Catholic "hostility" grew in Europe—most notably tied in with accusations of British mishandling of the potato famine in late 1840s Ireland and later Bismarck's *Kulturkkampf*—the proportion of Catholic immigrants grew. It seemed to many nativists that Beecher's predictions were coming true:

> In 1895 the Catholic population [of the United States as a whole], which in 1840 numbered little more than a million, had risen to 12,500,000 and the annual increase from approximately 72,000 in 1850 had jumped to over 350,000 in 1890.[28]

As Catholicism grew in America, Beecher's immigration proposals increasingly formed the cornerstones of anti-Catholic restrictionism both in the country as a whole and the Northwest specifically. The solution, according to Beecher, lay in the preservation of American Protestantism through compulsory, all-encompassing, state-funded Protestant education, control of Catholic immigration and a limitation on granting of citizenship to those able, and willing, to assimilate into Protestant America.

While Beecher's anti-Catholicism drew on what the Catholics hoped to achieve, Maria Monk's *Awful Disclosures of the Hotel Dieu Nunnery of Montreal* (New York, 1836) claimed to expose the prevalent dishonesty, corruption and debauchery of Catholicism. The fraudulent nun's[29] account tells the pathetic tale of her imprisonment, sexual exploitation and eventual escape from the Hotel Dieu. The appeal of the book lay in an already extant market for salacious anti-Catholic tales in an era of growing anti-Catholic sentiment.[30] The tales of escaped nuns became a favorite ploy of nativists—the practice was potentially lucrative as well as patriotic.[31] However, the significance of the book, as with most others in its genre, lies in its re-enforcement to the "American" public of the archaic, un-natural, stultifying, "foreignness" of Catholicism. As Catholic immigration increased and the Catholic Church countered nativist propaganda, nativism became more reasoned, if, arguably, little more subtle. Roman doctrine and reliance on ritual was depicted as a cause of the poverty, backwardness and superstition of Catholic immigrants. Where Monk pointed out the results of Catholicism for the individual, others indicated the results for society:

> Thus, as she [the Catholic Church]...brutalized human nature by her system of celibacy applied to the gentle, she demoralized it by her system of persecution of the intelligent, the sincere and the free. It is enough to make the blood boil to think of the blind folly that has caused the foremost nations of struggling humanity to be heirs of such hateful ancestry and that has so bred our instincts as to keep them in an unnecessarily long continued antagonism with the essential requirements of a steadily advancing civilization.[32]

From both Beecher and Monk emerged a perception of the gullibility and "shackles and chains of blind obedience...[and] the bound conscience of a priest-ridden and church oppressed people"[33] which continued to make the Catholics in America targets for nativists across the Union, from the Know-Nothings to the Ku Klux Klan. If it was the overly traditional and superstitious nature of the Catholic Church that excited nativist animosity, the opposite can be held to be contributory to opposition to Jewish immigration. As with the wave of anti-Semitism which was sweeping Europe at the turn of the century, in America opposition to Jews had an element of their perceived addiction to ritual which chained them to poverty and backwardness:

> The thing that marked him [the "Russian and Polish Jew"] most conspicuously was his religious orthodoxy. The long, unkempt beards, the trailing hair, the little curls about the ears—these carefully preserved stigmata of traditional Israel were merely the outward signs of lives that were lived strictly according to the teachings of rabbinical law....The graces and decencies of life had never been his portion; he was about as ignorant and stupid a human being as the earth contained. [34]

Nevertheless, it was in their ready adoption of, and adaptation to, the modern, industrial society that many anti-Semites discovered the most abhorrent of "Jewish traits". Nor was this peculiar to America. The processes of modernization—most notably industrialization, with its consequent growth in capitalization and economies of scale—when combined with urbanization created anxiety among the lower middle and working classes throughout industrialized western-European countries. Often these fears expressed themselves in the form of "nationalist" religious intolerance—nationalism being one of the constants that could allay this insecurity, and religion being one of the definitions of that nationality, as demonstrated, for example, in Austrian, German and French anti-Semitism.[35]

In America the process was magnified by the massive increase in immigration from the 1890s, with many of these immigrants fleeing the results of both industrialization and religious persecution. Initially the contemporary model of European religious intolerance would appear to be inapplicable to the Northwest. The area was not subject to the massive influx of "alien" Eastern Europeans, particularly the *Ostjuden*, against whom, for instance, the Austrian Christian Socialists agitated. Early Jewish settlers in the region were frequently adventurous single males. A contemporary observer commented that they were often too few and too scattered to establish congregations with the result that they were less detectable to both the resident population and modern historians:

> searching for traces of Jewish pioneer settlers in this country [the Western United States], [one] encounters much greater difficulties in the West than along our Eastern seacoast....Unlike the Eastern settlements, Jewish immigrants going westward commonly migrated in isolated, individual, or family groups, generally insufficient in numbers to establish congregations, till long after the first settlement, and many lost track of the Jewish community forever.[36]

At the start of the period the area did not have a resident Jewish population of any magnitude to target, unlike, say, Romania or Bohemia. Seattle had a Jewish population of less than 1 percent throughout the period. Portland's Jewish population fluctuated between 2 and 3 percent.[37] Since the federal Constitution precluded the establishment of a state religion, the issues which troubled the nascent German nation over the position of Jews in the state could, at least outwardly, be avoided.

Even by comparison with America as a whole, the area appears relatively placid. The Northwest's early Jewish population tended to assimilate well. Oregon's early German Jewish immigrants found little overt prejudice. The lawyer Joseph Simon became one of the state's leading Republican politicians of the 1870s, serving in the State Senate, later as a senator in Washington D.C. and as mayor of Portland. The merchant Solomon Hirsch, partner in the largest dry goods firm "west of the Mississippi River", Flieshner and Meyer, served as a leading state senator for 11 years and as United States Minister to Turkey for three. Earlier, Portland had two Jewish mayors in succession—Bernard Goldsmith and Philip Wasserman. Jews were highly prominent in the commercial life of the area with such figures as Ben Selling, Sigmund Frank, Nathan Strauss, Joseph Shemansky, Isaac Gevurtz and Aaron Frank dominating Portland's retail and hotel industries as well as contributing to the city's infrastructure and cultural life.[38] There was no equivalent to the much-publicized 1877 exclusion of Joseph Seligman from Saratoga Springs. There were no anti-Semitic riots as erupted in New York in the 1850's. There were no overt displays of anti-Semitic hatred as in the 1913 Frank case, where anti-Jewish sentiment overtook a vigilante mob in Atlanta and led to the lynching of the Jew, Leo Frank, although it was widely known that he was not guilty of the rape or murder of a "white" girl.

NON-PROTESTANT IMMIGRATION AND THE STATE

This is not to say that there was not mistrust of Jews as well as Catholics. Both were subject to xenophobia that fed off an underlying mistrust of them as members of "alien" groups. The association of Catholics with allegiance to a tyrannical, feudal, corrupt and repressive papacy was a potent nativist argument. Unlike other immigrants, with the exception perhaps of the Jews, the Catholics brought with them, and attempted to militantly replicate and propagate the seeming instruments of their repression within America. To the nativist, the Catholics were behind a high proportion of American misfortunes. There was a hierarchy who trained immigrants to willingly follow orders whose sole objective seemed to be to bring down the American state. By the 1920s the region's Klan could point to overwhelming evidence of a long-term national Catholic conspiracy:

> Who assassinated Abraham Lincoln? A Jesuit. Who instigated the anti-draft riots in New York during the Civil War? A Jesuit archbishop. Who deliberately plotted to burn the cities of Chicago, Cincinnati, Philadelphia and St Louis at the same time? The minions of a foreign pope. Who led three regiments of Catholic troops to mutiny during the Mexican War? Jesuit

> Priests. Who assassinated Presidents Garfield and McKinley, Mayor Harrison of Chicago, and attempted the lives of Theodore Roosevelt and Mayor Gaynor of New York City? Roman Catholics. Who pleaded guilty to the most gigantic dynamiting conspiracy in the history of this nation? The McNamara brothers, faithful followers of the Pope of Rome. Who have been for years and still are trying to make trouble and an open rupture between England and the United States? The Jesuits in Congress and in editorial sanctums. Who are in charge of some of the most important government positions today? The Jesuits. These Machia-villians are unsurpassed in audacity and intrigue.[39]

The Catholic immigrant may have seemed innocent enough, but as with other immigrant groups—like the Japanese or Jews—beneath the seeming assimilation lurked a master plan for domination. Cuckoo-like, the Catholic organizations were dedicated to the overthrow of the Protestant states. For example in 1921 the *New York World's* investigation of the Klan cited a bogus "Fourth Degree" oath of the seemingly innocent Knights of Columbus which claimed that:

> His Holiness, the Pope…hath the power to depose heretical kings, princes, States, Commonwealths and Governments, and they maybe safely destroyed…[And that the initiate would seek to] wage war, relentless war, openly and secretly, against all heretics, Protestants and Masons. [Also] hang, burn, waste, boil, flay, strangle and bury alive those infamous heretics; rip up the stomachs and wombs of their women and crash their infants' heads against the walls in order to annihilate their execrable race.[40]

In somewhat less blood-curdling language nativists also pointed out the expansion of the Catholic Church in America. With its national hierarchy and apparently unified network of churches, charities and educational establishments, the Catholic Church was a dangerously powerful and wealthy organization.

The Catholic Church in the Northwest not only controlled many schools but also hospitals, orphanages and other institutions that threatened the constitutional separation of church and state.[41] The then leader of the Ku Klux Klan in 1926, Hiram Wesley Evans, perhaps most unequivocally states this argument when he declared:

> We [the Ku Klux Klan] believe that its [the Roman Catholic Church's] official position and its dogma, its theocratic autocracy and its claim to full authority in temporal as well as

> spiritual matters, all make it impossible for it as a church, or for its members if they obey it, to co-operate in a free democracy in which Church and State have been separated....Thus it is fundamental to the Roman Church to demand a supreme loyalty, overshadowing national or race loyalty, to a power that is inevitably alien, and which at the best must inevitably inculcate ideals un-American if not actively anti-American.[42]

Nativists particularly amplified this sentiment in times of crisis, with the "loyalty" of the Catholic immigrant to "American" ideals and American interests coming under even greater scrutiny in times of war.

During the Civil War the imposition of a district conscription lottery in New York was met by rioting among the Irish population in July 1863, which led nativists to question the commitment of the Catholic establishment to the Union cause in spite of the undoubted bravery of many Irish volunteers.[43] Catholic apologists claim it was the option of a $300 payment for exemption—from which the bulk of Catholics would be excluded for reasons of poverty—which sparked the riots, rather than any feeling of opposition to conscription into the Union cause itself. There is, however, evidence that the Irish felt that the beneficiaries of the Union cause were those who were seen to be in direct conflict with their interests—most notably the wealthy Protestant elite and the blacks, with whom they already felt to be in direct competition for jobs.[44] Catholic Archbishop John Hughes of New York was accused of complicity in the disturbances by his refusal to speak out against the riots—he was at the time incapacitated by illness. Nonetheless, he had previously summed up the ambivalence of many Irish in his congregation when he wrote to Simon Cameron in 1861:

> The Catholics as far as I know, whether of native or foreign birth are willing to fight to the death for the support of the constitution, the Government and the laws of the country. But if it should be understood that, with or without knowing it, they are to fight for the abolition of slavery, then, indeed, they will turn away in disgust from the discharge of what would otherwise be a patriotic duty.[45]

This ambivalence was equally apparent in the Spanish-American War of 1898 and its colonial aftermath, when the Catholic community was seen as having divided allegiances. America was at war with a Catholic country and then engaged in the quelling of a "ferocious" uprising of a Catholic population. In the Northwest, the increasingly outspoken Oregon Catholic newspaper—the "firm, fearless and aggressive"[46] Portland-based *Catholic Sentinel*—went as far as to condemn American intervention in the war.[47] The paper also repeatedly published details of allegations of atrocities committed by American troops in the war's aftermath in the Philippines.[48] Northwestern Catholic loyalty was again under scrutiny with America's involvement in the First World War.[49] The *Sentinel* took an anti-Allied stance prior to America's entry. The *Catholic Sentinel*'s editor, Father John O'Hara, claimed that the Allies were instrumental in starting the conflict. He supported German Catholics and condemned "British bigotry" in his September 24, 1914, editorial. He continued this line, even as America's position became increasingly overtly pro-Allied, blasting "the British Orders in Council, the censorship, the blacklist and interference with neutral mails."[50] At one point, the *Sentinel* published claims that the war was the result of anti-Catholic, anti-Austrian feeling in Europe whipped up by Freemasonry in France and Switzerland.[51]

Accusations of the hypocrisy of the Allies in their condemnation of unrestricted submarine warfare remained alive in the Irish-dominated Catholic community of the Northwest well after American entry into the European conflict. In addition, the Portland, Swiss, Benedictine-edited, but most important, German-language, *St. Josephs-Blatt* claimed that British sabotage had led to the sinking of the Lusitania on May 7, 1915. It cited "congressman Hobson" whose cousin had been warned, by an obviously well-informed Cunard agent, that "under no circumstances" should she travel on the ill-fated liner.[52] The much-maligned and misinterpreted Bishop Augustine Schinner of Spokane pointed out British maritime atrocities, while condemning German U-boat activity, claiming that "three of our ships were sunk by British mines, entailing loss of life" which added to accusations of the Wisconsin-born bishop's "German image".[53]

Added to this, well-aimed German wartime propaganda increased anti-Catholic feeling by feeding fears that America's Catholics sought the imposition of Catholic/Central Power domination via invasion from Mexico. Claims were made that at the very least Catholics hoped to violently re-assert the papal domination, which had diminished during the Diaz era, of America's southern neighbor:

> We are informed and believe that the Roman Catholic Hierarchy is now and has been for more one year last past [sic] actively engaged within the territory of the United States, fomenting and inciting revolution in the Republic of Mexico, and attempting to bring about a state of war between the Republic of Mexico and the United States of America.[54]

Nonetheless, Catholics were not as unanimous in their views as their opponents suggested. The local Catholic press tended to reflect the national origins of American Catholicism. While German, Austrian and Irish Catholics generally favored the Central Powers, Polish, Italian, at least from 1915, and French Catholics tended to support the Allies.[55] However, rather belatedly sensing the mood of the country, the Catholic press itself generally altered its position to one of unanimous, visible, if arguably less than heartfelt, support for the Allied cause once America joined the war. The one outstanding local exception was the *St. Josephs-Blatt* that continued to celebrate German victories as late as March 1918. Nonetheless, ultimately this last bastion of Catholic belligerency ceased publication for over a year in April 1918 when it was felt the sympathies of the editorship were incompatible with prevailing public sentiment.[56] Even the *Sentinel*'s fiery editor, Father O'Hara, reluctantly conceded: "The period of debate is closed. Now that we are in the world conflict, it is the business of every American to do his share in prosecuting the war that this country may obtain an honorable peace."[57]

The Catholic community responded to the super-patriotism of the war years by attempting to demonstrate the obligatory "One Hundred Percent Americanism". For example, the Church advocated the purchase of war bonds and the flying of American flags on Catholic buildings, and also responded to Woodrow Wilson's appeal for chaplains for the armed forces. In August 1917, the National Catholic War Council (NCWC) was formed, joining a variety of local bodies, to "disseminate correct information [on the war effort]...among our Catholic citizens," raise money and generally mobilize Catholic support for the war effort.[58] The Knights of Columbus directed centers for American soldiers in Europe, attempted to organize facilities for de-mobilization and participated in the activities of the American Legion.[59] German-Catholic Americans were exhorted to show particular patriotism by their press—the sin of "hyphenation" was played down. The *St. Josephs-Blatt*, while continuing its seemingly pro-German line, held that

> Now duty calls, the voice of the heart must be silent though the heart strings should break. German Americans must be loyal under all circumstances....We have sworn allegiance to the land of our choice, and we owe it as a duty to our descendants, to our fellow citizens, and to ourselves, to keep the oath faithfully and inviolably.[60]

Accusations of Catholic disloyalty continued. Some prominent church leaders never could accept that the Vatican was neutral. Even after the war, one of Woodrow Wilson's most staunch allies in the Northwest—the influential Seattle Presbyterian, Mark A. Matthews—was horrified at the prospect of the President visiting the Vatican in 1919 claiming that:

> The Pope has been pro-German from the beginning [of the war] ...if the president visits that damnable dago, it will do more harm and produce more disaster in the Democratic party than any act he could commit. For God's sake [Vice-President Marshall] wire him and tell him to stay away from the infernal pro-German dago.[61]

Supporters of America's intervention deliberately misconstrued Catholic statements and intentions. For example, Spokane's Bishop Schinner's support for the Papal mediation in Europe led him to be charged with defeatism when he criticized Woodrow Wilson's rejection of the peace proposals in August 1917.[62] German and Austrian Catholics remained targets of suspicious "Councils of Defense" and their enthusiastic vigilante enforcers. Bogus Knights of Columbus and Jesuit oaths[63] re-surfaced and the perennial accusations of arms caches led to claims of the forcible searching of Church buildings and private homes.[64] Such accusations retained a certain potency. Even after the war the Catholics' loyalty was questioned. For example an article sympathetic to the Klan published in 1925 claimed that some 90 percent of all wartime deserters were Catholics.[65]

Many Catholics felt that their loyalty was beyond suspicion. Some outspoken Catholic critics continued to resent the pressure for rapid Americanization, claiming that the pressures for patriotic conformity represented little more than venomous, self-serving nativism:

> "Americanizers" [are] the latter day know-nothings...the man or woman who would tamely submit to a large part of what goes on under the name of Americanization is not fit to be in America...."Americanization" [demonstrates] the spirit of the boy who abuses his new puppy "so that he will know that he's my dog"....[It] may destroy the delicate vital bonds that are destined by nature to pass over from parent to children transforming the latter from selfish, greedy little hearts into generous, self-forgetting citizens who will labor for the common good.[66]

By and large, the "Super Patriotism" generated by American entry into the war tended to dissipate anti-Catholicism and focus public attention onto fears of "Prussian" militarism rather than the Vatican-Hapsburg alliance, or other such indications of "Papal-Hun" interaction, despite the best efforts of the anti-Catholic nativists.[67] Besides which, in the Northwest, the majority of German Catholics tended to live in rural areas and were protected from the worst excesses of "One Hundred Percentism" by their acceptance as a part of the community and their isolation. Nevertheless, for the Nordic anti-Catholics the war still offered an insidious message of the inferiority and undesirability of Catholic immigration—largely played down due to the war effort—but it was still to remain strong enough to inform understanding of the theories which were to underpin the 1921 and 1924 immigration acts.[68]

These theories relied on an interpretation of a tribal, racial reasoning for Anglo-Saxon Protestantism. This "Nordic world" was involved in one of its periodic "civil wars", a suicidal trial of strength, as such advocates of Nordic racial/religious theory as David Starr Jordan or Madison Grant saw it.[69] This was the mythical, heroic cleansing of ancient peoples celebrated by Wagner and

Tennyson. It was the outcome of the inherent, reasoned but aggressive need within the "Teutonic peoples" for dominance and expansive democracy—the result of their centuries old innate racial desire for personal freedom: "Ruskin once said that "war is the foundation of all high virtues and faculties of men." Another writer, Hardwick, declares that "war is essential to the life of a nation; war strengthens a nation morally, mentally and physically."[70]

However, the "inferior races" ignored these noble aims and merely sought to use the struggle for their own advantage. The Jews fed their purses through the exploitation of commercial opportunities generated by the war and in 1917 toppled the Tsarist regime, implementing an immoral and unnatural system designed to punish Gentiles—a system they longed to export throughout Europe and the New World.[71] The Japanese used the opportunity to continue to successfully expand their Asian territory into German protectorates in China.[72] Those peoples subservient to Catholicism's demands, most particularly the American-Catholics—"hyphenated" and therefore doubly untrustworthy—supported the Irish in their treacherous mutiny against Nordic Britain[73] and their post-war terrorist demands for a Catholic Irish Free State. To the Nordics this was taken as symptomatic of a more sinister plot—to divide and conquer the Anglo-Saxons, while emigrating en-masse to, and then breeding prodigiously within, the Protestant New World. The plan hinged on exacerbating frictions between the leading nations—"in order to separate the two great Protestant countries—our own and England", in this case, over the issue of the Irish Free State.[74]

To the Nordic nativist, the Catholic immigrant, like the Jew, with some exceptions, never fully assimilated into American society, he merely existed on the periphery of it—all the time owing allegiance first to the papacy and the Vatican's "American" representatives. Anglo-Saxon America's ideals were not his. His beliefs were interpreted by nativists as primarily pan-Catholic. Even when displaying their patriotism, it was often seen as that of hyphenated American-Catholics rather than One Hundred Percent Americans. For example, Father J.H. Sherry's eulogy of Catholic self-sacrifice and patriotic loyalty given to the 1917 National Catholic Education Association conference could not escape accusations of "hyphenation" when he zealously pointed out:

> Who was the first to lay down his life in the landing of Vera Cruz—Haggerty, an Irish Catholic. When we declared war on Germany who was the first to fall in defense of the flag and now lies buried in the broad Atlantic? Eopulucci, an Italian Catholic. But the Irish Catholic and Italian Catholic were above all, American Catholics. [75]

Bishop Augustine Schinner fed accusations of his pro-German sympathies when in an attempt to demonstrate his loyalty he stated that "Next to fighting to defend my faith, I would fight to defend my country."[76] In the Northwest, the Catholic Church vociferously fought allegations of less-than-total loyalty within the Catholic communities. The leading Catholic papers promoted demonstrations of their integration—detailing the "Preparedness" and "Americanization" schemes of such bodies as the National Catholic War Council, the National Conference of Catholic Charities and the National Catholic Educational Association. They also launched attacks on the anti-Catholic lobby as being divisive to the country in such times of crisis. For example in Portland Father O'Hara even went as far as to compare the actions of the "rebellious Irish" with the "freedom fighters" of the American Revolution. However, he could not resist also baiting the anti-Catholics by insinuating those who opposed the Easter Rising were not supporting Wilson's crusade for self-determination or acknowledging the rebellious roots of the United States. In the same editorial he claimed that the Philippines should be granted, what would amount to Catholic Home Rule:

> A hundred and forty years ago a handful of English subjects, distantly related to some of us, rebelled against England with the object of setting up an independent American republic. The British and American Tory publications of that day regarded those who had taken arms against England as ungrateful rebels who deserved to be hanged. The same publications were also vastly indignant because France, at war with England, aided the American revolutionists in their efforts to establish an independent republic. History has a habit of repeating herself. In this case she has done so with perfect exactness....
> Whereas when [Irish] Home Rule was wrung from the reluctant [British] government in 1914, there was a spirit of forgiveness, if not forgetfulness abroad....[Such] a bill was such as might be expected to be given to the Philippine Islands and [would not be]...unworthy [of]...a nation [such as the United States] which has given to the world statesmen, lawyers, soldiers, ecclesiastics of many denominations; a nation which leads the morality in the world.[77]

Given the prevalent anti-Catholic sentiment in the Northwest, O'Hara's aggressive and provocative tone did little to improve Catholic/nativist relations. Furthermore, the Catholic press cheerfully pointed out the rapid growth of their church in the area, which made it, throughout the period, the largest single religious denomination not only in the Northwest, but the country as a whole.

Just as Catholics were associated with allegiance to an "un-American" power, the same was true of a proportion of the Jewish element of the "new" immigration. The issue of anti-Semitism points out one of the fundamental regional differences in the restrictionist debates in the Pacific Northwest. The conservative nature of Oregon worked in favor of the assimilated Jewish population, enabling them to largely fend off the power of the Klan in the state and maintain a powerful political presence in the State and Federal legislatures, as well as in the commercial activities within the state. Jewish political activity in Oregon had frequently been associated with conservatism. Joseph Simon's Republican "political machine" had been open to accusations of sectionalism, self-interest and reactionism in the 1870s and his legacy was reflected in the political stance of Portland's Jewish commercial elite.[78] Although only ever representing a maximum of 3 percent of Portland's population in the early twentieth century, the city's Jewish population claimed 8 percent of the entries in Portland's directory of the social elite, the *Blue Book.*[79]

By contrast, the growing fear, and activities, of radicals in Washington fed the nativists' national association of Jewish immigrants with Bolshevism, revolution and social unrest.[80] As Henry Ford, one of America's most vocal anti-Semites, claimed, the Jew was motivated by a plan outlined in the *Protocols of the Elders of Zion.* This interpretation held that the ultimate Jewish aim was similar to the IWW's syndicalist objectives of "boring from within" to achieve their "un-American", revolutionary, aims:

> In Eastern Europe Bolshevism and Zionism often seem to grow side by side, just as Jewish influence molded Republican and Socialist thought throughout the Nineteenth century, down to the Young Turk revolution in Constantinople hardly more than a decade ago—not because the Jew cares for the positive side of radical philosophy, not because he desires to be a partaker in Gentile nationalism or Gentile democracy, *but because no existing Gentile system of government is ever anything but distasteful to him.*
> ...If it is anti-Semitic to say that Communism in the United States is Jewish, so be it; but to the unprejudiced mind it will look very like Americanism. [81]

Ford's obsession with Jewish plans for world domination followed in a tradition which had drawn on strains present in populist thought from Minnesotan Ignatius Donnelly's critique of utopianism[82] to Georgian Thomas E. Watson's disillusioned ventures into religious bigotry following the collapse of his agrarian reform dreams.[83] This early Populist anti-Semitism stressed the importance of Jewish involvement in the monopolistic trusts which threatened to strangle the predominantly extractive industries of the Northwest with their refusal to "free up" silver coinage, their suppression of prices by unscrupulous middlemen and merchants and their unfair elevator and transport charges. Fears of Jewish "Gold-Trusts" combined with the prevalence of Jewish supply merchants in the mining and agricultural areas to inform a view of Jews as a close-knit community of alien habits with peculiar rituals whose greed ignored international boundaries and national, let alone, regional, interests.[84] To his enemies, the Jew was "unalterably fixed in his instincts, character and thoughts by centuries of racial selection and development...[and] thinks first only for his own people, works only with and for them, cares entirely for their interests, considers himself always one of them, and never an American."[85] Alongside this, the industrial troubles of the post-war era and the growth in political insecurity caused by the "Jewish led" Russian revolution displayed themselves in the anti-radical strain of anti-Semitism.

The Northwest's Jews were accused of internationalism during this highly charged era of super-patriotism and xenophobia, both as agents of capitalist greed and as un-American revolutionaries. Underlying this was the nativist's fear that without a restriction on their immigration these undesirables would become as populous as they were in their "colonies" on the East Coast:

> Jews are either Bolsheviks, undermining our government, or are Shylocks in finance or commerce who control and corrupt Christians as borrowers or employees. It is repugnant to a true Christian to be bossed by a Sheenie. And in some parts of America the kikes are so thick that a white man can hardly find room to walk on the sidewalks.[86]

If the radical immigrant was repeatedly attacked for his religious-ethnic background, he was also, somewhat ironically, often condemned for his atheism. The atheistic socialist, Bolshevik or anarchist was not only a menace to the political stability of the state but also was portrayed as a threat to the moral tenor of society. Sometimes it was the stultifying nature of non-Protestant religions which were blamed for producing lawlessness, as with McKinley's assassin Leon Czolgosz's anarchism which the *Pacific Baptist* claimed came about 'as a reaction against the repressive nature of his Catholic upbringing'.[87] At other times it was the failure of his religion to condemn anti-social, even criminal, behavior. This link between an immigrant's religion and his criminality was particularly relevant with reference to the Eighteenth Amendment, especially in the Northwest where the temperance movement had won two early victories. Anti-saloon laws had been adopted in Washington State in 1912 and Oregon in 1916. Many Protestant groups shared a condemnation of the Catholic Church's attitude to alcohol, which was seen as at best ambivalent, if not positively hostile to prohibition. That in itself re-enforced Protestant hostility to Catholic immigration. It placed many Protestant churches alongside the Klan in their condemnation of the influence of aliens in American society and the un-American behavior of those whose criminal activities defied the Volstead Act.

Such infractions of the law were seen as typical of the morality of the renewed post-war stream of non-Protestant immigration—un-American morals, bred in un-American "colonies", unchecked by "un-American and un-scriptural"[88] churches. A typical view was expressed by the sociologist E.A. Ross in 1914:

> In the Neapolitan the intoxication of the lottery takes the place occupied by alcoholic intoxication in the Anglo-Saxon....It

> was frequently stated to the members of the Immigration Commission [Dillingham] in southern Italy that crime had greatly diminished in many communities because most of the criminals had gone to America. One Italian official at Messina stated that several years ago southern Italy was a hotbed of crime, but that now very few criminals were left. When asked as to their whereabouts, he replied, " Why, they are all in the United States."[89]

The statisticians drew a correlation between the immigrant and crime, statistics which were grasped by eager nativists in the Northwest. Albert Johnson's *Washingtonian* reported in 1921 that Raymond B. Fosdick, of the Bureau of Social Hygiene, had concluded "that [the] preponderance of crime in this country is augmented by unassimilated or poorly assimilated [and by inference, non-Protestant] races."[90] This added to the already extant nativist tradition of viewing the Catholic immigrant as morally undesirable. The Irish had traditionally been seen as more prone to drunkenness, a view which census statistics seemingly re-enforced. Table 2.3 shows how one immigrant group—in this case the Italians—propagated such a connection in order to further their own social standing. [91] The Italians, particularly the southern Italians, were seen as criminal and violent—"[as] ferocious and desperate men as ever gathered in a modern city in the time of United States—medieval criminals who must be dealt with under modern laws."[92]

Table 2.3: Arrests and Deaths Due to Alcoholism

Country of birth	Number of arrests for drunkenness and disorderly conduct (per 100,000)	Number of deaths from alcoholism (1900 census) per 100,000
America	285.9	2.4
Of which White	202.6	-
Negro	424.9	-
England	488.5	8.3
Ireland	1540.1	17.7

The other major Catholic nationality, the Poles, were viewed as superstitious, brutish and ignorant—

> Every [Slavic] married man...strikes his wife black and blue at least once a month, or spreads a box on the ear over her whole face, or else people are likely to say that he is afraid of his wife. Their popular proverbs corroborate this, as for example: " He who does not beat his wife is no man", " Strike a wife and a snake on the head ", "One devil is afraid of the cross, the other (the wife) of a stick." "The dog may howl, but the wife must hold her tongue." In one wedding-song the bride

> begs her husband: " Strike your wife only with good cause and when she has greatly vexed you." In another folk-song the young wife sings: "What sort of husband are you to me? You do not pull my hair, nor do you strike me!" [93]

Further, other non-Protestant groups were seen as equally morally suspect. Hackneyed prejudices were inherited from other areas of the Union. Jews were condemned for their all-encompassing and over-weaning avariciousness, Orthodox Russians and Greeks for their sub-servience and the Asian religions for their seeming fatalistic acceptance of filth and squalor.

At other times it was the immigrant's repudiation of religion which caused hostility. This happened within the non-Protestant communities themselves. The author of the IWW's notorious 1905 preamble, a certain Father Thomas J. Hagerty, found himself defrocked for his most notorious sermon.[94] This was hardly surprising, for the Industrial Workers of the World soon became notorious for their "Godlessness". They mocked Christian imagery and institutions—most notably, as at the Spokane "Free Speech Fight" of 1909, the Salvation Army.[95] The feeling that the denial of IWW rights to hold street meetings should apply to all bodies, regardless of their religious or political affiliation largely sparked this hostility.

Many of the Jewish leaders of American socialism—for example Benjamin Fiegenbaum, Morris Winchevsky and Emma Goldman—openly attacked religion, often most vehemently Judaism. This led not only to hostility from Protestant nativists, but also growing Jewish suspicion of the implications of free immigration for American Jewry.[96] The approach of Morris Hillquit, one the most eloquent Jewish spokesmen and elegant tacticians of contemporary American socialism, is instructive. Aware of the dangers inherent in alienating the Jewish and other religious establishments, Hillquit tried to stress the nature of contemporary socialism as concerned with the economic and political spheres—"It [socialism] is not concerned with institutions of marriage and religion."[97]

The "institutions of marriage", influenced the national immigration debate in a variety of ways. Not only were Jews implicated in the immoral "white slave traffic", so were their fellow "Asiatics", the Japanese and Chinese. This condemnation was re-enforced by the fact that immigrants were often the undesirable and, equally often, reluctant victims–prostitutes. However according to the 1910 census the Irish and English would appear to have produced the greatest number of prostitutes out of a, small, selection of European nationalities, as demonstrated in Table 2.4.[98] Nevertheless, ironically, nativist opposition was also re-enforced by the commonly believed insinuation that this criminal trade was carried on by immoral, licentious and avaricious non-Protestants, particularly Jews—"Next to his lust for money, the strongest passion in the Jew is his licentiousness."[99]

Table 2.4: Numbers of Prostitutes by Country of Birth

Country of Birth	Total Foreign born Resident in the U.S.	Arrested for Prostitution	Ratio of Convicted Prostitutes per 100,000 of U.S. Residents
Italians	1,343,070	14	1
Russians	1,184,382	34	2.9
Germans	2,501,181	38	1.5
English	958,934	75	7.8
Irish	1,352,155	112	8.3

All of the early twentieth century immigration acts refined the prohibition of this international trade and the 1910 Mann Act extended these prohibitions to internal state traffic. The declining birth rate among Protestant "native "Americans" led to condemnation of the fecundity of the "new" immigrants. For example, as early as 1868, Matthew Deady—an ally of Oregon's Jewish community—voiced this fear eloquently:

> These children of Shem [Oregon's nascent Jewish community]—at least the German part of them—are a domestic, home loving people. As a rule they marry young and faithfully obey the first commandment given to man and woman—"Be fruitful and multiply." How long will the cultivated American of Yanky [sic] descent, with his maximum family of one delicate child, successfully compete with this healthy and fruitful people for the lead and mastery in commerce and business.[100]

Deady was writing before the bulk of the "new", non-Protestant, immigration began to impact on the East Coast, let alone the West. Many others in America amplified his apprehension as southern and eastern Europeans and Asians arrived in increasing numbers from the 1890s on. These fears reached a crescendo in 1916 with the Nordic supremacist Madison Grant's *Passing of the Great Race*, which outlined the terrible threat the gradual erosion of America's Anglo-Saxonism by the incoming tide of "inferior" races. Central to this Nordic nativist insecurity was a dread of miscegenation. While this was of particular concern on the predominantly male, wage earner's frontier, in the Northwest this was largely associated with the threat of the Oriental immigrant and arguably had little, if any, direct religious component. Unlike the California model where, for example, Mexican Catholicism could provide direct linkage to, and evidence of, the undesirability of a large and physically recognizable population, in Washington in particular the very diversity and often insularity of the "New" immigration defied such simple religious/ethnic definition. Nevertheless, there were less overt examples. In the case of "East Indians", as with Jews, religion was used to distinguish racial/ethnic grouping. This interchanging of prejudice can be confusing. For example, objections to "Hindu" immigrants, particularly in the cases of the Bellingham, Washington, and St. John, Oregon, "anti-Hindu riots" of 1907 hinged more on the threat they posed to the area's wage levels than religious intolerance, per se.[101] Nevertheless, local objections also contained elements which drew on the "immoral" activities, more often than not the sexual behavior of immigrants. The Bellingham "anti-Hindu riot" of September 1907 was partly the result of public outrage at the dress of, and cohabitation of, both sexes in the "Hindu's" squalid barracks.[102]

More widespread was opposition to "free-thinking", often atheist radicals—who, if not actually foreign-born immigrants, were often associated with ideals influenced by "un-American" groups. For example a wartime visit for the Bureau of Immigration in August 1918 to the Puget Sound communitarian Home Colony claimed that of the "250 to 300" who were present at the time of the investigation "most were foreign-born" and only "a few" had applied for naturalization.[103] Although attacks were made on the sexual mores of radicals in general, it was often women, such as "The Rebel Girl", Elizabeth Gurley Flynn or Emma Goldman, who bore the brunt of such attacks. They were frequently condemned for "betraying their sex" by condemning what they called the "slavery of marriage" and condoning cohabitation, birth control, lesbianism and/or hatred of men.[104] One of the most striking examples of this opposition is the condemnation of "free love" within the Utopian, communitarian settlements of Puget Sound in the late nineteenth and early twentieth centuries. Accusations that the "so-called socialists...anarchists [and]...free lovers [of the Freeland Colony, were] living in lewd, open and notorious adultery."[105] This added to the popular perception of the moral undesirability of radical immigrants and the danger they presented to Protestant American society, particularly in the paranoid environment of post-war America.

RELIGIOUSLY BASED NATIVIST POLITICAL GROUPS IN THE NORTHWEST

While these accusations of immigrant disloyalty, immorality and criminality fed an undertone of prejudice in the Northwest it required direct challenges to the status quo for them to break surface and form coherent movements—movements capable of bringing pressures for the exclusion of undesirable, non-Protestant immigrants into the local, regional and national forums. Unsurprisingly, exclusionist tendencies were far greater in times of the larger "waves" of immigration or changes in the sources of immigrants, in times of economic hardship and social division, as well as in times of national crisis or war. This is demonstrated by the rise of the American, or "Know-Nothing", Party in the 1850s. This was the direct result of the largest wave of Irish immigration to date, which followed the Irish famines of the 1840s.[106] Similarly the Immigration Restriction League was formed in 1894, coinciding with the emergence of the massive wave of Southern and Eastern European immigration in the period 1890 to 1914. On the West Coast anti-Chinese feeling was to some extent fuelled by the completion of the trans-continental railroad, as well as the collapse of the mining speculation boom and the consequent strains which these events placed on the employment market of the area.

In order to be successful, restrictionist groups required not only cohesive, relevant arguments and achievable goals, but also national appeal, or, as with the anti-Chinese movement, effective political leverage or public sympathy outside the area. Most important the effective restrictionist lobby required the ability to remain relevant as circumstances changed—the ability to adapt and mutate—in both time and place. For example the Immigration Restriction League, which from 1894 until 1917 single-mindedly pushed for America to adopt a literacy clause to control immigrants, managed to ally itself with the growing "scientific" exclusionist thinkers in such organizations as the American Breeders Association and their successors in the eugenics movement. The anti-Chinese Sandlot Movement evolved into the Asiatic Exclusion League. However, the Know-Nothing Party, although remaining the byword for anti-Catholic exclusion, disappeared as a coherent party organization in 1860. To some extent it had failed to remain relevant as the abolitionist debate and the issue of secession from the Union overtook fears of Papal influence.[107]

Nevertheless, although the Know-Nothing Party's fiery ambitions were dowsed in the conflicts of the Civil War, embers of its constituent parts remained active throughout America. The Junior Order United American Mechanics[108] and the Scottish Rite Masons[109] continued beyond 1860 and their nativist theories, particularly anti-Catholic sentiments, informed the restrictionist organizations which re-emerged with the economic difficulties and the large proportion of Catholics in the mass-migration of the 1890s. These changes coincided with the Catholic Church taking a higher profile in American affairs. Democrat victories in 1890 and 1892 increased the number of Irish politicians in office. The massive October 1892 "Columbus" celebrations of the Catholic Church re-enforced the power of the "alien" Catholic Church in American society. Added to this, in 1893 the Catholic Church mounted a massive display of its influence in America at the Chicago World Fair and in the same year Archbishop Francesco Satolli, the first permanent Papal delegate arrived in America.

In response, the Protestant nativists rallied their forces. Two organizations emerged in the late 1880s dedicated to fighting for the Constitutional separation of Church and State. The first, the American Protective Association was fundamentally an organization of the Middle West, which spread to the West. The other, the National League for the Protection of American Institutions, the NLPAI, drew its main strength from the East Coast Protestant elite and remained within that elite stratum, even as its influence spread. These bodies differed fundamentally from their unsuccessful precursor. Where the Know-Nothings were dedicated to reducing the Catholic immigrants' options of integration into American society, their 1890s nativist successors sought to halt the results of that integration as well as limiting future Catholic immigration: "Whereas Know-Nothingism was due to the jealousy of the growing political strength of the [Irish] Catholic immigrant...APAism [sic] in the West was perhaps due to the envy of the growing social and industrial strength of the Catholic Americans." [110] Moreover, although both of these organizations had national ambitions and saw themselves as national bodies, they differed from the Know-Nothings in their attempts to wield pressure via lobbying rather than the establishment of a stand-alone third political party. While the NLPAI sought to unite Protestant anti-Catholic prejudice by appealing to the similarities between America's diverse Protestant religious groups,[111] the APA attempted to utilize the existing Republican Party organizational apparatus[112] in order to promote their anti-Catholic platform and disseminate their often spurious propaganda.[113] Such strategies had the effect that while the overall objectives of the APA were national, their policies and methods often appeared regional—the tone of the movement being dictated by the hostility, or otherwise, of the local population to Catholics.

The NLPAI remained primarily an elite and East Coast institution. The organization's roll call of members contained politicians such as Benjamin Harrison's vice-president Levi P. Morgan; writers such as James Fenimore Cooper; academics such as David Starr Jordan; financiers such as Cornelius Vanderbilt (Junior), John D. Rockefeller and J. Pierpont Morgan; and publishers such as George Putnam and Charles Scribner. The most important figure in the NLPAI in the Northwestern context was the railway and publishing magnate Henry Villard, whose spectacular financial reverses from 1884 probably contributed to his belief in a Catholic conspiracy.[114] The organization largely confined itself to putting high-level pressure on Congress to limit Catholic power. In September 1889, one nativist complained to another that the NLPAI consisted of men who circulated " a little printed stuff and then drop off in their easy chairs—and say they are too old for political work."[115] By contrast the APA attempted to influence political opinion at a more local level. APA recruiting drives in the Northwest began to be reported in early 1894. By March of that year the region's newspapers, most notably the Portland-based *Catholic Sentinel*, devoted increasing space to the movement's activities.[116]

As the organization gained more influence—growing from some 28 lodges in Oregon in 1894 to 178 lodges by 1896[117]—the APA's original anti-Catholic stance became increasing rabid, particularly in the already anti-Catholic Northwest. This growth was fed by the 1893 economic slump and the consequent industrial unrest, events which coincided with a shift in the APA's leadership away from the ageing Henry Francis Bowers to the more driven William "Whiskey Bill" Traynor. The organization portrayed the influence of Catholics as being behind many of Western America's ills. From an attempt to limit Catholic patronage in politics, the emphasis shifted to a declared ambition to outlaw the Catholic faith in the region. The original 1887 American Protective Association statement of principles made in Clinton, Iowa, claimed that the organization respected the constitutional right of "every man in this country...to worship God according to the dictates of his conscience." Nevertheless, the organization's anti-Catholicism was contained in its condemnation of "the right of any set of men to control and manipulate the political affairs of this country to the aggrandizement of any ecclesiastical power."[118] In March 1895 the movement began to make a real political impact in Oregon. The founding principles of the APA lodge in Corvallis upheld the association's 1887 creed with its seeming open-mindedness but with an even stronger caveat that excluded toleration of "any ecclesiastical powers not created and controlled by American citizens."[119] By October 1895 as the APA became more confident of its power, a Seattle APA lecturer—"a fellow named Lansing"—was advocating not only a halt on Catholic immigration but also the "banish[ing] of every Romish priest and prelate from our shores, tomorrow."[120]

In reality the APA proved something of a paper tiger. The power, or rather absence of *real* power, wielded by the organization is demonstrated in the 1896 election. The APA held itself to be "the strongest and purest political force that the Western world ever knew." APA leadership claimed that it held "the political balance of power in the United States, with its membership of over 2,500,000 persons, who influence nearly 4,000,000 votes."[121] Nevertheless, it failed to significantly influence the 1896 presidential campaign. Polarized by national organizations which fused with both Parties—the APA with the Republicans[122] and the Populists with the Democrats—the election has been seen as the first modern campaign, and arguably set the agenda for much of the "Progressive" era's reforms.[123] However, so typical of the period, the issue of immigration, which was to be so vital throughout the era, played only an oblique role in the election—in spite of the fact that both parties had immigration restriction as one of their political planks. Also, the place of Catholicism in the state was muddled and muddied by the need of both established political parties to rally disparate and often, what were to them, unfamiliar supporters, by a general concentration on a single issue and its perceived consequences. That issue was not anti-Catholicism, or even immigration; it was the money supply.

The fusion Democrat/Populist Party under William Jennings Bryan concentrated its campaign on the free-silver question, largely avoiding the equally controversial tariff and labor/immigrant aspects of the Populists' Omaha and St Louis platforms.[124] Conversely, the Republican/APA union concentrated on the damage which could be done to the economy by freeing up the money supply, while not wishing to alienate its wealthy East Coast core constituency by openly advocating restriction of what Andrew Carnegie saw as the "golden stream" of cheap immigrant labor. Furthermore, Bryan's overtly Protestant evangelical style and deeply held Protestant beliefs, as well as his agrarian program alienated some of the fundamentally urban Catholic vote.[125] Ironically, William McKinley's, at best, ambivalent anti-Catholicism[126] and accusations of support for him by, and from, Catholics threatened to separate the "kite labeled APA [from]—the tail, GOP."[127]

This division was illustrative of the pre-Klan position of anti-Catholic nativism in the Northwest. While commanding significant popular support, anti-Catholicism failed to concentrate that support into an effective political lobby. Although McKinley carried Oregon and lost Washington State, as Table 2.5

shows.[128] The 1896 Republican election campaign was a nativist disaster. The Oregon State Secretary of the APA, J.T. Haynes', prediction that "when it comes to the test we [the nativist organizations] will all pull together"[129] proved overly optimistic. Rather, what the 1896 election verified was that, although anti-Catholicism was a powerful force, particularly in Oregon, it was not sufficient, of itself, to propel nativism. Rather, the area's nativists demonstrated a fundamental failure to utilize anti-Catholicism as a political tool for little other than to provide a temporary forum for a few ambitious individuals. They failed to unite their disparate organizations into bloc support for one or other political party. Instead, other issues obscured anti-Catholic cohesion. The Junior Order American Mechanics (JOAM) maintained its allegiance to McKinley in the face of divisive APA accusations that he was a Catholic sympathizer. Urged on by Mark Hanna's skilful management of the dangers inherent to job security in free-silver inflation, the Junior Order viewed anti-Catholic issues as subordinate to reviving the economy.[130] Further, the Order was upset by the APA policy of allowing naturalized immigrants membership rather than restricting the movement merely to native-born Americans.[131] A "prominent member" of the Oregon Junior Order, Council Number Two, summed up the organization's mistrust of the APA at a meeting in Portland in March 1896:

> The membership of the APA includes a lot of foreigners, who are strangers to all American sentiments, and they are the people who are stirring up this hubbub about McKinley. If the APA wants to fight McKinley, let them go ahead and fight him. They will get no help from the Junior Order. That organization stands for Americanism. Its membership is composed of native-born Americans, and it does not take in the foreign-born riffraff that happens to be opposed to the Catholic Church. I don't see why the APA wants to oppose a good American like McKinley, but there is probably something behind it that does not show on the surface.[132]

Table 2.5: The Results of the 1896 Presidential Election in Washington and Oregon

Candidate	W.J. Bryan	W. McKinley	J.M. Palmer	J. Levering
Party	Democrat	Republican	"Gold Democrat"	Prohibition
Oregon	46,662	48,779	977	919
Washington State	51,557	39,124	1,499	805

In addition, as if these cleavages were not enough, the Orange Order, which composed much of the APA membership—including, the Canadian-born, Traynor himself—further divided the anti-Catholic vote by supporting Bryan. The Oregon APA's bankruptcy and subsequent collapse in 1898 re-enforced the organization's inability to unite nativists purely through anti-Catholicism, even in traditionally anti-Catholic Oregon.

However, the APA's anti-Catholic program lived on in the Pacific Northwest—surfacing throughout the first two decades of the twentieth century with tales of escaped nuns, attempts to form successor movements and perhaps most notably with the persistence of the question of state and parochial schooling. The education issue provided a nativist rallying point, just as it had in 1906 with the Japanese in San Francisco. Similarly, as anti-Japanese pressures had required the focus of land-ownership to intensify local feeling, anti-Catholicism found its point of convergence with the educational debate. The issue highlighted the religious differences between the alien Catholic and the "American" Protestant in increasingly fashionable "Nordic" terms—particularly given the performance of "Catholic" immigrants in the wartime IQ tests. The notorious IQ tests became a robust tool for the classification of races in the post-war era, largely reinforcing existing stereotyping. The emigrants from Catholic donor nations fared as badly as the majority of Southern and Eastern Europeans. This confirmed the traditional prejudice of Catholic ignorance—the consequence of the dominance of Catholic youth by a tyrannical priesthood and their inculcation of an unquestioning nature—"the Catholics, no matter where they dwell, are considered lower in the scale of mental cultivation and refinement than the Protestant....[This] degradation is due to their being deprived of the Bible by their priesthood." [133]

This prejudice also re-enforced doubts of Catholic commitment to principle of the separation of Church and State and the whole ideal of Americanization. The solution harked back to Lyman Beecher. By outlawing "Parochial Schools" of all denominations the curriculum could be controlled, "American" values promoted and, in theory, non-Protestant immigration restricted, or at least the undesirable affects limited—"the Bible and the Common Schools were the two stones of the mill that would grind Catholicity out of the Catholics."[134] The schools issue was by no means novel, or restricted to the West—in 1813 the Free School Society of New York had raised the question.[135] Nonetheless, it was seen as particularly relevant to the settling and governance of the "frontier" states. As early as 1835, the high priest of early anti-Catholicism, Lyman Beecher, had seen this educational battle as the "conflict which is to decide the destiny of the West...[a struggle which would result in the dominance of either] superstition, or evangelical light; of despotism or liberty."[136] If non-Protestant, parochial, education was not checked he held that "by immigration and Catholic education, we will become...a Catholic nation."[137] The educational power of the Catholic Church was the area in which the APA achieved some success. Nationally, the APA managed to cut substantially, if not entirely halt, the practice established by President Grant in 1870 of giving federal grants to religious, and most controversially, Catholic, schools for the aboriginal population—an aspect of the so-called Indian Peace Policy.[138] In 1895, in Portland the APA briefly dominated the school board and forced the firing of 9 Catholic teachers. While in Roseburg and the towns of the Willamette Valley the APA fought ambivalence, if not opposition, toward their anti-Catholic education policies within the school boards with decidedly varied success.[139] However, with the decline of the organization from 1896, the APA school board candidates were almost universally defeated and the anti-Catholic Holy Grail of halting Catholic influence by outlawing parochial schools was to remain beyond reach for a further two decades.

This was not due to a lack of will. As early as 1901 successors to the APA tried to breathe life into the campaign for a settlement of the "schools problem."[140] Ironically during the period of the Northwestern Catholic Church's greatest expansion to date—the decades from 1900 to 1920—the area's anti-Catholic groups, although as vocal as ever, remained fragmented. This was largely because the potentially unifying issue of parochial schooling was submerged as nativism turned its focus towards anti-radicalism, racial issues and super-patriotism. Various religiously motivated nativist organizations attempted to propagate the anti-Catholic cause but with even less political effect than the APA. Some achieved brief electoral successes. Dr. G. Davidson Buchanan's fervently anti-Catholic Federation of Patriotic Societies managed to get 28 out of its 33 candidates elected in the May 1916 Oregon elections.[141] However, the organization splintered shortly after the election. The APA's fragmentation illustrated the fragility of anti-Catholic parties in the period. Again, personal ambition often overtook commitment to anti-Catholicism. The defection of the successful Federation candidate "Cap" Perry shortly after the May election led to two separate organizations—Buchanan's Federation of Patriotic Societies and Perry's Federation of Patriotic Societies of Oregon—once again splitting the anti-Catholic vote in the November general election.[142]

This pattern of rapid rise, political impotence and divisions when in "power", followed by equally rapid decline, and often, disgrace became a feature of the Northwest's anti-Catholic organizations. One of the most spectacular illustrations was New York Congressman Charles Haines' Guardians of Liberty[143] that gained a following in the Northwest soon after its founding in 1911. However, despite, and to some extent because of, harnessing the propaganda potential of an escaped Mount Angel "nun"—Mary Lasenan—in 1913, the organization had largely ceased to exist by 1914 when it amalgamated with Buchanan's Federation. The editor of the *Silverton Journal*, J.E. Hosmer, was prosecuted and convicted for malicious libel over publishing the claims of Mary Lasenan. This brought the organization into disrepute because the Reverend Leon L. Myers of the Silverton Christian Church, who "saved" the "unfortunate nun", was the chief recruiting officer for the Guardians.[144] Nevertheless, even if these organizations achieved few tangible results they demonstrated that anti-Catholicism was still very much alive in the period.

What Northwestern anti-Catholic restrictionists lacked in the first two decades of the twentieth century was not sympathy, or even underlying support, it was the cohesion and political direction to make that support count. That cohesion required a broadening of the appeal to the "patriotic" electorate, an elaboration in which the halting of ever-expanding Catholic power could form one of a raft of nativist ambitions. Watson's *Menace* in 1915 could warn "a breathless world [that] next June there won't be any Catholic Church—it will have gone up in smoke, the smoke of the fires of patriotism."[145] But in reality, in the Northwest, the Catholic Church remained largely untroubled by nativist activity. Even in the ultra-patriotic atmosphere which continued after the war, the Northwestern Catholic Church felt safe enough to attack the fervor for "Americanization" that was prevailing across the country with its consequent hostility to Catholic immigrants:

> A great deal of iniquitous profiteering in patriotism is being carried out by commercial or political reactionary interests under the mask of "Americanization"....Deliberate efforts to promote popular hysteria and wild fears with the direct object of promoting reaction, are matters of common observation. Paid advertisements for Americanization by commercial interests with very doubtful patriotic motives have been carried by papers throughout the country. The dollar sign is too plainly stamped on many of these schemes.[146]

THE KU KLUX KLAN AND THE PUBLIC SCHOOL BILL

It could be argued that this confidence and complacency fed anti-Catholicism in the Northwest. That was certainly the view the region's Catholic Church took when ambushed by the success of the Ku Klux Klan in Oregon—"The campaign [against the Parochial School Bill] was lost in Oregon through the absolute apathy and inaction of many Catholics".[147] The church was not alone, Republican Governor Ben Olcott dismissed Klan influence as a spent force in September 1921.[148] However, the Klan rapidly expanded in the next six months. By February 1922 the Klan claimed 10,000 members in Portland alone, with large Klaverns in Pendleton, Eugene, Salem, Coos Bay, Corvallis, Astoria, Myrtle Creek, Marshfield, Roseburg as well as several smaller ones comprising a further 5,000.[149] In Washington, the Klan quickly established a base in Seattle with Klan Number 4 and major Klaverns in Spokane, Walla Walla and Tacoma.[150] Nationally, the Klan seemingly tapped the "patriotism" of the "White Protestant Race".

The second Klan was a broad church. It succeeded in drawing in anti-Orientalism, anti-Semitism, anti-Catholicism and the remnants of wartime One Hundred Percentism as well as post-war anti-radical hysteria and tying in fears of economic exclusion and declining moral standards with the frisson of secrecy and ritual to form a popular and potent force of "Americanism".[151] Nevertheless, this cocktail of nativist sentiments varied from area to area. Even in the individual states of the West the mix was variegated—the oaths, rituals and stated principles may have been national, but in reality, as with the APA, the motivation of membership was translated into a variety of different objectives. In Utah much of the support for the Invisible Empire can be seen as opposition to Mormon domination. In Indiana it relied more on the issues inherent in prohibition. In Texas it was Mexican labor.[152] In Oregon, the Klan's appeal has been seen largely as anti-Catholic:

> The Pope has probably never heard of Oregon, [where] the Catholics are, and always have been, in a hopeless minority [some 8.5 percent of the total population]:[153] but what are facts when politics are considered and the public mind happens to be in a state of acute inflammation?
> Without enough Negroes to man a Pullman car, without any alien problem worthy of a name, anti-Catholicism remained as the only possible leg upon which the Klan could stand.[154]

The Northwest Klan tied its fortunes with the passage of a schools measure. Buoyed up by growing anti-immigrant feeling—demonstrated most obviously in the 1921 Immigration Act which established the ideal of national quotas—the Klan inextricably linked immigration with the education system. To allow national parochial schools to continue was to send a welcome message to the ill-educated. It would encourage the propagation of a:

> stupendous army of downtrodden, landless peasants, illiterate for a thousand years, submerged and warped in mind and body and spiritual estate by their cramped existence and absolutism under which they have lived—the very flood from the cesspools of that old continent boiling and reeking with the filth of ten centuries of plundered, profaned and disinherited mankind.[155]

The continued existence of the parochial school in American society would encourage illiteracy and crime, it would discourage individuality and undoubtedly lead to the collapse of American democracy. This was a stand for American values, values which continued immigration could only destroy, for as a Klan spokesman explained:

> Many Americans are at the present being led away from the path of safety by sects and group—native to our country—who for group interests oppose education in public schools. How much greater is the danger, then, for those who lack the American viewpoint in all things. In the lands from which they came these foreign groups are almost entirely without individual consciousness [sic]. They live in groups, play in groups and think in groups—iron circumstances have shaped their minds in the same narrow groove.
>
> They do not think in terms of nationality, and so do not care or even know of the ideals of Americans, not the form of

> government under which they live. The children attend the public or parochial schools until their parents find them a job, when they must stop and help support the family. They go just far enough to feel above the station of their parents and yet to hate the customs and people of our country, because they feel there is something they do not yet grasp....This untrained and restless youthful energy is the cause of a large percentage of crime amongst children of the foreign born, which is 5,886 per million and 70 percent greater than of the children of native parents....
>
> Not less than ten millions of foreign descended children and not less than two millions of children of special groups in our nation [are] illiterate [and] constitute a menace to our very civilization which makes every real American shudder for the future of his country. We know those who are opposed to education prescribed and regulated by the state, and we know why they are opposed. Most of the hordes from the south of Europe are controlled by the Papal Roman Machine. It [the Papacy] knows that real education spells its doom.[156]

However, it could be held that to the majority of Oregon's population the schools debate, centerpiece of the Oregon Klan's crusade for Americanization, was either of little consequence or misunderstood and that anti-immigrant feeling, let alone anti-Catholicism, was not a major consideration.[157] In the November 1922 gubernatorial election, opponents of the measure claimed a large proportion of the Oregon electorate:

> voted for Pierce, not because of his bargain with the Ku Klux Klan involving support of their School Bill...but rather in spite of that bargain, because only by voting for Pierce could they escape voting for Olcott, who to them, at least, represented a continuation of conditions they were determined to change.[158]

Certainly, the scale of the "problem" was small and localized. In 1923 Oregon had 160,924 children in 2,623 public schools and 12,031 children in 92 private schools. Some 7,300 of those children were in Catholic schools. Two thirds of those private schools were in the Portland district.[159] Nonetheless, the evidence points to an "anti-Catholic" groundswell. The issues at stake in the banning of private educational establishments had formed a central plank of anti-Catholic nativism since Beecher's diatribes in the 1830s—the electorate must have been informed, if not necessarily in favor, of the arguments.

To some, the scale of the Masonic/Klan measure's support could indicate little other than a pervading anti-Catholic hostility. Dudley S. Wooten, organizer of the Catholic Church's opposition to the measure, described the mood as like being in a "vortex...[a] hurricane of hate".[160] The Compulsory Education initiative was adopted by a huge majority—some ten to one. Even the claims made of falsifying signatures on the original petition left some 16,000 valid petitioners, and they all signed their approval in a single day. The initiative received the approval of 62,024 voters and was opposed by a mere 5,688. Given these figures, the exaggerated claims of the sponsor of the petition, Robert E. Smith, that it had 50,000 signatures by the evening of June 15, 1922, are rather immaterial. The Lutheran Church's dismissal as invalid of some 34,000 of these signatures still left 16,000 valid signatures and the Initiative required only 13,000 to be adopted. Also 16,000 supporters at this point was still over 10,000 more than the opponents of the measure could raise.[161] Also, having passed that legislation the largely Protestant, Masonic dominated, Oregon legislature[162] went on to pass a law banning the wearing of religious "garb" by teachers in all public schools in the state and introduced several more overtly anti-Catholic proposals. The Religious Garb Act was introduced at the height of Ku Klux Klan power in Salem in January 1923. Attempts to pass legislation to disbar Catholic chaplains from state institutions, tax church property, prohibit the importing of sacrament wine and eliminate Columbus Day all failed, although their very introduction shows the tenor of the State Legislature at the time:

> Oregon is getting some fine advertising, which if it does nothing else, calls attention to our "inferiority complex" for if we haven't got ability enough to reduce taxation we can certainly capitalize fanaticism and safeguard ourselves from the "tyrant of the Tiber", if not from flesh and the devil. Consolidation, economy and taxation are all right in their way, but the paramount issue is – "to hell with the Pope."[163]

Nevertheless, as with 1896 presidential campaign, the issues in the 1922 Oregon gubernatorial primaries and race were more complex than purely anti-Catholicism, or even Americanization. The skilful political machinations of Exalted Cyclops Frank Gifford enabled the nativists to use this complexity to their advantage. Many opponents thought the schools issue had been defeated with the narrow failure of Klan backed Charles Hall to gain the Republican ticket in the 1922 gubernatorial primary. They were taken by surprise and were consequently slow to organize resistance when the normally Republican-affiliated Klan decided to put its muscle behind a Democrat candidate, Walter Pierce, in staunchly Republican Oregon. Hall had introduced the Scottish Rite Masons' version of the School Bill in the gubernatorial primary campaign. His failure to gain the primaries—he was defeated by a margin of 500 votes, out of a total of 116,000—meant that many saw the issue as having died with him. Exalted Cyclops Gifford managed to persuade Pierce to back the School Bill and thus combined the Klan and Protestant "vote" with the Democrat vote.[164] Also, events conspired against Ben Olcott. The crash of the export market for wheat forced generally low farm prices lower; this combined with a national depression and rail strike made many farmers hostile to the generally liberal Olcott, who it seemed was wrong-footed by Pierce's adoption of the issue of tax cuts. Pierce stood on a "populist" platform which promised a halving of taxation, reduced telephone rates and aid to struggling farmers. Some contemporaries saw the issue of tax as central to the election.[165]

This revenue-cutting platform sat unhappily with the School Bill, which Pierce was forced to accept as a part of his pact with Gifford, knowing that it would place an additional 12,000 pupils in the publicly funded public school system. Nevertheless, Pierce still claimed—"There is only one problem, one issue before the voters of Oregon today. That is the tax problem"—and the electorate believed him:

> Governor Olcott...gave the Klan credit for landing [him] in political discard....[But] his downfall was really due to the solid vote of the taxpayers against the increasing costs of Oregon's administration....The issue was clean cut: Pierce promised tax relief; Olcott's managers said it could not be done by a governor. The taxpayers took Pierce's word for it, in the absence of any definite word from Olcott.[166]

Also the Klan associated[167] Portland Mayor George Louis Baker claimed that a 1,000 strong longshoreman strike in October 1922 was the initial stage of a revolution, a fact he re-enforced with claims that 25,000 armed "Wobblies" were marching on the city. Although some saw Baker's fears as exaggerated and his actions as out of proportion,[168] to a generally conservative public, with the example of the Seattle General Strike fresh in their memory, his prompt and harsh action seemed to illustrate the effectiveness of the Klan's campaign for strong "American" governance.[169] By contrast Olcott's staunchly declared anti-Klan stance, although perceived by his supporters as principled and necessary, was seen by some as indicative of his political incompetence[170] and by others as attacking what was a "seemingly harmless" American organization which was merely defending American values.[171]

There is also some truth to the claims that the Klan fought a disingenuous campaign. Klan-backed nativists may have regarded the elimination of parochial schools as a method of reducing the influence of an alien presence propagating itself in American society. They may have seen the measure as enabling "the assimilation and education of our foreign born citizens in the principles of our government, the hopes and inspirations of our people."[172] Nevertheless, the nativists largely dropped the public anti-Catholic haranguing of previous champions of compulsory public schooling in favor of a more stealthy approach.[173] Initially the 1922 School Bill was portrayed as merely imposing compulsory education "within a public school of the district" for all children aged between eight and sixteen years old, under penalty of a fine ranging from \$5 to \$100.[174] They played down the religious aspects of the issue with the result that opponents of the measure claimed that:

> Many [of those who voted for the Initiative] were under the belief that it was nothing but a compulsory education bill, and did not know it would destroy all private schools in the State. Those thus deceived now declare they never would have signed if they had understood the bill.[175]

The bill's supporters effectively neutralized opposition by claiming that the "wholesome law" had three fundamental, simple, purposes:

> 1. To prevent the public schools from falling into decay because of the encroachments of private schools;
> 2. To ensure education of children in the subjects adopted by the public schools, and
> 3. To prevent using children as work animals while they grow up in ignorance.[176]

Given these arguments, opposition to the bill was depicted by the measure's supporters as motivated by "alien" sentiments. Opponents of parochial schooling could claim it represented a means of discriminating against the non-Protestant population, and particularly Catholic immigrants, painting it as unrepresentative of the American population in general, pointing out "This is not a Protestant country. It is not even a Christian country, for the [1920] census shows that 65 per cent of the population has no religion of any kind. Neither is it a Catholic country, but there are 18 million Catholics in the Republic." [177] To the nativist, this argument merely re-enforced perceptions of the non-Protestants' inability to assimilate, these were American schools, on American soil, teaching American values, in an American way—"One Country, One Flag, One School."[178] Restrictionists had long regarded the public school education system as "one great assimilative agency [designed]...to prevent the immigrant child from...associating with others equally foreign with [sic] himself "[179], besides which in the eyes of the Klan and its supporters, "America was Protestant from birth".[180]

Opponents could object to the religious discrimination inherent in the premise underlying the measure, claiming: "It is merely a part of the propaganda of the Anglican Church to justify its apostasy, and [an opportunity for]...Protestant apologists to defame the Catholic Church. The mere mention of this subject was calculated and intended to raise a religious issue."[181] But, this was easily dismissed by nativists as being the claims of aliens who sought "the gradual and insidious absorption of the public school for their own purposes."[182] By demonstrating their wish to educate their children outside the "American" system they were seen as condemning that system. Fighting the bill set the Catholic Church, in particular, against the will of elected "American" officials and singled them out as "alien". Even members of the Catholic Church realized this:

> They [American Catholics] think and reason along different lines upon public questions involving religious issues; they occupy an attitude of detachment and isolation towards the outside world, they fail to make themselves an integral factor in the formation and control of public opinion; they seem to be separate and apart from the general movements which engross and direct the interests of their Protestant and non-Catholic fellow-citizens.[183]

Sensing the isolated position in which opposition to the School Bill had left the Oregon Catholic Church, Archbishop Edward O'Dea of Seattle determined that the fight against Initiative 49, Washington's equivalent proposal, should take a different form from that adopted by Archbishop Christie, Dudley Wooten and Bishop McGrath, in Oregon. As well as using the methods that had failed to halt the Oregon School Bill, O'Dea steered opposition away from seeming overtly Catholic. In an attempt to break any potential alliance, the Seattle Klan's paper—*The Watcher on the Tower*—pointed out that a coalition of Jews and Catholics opposed to Initiative 49 was hypocritical, bearing in mind the traditional animosity of Catholics to Jews. Catholics had rarely supported Jewish interests, indeed:

> The ability displayed by young Hebrews is only conspicuous in Protestant countries where they enjoy freedom of thought. If you have ever seen flocks of them arriving from your European Catholic centers you would realize that they owe your church nothing but resentment. The Hebrew in England and America is treated as a man. In Roman Catholic Europe he is treated as a dog and a parasite. For political reasons you may veil your hatred for B'nai B'rith, but it is a horrible partnership doomed to a disastrous conclusion.[184]

In co-ordinating the anti-initiative campaign, Archbishop O'Dea attempted to distance the issue from being seen as purely applicable to the Catholic population. He allowed and encouraged others, in particular the American Federation of Labor and the "Organization of Friends of Educational Freedom", to appear to be leading the campaign to preserve private schools.[185] The officers of these groups made displays of being pointedly "non-Catholic". By doing this he hoped to focus attacks on the constitutionality of the measure rather than the morality of the issue. This stance was aided by the national publicity surrounding the deliberations on the Oregon School Act by the Oregon District Court, and later, United States Supreme, Court over the appeals of the Sisters of the Holy Names and Portland's Episcopalian Hill Military Academy.[186]

Opponents of the Klan's campaign attempted to demonstrate that the forces aligned against the measure were the true forces of Americanism—"he who shouts for the Stars and Stripes and makes great outward demonstrations but who does not respect the equal rights of his neighbor is not a true American."[187] The Catholic Church increasing displayed itself as inclusive and tolerant, the last bastion of the truly American ideal of the melting pot. O'Dea encouraged a view of the anti-initiative alliance as the antidote to the bigotry of the Klan as his use of the following pamphlet demonstrates:

> I believe that my country has a divine mission; that we are ordained to complete the unfinished work of the ancients; that here the good and true of every race will form a people so strong and determined in the right, so armed with high purpose and resolve, so vast in vision and accomplishment that the day will not suffice for the good that they would do; that the Frank and the Celt, the Briton and Scot, the Teuton and Pole, the Latin and Jew, the Negro and Indian, the Norse and Slav...who come as their fathers came, to kneel at the same shrine, to obey the same laws, to make a home with us and live in the faith of our fathers, to be blood of our blood, are, like us, members of the family of men, the light of whose lives will add glory to the work we seek to perpetuate.[188]

His aim was to demonstrate the assimilation of Catholics into Northwestern society. He hoped to illustrate their patriotism by demonstrating that the attacks on religious freedom inherent in the measure affected "the good name of Washington...[and] serve no purpose but to occasion discord and strife in the community to the great injury of our cities and the state we love."[189] This was an effective message in Washington, where nativism was largely motivated by a fear of radicalism and revolution. By contrast, the Klan used the same methods as they had in Oregon and targeted what was, by Washington standards, fundamentally conservative Catholicism. Archbishop O'Dea had already attacked the Klan's Oregon measure as radical: "This is sovietism with a vengeance, disguised scarcely at all. It is a flat endorsement of the doctrine that the child is the property of the state and the parents' rights in the child are secondary. It is socialism in its most elemental form."[190] Although a link was often seen between radicalism and Rome, and more especially Judaism and radicalism, the attempts to motivate Washington's nativist forces could not rely on the same groundswell of opinion. Cosmopolitan Seattle in 1924 was not conservative Portland in 1922.

In 1922, King Kleagle "Major" Luther I. Powell may have established an effective base in Seattle but his organizational abilities were not as honed as those of Oregon's Exalted Cyclops Gifford. For example, the Seattle based *Watcher on the Tower*'s anti-Catholic message never reached the circulation figures or influence of Lem Dever's *Western American* and proved poor opposition for Hearst's anti-Klan *Post-Intelligencer*. It folded less than a month before the vote on Initiative 49, a vote in which the Washington Klan's leading journal would have played a crucial role.[191] The contrast between the successful passage of the Schools measure in Oregon and its failure in Washington State could be taken as indicating a less virulent form of anti-Catholicism existed in the latter. However, not only was the Washington campaign more sensitively and effectively organized—largely due to the lessons learned from the Oregon experience—but also the environment which had enabled the swift acceptance of the Klan's measure in Oregon was not the same that in its northern neighbor. The alliance that had united pressure—and finance—for anti-Catholic measures in Oregon, was never as strong in Washington. What strength it had, it drew from the "might" of the Klan in Oregon. Given the leading role the Oregon Klan played in the Washington Invisible Empire, the decline of the national Klan and Gifford's organization indicated a cooling of anti-Catholic fervor throughout the region. The autocratic Exalted Cyclops himself was feeling the adverse effects of rapid expansion and his seeming success. The Klan lost more Oregon school board elections in May 1923 than it won.[192]

Gifford's patronage machine was breaking down. His Oregon subordinates were questioning his growing personal wealth and "unorthodox" accounting methods. Oregon Klan membership declined from a peak of 17,000 at the end of 1922 to some 5,000 by 1924.[193] In May, 1923, the Federation of Patriotic Societies and Orange Lodges, feeling Gifford had hijacked anti-Catholicism, sought dis-association from their previous alliance, and in the ensuing highly public squabble the unity of anti-Catholicism was further divided.[194] Disillusioned by his discoveries of self-serving corruption in the epicenter of Klan activity in Atlanta, Georgia, as well as by the machinations of Gifford, the editor of the *Western American*, Lem Dever, fled the organization. He then published his damaging, if self-servingly unreliable, account of the corrupt and cynical nature of the Oregon Klan in the autumn of 1924.[195] This exposé came at the end of a lengthy power struggle within the Oregon Klan that had been gleefully blown up by the Klan's enemies. The organization was increasingly seen as a joke. Support for Klan policies evaporated as the increasingly comical fights between the Goblins, Dragons and Kleagles became more public:

> The King Kleagle [Luther I Powell]: "You're a Kaiser and a steamroller politician!"
> The Grand Dragon [Fred L Gifford]: "You're connected with the Simmons' gang!"
> The King Kleagle: "You're a pro-Catholic autocrat!"
> The Grand Dragon: "You're a treacherous, disloyal backbiter who has turned upon the hand that fed you the moment you were disconnected from the $ train![196]

Added to this Walter Pierce increasingly showed patronage to Democrats rather than Klan members and was threatened with recall in June 1923—"Governor Pierce started to carry out his compact with the Klan by naming Klansmen to office, but they proved so inefficient and created so much trouble that he washed his hands of the smut."[197] The defeat of Initiative 49 in Washington can be seen as indicative of the spectacular internal revolt and disintegration of the Klan. By mid-November the slow implosion of the Oregon Klan was followed by discontent in Washington as "several hundred" Washington Klansmen publicly bemoaned the "tyranny, despotism and autocracy" of Atlanta, not Rome.[198]

RELIGIOUS AFFILIATION AND IMMIGRATION RESTRICTION

The failure of Initiative 49 may have demonstrated that the Klan's mission to preserve America's Protestant values could not be extended across the Northwest, let alone the nation, but it still served to highlight that the forces of religious bigotry and opposition to alien influence commanded a strong position. As it was, in November 1924, Initiative 49 may have been defeated by a margin of three to two, nearly 60,000 votes, but still over 130,000 voters actively supported the measure and its initial proposal had received over 55,000 signatures.[199] Significantly, this was also seven months after a federal district court had declared the measure unconstitutional. Furthermore, opposition to the schools issue did not illustrate support for non-Protestant immigration. To many, the issue simply represented an unwarranted increase in state intervention, and a consequent rise in the tax burden. Others opposed the measure because they had an interest in preserving their own private schools, as demonstrated by the Episcopalian Hill Military Academy's attack on the Oregon law.

To other groups the measure represented an "un-American" form of discrimination, as the AFL claimed. The alliance of groups that opposed the issue was not necessarily an alliance of groups opposed to immigration restriction. Groups which had been vociferous in their condemnation of the measure had been equally vocal in their condemnation of open-door immigration. The Episcopal Church had publicly voiced its opinion that Catholic immigration was not desirable.[200] The AFL had supported immigration restriction since the 1890s on account of opposition to the "padrone system" and the non-union stance of many southern and eastern European immigrants and their use as strikebreakers.[201]

Also the assumption that all *Catholic* support for the retention of their independent schools necessarily indicated universal support for free immigration can be seen as erroneous. The "New" immigration brought problems for the integrated nature of an American Catholic Church with struggles over the language of the liturgy and, indeed, the language of education. In the 1880s and 1890s the dominance of the church by Irish-Americans had led to disputes over the congregation it represented and the course it hoped to adopt. Polish, Italian and, most particularly, German-Americans within the congregations and the hierarchy objected to the rapid Americanization measures put forward by the Irish "progressives"—most notably Archbishop Ireland of St. Paul, Cardinal Gibbons of Baltimore and Bishop Keane of Richmond.[202] The progressives sought integration and even went as far as to voice support in 1893 for the public schools and the desirability of separation of church and state.[203]

Similar divisions were apparent between the Orthodox Jews and their Reform counterparts. Reform Jews tended to be earlier, often German, immigrants and they were largely better assimilated, frequently relatively affluent and with closer business, social and cultural ties with local society in general than the predominantly Eastern European Orthodox Jews. In many ways their attitudes and aspirations were very similar to those of Americanizing Irish Catholics. The Reform Jews were less interested in protecting free immigration than many of the Orthodox. They had been in America longer and their ties with the "Old Countries" were less immediate and apparent.[204]

As a part of their vision of Catholic integration, these Americanizing non-Protestant progressives obviously sought immigrants who would be readily assimilable into American-Catholic or American-Jewish society as they saw it. As Cardinal Gibbons, in grandiloquent Old Testament mood, put it at the investiture of Archbishop Katzer of Milwaukee in 1891:

> Woe to him who would breed dissension among the leaders of Israel by introducing a spirit of nationalism into the Camp of the Lord....We owe our allegiance to one country and that country is America. We must be in harmony with her political institutions. It matters not whether this be the land of our birth or the land of our adoption.[205]

It has been argued that the established Catholic Church—more often than not Irish parishes—acted as a force for Americanization by inculcating American culture and "democratic" ideals, at least in the initial stages of the "New Immigration".[206] Nonetheless, the more "conservative", often "continental" European, element of the Catholic clergy and congregation saw the "Americanization" movement as influencing the "defection" of substantial numbers of recent immigrants from the church. Rapid "Americanization" removed the surety and safety previously provided by the "national" churches—the ties of familiarity in ritual, language, fraternity and culture.[207] To them rapid "Americanization" left the immigrant in a state of limbo in which the church became as alien as the rest of American culture.

In the Northwest this was not initially the situation. Where all immigrants were "recent" the co-operation and "overlap" in national parishes tended to be greater. For instance, the Italian and German Catholic congregations of Portland shared St. Michael's chapel until St. Joseph's church was built for the Germans in 1901.[208] Nevertheless, as immigrants naturalized and Americanized it became apparent to many that there was a good chance the new immigrant would lose his faith, as many as 10 million already had, and this being the case, would it be worth opposing restriction? To many established Catholic Americans, freedom to immigrate was no longer worth unquestionably protecting as such.[209]

Moreover, it would be facile to regard the Catholic attitude as either immovable in its homogeneity or as immune from national and intra-national influences. Catholic attitudes to immigration did not formulate in a vacuum. In an era when the immigration debate informed and occupied attention, and not only in America, the detrimental aspects of immigration were as apparent to Catholics as they were to Protestants. In 1924, the New Jersey American Legion's campaign for a "standard American" history textbook was supported by both the regional Knights of Columbus and Jewish Alliance.[210] To the vast bulk of the American population, Catholic, Protestant or Jewish, immigration restriction legislation was inevitable, as inevitable in this era as prohibitions on child labor, or the regulation of trusts. Since the foundation of the Republic, immigration had been controlled, further restriction was desirable, it merely required "equitable", "scientific" formulation. To Catholics from the "Nordic" nations—Britain and Germany, in particular—the exclusion of the Southern and Eastern Catholics could be seen as justifiable with regard to the development of American secular society. The demands such immigration placed on the welfare, public order and education systems of the country could not be ignored, even if much of the pressure frequently came from sources which relied on theories evolved from Darwin and his disciples.

In 1901 Cardinal Gibbons advised his countrymen to remain in Ireland as America was already "overrun with immigrants".[211] The Cincinnati *Catholic Telegraph* went further when it declared that the "scum population of Eastern Europe [presumably including Austrian and Polish Catholics] should be starved to death at home rather than that all the rest of the civilized world be made rotten."[212] By 1911, the Dillingham Commission's report had even persuaded the Northwest's Know-Nothings worst enemy, O'Hara, that some form of restriction was necessary and the *Catholic Sentinel* briefly advocated immigrant limitation.[213] Catholic opposition to immigration restriction had a more fluid quality than many later accounts have obediently portrayed—it was neither entirely constant, nor entirely unified.

The fundamental conservatism of the Catholic Church, its understandable opposition to the anti-clericalism and humanism inherent in the emerging left-wing successors to European liberal philosophies—anarchism and socialism—can be seen as briefly allying it with many nativist views. For example, American Catholic bishops had campaigned for Henry George's *Progress and Poverty* to be placed on the index in the mid-1880s and the church had defrocked Father Edward McGlynn for supporting George's New York mayoral campaign in 1886. Nevertheless, the *Catholic Northwest Progress* later echoed George's sentiments in citing Pope Leo XIII's condemnation of the "small number of very rich men [who] have been able to lay upon the teeming masses a yoke little better than that of slavery."[214] It has been claimed that the "conservative" Catholic lobby was solid in its opposition to the "radical" reforms of the Progressive era, reforms which often meant that even "assimilated" Catholics felt that they were being condemned as inferior.[215] This increasingly informed its opposition to immigration restriction—it was not so much the actual restriction they opposed as much as the reasoning behind it. As early as 1890 the *Sentinel* was warning that:

> In these times of Know-Nothing revival, every legislative measure looking toward the restriction of foreign immigration should be regarded with suspicion....We know that it is difficult to frame such a measure that would not admit of the operations of prejudice and injustice, but if a bill be not wholly proof against such operation it ought not to become law.[216]

This mistrust is seen as being re-enforced by the emerging "anthropological" concentration on the Nordic/racial line against immigration which from the mid-1890's fed Catholic fears that immigration restriction was motivated as much by anti-Catholicism as it was by anti-radicalism or the claims that it would protect America's health and living standards. For example, many Catholics joined the largely East Coast, Jewish led, nation-wide condemnation of the restrictionist emphasis on a literacy test from its 1896 congressional inception.[217] They saw it as poorly disguised prejudice against the predominantly Catholic "new" immigration—"the greatest force of all [backing] the [1913 literacy test] bill is secretly organized religious prejudice".[218] All the same, as one hundred percentism built up momentum, pragmatic considerations prevented organized Catholic opposition to the final passage of a literacy clause in the 1917 Immigration Act. Other Catholics went further; the (Catholic) *Fortnightly Review* roundly, if retrospectively, condemned the sentimentality of Catholic opposition to the literacy test as ignoring the real economic and social consequences of unfettered immigration.[219] Also while some more conservative Catholics denied nativist claims that immigrants lowered wages and took "American" jobs, others saw the dangers of free immigration to the economy. Supporters of free immigration saw the immigrant as vital to American prosperity, performing jobs essential to the economy, which Americans felt beneath themselves—Italians "left New York its subway which Americans would not have dug."[220] Others condemned unlimited immigration as supporting the "industrial feudalists" who exploited cheap labor and in so doing denied the immigrants their basic human rights.[221]

The reaction of the Northwest's small Jewish population to the threat of increased immigration was equally divided. Much of the contemporary anti-Semitic literature, notably the fraudulent and scurrilous *Protocols of the Elders of Zion*, portrayed the Jews as international in their objectives, and single-minded in their efforts to achieve them. In fact American Jewry was far from unified.[222] The initial Jewish settlers in the Northwest had, as already observed, often encountered little difficulty in assimilating. Largely Bavarian in origin, German speaking, urban and, often relatively, urbane, their reaction to the threat of large-scale immigration, even of their co-religionists, was mixed. Some historians largely deny the existence of animus as on the East Coast. They see the travel from the point of arrival on the East Coast, frequently after some time in that area, acting as a crash course in Americanism for many *Ostjuden*, sloughing off the irritating and embarrassing Old World traits and smoothing assimilation.[223]

Nevertheless, just as "assimilated" German, Austrian and British Jews at the turn of the century demonstrated a certain embarrassment at the mounting numbers of illiterate, impoverished, rural and largely Yiddish-speaking, Orthodox Jews arriving from Eastern Europe, the same was true of their American counterparts, a fact which even their opponents recognized:

> No descendant of the *Mayflower* is prouder of his American origin than the Jew whose ancestors have lived in this country for two or three generations. It is impossible to say an unkinder thing to such an American aristocrat than to confuse him indiscriminately with the recent arrivals from Poland and Russia.[224]

Similarly, the settled and generally successful, or at least aspiring, often second-generation, Northwestern Jewish population sensed little in common with the "new" Jewish immigrant. The example of Portland in the first decade of the twentieth century is instructive, not only for Jewish immigrants, but also for immigrants in general.[225]

By 1905, a mere three years after the foundation of Portland's first Orthodox synagogue, Russian members of Portland's five B'nai B'rith lodges outnumbered German members.[226] The 1904 records for the lodges of German Jews demonstrate that they concentrated a proportion of their not inconsiderable funds on aid to altruistic ventures for kindergartens, a "settlement house" and a "relief board" for Jewish immigrants as well as supporting other lodges. By 1907 the same sources demonstrated that they felt that all B'nai B'rith lodges should support themselves independently and that the existence of Jewish aid societies discouraged integration and added to anti-Semitism. Although not actively hostile,[227] the local and regional Jewish population had aided their co-religionists in employment, funding and social support while they had remained relatively similar in background to themselves, or if different, relatively few in number.[228] Having shed many of the outward signs of their Jewish origins[229]—either in the first or second generation, or even prior to departure for America—they had little reason to encourage the arrival of large numbers of immigrants whose only similarity was a supposed commonality of religion. Why continue to encourage their co-religionists to arrive when it was of little benefit to themselves? The arrival of large numbers of Eastern European Jews would threaten their position in local society, their integration. For as a local rabbi recalled from his youth "Before the mass of Eastern European immigration hit Portland...physically and socially Jews lived and worked next to Christians; they had a firm sense of belonging; they were Northwesterners body and soul."[230] This argument was doubly powerful when it is considered that this religious proximity was, to many of the "assimilated" Jewish population, perceived as being as closely related as Protestantism was to Catholicism and that contemporary America demonstrated an increasingly hostile reaction to Jewish immigration.[231] The growth of national anti-Semitism, particularly after the Frank case, tended to unify the national Jewish community. The effects were noticeable even in Portland—in 1918 the Orthodox and Reform B'nai B'rith lodges united.

It could be held that Portland's Jews adhered to their religious obligation to aid other members of their faith. There were some distinguished examples of this philanthropy, such as Ben Selling. Nonetheless a certain reluctance was discernible in the tailing off of active encouragement of Eastern European immigration from the middle of the first decade of the twentieth century. In a mirror image of contemporary Protestant restrictionist movements, self-interest sometimes clashed with principle to reduce the seeming effectiveness of resistance to immigration restriction as well as opposition to immigrants. Whereas the networks of mutual interest generally remained strong amongst first-generation immigrants—as attested by the strength of religious, racial or national organizations—these bonds frequently strained and broke as immigrants assimilated linguistically, culturally and economically and began to consider themselves "American". As with other immigrant groups, as the Jewish population integrated their motives became more personal and familial rather than communal or religious. A prime example of this is the willingness of the wealthy owner of street-car advertising company, Jesse Winburn, to donate $5,000 to what became a Klan-backed Democrat campaign. Winburn was a practicing Jew. Given his religion it is highly surprising that Winburn was asked to act as "Klan candidate" Walter Pierce's campaign manager in 1922.

It was Portland's elite Jewish community which voiced hostility to Winburn taking the position and persuaded him to resign through the intercession of the highly respected East Coast, Jewish, anti-restrictionist lawyer Louis Marshall. Winburn defended his actions by claiming that he supported Pierce's populist fiscal platform, not his association with the bigotry of the Klan. In this the Americanizing rabbi Jonah Wise and other community activists felt much the same, however none actively backed him. It is telling that the underlying focus of the objections raised by Portland's "society Jews'" were largely based on the effects of the Klan's potentially damaging egalitarian taxation proposals rather than the organization's much publicized hostility to Jewish immigrants.[232] Similarly, this incident brings the Klan's commitment to "Pure Protestantism" into question. The organization was not only willing to utilize a practicing Jew, Winburn, as its preferred candidate's campaign manager, but also endorsed a Catholic as its regional leader's secretary:

> When elected EC [Exalted Cyclops] Gifford picked Mr P[arker] as Secretary of the Portland Klan. Mr P, it is said, was recommended by Mr O'B, a prominent Roman Catholic railroad official. Mr P was born and raised a Roman Catholic,

> but he himself was a Protestant. He was also a Mason, like Gifford. His Roman Catholic record was immaterial to Gifford, whose family affiliations had been similar [Gifford's wife was Catholic].[233]

Amongst the higher echelons of the Klan of this era, the "Invisible Empire" has frequently been portrayed as representing little more than a cynical, but profitable, financial venture. The Oregon Klan stretched the principles of the organization's condemnation of non-Protestants in order to form the Royal Riders of the Red Robe in the region.

This body was a Klan—inspired and led—fraternity which was founded to admit "suitable" aliens whom it was felt would be capable of assuming the principles of "Klansmanship" and "One Hundred Percentism". These were pronounced by Gifford to be Klansmen in waiting and seen as valuable, and no doubt lucrative, junior allies, who upon naturalization would be faithful Klansmen. Although the Klan's hierarchy claimed that these affiliates would come from purely "Nordic" stock, some of the lower ranks claimed that the reality, indeed, the motivation was somewhat less pure:

> In the [1922] primary it became apparent that, while the Klan has wielded un-questioned influence, there had also been the loss of about 7,000 Protestant votes—votes of aliens and Jews and others who were not eligible to membership in the Klan....[So] The Royal Riders of the Red Robe came into existence...in contravention of the provisions laid down in the laws of the Klan. Aliens and Jews were invited to join it....The RRRR existed only in Portland and Astoria in any strength. They existed nowhere in the US outside of Oregon.[234]

An alien, and probably a Jew, Dr. Martin W. Rose, led the organization. Nevertheless, while the Riders certainly had Jewish members, Catholics were explicitly barred from membership. Again, this raises questions about both the Klan's position and the Jewish community's stance on the importance of the issues of aliens' religious affiliations.

Thus although it would be convenient to regard pressures for immigration restriction in the Northwest as a Protestant phenomenon, closer analysis shows that the situation was not that simple. There are more subtle religious divisions. Those religious groups which had been "assimilated" into local society—such as Portland's German Jews or Catholics—were understandably reluctant to see that status threatened. While rarely advocating restriction they occasionally acted more out of self-preservation than altruism, with the result that until they felt their own position was threatened, they showed little effective religious solidarity. The same could be argued of the Protestant nativist groups. In general, opposition to Jews and Catholics of the "old" immigration tended to be aimed at religion in the abstract, rather than at the individual. It was frequently focused on a condemnation of ritual and hierarchy. In the "new" immigration it was often the other way around.

As the period progressed the nativists' target was the non-Protestant aliens' ability to assimilate and the results of that assimilation for American society. This would imply that race and nationality played a predominant role in objections to the "new" immigration, re-enforcing, if not largely replacing, the function played by religion in the "old". Given this it is hardly surprising that immigration restriction was supported, or opposed, more strongly, by relatively unified religious groups when the Nordic argument came to the fore in post-war America. Individual Catholics in 1898 and 1899 could choose whether or not to reiterate the *Sentinel*'s condemnation of American activities in the Philippines. They could not help being of Austrian or German descent in 1917-18. Collusion between non-Protestant and, indeed, Protestant organizations occurred largely when their interests had some commonality—other than simply Christian community—as with the threats to their own well-being or their acceptance as "Americans" implicit in the School Bills.

In 1913 a certain Father Salvatore Cianci could claim that—"To forbid immigration means to go against the instincts and needs of the people, who like the birds, immigrate [sic] where they hope to find more abundance....[They] are simply obeying the command of God to 'fill the earth.'"[235] Protestant nativists might point to this as indicating solid Catholic support for free immigration. Nevertheless, it was largely the efforts of a German Catholic that led to the expulsion of the Chinese from Tacoma in 1885. It was the Irish-led pressures which generated hostility to Asians in Portland in the 1880s. Equally, there is little evidence of Catholic, or, for that matter, Jewish opposition to the moves to bar the Japanese from citizenship or halt their immigration. There was Protestant opposition. In reality, Northwestern nativism—at least in its religious guise—was largely a matter of individual conscience. That conscience was largely determined by the time of the immigrant's arrival and consequent social status, rather than religious affiliation in spite of the best efforts of leaders of the various faiths to persuade their congregations otherwise. At its most base, this nativism was little more than political opportunism. Nothing demonstrates this more clearly than Lem Devers' attempt to rehabilitate himself. The editor of the once-powerful Portland Klan's journal *The Western American* went from issuing dire warnings of the dangers of a flood of foreign-born Catholic or Jewish immigrants to claiming that he had:

> often argued that the average foreign born citizen knows more about the Constitution and Government of our country than the average native born....Many times I emphasized the truth that the Jews and Catholics compose a great bloc of bully good Americans, and that it was a cowardly outrage to discriminate against them or in any way hate them because of race or religion.[236]

There can be few more telling indications of the political opportunities religious divisions, or indeed religious tolerance, could offer.

NOTES

[1] Taken "From *The Tablet* 26 December, 1914" cited in A.H. Beach, "Quotations and Extracts taken from Roman Catholic Papers and Periodicals" *Watcher on the Tower* October 6, 1923 p.9.

[2] Frederick Jackson Turner, *The Frontier in American History* (New York, 1958) p. 305.

[3] Thomas J. Ferraro, "The Souls of Catholic Folk" in Stephen Fender (ed.) *American and European National Identities* (Keele, 1996) p.75.

[4] Lynn Dumenil points to statistics which claim that in the 1920s 62 percent of white women and 73 percent of Black women were on Church rolls in the 1920s. For men it was 49percent of whites and 46 percent of Blacks. Lynn Dumenil, *The Modern Temper: American Culture and Society in the 1920s* (New York, 1995) p.173.

[5] For an analysis of the issues involved in this secularization see Robert S. Lynd & Helen Merrel Lynd, *Middletown: A Study in Modern American Culture* (New York, 1929) pp. 313-331 and Robert Handy, "The American Religious Depression, 1925-1935" *Church History* 29 (March, 1960) 3-26.

[6] For example see David M. Buerge and Junius Rochester, *Roots and Branches: The Religious Heritage of Washington State* (Seattle, 1988) pp.43-46.

[7] Figures taken from A.M. Carr Saunders, *World Population* (London, 1936) cited in Eric Hobsbawm, *The Age of Empire 1875-1914* (London, 1988) p.344.

[8] Figures taken from *Statistical Abstract of the United States, 1920* (Washington, D.C., 1921) pp.100-101.

[9] Figures taken from Alex Toth, *American Catholicism and Immigration* (Unpublished Paper MSS 2400, held at the Oregon Historical Society, 1973) pp.1-5.

[10] Figures taken from the 1916 *Official Catholic Directory* cited in the *Catholic Sentinel* 20 April 1916.

[11] "There are no official figures as to the number of Jews in the United States, for the Jews themselves have strenuously—and successfully—opposed any attempt to enumerate them; this is the reason that the United States Census does not enroll our people according to religion, but according to nationality. Our great Jewish population therefore appears in the documents of the Census Office as "Russian," "Austro-Hungarian," "German," and the like. But the highest Jewish authority, the *Communal Register*, estimates—on apparently excellent grounds - the Jewish population of New York City at 1,500,000; and numerous statisticians who have exhaustively studied the subject figure that the Jewish population of the United States ranges from 2,500,000 to 3,000,000." Burton Jesse Hendrick, *The Jews in America* (New York, 1922) pp.4-5.

[12] See *Catholic Sentinel* April 20th, 1922.
[13] Immigration accounted for only part of the increase; for example some 19,000 converts were received into the Catholic Church in the year to April 1916, see *Catholic Sentinel* 20 April 1916.
[14] Josiah Strong, *Our Country: Its Possible Future and Its Present Crisis* (New York, 1885) cited in Donald W. Kinzer, *An Episode in Anti-Catholicism: The American Protective Association* (Seattle, 1964) p.19.
[15]Figures available in *World's Work* 18 (October, 1909) 1209-1210.
[16] Figures taken from the *Official Catholic Directory* (New York, 1890) pp.119 & 312; *Official Catholic Directory* (Milwaukee, 1900) pp.120 & 407; *Official Catholic Directory* (Milwaukee, 1910) pp.147 & 620, *Official Catholic Directory* (New York, 1920) pp.138, 585 & 600; and *Official Catholic Directory* (New York, 1930) pp.164, 231, 607 & 621.
[17]Figures taken from Department of Commerce, Bureau of the Census, *Religious Bodies 1916: Part I Summary and General Tables* (Washington, D.C., 1919) and United States Department of Commerce, Bureau of the Census, *Religious Bodies 1926 Volume I, Summary and Detailed Tables* (Washington, D.C., 1930).
[18] Figures extrapolated, on an average of 4 members per household, from Wilfred P. Schoenberg, *A History of the Catholic Church in the Pacific Northwest 1743 to 1983* (Washington, D.C., 1987) p. 469.
[19] *Annual Reports,* Archives of Archdiocese of Seattle, Box 77, file 144 (St. Joseph), Box 80, file 148 (St. Stanislaus) and 149 (St. Rita).
[20] Brouillet wrote of the incident in a letter to Colonel Cornelius Gilliam from Walla Walla on March 2 1848. The letter is cited in full in William I Marshall, *The Acquisition of Oregon and the Long Suppressed Evidence About Marcus Whitman* Volume II (Seattle, 1911) p.212 et seq.
[21] Henry Harmon Spalding in January 1848—George N. Belknap, "Authentic Account of the Murder of Dr Whitman: The History of a Pamphlet" in *Papers of the Bibliographical Society of America* vol. 55, (1961) pp.319-346 cited in Wilfred Schoenberg, *Defender of the Faith: The 123-Year History of the Catholic Sentinel Newspaper of Portland, Oregon* (Portland, 1993) p.6.
[22] For example see Belknap, op.cit. and Edwin O'Hara, *A Pioneer Catholic History of Oregon* (Portland, 1911) pp.145-170 for the pro-Catholic stance, or Eliza Spalding Warren, *Memoirs of the West, The Spaldings* (Portland, 1916) for the Protestant point of view.
[23] Beecher's fiery preaching was held as instrumental in violence which led to the burning down of the Mount Benedict Ursuline convent in Charlestown, Massachusetts, in 1832, although he distanced himself from any responsibility.
[24] Lyman Beecher, *A Plea for the West* (Cincinnati, 1835) pp. 97-98.
[25] For details of the incident see George W. Fuller, *A History of the Pacific Northwest; With Special Emphasis on the Inland Empire* (New York, 1931) p.364 and Edward J. Kowrach (ed.), *Historical Sketches of the Catholic Church in Oregon by the Most Reverend Frances Norbert Blanchet* (Fairfield, Oregon, 1983) p.137.

[26] *Catholic Sentinel* 16 August 1895.
[27] Beecher and other nativists viewed with horror the expansion of Catholic immigration. They saw their suspicions of conspiracy coming close to reality with the emergence of groups from the late 1830s such as the Leopoldsverien, the German Auswanderungs, the French Society for the Propagation of Faith and the Irish Colonization Association which nativists saw as dedicated to the emigration of Catholics to the New World.
[28] C. Easton Rothwell, *The Ku Klux Klan in the State of Oregon* (BA Thesis, Reed College, Oregon, 1924) p.20.
[29] Maria Monk was born to a Protestant family in Quebec around 1817. She was left brain damaged by a childhood accident with the result that her behavior was erratic and she was admitted to the Magdalene Asylum in Montreal, where she became pregnant. She left the asylum to become the mistress of William K. Hoyte, the head of the Protestant Canadian Benevolent Society who traveled with her to New York where the *Awful Disclosures* were concocted. After a legal wrangle over the proceeds of the book, Monk ran away to Philadelphia with an unknown man. She died in 1849, at the age of 33. See Maria Monk, *Awful Disclosures By Maria Monk of the Hotel Dieu Nunnery of Montreal* (New York, 1836).
[30] The book went into several editions and had sold some 300,000 copies prior to the Civil War. A sequel was published in 1837—*Further Disclosures by Maria Monk Concerning the Hotel Dieu.*
[31] In order to increase revenue when sales of the book started to decline, Maria was introduced in a tearful stage-managed "re-union" to another "victim" of the Hotel Dieu who had published her story—"Saint" Francis Patrick. In 1913 in the Northwest, Mary Lasenan was brought forward to testify to audiences in the area that she had witnessed and participated in orgies and infanticide while held in Oregon's Mount Angel Convent.
[32] Francis Galton, *Hereditary Genius* (London, 1887) pp. 358-359.
[33] Part of the "True Oath of the APA" cited Rothwell, op.cit. p.24.
[34] Hendrick, op.cit. pp.31-33.
[35] For an analysis of modern European anti-Semitism see Richard S Levy, *Anti-Semitism in the Modern World: An Anthology of Texts* (Lexington, Massachussetts, 1991) pp.1-11; Jacob Katz, *From Prejudice to Destruction: Anti-Semitism, 1700-1933* (Cambridge, Massachusetts, 1980) pp.245-292; and Albert S. Lindemann, *Esau's Tears: Modern Anti-Semitism and the Rise of the Jews* (Cambridge, 1997) pp.273-347.
[36] Max J. Kohler, "Some Jewish Factors in the Settlement of the West" *Publications of the American Jewish Historical Society* 11 (1903) 23.
[37] See Karyl Winn, "The Seattle Jewish Community: A Photographic Essay" *Pacific Northwest Quarterly* 70 (1979) 69 and William Toll, "Fraternalism and Community Structure on the Urban Frontier: The Jews of Portland, Oregon—A Case Study" *Pacific Historical Review* 47 (1978) 373.

[38] See E. Kimball MacColl, *The Growth of a City: Power and Politics in Portland Oregon, 1915-1950* (Portland, 1979) pp.48-54, Gordon B. Dodds, *The American Northwest, A History of Oregon and Washington* (Arlington Heights, Illinois, 1986) pp.78-79 and William Toll, *The Making of an Ethnic Middle Class: Portland Jewry over Four Generations* (New York, 1982) pp.85-88. For a general history of early Jewish settlers in the Far West see Harriet and Fred Rochlin, *Pioneer Jews: A New Life in the Far West* (Boston, 1984) especially pp.107-139.

[39] "Our liberties are in Danger" *Watcher on the Tower* 13 October 1923, p.7.

[40] The *New York World* 14 September 1921 pp.1-2.

[41] For a concise account of the major Catholic charitable institutions in the region see Buerge and Rochester, op.cit. pp.138-44.

[42] Evans, op.cit. 45-46.

[43] For an account of Irish, Italian and other foreign-born soldiers in the Civil War see William L. Burton, *Melting Pot Soldiers: The Union's Ethnic Regiments* (New York, 1998).

[44] Although it was utilized by nativists against them this sentiment was not limited to the Irish. Other Union soldiers felt hostility to the abolitionist cause. See Susan-Mary Grant, "For God and Country: Why Men Joined Up for the American Civil War" *History Today* 50:7 (July, 2000) 25.

[45] Cited in John R.G. Hassard, *The Life of the Most Reverend John Hughes, DD, First ArchBishop of New York With Extracts from His Private Correspondence* (New York, 1866) p.437.

[46] Catholic archbishop Alexander Christie of Oregon in a letter in the *Catholic Sentinel* 20 July 1899.

[47] *Catholic Sentinel* 15 April 1898.

[48] *Catholic Sentinel* 4 June, 6 November and 3 December 1902.

[49] For the attitudes of and to the foreign-born at the time of the First World War see Nancy Gentile Ford, *Americans All! Foreign-born Soldiers in World War I* (College Station, Texas, 2001) especially pp.16-45.

[50] *Catholic Sentinel* 24 August 1916.

[51] See "Lumen" in the *Catholic Sentinel* 13 May 1915.

[52] See *St Joseph-Blatt* 28 May 1915 cited in Steven W. Harmon, *The St. Josephs-Blatt, 1896-1919* (New York, 1989) p.129.

[53] *Spokane Spokesman Review* 3 April 1917

[54] Gilbert O. Nations, editor of the anti-Catholic *Protestant*, to Woodrow Wilson cited in the *Catholic Sentinel* May 4 1916.

[55] An idea of the national origins of the American Catholic Church is provided by the national composition of the hierarchy in 1914. Of 133 American-Catholic cardinals, archbishops and bishops, 53 were foreign-born—Ireland produced 28 of the American Catholic hierarchy—of the rank of bishop and above—Germany produced 6; France 5; Belgium and Holland 3 each; Switzerland and Italy 2 each; and Luxemburg, England, Canada and Austria 1 each. Figures extrapolated from Elizabeth King McKeown, *War and Welfare: A Study of*

American Catholic Leadership (PhD Dissertation, University of Chicago, 1972) p.64.

[56] Even the last edition before suspension of publication carried both the Allied and German versions of the Somme salient activity. See *St. Josephs-Blatt* April 12, 1918 cited Harmon, op.cit. pp.182-183.

[57] *Catholic Sentinel* April 10 1917.

[58] See McKeown, op.cit. p.162.

[59] For example see the *Catholic Sentinel* May 28, 1920 and March 3 1922 which detail Knights of Columbus activities in France and American Legion lauding of Catholic war efforts, respectively. See also the *Catholic Northwest Progress* January 9, 1920 which reported plans for a Knights of Columbus college in Seattle to re-train 500 ex-servicemen on a non-sectarian basis in a variety of trades.

[60] *St. Josephs-Blatt*, March 29, 1918 cited in Harmon, op.cit. p. 178.

[61] Dr. Mark A. Matthews cited in Dale E. Soden, *The Reverend Mark A Matthews: An Activist in the Progressive Era* (Seattle, 2001) p. 149.

[62] See *Spokane Chronicle* August 31, 1917.

[63] See *New York World* September 16, 1921, pp.2-4.

[64] For examples see *Catholic Northwest Progress* March 26, 1920 which details wartime anti-Catholic activity from the Knights of Columbus oath to accusations of arms caches.

[65] See William R. Pattangal, "Is the Ku Klux Klan Un-American?" *Forum* September, 1925 325 cited in Paul A. Fisher, *Behind the Lodge Door: Church, State and Freemasonry in America* (Rockford, Illinois, 1989) p.101.

[66] Arthur Preuss, "Americanizing the Immigrant" *Fortnightly Review* [Chicago] 25 (May 15th, 1918) 156-159.

[67] Much of the anti-Catholic feeling was whipped up by journals such as the *Menace* which underwent a revival in fortunes in the early days of the war, reaching its highest circulation in April 1915 but reduced by two-thirds as anti-Germanism and anti-radicalism replaced anti-Catholicism. See John Higham, *Strangers in the Land* (rev.ed. New York, 1994) pp.200-201.

[68] Although Madison Grant's 1916 edition of the *Passing of the Great Race* outlined the superiority of the Teutonic peoples, the revised 1918 edition skirted the issue—a patrician nod towards One Hundred Percentist sentiment. Subsequent editions returned to the overtly pro-German original thesis.

[69] Early twentieth-century racial theorizing confused racial and religious traits—religion sometimes formed a racial trait, informing the behavior of both Jews and Catholics creating subservient races. Conversely "wherever an Englishman goes…it is a British deed which he does, British history that he makes. Thus, too, a Jew is a Jew in all ages and climes" David Starr Jordan, *The Human Harvest* (Boston, 1907) pp.40-41.

[70] Ibid. p.117. However, Jordan disagreed with these sentiments, citing them merely to point out his abhorrence of the cult of bellicosity sweeping turn-of-

the-century Europe. "War can only waste and corrupt…the death of the strong is a true cause of the decline of nations." Ibid. pp.117 and 119.

[71] See Ford, op.cit. pp.125-145 and 187-201.

[72] See Valentine Stuart McClatchy, *The Germany of Asia* (Sacramento, 1920).

[73] "If we have not misunderstood the remarks of our morning and evening contemporaries in this town, the majority of them regard the Irishmen who have taken arms against England as ungrateful rebels who deserve to be hanged. The same papers are also vastly indignant because Germany, at war with England, has aided the Irish revolutionaries in their effort to establish an independent Irish republic." *Catholic Sentinel* May 11, 1916.

[74] Dr. Leighton Parks of New York's St Bartholomew's Episcopal Church cited in the *Catholic Northwest Progress* May 27, 1921.

[75]National Catholic Educational Association, *Proceedings of the Fourteenth Annual Meeting* (Buffalo, 1917) p.404 cited in Richard M. Linkh, *American Catholicism and European Immigrants (1900-1924)* (New York, 1975) p. 138.

[76] Bishop Augustine Schinner of Spokane cited in *The Spokane Spokesman Review* September 15, 1917.

[77] *Catholic Sentinel* May 11, 1916.

[78] The Jewish community was not unanimous in its support of Joseph Simon's conservatism. Such important Jewish figures as David Solis Cohen and Solomon Hirsch became critics of his stance and favored a more reform based program for the Republican Party in the 1890s. Also, as Southern and Eastern Jewry began to filter through to Oregon in the first decade of the twentieth century, it was originally met by the philanthropic solidarity which was a feature of East Coast Jewish communities. However, once Portland's Jewish population began to escalate (from 5,000 in 1910 to 10,000 by 1930) and they began to appear more numerous in South Portland's poorer immigrant areas, the commonality of interests disappeared and cracks appeared in their political cohesion. This was apparent in Rabbi Jonah Wise and other community activists favoring of the taxation proposals of the early 1920s even if they had the backing of the Ku Klux Klan and the opposition of the Jewish mercantile elite.

[79] Although this figure declined in the 1920s to "less than five percent" as national anti-Semitism took effect. See *Portland Blue Book and Social Register* (Portland, 1930) cited in Toll (1982), op.cit. p.134.

[80] See Hendrick, op.cit. pp.134-171.

[81] Henry Ford and W.J. Cameron, *The International Jew, The World's Foremost Problem* (Dearborn, Michigan, 1922) pp.62-63& 130.

[82] Ignatius Donnelly, *Caesar's Column* (New York, 1891) lays out a Jewish plot for world domination.

[83] Watson's anti-Semitism was similar to his anti-Catholicism. He saw the danger of massive Jewish immigration altering, by deliberate policy, the demographics of the country: "From all over the world, the children of Israel are flocking to this country and plans are on foot to move them from Europe en

masse...to empty on our shores the very scum and dregs of the *Parasite Race*." *Watson's Magazine*, 21(1915) 296

[84] For an examination of Populist anti-Semitism in context see Walter T.K. Nugent, *The Tolerant Populists: Kansas Populism and Nativism* (Chicago, 1963) pp. 5, 13, 14-16, 20-21, 180 & 231.

[85] Hiram Wesley Evans, "The Klan's Fight for Americanism" *The North American Review* 223 (March, 1926) 40.

[86] Reverend Rueben H. Sawyer to a Portland Ku Klux Klan meeting reported in the *Oregon Voter* May 27, 1922 p.15

[87] Malcolm Clark, 'The Bigot Disclosed: Ninety Years of Nativism' *The Oregon Historical Quarterly* 75 (June, 1974) 140.

[88] Austin H. Folly, "Who is My Neighbor?" *Assembly Herald* April, 1913, 196 cited in Salvatore J. La Gumina, *Wop!: A Documentary History of Anti-Italian Discrimination* (New York, 1973) p.179.

[89] Edward Alsworth Ross, *The Old World in the New; The Significance of Past and Present Immigration to the American People* (New York, 1914) pp.105-107.

[90] *The Grays Harbor Washingtonian* January 1, 1921.

[91] Figures extrapolated from The Department of Commerce and Labor, Bureau of the Census, *United States Census, 1910: Prisoners and Delinquents* (Washington, D.C., 1912) p.415, Tables 51 and 112, cited in Antonio Stella, *Some Aspects of Italian Immigration to the United States* (New York, 1924) p.59.

[92] Immigration Commission, *Reports: Immigration and Crime* vol. 36 (Washington, D.C., 1911) cited in La Gumina, op.cit. p.113.

[93] Ross op.cit. pp.129-130.

[94] See Donald E. Winters, *The Soul of the Wobblies: The IWW, Religion and American Culture in the Progressive Era, 1905-1917* (Westport, Connecticut, 1985).

[95] Fred W. Haslewood, "Barbarous Spokane" *International Socialist Review* 10 (February 1910) 705-713 and Glen J. Broyles, "The Spokane Free-Speech Fight, 1909-1910: A Study in IWW Tactics" *Labor History* 19 (Spring, 1978) 238-252.

[96] See Gerald Sorin, *The Prophetic Minority: American Jewish Immigrant Radicals, 1880-1920* (Bloomington, Indiana, 1985) pp.88-104.

[97] Quoted in Irwin Yellowitz, "Morris Hillquit, American Socialism and Jewish Concerns" *American Jewish History* 68:2 (December, 1978) 164.

[98] Figures extrapolated from Antonio Stella, *Some Aspects of Italian Immigration to the United States* (New York, 1924) p.60. These figures must be viewed with some scepticism. Stella's objective in his book is to point out the unfair way in which Italian morality was being portrayed in the immigration debate in the early 1920s. Also these figures are for arrests. Given the autonomous nature of immigrant "colonies", the relatively low levels of policing within them, it is hardly surprising that less Italians were arrested than English or Irish. It is interesting, given his selectivity, that Stella is willing to cite another Catholic

nation, albeit a nation with a long tradition of emigration to America, Ireland, as producing a high level of prostitution in defense of his fellow Italians.

[99] Anon. *The American Jew* (New York, 1888) cited in Michael Selzer and Herbert Gold (eds.), *Kike!* (New York, 1972) p.50.

[100] Judge Matthew Deady cited in Eugene Kimbark MacColl, "Eight Unique Contributions to Oregon Public Life", A Talk to Oregon Jewish Museum Group, July 23, 1992. Typescript Oregon Historical Society, MSS 2440—1 p.8 "In an article that [Judge Matthew] Deady published in San Francisco in 1868...he noted that the cities [sic] merchants and business men are principally Jews and American, an interesting distinction, unless he assumed that Portland's 467 Jews in 1870 were foreign-born, which they were not—only 46 percent [were]." Ibid.p.7

"One of the Jewish congregations is of the reformed practice [Temple Beth Israel], the other [Ahavai Shalom] was in the process of formal organization to meet the needs of the expanding Polish population. Both of them represent comparative wealth, and are growing in numbers." Ibid. p.6.

[101] See "The Hindu, The Newest Immigrant Problem" *The Survey* 25 (October 1, 1910) 2-3, "Race riots on the Pacific Coast" *The Outlook* 87 (September 21, 1907) 99 and Agnes Foster Buchanan, "The West and the Hindu Invasion" *Overland Monthly* 51:4 (April, 1908) 303-308.

[102] See James A. Halseth and Bruce A. Glasrud (eds.), *The Northwest Mosaic: Minority Conflicts in Pacific Northwest History* (Boulder, 1977) p.146.

[103]See United States Congress, *House Reports; Communist and Anarchist Deportation Cases, Hearings*, 66th Congress, 2nd Session pp.105-106.

[104] An example of the moral tone adopted by "patriots" is the entry for Emma Goldman in Elizabeth Dilling's *The Red Network: A "Who's Who" and Handbook of Radicalism for Patriots* (Kenilworth, Illinois, 1934) list her as "Anarchist-Communist; free love exponent...her book "Living my Life" tells of her intimate relations with Berkman, Ben Reitman *and many other men*." ibid. p.285.

[105] Quoted in the hearing to dissolve the Freeland Colony in 1907 at Skagit County (Washington State), Superior Court (file 4823), cited in Charles Pierce Le Warne, *Utopias on Puget Sound 1885-1915* (rev.ed. Seattle, 1995) p.107.

[106] See Ray Allen Billington, *The Protestant Crusade, 1800-1860: A Study of the Origins of American Nativism* (New York, 1938).

[107] See William G. Bean, "An Aspect of Know-Nothingism—The Immigrant and Slavery" *South Atlantic Quarterly* XXIII (1924) 328-329. Bruce Levine, ("Conservatism, Nativism and Slavery: Thomas R. Whitney and the Origins of the Know-Nothing Party" *The Journal of American History* 88:2 (September, 2001) 455-489) argues that as early as the 1840's slavery was a divisive issue to the Northern nativists of the Know-Nothing movement.

[108] While the Mechanics remained committed to the principle of white protestant workingmen's solidarity, which entailed a logical element of immigration exclusion, the secret of their survival lay more in their mutual structure and

insurance policies than in their anti-immigrant arguments. See Higham, op.cit. p.59.

[109] For an overtly pro-Catholic analysis of the role of Masons in American anti-Catholicism see Fisher op.cit.

[110] Humphrey J. Desmond *The APA Movement* (Washington, D.C., 1912) pp.9-10.

[111] "The Protestants are divided into numerous friendly divisions, agreeing to the great essentials of religious beliefs, but differing on minor points." The Reverend Thomas J Morgan, Baptist minister and member of the Board of Administrators of the NLPAI, cited in the *New York Times* June 9, 1894.

[112] For an account of the political machinations of the APA within William McKinley's 1893 Ohio gubernatorial campaign see letters to the editor *The Nation* November 9 and 23, 1893. For the later schism with the Republicans, see Kinzer op.cit. For the breakdown in Northwestern Republican affiliations see the *Oregonian* April 14, 17, 23 and 26, and May 3, 1896.

[113] As Ignatius Donnelly, himself no friend of American Catholicism, said of "Professor" James Sims' APA lectures: "I want to say to my friends, that I do not believe in some of the authorities quoted by the professor; I doubt their authenticity. When he comes up here and admits that the APA organization sent out an encyclical of the Pope that was bogus and published documents which were forgeries, he casts doubt on every document he may produce. False in one thing, false in all." Cited in Desmond, op.cit. p.56.

[114] See *Congressional Record* June 14, 1894 pp.6311-6312. For biographical details of Villard see Dietrich G. Buss, *Henry Villard: A Study of Transatlantic Investment and Interests, 1870-1895* (New York, 1978) and Carlos A. Schwantes, *The Pacific Northwest: An Interpretive History* (Lincoln, Nebraska, 1989) pp.139-147.

[115] Andrew Powell to Henry Baldwin cited Higham, op.cit. p.359.

[116] For details of the early activities of the APA in Seattle and Portland see the *Catholic Sentinel* March 8, 1894.

[117] Figures taken from the *Oregonian* April 23, 1896.

[118] Henry Francis Bowers, 1887 cited in Pam Epstein, *The American Protective Association* reproduced at http://iberia.vassar.edu/1896/apa.html p.5.

[119] "The Objects of the American Protective Association" cited in the *Oregonian* March 3, 1895.

[120] The *Catholic Sentinel* October 17, 1895.

[121] W.J.H. Traynor "Policy and Power of the APA" *North American Review* 475 (June, 1896) 666.

[122] Although Traynor originally advocated alliance with the Republicans, McKinley's refusal to adopt an anti-Catholic platform and the claim that "political affiliation shall not be entertained in connection with membership of this body" (H.G. Mathies, State Secretary, Oregon APA cited in *Oregonian* March 4, 1894) meant that the fusion of the organization with the party never really held any weight.

[123] Elizabeth Sanders, *The Roots of Reform: Farmers, Workers and the American State, 1877-1917* (Chicago, 1999) argues that a "soft alliance" of agrarian pressures with industrial labor emerged as a result of the Populist movement, particularly in Bryan's 1896 campaign. This coalition dictated the issues which dominated the reform movement from that election until America's entry into the First World War.
[124] For analysis of the Populist programs see Lawrence Goodwyn, *The Populist Moment: A Short History of the Agrarian Revolt in America* (Oxford, 1978) pp.107-109 and 293-310.
[125] See Gwendolyn Mink, *Old Labor and the New Immigrants* (Ithaca, New York, 1986) pp.129-157.
[126] "As far as McKinley is concerned, it is more likely that the organization [the APA] will work against him. He has been silent when interrogated on the immigration and sectarian school questions, while other candidates have given more or less favorable replies. My personal opinion is that the choice of the order will be either Harrison or Allison." J.T. Hayne, Oregon State Secretary of the APA cited in the *Oregonian* April 23, 1896.
[127] The *Cheyenne Leader*, a Democrat paper, cited in Desmond, op.cit. p.32.
[128] Figures taken from the *World Almanac Encyclopedia* IV (40) (New York, 1897).
[129] The *Oregonian* April 23, 1896.
[130] The *Oregonian* followed the nativists divisions with an earnestness which forgave them their almost comical divisions. For the position of the JOAM see the *Oregonian* January 26,1894. For the APA position over McKinley see the *Oregonian* March 6, April 17 and 26 and May 3, 1896. For the APA/JOAM split see the *Oregonian* April 23 and May 3, 1896.
[131] This was a prevalent view amongst nativists. As the Reverend Williams of St. Barnabas' church Omaha put it in 1893: "Their [the APA] backbone, if not their brains, is made up of Englishmen, Canadians, Irish Orangemen, Scandinavians, Germans, etc., etc." cited Desmond, op.cit. p.46.
[132] The *Oregonian* April 23, 1896.
[133] *The Cincinnati Catholic Telegraph* November 8 and 15, 1838 cited in Sister Mary Evangeline Thomas, *Nativism in the Old Northwest 1850-1860* (PhD Thesis, Catholic University of America, Washington, D.C., 1936) p.106.
[134] Richard J. Gabel, *Public Funds for Church and Private Schools* (Washington, D.C., 1937) p.487.
[135] See William O. Bourne, *History of the Public School Society of the City of New York* (New York, 1870) and Arthur Jackson Hall, *Religious Education in the Public Schools in the State and City of New York* (Chicago, 1914); Gabel, op.cit; and Billington op.cit. pp.144-155.
[136] Beecher, op.cit. p.12.
[137] Ibid. p.184.
[138] See Robert H. Keller, *American Protestantism and United States Indian Policy, 1869-1882* (Lincoln, Nebraska, 1983) and Desmond, op.cit. pp.94-100.

[139] See the *Catholic Sentinel* March 26, April 4, July 4 and 18, 1895.
[140] Major Alfred J Sears wrote to the *Oregonian* about "a new contest, Jesuitical, treasonable in its methods, is now being made against the [American public school] system" *Oregonian* May 29, 1901. For details of Sears' crusade see *Catholic Sentinel* May 30, 1901.
[141] See *Catholic Sentinel* June 15, 1916, and the *Oregon Voter* June 17, 1916.
[142] See Lem A. Dever, *Behind the Mask:, Confessions of an Imperial Klansman* (Portland, 1924) pp.42-43 and Clark (1974) op.cit. 145-6.
[143] For a statement of the principles of the organization see *Catholic Sentinel* April 18, 1912.
[144] See the *Silverton Journal* June 13, and July 18, 1913.
[145] Tom Watson cited in the *Catholic Sentinel* May 26, 1915.
[146] *Catholic Northwest Progress* May 28, 1920.
[147] Dudley C. Wooten cited in the *Catholic Northwest Progress* May 30, 1924.
[148] "Because of wholesome conditions in Oregon, with little discontent and a satisfied people, the Ku Klux Klan, although endeavoring to invade the state, has made little or no progress and I am informed it is now folding its tent like the Arab and as silently stealing away. The Klan has been taken lightly here, and because of the fact that it has made practically no impression on our people or our institutions, the executive office of this state has deemed action or any particular comment unnecessary." Ben Olcott in a letter to the *New York World* September 13, 1921 subsequently published, with some irony, in the *Oregonian* May 15, 1922.
[149] The *Oregonian* October 27, 1924 used Grand Dragon Fred L. Gifford's own figures to draw up these estimates of Klan strength in Oregon. The *Oregonian* was hostile to the Klan, rejoicing prematurely, when in September 1921 King Kleagle Major Luther Ivan Powell returned to Atlanta, seeing it—like Governor Olcott—as a victory for forces opposed to the Invisible Empire. However in November, 1921, the paper reassessed its position with an investigation of a report on the Pendleton Klavern which seemed to be thriving (see *Oregonian* November 4, 1921). The *Oregon Voter* estimated that there were 58 chartered Klaverns in Oregon by the end of 1923, cited David A. Horowitz, *Inside the Klavern; The Secret History of a Ku Klux Klan of the 1920s* (Carbondale, Illinois, 1999) p. 6.
[150] The Washington State Klan has always been regarded as somewhat peripheral to the Oregon Klan during the period. Contemporary and historical analysis of the Klan in the state has reflected this. For an estimation of Washington State Klan numbers see Jackson, op.cit. pp.192-195.
[151] For the Klan's own version of its crusade see Evans, (1926) op.cit. 33-63. For a contemporary analysis of the reasons behind Klan growth in the Northwest see Rothwell, op.cit. and Waldo Roberts, "The Ku Kluxing of Oregon" *Outlook* March 14, 1923 490-491.

[152] For an analysis of the various objectives of the 1920s Klan in the West see Shawn Lay (ed.), *The Invisible Empire in the West: Towards a New Appraisal of the Ku Klux Klan of the 1920s* (Urbana, Illinois, 1992).
[153] There were 67,123 Catholics in Oregon according to the *Fourteenth Census of the United States, 1920,* Vol II : *Population: General Report and Analytical Tables* (Washington, D.C., 1922) p.46.
[154] Roberts (1923) op.cit. 491.
[155] John A. Jeffrey, "The Public School" *Watcher on the Tower* September 22, 1923 p.11.
[156] Ibid. p.12.
[157] See Roberts, op.cit, 491.
[158] Ibid.
[159] *Oregon Voter* September 16, 1922 p.16. See also Superintendent of Schools for the State of Oregon, *Reports* (Salem, 1924) cited in Rothwell, op.cit. p.107.
[160] Dudley S. Wooten, *Remember Oregon* (Denver, 1923) p.5.
[161] See Rothwell, op.cit. p. 114 and *Catholic Sentinel* June 22, 1922.
[162] *Oregon Voter*, December 30, 1922.
[163] The *Capital Journal* cited in George S. Turnbull, *An Oregon Crusader* (Portland, 1955) p.164. See also the *Catholic Sentinel* January 11 and February 22, 1923, the *Portland Telegram* February 19 and March 5, 1923.
[164] See the *Oregonian* May 16 and 17, 1922, *Portland Telegram* May 20, 1922, *Oregon Voter* May 27, 1922 p.4 and September 16, 1922 pp.4-11 and *Catholic Sentinel* June 22, 1922.
[165] See Turnbull, op.cit. p.150.
[166] *The Marshfield Sun* January 4, 1923. See also the *Oregon Journal* October 5, 1922 cited in Clark (1974), op.cit. p.189.
[167] George Luis Baker was a populist, Republican backed supporter of the "common man". His background was German-Irish. Although allegations were made that he was a member of the Klan, it is more probable that he merely tolerated Klan activity as it fitted his vehement hatred of radicals and bootleggers. Dever (op.cit. p.35) claims that Gifford blackmailed Baker for his support. See MacColl, op.cit. pp. 140-143 & 174-176.
[168] See labor attorney Burl A. Green's first hand account of the "Revolutionaries" objectives in B.A. Green, "Portland's Mayor-Made Revolution" *The Nation* 115 (December 6, 1922) 605.
[169] Mayor Baker's anti-revolutionary credentials and vigilante activities led many, including Lem Dever, to see him as a member of the Klan—an accusation he denied, see Dever, op.cit. p.40.
[170] See the Republican editor's comments in the *Portland Telegram* May 20, 1922.
[171]See the letter of David Beattie to the editor of the *Portland Telegram* July 21, 1922 and the *Oregonian* May 16 and 17, 1922.
[172] Secretary of State of Oregon, *Proposed Constitutional Amendments and Measures* (Salem, 1922) p.23.

[173] This is of the rhetoric of "Dr. Drake" who ran for School Director in June 1916 (cited in the *Oregon Voter* June 17, 1916 pp. 194-195) and that of George Estes, *The Old Cedar School* (Portland, 1922).
[174] Compulsory Education Bill, 1922, Amendment to Section 5259 cited in A.B. Cain, *The Oregon School Fight* (Portland, 1924) p.5.
[175] The Civil Rights Association, *Twenty Four Reasons* (Portland, 1922) cited in Lawrence J. Saalfeld, *Forces of Prejudice in Oregon, 1920-1925* (Portland, 1984) p.68.
[176] Estes, op.cit. p.6.
[177] Dudley G. Wooten to the Hon. J. Speed Smith, Chief Examiner, US Naturalization Service, Seattle, March 1, 1923. The Archives of the Roman Catholic Archdiocese of Seattle, Education. O'Dea and Wooten on Oregon School Law, RG 640, Box 6—Correspondence.
[178] Dean Collins, "Prisoners of Freedom" cited in the *Oregon Voter* October 14, 1922 p.21.
[179] Henry Pratt Fairchild, *Immigration: A World Movement and its Significance* (New York, 1913) p.410.
[180] "She must remain Protestant....We of the old stock Americans could not work...if we become priest-ridden, if we submit our consciences and limit our activities and suppress our thoughts at the command of any man, much less of the man sitting upon the Seven Hills thousands of miles away." Evans, op.cit. 54-55.
[181] Wooten to Speed Smith, Archives of the Archdiocese of Seattle, op.cit.
[182] Estes, op.cit. p.8.
[183] Wooten, op.cit. p. 11.
[184] *The Watcher on the Tower* June 20, 1923 p.6.
[185] See the *Catholic Northwest Progress* May 23, 1924 for the opposition of the "Protestants, Jews or atheists" within the AFL leadership. See the *Catholic Northwest Progress* May 16 and 23 and the *Oregonian* March 31, 1924 for the position of other groups opposed to the measure.
[186] For the arguments in the Oregon court see Cain, op.cit. pp.132-156. For the decisions of the Courts see the *Oregonian* June 2, 1925 and Saalsfeld, op.cit. pp.88-94.
[187] *Seattle Post-Intelligencer* October 2, 1924.
[188] Pamphlet by J.W. Guinan, *My American Creed* (Detroit, 1923) in collection number 640, The Catholic Archdiocese of Seattle, file 208-4.
[189] *Catholic Northwest Progress* May 23, 1924.
[190] *The Tacoma News Tribune* November 17, 1922.
[191] See Clark (1974), op.cit. 179 and Jackson, op.cit. p.194.
[192] See *Oregon Voter* June 23, 1923 p.7.
[193] See Rothwell, op.cit. pp.138-139.
[194] See the *Oregon Voter* May 12 p.37, July 28 pp.26-27 and August 25, 1923 pp.13-15, and the *Oregonian* June 12,16 and 23 and November 23, 26 and 27, 1923.

[195] Dever, op.cit.
[196] The Portland *Telegram* November 26, 1923.
[197] The *Capital Journal* (Salem) August 16, 1927. See also the *Oregon Voter* April 7, 1923 p.6 and June 23, 1923 p.7.
[198] *Seattle Post Intelligencer* November 26, 1924.
[199] Figures extrapolated from RG 640, Initiative 49, 1924, Folder 208-16, Archives of the Archdiocese of Seattle, and Schoenberg (1993), op.cit. p.529
[200] See the *Catholic Northwest Progress* May 27, 1921.
[201] See Samuel Gompers, *Seventy Years of Life and Labor* Vol. II (New York, 1925) pp.151-173.
[202] The Irish/German debate is most comprehensively, if largely from a pro-German perspective, in Anton H. Walburg, *The Question of Nationality in Its Relation to the Catholic Church in the United States* (Cincinnati, 1889). For an Italian perspective see Henry J. Browne, "The "Italian Problem" in the Catholic Church of the United States, 1880-1900" *Historical Records and Studies of the United States Catholic Historical Society,* 35 (1946). For a general overview see John Meng, "Growing Pains in the American Catholic Church, 1880-1908" *Historical Records and Studies of the United States Catholic Historical Society* 36 (1947) 17-67. For a local context see Toth, op.cit.
[203] See Linkh, op.cit. pp.1-15.
[204] This attitude is demonstrated in the pro-Americanization stances of Rabbi Jonah Wise of Portland's (Reform) Beth Israel synagogue and his congregant, Grand Master of Oregon Masons and Jewish activist, David Solis Cohen. See Ellen Eisenbert, "Beyond San Francisco: The Failure of Anti-Zionism in Portland, Oregon" *American Jewish History* (September, 1998) 313-315 and Toll (1982), op.cit. p.132.
[205] Cardinal James Gibbons of Baltimore quoted in the second volume of his autobiography, *A Retrospective of Fifty Years*, which was published in 1916 and was no doubt included as a measure of his commitment to "American" principles. Cited Linkh, op.cit. pp. 9-10.
[206] See JoEllen McNergney Vinyard, *For Faith and Fortune: The Education of Catholic Immigrants in Detroit, 1805-1925* (New York, 1998).
[207] For the issues of immigrant religious security see Oscar Handlin, *The Uprooted* (rev.ed. New York, 1990).
[208] See Toth, op.cit. p.14.
[209] See Linkh, op.cit. pp.8-11.
[210] For an account of these "compulsions toward conformity" see Jonathan Zimmerman, "Each Race Could Have Its Heroes Sung": Ethnicity and the History Wars of the 1920s" *Journal of American History* 87:1 (June, 2000) 92-111.
[211] See the *New York Times* August 25, 1901.
[212] Mary Stanislas Connaughton, *The Editorial Opinion of the Catholic Telegraph of Cincinnati on Contemporary Affairs and Politics, 1871-1921* (Washington, D.C., 1943) p.203 cited in Linkh, op.cit. p.168.

[213] Edward Roddy, *The Catholic Newspaper Press and the Quest for Social Justice 1912-1920* (Unpublished PhD Thesis, Georgetown, 1961) p.194.
[214] *Catholic Northwest Progress* July 23, 1920.
[215] For the attitude of the Catholic Church to progressivism see Aaron Abell, *American Catholic and Social Action* (Garden City, New York, 1960) pp.137-88 and Roddy, op.cit.
[216] *The Catholic Sentinel* 23 January, 1890.
[217] See Henry Beardsell Leonard, *The Open Gates; The Protest Against the Movement to Restrict European Immigration, 1896-1924.* (PhD Thesis, Northwestern University, 1967) pp.133-190.
[218] *Catholic News* February 14, 1914 cited in Linkh, op.cit. p.172.
[219] *Fortnightly Review* 31, (May, 1924) 178.
[220] Frederick Siedenburg, "The Immigrant Problem" *Catholic Mind* 12 (September, 1915) 497 cited in Linkh, op.cit. p. 170.
[221] *Catholic Northwest Progress* July 30, 1920.
[222] For a general appraisal of Jewish reaction to the new immigration see Avraham Barkai, *Branching Out: German Jewish Immigration to the United States, 1820-1914* (New York, 1994) pp.125-142.
[223] See Ellen Eisenberg, "Transplanted to the Rose City: The Creation of East European Community in Portland, Oregon" *Journal of American Ethnic History* 19:3 (Spring, 2000) 82-97.
[224] Hendrick, op.cit. pp.5-6.
[225] See Toll (1978), op.cit. 369-403.
[226] While Toll (1978), op.cit. p.395, claims that by 1905 Portland had five B'nai B'rith lodges and that the city's first Orthodox synagogue was founded in 1902, Robert A Rockaway, *Words of the Uprooted: Jewish Immigration in Early 20th Century America* (Ithaca, New York, 1998) p.174 claims there were three Orthodox synagogues (but only one Reform Temple) and only four lodges in Portland by 1905. In view of the specific and local nature of Toll's study, these are the figures cited.
[227] For example, Ben Selling, "self-appointed champion not only of Russian Jews, but of suffering humanity everywhere" (Rabbi Julius Nodel cited McColl, op.cit p.50), was famous for his philanthropy—much of which was aimed at the Jewish immigrant community see ibid., pp.48-54. The local Jewish organizations also supported the contemporary movement to distribute immigrants from the East Coast urban colonies—particularly New York—see the correspondence between the New York office of the Industrial Removal Office and Alex Grubman in Portland during 1905 and 1906 cited in Rockaway, op.cit. pp.173-176.
[228] Estimates of Portland's Jewish population indicate that it rose from some 3,000 in 1905 to 5,000 in 1910 to 10,000 in 1930. Given the relative youth of the population, the near equality of the sexual distribution and their settled, relatively affluent nature, this growth does not indicate massive immigration. As with much of Oregonian nativism the fears of immigration were more potential

than real. Figures taken from Rockaway, op.cit. pp.173-174, McColl, op.cit. p.54 and Toll (1978), op.cit. 394-398.
[229] Oscar Handlin, *Adventures in Freedom: Three Hundred Years of Jewish Life in America* (New York, 1954) pp.109-112.
[230] Julius J. Nodel, *The Ties Between* (Portland, 1959) p.71.
[231] See Zosa Szajkowski, "The Attitude of American Jews to East European Jewish Immigrants 1881-1893" *Publications of the American Jewish Historical Society* 40 (March, 1951) 222 & 240.
[232] See Toll (1982), op.cit. p.133.
[233] Dever, op.cit. p.23.
[234] "Former Klan Member", Ben Titus, Manuscript 22, Ku Klux Klan Records, Oregon Historical Society, Dosier GD pp.12-13.
[235] *Catholic News* October, 1913 cited in Linkh, op.cit. p.170.
[236] Dever, op.cit. p.24.

3

THE EXCLUSION OF RADICALS

> Too many Americans are unfamiliar with the Constitution; and we should see to it that foreigners who wish to become American citizens should know it and believe in it, and if they do not square with it we should not allow them to become citizens. It is our country, our constitution and our government....We have been too liberal—liberal to the point of looseness—in admitting to citizenship men and women who are not in sympathy with our institutions, and citizens of this class are largely responsible for that form of radicalism in America which is now urging us to abandon the paths of our fathers, discard the constitution and get up a new kind of government in America. In answer to these tempters and betrayers...I offer the Constitution.[1]

"BINDLE STIFFS" AND "SCISSOR BILLS"

At the turn of the twentieth century throughout America, the image the Pacific Northwest presented was one that was predicated on the optimism and superlatives of the area's boosters and promoters. The huge expanse of the region was represented as being populated by industrious, healthy, wealthy and happy bucolic workers who labored, at one with nature, in the region's unsurpassed scenery:

> Our people are concerned with growing big orchards, shipping fruit, netting and canning salmon, plowing the fields and planting wheat, building barns and selling land. Even though we apparently have little time to enjoy our scenery and write poetry, yet our scenery has its effect upon the people. One who lives in Oregon cannot help but be influenced by the snow-capped mountains, stately forests of firs and pines and its splendid streams.

The Northwest promoted itself as a rural area and sought to attract "intelligent, industrious, hardworking, experienced farmer[s]...ambitious to make a home [for themselves]", who would purchase or reclaim land, for as the promotional literature pointed out—"It is the land, not the cities or towns, which needs more people."[2]

It appeared as the period of this study opened that the reality was going to be somewhat different. The region's dominant industry, lumber, was expanding. By 1914, a half of all privately owned commercial timberland in the United States was in the Pacific Northwest and the region was well on the way to overtaking the Great Lakes region as the nation's leading supplier of timber.[3] The Northwest witnessed the emergence of huge speculative timber estates—a quarter of all the vast expanses of timberland in the region belonged to Weyerhaeuser, the Northern Pacific or Southern Pacific Railroads. This new style industrialization required higher capitalization for land, timber rights, machinery and payroll. Highly mechanized, integrated milling plants emerged to process and add value to the increasing footage of timber. All this led to a general escalation of scale moving the entire process away from the self-employed lumberjack, since these operations required large numbers of laborers to remain profitable. Similarly, expansion of the salmon, fruit and meat canneries and the increased scale of the fruit and grain harvests increased the need for large-scale labor forces. Other industries were emerging and expanding—sucking in ever increasing numbers of skilled, semi-skilled and un-skilled labor. The region's major metropolis, Seattle, witnessed the evolution of new manufacturing industries largely based around the newly emerged boatyards. These vast employers had expanded from small-scale enterprises supplying local needs at the opening of the period, to sizeable concerns winning one in four of the vastly expanded government shipbuilding contracts during the First World War. Expansion took place also in mining, smelting and processing in the Kootenays, the Inland Empire and the Newcastle districts, as well as other regions.

The majority of this industrialization took place north of the Columbia River. Oregon remained predominantly a rural area, populated by residents who in many cases clung to the view of themselves as yeoman farmers or self-employed lumbermen, although pockets of industry became more and more common as the period progressed. Washington, by contrast, had no such vision of itself. It was the product of the symbol of the industrial age—the railroad—and arguably saw itself as an emerging industrial state. As such, at the beginning of the period, both states demonstrated an increasing need for workers—more or less permanent, more or less skilled, but definitely plentiful and hopefully cheap. This expansion of the wage-worker economy in the Northwest created tensions which mirrored the radicalization of industrial labor across the rest of the nation. The West had always had a reputation for radicalism, but in the Pacific Northwest there were also emerging features which were unique to the region, features which made this radicalism all the more significant and in many cases even less welcome.

The Northwestern workforce throughout the early twentieth century demonstrated a curious duality. A growing radicalism sat alongside a staunch conservatism. The one the product of the itinerant workforce roaming the woods, mines and fields of the region—born of desperation, insecurity and, increasingly, persecution. The other was the product of self-employed, self-sufficiency evolving from a belief in the region's unlimited potential. The one was a product of pessimism, a foreign import—the result of the undesirable immigrant. The other was American optimism—something worth protecting. It is hardly coincidence that the area's most adamant congressional restrictionist, Albert Johnson, powerfully embodied an aspect of this latter view, this regional pride. His career is illustrative. Originally a journalist, he moved from Springfield, Illinois, to Tacoma—" a city of destiny with opportunities and possibilities beyond that of any place in the universe"—to edit the *Tacoma Times* in 1898.[4] Although arguably himself a product of Washington's wage-worker frontier, his congressional career, particularly in its most notable phase—the early 1920s—was dedicated to the same principles as, and aided by, the leading lights of the East Coast's elitist, patrician, staunchly conservative, nativist lobby. This commonality of interest stemmed not only from his fear of neo-feudalism with Japanese "coolie" labor entering the area but also from his opposition to what he saw as the subversion of Western labor by alien influences.

A perceived shift from self-employment and individual ownership of the means of production, to wage-working and contract in the region, brought with it increasing complexity for the relationship of labor and capital. Added to this national problem was the continuing myth of the rugged individualist of the frontier, that peculiarly Western phenomenon, intensified by the perception that that very frontier was fast disappearing. It has been argued that in the Northwest the influence of the frontier often made it a more polarized, more visibly violent, struggle.[5] This violence distanced workers' politics in the industrial areas of the region from those of the rest of the Union. The 1886 Haymarket bombing in Chicago and the seemingly futile violence of the Pullman strike (1893-94) had largely moved American unionism towards a more "American", conciliatory, less inclusive and less radical approach centered in individual crafts with

Samuel Gompers' American Federation of Labor setting the tone.[6] The conviction of foreign-born anarchists for the fateful bomb had re-enforced a latent connection between immigration and radicalism, which in turn inspired a move to make American unionism less confrontational, more pragmatic and less antagonistic in an effort to distance itself from the "foreign" anarchist and socialist threat. [7]

After 1886, the AFL steadily replaced the more broadly based and idealistic Knights of Labor (KoL) across the nation. Nevertheless, on the wage-working frontier of the Northwest the AFL was slow to reach a dominant position despite the rapid collapse of the KoL in urban areas, arguably in some measure, due to their association with the Chinese expulsions in Tacoma and Seattle. The AFL made consistent attempts at organizing Northwestern labor throughout the last decades of nineteenth century, to little avail. Frontier individualism, particular working patterns, rough working conditions and frontier ethos inclined the mobile "bindle stiffs", and occasionally even sedentary "home guards", towards a radicalism that had little in common with the "business unionism" of the AFL. The radical Western unions—most notably the Western Federation of Mine Workers—and its more general wing the Western Labor Union—saw Gompers' "business unionism" regime as too exclusive, conciliatory and outdated. Gompers' AFL in turn had already dismissed the radical unionists in no uncertain terms—"Economically, you are unsound; socially you are wrong; industrially you are an impossibility."[8] Gompers attacked the divisions which the existence of radicals caused within the labor movement. Opposition to such "dual unionism" remained a feature of AFL policy throughout the period. The result was a stand off, dividing the positions of unions in the Northwest into the "American"-type craft unions of skilled workers and the radical, revolutionary, industrial unions associated with "European" influence—the radical immigrant.

Although ideology excluded many of the wage-workers in the Northwest from AFL membership, many were also excluded by the demographic and industrial structure of the area. The craftsmen and artisan workers of the Northwest were relatively affluent, settled and secure by comparison with many regions of the United States—seemingly ideally suited to the AFL's aspirant, craft-based unionism. The Pacific Northwest had a relatively high wage rate. In 1890, the mean daily wage of selected blue-collar workers was $3.02 in the Pacific region, compared with $2.34 for the New England region or $2.75 in the West North Central region.[9] In 1903-04, the average income in Washington State was $789 per annum, there was 40 percent wage-earner home ownership and 80 percent of the population were married.[10] Underlying this stable majority—the "scissor-bills" as the itinerant laborers called them—there was also a large indigent, migratory labor force which was generally associated with what was often seasonal work in the lumber industry, the fish canneries and the agricultural and horticultural harvest. By their very nature these workers are more difficult to quantify. Some idea of their number is given by the fact that one source estimates that by 1910 over 63 percent of all wage-earners in

Washington State were employed in the lumber industry—although only a proportion would have been made up of the impoverished, migratory "timber beasts" and other itinerant bindle stiffs.[11]

It could be argued that these itinerant laborers were more visible in the wage-earners' frontier of the Northwest. Since in many cases the distances traveled in the region in search of work were often greater than in other regions, these bindle stiffs rapidly became a defining feature of the Pacific Northwest's workforce:

> Broadly speaking, there are three distinct classes of casual laborers: First, the "harvest stiff" of the middle West who follows the ripening crops from Kansas to the Dakotas, finding winter employment in the North, Middle Western woods, in construction camps or on the ice fields. Then there is the harvest worker of "the Coast" who garners the fruit, hops and grain, and does the canning of California, Washington and Oregon, finding out-of-season employment wherever possible. Finally there is the Northwestern logger, whose work, unlike that of the Middle Western "jack" is not seasonal, but who is compelled nevertheless to remain migratory. As a rule, however, his habitat is confined, according to preference or force of circumstances, to either the "long log" country of Western Washington and Oregon as well as California, or to the "short log" country of [the "Inland Empire" of] Eastern Washington and Oregon, Northern Idaho and Western Montana.[12]

The loss of work in the one of the region's "island" communities—the logging, salmon cannery and mining towns, which were by the nature of the industries which dominated them dispersed and isolated—more often than not meant leaving that community and travelling a significant distance to the next. Local slumps in lumber demand, adverse weather conditions in the harvest season or a poor salmon yield could put large numbers of "casual laborers", hoboes and tramps into, onto or even beneath rail freight cars, criss-crossing the region for work:

> His [the "Nomadic worker of the West"'s] anomalous position, half industrial slave, half vagabond adventurer, leaves him infinitely less servile than his fellow worker in the East....His mobility is amazing. Buoyantly confident of his ability to "get by" somehow, he promptly shakes the dust of a locality from his feet whenever the board is bad, or the boss too exacting, or the work unduly tiresome, departing for the next job, even if it be 500 miles away...."Freight trains run

> everyday" and his ingenuity is a match for the trainmen and the special police.[13]

The region's extractive economy was arguably more volatile than the Eastern or Mid-Western manufacturing-based economies. It was certainly more weather dependent and seasonal. Even when the region's economy was stable, job security was never long-term. In 1914, the average worker in one of the region's lumber camps could expect a job to last 15 to 30 days; 30 days in the canneries; 60 days in a mine; 10 days on a construction site; and a mere 7 in the fields and orchards at harvest time. In 1913 and 1914 in two Northwestern rail construction camps laborers worked an average of between 10 and 12 days a month.[14]

Each of these industries employed a significant, frequently predominant number of foreign-born and these were often disproportionately from the Oriental or "new [European] immigration". The Dillingham Commission provides perhaps the most relevant source of data. The information the Commission recorded in the coalmines of Colorado, Wyoming and Washington shows them as having nearly 5,500 foreign-born workers, as opposed to just under 1,500 native-born. Southern and Eastern Europeans made up the largest groups. The report found nearly as many Italian miners as there were total native-born. Slovenes, Poles and Croats formed large contingents, as did both the Chinese and Japanese. On the railways the Report found that in America some 92 percent of section hands were foreign-born. In the Northwest this was not quite as exaggerated. For example, in 1909 the Oregon Short Line employed just under 400 "Americans" but over 2,300 foreigners—largely Greeks, Italians, Japanese and Koreans.[15] Similarly, in the Washington sugar-beet harvest the Report claimed that "the Japanese do about 95 percent" of the field labor although the Commission claimed that Volga Germans were becoming an increasingly important source of labor.[16] In the lumber industry the report had no data later than 1900. The figures that were available showed that of the one in ten lumber mills in Washington and Oregon that sent data, a little under 40% of employees were native-born. At this point the "Nordics" predominated and "Russians, Poles and Italians…were still few in number."[17]

What is striking about the Dillingham Commission's findings is that in all the region's industries in which foreign-born labor of the "new immigration" predominates, they are dominant only at the un-skilled or semi-skilled levels, very rarely at the management levels. For example in the coalmines of Colorado, Wyoming and Washington, those of English, Welsh, Irish, Swedish and Canadian stock—whether native or foreign-born—made up over 80 percent of the "superintendents, bosses and foremen". Italians, Japanese and Slovenians, although composing almost four times the total numbers of employees, made up less than 5 percent.[18] The timber industry showed similar demarcation, frequently following stereotypical views of the workers national origins, as Frederick Mills' 1914 report on a central Californian lumber camp indicates:

> The work in the woods is almost exclusively in the hands of what might be termed the Northern type, the American, German and Swede predominating. Practically all the work of timber felling, [the most prestigious and best paid of timber work] the swinging of the axe, is done, strangely enough by Swedes, while much of the patient work of sawing is done by Germans....Several Scotchmen, [sic] three Italians and two Russians are included in the force of the logging camp proper. These Italians, it is interesting to note, are the only ones out of hundreds that have been tried, that have shown an ability to do independent, responsible work.
>
> The [company rail] construction crew are a mixed lot of Scotch, Irish and American casuals, with several Greeks and Italians. The grading crew [those who cleared obstructions from the area into which the valuable giant trees were to be felled] the lowest class of un-skilled workers, consisted of five Greeks, one Italian and two Americans.[19]

This latter group of casual workers was particularly difficult to unionize as their mobility, the isolated areas in which they worked and the "un-skilled" nature of their work largely excluded them from membership of AFL-affiliated unions. Added to this they were frequently from the new immigrant groups, and thus subject to the nationwide prejudices of the period. These were members of a workforce whose working conditions, interaction with other, often disillusioned, under-classes and consequent social exclusion led them towards a more revolutionary political motivation. They considered their place in society could not be changed by piecemeal Progressive reform. As a leading Seattle Fabian put it, this was an area where "reform was impractical and revolution necessary".[20] Lacking any other means of cohesion, to many of these workers the siren call of class solidarity to forward the cause of revolutionary socialism placed them at odds with the Gompers-style aspirations of a working partnership with capital. To them revolution was only achievable from a position of unified strength and conciliation was unrealistic and undesirable. It was among this group that the area's radicalism found its most enduring roots, especially in Washington.

It was these typically Western, indigent workers who formed the grass-roots support for Eugene Debs' Socialists and the anarcho-syndicalist Industrial Workers of the World. As the communist William Z. Foster, himself a Western hobo and, at this point (1905-16), a "Wobbly", recalled in his memoirs of the period:

> The floating Western workers usually had no homes or families and often no religion. They were voteless and took little or no interest in the political and social life of the cities, where they crowded the [often Japanese] lodging houses in the

> "slave markets" and "skid roads"...Their whole world tended to make them militant fighters, and the heroic strikes of the Western metal miners, lumber workers and farm hands wrote many of the most glorious pages of American labor history...The Industrial Workers of the World, from 1905 on, was the true organization of the floating workers...[it] was the bone of the bone, the flesh of the flesh of the floating workers. It shared their utter contempt for the home guard, the politician and the preacher.[21]

It was these organizations which contained the most vociferous defenders of internationalism. They were composed of under-classes whose race or nationality was frequently immaterial. They did not perceive their enemies as entering the region from Europe or Asia. Nativists saw these organizations as being either dangerously tolerant of, allied to, if not composed of, the most obvious examples of un-assimilated alien immigrant workers.

TECHNOLOGY, SOCIAL CHANGE AND THE ATTITUDE TOWARDS THE IMMIGRANT, 1890-1924

It was not only political, demographic and social events that changed the attitude toward the immigrant worker, for these changes brought others in their wake. As the region's industrial base developed there was also in some regions a seemingly contradictory reduction in the requirements for itinerant laborers. Never popular, they were considered an unpleasant necessity; a fact that was concealed only until the harvest was over:

> At the beginning of the harvest the word goes out to trainmen that the "hoboes" are to be unmolested. They go out into the harvest without funds and their labor is a vital community need. After the crops are harvested the attitude of town authorities and railroad officials suddenly changes. The harvest hands straight away become "bums". They are arrested, thrown into jail, and fined....[Each incident] is only one of a hundred true stories that help to explain the IWW.[22]

It is notable that the Northwestern support for an open-door immigration policy diminished as mechanization developed and an increasingly sedentary workforce emerged—removing the necessity for a volatile, unreliable and increasing undesirable "foreign" workforce. The reliance on the previously ubiquitous itinerant laborer gradually diminished as the period progressed.[23]

By 1924, the need for a "casual", itinerant, floating labor force in the region was vastly different from what it had been in 1890. Technological advances in harvesting—the combine harvester, the shift to bulk transport from the old hand-stitched burlap bags and other practical advances—gradually eroded the need for vast numbers of laborers in the grain fields. Throughout the period, the region's wheat harvest labor force dropped by as much as two-thirds, although the horticultural and soft fruit harvest remained just as labor-intensive as it always was.[24] The increasing use of electricity instead of hydraulic power in mines enabled work, and employment, to continue all year round—even in frozen conditions. On the railroads, the completion of the majority of spur lines by the mid-1910s and the emergence of modern earth-moving and construction plant saw a large employer of the floating, frequently foreign-born, worker gradually withering away. In the early twentieth century the size of the temporary workforce gradually diminished, but it was still viewed as essential—even if it brought with it the specter of undesirable radicalism.

Technology also encouraged a shift in the nature of the remaining travelling workforce. At the beginning of the period the rail system, which had emerged in the region with revolutionary consequences in the 1880s and 1890s, enabled the transcontinental shipping of goods and people. It also fuelled the extractive industries of the Northwest, providing both markets and the labor to supply those markets. The ever-increasing efficiency, affordability and reliability of the gasoline engine and from the middle of the second decade of the twentieth century, the vast expansion in the regional all weather road network foretold a new form of personal mobility. The two states were among the first to actively encourage the development of road systems in spite of railway objections.[25] The era of the itinerant laborer was drawing to a close and the region's authorities aided this transition. In many districts the original rough planking roads of the 1890s gave way to gravel versions in the early 1900s and finally tarmac or concrete as local Chambers of Commerce, Granges and other interested parties raised funds to improve access to their areas and markets. Each settlement seemed to have a "Good Roads Committee" dedicated to building, re-routing, maintaining, re-grading and improving their own region's roads.[26] By 1919, Oregon had overcome its reliance on the railroad and introduced the first gasoline tax in the Union to fund highway building, improvement and maintenance. Washington followed suit in 1921. The growth of car ownership climbed steadily during the second decade of the twentieth century and took off in the third. For example, in 1916 Multnomah County, Oregon, had fewer than 10,000 cars registered, by 1920 there were 36,000 and by 1929 some 90,000.[27] It was now becoming increasingly possible for those working in isolated regions to return home to their families more or less when and where they liked.

In addition, the regional and Federal response to the wartime lumber strike had resulted in a general improvement in both the wages and the conditions within the lumber camps. Somewhat ironically, the government sponsored Loyal Legion of Loggers and Lumbermen (the Four L's), and their military protectors the Spruce Production Division, had wrung many of the original IWW demands from even the most bull-headed of the lumber lords. The eight-hour day, reasonable living conditions, even including, in some cases, clean sheets and hot showers, seemed well on the way to becoming the norm. These were the issues that had appeared insurmountable at the opening of the period and their resolution calmed the woodland working environment. The gradual shift in the logging camps away from the unspeakably squalid, un-hygienic laborers' slums of the 1890s to 1910s attracted those who sought more stable employment. The day of the legendary IWW bindle stiff was showing signs of drawing to an end, for as one of America's leading radicals later put it: "The decline of the IWW as an organization kept pace with the diminishing role of the floating workers in the West through the introduction of farm machinery, the completion of the building of the railroads, the tendency of the workers to "settle down" in the lumber industry, etc."[28] The region's population was becoming increasingly settled with the consequence that its attitudes towards the itinerant hardened. Many working within the industry saw changes which represented considerable progress in their working environment and as a result resented the entrance of any whose political beliefs or un-willingness to work jeopardized these gains.[29]

An open immigration policy had long been held up as the objective of the capital classes. Massive immigration meant competition in the labor market, which in turn meant lower wage bills and management-dictated working conditions. However, there was a gradual evaporation of business support for unrestricted immigration on the East Coast. In patrician circles this had long been spurred on by fears of race suicide. At the start of the period it was a dread of the submergence of the Anglo-Saxon amid hordes of immigrants who "fomented discontent and distributed dirt, garlic and trampdom everywhere."[30] By the end of the period, the growing doubts of this patrician, industrial elite had become generally accepted and the population had been convinced of the sense of restrictive policies. As the racial restrictionist DeCourcey Ward crowed in 1925—"It [the 1924 Act] expressed the conviction of the American people that immigration is a long-time investment in family stocks rather than a short-time investment in productive labor."[31] In the more pragmatic society of the commercial manufacturer, the growing doubt over the social consequences of continued open-door immigration was fed by a more prosaic feeling that machinery was becoming increasingly more reliable, cheaper and therefore more desirable than the flood of dubious immigrants. It was simply stability, for—"Machinery "stays put." It does not go out on strike, it cannot decide to go [back] to Europe, or take a job in the next town."[32] Such sentiments spread west. The "box-car hobo" was becoming considered less than vital to the Palouse harvest or the seasonal work of the logging camp.

Technology's influence was not indiscriminate. Mechanization seemed to favor the racially "desirable" immigrant over the "undesirable", for its effects re-enforced the racial restrictionists' arguments that the inferior Mongolian, Slavic and Mediterranean races were the ones least-suited to a modern, industrial world. This was as true of the Northwest as it was of the rest of the country—it was the un-skilled immigrant whose jobs disappeared. For instance, the region's salmon industry had always had a strict racial hierarchy of employment. The fishermen themselves were overwhelmingly Swedish, Norwegian and Finnish (i.e. desirable Nordics) although Italians also featured heavily. The membership records for the Fisherman's Protective Union of the Pacific Coast and Alaska for 1908 show that Italians made up some 23.6 percent of members. Swedes, Finns and Norwegians made up 53.3 percent.[33] Conversely, the vast majority of cannery workers were Chinese—and later Filipino, Japanese and in some cases aboriginal American. "No Orientals are engaged in salmon fishing for the canneries. [In fact they were banned from fishing in both states by 1915]. Their labor...is entirely within the canneries....[Whereas] White men have always been employed...[within the canneries] as engineers, firemen and mechanics."[34] It is telling that much of the mechanization that emerged in the period was aimed at replacing these Asians rather than the "White men". For example, the mechanical fish gutter, used in some Northwest canneries from 1905 onwards, gained the name of the "Iron Chink", for one machine was able to replace some ten of what Rudyard Kipling referred to as those "blood smeared yellow devils".[35]

Similarly, after the technological advances in the woods of the 1880s and 1890s—the introduction of steam donkey engines, steam winches and their mass of cables, blocks and lines—the mechanization of the 1900s was aimed at speeding up the milling processes rather than the felling and extraction. This meant machinery replacing the Asian, Southern and Eastern European manpower of the mills and yards rather than the Scandinavians who worked in the woods.[36] It was the Japanese, the Greek and the Italian gangs building and maintaining the railroads who were replaced by the steam shovel and its largely native-born, or Nordic, crews. To many of the region's residents, as the immigrant's utility diminished, his radicalism became more apparent.

Immigration was a significant issue in relation to these perceptions of radicalism. Although it may be held that such anti-immigrant pressures could be found in any region of the United States during this period, arguably it is the Northwest that emerged as the most vociferous and adamant area in the fight for radical deportation and, by extension, radical exclusion. There are two fundamental reasons for this. First, as already indicated, the Northwest's essentially extractive economy with its vast areas, its island communities and its lack of financial autonomy were ideal breeding grounds for the type of disaffected, revolutionary radicalism which was most feared by the nativists. Second, the apparent coincidence that increasingly intractable and violent radical activity in the region built to a crescendo at the same time as the enervated era of super-patriotism of wartime and the immediate post-war period in America. This led to a gradual, if temporary, alliance of three broad groups of anti-radical nativists—the unions, the employers and what can best be described as the communities. Each of these groups evolved a strategy at different times and for different reasons that relied on portraying the radical as alien—the outsider—someone who could and should be excluded. In order to understand this concurrence it is essential to determine the key motivation of anti-radicalism within each of these groups—what led to the increased passions associated with the issue, what caused the seeming escalation of violence and why the nativists evolved a strategy of exclusion rather than containment.

UNION ANTI-RADICALISM

Of all the groups mentioned above, it was the unions which had traditionally displayed the most intractable opposition to mass immigration. The "American" unions fought for immigration regulation to protect wages and strengthen union solidarity. The fraternal, mystic, Knights of Labor were generally in favor of the unionization of women and blacks and yet, despite this seemingly inclusive charter, the Knights had enthusiastically joined Denis Kearney's fight for Chinese exclusion in the 1870s and 1880s. It was the Knights that organized and led the Tacoma expulsion in 1885. In 1885, it was members of the KoL who, following the example of miners at Rock Springs, Wyoming, committed the murder of three Chinese hop-pickers at Squak in the Issaquah Valley, east of Seattle. They led the attack on Chinese miners in Newcastle, Oregon, in the same year, as well as many other acts of violence.[37] Ironically, some resented the KoL's anti-Chinese campaign, seeing it as representing an un-American form of radicalism:

> In 1885 an attempt was made by the Knights of Labor, an organization mainly composed of foreigners, to expel them [the Chinese] from the [Washington] territory...[as] the herding in cities of hordes of Chinamen was becoming a serious menace to society and to the working classes an ever-present source of uneasiness.[38]

In some measure it was this concentration on the exclusion of the Asian, as a threat to the American laborer, that accounted for the area's seeming tolerance of the European immigrant in the period before America's entry into the First World War. In many cases the European immigrant was not seen as a threat to the working conditions of the native-born laborer in the same way as he was on the East Coast. Organized labor, particularly in Washington, did not have the AFL's attitude to European immigration.

As the American Federation of Labor overtook the KoL, such instinctive, reactive—and frequently violent—policies of opposition to immigration which Western unionism had demonstrated started to be replaced by a more reasoned, targeted and quantified strategy. The AFL as a body had advocated the adoption of a literacy test—"stricter civil and educational qualifications for naturalization"—since 1896. Samuel Gompers, himself an English Jew, had personally opposed free immigration since 1892 and actively supported literacy tests.[39] In 1897, at its Nashville conference the Federation voted by 1858 to 351 for restriction.[40] The expansion of union membership in the period exaggerated rather than diminished the hostility towards the cheap immigrant labor and the new immigration in particular. As Isaac A. Hourwich put it in his attack on the logic of the restrictionist economic creed—the immigrant was caught in a cleft stick, he was a valuable a tool for union organization:

> The change in public sentiment from 1894, when the "ignorant foreign workmen" were accused of organizing labor unions, to 1910, when the "ignorant foreign workmen" were accused of keeping away from labor unions, is symptomatic of the progress of organized labor during the intervening period. In 1894, when the "ignorant foreigners" comprised mainly the races of the old immigration, trade unionism was still weak; after 18 years of "undesirable immigration from Southern and Eastern Europe", organized labor has gained in numbers and won public recognition.[41]

The Northwest's AFL-affiliated unions followed suit condemning what they saw as the importing of Chinese and Japanese as cheap labor and strike-breakers. AFL-affiliated unions had agitated for the dismissal of Chinese workers in the Tacoma and Port Blakely lumber mills in the 1880s. This anti-Asian element continued through until the 1920s when many AFL-affiliated unions were prominent members of the coalition that formed the influential Japanese Exclusion League in the area. Race was a prominent issue. Of the more than 100 AFL-affiliated locals in Seattle in the 1920s only nine had ever admitted any African or Asian workers, and Puget Sound would probably have been the least racially exclusive region of the Northwest.[42] By contrast, the IWW had seemingly always operated an inclusive policy towards membership, rejecting the Oriental exclusion arguments of Gompers and Debs: "The IWW welcomes alike the American-born and the Asiatic, although the latter is turned down by craft unionists and political socialists."[43] The majority of Oregon's IWW "Idle Army" which marched up the Willamette Valley in 1914 were foreign-born and "many could barely speak English".[44] Perhaps most tellingly, an IWW leader in the Pacific Northwest told a 1925 race-relations survey that Chinese made up nearly a half of Portland's "Wobblies".[45]

It would be difficult to separate the "mainstream" American unions' response from that of the Northwest's "community" in general, but it is worth analyzing the reaction of the Puget Sound and, to a lesser extent, the "Inland Empire's" response separately. These two areas indicate an increasing disenchantment with, and distancing from, radicalism in what has traditionally been viewed as an area tolerant of the radicals' causes. The period before the Seattle General Strike was to some extent marked by a running battle for dominance of the West's unions between the exclusivity of the AFL's "American", apolitical, "voluntarism" and the industrial, class-consciousness based approach of the Industrial Workers of the World, the Western Federation of Miners (WFM) and the Western Labor Union (WLU). In Seattle and some eastern regions of Washington this was less pronounced. Some historians have seen this as the result of a mediating stance taken by the Socialist Party in the region.[46] The Washington Socialists did not adopt Debs' antagonism towards the syndicalist IWW, nor did they feel stung into hatred of the AFL by Gompers' swingeing attacks on socialism's practicality. Rather, James A. Duncan, the secretary of city's Central Labor Council, and the *Union Record*'s Harry Ault both saw no danger in mixing their AFL affiliations with socialist or syndicalist ideas. The Labor Council, which represented 110 AFL-affiliated unions in the city, even put up its president Hulet Wells as a socialist mayoral candidate in 1915.

Similarly, from 1902, the "radical" Western Federation of Miners and the American Labor Union, both especially powerful unions in Spokane and the Inland Empire, were directly associated with socialism. As with the socialists, and—even more—the IWW, class-consciousness was more or less central to Puget Sound and eastern Washington's "mainstream" unionism. The unique mix of pragmatism and dogma ensured a general, if frequently strained, tolerance. As the "Progressive" Labor Council secretary James A. Duncan saw it, the AFL needed the IWW as a source of perpetual renovation of ideas, for:

> After an idea gets really old with the IWW then the AF of L begin thinking about it...those radical ideas are being rapidly absorbed by the AF of L and what some of us consider radical today will be conservative tomorrow....[I] see no reason why one has to join the IWW to carry out those ideas. Good ideas we can absorb. Some of the bad ones they can keep.[47]

Fundamental to this was the ever-evolving concept of a fraternity of labor. A worker was a brother—progressively, more and more, regardless of his national origin. Increasingly, the Seattle Central Labor Council, as with the IWW, viewed xenophobia and discrimination as a divisive tool of their class enemies. As an IWW sympathizer writing to the Seattle *Union Record* saw it, "Teaching race hatred has been the foundation rock on which the capitalists have been able to induce the workers to sanction and enlist in war....Yours for one big union, with nobody that works barred no matter what his or her color, race or creed."[48]

Nevertheless, unlike the IWW, Seattle's Central Labor Council AFL-affiliated unions in particular saw some workers not as brothers, but lackeys of the oppressing classes, damaging the interests of American workers by undercutting wages, strike-breaking and alien behavior. Although the labor movement was frequently bound together by its hatred of Asian immigrant labor—first Chinese, and then Japanese—in the larger metropolitan regions of Washington it was, in the pre-war era, unlike the stance taken by the national leadership of the AFL, marked by a general tolerance towards the "new immigrant".[49]A large measure of this tolerance can be seen simply as a response to the low levels of the "new" immigration in the region—the "new" white immigration was not the primary threat. In 1920 Seattle had some 80,000 foreign-born among its 315,000 residents. Unlike the situation in the cities of the Middle West and East, the "old" immigration still vastly outnumbered the "new". For example, the combined population of those resident in Seattle born in Britain, Ireland, Germany and Scandinavia—the major "old" donor countries—totaled a little under a half of the foreign-born. If the Canadian-born were added in it became closer to two-thirds. The combined Italian, Polish, Russian, Austrian and Hungarian populations—the countries which provided the largest proportion of "new" immigrants coming to the Northwest—made up only marginally over 10 percent. The situation was similar for Spokane and Tacoma.[50]

This situation changed in the post-war era. Seattle's general strike and its "defeat" disrupted this cozy consensus between radical and mainstream unionists. It led many interested parties to advise the Washington labor movement to break its connections with the radicals. Frequently this advice was accompanied by some measure of coercion. The reappraisal was led by the Seattle *Star's* vitriolic attack on the "gang of criminal, un-American leaders" and it was not long before the national and regional mainstream press insisted that the strike had failed and in reality the debacle was nothing short of a failed revolution.[51] Some local observers pushed the image of the defeated general strike as the failure of the region's radicals to gain control and "crucify the American Federation of Labor."[52] It has been suggested—largely by radicals, such as Harvey O'Connor or George Vanderveer—that the object of such conservatives was to press home the advantages won by the "breaking of labor solidarity" and to ensure the destruction of any possibility of Seattle becoming a "closed shop city".[53] The "savior" of Seattle, Ole Hanson, at the beginning of his brief spell as the nation's media darling and oracle on all things Northwestern, summed it up when he advised that "Labor must clean house" and insinuated that such a Herculean task would require a return to American values. [54]

Certainly, the employers were euphoric at the failure of the strike, and there was much talk on their behalf of an "American Plan" of industrial relations. Not for the first time, this plan drew on nativist sentiment, patriotic common sense, to prize workers away from industrial disruption. The "American Plan" drew on the residues of conformity that the federal government and its formal, and informal, agencies had encouraged in the wartime super-patriotism. Although less explicitly founded on anti-immigrant sentiment than on opposition to the IWW, Socialist or Communist Party, it served to establish an "American" way of unionizing. It re-iterated the wartime virtues, the "patriotic" principles of self-reliance, market forces, individualism and their expression through the "open shop". Seattle's employers, with their Associated Industries of Seattle, led the way in what was to become a national campaign. Their objectives were un-ambiguous: "We are for the open shop, the fair, square American plan of industry which permits the union man as well as a non-union man to find a job."[55] The Queen City of the Northwest became the first of some 240 American cities to launch a coordinated open shop campaign.[56]

In the months after the collapse of the Seattle strike, the major unions of Washington appeared to actively protest against this policy. With considerable bravado the Central Labor Council seemed to continue to pursue an aggressively unapologetic radical course. They were not going to adopt the anti-radical stance of the national leadership of the AFL. Initially, the Seattle Central Labor

Council stood by their "un-American" radical co-workers belligerently claiming that:

> all the employers who hate labor and all those who love to lick their boots, [should be aware] that we know exactly what they mean by "bolsheviki", exactly what they mean by "cleaning house"...Organized labor in Seattle was never so proud of itself, that it appreciates the reds more for the enemies they have made, that it has no intention of cleaning house to please its opponents and that the general strike is permanently in the arsenal of labor's peaceful weapons.[57]

But all was not as it seemed. This apparently solid support for their more radical brothers was as untenable as it was hollow. The majority of the nation's labor was keen to demonstrate its Americanism, no matter how important it was to uphold principle. For example, Gompers took to lecturing at military institutions until his death in 1924 and the AFL formed a high-profile alliance with that outspoken bastion of anti-radicalism, the American Legion.[58] Similarly, when threatened with expulsion from the AFL, James A Duncan broke with the radicals at the June, 1919 Washington State Federation of Labor conference and Seattle labor allied itself with the Grange—itself, hardly a radical organization—in order to stave off radicalization.

Meanwhile, the Seattle Labor Council claimed they would maintain their original decision to back other radical organizations in calling for a general strike to gain a re-trial for the San Francisco anti-capitalist bomber Tom Mooney if his status was not clarified by Independence Day, 1919. This belief in direct action belied the image the Labor Council's candidates for the City Council presented to the arch-anti-radical Ole Hanson in March, 1919. He saw them as "decent, fairly conservative labor men" but could not resist gloating over their disastrous polling among the hopelessly divided labor voters in the election.[59] Even when the central leadership was determined about an issue, many of the union locals simply acted in their own interests. Several unions merely refused to take part in the proposed general strike. Significantly for the region's nativists the old fraternity of labor also began to deteriorate in spite of the mythical retention of solidarity. At the end of February, 1919, the Council rejected the prohibition on blacks and Asians in AFL unions by passing a motion that theoretically removed barriers to union membership—and presumably opposition to immigration. As late as April, 1919, there was evidence that they could not compel unions to initiate the policy. In practice the policy was never instigated.[60]

COMMUNAL ANTI-RADICALISM

It is arguable that in the Northwest, the fragility of society, the shallow-rooted nature of what cohesion there was, made the area all the more sensitive to the threats posed by the revolutionaries. Although many arrive Northwest hoping to create a radically more equitable future, the g social and familial ties and in time an increasing civic pride, often strong objections to such utopian idealists. This was especially the ca when their actions threatened the stability of the locality. The inhabitants of the insular settlements of the Northwest were particularly aware of the damage that radicalism could do to their small communities. It could also be argued that the itinerant workers, particularly the unapologetic radicals, were an unwelcome reminder of the all-too-recent brash roots of the region. There had always been an ambivalence, a selectivity, in the attitude towards the region's original settlers. The rapidity of settlement did not allow for an acceptance of the reality of the past; the region's history was redecorated—sanctified and sanitized—this was the great Northwest. When coupled with the growing fear of radicalism, this orthodoxy became exaggerated. The motives of pioneers became dynastic, inspired and mythical in the retelling. There was a preference for the fêting of the divinely inspired, selfless, cultured missionary over the avaricious, unwashed, pillaging, mountain man. The region frequently displayed the arriviste's conservatism and love of conformity. It was hardly coincidence that the celebrated "Wobbly", William "Big Bill" Haywood, was first arrested for smoking in public in North Yakima, or that two girls found themselves detained as radical aliens in Seattle simply for wearing cropped hair and overalls.[61]

Added to this prurience was another, patronizing, thread of conformity. Many communities were dependent on a single industry and a considerable proportion of these were reliant on a single company. In Oregon the bulk of these "company towns" were often little more than glorified logging camps. In Washington there was more of a variety in the industries involved ranging from the DuPont's eponymous explosives plant to the copper mining town of Holden or coalmining at Newcastle. Unlike Oregon's small camps of under 50 men, Washington had some significant company towns, such as the Northern Pacific Coal Company's Roslyn which boasted 4,000 employee/inhabitants in 1900. These peculiarly Western company towns were largely bachelor communities of un-skilled or semi-skilled workers who were more often than not on the lowest rates of pay. Even if the workforce were not subject to the all-too-common abuses of the company shop, scrip, rack-renting, involuntary deductions, unfair contracts or other monopolistic practices, the company town workers could still find themselves with terrible accident rates, few recreational facilities and arguably, most importantly, without access to the regulatory institutions of local government or conventional craft unions. These company-towns were ideal breeding grounds for radicalism. Further to this the employers often sought the cheapest labor available and Asians, Greeks, Russians and other immigrants frequently formed large proportions of the workforce. In the majority of the region's lumber towns foreign-born made up over half the population and racial animosity and abuse was common.[62]

Many of these settlements, such as Pope and Talbot's imitations of New England propriety at Port Gamble and Port Ludlow or E.S. Collins', Methodist,

Ostrander—even before prohibition—adopted a repressively paternalistic attitude which frowned on alcohol, let alone radical politics and had an established practice of expelling "trouble makers".[63] These were not the large steel, textile or mining cities of the East Coast and Middle West—the immigrant radical was far more visible. The institutions were less established, less financially and managerially autonomous and the economy less robust. At its heart the Northwestern establishment maintained that conformity was profit and cohesion, whereas radicalism was division and disintegration:

> Peace is necessary for commercial advancement....Many working men own their own homes. They want the town to grow and prosper; they want the community to be happy and free from bickering; they want their residence property [sic] to increase in value; they want their positions to be permanent. These men know that alliance with such uncertain and unstable organizations, as the IWW, cannot bring about these things.[64]

As this radicalism became more widespread, in many of the region's isolated communities the authorities response to such outsiders evolved into one of expulsion—"A city in self-protection has but two course to pursue. One is to pay no attention to the [radical] street speakers; the other is to drive the disturbers out."[65] The evolution of such a policy is crucial to the immigration debate in the region. The initial policy of mass arrests—as in Spokane in 1908-09—proved counter-productive against the radicals. It merely created martyrs, inspired a bond of solidarity bred of hardship. This romanticized the movement and excited a further influx of those willing to show their dedication to the cause—a cause which made many nativists regard such radicals as totally alien to themselves and seeking aims wildly at odds with their own aspirations. Many locals saw the alien IWW "disturbers" as radicalizing local workers, turning their justifiable grievances into ammunition to be used to achieve revolution. They saw this radicalizing as incremental, particularly in the harsh logging camps where the imported workers arrived and then proceeded to:

> grumble because there were no shower baths, which they [the logging camps] never had. They also complained about having to carry their blankets, which they had always carried. And they even thought the camp should supply them with clean sheets. The loggers did not get those luxuries, but thinking of them seemed to lead them to other expensive tastes, and persistently they talked about working only eight hours a day and being paid more. By the end of the summer they had decided that the woods belonged to them as much as the operators, and they should have a share of the profits. By fall they had decided that the operators were unnecessary and

> should have their lands and camps taken away to run by the loggers.[66]

These imported "disturbers" had no regard for property, law or decency. They mocked "decent folks'" attempts to better themselves, condemning them as "lackies of the system". They attacked the Salvation Army, calling them "Jesus Screamers" and "Sky Pilots", mocking their piety and turning the words of their hymns into anarchist anthems. They wantonly relished breaking the law. At the height of the Spokane "fight" some 600 Wobblies flocked to the city, eager to stand on the soapbox, denounce the system and serve their sentences in jail. Added to this they created financial and logistical problems for the city that they pragmatically and seemingly gleefully, exploited. The IWW's paper, the *Industrial Worker*, delighted in reporting the authorities' failure to deter Wobblies by imprisonment and enthusiastically pointed out how arrests in Spokane could be made to serve the revolutionaries' cause:

> No more will we live on bread and water at the cost [to the city] of two cents a day per man; but we will go on the chain gang and get three square meals a day at the cost of seventy five cents a day per man...Don't think we will build the new Monroe bridge, we understand how to work too well to make any monuments to free speech...The effects of organization upon the rock pile was remarkable....We simply went through the motions of working. For instance, two men chained together pounded for four days upon one rock when it accidentally broke. To break that small rock cost the city of Spokane about four dollars in food alone...besides the other expenses of guards etc.[67]

Elizabeth Gurley Flynn estimated that at the height of the dispute the imprisonment of the free speech fighters was costing the city of Spokane $1,000 a week.[68]

A more effective use of local resources—and more telling technique from the perspective of nativism—was the policy of deportation that had been used in the Northwest from the emergence of the "IWW problem" with various degrees of brutality in Eugene, Florence and Coos Bay among other places. It was a relatively inexpensive way of removing the disruptive influence. More important it demonstrated the externalizing of the problem. The radical was seen as arriving in the area, an immigrant. The radical was by definition not of the community, he was foreign. The Hoquiam and Raymond lumber strike that followed the Aberdeen free-speech fight in 1912 saw a clear indication of the perceived foreign-ness of the radical. The Finnish and Greek workers were deported because, as one leading lumber man succinctly explained, "The mill men [became] inclined to import men with families...and do away with the Finns and Greeks. I feel we owe it to our country to do the same."[69]

Also, as outsiders, foreigners and immigrants, different measures could be applied to the exclusion of these nuisances. Measures that would usually have been frowned upon were legitimated—most notably violence. Violence was seen as accompanying the IWW. They were uncouth and violent people. If it was the "establishment" that beat, tarred and feathered or "necktied" the Wobblies, it was generally justified as a community's response to dangerous outsiders who would understand no other warnings. For example, in Aberdeen in March, 1912 a crowd of 100 watched without intervening as two IWW organizers were beaten by "masked vigilantes" before their expulsion beyond the city limits.[70] The IWW accused the local "Special Police" of "club[bing] our members to death".[71] Although there is no corroboration of these claims, the use of high-pressure water hoses, blackjacks and clubs were claimed by the IWW and their sympathizers to be more or less standard practice. The *Oregonian* rather approvingly reported that—"The citizens' police have armed themselves with wagon spokes and axe handles for use as clubs, and these weapons have proved most effective."[72]

There was little new or unique in this violence. Far more violent acts against radicals had been, and would be alternately, approved, tolerated or ignored by the national and regional press. The arrival of the IWW in a region was frequently seen as heralding a breakdown in civil order in that area. Violence on one side was the excuse for retribution by the other. Elizabeth Gurley Flynn detailed police brutality in the Spokane Free Speech Fight, claiming beatings, rapes and torture in custody as so frequent that they were almost routine and claimed that the shooting dead of "the unspeakable [police] Chief Sullivan", which swiftly followed the end of the fight, was the direct retribution for his cruelty.[73] The IWW accepted that their position generally attracted little outside support and there is some evidence that the leadership sought to break the cycle of retribution. At the height of the Gray's Harbor violence the *Industrial Worker* stoically claimed: "We must be prepared to meet these new tactics and we must not meet them with axe handles because we have a queer faculty that there is no such things [sic] as equality before the law."[74]

These words proved prophetic. It was the Everett "massacre" that marked the nadir of anti-radical violence in which the fists and clubs were replaced by firearms for both deputies and Wobblies on November 5, 1916, leaving some 56 men from both sides killed or wounded. Although there is little doubt that they were the instigators of the violence, Sheriff Donald McRae and his deputies suffered no prosecution. Indeed, they continued with their campaign of torture and brutality against any radicals they could find within the city limits.[75] Conversely, some 74 "Wobblies" were arrested on the *Verona*'s return to Seattle to face charges of "having assisted, counseled, aided and abetted and encouraged some unknown person to kill [deputy] Jefferson Beard on the 5th of November, 1916".[76] As the consequences of Sheriff McRae's violence became apparent, the region's radicals were galvanized into action, particularly in left-leaning Seattle. Huge meetings in favor of the prisoners took place at the Dreamland Ice-rink and the "progressive" secretary of the Seattle Central Labor

Council, James A. Duncan, coerced the body to provide advice and funds—albeit, totaling a miserly $100—for the defense.[77] The mass rally of November 19 demonstrated the diversity of support. Religious leaders, IWW organizers, local politicians and members of the business community condemned the violence of McRae and his deputies.[78] The city's controversial mayor Hiram Gill sent three hundred blankets and a supply of tobacco to the 74 IWW prisoners. He even went as far as to exonerate their actions by claiming:

> In the final analysis it will be found that these cowards [McRae and his deputies] in Everett who, without right or justification, shot into the crowd on the boat, were the murderers and not the IWW's....If I were one of the forty IWW's who was almost beaten to death by 300 citizens of Everett without being able to defend myself, I probably would have armed myself if I intended to visit Everett again.[79]

Such official support was brief, the situation only worsened for the IWW in the wartime patriotic frenzy and the post-war anti-radical frenzy. The campaigns against the saboteur, "slacker" and "skulker" centered attention on the internationalist, pacifist and class war aspects of the radicals. The Espionage Act of 1917 was revised to give the authorities, and their deputies, almost open-ended powers to fight "alien enemies." Three of the leading lights of the Socialist Party—Victor Berger, Charles Schenck and Eugene Debs—were among those imprisoned for their opposition to the war following highly public trials, re-enforcing the alien/radical connection, although only Berger was foreign-born. Postmaster General Albert S. Burleston used the postal provisions of the re-invigorated 1917 Espionage Act to effectively ban the IWW and Socialist press. The feeling that there was a radical conspiracy was particularly tangible in the Northwest. The Seattle region's plague of strikes in the second half of 1917 and early 1918, in industries as diverse as streetcars and laundries, metalworking and longshoremen, increased the hatred of the alien radicals. There was a widespread perception that such radical beliefs were at odds with those of the genuine American community and damaging to the American war effort. The region's patriots began to advocate extreme measures. The Seattle Employers Association pressured for "the [state] legislature [to] make it a criminal offense...for any able bodied man to remain willfully idle...[because] such idleness breeds disloyalty, treason, sedition, anarchy and vice."[80] Pleas were even made for the importing of less radical "Oriental labor".[81]

The all-enveloping environment of wartime super-patriotism fed a deepening association of radicalism with the enemies of America. It became increasingly clear to nativists that the three American Legionnaires who died in the melee with Wobblies at the 1919 Armistice Day parade at Centralia were killed in the service of their country, just as surely as the 50,000 American heroes who had perished in the trenches of France. Radical opponents of war had condemned America's armed forces as the "Implements of civilized slaughter...uniformed parasites." Anyone who had served in the U.S. forces forfeited the right to membership of the IWW. The organization had advocated that the "average American citizen should "risk starvation rather than don the [doughboy's] uniform."[82] They promoted the class struggle at home. It was *their* "aggression", the fact that *they* were armed, that led to the tragedy—rather than the legionnaires' storming of the IWW hall. As a local U.S. senator put it,

> A few days ago the nation was startled and shocked by the news of that American citizens had been shot down in Centralia, Wash., by the IWW. [It is worth noting that the majority of the Wobblies were also citizens. It indicates the prevailing sentiment that they are, by implication, assumed to be aliens.] The boys killed had donned the uniform of the United States and offered their lives in the Nation's defense. They were shot down while marching in a patriotic parade celebrating the victory they had done so much to win....They were shot down by a destructive element that had no respect for law and no love for orderly government. The shots that killed these boys were really aimed at the heart of this nation.[83]

Such an overt indication of the real objectives of the radicals meant that it was a patriotic duty to oppose, even violently, the alien radical. To the nativist the United States was engaged in a war with radicalism. It was a struggle on behalf of the "American way", for this was "the most enlightened [nation] the sun ever shone upon and any one who talks slightingly of it is a traitor....Out here in the far Western Coast red radicalism showed its hand and for years to come Centralia will be referred to as the Lexington of industrial liberty."[84]

The reaction of the mainstream of public opinion to the Everett and Centralia "massacres" indicates not only the hatred and fear the alien Wobblies inspired, but also the pressure which was building up at the delay, cost, duration and impotence of legal remedy to the IWW problem. For example, the Everett trial, in 1917, of the single Wobbly—Thomas Tracy—was estimated to have cost the state over $20,000. The case lasted for two months and then the defendant was acquitted.[85] Little seemed to have changed in the legal position vis-à-vis the radical threat in the ten years that separated the Spokane Free Speech Fight from the Centralia shootings. There was a growing realization that the existing measures were at best temporary in their resolution of the problem. Pressures grew to extend the ideal of local deportation to a national campaign. In times of Wobbly activity, relief was expressed each time the radicals were "expelled" from an area, but still neighborhoods were forced to live in a state of determined insular preparedness, frequently guarding the rail and road routes into their communities and fearing the return of the ostracized militants. The threat of an influx of radicals was enough to create panic. Aberdeen declared martial law in 1912 when a rumor spread that 250 Canadian Wobblies were on their way to re-enforce local free speech agitators. [86]

This pressure for a comprehensive policy of isolating and excluding the radical received a boost with American entry into the Great War. Outspoken and active pacifism, the continual industrial disputes—especially in the lumber industry—the radicals' overt *hyphenation* and later their conspiratorial contact with the "treacherous" Bolshevik regime increased the national sense that radicalism was a foreign trait. Between 1918 and 1919, nativist prejudice smoothly repositioned itself, moving from the condemnation of the wartime fifth columnist to the hunting of the Red terrorist. The similarities which prompted such an effortless transition were obvious—both wartime traitor and revolutionary terrorist wanted America to be dominated by a foreign power. As late as 1919 the two were synonymous—the nine bombs of June 1919 were seen as "connected with Russian bolshevism, aided by Hun money."[87] During 1919, fourteen states, including Oregon and Washington[88] followed Idaho's 1917 example and enacted legislation which enabled them to prosecute individuals purely for membership of radical organizations. Although Governor Ernest Lister vetoed an attempt by the Washington State legislature to pass anti-syndicalist legislation in 1917, the events of the following year meant that the measure was adopted with great enthusiasm in 1919. The mood of the state is demonstrated by the fact that under this legislation some 86 Wobblies were convicted in three months. Nevertheless, Congress appeared resolutely unwilling or unable to legislate upon a similar federal measure.

In spite of their seeming "friends" in Congress it was evident that the IWW were becoming increasingly excluded politically and socially. The perception that they were all foreign was re-enforced by their popular image. They had largely become representative of " a social class with fewer legal or social rights than [are] conventionally ascribed to American citizens"[89]. Their mobility would have disenfranchised them had they not already opted to ignore the ballot box. Rather unsurprisingly, the Wobblies demonstrated little concern for the niceties of that society. Their impertinent, if often playful, attacks on "American decency" further aggravated and alienated an already hostile resident population. They relished tormenting, Scout-in-chief, Robert Baden-Powell in Portland during his 1912 American tour. They launched a tongue-in-cheek campaign as the agents of prohibition and guardians of morality in the 1923 lumber strike. Perhaps most notoriously, they unrelentingly baited that most virtuous of Christian institutions—the Salvation Army—throughout the period.[90] It was America's entry into the European conflict that really widened the gulf between the radicals and their opponents. Although the IWW's leadership spurned the actively pacifist stance of Debs' Socialists as being too politically motivated, they made no secret of their opposition to the war and the potential they saw as inherent within the conflict to bring down the "capitalist class":

> Capitalism is a hydra with many heads. War is but one of them...If the working class had the power to cut off one of

> these heads it would have the power to kill the monster outright...The time for talk is past: the time for action is here—ACT. If each one of us will do his bit, Capitalism will be at our mercy within a month. Stir up the smoldering flames of discontent until the conflagration can be seen around the world.[91]

Such ambitions were taken at face value in the increasingly paranoid climate of ultra-patriotism engendered by the war: "The heart of the current condemnation of the IWW is that it is a viciously unpatriotic organization."[92] The *Congressional Record* reported their unpatriotic stance, the plea for workers to ignore the call to arms:

> The question of preparedness is also being considered—what preparations have been made or are necessary to pursue a war to successful conclusion? To the profit gluttons of big business it means battleships, canons, shrapnel and machine guns and other things which are essential to the slaughtering of slaves....Make the slogan "Rebellion sooner than war." Don't make yourself a target in order to fatten Rockefeller, Morgan, Carnegie, the Rosthchilds, Guggenhiem and the other industrial pirates....Don't become hired murderers. Don't join the Army or the Navy....We are confined to no country, no flag....We are revolt. We are progress, we are revolution.[93]

The IWW's class-consciousness may have provided a coherent explanation for many of the casual workers' miseries. The idea of "the bosses" being crippled by an over-whelming general strike could provide a goal and hope for the future, but there can be little doubt that the bulk of the IWW were simply workingmen who found a camaraderie and empathy with others through membership of the organization, safety in the "Union Hall" and "Jungles" with fellow itinerant workers.

Many of the region's Wobblies were frequently more ambivalent than hostile to the war; more cynical than revolutionary and more gregarious than syndicalist, but nonetheless they felt little of the patriotism of the "American" people. As "one of the most influential of the IWW leaders" eloquently explained to Professor Carleton H. Parker of Washington State University:

> You ask me why the IWW is not patriotic to the United States. If you were a bum without a blanket; if you left your wife and kids when you went West for a job and had never located them since; if your job never kept you long enough in a place to qualify you to vote; if you slept in a lousy, sour bunkhouse, and ate food just as rotten as they could give you and get away with it; if deputy sheriffs shot your cooking cans full of holes

> and spilled your grub on the ground; if your wages were lowered on you when the bosses felt they had you down; if there was one law for Ford, Suhr and Mooney [Californian IWW activists convicted of murder], and another for Harry Thaw [a millionaire sensationally acquitted of murder on grounds of insanity]; if every person who represented law and order and the nation beat you up, railroaded you to jail, and the good Christian people cheered and told them to go to it, how in hell do you expect a man to be patriotic? This war is a businessman's war and we don't see why we should go out and get shot in order to save the lovely state of affairs that we now enjoy.[94]

It was in the Northwest's lumber industry in particular that the IWW revealed its most "unpatriotic" side. Calls for workers to spike timber or sabotage machinery, coupled with threats of a general strike throughout the summer of 1917 were seen by nativists as either the actions of fifth columnists or presaging a revolution. The situation appeared grave. Stories of arson, spiked timber, bearings filled with sand or lemon juice, "slowing up on the job" and other forms of sabotage were printed in the region's press. Dire warnings of the consequences were given in Congress:

> Some drastic measures will have to be used with the IWW....An incident occurred a few weeks ago at Aberdeen, Wash[ington]....A great spruce log was taken into one of the lumber mill to be sawed into lumber for airplanes. The great belt saw moved forward, and the saw broke into a thousand pieces. It had run into an iron hasp that had been driven into the log before it was brought there....the people of the localities in that section are getting desperate and they propose to take the law into their own hands unless something is done to suppress this evil that is traitorous in its conduct and most disastrous in its effect...threatening the success of our armies and our arms.[95]

"By the middle of June thirteen camps had been shut down near Hoquiam [Grays Harbor]."[96] By mid-July 1917, some 3,000 mill workers and loggers were out on strike in the Gray's Harbor region alone joining a joint AFL/IWW strike which brought out an estimated 90 percent of all loggers in the "Long Log" districts of Western Washington. The majority of this militancy was attributed to "Huns", "Russians" or other "aliens". Their purpose was simply to destroy America's ability to wage war and many patriotic nativists held that they were succeeding. Their action virtually halted the region's production of the scarce Sitka spruce so vital to aircraft production. As one Wobbly gleefully commented—"not a stick of spruce was produced."[97] It became the region's patriotic duty to provide this “clean clear spruce that builds the battle fleets of the air, th[os]e war eagles that carry the glad tiding of freedom to all the world”.[98] With this in mind, the lumber barons felt little compunction in expanding to epic proportions the threat the IWW’s militant actions represented to America’s war effort.

The area continued to lead the nation’s anti-radicalism after the war. Communal experiences gained during the Free Speech Fights and the wartime strikes gave the area’s anti-radicals a comprehensive idea of the “real issues” underlying the Seattle General Strike, the Centralia massacre and the Red Scare. More important it gave them a dogged persistence to see the issue of alien radicalism resolved. It is telling that after Mitchell A. Palmer’s anti-Red crusade had come to be viewed as an embarrassing over-reaction in many other regions of the country, the sentiments that had inspired it were still being used as a means to political power in the Northwest. The link between radicals and undesirable immigration was forged of sterner stuff in the Northwest than other regions. Not only did such politicians as Ole Hanson or Albert Johnson continue to use the issues of radical exclusion as a means to further power, but the region’s increasingly powerful Ku Klux Klan saw the potential in anti-radicalism. As late as 1922, when the IWW and other forms of radicalism were showing signs of terminal decline, the resurrection of xenophobia inherent in the opposition to the Wobblies in particular was still considered a powerful device in the Northwest. Where the IWW was fundamentally internationalist, unpatriotic and alien, the Klan was all-American:

> Quite recently the governor of Oregon [Ben Olcott] issued a proclamation taking a stand against the Ku Klux Klan....We are not attempting to defend it but ask why it is that such a “hue and cry” should be raised against a seemingly harmless organization while a group of renegade disorganizers, the IWW’s, are allowed to carry on their work of destruction unhindered. This society [the IWW] publishes and distributes all over the country literature which is most un-American—in fact it could hardly be otherwise considering the nationality of the most of the “wobblies” as we call them—literature which is undermining American ideals and America herself and is becoming more of a menace day by day.[99]

The Ku Klux Klan saw the potential in the hackneyed national stereotypes of Eastern European revolutionaries, Italian anarchists, Jewish socialists and Irish terrorists as a method of feeding the link between the immigrant and radicalism. The “alien” radical was a potent bogeyman embodying “Revolution with a foreign accent.”[100] For example, in 1922, the leading politicians of the East were condemning, or at least distancing themselves from, the “deportations delirium” of Palmer’s brief bid for xenophobia-fuelled power. Simultaneously, the Invisible Empire in Washington was assuring its supporters that—“The Klan is pledged in opposition to the IWW and the Bolshevik, and every IWW organizer in the United States is under the eye of a Klansman."[101]

The longevity and virulence of this phobia can in some cases be explained by the Northwest's scattered demography and peculiar industrial pattern which served to highlight the connection between the alien and radicalism in the area. This was small-town intolerance—those who were not from the insular communities were alien, and those who sought radical objectives must also be alien, therefore radicalism was an alien import and the obvious way to halt it was to stem the tide of aliens. Ironically, also in the area's larger cities—most notably Seattle and Spokane—tolerance of radicalism, as aspects of individualism, seemed to attract further radicals. Washington was gaining a reputation as something of a radical center. For example, during the 1909 Spokane fight many liberals—from town councilors, members of the AFL, to churchmen—supported the fight on the grounds of individual liberty. This certainly served to prolong the fight as well as bringing it a national notoriety. The free speech fight became the focus of many radical journals—from the IWW's *Industrial Worker* to the *International Socialist Review*. It dominated the headlines and editorials of the local and regional press of all political leanings—from the Republican *Oregonian* to the labor orientated *Seattle Union Record*. Spokane elected a former Wobbly as city commissioner in 1911 and by 1912 Washington had a socialist representative in Olympia.[102] It also served to attract other radicals—who if not necessarily foreign-born were certainly portrayed as being alien in the nativist press.

As early as the 1880s Washington had become the destination of idealist communitarians—although unlike other areas of America these were often politically motivated rather than being founded on a national or religious basis.[103] The influence of these colonies was greater than is often appreciated. If many of their objectives remained beyond achievement, they still served as reservoirs and exchanges for radical thought, producing a range of influential figures in the political life of the state. The anarchist Home Colony was typical. Its diverse political, social, religious and sexual beliefs were published in the aptly named paper it published—*Discontent: The Mother of Progress.* It played host to and feted such notorious figures as the Russian-born Jewish anarchist "Red" Emma Goldman and David Caplan, one of those convicted of the infamous 1910 Los Angeles McNamara bombing. The Puget Sound colonies were rarely out of the regional news, frequently raided and always suspect.[104] Nevertheless, out of the motley assortment of free-lovers, pantheists, vegetarians and nude bathers emerged such influential idealistic figures as "Harry" Ault, from 1912 to 1928 the editor of America's first mass-circulation, union-owned newspaper—the *Seattle Union Record*—and Jay Fox who worked under him. These utopias also produced committed reformers like George E. Boomer, the editor of several radical papers throughout the state, and the socialist councilman and mayoral candidate for Bellingham, John Cloak, as well as several other local and national socialist candidates.

It was not merely isolation and relatively cheap land that attracted them, it was the area's marked tolerance—"We find this state [of Washington] to be particularly adapted to the work [of establishing "utopian" colonies] on account of the fact that the people are, mostly, well disposed towards Socialism."[105] Election results illustrate this left-wing sympathy. In 1894, 23 Populists were voted into Olympia, giving Washington a Free-silver/Populist/Democrat dominated State legislature. John R. Rogers, a Democrat/Populist of radical credentials, was voted into the Governorship in 1896, 1898 and 1900. In 1911, Judge Richard Winsor of Seattle was appointed the nation's first socialist schools director and in 1912 Mason County sent Washington's first socialist to Olympia. By 1913 the Washington city of Pasco had elected an entire municipal slate of socialists to office.[106] The state averaged 55 percent for Bryan in 1896 and Washington returned a higher vote for the socialists than the nation as a whole in the second decade of the Twentieth century. In 1912, some 40,000, over 12 percent, of all Washington ballots cast were for Eugene Debs. The national average was a little under 6 percent. Publications also indicated a leftward leaning. By 1903 even the indefatigable, uncompromising and abrasive Hermon F. Titus' hard-line revolutionary *Socialist* was selling to some 7,000 subscribers, making it the third largest American socialist publication.[107]

Nonetheless, a steady program of progressive legislation and internal wrangling between the revolutionary "Reds" and reform "Yellows" of the left ensured that the radicals' influence steadily declined in the period and they remained a minority in the bulk of the region outside Seattle. In Spokane the split condemned the powerful socialist element to the sidelines from as early as 1909. Similarly, in 1913 in Tacoma a "progressive" socialist party sheared some 2,000 from the estimated 6,000 socialist votes. Even in Pasco the socialist's municipal triumph endured for less than a year. This neutering of socialism served to both isolate and "radicalize" the radicals. In Seattle the influential, if despotic and eccentric, leader of the United Wage Workers of Washington and editor of the Seattle, later Toledo, *Socialist*, Dr. Hermon Titus advocated an "uncompromising, unpatriotic, class-conscious, militant, revolutionary" Marxism.[108] This "gang of red-flag worshippers and anarchists" became ever more associated with un-American ideals. For example, in 1913, the *Seattle Times* report of the quelling of a riot of drunken sailors inflamed by an IWW speaker in Seattle's skid row serves to illustrate the enduring "foreign-ness" of Seattle's radicals. The editor, "Colonel" Alden J. Blethen, stated the nativist view point—"Anarchy, the grizzly hydra-headed serpent which Seattle has been forced to nourish in its midst by a naturalized chief executive [British-born, mayor George F. Cotterill]...was plucked from the city and wiped out in a blaze of patriotism last night."[109]

With the influence of the First World War, the Russian Revolution and the Red Scare, these processes of alienation and demonization increased, culminating in the region with the reaction to America's first general strike and the violence in Centralia in November 1919. For a variety of reasons—ranging from economic or political self-interest, to a genuine fear of revolution—

"patriotism" increasingly demanded a linkage of "organic" labor politics with America and its revolutionary counterparts with the immigrant. The highly publicized swansongs of socialist radicalism in Seattle and syndicalist radicalism at Centralia re-enforced these views. Although the forces released and people disaffected by these seeming collapses proved too weak to propel (Ole) Hanson's presidential ambitions, Albert Johnson shepherded them into an effective congressional alliance—an alliance of political, media and commercial interests strong enough to force through his dreams of immigration restriction. The Northwest's role in the formation of this alliance lay in its unrelenting support for such exclusion from at least the first decade of the twentieth century. By the time the rest of the nation caught up with the Northwest's expulsive enthusiasm—with Palmer's deportation frenzy—the Northwest was used to patriotic exhortations "to show their Americanism" and remove this "part of our community which is, in fact, defying our government."[110]

No one was more sensitized to these warnings or took them more seriously than the self-proclaimed hero of the Seattle general strike, mayor Ole Hanson. Hanson claimed he had defeated these striking "aliens from Russia and Finland"—although the leadership was overwhelmingly naturalized-American—and imagined he had "deported them…[back] to their European homes."[111] The anomalies present in such claims demonstrate the essence of anti-radical nativism in the region—radicalism *was* a foreign phenomenon whether or not the advocates or activists were foreign-born. The link was almost undeniable in the minds of most Northwestern nativists. Radicalism was the product of undesirable immigration, for as Albert Johnson pointed out:

> The outbreaks of the Industrial Workers of the World and the growth of socialism…may be directly charged to the great incoming heterogeneous mass of undesirable wage-cutting inhabitants, many of them admittedly temporary inhabitants, who, before they have learned to speak our language and before they know our customs and institutions, are taught by foreign-born agitators to hate the United States.[112]

THE EMPLOYERS' ANTI-RADICALISM

There can be little doubt that it was in the interest of the employers, particularly those in the beleaguered wartime lumber industry, to propagate and manipulate this patriotic fervor. The war provided one of those infrequent opportunities for a lumber boom. Disaster, discovery or conflict had done so in the past as with the 1906 San Francisco earthquake, the Klondike gold rush and the Spanish-American War for example. The Northwest's lumber owners did not want to see their competitors in the Southern Pine Region pick up the sudden bonanza represented by the lucrative military contracts, particularly for the vital

Sitka. The veteran Wobbly Ralph Chaplin explained the IWW's version of what was happening:

> As soon as this country had taken its stand with the allied imperialists the price of lumber, needed for war purposes, was boosted to sky high figures. From $16.00 to $116.00 per thousand feet is quite a jump; but recent disclosures show that the Government paid as high as $1200.00 per thousand for spruce that private concerns were purchasing for less than one tenth of that sum. Gay parties with plenty of wild women and hard drink are alleged to have been instrumental in enabling the "patriotic" lumber trust to put these little deals across...Uncle Sam needed the wood and the lumber interests [wanted] the money.[113]

In spite of Chaplin's cynical allegations, the lumber barons remained determined to marry anti-radical patriotism to production. As one student of wartime industrial action, and a former member of a wartime government Labor Board explained, much of the blame for the perception of the IWW's aims in the region was down to the wish of the employers to isolate the radicals, for—

> [A]n impartial study of the things it [the IWW] actually did during the war...its work in the field...will show: (1) That the large majority of its members were, and are, ignorant of its subversive doctrines. (2) That during the war its functions were those of the ordinary trade union, even though its leaders expressed extremely radical and frequently revolutionary opinions....That employers made the existence and doctorines [sic] of the IWW excuse for illegal and violent effort toward any organized effort to improve wages, hours, or working conditions, whether by members of the IWW, the AFL or otherwise.[114]

The strikers were portrayed as being disloyal extremists—unpatriotic Wobblies—although the vast majority of striking loggers were not members of the "alien" IWW. Estimates of the maximum Wobbly strength in the Northwest lumber industry would indicate that between 2,000 and 3,000 men held the syndicalists' red membership card throughout the period. Further, many of these cards would have been inactive as the owner may have left the region, been injured or even settled down as a "scissor bill". Coupled with this a large proportion, if rarely the majority, of the workers were American citizens and their motivation was an improvement of conditions and pay rather than German victory in Europe or the overthrow of American democracy. Carleton H. Parker held that the lumber workers' action was fundamentally "a strike to better conditions. The IWW are only the display feature. The main body of opinion is from a lot of un-skilled workers who are sick of the filthy bunk-house and rotten grub."[115] Some indication of the influence of the depth of grievance is demonstrated by the fact that at the height of the Northwest's lumber dispute some 20,000 loggers were on strike.[116]

Nevertheless, the lumber barons' attitude was not purely predicated on self-interest and deception. The mobility, militancy, evangelism, vociferousness and inter-changeability of membership cards meant that IWW numbers always appeared greater than they actually were.[117] Regardless of the apologies of liberals like Parker, the bosses maintained that the strike in a time of national emergency could not be the action of patriotic American workers. The appearance of the notorious black cat sticker and the barrage of threats of sabotage induced a siege mentality in the lumber barons' minds. The embattled employers' view was that the Wobblies' radical creed gave them gave them the super-human strength of the fanatic and made them oblivious to patriotism or common morality:

> Numerically the Industrial Workers of the World organization is not strong. I do not think its membership exceeds 200,000 and yet its name is a source of terror and fear for the same reason that a mad dog in a crowded thoroughfare or a murderous maniac at large might terrorize a large community....They know no flag except the flag of revolution....If German troops were upon our shores they would furnish information that would aid in their efforts to subjugate our people....They attempt to close every mine, shut down every factory and manufacturing plant, stop every train, prevent the planting of all crops or the reaping of the harvest. They terrorize the honest wage earner, and do not hesitate to assassinate him if they cannot secure his allegiance.[118]

Suspicion of workers' motives was closely tied in with immigration. The employers were now wary of those they had previously regarded as their main defense against radicalism—the immigrant laborer. The situation in the Northwest's woods demonstrated that control of unionism by the importing of foreign labor was now a risky strategy. For, a few years later a historian pointed out:

> the hordes of immigrants, whose admission to this country they [the employers] had encouraged as a means of curbing the demands of organized labor, might prove to be a greater menace to the existing economic order here than even the most extravagant claims of the [American] labor unions.[119]

This growing mistrust served to re-enforce the suspicions of what motivated strikers, particularly in the lumber industry, which had always been seen as notable for the amount of foreign-born workers within it:

> Much of the labor done in the lumber mills is heavy and is done under bad conditions. The yard work in bad weather and the handling of timbers in the streams are particularly unattractive. Because of this fact, a large share of the work connected with the lumber industry has always been done by the large immigrant class in the population....Any class of new immigrants capable of doing the heavier work around the lumber mills has readily found employment.[120]

The Dillingham Commission (1911) had found that foreign-born whites had made up between 40 and 60 percent of loggers in the northwest in the period between 1890 and 1910 and there is little reason to suggest that this trend changed in the next decade. Some 14 percent were Germans. There were high proportions of Nordics—largely Finns and Swedes—as well as a considerable numbers of Greeks, Italians, Slovaks, Dalmatians and Russians.[121] The war merely exaggerated these perceptions. The region's overwhelming patriotic response to the call for volunteers—Oregon had the greatest per capita percentage of volunteers of any state in the Union—and later the impact of conscription meant that many imagined the region's remaining workforce to be made up of aliens and shirkers.

The lumber barons' campaign fitted the prevalent mood of the nation—war fever. A large proportion of the American public *wanted* to believe that the radicals were fifth columnists. Regional Councils of Defense, Patriotic Societies and other vigilante groups needed targets and the over-whelming majority of foreign-born who originated from the Central Power states of Europe either demonstrated active support for the American war effort or remained stolidly mute over their true feelings. American patriots, detached from the military conflict by thousands of miles, required a visible, tangible enemy and the IWW was the obvious foil. Portland's *Oregonian* stated the nativist case in no uncertain terms—"US defeat in War the Plan of the IWW" was the headline of an article which re-iterated prevalent charges of sabotage and the internationalist defeatism that lay behind the lumber strike of 1917.[122] In the words of the historian of a leading wartime patriotic vigilante group, the American Protective League—"If they [the IWW] were not all Huns, they had the foul Hun imagination, and also the methods of the Hun."[123] As Professor Carleton H. Parker of Washington University—economist, academic theoretician of industrial relations, roving government IWW "expert" and co-architect of the Northwest lumber industry's wartime radical policy—put it:

> Some important portion of IWW terrorism can be traced directly back to the inarticulated [sic] public demand that the IWW news story produce a thrill....The current analysis of the IWW and its activities is an example of this perverted and unscientific method....[To the "Americans"] The organization

> is unlawful in its activity, un-American in its sabotage, unpatriotic in its relation to the flag, the government and the war.[124]

Many were swept along in the patriotic condemnation of the radical. American labor in its more conventional guise saw the dangers of international socialism. The elder statesman of conciliatory unionism, Samuel Gompers, claimed that Bismarck had invented international socialism for Germany to gain an international hegemony—"he [Bismarck] anticipated the advantage to the German Empire…[and] promoted internationalism among the peoples of other countries, but nationalism for Germany." He also accused the American socialists of receiving "large donations which could be traced to the German Imperial Treasury."[125] The nativists charged the IWW with being funded and supported by Germany. Utah's Senator King claimed:

> Members of this organization are in the employ of Germany. Certain it is that many of them are supplied with an abundance of gold and denounce this country and speak approvingly of Germany. In some sections where Austrians were employed, the IWW's urged them to strike using as an argument among others that they were producing materials which would be used by the allies and this country against their countrymen: that is the Austrians and Germans.[126]

It became simple for the enemies of the radicals to utilize patriotism in order to dismiss their arguments and to silence them. Although the jury dismissed the prosecution allegations that Hulet Wells and Kate Sadler's outspoken stance against conscription was backed by German funds, it took a Seattle jury a mere half hour to sentence the secretary Louise Olivereau to ten years under the Espionage Act for the distribution of anti-war leaflets. The jury was convinced, in spite of her protestations, that her actions were taken on the behalf of her IWW employers, and, the prosecution assured the court, that they in turn were funded from Berlin.[127]

The foreign-born, especially Scandinavians—largely Finns and Swedes—and, of course, Germans were of particular interest to patriots.[128] The patriots in the region went to the job of maintaining "security" with relish. A good example of this is the nation's foremost vigilante group, The American Protective League (APL). This was an organization of "250,000 American businessmen [turned]…detective to help win the war". It became a considerable force in the area. The APL's operatives reported that Portland was a "good place for roses, but a poor place for alien enemies." In Washington the patriots detected some

> 302 cases of disloyalty and sedition, nineteen of sabotage, twenty-four of anti-military activity, fifteen of propaganda, as well as 116 cases under the selective service [conscription] regulations and 124 ["shirkers"] under the "work or fight"

> order...[added to this] many IWW were jailed and many more were inducted into the Army. [However this did not necessarily lead to them reforming their ways as] Some of the latter tribe have been court-martialled since entering the army.[129]

The region developed a sophisticated mix of coercion and persecution in order to further alienate radicals. Some of this was the result of federal intervention. Government contracts contained clauses that stipulated conditions under which goods were to be produced, including the vital eight-hour day. The national government also sent Colonel Brice Disque, veteran lumber procurer of the Philippines, with one hundred "officers" and 25,000 federal troops/"workers", the Spruce Production Division, to support the Loyal Legion of Loggers and Lumbermen (the "Four L's"). Their job "as one of Uncle Sam's long range guns" was "bombing pro-Hunism out of the Northwest's forests."[130] This was to be achieved by means of a hybrid union/patriotic society/fraternity that once again stressed the lumber barons' linkage of production and patriotism. Their oath demonstrated the patriotic duties:

> I the undersigned, in consideration of my being a member of the Loyal Legion of Loggers and Lumbermen, do hereby solemnly pledge my efforts during the war, to the United States of America, and will support and defend this country against enemies both foreign and domestic....I further swear, by these presents [sic], to faithfully perform my duty toward this company by directing my best efforts, in every way possible, to the production of logs and lumber for the construction of Army airplanes and ships to be used against our common enemies. That I will stamp out any sedition or acts of hostility against the United States Government which may come within my knowledge, and I will do every act and thing [sic] which will in general aid in carrying this war to a successful conclusion.[131]

In return Disque negotiated with the lumber barons to gain an industry-standard eight hour day, time and a half for overtime, a uniform charge for board and to provide a weekly change of bedding at a nominal charge.[132]

While the employers, often reluctantly, had to agree to these concessions to worker comfort that were built into government contracts—not least the eight hour day—they gained a compliant and increasingly productive workforce. The region's lumber production soared from some 2.5 million board feet a month in September 1917 to over 20 million by the end of the war. This was over double what Colonel Disque had estimated was needed by the military.[133] The workforce gained more constant employment, under better conditions—although they lost many of their rights to organize. They also had reached an all time maximum for wages—50 cents per hour in the mills and 55 per hour in the woods and labor turnover "which had been over a thousand percent per annum, was substantially reduced."[134] By the time of the armistice the Four L's had an estimated 110,000 members in a thousand locals in Washington, Oregon and Idaho and its journal—*The Four L Bulletin*—had a circulation of 90,000 per month.[135] This represented a coup for the lumber baron, local workforce and nativist alike.[136]

The Northwestern approach with the Four L's was at variance with the national attempts at incorporation practiced in other regions. Whereas the National Association of Manufacturers, the Chambers of Commerce, Henry Ford and other employers in other industries in other regions famously put patriotic slogans in pay-packets, organized night schools and generally attempted to persuade the foreign-born of the advantages of American life, the lumbermen totally ignored these evangelical avenues.[137] In reality, in the forests and mills, *production* united employer and employee. As long as both sides strived for this common goal, patriotism was really a secondary issue to job stability, unity and profitability. The nativist—who existed among both employers and employees—had succeeded in further isolating and alienating the revolutionary threat to American democracy. Once isolated these radicals could be identified, arrested and imprisoned.

Nevertheless, the Four L's did not resolve the problem of what to do with the alien radicals. It was all very well to protect the woods and lumber mills from these revolutionaries by oaths and soldiers, but the radicals still remained in the area—albeit subdued or imprisoned. Mass imprisonment, as at Spokane in 1909-10, was costly and seemed to attract radicals to the area rather than repelling them. Regardless, the Northwest now embarked on a campaign which would dwarf the previous anti-radical roundups. Governor Lister acting with Washington's Patriotic League, threatened the IWW with the use of soldiers if they moved into the harvest fields and from July 1917 started a program of mass arrests using the widest possible interpretation of emergency powers granted under the 1917 Espionage Act.[138] The Department of Labor in Seattle, under local Immigration Bureau Chief Henry M. White, took over the city's persecution of the IWW. Within two weeks in January, 1918 immigration officials, police and the specially formed vigilante groups in collaboration with local employers had arrested 100 Wobblies in Seattle and similar high yielding raids took place in Tacoma, Spokane and Bend.[139]

The ending of the Great War saw a major increase in national industrial strife. In the year after the Armistice some 4 million American workers went out in over 3,500 bitterly fought strikes.[140] The causes were diverse. Some 4 million servicemen were leaving the armed forces. American opinion demanded that the "doughboy" was swiftly de-mobilized. He was. Some 600,000 left the services by the end of 1918, to be joined by the entire 4 million by the end of 1919. Promised "Anything You Want", the returning hero from the Northwest found himself leaving the army with a meager $60. Pushed into a shrinking economy he discovered a consequent reduction in employment opportunity as the region's wartime contracts dried up. He also found a more aggressive and organized labor movement, determined to protect its members' jobs. The taste of power that organized labor had gained with the conciliatory attitude of the wartime government to industrial relations led to an increased drive within the labor movement for powers of collective bargaining. They had seen the dollar's purchasing power decline to 45 percent of its pre-war value. Between 1913 and 1919 the cost of a basket of basic goods had risen by almost 100 percent. By contrast, over the same period wages had increased by less than 10 percent.[141] The AFL wartime truce ended as the obedient American workers felt that their patience and patriotism, their no-strike pledges and moderate wage demands, should be rewarded by increases in earnings that would meet the inflationary conditions unleashed by America's massive war effort.[142]

While their order books had filled and their profits had grown as a result of the benefits of an economy on a war footing, the employers had been in a tolerant mood. They had even made concessions to the workforce—in working conditions, hours and unionization. The unions assumed this would continue. Union membership grew. In November 1918 there were 4.5 million union members in the national workforce. By 1920 union membership had doubled from the pre-war figure to a brief high point of 5 million, almost 19 percent of the total workforce. Somewhat ironically, the industrialists had also benefited from the industrial relations policy of Woodrow Wilson's wartime administration. The concessions made to labor had been matched in a wartime relaxation of progressive checks on industrialists. The pre-war robber barons became the agency of America's wartime production miracle. On the eve of American entry into the conflict, Wilson himself had realized this anomaly:

> Every reform we have won will be lost if we go into this war. We have been making a fight on special privilege....War means autocracy. The people we have unhorsed will inevitably come into control of the country for we shall be dependent upon the steel, ore and financial magnate. They will run the nation.[143]

Some of the more reactionary industrialists and their supporters saw Wilson's administration as having gone too far in the search for industrial and later military peace. He was seen as attacking the sacrosanct principles of small government and individualism. His conservative opponents resented his internationalism and saw his vision of the post-war world as "pink" if not actively pro-Bolshevik:

> President Wilson, in his ignorance—an ignorance constantly nurtured by the pinks and red sympathizers who were his advisers...was an unconscious ally of bolshevism...endlessly prating about "democracy" and "internationalism" and constantly enthroning "peoples" and deprecating governments.

> Unwittingly, perhaps: doubtless misled by his radical-minded advisors, the advance agents of the new socialist revolution and the new program of the pinks in the United States.[144]

Industrialists sought a return to their heyday—the Gilded Age—where the executive and legislature had supported them unequivocally in a *laissez-faire* paradise prior to the incremental controls imposed by the progressives—a period before "the employing class was arrayed [by the muckrakers] as defendant before the bar of public opinion."[145] The business lobby was in no mood to compromise with newly empowered American unionism. Increasingly they stressed their age-old opposition to radicalism dressed up in the by now familiar combination of patriotism and xenophobia which both inspired and justified their intransigence.

The situation was even more volatile in the Northwest; the battle lines were even more distinctly drawn. The cease-fire in industrial disputes which Gompers' AFL had negotiated with central government seemed to have bypassed the Seattle region's unions. The underlying radicalism of the city combined in a volatile mix with the massive expansion of the city's industrial output in the war years, consequent housing shortages and an increase in prices that was higher even than the national average. In mid-June 1917, 900 of city's laundry workers had struck, joining the 100 or so street-car operatives and 200 metal workers already on strike. By the end of the year the trainmen of the Puget Sound Traction, Power and Light Co.; the meat packers at the city's massive Frye plant; the Candy and Cracker Co.'s workers; the waitresses and telephone exchange workers; along with some 12,000 shipyard workers had all been—or were still—out on strike.[146] Many of these strikes smoldered on into 1918 and during that year the longshoremen came out, the meat packer's action expanded into three further plants and the shipyard workers displayed ever-increasing levels of militancy. Seattle's veteran socialist, Hulet Wells understated the case when he commented that—"The radical labor sentiment which existed in Seattle at the close of the war was not typical of the country as a whole."[147] Many in the region agreed with the *Business Chronicles*' assessment that in the post-war era Seattle was the "most labor-tyrannized city in America" and the most likely site for what was felt to be the inevitable attempt at an American Bolshevik revolution.[148]

The October Revolution resonated throughout the world, not least America. American public opinion during the war had been put in the "charge of drill sergeants…goose-stepped…[and] taught to stand at attention and salute"[149] the One Hundred Percent Americanists. Victory over the central powers meant that the American public largely replaced the "evil Hun" with the Bolshevik menace. The Bolshevik regime had always been condemned. During the war, Americans could damn communism for the "betrayal" of their allies by the Bolsheviks at Brest-Litovsk. When the war ended the condemnation of the "un-democratic", violent and above all un-American nature of communism continued. The seemingly un-stoppable threat of the post-war expansion of communism inspired many of America's radicals and infuriated and terrified the establishment. The world was unsettled by events as ominous as Bela Kun's behavior in Hungary, the Kapp Putsch in Berlin or the general strike in Buenos Aires. To conservatives, "patriots" and nativists in enervated wartime and post-war America, unionism, communism and syndicalism became regarded as one. They were both the harbingers and tools of revolution. The Northwest was used to this. As early as March, 1917, the commandant of Seattle's Fort Lawton saw militant unionism as representing the primary threat to the region's stability: "Gentlemen, it is not Germany that our government fears...What it fears is industrial revolution which may be upon us in forty-eight hours, and you [of Seattle's Harvard Club] are the men to suppress such a revolution."[150]

He had some grounds for this belief. For after the Russian Revolution, in radical and disaffected Seattle the city's union organizations were at variance with the AFL, which remained largely true to its craft-based principles. Where Gompers had condemned Bolshevism "completely, finally and for all time"[151], Seattle's Central Labor Council had sent congratulations to the Soviet government. Seattle's longshoremen had refused to handle weapons bound for Admiral Kolchak's "White" forces in Siberia. The Council's mouthpiece, the *Union Record*, supported the labor protest over American troops in Siberia even when demonstrations had twice escalated to riot proportions. It also published, translated and annotated Lenin's speeches and urged the American emulation of Russia's revolutionary example: "Workers, your hour has struck! In Russia, in Austria and in Germany the producers are taking their heritage, long past due. In England, the toilers prepare to assume "a place in the sun" [with the Khaki Election]. In America—aye, there's the rub."[152] Such an outspoken stance polarized local opinion. Just as the lumber barons had found a fundamentally sympathetic audience in the region for their portrayal of the 1917 lumber strike as the attempt by German agents to disrupt the vital supply of lumber for America's war production, so in light of their self-confessed Bolshevik sympathies it was not difficult for the conservatives of the region to portray Seattle's labor movement as motivated purely by a wish for their own Communist revolution.

When the famed General Strike erupted on February 6, 1919, the strikers were swiftly pounced on by the conservatives and condemned as unpatriotic. The sympathy strike for Seattle's 28,000 shipyard workers became a battle with alien Bolsheviks who wanted to "take possession of our American Government and try to duplicate the anarchy of Russia."[153] Before, during and after the strike conservatives attempted to demonstrate the "foreignness" of both the concept of militant unionism and the strikers. The Seattle *Star*—the paper which advertised itself as having the "greatest daily circulation of any paper in the Pacific Northwest"—exemplified this. It started its campaign for the defense of patriotic virtues by informing "the common-sense union men of Seattle...[that] these false Bolsheviks haven't a chance to win anything for you in this country, because this is America—not Russia."[154] It then went on to point out:

> We call this thing that is upon us a general strike, but it is more than that. It is to be the acid test of American citizenship—an acid test of all those principles for which our soldiers have fought and died. It is to determine whether this is a country worth living in and a country worth dying for. The challenge is right up to you—men and women of Seattle. Under which flag do you stand?[155]

The *Star*'s message was taken seriously and rumors abounded of the revolution taking place: the city's water supply was apparently going to run out because the revolutionary strikers had blown up the Cedar River Dam; buildings were being dynamited and private property confiscated. None of these rumors were true. Nevertheless, to a populace fearful of marauding hordes of revolutionaries the headlines created something of a frenzy—law was about to break down, services would collapse and a Red Terror would emerge. The panic had already created a demand for weapons which gun shops found impossible to fill. A mixture of genuine fear of violence and disruption mixed with an increasingly generous dose of political opportunism, led the authorities to overplay the threat of revolution.

Anarchists and traitors, the city's conservatives increasingly held that the strike was bound to spread and the strikers were certain to resort to violence. Mayor Ole Hanson—who according to rumor had been assassinated—swore in, and armed, extra police and attempted to get the genuinely dying Governor Ernest Lister to call out the National Guard. He was pre-empted by the State Council of Defense Chairman—Henry Suzzallo—and State Attorney General Vaughn Tanner, who had managed to persuade the Secretary of War Newton Baker to dispatch the 13th Division of the First U.S. Infantry to Seattle and Tacoma. In the early hours of the morning of February 6, they arrived to join the 950 marines and sailors already in the city.[156] On February 7, Mayor Hanson put the general public at ease by writing a proclamation published in the *Star*. Some saw his confidence as shallow, for the paper was delivered free from trucks armed with machine guns. Nevertheless, he assured all that Seattle was safe, for he had already mobilized "fifteen hundred policemen [and] fifteen hundred regular soldiers…[and could] secure if necessary, every soldier in the Northwest to protect life, business and property."[157] The somewhat banal reality was that the police were called out to less than a third of their normal average of cases, the majority of schools and all hospitals remained open and food, fuel and electricity were readily available.[158]

The crucial aspect of the anti-radical scaremongers was the un-American nature of the strikers and their objectives. Seattle's left-wing community had always been considered by its enemies to be of dubious loyalty, for as America's top-selling weekly the *Saturday Evening Post* explained, the October Revolution was planned in Seattle "while Lenine [sic] and Trotsky tarried in the city's midst, en route to Russia."[159] This Bolshevik connection was also apparent to the city's residents. The eloquent and colorful Presbyterian urban missionary,

Dr. Mark A. Matthews, claimed that the Kerensky regime's demise had been "planned, schemed and executed in the city of Seattle...[by the] pro-German forces—the IWW fiends." [160] The "failure" of the strike was down to the true patriots holding their nerve. "Holy Ole" [Hanson], as the *Union Record* began calling him, took to driving with a huge Stars and Stripes arranged over his car—an outward sign of his "two-fisted" patriotism with which, as he informed the country, he had averted revolution. His view of events was that revolution had been averted by swift, decisive action:

> The sympathetic revolution [in Seattle] was called in the exact manner, as was the revolution in Petrograd. Labor tried to run everything...except for a few things which were exempted. We refused to ask [for] exemptions from anyone. The seat of government is at City Hall. We organized 1,000 extra policemen...and told them to shoot on sight anyone causing disorder....They [the strikers] knew we meant business and they started no trouble....This was an attempted revolution which they attempted to spread all over the United States. It never got to first base, and it never will if the men in control of affairs will tell all traitors and anarchists that death will be their portion if they start anything....Let us clean up the United States of America.[161]

Americanism as an anti-radical policy worked. It was not only an offensive weapon with which to beat the radicals, it was also a defensive weapon with which to deflect any blame for the consequences of post-war decline in the regional economy. A spectacular wartime boom propelled Seattle from an expanding lumber town to a city of heavy industry, one of the largest shipbuilding centers in the Union—drawing in labor from wherever it was available. The war created an industrious workforce working towards the patriotic goal of supplying a seemingly insatiable need for shipping. These shipyards bragged they could construct a steel freighter in 78 days. Seattle's shipyards filled some 26.5 percent of the Emergency Fleet Corporation's almost $3 billion worth of contracts. This boom period abruptly closed with the Armistice. The evaporation of lucrative "cost plus" government contracts inevitably led to the closure of many of the yards—most notably the largest, the high-capacity Skinner and Eddy yard. The city's "industrial" workforce shrank from some 40,000 at the start of 1919 to a little over 13,000 by 1921.[162] To the anti-radicals, particularly those attempting to reduce their workforces, this collapse was not simply the result of the outbreak of peace removing government contracts, but rather it was indicative of the image of Seattle. The evaporation of Seattle's industrial base was the consequence of the refusal of America to deal with a "Red Seattle" dominated by un-American ideals.

To the "patriots", the conservatives, the nativists, the strike came to be seen as an un-American tool. At the height of the Red Scare, J Edgar Hoover—

then head of the Justice Department's General Intelligence Division—claimed that following Seattle's "attempted revolution" at least "fifty percent of the influence behind [the strikes across the nation was] traceable directly to communist agents."[163] "Run the Reds out from the land whose flag they sully" boomed the AFL's new ally, the American Legion in 1919.[164] It became even more important for the region to re-iterate its Americanism. Asserting this patriotism was becoming increasingly shrewd as America entered what John Higham has termed the "Tribal Twenties" where racial, religious and anti-radical nativism congealed and increasingly took on a more aggressive stance with such organizations as the revitalized Klan.[165] Early shoots of such sentiments provided the grassroots support for the region's patriotic nativists—whether they were laborers or management. Nevertheless, given the apparent importance of the revolutionary threat that had been so comprehensively defeated, there was, as Harvey O'Connor pointed out, an embarrassing shortage of revolutionary anarchists, traitors and Bolsheviks in Seattle's prisons. The *World's Work* explained this shortfall claiming that "the aliens who started the disturbance have been deported to their European homes."[166] This was, in large measure, wishful thinking on the nativists' part. The arrests for deportation became a significant reality only after a bomb exploded outside Attorney General Mitchell A Palmer's house on June 2, 1919. Enraged, and with one eye on the presidency, Palmer authorized his crusade to eliminate America's "Red Web", feeding the Northwestern nativists' extant desire to see the region cleansed of the perennial radical problem that so blighted the lives of the genuine "patriots". Many in the region saw the dangers of radicalism more clearly than the rest of the nation. In the weeks following June's mysterious bombings, it was Washington State's Progressive Senator Miles Poindexter who expressed a fear that there was a "real danger that the government will fall" under the radical threat.[167]

THE NORTH WEST AND FEDERAL EXCLUSION OF RADICALS

Even before Palmer's raids started, the Northwest's conservative restrictionists had demonstrated a persistent, relentless, single-mindedness in their pressure for alien radical deportations and exclusion. It is telling that the Northwest is the only area which warrants detailed analysis of "de-naturalization" as a response to immigrant radicalism in the one significant contemporary study of the immigrant and the American legal system—the 1923 *The Immigrant's Day in Court* by the sociologist Kate Claghorn. Claghorn details the highly publicized Olsson case which dominated the press in Seattle in the winter of 1912-13. This case in many ways presaged the national wartime campaign of Americanization with its hatred of "hyphenism". Tacoma "Wobbly" Leonard Olsson—who by his own admission was "a frequenter of assemblages…as a speaker…for radical changes in the institutions of this country"[168]—was found guilty of naturalization fraud. His conviction rested on

Judge C.H.Hanford's assertion that Olsson's political affiliations precluded him genuinely swearing allegiance to the American flag—"Those who believe in and propagate crude theories hostile to the Constitution are barred [from American citizenship]."[169] Claghorn also deals with the less publicized but equally telling decision in 1918 to deprive Carl Swelgin of his citizenship in Oregon, again as the result of his membership of the IWW.

Both cases illustrate the region's legitimization of hostility to radicals, the belief in guilt by association when dealing with the organizations of the left. For some in the region it was not enough to revoke or prevent naturalization, any legislation dealing with radicalism should eject such aliens from the country. Such sentiments led Congressman Albert Johnson to claim that "that the joining of an organization such as the Industrial Workers of the World by an alien is of itself the overt act sufficient to warrant deportation."[170]As the then Assistant Secretary of Labor Louis F Post damningly put it:

> [T]he forest-region influences of the Pacific Northwest thrust through Congress the comprehensive law of 1918...[that] compel[ed] the Secretary of Labor to deport aliens for mere membership in the IWW without any proof of individual culpability.[171]

Post's condemnation was founded on this casual presumption of guilt. Misgivings over the very concept lay at the heart of Secretary of Labor William Wilson's circumspection over the issue of the deportation cases. The government's attitude was that the existing legislation was sufficient for the control of alien radicals and that it required a careful application:

> Even if some aliens are anarchists and lawless, I can see no justification for making the Department of Labor so....We will not arrest, detain or deport any alien simply for joining the IWW, but we will arrest and detain until we can deport, any alien, whether a member of the IWW or not, who is found advocating or teaching the unlawful destruction of property...anarchy or the overthrow of the government by force...or who is in any manner subject to deportation under the immigration laws.[172]

Many of the Northwest's anti-radicals felt that they were the only Americans who truly understood the true motives and therefore the real dangers of the alien revolutionary. Even before the June bombings which sparked the Justice Department's round-ups, the behavior of radicals in the Northwest with the free speech fights, lumber strikes and war time labor militancy assured a more entrenched and polarized attitude within the region. There were frequent calls for increased powers for vigilante groups:

> The recent outrages perpetrated on it [the American flag] by the IWW, socialists and anarchists make it our duty to urge such actions as suggested in our resolutions [among which was request that the vigilante groups of Spanish War veterans' be given the ability to vet]...the names of all persons applying for citizenship...to investigate the character and record of such aliens, [since]...many foreigners seeking refuge here are already inflamed with the poison of anarchy and have no respect for our government.[173]

The failure of Seattle's revolution merely confirmed the suspicions of the region's nativists. To Northwestern conservatives the radicals had proved their destructive, revolutionary and "Un-American" aims time after time. Exaggerated tales of radical opposition to all that true patriots held dear were found in their "violence" at Spokane, Aberdeen and Everett; in their sabotage of the vital wartime spruce industry; in their revolutionary, Bolshevik ambitions for the communist dictatorship in Seattle. They had forfeited their right to be treated as Americans, if indeed they ever had been. The solution was once again ejection. Once again the federal authorities refused to comply. No alien "anarchists" were deported from the United States in the year to June, 1917 and only two were deported the following year, this figure rose to a mere 37 in 1919.[174] A mere 9 out of 129 Wobblies arrested on the Seattle waterfront by the local Office of Naval Intelligence between October, 1917 and April, 1918 were even charged.[175] Even when Seattle's anti-radical forces had faced down the threat of the revolutionaries, their demands for the ejection of these aliens met with little concrete success. The federal authorities continued to block their attempts to have these obvious undesirables deported. In May, 1919, Seattle's Immigration Commissioner, and ever-enthusiastic red-hunter, Henry White arrested and sent to New York for deportation 54 Italian and Russian radicals from Puget Sound's mining district. Of these, 14 were immediately freed on arrival at Ellis Island, 12 chose to leave America rather than endure continued detention and a mere three were convicted of any "crime" worthy of deportation.[176]

Most worryingly many nativists felt that the region's radicals seemed to be recovering from their "defeat" in the general strike. For example, in July, 1919, Seattle's Labor Council had been one of three organizations to threaten a second general strike if the infamous San Francisco Preparedness Day bomber, Thomas Mooney, was not given a retrial.[177] Arguably, what really increased the pressure for some resolution of what was now considered a perennial problem in the area was the violence of the events in Centralia in November, 1919. The opposition was once again centered on the fear that itinerant agricultural, lumber and fishery workers would congregate in the urban areas, most notably Spokane and Seattle, during the winter months. The cheap, frequently Japanese run, boarding houses and IWW halls came to be seen as nests of radicalism. Unsurprisingly, many Northwesterners were at the forefront of Attorney General A. Mitchell Palmer's crusade for the eradication of left-wing radicalism. The region was zealous in its arrest of "Reds", although in the area it was more the IWW than the Communist Party—"the former [the IWW] constitutes the same menace in the West as the latter [the Russian Workers' Union] does in the East....[Seattle's Immigration Bureau claimed] that the organization is anarchistic and revolutionary in its teachings."[178] The scale of the region's anti-radicalism ambitions was impressive. From as early as January 1918 the local immigration center in Seattle, under commissioner Henry M. White, had stated its objective was to remove an estimated 5,000 local Wobblies. In order to achieve this the region was creative in its interpretations of the immigration law. Wobblies were accused of being public charges, threatening the sanctity of property or the safety of the Federal Government, rather than charged simply as members of the IWW—although there can be little doubt that in most cases this was the real reason for their arrest.

Washington State had become the proving ground. The nativist remained convinced that the success or failure of such cases was dependent on the "whim" of judges. In 1918, Judge Augustus Hand drew a nice distinction between "active" and "inactive" membership of the IWW in the Nelson case. While the "inactive" Wobbly was considered the dupe of higher forces, the active one was an altogether different proposition. He was a revolutionary, an advocate and teacher of the unlawful destruction of property, sabotage and class hatred. Hand found Sam Nelson "inactive" and thus ineligible for deportation and this distinction remained one of the acid tests for deportation. The "Hollander, De Wal" was found to be "active" and deported. Sometimes the entire armory of deportation clauses had to be used. The "Wobbly" John Morgan was acquitted of charges of anarchy and liability to become a public charge, but deported on grounds of advocating the destruction of property. A "Czecho-Slovak" [sic] Wobbly with $100 "in his pocket" and $700 "in a Canadian bank" admitted he had "asked for a night's lodging in a police cell" and found himself deported as a result.[179] Given the uncertainty of the courts, more imaginative methods were employed by the regional immigration authorities. For instance, provisions within existing immigration legislation allowed the authorities to deport those who had been resident in the United States for less than five years. Wobblies who crossed and re-crossed the fluid Canadian-American border in search of logging, fisheries and harvesting jobs, could be, and frequently were, therefore detained for deportation as itinerant aliens liable to become a public charge. Nevertheless, given the ingenuity used, to the nativists the results were paltry. By November 1919, 697 aliens had been arrested nation-wide. Sixty were deported—all except three of them were deported as a radical threat to property, the government or general law and order.[180] Of a total 150 Wobblies arrested in Seattle during the Red Scare, 27 were deported.[181]

In their efforts to rid the country of alien radicals, at the height of the paranoia, Palmer's supporters managed to get Albert Johnson appointed chairman of the influential House Immigration and Naturalization Committee. Johnson, the high priest of restrictionism, was determined to carry through what he saw as the will of his region, if not the country. He felt that the Wilson administration was unsympathetic to the Northwest's escalating radical problem. From his new position he felt able to counteract the " polite parlour Bosheviks" within the Labor Department whom he saw as lending "comfort and sympathy…and giv[ing] advice to revolutionaries, which can only serve to get all hands into trouble sooner or later."[182] Johnson's aversion to the Labor Department had some justification from a nativist perspective. Between November, 1919 and April, 1920 the attorney general's office issued warrants for the arrest of 6,350 alien radicals nationwide. About 3,000 arrests were made. Some 2,500 of those arrested were members of the Communist Party and the remainder were members of the Union of Russian Workers. Secretary Post upheld the deportation order for 762.[183] Just before Christmas, 1919 the former troop transport the *Buford*, left Ellis Island for Russia on the first of what was hoped would be a series of "Soviet Arks".[184] On board were 249 of these deportees—"blasphemous creatures who not only rejected America's hospitality…but also sought by a campaign of assassination and terrorism to ruin her as a nation of free men".[185] A further eleven of the 762 were sent by other means to a variety of destinations. The remainder were detained and then eventually freed.

Secretaries Wilson and Post seemed dedicated to blocking the anti-radical crusade. Johnson was furious, he claimed that—"While [Palmer's]…Justice Department hunts down dangerous aliens, [Secretary Post's]…Department of Labor considers it its duty to protect them instead of the public."[186] He felt that the Labor Department's attitude amounted "a negative endorsement of the legality of the IWW."[187] The reluctance of the Labor Department to enforce the existing deportation legislation stemmed from a combination of difficulties imposed by the political situation in Russia—with the outbreak of civil war—and worries over the humanitarian and constitutional implications of such expulsions. Those who supported the deportation policy pointed to radical claims that Russia was a workers' paradise. Why should they not want to go? Hadn't those radicals claimed that "To all appearances Russia is breaking with the chains of autocracy…in place of Russian refugees seeking shelter in the United States from tyranny at home, will it be persecuted Americans who will be driven to Russia for a haven of refuge from the iron heel of American plutocracy?"[188]

In a final attempt to tighten the legislation on deportation, Johnson and other nativists forced the Immigration Act of May 1920 over the objections of a reluctant Labor Department. Nevertheless, although this act clarified the position on the repatriation of alien radicals, by the time of its adoption the Labor Department had freed all aliens in detention.[189] Little had changed in spite of Johnson's efforts. To the nativist, the legal system still appeared to be designed to protect the alien radical. Increasingly, they felt that the only way to achieve a permanent solution to the radical problem was through national immigration restriction, legislation that could stop radicals entering the country rather than relying the frequently ineffective methods of deporting them. In order to achieve this, nativists needed to re-enforce the foreign nature of radicalism.

The area had a history of associating foreigners with radicalism and violence. A variety of foreign groups were associated with such radicalism. Irish and German immigrants had been associated with the radical organizations dedicated to the expulsion of Chinese labor in Portland, Tacoma and Seattle in the 1890s. The utopian communitarian communities of the first two decades of the Twentieth century in Puget Sound were viewed as predominantly populated by radical, immoral, foreigners.[190] Nativists pointed to the IWW being "riddled with foreigners." There were many Italians, Germans and Irish among the leadership; Greeks, Finns and Russians among the rank and file. It was a Swede, Joel Emmanuel Haggland—Joe Hill—veteran of the free speech fights, who created the Wobbly anthem "Hallelujah, I'm a Bum" prior to his 1915 "martyrdom" in Utah. An Italian immigrant, Joseph Ettor, was one of the most influential Wobblies in the Northwest region.[191] He organized the 1907 Portland lumber strike that arguably established the *modus operandi* for future IWW action in the region. He went on to be involved in most of the important national incidents of radicalism from the Lawrence Textile strike of 1912 to the Paterson trial of 1913 to the Mesabi Range Strike of 1916.

To the nativists, wherever there was radical violence, there you would find the foreign-born. Frequently the local press would find some link between an act of violence and the alien. In 1900, the region's Baptists blamed the anarchist assassination of President McKinley on the gunman's Polish Catholic upbringing.[192] Two Irish-born Wobblies were among those charged after the fighting in the Astoria Hotel in Centralia in 1919.[193] Ole Hanson put "unassimilated aliens" at the top of his list of "the [eight] major causes of …unrest and anarchy" in the United States.[194] But it is perhaps the Presbyterian minister Mark A. Matthews who best expressed the association of the foreign-born radical with all that was abhorrent in American society. He saw the large part of Seattle's radical problems as the predictable result of the unchecked invasions by "The foreign elements – the IWW forces, the vice syndicate fiends, the pro-German element and the German spies."[195]

Jewish, German and Russian immigrants were regularly associated with socialism and Bolshevism, particularly after the First World War and the Russian Revolution. The regions within the Northwest rejected the calls for Americanization of the workforce advocated by such East Coast reformers as Francis Kellor and opted for an aggressive exclusion policy long before the nation perceived a failure within the wartime efforts to produce conformity in the foreign-born. The activities of radicals in the region produced a sustained disillusioned xenophobia in a variety of communities before the emergence of Palmer's crusade let alone its continuation by such groups as the Ku Klux Klan. For example, the 1912 Aberdeen free speech fight resulted in a successful drive to Americanize the workforce and expel the Finnish and Greek workers who had been seen to form the backbone of IWW support in the region.[196] All these prejudices and preconceptions were applicable to most areas of the Union which were undergoing industrial strife and immigration during the period. Various events from the Haymarket bombing to the Russian Revolution brought foreign radicalism to the national press' attention and served to re-enforce the national prejudice. Nonetheless there were features peculiar to the region which go some way to explaining the vehemence of anti-radicalism in the area.

The radical threat in the Northwest was not solely seen as emanating from Europe. The absence of America's rigid two-party system, the influence of British socialists and the, at least occasionally, pragmatic rather than confrontational attitude of British Columbia's administration, all contributed to a strong pro-labor bloc in the province. Socialism was not "un-Canadian". Nativists claimed that Canadian radicalism infected American workers—Canadians claimed the opposite. There was certainly interaction, the IWW's Spokane-based *Industrial Worker* was circulated on both sides of the border. To the leading Seattle socialists, the opposite was true. Canadian socialism's frequent moderation acted as a spur to the Northwest's radicalism.[197] Ironically, many American socialists saw their Canadian counterparts as collaborators with the forces of the workers' oppression. The Americans' isolated position radicalized them, demonstrated in a dogmatic adherence to principle. For example, Dr. Hermon Titus' refused to treat with the Canadian Socialist National Executive Committee when they attempted to mend the rural/urban schism they saw as crippling Washington socialism.

Given the porous nature of the Canadian border—most notably in the boundary-defying integration of mining, farming and lumber of the Inland Empire and the Kootenays, with its commercial center in "radical" Spokane—this foreign socialist element frequently provided another strand of alien radicalism which was absent in many other areas of the Union. A large proportion of the area's workers migrated over the border to work in the forests and farms of British Columbia, returning when the season was over. The supposed internationalism of radical thought and the area's long-standing mistrust of their northern neighbor made many Northwesterners fearful of the power of Canadian radicalism, or so the nativists hoped. After all, it had been Canadian Wobblies that the conservative Aberdeen community saw as the bogeyman in 1912.

It is also perhaps worth noting that some within the radical organizations saw the continuation of open immigration as hastening the end of their halcyon days. A mythology was increasingly growing around the transient laborer as mechanization; population growth and the automobile caused his utility and numbers to die back in the 1920s. Throughout the period a number of histories, studies and reports showed increasing sympathy for the "casual" and his plight.[198] In a mirror image of the fear his presence inspired in the settled communities of the West, the legendary hobo of the woods, harvest fields, mines and fisheries of the Pacific states was seen as threatened with extinction by the mass immigration of "non-American types". Once the Red Scare had ended and the threat of revolution subsided, many felt that the Wobbly rebel was as "American" a hero as the prairie settler or the Indian hunter. To add to this heroic image there emerged a genre of "tramping" autobiographies, of which William H. Davies' 1917 *Autobiography of a Supertramp* was probably the best known and most widely read.[199] In the vast majority of these works the hero was a young British, Canadian or American-born man of settled, urban background whose wanderlust got the better of him. These sanitized tales turned the desperate "bay rum soaked bindle stiff" into a young "tramping casual" who voluntarily embarked upon a turn-of-the-century proletarian American version of the "Grand Tour". He spent the last part of his youth adventurously riding the rails in the "side-door Pullmans", experiencing the camaraderie of the "jungles", flop houses and skid rows, showing contempt for the "homeguards" while feeling the harshness and hostility of authority. All this took place while he working his way from coast to coast—most often, as with his pioneer antecedents, from East to West. When he tired of this, met his love or was incapacitated he settled down and wrote of his exploits explaining the "casuals'" sub-culture to a growing readership.[200]

In the Northwestern context this hero emerged most clearly in works which called themselves fiction. The setting of these works was almost always sylvan or rural and the un-skilled industrial truth for the vast majority of the region's itinerants was often concealed in a haze of nostalgic yearning for bygone craftsmanship. The fictitious "itinerant" was frequently portrayed less as the lumberyard worker, fruit grader or fish packer, than as the virile, hard living, but basically honest, lumberjack or the taciturn, respectful, annual visitor welcomed onto the isolated Palouse farm for the harvest.[201] Nevertheless, uncompromising radicalism—born of grim, more often than not, violent, experience—was central to his character. Here was a man governed by principle and that principle was solidarity with his fellow workers. Crucially, this new breed of left-wing hero was typically either Scandinavian, German or Irish and as such was threatened by the immigration patterns of his time as surely any other "American". As early as 1914, one observer of the Western itinerant labor force claimed that the region's idealized independence of spirit, freedom, fellowship and mobility would disappear with the continuation of mass immigration, for

> It seems to be a characteristic of the [Western] American type worker to take no lip from the boss. He is seldom so tied to a job but that he will throw it up if the boss curses him....The job is not dear to the heart of the transient worker. This independent attitude does not hold true of the Oriental and to a less extent than among workers of the American type does it hold true of the "New Immigration".[202]

NOTES

[1] The journal of the Seattle Ku Klux Klan, *The Watcher on the Tower* June 20, 1923.
[2] Oregon State Immigration Commission, *The Oregon Almanac, 1915* (Salem, 1914) pp.54, 319 & 320.
[3] Timber figures taken from Dorothy Johansen and Charles M. Gates, *Empire of the Columbia: A History of the Pacific Northwest* (New York, 1957) pp.383-399, unless otherwise stated.
[4] See the Grays Harbor *Washingtonian* April 1, 1934.
[5] See Carlos A. Schwantes, "Perceptions of Violence on the Wageworkers Frontier: An American-Canadian Comparison" *Pacific Northwest Quarterly* 77 (1986) 52-71.
[6] As one labor historian put it, "The labor movement lay stunned after its brief flirtation with anarchy [the Haymarket massacre]. The union men drew away from the anarchist agitators and taking their information from the capitalist press only, concluded that socialism and anarchism were the same thing, and would if tolerated, lead the movement to ruin and disaster." Paul W. Brissenden, *The IWW* (New York, 1957) p.39.
[7] For a definitive, if lengthy, contemporary insight into the co-relation of immigration and radicalism centered on the Haymarket affair see Michael J. Schaack, *Anarchy and Anarchists* (Chicago, 1889).
[8] Samuel Gompers to the 1893 Labor Convention in Chicago cited in Samuel Gompers, *Seventy Years of Life and Labor* Vol I (New York, 1925) p.397. However, there are examples of common interest between the radicals and the AFL. For example, AFL activists were eager to defend IWW pressures for free speech rights in Spokane in 1908-09 and the AFL unions joined IWW workers in the 1917 Cascades lumber strike.
[9] The only region with a higher mean wage was the "Mountain region" with $3-25 a day. Figures taken from the *Aldrich* report cited in Richard White, *It's Your Misfortune and None of My Own: A New History of the American West* (Norman, Oklahoma, 1991) p.279.
[10] Figures taken from Carlos A. Schwantes, *Radical Heritage: Labor, Socialism and Reform in Washington and British Columbia 1885-1917* (Moscow, Idaho, 1979) p.19
[11] See ibid. p.20.
[12] Ralph Chaplin, *The Centralia Conspiracy* (Seattle, 1920) p.9.
[13] Cloice Ray Howd, *Industrial Relations in the West Coast Lumber Industry U.S. Department of Labor Statistics, Bulletin No. 349* (Washington, D.C., 1924) p.54.
[14] Figures taken from Carleton H. Parker, *The Casual Laborer and Other Essays* (New York, 1920) pp.77-79.
[15] The Immigration Commission, *Reports: Immigrants in Industries, Japanese and Other Immigrant Races in the Pacific Coast and Rocky Mountain States vol. 25* (Washington, D.C., 1911) pp.7 & 317.

[16] Ibid. p.148.
[17] Ibid. p.345.
[18] Ibid. p. 317.
[19] Frederick C Mills cited in Gregory R Woirol, *In the Floating Army: F.C. Mills on Itinerant Life in California, 1914* (Urbana, Illinois, 1992) p.57.
[20] Hermon F Titus, "Revolutionary Socialism and Reform Socialism" Toledo *Socialist* January 7, 1906 cited in Schwantes (1979), op.cit. p.96.
[21] William Z. Foster, *Pages from a Worker's Life* (New York, 1939) p.108
[22] *Congressional Record* 65th Congress, 2nd Session, p.5494.
[23] For an analysis of the decline of migratory labor see Carey McWilliams, *Ill Fares the Land: Migrants and Migratory Labor in the United States* (Boston, 1942) pp.34-60.
[24] See James F. Shepherd, "The Development of Wheat Production in the Pacific Northwest" *Agricultural History* 49 (1975) 258-271.
[25] See Jonathan Dembo, "Dave Beck and the Transportation Revolution in the Pacific Northwest 1917-1941" in G. Thomas Edwards and Carlos A. Schwantes, *Experiences in a Promised Land: Essays in Pacific Northwest History* (Seattle, 1986) pp.339-352.
[26] For an account of the early rural pressures for improved roads, see Marilyn P. Watkins, *Rural Democracy: Family Matters and Politics in Western Washington, 1890-1925* (Ithaca, New York, 1995) pp.80-83.
[27] Figures taken from Carl Abbot, *Portland: Planning, Politics and Growth in a Twentieth century City* (Lincoln, Nebraska, 1983) p.93.
[28] Foster, op.cit. pp.108-109.
[29] For a knowledgeable and personal account of the improvements in the Northwest forestry industry see James Lemonds, *Deadfall: Generations of Logging in the Pacific Northwest* (Missoula, Montana, 2001) pp.7-23.
[30] *Age of Steel* August 30, 1890 p.9.
[31] Robert DeC. Ward, "The New Immigration Law and its Operation" *Scientific Monthly* 21 (1925) 53
[32] K.H.Condit, 'Immigration or Machinery' *American Machinist* LVIII (1923) 393 cited in Higham op.cit. p.317. See also Morrel Heald, "Business Attitudes Toward European Immigration, 1880-1900" *Journal of Economic History* 13 (1953) 291-304.
[33] The Immigration Commission, vol. 25 op.cit. pp.389
[34] Ibid. pp.389-90.
[35] For an account of the manual salmon canning on the Columbia see Rudyard Kipling, *American Notes* (Boston, 1899) pp.59-60. For details of Edmund A. Smith's "Iron Chink" see Carlos A. Schwantes, *Hard Travelling: A Portrait of Work Life in the New Northwest* (Lincoln, Nebraska, 1994) p.117 and Patrick W. O' Bannon, "Technological Change in the Pacific Coast Canned Salmon Industry, 1900-1925: A Case Study" *Agricultural History* 56:1 (1982) 151-166.
[36]See Richard A Rajala, "Bill and the Boss: Protest, Technological Change and the Transformation of the West Coast Logging Camp 1890-1930" *Journal of*

Forest History 33 (1989) 168-179; and Andrew Mason Prouty, *More Deadly than War: Pacific Coast Logging, 1827-1981* (New York, 1989).

[37] See A.A. Sargent, "The Wyoming Anti-Chinese Riot" *Overland Monthly* 4 (November 1885) 510 and for the Squak massacre see the *Washington Standard* September 11, 1885.

[38] Hubert H. Bancroft, *History of Washington, Idaho and Montana* (San Francisco, 1887) p.294.

[39] See Gompers, op.cit. Vol II, pp.151-173.

[40] Figures cited in Prescott F. Hall, *Immigration and Its Effects Upon the United States* (New York, 1907) p.312.

[41] Isaac A. Hourwich, *Immigration and Labor: The Economic Aspects of European Immigration to the United States* (New York, 1912) p.333.

[42] See Dana Frank, "Race Relations and the Seattle Labor Movement, 1915-1929" *Pacific Northwest Quarterly* 85 (Winter, 1994) 35

[43] "Industrialism is not Syndicalism" *Industrial Worker* January 9, 1913 p.2

[44] The *Oregonian* January 12, 1914.

[45] See Paul Buhle and Dan Georgakas, *The Immigrant Left in the United States* (New York, 1996) p.276.

[46] See Dana Frank, *Purchasing Power: Consumer Organising, Gender and the Seattle Labor Movement* (Cambridge, U.K., 1994) p.20.

[47] James A. Duncan cited in Robert L. Friedheim, *The Seattle General Strike* (Seattle, 1964) p.48.

[48] Seattle *Union Record* August 11, 1919.

[49] See Carlos A. Schwantes, "Leftward Tilt on the Pacific Slope: Indigenous Unionism and the Struggle Against AFL Hegemony in the State of Washington" *Pacific Northwest Quarterly* 70 (1979) 24-33

[50] Figures taken from Department of Commerce, Bureau of Census, *Abstract of the Fourteenth Census of the United States, 1920* (Washington, D.C., 1923) pp.314-319

[51] The Seattle *Star* February 10, 1919.

[52] The Reverend Mark A. Matthews, "An Appeal to the Patriots of Seattle" 1919, cited in Dale E. Soden, *The Reverend Mark A. Matthews: An Activist in the Progressive Era* (Seattle, 2001) p.153.

[53] For example, see Harvey O'Connor, *Revolution in Seattle* (New York, 1964) pp.154-158.

[54] Ole Hanson cited in the *New York Times* February 11, 1919.

[55] Frank Waterhouse, the first president of Associated Industries, cited in Friedheim, op.cit. p.158.

[56]See Alan M. Wakstein, "The Origins of the Open Shop Movement, 1919-1920" *Journal of American History* 51:4 (December, 1964) 460-475. For a concise analysis of the decline of labor's power in the 1920s see Mark Perlman, " Labor in Eclipse" in John Braeman et al. (eds.), *Change and Continuity in Twentieth century America: The 1920s* (Columbus, Ohio, 1968) pp.103-145.

[57] Seattle Central Labor Council declaration of March 6, 1919 cited in O'Connor, op.cit. p.157.
[58] See Gompers, op.cit. Vol.1, p.440.
[59] Ole Hanson, *Americanism versus Bolshevism* (New York, 1920) p.96.
[60] See the Seattle *Union Record* April 23, 1919.
[61] See William D. Haywood, *Bill Haywood's Book: The Autobiography of William D Haywood* (New York, 1929) pp.228-229 and the Seattle *Union Record* September 1, 1917.
[62] For example see Robert E. Ficken, *The Forested Land, A History of Lumbering in Western Washington* (Seattle, 1987) pp.133-136.
[63] For further details see James B. Allen, *The Company Town in the American West* (Norman, Oklahoma, 1966) pp. 167-169 & 175-180.
[64] *Washingtonian* May 11, 1912.
[65] *Washingtonian* November 26, 1911.
[66] Archie Binns, *The Timber Beast* (New York, 1944) p.154
[67] "On to Spokane March First" *Industrial Worker* February 19, 1910, 1
[68] Elizabeth Gurley Flynn, *Rebel Girl: An Autobiography, My First Life (1906-1926)* (Rev.Ed. New York, 1973) p.111.
[69] Alex Polson of the logging company Merrill, Ring and Polson to his partner R. Merrill on the April 19, 1912 cited in Ficken, op.cit. p.136.
[70] The *Oregonian* March 22, 1912.
[71] *Industrial Worker* November 23, 1911 p. 1.
[72] *Oregonian* November 25, 1911.
[73] Elizabeth Gurley Flynn, "The Shame of Spokane" published both in the *Industrial Worker* December 10, 1909 p.1 and the *International Socialist Review* January, 1910 p.611. See also Flynn (1973), op.cit. pp.106-111.
[74] *Industrial Worker* November 23, 1911 p. 1.
[75] See the Seattle *Union Record* November 18, 1916.
[76] They were later acquitted when the interest of the nation shifted to the more bloody struggle in Europe at the conclusion of the trial on April 2 1917. See Lowell S Hawley and Ralph Bushnell Potts, *Counsel for the Damned* (Philadelphia, 1953) pp.76-78 and pp.191-212
[77] See the Seattle *Union Record* November 11, 1916 and the Industrial *Worker* January 27, 1917.
[78] See Seattle *Union Record* November 25, 1916.
[79] The *Seattle Times* November 8, 1916.
[80] *Seattle Municipal News* December 29, 1917 cited in Richard C. Berner, *Seattle 1900-1920: Boomtown, Urban Turbulence to Restoration* (Seattle, 1991) p. 238.
[81] *Seattle Times* May 3, 1917.
[82] See "Patriotism, a Menace to Liberty" in Emma Goldman, *Anarchism and Other Essays* (rev.ed. New York, 1911) pp.141 & 148 and *Statement of the General Executive Board of the I.W.W. on War* cited in full at http://digital.library.arizona.edu/bisbee/docs/053.php

[83] Senator [Wesley] Jones of [Yakima] Washington State *Congressional Record* 66th Congress 2nd Session p.448.
[84] The *Centralia Chronicle* November 15, 1919.
[85] See Anna Louise Strong, "The Verdict at Everett" *Survey* (May 19, 1917) 38.
[86] See *The Washingtonian* November 26, 1911.
[87] The *Washington Post* July 3, 1919.
[88] For details of the Criminal Syndicalist laws see *Congressional Record* 66th Congress, 2nd Session pp.998-999.
[89] Carleton H. Parker, "The IWW" *The Atlantic Monthly* (November, 1917) cited in Parker (1920), op.cit. p.17.
[90] See the *Oregonian* July 18, 1913 for the Baden-Powell incident, ibid. April 26, 1923 and "The IWW closes the Saloons" *Nation* May 23, 1923 p.588 for the prohibition stance and the *Industrial Worker* October 28, 1909 for the Spokane origins of the Salvation Army hatred.
[91] *Solidarity*, the official IWW publication, July 7 and August 18, 1917 cited in Alexander M. Bing, *War-Time Strikes and Their Adjustment* (New York, 1921) p.256.
[92] Parker (1920) op.cit. p.100.
[93] The IWW publication *Solidarity* cited in the *Congressional Record* 65th Congress, 2nd Session, pp.6092-6093.
[94] Cited in Cornelia S. Parker, *An American Idyll: The Life of Carleton H. Parker* (Boston, 1919) p.144.
[95] Senator Wesley Jones in *Congressional Record* 65th Congress, 2nd Session p. 3821.
[96] Seattle *Times* July 14, 1917.
[97] James Rowan, *The IWW in the Lumber Industry* (Seattle, 1920) p.54. See also the *Oregonian* July 15, 1917.
[98] *Four L Monthly Bulletin* cited in Vernon H. Jensen *Lumber and Labor* (New York, 1945) p.130.
[99] Letter from David Beattie to the Editor of the Portland *Telegram* July 21, 1922
[100] Sally M. Miller, *The Immigrant Radical* (New York, 1974) p.17.
[101] *Colfax Gazette* December 1, 1922 cited in Craig Holstine, "The Ku Klux Klan in Whitman County in the 1920s" *Bunchgrass Historian* 9:3 (Fall, 1981) 21.
[102] See Charles Pierce LeWarne, *Utopias on Puget Sound: 1885-1915* (rev.ed. Seattle, 1995) p.238 and Schwantes (1989), op.cit. pp. 278-9.
[103] See LeWarne, op.cit. pp. 3-15.
[104] For an irreverent account of the Home Colony see Stuart Holbrook, "The Anarchists at Home" in Brian Booth (ed.), *Wildmen, Wobblies and Whistle Punks* (Corvallis, Oregon, 1992) pp.97-121.
[105] E. Pelton, one of the founders of the Puget Sound, Equality commune, to Henry Demarest Lloyd, 14 December 1897, cited in Schwantes (1979), op.cit. p.88. For the tolerance of the region see Booth op.cit., pp.97-111.

[106] See Schwantes (1979), op.cit. pp.206-209.
[107] Ira Kipnis, *The American Socialist Movement 1897-1912* (New York, 1952) p.177.
[108] O'Connor, op.cit. p.15
[109] The *Seattle Times* cited in ibid.pp.22-23.
[110] Seattle *Star* February 7, 1919.
[111] See citation in O'Connor, op.cit. p.144. For further details on mayor Ole Hanson see Terje I. Lieren "Ole and the Reds: The Americanism of Seattle Mayor Ole Hanson" *Norwegian American Studies* 30 (1985) 75-95.
[112] Albert Johnson cited in the Gray's Harbor *Washingtonian* August 12, 1920.
[113] Chaplin, op.cit. pp.17-18.
[114] Bing, op.cit. p.256.
[115] Carleton H. Parker cited in Cornelia Parker, op.cit. p. 136.
[116] See the *Oregonian* September 25, 1917.
[117] For details of IWW lumber worker membership see Robert L. Tyler, *The Rebels of the Woods: The IWW in the Pacific Northwest* (Eugene, Oregon, 1967) p.26-9.
[118] Senator King of Utah cited in the *Congressional Record* 65:2 pp. 6090-6091
[119] Nelson P. Mead, *The Development of the United States Since 1865* (New York, 1930) p.417.
[120] The Immigration Commission, Vol. 25, op.cit. pp.343-344.
[121] See ibid. p.344-5.
[122] See the *Oregonian* May 11, 1918.
[123] Emerson Hough, *The Web: A Revelation of Patriotism, The Story of the American Protective League* (Chicago, 1919) p.140.
[124] C.H. Parker op.cit. pp. 93-94.
[125] Gompers, Vol. II op.cit. p.388 and 391.
[126] *Congressional Record* 65th Congress, 2nd Session p.6091.
[127] For a resume of the Olivereau case see Jessie Lloyd , "One Woman's Resistance" in O'Connor, op.cit. pp. 248-261 and Robert L. Friedheim, "The Seattle General Strike of 1919" *Pacific Northwest Quarterly* 52 (July, 1961) 83. For details of other associations of radicalism and "the Hun" see the *New York Times* July 17, 1917 and the *Oregonian* October 1, 1917.
[128] See O'Connor, op.cit. p.100.
[129] Hough, op.cit. pp. 447- 448.
[130] *Four L Monthly Bulletin* Jensen, op.cit.p.130.
[131] Four L's oath cited in Howd, op.cit. p.78.
[132] See Jensen, op.cit. p.132.
[133] Figures taken from Tyler, op.cit. pp. 102 & 109.
[134] Figures taken from United States Department of Labor cited in Jensen, op.cit. p.137.
[135] Bing, op.cit. p.271.

[136] For a list of the Legion's accomplishments see Brice P. Disque, "How We Found A Cure for Strikes in the Lumber Industry in the Pacific Northwest" *System* (September, 1919) pp.379-384.
[137] See Higham, (1994) op.cit. pp.242-250.
[138] See the *Oregonian* July 8, 10 & 17, 1917
[139] See William Preston, *Aliens and Dissenters: Federal Suppression of Radicals, 1903-1933* (Chicago, 1963) pp.165-166.
[140]Figures taken from Florence Peterson, "Strikes in the United States, 1880-1936" *US Department of Labor Bulletin* 651 (Washington, D.C., 1938) 21. For a concise analysis of the post-war increase in industrial strife see Lynn Dumenil, *The Modern Temper; American Culture and Society in the 1920s* (New York, 1995) pp.58-71.
[141] *Bulletin of the United States Bureau of Labor Statistics* no. 357 (May, 1924) 466.
[142] For a comprehensive analysis of the wartime labor strategy see Valerie Jean Connor, *The National War Labor Board, 1918-1919: Stability and Social Justice in the Voluntary State in World War One* (Chapel Hill, North Carolina, 1983).
[143] Woodrow Wilson to Josephus Daniels in Ray S. Baker, *Woodrow Wilson: Life and Letters* Volume VI (New York, 1939) p.506
[144] Blair Coan, *The Red Web* (Boston, 1925) p.14.
[145] Selig Perlman and Philip Taft, *Labor Movements* (New York, 1935) p. 164.
[146] For details of these industrial actions see O'Connor op.cit. pp.114-123.
[147]Hulet M. Wells, "I Wanted to Work" unpublished auto-biography cited in Richard C. Berner, *Seattle 1900-1920: Boomtown, Urban Turbulence to Restoration* (Seattle, 1991) p.254
[148] Cited in O'Connor, op.cit. p.130.
[149] Frank Cobb [editor of the *New York World*], "The Press and Public Opinion" *New Republic* 21 (December, 1919) 144.
[150] Captain Bunn of Fort Lawton cited in the Seattle *Union Record* March 31, 1917.
[151]"The Truth About Soviet Russia and Bolshevism" *The American Federationalist* 37 (February, 1919) 167
[152] Seattle *Union Record* November 16, 1918.
[153] Ole Hanson, *Americanism versus Bolshevism* (New York, 1920) p.24
[154] Seattle *Star* February 4, 1919.
[155] Seattle *Star* February 5, 1919.
[156] See Patrick Farrell, *The Campus Kaiser: Henry Suzzallo, Militarism, the University of Washington and Labor Politics, 1915-1920* (Seattle, 1999) pp.7-9 cited at http://faculty.washington.edu/gregoryj/strike/strikehome.htm
[157] Ole Hanson in the Seattle *Star* February 7, 1919.
[158] For details of the day-to-day management of the strike, albeit from an overt pro-labor stance, see Anna Louise Strong, *The Seattle General Strike* (Seattle, 1919) p.46

[159] *Saturday Evening Post* April 12, 1919 cited in O'Connor, op.cit. p.143.
[160] Dr. Mark A. Matthews cited in Preston, op.cit. p.152.
[161] Ole Hanson in the *New York Times* February 9, 1919.
[162] Figures taken from Gerald B. Nelson, *Seattle: The Life and Times of an American City* (New York, 1977) pp. 32, 53 & 61.
[163]J. Edgar Hoover to a public hearing, cited in the *New York Times* April 25, 1920.
[164] *American Legion Weekly* I November 14, 1919, 12.
[165] Higham (1994), op.cit. pp. 264-299.
[166] *World's Work* April, 1919 cited in O'Connor op.cit. p.144.
[167] See the *New York World* July 19, 1919.
[168] Leonard Olsson cited in Kate Halladay Claghorn, *The Immigrant's Day in Court* (New York, 1923) p.320.
[169] Federal Judge C.H. Hanford May 10, 1912 cited in the *Washingtonian* 11th May, 1912. See also Lowell S. Hawley & Ralph Bushnell Potts, *Counsel for the Damned: A Biography of George Francis Vanderveer* (Philadelphia, 1953) pp. 142-145. Hanford's ruling was reversed on appeal by Judge Augustus Hand the following year.
[170] Albert Johnson cited in House Report 504, 66th Congress, 2nd Session, p.7.
[171] Louis F. Post, *The Deportations Delirium of 1920* (Chicago, 1923) p.65.
[172] Secretary of Labor William Wilson cited in Louis F. Post, *The Deportations Delerium of Nineteen-Twenty* (Chicago, 1923) p.66.
[173]C.D. Felter, a member of the Camp Number 7 of the Grand Army, Spanish War veterans, cited in the *Washingtonian* May 3, 1912.
[174] *Appendix to the Congressional Record* 66th Congress, 2nd Session, 9280
[175] Post, op.cit. p.187
[176] For details see O'Connor, op.cit. p.154 and Preston, op.cit. pp.180-215.
[177] See Seattle *Union Record* January 25, February 1 and 22, 1919.
[178] "IWW Deportation Cases" *Hearings Before a Subcommittee of the Committee on Immigration and Naturalization, House of Representatives, 66th Congress, 2nd Session* p.82.
[179] See ibid.
[180] See *Arrests on Deportation Warrants,* p.2 in House Documents 66th Congress, 2nd Session, vol.97, Document No.317.
[181] Claghorn, op.cit. pp.346-357.
[182] *Congressional Record* 66th Congress, 2nd Session 9247.
[183] Figures taken from Jane Perry Clark, *Deportations of Aliens from the United States to Europe* (New York, 1931) pp.220-221.
[184] For details of the voyage of the *Buford* see Post, op.cit. pp.1-12.
[185] *New York Times* December 22, 1919.
[186]Congressman Albert Johnson (Washington) cited *Congressional Record* 67th Congress, 1st Session 9279.
[187] Albert Johnson cited in House Report 504, 66th Congress, 2nd Session p.11.

[188] *Solidarity* March 17, 1917 cited in the *Congressional Record* 65th Congress, 2nd Session p.6093
[189] *Congressional Record* 66th Congress, 1st Session 3369, 3373 and 3376.
[190] See United States Congress, *House Reports; Communist and Anarchist Deportation Cases, Hearings*, 66th Congress, 2nd Session p.105-106.
[191] For Ettor's own standpoint see Joseph Ettor, "The IWW versus the AF of L" *The New Review* 2 (May, 1914) 279–283.
[192] See Malcolm Clark, "The Bigot Disclosed: Ninety Years of Nativism" *The Oregon Historical Quarterly* 75 (June, 1974) 140
[193] See Robert L. Tyler, "The IWW and the West" *American Quarterly* XII (Summer, 1960) 182.
[194]Hanson, op.cit. p.243.
[195] Dr. Mark A. Matthews cited in Soden, op.cit. p.143.
[196]For contemporary comment see the Aberdeen *Daily World* April 6, 1912. See also Philip J. Dreyfus, "The IWW and the Limits of Inter-ethnic Organizing: Reds, Whites and Greeks in Grays Harbor, Washington, 1912" *Labor History* 38:4 (1997) 450-463.
[197] For example, see the *Oregonian* July 13 and 14, 1917.
[198] For a discussion of the image of the transient laborer in American society see Eric H. Monkkonen, *Walking to Work: Tramps in America 1790-1935* (Lincoln, Nebraska, 1984) pp.1-17.
[199] Davies classic account of his adventures in America was first published in London in 1908. The first American edition came out in 1917. Perhaps one of the best of these memoirs is the reminiscences of Charles P. Barth in his *Hobo Trail to Nowhere* (Philadelphia, 1969). This details a long term hobo career in the Northwest, citing details of "riding the rods", "jungles" and the "main stems" and "skid rows" of Seattle, Portland, Spokane and other cities in the region.
[200] See Nels Anderson, *Hobo: The Sociology of the Homeless Man* (Chicago, 1922) p.2.
[201] For two examples of this genre see Binns, op.cit. and Matthea Thorseth, *The Color of Ripening* (Seattle, 1949) which although written after the period, and arguably influenced by the chastening experiences of the 1930s, are frequently autobiographical in foundation and display a sentimental attachment to the Wobbly cause which was already emerging in the early 1920s.
[202] Frederick C. Mills writing a 1914 report gleaned from "under-cover" work as an itinerant laborer in the farms and lumber camps of central California for the California Immigration Commission cited in Gregory R. Woirol, *In the Floating Army: FC Mills on Itinerant Life in California, 1914* (Urbana, Illinois, 1992) p.30.

4

RACE AND RESTRICTION

In many ways, race can be seen as the underlying cause of immigration restriction not only in the United States as a whole but in the Pacific Northwest region as well. Race had always been one of the definitions of suitability for American citizenship. It had justified continental expansion by defining and legitimating the white Protestant pioneers, not only with relation to the aboriginal population but also with regard to Mexicans, blacks and on the West Coast particularly, Chinese and other Asians. Race had justified war and forced re-location, imprisonment, enslavement, persecution and exclusion. Race, in many respects, became the badge touted to justify white territorial expansion, to demonstrate "American" superiority on the continent. The racial questions that had formed the basis for the national schism over slavery had been forcibly sidelined, if not resolved, by the Fourteenth Amendment. The racial issues that were inherent in the appropriation of aboriginal lands had all but resolved themselves as native resistance to relocation was quashed by treaty, force of arms or disease—or a mixture of all three. Nonetheless, at the turn of the twentieth century, race re-emerged as a vital issue, if indeed it had ever truly disappeared. Most important, in terms of this study, it was race that largely defined the threat that continued open immigration represented to the future of America.

The much publicized *new immigration* represented an essential change in the origin of America's immigrants, but such changes had occurred before—as with the escalation of German and Irish immigration in the 1850s. What made this different was the scale. In Europe and Asia, huge numbers of potential "Americans" took advantage of the relaxation in emigration legislation, the expansion of world trade and the revolution in trans-continental and trans-oceanic transport. In light of the arrival of seemingly unlimited streams of immigrants, many resident Americans began to convince themselves that they faced an unprecedented crisis. This crisis was reflected in the very processes of recording immigration and the analysis of that raw data. Changes occurred both in the nature and quantity of information gathered on the immigrant. Increasingly sophisticated statistical methods were employed to lend empirical evidence to perceived changes in America's population.

The federal decennial census investigated, correlated and extrapolated figures on increasingly diverse aspects of American life. These developments are demonstrated by an increase in the volume of data collected. In 1860 the census data was published in five volumes, whereas by 1890 it took 32.[1] Funding for research into immigration grew, as with the voluminous, wide-ranging—and consequently expensive—Dillingham Report of 1911, which cost a little under $1 million. Novel methods of analyzing demographic information were employed, from the wartime IQ tests, to the emergence of pyramids of national preference promoted throughout the period by such figures as Henry Cabot Lodge, William Rossiter, Clinton Stoddard Burr and Captain John B. Trevor. One common feature emerges from this escalation of information: there was an increasing concentration on race in the methodology behind the analysis of all aspects of immigration. It is apparent in the redrawing, subdividing and extrapolating of ethnic boundaries that increasingly enabled restrictionists to apply "scientific", statistical, rational explanations to a range of desirable or less-desirable traits found among the old and the new sources of immigrants, from their levels of poverty to their political beliefs; from their intelligence to their fecundity.

It is hardly coincidence that these racial theories crystallized as the immigration pattern seemed to change—the one largely defined the other. Arguably, while the immigration pattern was considered over-whelming desirable, the sub-division of the ethnicity of immigrants beyond obvious physical traits of color or physiognomy was of marginal importance. Before the explosion in their immigration, during the last three decades of the nineteenth century, an Asian was immediately recognizable as an Asian, regardless of nationality. Similarly, a European was generally regarded simply as a European, wherever his birthplace. The numbers, particularly on the "frontier", were small enough to make subdivision of races of little consequence. By the beginning of the period of this study, this was changing. On the East Coast there was an increasingly perceptible shift away from the North and West European donor countries—the Anglo-Saxon, German and Scandinavian. This shift coincided with a perceived rise in Japanese immigration on the West Coast. To the restrictionist, both were seen as undesirable. Both threatened the nativists' perception of what races should make up the "American" population. Consequently, both required legislation to exclude them.

Put crudely, the East and West Coast of the country had simple objectives: to halt the flow of immigrants who threatened to alter the ethnic makeup of the nation. In order to achieve this, it was necessary to define such undesirable immigrants. For nativists on both coasts new refinements of racial classification produced a happy coincidence of interests, one which was exploited by an unlikely, but effective, alliance in Congress. On the Atlantic coast, it was seen as essential to categorize the "new" immigrants in order to isolate them from the more desirable streams of immigration. On the Pacific Coast it was crucial to include the Japanese with the already excluded Chinese. Following in a tradition of Western animosity to Asian immigrants, the exclusion of Japanese immigration was the most visible and consistent of all Northwestern restrictionist aims, in the first decades of the twentieth century. The vehemence and violence of the Northwest's hostility to Asian immigration proved enduring, even at the time of the area's greatest efforts to attract settlers. Unlike the hostility to Catholics, Jews or blacks, opposition to Asians was born out of the geographic position of the region, rather than being based largely on imported prejudice. It is perhaps worth starting any examination of the role of the Northwest in the racial issues of immigration by exploring the national and regional position.

THE CONTEXT, NATIONAL AND REGIONAL INFLUENCES

Just as the East Coast's traditional trade links were with Europe, so the West Coast's were increasingly with Asia. The region's initial wealth had been founded on a fur trade bonanza that had had its genesis in Cantonese merchants' near insatiable, and for the trappers highly lucrative, desire for sea otter pelts. These trading links grew. By the end of the first decade of the twentieth century, more than $21 million of Seattle's total imports, with an estimated worth of over $28 million, were from China and Japan and this trade had grown from some $6 million at the turn of the century.[2] As on the Atlantic seaboard, the passage of goods between continents became increasingly linked with the movement of people. Asian immigration arrived via a direct shipping route across the Pacific. Consequently, as the East Coast's fears of "race suicide" hinged on "American" submersion in a tide of alien European immigration, so the West assumed that any deluge would be Asian in origin.

The threat of a flood of Asians was more real, immediate and instinctive in the region. Given this concentration on Asia, it is hardly surprising that the racial motive for immigration restriction on the West Coast is almost exclusively bound in with the Asian. During the period of this study it was largely aimed at excluding the Japanese, the Chinese having already been excluded by the 1882 Chinese Exclusion Act and subsequent laws. The black population of the region was largely native-born. Other colored immigration, although often considerable—as with the Filipinos or East Indian "Hindus"—only rarely achieved the numbers or attention that the Japanese immigrants received. If they did, they were usually subjected to the same pressures for exclusion, finding themselves linked with the "Japs" either as Asiatics, Mongolians or merely other "Little Brown Men".

This pressure for Japanese exclusion is often seen as a California phenomenon, growing out of the San Francisco sandlot movement, and following "Mongolian" immigrants wherever they settled. Certainly the vast bulk of Asian immigrants, initially Chinese, settled in California—for example the 1850 United States census reported a mere two Chinese in the Oregon Territory, against some 626 in California. By the 1860s the lure of gold had induced the Chinese to travel north, so much so that the 1880 census recorded 3,186 Chinese in the Washington Territory and 9,510 in Oregon. Nevertheless, the same census gives California over 75,000.[3] Given the preponderance of Chinese in California it was likely that this would be the epicenter of anti-Asian pressures. Some idea of the California flavor of this anti-Chinese discrimination is demonstrated by the arrival in 1861 of the 2nd Infantry, California Volunteers in Fort Colville on the Upper Columbia, where

> Within four days after their arrival...they burglarized the only laundry, ran the Chinese proprietor out of town and stole every stitch of apparel in the place, leaving most of the citizens with only the clothing on their persons. Soon afterwards Lt. John M. Henry came downtown and, with a common butcher [sic] knife, killed [the Chinese] John Burt.[4]

By contrast, some years later the editor of a local paper disapproved of these actions and hoped that such persecution would not "discourage" the Chinese. He claimed apologetically that

> Colville feels the loss of her Chinamen, they having been the principal consumers of their productions...nearly every dollar they made was money put into circulation and the benefit of which could never have been felt had it not been for them. It is hoped that since the Chinese Poll Tax has been removed they will remain.[5]

Nevertheless, by the 1880s, after the Chinese Exclusion Act, the Northwest was demonstrating its own virulent hostility to Chinese. Not content with banning their immigration, Northwestern nativists attempted to expel their existing Chinese populations. This urge was powerful enough to secure the forceful eviction in 1885 of all except 200 of Tacoma's 700 Chinese, most of who ended up, via Portland, in San Francisco. The following year, attempts to imitate Tacoma's evictions resulted in a declaration of martial law in Seattle and the mobilization of militia companies and a doubling of police forces in Portland. The feeling was so widespread that the violently anti-Chinese anarchist International Workingman's Party claimed 2,000 members in the region by 1886 and this was by no means the region's only "anti-coolie" organization dedicated to the expulsion of Chinese.[6] The original sentiments may have been imported from California, but in the Northwest the anti-Chinese movement swiftly established a tradition of racially motivated nativism which, although often drawing on its southern neighbor's example, frequently refined and re-invigorated the prototype.

The influence of California on the Northwest should be placed in a national context. In the post-Civil War era the East Coast was aware of the problems inherent in Chinese immigration, even though the nation's Chinese population was almost entirely confined to the West. By 1879 some 102,000, 97 percent, of America's 105,000 resident Chinese, lived in states west of the Rockies.[7] All the same, the threat of growing Chinese immigration was increasingly seen as a national problem, indicative of the considerable social dilemmas inherent in federal integration and post-war reconstruction. In 1874, President Ulysses Grant typified this concern when he voiced the fear that the Chinese immigration represented a re-introduction of slavery. In areas where the Asian was little more than a mythical being, the importing of coolie labor and the conditions of their servitude re-activated abolitionist sentiments. Nevertheless, initial efforts to include the "Celestials" in American society, the mirror of the motive of abolitionists, met with decidedly cool receptions.

For a variety of reasons the Asian never received the wide-ranging support offered to the Black. In 1870, the Radical Republican Senators, Charles Sumner and Lyman Trumbull attempted to amend the naturalization laws to allow for Chinese citizenship but they were comprehensively defeated. In the Northwest 50 years later the reason for this defeat was still apparent. The "Negro", by virtue of his resident status and his resilience, had long since earned his freedom—the Asian was still regarded as interloper—"Of course we fight the niggers now and then, but we fought to make them free. We haven't fought yet to make those little yellow sons of bitches free."[8] Many have seen this as a display of anti-Asianism that was peculiar to the West, a prejudice which Eastern politicians supported with a patronizingly half-hearted pragmatism based on hopes of future Western compliance in ventures on Capitol Hill. This view is questionable.

Arguably, at this stage the issue of Chinese immigration should not be seen as political horse-trading in order for a dominant East to pacify and utilize the West, but rather as the outgrowth of a genuine national perception that the Chinese represented a threat to American institutions. The Chinese were perceived as racial contaminants, and there is evidence that even in the traditionally more tolerant Northern areas there was a fear that a flood of Asian blood would cause untold and irreversible damage to Americans and American institutions. For example, in 1865, when evangelical Yankee inclusiveness was blooming throughout the Union, the editor of the *New York Times* warned that allowing continued Chinese immigration would create a new race problem:

> We have four millions of degraded negroes in the South ...and if there were to be a flood-tide of Chinese population—a

> population befouled with all the social vices, with no knowledge or appreciation of free institutions or constitutional liberty, with heathenish souls and heathenish propensities, whose character, and habits, and modes of thought are firmly fixed by the consolidating influence of ages upon ages—we should be prepared to bid farewell to republicanism and democracy.[9]

The Northwestern view on this contrast of black and Asian was most succinctly put by the Oregon Democrat and Progressive George E. Chamberlain, who unequivocally claimed: "As between the Chinese and the Negro, I believe the latter the lesser of two evils."[10]

Conversely, many see the Western hatred of the Asian immigrant as being imported from the East—an aspect of, an outgrowth of, Southern defeat. In the context of Reconstruction it has been suggested that the considerable westward exodus of those fleeing the defeated South, fearing the consequences of reconstruction—and most particularly the racial consequences—significantly influenced the West's attitudes to immigration and the internal migration of non-Europeans.[11] The discouraging of free black settlement was seen as a means to avoid the spread of sharecropping poverty and its corollary, the lien system, which many of the immigrants left behind in the post-war South. This refugee thesis can be over-emphasized. There is evidence that points to the racial attitudes being already solidly enshrined in the Northwest before the start of the Civil War.

In Oregon, the powerful Democrat "Salem Clique" dominated the 1857 Constitutional conference, but they saw the acceptance of slavery within the state as being dangerously divisive—both nationally and locally—and left the decision to a referendum. Even to the Portland-based "anti-Democrats", free-soil sympathies had less to do with abolitionism than what they saw as the inevitable degradation of white labor by the institution of slavery. The conference discussions accepted the idea of free-soil as the most effective method of racial exclusion. Even so, delegates of all political hues at one point challenged each other to call for more stringent guides to the state's racial purity. They ended up excluding not only the aboriginal population from the franchise but also the, at that time, negligible Chinese element as well.[12] In the following referendum, the state's electorate upheld these ideals. The result was an almost 70 percent vote for free soil. The original Oregon State Constitution of 1857 clearly demonstrated a wish to reduce to a minimum the perceived problems arising from race via a policy of exclusion, stating:

> No free negro or mulatto, not residing in this State at the time of the adoption of this Constitution [November 9, 1857], shall come, reside or be within this State, or hold any real estate, or make any contracts, or maintain any suit therein; and the Legislative Assembly shall provide by penal laws for the

> removal by public officers of all such negroes and mulattoes, and for their effectual exclusion from the State, and for the punishment of the persons who shall bring them into the State, or employ or harbor them.[13]

It is tempting to attribute Oregon's retention of one of the lowest black populations in the Union—rising from a mere 128 in 1860 to 1,186 in 1890 and 2,144 in 1920—to a legacy of this initial racial hostility. This interpretation is re-enforced by analysis of proportion of blacks in the total State population which remained relatively constant at around 0.3 percent. Washington State was guided at its foundation, in 1889, less by the Dred Scott decision than by the Fourteenth Amendment. It had an equally low proportion of blacks within its total population, some 0.4 percent in 1890 rising to 0.5 percent in 1920.[14] Rather than seeing the low level of black migration into the area as the result of regional hostility, it is probably more productive to view black migration in the period as being limited by economic constraints. The main reservoir of the nation's black population—the South—was increasingly suffering from an immobility induced by the Jim Crow laws and the results of the lien system. Those who migrated North and West, particularly in the First World War era, tended to settle in urban, industrial areas and the "wage-earner's frontier" of the Northwest was unappealing when opportunity generally lay closer to home and family.

This was not the case with the Asian immigrant. The Northwest held a particular allure for first the Chinese and later the Japanese. As has been noted already, trade routes were well established by the period of this study. "Coolie" labor was as much a part of the construction of the West as black labor had been in the rural South, or the "new" European was becoming in the urban North. The ubiquitous coolie worked on the railroad, the salmon cannery, the lumberyard, the mine and in a variety of other industrial and domestic positions. John Chinaman may have been unpopular with the laborers of the region, but his employers saw him as essential. Even so, the growing popular antagonism won over: 1882, 1892, 1902 and 1904 federal prohibitions on Chinese immigration fundamentally changed what had become an almost traditional Asian distribution in the region. The Chinese population declined from 4.8 percent of the total population of Oregon and the Washington Territory in 1880, to 0.6 percent of the two States populations' in 1910.[15] All the same, anti-Asianism remained a potent force in the region due to growing numbers of Japanese immigrants.[16] The Japanese population grew, in relation to the total population of the two States, from 0.1 percent in 1890 to 0.8 percent in 1910 and 0.9 percent in 1920.[17]

As with the anti-Chinese pressure, the anti-Japanese movement originated in California, again largely due to the vast bulk of Japanese entering through San Francisco and settling in that state. In December 1913, California had a Japanese population of 59,755, making up 2.9 percent of the State's population and 62 percent of the nation's total Japanese population. On the other hand, the employment opportunities and Seattle's trading links with Hawaii soon led to the city becoming the second most important point of arrival for Japanese, with the consequence that in 1913 Japanese comprised 1.06 percent of Washington's population, which totaled 15.4 percent of the nation's Japanese.[18] More important, Japanese dominated the foreign-born immigration into both states. Japanese immigrants made up the largest single ethnic group among Washington's foreign-born immigrants between 1899 and 1910—almost 26,000 out of nearly 112,000. They made up the second largest in Oregon—some 4,500 out of just under 29,000.[19] In Seattle the Japanese population grew from 125 individuals in 1890 to 2,990 in 1900. By 1900, they represented the largest non-white group in the city, nearly 4 percent of Seattle's total population.[20]

The position and perception of these Asian immigrants was different from that of other incomers. Not only were they obviously ethnically recognizable, their numbers were perceived to be increasing and this was compounded by the fact that, unlike the migrant blacks, they were linguistically and often religiously exotic—few spoke English; a minority were Christian. Perhaps most important they were seen by many of those already resident in the Northwest as having been specifically imported to provide direct competition in a diverse range of industries. In the West, Catholics and blacks were viewed as an existing, if frequently undesirable, part of America's cultural mix. Their presence in the region, however unwelcome, from the very founding of the American society in the area, gave them a certain legitimacy. More or less sincere efforts may have been made to prevent further encroachments of Catholic power in the Northwest by limiting their immigration, but few realistically sought to expel all the Pacific Coast's resident Catholics. Similarly, the region's Jews and blacks may have been regarded as inferior or objectionable, but even their relative scarcity never led to calls for their expulsion—rather, it generally increased the ease with which they could be absorbed into local society. By contrast, the Asian continued to be regarded as an interloper.

The fact that Asians were largely limited to the West Coast, and almost exclusively arrived in the region after the establishment of Oregon's statehood in 1859, removed the historical acceptance of their presence. Whites who settled in the region rarely had any previous experience of Asians from their original homelands—as Southern American migrants had with blacks, or European immigrants had with Jews. Neither were they used to Asians as a presence historically associated with the region—as with the aboriginal population of Native Indians and arguably, for most, the Catholic population. This made his appearance, culture, language and, above all, race all the more alien and his presence more unwelcome. The Asian had no "historical right" to residency, he was not conquered or "compounded". There was rarely a call that the "Black/Jew/Catholic must go!" as there was for the Chinese, or later the Japanese. What opposition these non-Asian groups encountered was more often a divided plea not to let them continue to arrive. This more visceral antagonism was reflected in legislation. Unlike the Jew, Catholic or Black, the Asian could not naturalize. Remaining an alien, the Asian immigrant could never gain political representation. What political voice Asians in America could demonstrate frequently came through diplomatic pressure from the governments of their native lands, and this in itself often served to re-enforce feelings of their uncertain loyalty to America. Rather than representing a potential source of political power, first the Chinese and then the Japanese represented a target for ambitious politicians—a constantly re-emerging scapegoat.

THE JAPANESE IMMIGRANT AND LABOR

The initial similarity between the anti-Chinese and anti-Japanese campaigns is attested by the early interest of the leader of the California Workingman's Party in the issue. Denis Kearney managed in 1892, while the numbers of Japanese entering the country were still relatively small, to transfer the continuing hostility to the Chinese over to the Japanese—although there can be little doubt the distinction between the two nationalities was lost on the bulk of the population. He managed to draw attention to two of what would become the major objections to their arrival—their willingness to work for lower wages and their suspect morality:

> the foreign Shylocks [Japanese labor contractors, who are referred to later, with some accuracy, as "absentee money-lenders"] are rushing another breed of Asiatic slaves to fill up the gap made vacant by the Chinese who are shut out by our laws....Japs...are being brought here now in countless numbers to demoralize and discourage our domestic labor market and to be educated...at our expense...We are paying out money [to allow] fully developed men who know no morals but vice to sit beside our...daughters [and] to debauch [and] demoralize them....The Japs must go![21]

Kearney's objections to the labor contractors are significant. A total of 1,380 Japanese entered the United States in the year from June 1892. This rapidly escalated; from 1899 to 1900 the Japanese government issued passports to 12,635 laborers and from 1902 to 1906 United States statistics indicated that some 35,000 Japanese laborers entered the country. The position in the Northwest reflected this. In 1891, the Portland-based labor contractor Shinzaburo Ban had started to import Japanese laborers for work on Northwestern railway construction. In 1892, 400 Japanese were working on the construction of the Union Pacific line from Huntington, Oregon, to Granger, Wyoming. By 1906 the railroads employed 13,000 or one third of all Japanese in the United States and 26 percent of all of Oregon's resident Japanese.[22] This figure had dropped to 10,000 by 1909, but many Japanese had moved into alternative employment. Some 38,000 Japanese were employed as agricultural laborers, 3,600 in the salmon canneries and 2,200 in the sawmills.[23] These laborers continued to arrive in deliberate contravention of 1885 and 1891 American immigration legislation, which prohibited the importing of contract labor, and the Japanese government's attempts from 1898 to regulate the trade via a quota system on passports. Nevertheless, the labor contractors circumvented this legislation to continue their lucrative trade by the importing of labor via Hawaii and Canada, as well as the use of corruption and fraud within Japan.

A mixture of economics and racism underpinned the objection to Japanese labor. The "Asiatic" worker was seen as coming from countries where the standard of living was considerably lower than that of the United States. Objections followed the course of the earlier anti-Chinese agitation. The Japanese laborer was seen as willing to work at lower rates of pay than his native-born American counterpart, in worse conditions and for longer hours—"Reilly can *outdo* Ah San, but Ah San can *underlive* Reilly."[24] The Japanese laborer was seen as clannish in the workplace and owing his allegiance solely to his contractor. Although this aloof appearance was in itself often the result of his poor grasp of the language and culture, these shortcomings in turn aggravated residents and ensured his ostracism due to his alien appearance, language and customs. The Japanese were viewed as overly subservient—particularly when imported as strikebreakers—and this added to a perception among labor nativists that they were incapable of unionization.

As the Japanese in the Northwest expanded into industries other than domestic service and railroad construction, they started to compete with the area's resident labor force with the consequence that they were seen as reducing wage levels and ousting white laborers from their jobs. By the end of the first decade of the twentieth century it had become generally accepted that the Asian could and would work for less than his white counterpart:

> Where the Japanese have been employed they have, without exception, been paid lower wages than men of other races engaged in the same occupations. In the one [lumber] mill investigated where they were employed in skilled and semi-skilled positions, also, their wages were considerably lower than those paid to white men employed in similar positions in other mills....While white men are paid $ 1.75, $2, and $2.25 as common laborers, Japanese are paid $1.50, $1.60, and $1.75, and rarely $2, and in one mill employing a large number they receive only $1.25 per day....
>
> While the Japanese have never been employed in the majority of the mills and have been discharged from some others, this has been due chiefly to the race feeling exhibited against them and seemingly closely connected with the fact that they are of a different race and tongue and have always worked for lower wages than were paid to white men.[25]

These claims however are disproportionate to the numbers involved. In 1909 the (Dillingham) Immigration Commission claimed that of Washington's 1,263 lumber and shingle mills, only 67 employed Japanese and that "only a few in Oregon" employed Japanese. The same investigation discovered that the Japanese comprised an estimated 2,400 to 2,500 out of the entire 58,815 employed in the lumber industry in Oregon and Washington.[26] Nevertheless, the arguments of the anti-Japanese movement relied less on the actual position than the possibilities inherent in continued Japanese immigration.

The region's anti-Japanese labor activists saw the threats posed by continued Japanese immigration to be self-evident. The attraction of Japanese workers for employers was equally obvious. Not only could they be employed at lower rates of pay, but they could also be used to drive down rates of pay for other workers. Employers in the Northwest also contributed to their workforce's hostility to Japanese labor in other ways. As with Eastern and Mid-Western industrialists, Northwestern management saw the potential of ethnic conflict as a method of reducing the workforces' solidarity. The logging industry reveals instances of laborers' unity being deliberately targeted by a management policy of heightening the racial tensions inherent within the multi-ethnic workforce. One of the region's lumber foremen understood the principle—"I don't think the races can ever mix....[Yet] I think if we had an all-Jap crew we would have as much trouble with them as we do with the whites because the Japs would get cocky if they thought you could not get along without them. But if you keep a mixed crew you never have any trouble."[27]

Invariably male, and normally single, the Asian immigrant laborer could also be housed, fed and "entertained" by the company—allowing for additional profits and "perks" for the invariably white shop floor managers. This was particularly common in the frequently self-contained, isolated extractive industries of the Northwest. The region's salmon canning industry represents the most obvious example. Traditionally the skilled but unpleasant work of gutting and cooking the fish, as well as soldering the cans had been dominated by Chinese workers, shipped in, paid and managed by a Chinese labor contractor.

As the Chinese population aged and their numbers decreased, Filipinos and Japanese, and, from the 1930s, Mexicans, increasingly took their place in the Oregon, Washington and Alaskan industries. These companies frequently increased their already considerable profits by over-charging their captive workforces for basic commodities. Exposures of the conditions within the industry served to re-enforce racial prejudices about the feudal nature of Asian workers, their stupidity, their "natural" ability to tolerate poor working conditions and the corrupt nature of the Asian labor contractors.[28] The isolated locations and harsh, unpleasant working conditions of the canning industry held few attractions for native-born workers and relatively few worked within it, at least at the same level as the Asians:

> White men have always been employed as "company men" to fill office positions [in the canneries]....It is only in recent

> years that any large numbers have been employed at cannery work...such work was formerly distasteful to them, chiefly because it was a Chinese industry.[29]

In addition, the seasonality of the work and spiral of poverty into which many of the industry's out-of-season unemployed, debt-ridden workforce was plunged led to job competition, criminal behavior and wage-cutting, particularly with Seattle and Portland's other migrant laborers. It was estimated that two-thirds of the region's employees in agriculture, logging, construction, fisheries and canning were laid off between November and March each year.[30]

As the wage differential between Japanese and "white" workers began to diminish from the early 1910s, many employers increasingly viewed the Japanese as a reliable, dextrous and industrious workforce—"they can sure jump around and work fast."[31] Some employers even saw Japanese as superior to white workforces in spite of the risks inherent in growing labor agitation for their exclusion from the workplace:

> In 1921 we attempted to change to an all-white crew. We had ten Japs then and used them on the sorting tables and as lumber pilers. Well, we fired all the Japs but ten days later we began hiring them back again. During that ten days we had four crews—one working, one coming, one going and one being hired. Some of the whites would only work two hours and wouldn't even work then. So we hired our Jap crew back then and they have been with us ever since. If they quit I would hire Japs to take their place.[32]

The post-war growth of labor radicalism fed restrictionist pressures among employers aimed at Eastern Europeans, while labor fought for the exclusion of the Asians from both the country and the workplace. To the white workforce their seeming subservience, lack of solidarity with other workers and willingness to tolerate poor working conditions made the Japanese more or less willing lackeys of the employers. For many immigrants, including those from Southern and Eastern Europe, support for the anti-Japanese movement signaled membership of the white working community. Opposition to Asian labor proved an immigrant's commitment to retaining America's standard of living, for the presence of Asian labor had always threatened to "degrade all white working people to the abject condition of a servile class."[33] It was a valuable tool for the union movement. Many felt that the causes of unionization were well served by the presence of a common enemy: "Everett [is]...fast coming to the front as a union town. The anti-Jap agitation is the chief incentive, and it is a powerful one."[34]

The inclusion such membership provided was particularly important for "new" immigrants. In the Northwest, the relative scarcity of Southern and Eastern Europeans, Mexicans or blacks simplified the racial hierarchy. A clear illustration of this racial divide is given by the Seattle Labor Council's reaction in 1915 to the housing by two Seattle labor contractors of imported Greek, Russian, Italian and Austrian laborers in a "tent city" on the outskirts of the city. These unfortunates were worked between 10 and 16 hours a day. When the Russians were provoked by the appalling conditions to strike, the Council's weekly, the Seattle *Union Record*, sympathetically covered the events, raised a plea for food and supplies and applauded the arrest and charging of one of the exploitative contractors. These were European workers. The *Union Record* did not seek to condemn them for the jobs they were stealing, the precedent they set to other employers or their non-union status. When at the same time Seattle's Butler Hotel's decided to replace its "working girls...with cheap Japanese labor" the *Record* roundly condemned the action. By contrast these "Mongolians" were non-union, subservient, enemies of the American worker. [35]

Such a reaction was largely dependent on numbers. In the areas within the region where Greek, Russian or Italian workers were scarce, they were frequently considered by fellow workers to be infinitely preferable to Japanese workers. The area's unions often accepted any "white" members in their attempts to demonstrate a solid front to the employers' use of Asian labor. This was not always voluntary, frequently there was no option. For example, in 1923-24 in Lake Stevens, Washington, the local Four L's Union pressed for a closed shop of all white residents to oppose the employment of some 12 Japanese laborers in Rucker Brothers lumber mill. Those who did not join the protest "were liable to be hailed and scoffed in the street"—if not worse.[36]

There was little new in this unionized anti-Asianism. The Workingman's Party, which had co-ordinated anti-Chinese pressure in California in the 1870s, was largely a response by Irish laborers to the increasing numbers of Coolie laborers entering the State. Anti-Chinese pressure in Washington was similarly motivated by increasing numbers of Chinese flooding into the state's cities, with the completion of the region's major railroads. In these violent, economically turbulent environments they increasingly came into competition with the local workforce. In the 1880s, the attempted evictions of the Chinese populations of Tacoma and Seattle, the massacre of Chinese miners in Washington's Squak Valley and the general escalation of anti-Asian violence throughout the region often received more or less overt approval from the Knights of Labor. Labor organizations backed the removal of Chinese employees from many of the region's lumber mills, mines and fisheries and threatened employers of Chinese domestic servants.

The AFL played an increasingly dominant role in the ultimately successful campaign for the outlawing of Chinese immigration. Taking on the mantle from the KoL, support for open Asian immigration was equated with stealing the means of making living from genuine "American" workers. Samuel Gompers claimed that—"Every incoming coolie, means a displacement of an American and a lowering of the American standard of living."[37] At a more local level, the AFL-affiliated *Seattle Union Record* pointed out the dangers to the union movement of Asian labor—"Does a Chinaman do your washing? If so you are not carrying out the principles of unionism."[38] With the successful "permanent" exclusion of the Chinese threat from 1904, the labor organizations turned to the exclusion of the Japanese. It was largely labor organizations which composed the 200,000-strong membership of the Asiatic Exclusion League—at its 1905 inception, some 195 of the 231 affiliated groups in its membership were labor unions.[39]

The anti-Japanese groups fuelled and fed off the flourishing racial defensiveness and xenophobia of the times. The increasingly powerful California anti-Japanese labor movement under, the Norwegian-born, Olaf Tveitmoe's "thick-fisted, bull-necked" leadership rapidly spread into Washington and pushed the AFL further towards racial exclusion, as if it was needed, by goading Gompers away from "dodging the issue."[40] The American Legion thought it necessary to be "extreme and radical…to awaken the public to the Japanese danger." It claimed it "would make the position of the alien Oriental economically so undesirable that he would return to own land of his own will."[41] Demands for the removal of Asian laborers became more concerted and vociferous as the workforce sensed the real power of solidarity in the region during the war. As the order books filled, the workforce radicalized and the employers were forced to accept many of their demands. This position continued in the brief post-war boom, particularly in the militant unionism associated with the lumber industry: "They don't hire Japs in the other mills because the whites kick. About 3 years ago [1920] the Bay City Mill was going to take on some Japs. But the whole crew quit and told the company that if they hired Japs they would have to get a new crew. So the company did not hire them."[42]

Even the American Socialist Party adopted an anti-Japanese stance in 1907, for as Jack London laconically explained—"I am first of all a white man and only then a Socialist."[43] This nativism was not universal in the labor movement. The Industrial Workers of the World, seeing themselves as excluded from much of society took a more inclusive position. What mattered to the Wobblies was the overthrow of the capitalist system. They famously adopted an internationalist approach to membership. Their condemnation of "a [racist] state of affairs which allows one set of workers to be pitted against another set of workers in the same industry" distinguished them from the staunchly nativist AFL, especially when they advocated unity "with the Japanese to wring more wages and shorter hours from their common enemy—the employer."[44] This position had followed on from the Wobblies' industrially motivated antecedents—the United Mine Workers and the Western Federation of Miners. By the first decade of the twentieth century, these organizations had abandoned their earlier hostility to Asian competition, rationally accepting that the "brown and yellow men are here and are competitors in the labor market for jobs…[but] that the time has come when race and creed prejudice must be banished from the councils of organized labor."[45]

Seattle's Central Labor Council "went on record as favoring the admission of Japanese to all labor unions affiliated with the American Federation of Labor."[46] Nevertheless, while this pragmatism accepted the presence of Asian labor it was not a statement for free immigration, rather it was considered a sad testimony to the powerlessness of labor:

> The workers cannot keep them [the Japanese] out, because the working class does not compose the organized or dominant part of society. The organized part of society that controls [the country] today is the employing class, and it is at their will and desire that exclusion or admittance will be regulated.[47]

Support for the rights of resident Japanese laborers was not necessarily support for free Japanese immigration. Socialism may have required a brotherhood of man, and anarchism may have sought the destruction of artificial boundaries, but the less immigrants there were, the less the competition for jobs and the more power the worker had. One source claims that even the IWW succumbed to a variant of this argument and advocated Asian exclusion in the early 1920s.[48]

JAPANESE IMMIGRATION AND COMMUNITY

In many instances, the arrival of Japanese was seen as inducing community disintegration. The homogeneous makeup of neighborhoods was threatened by this "racial indigestion." In company towns such as Aberdeen, Washington, this was blamed on the establishment by corporations of "a form of vicious paternalism which is greatly accentuated by the Oriental and foreign element...[and which] results in the drowning of initiative and individualism."[49] In this respect, opposition to Japanese immigration differed little from objections to the "new" immigration in the country as a whole, or indeed from the Western anti-Chinese agitation of the 1870s and 1880s. Even in the early twentieth century, in the Grays Harbor region, where there had traditionally been a higher proportion of "New" European immigrants—largely Finns, Russians and Greeks—and the Asian laborers had largely been expelled, the local workforce still used racial divisions and condemned the non-Nordic workers as "blacks". In urban areas, nativist hostility was often linked to the growth of immigrant colonies which were seen as disease—and crime—ridden, as well as divisively and stubbornly un-American in ethos, language and appearance. Nearly ten years after the violent expulsion of Tacoma's Chinese a commentator explained how the "Celestials" living conditions had contributed to their treatment:

> The chief nests of the Chinamen in Tacoma were along the waterfront...[in which lived] a miserable combination of men, women, children, hogs, chickens and ducks. Living in horrible degredation—not greater, probably, than is customary among American Chinese, but horrible for the contemplation of the Tacoman in his own city. Their sewer system was the only cleanly thing about the dens, and this was so only because the

> ocean tides furnished the only means of disposing of their garbage.[50]

As Asians, the same was held to be true of the Japanese. The 1919 influenza epidemic was seen by nativists as hitting Japanese victims disproportionately as a result of their insanitary living conditions:

> Their ["American"] neighbors, in this [the Hood River] valley, [are people] who find time to make their homes match in some degree the [beautiful] settings in which they are placed, not unnaturally resent the indifference displayed by the Japanese, and there is every reason to believe that the heavy death roll [sic] that followed the visitation of the influenza early this year can be explained by the miserable condition of their [the Japanese residents'] houses.[51]

More significantly, in March, 1900 the case of Chick Gin, a Chinese bubonic plague victim in San Francisco's Chinatown, sparked a resurgence in anti-Asian pressure which had lain dormant since the renewal of decennial restrictive measures in 1892.[52] It was this threatened epidemic which led Mayor James Duval Phelan to take up the anti-Japanese crusade and from this point the issue of Japanese immigration exclusion began in earnest:

> The Japanese are starting the same tide of immigration which we thought we had checked twenty years ago...The Chinese and Japanese are not bona fide citizens. They are not the stuff of which Americans can be made....Personally we have nothing against Japanese, but as they will not assimilate with us and their social life is so different from ours, let them keep a respectful distance.[53]

The Northwest's largest Japanese "colony", Seattle's Japantown, Nihonmachi, can be seen as a case in point. It acted as a center for Northwestern Japanese with "alien" restaurants, shops, a temple, a language school, theatre, banks, bathhouses and brothels, and from 1920 the second largest gambling house on the West Coast.[54] Some idea of the regional dominance of Seattle's Japanese is given by a 1909 comparison of the Japanese-owned businesses in the region's major cities. Seattle had a total of 478, Tacoma 63 and Portland 97.[55] As with the "new" immigration on the East Coast, particularly the Eastern European Jews, the Japanese were condemned as an urban population. For all their urban roots, a significant proportion of the Progressives favored a pastoral society, for as David Star Jordan put it, "the stability of national character comes from firmness of foothold in the soil".[56] This was the era of the Country Life Movement, yet another manifestation of the Jeffersonian, Jacksonian, hankering for a bucolic innocence that urbanization was seen as extinguishing, rapidly. The city was the center of poverty, crime and disease. Once again nativists used statistical evidence to back their suspicions.

The 1909 investigations for the Dillingham Commission discovered that somewhere between a quarter and a third of the 80,000 "gainfully occupied" Japanese on the West Coast were engaged in "city trades and businesses". While some 12,000 to 15,000 of these Japanese were employed in domestic service, there were some 10,000 or 11,000 engaged in business for themselves or working for "those who were thus employed".[57] What they all had in common was that they catered for, and largely employed, Japanese. Although this meant that they did not actively seek existing "American" businesses' customers, it laid them open to accusations of clannishness, underbidding and employment discrimination. For instance in 1909, the California Labor Commission claimed that a mere 61 whites were employed in the 2,548 Japanese businesses investigated.[58] There is little reason to suspect the position in the Northwest was any different, as the majority of the region's Japanese businesses were either small enough to employ only family labor or relied on staff who generally boarded with their employers.

As the numbers of Japanese businesses expanded, so conflict with white traders became more frequent. Japanese were accused of ring bidding to exclude Italian produce in Seattle's expanding vegetable markets.[59] The Seattle Barbers Union claimed it was forced to lower its minimum rate to meet Japanese competition. In 1914, the complaints by white garment dyers and pressers, laundrymen and grocers of unfair competition from Japanese businesses made their leadership incensed enough to lobby Congress to "prevent all members of all colored races...except American Indians and Negroes born in the United States, from becoming citizens, or engaging in business in any capacity in the United States in competition with a citizen of this country."[60] Japanese were charged with reducing property values in the areas in which they set up businesses:

> Once a group has been formed, common language, acquaintance, shops and amusement places cause other Japanese to join it. Available buildings then command high rents so far as the colony spreads. These high rents and prejudice, in turn, cause other races to move elsewhere. As this shifting process takes place, the values and rentals of property lying near the "Japanese Quarter" fall because of little demand for it, until it, too, is vacated for the expansion of the colony.[61]

It was also held that the very presence of Japanese was "detrimental to the social and moral life" of communities and there were instances of "non-Caucasians" being barred from residency in certain areas—as in the Lake Washington and Mount Baker districts of Seattle in 1921.[62]

The bulk of Japanese arrived at a time when the Northwest's larger cities were undergoing social upheaval. The Northwest's lumber, mining and fishing towns developed a reputation for hard work and hard play. The gradually improving profitability of the extractive industries from the late 1890s was reflected in local businesses scrambling to cater for the most basic recreational needs of the growing numbers of workers. The never-closing saloon provided gambling tables, obliging women and narcotics and became synonymous with Seattle's Skid Row district or Everett's Hewitt Avenue. Even before the advent of wartime One Hundred Percentism or the moral guardianship of the Klan, the region had a prurience which sat at odds with its rough frontier mentality. The moral pendulum bounced from the victorious Mayor Hiram Gill's pragmatic endorsement of a contained, "restricted [red light] district" for Seattle in his 1910 campaign and the fire and brimstone condemnation of Everett's population by the evangelist Billy Sunday in June of the same year. Gill's 1910 acceptance of 700 working women being employed in Seattle's Midway brothel was indicative of the "whiskey, sawdust and fish" mentality that an increasingly influential, reforming, middle class sought to eradicate. Rational, Protestant morality coalesced into American indignation. The immorality of those who condoned such un-checked workers' playtime was vilified as un-American. Gill was removed from office in 1911 for his "lewd partnership with breakers of the law...[which was] wholly at variance with the spirit and genius of American political institutions and American law".[63] Billy Sunday's initial Everett sermon addressed the subjects of "Home, Booze and Native Land."[64]

Asians were frequently seen, with some degree of accuracy, as providing the "raw materials" for these immoral trades. In the prurient muckraking reports of the day, almost all of the accounts of the Northwest's brothels had a reference to at least one "China Mary", although from the 1890s it was increasingly likely she was either Japanese, Filipino or Korean. This Asian prostitute was considered particularly dangerous. Lacking the grace, sensitivity and gentleness of the fallen white woman, she was more likely to have arrived in her unfortunate position to indulge her own appetites. Even if her fall was involuntary, there was often an additional reason to denounce her. For example, she was frequently condemned for having a more virulent strain of venereal disease than that of her infected white counterpart or as attempting to dupe young, innocent white men. As Horace Greeley had claimed in 1854, "the Chinese are uncivilized, unclean and filthy...every female is a prostitute of the basest order."[65] Although much of this probably stemmed from the ubiquitous prejudices of Asian decadence, theories of Asian cruelty and avarice, there was some basis in fact.[66] The problem was of great interest to the local Japanese community. It exercised the American-Japanese leadership who were anxious to avoid the fate of the Chinese:

> Lately [1891] in the cities of California, Washington, and Oregon in America, Japanese women who ply the infamous trade, namely, prostitution, are increasing in number by the

> months [sic]....These women are a blot on our national image and national morality....The reasons for the ban on Chinese immigration and the call for the expulsion of the Chinese were many and varied, but the *main one was that Chinese women were prostitutes*....It is evident that, if this notorious vice spreads, America will adopt measures against us in the same manner as she did formerly against the Chinese.[67]

As early as 1891, according to the Japanese consul in San Francisco, there was very good reason for this fear. Seattle had around 250 Japanese residents of which, according to consular research, only 10 had legal work; 71 were recorded as prostitutes and the remainder, he claimed, were either pimping or professional gamblers. He also estimated that there were a further 30 Japanese pimps in Spokane and some 40 to 50 in Portland.[68] Throughout the period, the Asian was always seen as the perpetrator of the white slave trade that fixated and entranced with sheer horror the middle-class whites of both sexes across the western world. It was not only the white slaves they traded in. There are numerous accounts of Japanese, Korean and Chinese sailors supplementing their wages, and satisfying their appetites, by shanghaiing women from their home ports and selling them on arrival in America. There are accounts of Asians selling their wives, daughters and sisters into prostitution. It was a lucrative trade, an Asian prostitute could fetch as much as $1,000.[69]

Even without such considerable financial incentives the Asian, being led in his life by baser, more bestial impulses, was considered to have a less highly developed sense of morality than his white counterpart. He was seen as seeking the corruption not only of his own, often compliant, womenfolk but also innocent white women. However, it was more frequently the nativists in Britain, with the racial imperatives that legitimated empire, who raised accusations of Asian immorality. When such indictments were made in America they tended to center on areas where Asians formed a significant, if not dominant population—more on San Francisco's Chinese population and the Japanese in Hawaii rather than the Northwest's generally cowed and scattered Asian communities.[70] Even in Seattle where the Japanese had a considerable stake in the sex trade, as the period progressed, the objection to this aspect of their behavior was generally muted or the race issue removed and the question handled as an aspect of the city's overall vice problem.

Curiously, while the Japanese sexual impropriety was underplayed, by contrast towards the end of the period, during virtuous "Normalcy", the Japanese became increasingly associated with the bootlegging and narcotics trades in the Northwest. In 1923 at the height of anti-Japanese feeling in Oregon, House Bill 205 was passed to "require all foreign owners of business [to]...post conspicuously a notice of their nationality....Because 95 percent of all [the largely Japanese] alien owner soft drink establishments have been found [to be] bootlegger joints."[71] This accusation can be seen as symptomatic of the ease of using the Japanese as a scapegoat. It can be seen as an effort to distract attention from the vast network of corruption the attempts to enforce the Volstead Act brought in their wake—particularly in Seattle's police force. Focus on the Japanese distributors distracted attention from the graft taking place in higher circles.[72] It can also be seen as stemming from the Japanese inheriting the image of the opium-smoking Chinese coolie.

Opium smuggling was considered a major problem in the Northwest. The lax attitude of the Canadian authorities led to a lucrative trade developing, especially around Puget Sound. However, unlike the picture of the pathetic Chinese opium addict, in Seattle the Japanese were seen as more cynical—pushing, rather than using narcotics. As one Federal narcotics agent claimed, "The Chinese are the worst violators of the Narcotics Law—the Japs next. The Chinese use the most narcotics of any nationality—usually [they] smoke it. The Japs use the least, but they do sell it." There was also a more sinister, if more paranoid, and peculiarly Japanese, element to these accusations. The same source claimed that as a potential undercover agent for Japanese narcotics he was told that—"In a short time all Americans will be using dope and it will be easy for Japan to whip them then."[73]

While accusations of bootlegging and narcotics trading grew throughout the period in question, the problem of Japanese sexual impropriety seemed to recede. From 1907, Japanese women began to enter the Northwest in increasing numbers, overwhelmingly as potential brides. The result of this influx was that a greater number of the male population formed families resident in the area. This increase in the number of Japanese women points out a similarity between the Japanese and the "new" European immigration. Although, in most immigrant groups to America, males tended to arrive earlier than females, leading initially to predominantly male immigrant populations, this was particularly pronounced in the Japanese population. In 1910, the ratio of male to female among America's foreign-born population was 131 males to every 100 females.

The differential in the sex of immigrants was more pronounced in the "new" European immigration ranging from a ratio of 191 males to every 100 Italian females, to 137 males for every 100 Russian females.[74] The figures for Japanese are far more striking, as Table 4.1 illustrates.[75]

Table 4.1: Japanese Population in Washington and Oregon, 1900-1920

Year of Census	Total population	Japanese Population	Male Japanese	Female Japanese
1900				
Oregon	413,546	2,501 (0.6%)	2,405 (96.2%)	96 (3.8%)
Washington	518,103	5,617 (1.1%)	5,432 (96.7%)	185 (3.3%)
1910				
Oregon	672,765	3,148 (0.5%)	3,124 (91.4%)	292 (8.6%)
Washington	1,141,990	12,929 (1.1%)	11,241 (96.9%)	1,688 (3.1%)
1920				
Oregon	788,890	3,022 (0.5%)	2,722(67.7%)	1,300 (33.3%)
Washington	1,356,621	16,214(1.3%)	11,173 (65.3%)	5,041 (34.7%)

In 1910, using the same basis, the ratio in Washington State and Oregon works out at about 720 Japanese males to every 100 Japanese females, and this had grown from some 2,600 males to every 100 females in 1900.

These discrepancies were used as an indication by exclusionists of the migrant rather than immigrant status of Southern and Eastern Europeans. Leaving their dependents at home, these immigrants obviously displayed little intention of making America their permanent residence.This reasoning re-enforced labor accusations that the Japanese, like the Chinese, were simply economic migrants, that they were willing to work for less since they had no families to support, and that they merely intended to return to Japan as soon as they had accumulated sufficient wealth. They were seen as even more "blatant" in this than the "new" Europeans, and the anti-Asian lobby exploited this from the outset of anti-Chinese agitation. There was an enduring hatred of Asia, as an apologist for the Wyoming anti-Chinese riot demonstrated in 1885:

> There exists in narrow minds prejudice against Jews, against Irishmen, against Hungarians, and others and it is alleged triumphantly that our theories call for the exclusion of these [as well as the Chinese]. If the cases were parallel, the deduction would be sound. But there are, on the contrary, only slight and accidental resemblances between the immigration of other foreigners and Chinese. The former come voluntarily, to make a home with us; they bring their families with them; they soon sink into the body politic, and their children are not distinguishable from native born; they do not come, or threaten to come, in countless hosts like the swarms of Attilla; as a rule they bring no strange diseases, and have no unnatural vices.[76]

The Japanese themselves initially recognized the temporary nature of their migration to America. The Japanese term used for the first wave of migrants was *dekasegi*, meaning "empty handed", insinuating "poor". The underlying message was the "hand" would be filled and the migrant would return home:

> In the past the majority of Japanese in America and Canada were under the sway of the *dekasegi* spirit. We crossed the vast Pacific in order to earn money. The land here was only a temporary place to earn a living, a travel lodge as it were, with our real home being in Japan where the cherry blossoms bloom.[77]

Even those who intended to remain in America found themselves open to the ubiquitous nativist accusation that immigrants sent their earnings home rather than allowed them to circulate in the local economy. In 1910, the Dillingham Commission contrasted "Nordic", Italian and Japanese farmers in the "Vicinity of Seattle and Tacoma" who returned money to their native countries. Only 2 out of 35 Nordics interviewed sent money abroad, whereas 43 of the 77 Japanese, and 7 out of the 11 Italians did so. On average, the "Nordics" returned the least, under $20 per head, while the Italians returned under $40. The Japanese returned over $230 each.[78]

This export of resources was seen as evidence of a continued tie between the American-Japanese community and their native land. From the time of the 1906 San Francisco schools crisis, and the resulting growth in anti-Japanese sentiment, the Japanese government began to exert increasing pressure on her nationals abroad in order to change this attitude. Acting through consuls the Japanese government attempted to aid and influence Japanese emigrants via the Japanese Associations.[79] This was done largely through the Associations' control of the registration process, which was one of the conditions of the 1907 compromise—the "Gentlemen's Agreement". This compliance led to accusations, as with anti-Catholic sentiment, that the Japanese owed allegiance to a foreign power:

> A patriotism possesses them [the Japanese] that is second to that of no other country or race, and inspires them with a passionate determination to extend the governmental, commercial and cultural influences of Nippon into all parts of the world with which the mother country comes into close communication.[80]

JAPANESE IMMIGRATION AND AMERICAN SECURITY

To some nativists, the Gentlemen's Agreement represented the relinquishing of America's sovereign right to regulate her own immigration, and to a nation which was seen as an increasingly real economic and military threat in the Pacific—particularly in light of the Japanese defeat of Russia in 1905. At the first annual convention of the Anti-Asiatic League, held in Seattle, February, 1908, a memorial addressed to Congress was adopted which declared hostility to "any ["Gentlemen's"] agreement which will permit the ruler of any foreign country to make stipulations as to what class of persons and in what numbers shall leave said foreign country for the purpose of immigration to the United States."[81] This perception was re-enforced in the nativist mind by the knowledge that the registering of America's Japanese was, from 1910, left up to the increasingly powerful, and seemingly autonomous, Japanese Associations. In spite of this, many Japanese saw this registration as not only laying themselves open to military service but also as a reiteration of the alien stigma they sought to slough off. A considerable proportion of Japanese certainly had no wish to pass such a burden onto their children. Consequently, in reality the Associations' success in registering the Northwest's Japanese population was limited. For example, out of a total of 2,345 Japanese births in the State of

Washington for the years 1915 to 1917, only 1,770 were registered with the Japanese consulate in Seattle.[82]

In addition, to nativists, the omnipresent sinister militarist machinations of the Japanese government were apparent in the activities of the Associations. Many nativists saw these organizations as "organs of the Mikado", organizations which demonstrated the true intentions of the Japanese population in America. Not only did America's Japanese owe allegiance to a foreign ruler, but that ruler's expansionist intentions were all too apparent. Unlike the Native American Indian or the black, the Asian had been feared, seen as a being capable of becoming a sophisticated military force since the ravaging of Europe by the Mongol hordes. This applied particularly to the Japanese, who were to many exclusionists a militarist race—a fact increasingly evinced by their imperial ambitions in Asia and their perceived clannishness, their unquestioning obedience to the "Mikado", and their proclivity for group activities. Initially, the Western European powers regarded the development of Japan's military capabilities as a worthwhile export market for services and hardware. France and Germany competed for contracts to train the Japanese army, while Britain developed the Imperial Navy. Such ventures also held the potential to create a valuable extension of their spheres of influence.[83]

In America, the reaction was different, particularly on the Pacific coast. Japanese adoption in 1873 of European-style peacetime conscription for all males aged between 17 and 40 was increasingly viewed as an indication of Japan's militarist nature. More worryingly, was the fact that all these men, regardless of domicile, were liable for military service. To the nativist, this meant that in the event of military conflict Japan already had growing numbers of potential "troops" on American soil. Why else was this potential army largely concentrated in the most likely invasion area—the Pacific coastline? Nativists periodically claimed that the Japanese were amassing armies and operating as fifth columnists in Hawaii—an American territory since 1900. At the very best the Japanese-Hawaiians were considered of dubious loyalty: "Scores of intelligent, conservative, solid Americans...told me they did not believe a single Hawaiian-born Japanese could be trusted to fight for America against Japan or to take the American point of view in any matter of controversy with Japan."[84]

This potential disloyalty was coupled with fears of the superstition and under-lying savagery of the Asian. It was apparent to the white supremacist as early as 1900, with the slaughter of defenseless missionaries and "empowering" traders in the Boxer Rebellion, although the deliberate conflation of all Asians ignored the Japanese role alongside American marines as the largest contingent of the "European" relief force. Similarly, this mistrust was re-enforced by the knowledge that American soldiers were being killed in the Philippines in their efforts to ready the islands' population for the complexities of democracy, for civilization. Throughout the period, the Asian was seen as silently plotting, biding his time and readying his forces in preparation to launch a race war. Unlike the other colonized groups, the Asian was seen as a real threat, increasingly possessing both the means and mentality to wage effective war:

"The brown and yellow races possess great military potentialities. These...are unlikely to flame out in spontaneous fanaticism, but...are very likely to be mobilized for political reasons like revolt against white dominion."[85] Nevertheless, it seemed that some Europeans were oblivious to this obvious threat. They continued to commit racial treason by according Japan equal status in treaties and alliances and even supplied them with the military expertise and equipment which would certainly lead to their own destruction.[86]

The underlying racial assumptions on which the early twentieth-century Anglo-Saxon world based its presumption of superiority in turn spawned a vogue for threatening Asian villains. The most famous example is probably Sax Rohmer's 1913 creation of the evil genius Dr. Fu Manchu fed a trend which went from popular fiction to film. This inhuman criminal mastermind represented "all the cruel cunning of an entire Eastern race...the yellow peril incarnate in one man".[87] On the West Coast, there was a ready market for the imitation of such writers as H.G. Wells with their warnings of the "Yellow Peril" and assumptions of Asian race hatred.[88] This trend reached its shrillest pre-war tone in the works of Homer Lea, most notably his ripping *Valour of Ignorance* (New York, 1909). Its depiction of Japanese military expansion first into the Philippines and then California, Oregon and Washington State relied on a fashionable racial "Darwinist" premise. This premise was made all the more authentic after the 1911 revolution by Lea's personal knowledge gained from his near mythological status as a former general in the Chinese army and advisor to Sun Yat-Sen.[89]

It was not merely in fiction that the fear of Asian invasion loomed. Japan's increasing naval capabilities had represented a serious concern to Washington ever since their successful engagement with China (1894-95). It had been made even more frighteningly potent by the Japanese navy's daring and decisive demolition of the Russian fleet at Tsushima in 1905. These two victories challenged European, and therefore American, certainties of their own supremacy. This was an era of naval strategy dominated by the capital ship theories of Alfred Thayer Mahan in which control of oceanic movement was global domination. An Asian naval power was an anomaly; consequently the size of Japan's fleet was worrying enough to influence directly the immigration debate in the crucial 1921 Immigration Act. While wishing to avoid affronting Tokyo by excluding Japanese immigrants, the Americans sought to limit the Imperial Navy's capital ships in the concurrent naval negotiations taking place in Washington. The result was that federal government delayed a legislative response to West Coast proposals for Japanese exclusion until 1924.

On the West Coast the threat was considered more immediate. It had been for some while. In 1897, Japan had sent a battleship to "prowl" Hawaiian waters making her presence felt to Americans in the region and there was a real fear that Japan had intentions to annex the islands itself.[90] Hearst's *San Francisco Examiner* had ominously warned, even prior to the saber-rattling excursion of Theodore Roosevelt's "Great White Fleet", that "Japan Sounds Our Coasts. Brown men have maps and could easily land."[91] Former San Francisco mayor and leading anti-Japanese activist James Duval Phelan noted the weakness of California defenses. Richmond Pearson Hobson, the naval "hero" of Santiago de Cuba in the Spanish American War and Democratic congressman for Alabama, warned via the Hearst juggernaut that "Absolute control of the Pacific Ocean is our only safety [for a Japanese army of]...1,207,000 [?] could conquer the Pacific Coast."[92] By 1907 the threat was considered real enough for the United States navy to add Japan to a list of potentially hostile powers and draft "War Plan Orange" to deal with the threat.[93]

In the war years the paranoia of One Hundred Percentism fed the theme of Japanese territorial ambitions on the West Coast. The propaganda war prior to American entry had included an element that sought to break up any potential alliance of America and Japan, which it was felt would follow if America entered the war on the Allies' side. German propaganda fed the threat, warning of Japanese armies in California and Mexico poised to attack the undefended Pacific Coast. The Kaiser's personal phobia of the "Yellow Peril" led to this being a favorite component of the German propaganda machine even before the outbreak of the war in Europe. After American entry into the war in 1917, the Hearst papers, film—notably the picture *Patria*—and German agents, George S. Viereck and Franz von Papen in particular, added fuel to this phobia of invasion.[94]

As early as 1913, Heinrich Werner told reporters that "Japan has a well trained, highly efficient, standing army of 40,000 men [in California and Mexico]."[95] In the Northwest, these fears hinged on the threat not only of invasion by sea, but also by land, from the south—from California, and also from the north, from Alaska. In 1914, the restrictionist Congressman Albert Johnson of Washington pointed out the strategic necessity of a rail connection, what he termed a "covered way", between Washington State and Alaska in order "to protect this country from capture by the Japanese. [For Johnson]...shows that it would be an easy matter for the Jap navy to swoop down upon Cordova or Valdez or Skagway and grab Alaska by the feet and hang on until Kingdom Come. He then spends a lot of time endeavoring to lead us to believe that Japan has such an intention."[96]

Rather than quieting American nervousness about Japanese militarism, the war added to it. Against a background of American, New Zealand and Australian fears, Britain had invited Japanese intervention in order to activate Japan's treaty obligations. From August, 1914 the Royal Navy's Pacific presence was bolstered by the support of the Imperial navy.[97] Although Japan was one of America's allies during the war, her blatant territorial ambitions with the notorious "Twenty-one Demands" and, after the war, the Shantung question intensified post-war feelings of Japanese militarism.[98] When some 9,000 Americans served alongside 72,000 Japanese in their abortive attempt to aid Admiral Kolchak's White Russians in Siberia, the American commander saw the Japanese as unnecessarily cruel and their motives in the region as being less than selfless.[99] There was a feeling that Japan had entered the war merely to share in the spoils of the peace. In 1920 a West Coast nativist succinctly pointed out what he considered Japan's true motivation: "In following her established policy in the Far East, Japan has not only showed herself an apt pupil of Germany, her arch instructor, but has also proved herself an unfaithful partner to her allies, deliberately taking advantage of their necessities to feather her own nest."[100] The strength of these misgivings enabled Henry Cabot Lodge to manipulate Congress into viewing Ambassador Hanihara's 1924 plea to reconsider Albert Johnson's Japanese Exclusion Bill[101] into a "veiled threat" of conflict which swung the previously hostile Senate vote towards favoring of total Japanese exclusion.

Running alongside the nativists fears of Japan's bellicose plans were less violent but more insidious fears of Japanese domination of America by means of demographic, and therefore economic, supremacy. Contemporary racial assumptions, most notably those based on an anthropological corruption of Darwinian theory, gave a seeming scientific basis to the West Coast fears of Japanese domination. The main fear was that of Asians out-breeding the "American" population, as one California farmer complained: "I live on the farm where my six children were born. They go to the country school. Three years ago all their playmates were white children. Now all the children in that school except mine and those of one other farmer are Japanese."[102] West Coast nativists were quick to adopt the fashionable theory of "race suicide", which held the superior traits of the dominant white population to be sensitive and fragile. To the Nordic nativist, the natural morality, grace and humility of white women and the intelligence, self-control and discrimination of white men precluded, and made abhorrent, the bestial indulgence of their sexual urges. Consequently, the inferior races untroubled by such delicacy, increased disproportionately.[103] Along with blacks, Slavs, Jews, Chinese and any other undesirable components in American society, the Japanese were condemned for their prolificacy:

> A study of the vital factors affecting the several race stocks in California, as shown by the Vital Statistics records, leads to the conclusion that there is no race within our borders that can compare with the Japanese in rate of reproduction and vitality. Their birth rate is high, and their death rate is low. Japanese mothers have stillbirths less frequently than women of any other race in the State, and infant mortality is lower than for any race, except the Chinese. In 1920 alone, the Japanese increased their population 5.4 percent by reproduction, while the white race increased 0.5 percent, one-tenth as fast.[104]

This prolificacy among the Japanese population became an all-pervasive and potent nativist argument. Oregon's influential Davey Report of 1920 claimed that while the married Japanese population of Hood River county made up only 1.5 percent of the total population, they accounted for some 10 to 20 percent of the births in the area between 1916 and 1919—the consequences for the region were obvious. As with the international conspiracies of the Jews and Catholics, this prolificacy was part of a deliberate plan formulated in Japan to allow domination of America, for as an expert witness—"who taught in the public schools of Japan for six years"—told Portland's Nordics in 1920:

> Every [Japanese] girl (school girl) is thoroughly drilled in the doctrine that, should she become a picture bride in America, or an immigrant to other lands, her loyal duty to her Emperor is to have as many children as possible, so that the foreigners' land may become in time a possession of Japan, through the express will of a majority of the people.[105]

The Davey Report goes on to give a more rational, if—to their opponents—no less distressing, reason for Japanese fecundity. The report's examination of the age of Japanese women in Oregon found that—"nearly all Japanese families now in Oregon are at the stage of highest productivity."[106] Added to the prospect of an upsurge in numbers within the Japanese community was the dread of the "mongrelization" of the West, the inter-breeding of white and Asiatic. To the nativist such breaches of the laws of racial hygiene were a chilling prospect:

> Near my home there is an eighty-acre tract of as fine land as there is in California. On that tract lives a Japanese. With that Japanese lives a white woman. In that white woman's arms is a baby. What is that baby? It isn't Japanese. It isn't white. I'll tell you what it is. It is the germ of the mightiest problem that ever faced this state; a problem that will make the black problem of the South look white. All about us the Asiatics are gaining a foothold.[107]

LAND TENURE, CITIZENSHIP AND IMMIGRATION

As with the East Coast arguments against Southern and Eastern Europeans, Japanese exclusion arguments hinged on this growing number of aliens being able to assimilate into American society without disastrous effects for the "native" population. The *dekasegi* spirit, the preponderance of males to females, language, education, culture and allegiance were all seen as stumbling blocks to Japanese assimilation—reasons not only to exclude them from citizenship, but also from entry. The Japanese tried pragmatically to eliminate these causes of white hostility. Realizing the enmity of "native" labor to Japanese competition, the Japanese government sought to encourage other classes of emigrants. In the wake of the Gentlemen's Agreement, Tokyo ceased issuing passports for laborers and began issuing passports for wives, including the notorious "picture brides". The Associations had misjudged the depth of anti-Japanese sentiment. The increase in Japanese women emigrating was resented, not only as representing further immigration—and of a more ominous kind as it created potential for the virtually unlimited expansion of the Japanese community within America—it was opposed also as an unwelcome example of the Asian's disdain for individuality. The practice of sending for "Picture Brides"—brides unseen by their future husbands except in photographs—was held to be at best distasteful, and at worst a form of prostitution. Further, those with highly developed Western concepts of femininity were offended by the use of Japanese women as "cheap labor" or "beasts of burden" once they had arrived.[108]

In order to both limit numbers and ensure that these women would not become a burden on their new country, the right to "import" these wives was strictly limited to those who could demonstrate financial solvency. This solvency was based on a rule of thumb that the potential husband was required to demonstrate to the local Japanese Association that he had at least $800 of liquid assets in order to qualify to send for a mate. With such financial pressure, for many of America's Japanese immigrants agriculture represented one of the few options open that could generate the necessary capital: "As soon as a Jap can produce a lease, he is entitled to a wife. He sends a copy of the lease back home and gets a picture bride and they increase like rats."[109]

Although having an element of risk, farming enabled reasonable income with generally low capital investment. The risks were offset by the fact that the returns were relatively fast. A significant proportion of Japanese immigrants had agricultural backgrounds. The Dillingham Commission found that of 53 Japanese farmers surveyed in the Seattle/Tacoma region, some 32 had previous experience of agriculture; 22 were farmers in Japan; 6 had farmed for their fathers in Japan and 4 had been farm hands.[110] The majority of the region's immigrants came from rural areas of Japan—largely from the farms and fishing villages of the Yamaguchi, Hiroshima and Oshima regions. They welcomed the long-term purpose, relative stability and "sense of belonging" which land tenure gave.

The Japanese government and the leaders of the Japanese community hoped that this scheme encouraging settlement would go some way to alleviating growing anti-Japanese pressures. Japanese assumed that a considerable amount of nativist hostility was due to the transitory nature of their migration, as a California senator had claimed in 1905: "[The Japanese are]...mere transients [who] do not buy land [or] build or buy houses...They contribute nothing to the growth of the State. They add nothing to its wealth, and they are a blight on the prosperity of it, and a great and impending danger to its welfare."[111] Under the leadership of such optimistic individuals as Abiko Kyutaro, the Japanese community was urged to settle and assimilate through agriculture, sending for wives, striving for the elimination of "immorality" in the eyes of their American neighbors. There was significant pressure for instigating measures which would encourage Americanization. Through his paper the *Nichibei Shimbun* (*Japanese American News*), with the slogan "Settlement on Land and Permanent Residency", Abiko consistently implored laborers to take up agriculture. In order to aid Japanese agriculture, the newspaper also published the *Nichibei*

Nenkan (*American-Japanese Yearbook*) which from 1905 to 1910 acted as a newsletter for Japanese farmers, giving agricultural costings and a directory of addresses.

Abiko pointed to the experiences of Japanese in Utah and Idaho, where he claimed there was no great exclusion movement, rather the Japanese were accepted. He held that this was because of their close co-operation as contract growers for "native"-owned businesses such as the Utah Sugar Company. With this in mind he set up the Yamoto community on 3,200 acres of undeveloped land in Livingston, California, in 1906 and a further 2,000 in Cortez, California, in 1919. These communities were divided into 40-acre parcels that were resold to those wishing to farm. Thus the period 1908 to 1923 particularly was marked by the movement of Japanese into agriculture on the Pacific slope. In 1900, 37 Japanese farmers were working 4,674 acres in California. By 1913, 6,177 farmers worked 281,687 acres and in 1920 nearly 8,000 Japanese farmed some 458,056 acres and agriculture involved half of the California Japanese population. The situation was similar for Washington State and Oregon.[112]

In the Pacific Northwest, as in California, the Japanese ventures in agriculture often encouraged rather than quieted nativist pressures for their exclusion. Initially many Japanese had entered agriculture in the area by reclaiming logged-off land for landowners. In return for this arduous, and often dangerous, reclamation work the Japanese would receive a small portion, normally between five to seven acres, of un-cleared land. However, as the Japanese realized the potential of agriculture in the region they sought to buy or rent better land. Frequently the prices charged to Japanese were higher than the market average: "the relation between Japanese tenancy and relatively high rents is the most striking thing in the Northwest. It is all the more significant for it is one of the well-nigh universal facts. The Japanese have been the highest bidders for land."[113] This was largely because the Japanese tended towards market gardening, fruit farming and other labor-intensive forms of horticulture.[114] These undertakings normally generated higher returns than the more extensive arable or livestock ventures which the earlier European farmers favored.

This concentration on horticulture meant that the Japanese were rarely in direct competition with the European livestock farmers; they "simply fill[ed] the gap created by the unwillingness of other farmers to engage themselves in certain kinds of farming."[115] For example, as late as 1921, 8,500 "Caucasians" leased 350,000 acres in Washington State for dairy farming. A mere 87 Japanese milked cows on 6,595 acres of Washington. This equates to the Japanese making up 1.02 percent of Washington State's tenant dairy farmers on 1.8 percent of Washington's *leased* dairy land,[116] and these figures exclude "Caucasian" farmer-occupiers.[117] Nevertheless, as with figures cited by both the Japanese and their opponents, the importance lies in the general perception. Although the Japanese may have made up a minuscule proportion of the region's dairy farmers, the concentration of Japanese dairy farmers in the White River valley with its strategic position led to their dominance of the Seattle milk market. It is estimated that in the early 1920s they controlled over one half of the city's raw milk sales. This high visibility, and presumably high profitability, was arguably more important in the generation of nativist hostility than the numbers of Japanese farmers, their proportion to other ethnic groups in the industry or the acreages they farmed.

The Japanese willingness to pay high rents meant that in many cases the initial response of resident farmers to Japanese leasing was positive:

> it is said that those who have rented their farms out to the Japanese are realizing more money each year than they did when running the farms themselves....One farmer at least says he is receiving $2,000 a year for 120 acres....[Also, in Pleasant Home, some] 22 miles from Portland there are four farms rented to the little brown men and their owners are taking life easy and getting as much money as if they worked and worried themselves.[118]

Given the limited acreage of suitable land in an area of variable rainfall and topography,[119] the boom caused by the limited Japanese population began to tail off and the consequent enthusiasm of farmers for the Japanese waned.

The type of agriculture in which the Japanese specialized meant that they tended to concentrate in areas of high fertility, good communications and reliable rainfall, or with suitable irrigation potential—the most desirable land. The Japanese were accused of colonizing the region's most productive areas such as the Hood, Willamette, Yakima, Puyallup and White River valleys. In response nativists were swift to defend these "heart-lands of the white pioneers" from the "little brown men" when the issue came to head in 1919:

> Japanese farmers have swarmed into the Hood River Valley like an army of conquest...The Japanese have peacefully run out dozens of small ranchers who sought to make the Hood River Valley their permanent home....Noting that the beautiful valley was becoming so thickly settled with Orientals that before long no white family could live in it, a number of Hood River citizens recently organized the anti-Asiatic club.[120]

The passions of Hood River residents had been roused with the attempted purchase of 13,800 acres in Jefferson, Crook and Deschutes counties, Oregon, for the California–Japanese "Potato King" George Shima (Kenji Ushijima). Shima (1824-1926), who by 1913 already had some 28,000 acres under contract in California, sought to use the land to raise seed-potatoes in association with George L. Burt's Portland-Deschutes Company. Aware of the sensitivity of the residents the partners took steps to avoid any racial hostility and it was agreed that Burt was to purchase the land. When the partners announced that they proposed to use Japanese potato "experts", local antipathy gathered pace and

Shima's role became more apparent. Rumors of a Japanese "invasion" rose to such a pitch that they killed the proposed purchase.[121] The incident brought the issue of alien land tenure back into the public interest.

Wartime demand for produce had masked the issue. Japanese rental of land had continued in spite of obvious hostility throughout the region. Indeed, the acreages leased to Japanese increased significantly in the period. In 1909, Japanese farmed some 7,000 acres of Washington in 325 holdings and this was within a state where alien landownership was prohibited. By 1921 Washington's Japanese were farming some 16,000 acres in an unspecified number of holdings.[122] In Oregon the acreage leased increased from some 3,000 acres in 1909 to nearly 8,000 acres by 1920.[123] While claiming that in the Hood Valley prior to the Shima affair the local populace had raised "no great hue and cry, either in favor or against...a law prohibiting Japanese ownership of land in California", Oregon had attempted to introduce similar legislation in 1917.[124] This legislation was withdrawn, ostensibly because of diplomatic issues involved in American entry into the war: "The "consequence" if not the direct purpose of the Oregon and Idaho [Alien Land] legislation was to embarrass the United States...[for they represented] a professed intention to assert state rights regardless of the national interests and engagements."[125]

The successful passage of Alien Land Laws in California in 1913, amended in 1920; in Washington State in 1921; and Oregon in 1923 highlighted the position of the Japanese in America.[126] The justifications used for these discriminatory laws were varied, ranging from claims of intensive Japanese farming methods depleting soil fertility to accusations of Japanese farmers forming cartels or even the agricultural successes of the "little brown men" being the result of Japanese government subsidies.[127] However, the restrictionists were eventually forced to accept and press the racial arguments in view of their inability to prove deterioration in Japanese agricultural production and failure to confirm accusations of much other than community solidarity, family labor, skilful marketing and industrious, frugal lifestyles:

> We raise a hue and cry against them [the Japanese] and demand their exclusion...simply because we are jealous of their success and we fear their competition...there is a strong antipathy against the Japanese among small farmers, mechanics, laborers and salaried classes in general. A large part of this is racial and does not depend upon economic facts. In its crude form it is expressed in the emphatic pronouncement, "We don't want any damned Japs in this country at all."
>
> ...Those who give reasons for that verdict say that the Japanese cannot become a part of American life, socially or as loyal citizens, because their lines of thought, purpose and aspirations are Japanese, their standards of living are not ours; their commercial purposes are in the interests of Japan and not

> the United States, and their national sympathies are the same way; their methods are crafty and deceitful; they are leeches on the national body, sucking out its best blood and poisoning the body upon which it feeds.[128]

The issue of Japanese land-ownership illustrates the truly racial basis of opposition to the Japanese. In 1905, while the Japanese rented, or owned little land they were condemned as "a great and impending danger to...[America's] welfare."[129] By 1919, the Hood River Anti-Asiatic Association saw "Japanese ownership of land...as a menacing our welfare and threatening the ultimate domination of our Home Land by Asiatics."[130] The conflation of race and patriotism—that ubiquitous feature of post-war America's "Tribal Twenties"[131]—was as visible in the Northwest as it was anywhere in America. The various organizations that vocally staked a claim to be the arbiters of true Americanism, all used the issue of Alien Land tenure. For example, the American Legion condemned the situation where—"While the soldiers were gone the Japanese came in and rapidly acquired valuable land and control of hotels and small businesses. The returning soldier found himself without a job and thousands of Japanese fattening on the land."[132] Absorbing this message and elaborating it into a political program, the Klan called for "an absolute exclusion of all Japanese who may seek to come here...[and] control the entire acreage of irrigated lands...[turning the West into] a little Japan."[133]

The Alien Land Laws highlighted the position of the Japanese in America. These laws were predicated on race. Land-ownership or leasing was limited to those who were already citizens, or who had declared a wish to naturalize—i.e. all except Asian immigrants and American aboriginals. Foreign-born Japanese were "aliens ineligible for citizenship" and as such their tenancy, or ownership, of land was considered to be detrimental to the state:

> It is obvious that one who is not a citizen and cannot become one lacks an interest in, and the power to effectually [sic] work for the welfare of, the state and so lacking, the state may rightfully deny him the right to own and lease real estate within its boundaries. If one incapable of citizenship may lease or own real estate, it is within the realm of possibility that every foot of land within the state might pass to the ownership of non-citizens.[134]

Coupled with this it was felt that, as with Japanese laborers, any concentrations of Japanese farmers would increase displays of their natural aggression which lay dormant when they were in a minority:

> They [the Japanese] are alright [sic] so long as they are few in a community. They patronize American businesses and are very agreeable in their dealings, but let them increase

> sufficiently and there is a vast change. They lose their docility, become very arrogant, set up their own stores, warehouses and business connections, discontinue pleasant intercourse with the whites.[135]

A survey conducted in California in 1920 demonstrated that a majority of those questioned sought to limit Japanese immigration by means of prohibitions on alien agricultural tenancy and land-ownership. Out of a total of 756 people queried over the 1920 amendment to the California land Act (Initiative Measure No 1) by the University of California and Occidental College in 1920 the following replies, as shown in Table 4.2,[136] were given. There is no reason to suspect that the same reasoning did not apply in the Northwest, especially when viewed in light of the following Oregon editorial:

> California legislators have begun to grapple with the problem that will probably be up for solution for many years to come. It may be unfortunate that racial prejudice has been aroused there in those sections where the Japanese form such a large part of the population [and] has caused a hasty reaction on the part of the lawmakers. And as yet a law that tends to prevent Japanese immigration to this country is undoubtedly a wise one.[137]

Table 4.2: Voting Patterns for California Initiative Measure Number 1, 1920.

	"Did you read the initiative prior to voting?"	"Was it your intention to stop immigration by this measure?"	"Would You vote in the same way now?"
"Professionals"			
Yes	156	81	109
No	40	101	31
"Laborers"			
Yes	60	137	116
No	126	45	19
Farmers			
Yes	124	104	107
No	65	68	25
Women			
Yes	79	92	98
No	103	86	38
Total			
Yes	419	414	430
No	334	300	113

The land laws re-enforced Japanese feelings of their persecution and prejudice under the American legal system, which did little for the image of America as the *dekasegi* paradise, but the measures failed to halt Japanese immigration. Japanese alien status in 1919 did not preclude them from immigration into America—it merely meant they could not naturalize. They remained in a form of limbo caused by the Gentlemen's Agreement and the 1911 Commerce and Navigation Treaty, which excluded them from the provisions of restrictive legislation that followed in the period to 1924. They were not subject to the provisions of the Chinese Exclusion Acts. They had remained outside the "Asian Barred Zone" established by the 1917 Immigration Act and the quotas of the 1921 Act. The limitations on their entry were determined, under the 1907 Gentlemen's Agreement, by the issuance of passports from the Japanese government and these were in regard to the occupations and sex of immigrants rather than their numbers. Their status under American naturalization law provided a loophole by which tenancies could be continued. Under the initial 1913, California Act, those Japanese who did not have access to, or trust, American citizens willing to rent the land for them, could apply through their American-born children.

While foreign-born Japanese, the *Issei*, were ineligible for naturalization, their American-born offspring, the *Nisei*, were eligible. Thus when the California Law precluded the renting of land, many Japanese merely applied for tenancies in the names of their "American" offspring. In cases where these *Nisei* were minors, the land would be held in "trust" or guardianship by their Japanese parents. Whereas Japanese ownership of land may have proved difficult to sustain in court in the wake of a successful Alien Land Law, the example of California demonstrated that leasing was an altogether safer proposition. Those California Japanese who died between 1913 and 1920 without having transferred their lands to naturalized children or nominal white owners exemplified the dangers inherent within the legislation. Their surviving relatives frequently saw the land sold at public auction for values substantially below their real worth.

There can be little doubt that the hostility to Japanese residents, and further immigration, which expressed itself in the 1913 California Act and Oregon's 1917 attempt at an Alien Land Law, had significant impact on the long-term views of Japanese immigrants. Leased land—even when the rental period could not exceed three years, as the 1913 California act stipulated—was still seen as a profitable prospect. With the increasingly vociferous anti-Japanese lobby baying for their expulsion the Japanese residents on the Pacific Coast realized that farming in America should be viewed as a short-term activity. Over the next six years, this impression was somewhat dulled by the effects of international events on the region. Before the explosion of feeling caused by the 1919 Shima-Deschutes affair, anti-Japanese activity in rural areas of the Northwest was diminished by the wartime agricultural boom which meant even higher returns were available to those people willing to rent land to the Japanese. Nevertheless, the acreage of land owned, rather than leased, by Japanese in Oregon declined in the period 1913 to 1919 by almost a third and "American" buyers purchased several large tracts of Japanese land in the state.[138]

So, although the 1913 California Act made Japanese farming ventures less secure, it did not entirely preclude them. The 1920 California amendment and the more comprehensive Washington and Oregon laws went further.[139] While addressing many of the loopholes of the previous law, to many nativists they still did not go far enough. There were indications that the region's Japanese remained unaffected by the new measures. For instance, in California although the number of Japanese tenancies may have declined between 1920 and 1930, the number of Japanese landowners actually increased in spite of a declining Japanese population. [140] Also, in Oregon, in spite of American Legion protests, land was openly sold to un-naturalized Japanese before the May 25, 1923, deadline and through their *nisei* children after.[141] Nevertheless, by 1942 the average American Japanese farm was 45 acres, the American norm was 300.[142] It is worth considering that the overall decline in Japanese land tenure through until the 1940s may well have been exaggerated by the processes of mechanization. These changes enabled larger holdings to be managed by fewer individuals in areas of agriculture such as wheat, forage and root crops, fields in which whites were dominant. This also buoyed up land prices, encouraging Japanese sales.

Utilizing the sentiments aroused by the passage of the Anti-Alien Land Laws, nativists launched a determined campaign for federal exclusion as the only means of halting the "Japanese Menace", a means of negating the necessity for these "piecemeal measures". Consequently, after 1922 the nativist arguments for Japanese restriction became increasingly linked with the naturalization laws. The decisions of the Ozawa, Yamashita and Kono cases judged that as the Japanese were neither of white nor "African" origin they were ineligible for citizenship. The issue had been most baldly decided in the Supreme Court decision in November, 1922, which upheld the contemporary racial thinking on the racial status of the Japanese when it ruled:

> The appellant in the case now under consideration [Ozawa], however, is clearly of a race which is not Caucasian and therefore belongs entirely outside the zone on the negative side [regarding naturalization]. A large number of the federal and state courts have so decided, and we find no reported case definitely to the contrary. These decisions are sustained by numerous scientific authorities, which we do not deem it necessary to review. We think these decisions are right, and so hold.[143]

THE NORTHWEST AND FEDERAL PRESSURE FOR JAPANESE EXCLUSION

With the vital support the Ozawa clarification loaned to the anti-Japanese movement the AFL, the American Legion and the National Grange began a nation-wide campaign for "the enactment without delay, of laws, and the negation of treaties if required, for the permanent exclusion as immigrants or permanent residents of the United States of all persons ineligible under the laws thereof to citizenship."[144] The Japanese Exclusion League spearheaded the campaign in Congress. The League represented the main anti-Japanese lobbying organization representing a diverse range of national and western bodies.[145] Their aim was uncompromising:

> Absolute exclusion for the future of all Japanese immigration not only male but female, and not only laborers, skilled and unskilled, but 'farmers' and the men of small trades and professions, as recommended by Theodore Roosevelt [in the Gentlemen's Agreement]....Permission for temporary residence [would be granted] only for tourists, students, artists, commercial men, teachers, etc. [146]

This resolution was sent to all California delegates in Congress, President Warren Harding and Secretary of State Charles Evans Hughes. However, it was the Northwestern representatives who acted upon the proposals. The measure was adopted under the guise of the proposition that "no alien ineligible to citizenship should be admitted to the United States" by California's John E. Raker in his amendments (HR 12193) to Albert Johnson's June 1922 Bill (HR 12169) "as a model for future thinking on immigration".[147] In February 1923, Johnson introduced a further restriction bill which was amended the following day by his fellow Washingtonian, Representative John F. Miller, to exclude, specifically, the Japanese.[148]

The Northwestern position was unequivocally stated in a memorandum to all senators and congressmen from the Oregon legislature. This document attempted to point out the urgency of the issue when Congress seemed to be stalling on the passage of the Johnson-Miller Bill:

> [T]he State of Oregon is vitally interested in this problem, because in this State there are more than 17,000 aliens who are unable to speak English or write their own name...the cost to the Government of our alien population by reason of their violation of the eighteenth amendment and the Harrison Narcotic Act, as well as of the Volstead Act, by thousands of these aliens is burdensome in the extreme....Further the legislature of the state of Oregon is unalterably opposed to further immigration into the United States in excess of the

> present quota, and further recommends that our laws be so amended as to restrict the entrance into the United States of all Asiatics and Southern European internationals [sic]...[Oregon also called for a] rigid exclusion of all further immigration until such time as we may fully assimilate those within our borders and give to American labor and American laws the right which is their due.[149]

Oregon's effort had little effect and the bill never reached a vote. Undeterred, Johnson proposed a further unsuccessful Bill (HR 6540) the following year prior to the passage of his successful March 1924 Bill (HR 7995). This persistence and tenacity in the Northwestern anti-Japanese lobby can be seen as stemming from a series of issues which were peculiar to the area.

Unlike California's anti-Japanese advocates James D. Phelan or Hiram Johnson, the Northwest had a Congressman who had been elected on a specifically restrictionist, and therefore anti-Japanese platform. Washington's Albert Johnson claimed that viewing:

> The coolies [Japanese laborers arriving in Puget Sound]... treated like peons, and herded away to work on the section gangs of the railroads...[and being] satisfied...that inducements were offered to bring those Japanese laborers here...[committed him to restriction and] with the *Tacoma Daily News*, I began to call attention to the situation in every way I could...How could I know that in 1912—fourteen years later—I would be elected to Congress, with the restriction of immigration as the chief plank in my platform.[150]

Johnson remained true to this election pledge. He regarded his "patriotic duty" to be the rationalization of America's immigration legislation and his consistent pressure, initially for a total halt to immigration, and later for a quota plan in large measure, lay behind the restrictionist 1921 and 1924 Immigration Acts.

Aside from legislating for the return of hotel keys via post and establishing a tradition of boosting Northwestern salmon, Johnson's congressional career revolved around immigration restriction, culminating in his appointment as Chairman of the House Immigration and Naturalization Committee in 1919, a position which he used to promote his restrictionist agenda. Sometimes Johnson showed little interest in equanimity, as the following incident illustrates:

> Mr. Galbraith reports that last year his father was called to testify before the Congressional Investigating Committee in Tacoma of which Representative [Albert] Johnson was chairman. His father could only be in the city 3 days and notified the Committee accordingly...5 minutes after his

> testimony had begun some member of the Committee moved that they adjourn...until the following day.
> [The same thing happened on the following day and Mr Galbraith claimed] "Look here, you wouldn't let me talk yesterday or the day before because I was saying things in favour of the Japs. But I was telling the truth..."[He continued to relate his experiences with the Japanese only to interrupted by] Representative Johnson who said: "Galbraith we don't want your report on the situation at all. We don't want to hear that side of the question and you might as well go home." [151]

With characteristic single-mindedness Johnson saw the Gentlemen's Agreement as inefficient, difficult to operate and largely pointless. Increasingly he came to regard total Japanese exclusion as essential:

> I believe that all quotas should consist only of persons eligible to citizenship under our present naturalization laws. An amendment to that effect would end the difficulties which arise from our "Gentlemen's Agreement" with Japan. There is no reason why we should admit to become residents of the United States [those] who never can become citizens of the United States.[152]

Johnson saw himself as one of the foremost immigration experts in the country. He utilized his journalistic background and talent for self-promotion to gain considerable local kudos for himself. The local press billed him as "the man from Hoquiam" and he found little difficulty in getting himself constantly re-elected from 1912 to 1932. His monomania in Congress managed to assure that the issue of immigration restriction remained of disproportionate influence, even in an area where wartime nativism produced some of the most virulent xenophobia in the country. For although to some extent anti-Japanese feeling was driven by sentiments inherited from California, there was also a fear that without state legislation the Northwest might become a refuge for exiled California Japanese. As Ben Dorris, "chairman of the legislative committee of the American Legion", put it in 1923—"Oregon is now the only state on the coast not having an anti-alien [Land Law] of this nature. Without such a law Oregon will soon become a Mecca for the ineligible alien."[153]

While this reactive explanation seems to account for the chronology of the legislation, it ignores other important facts. The principle of prohibitions on alien land tenure was already well established in the Northwest. Washington had prohibited the ownership of land by non-citizens in its initial constitution of 1889 and put forward plans for a bill to extend this to the renting of land in March, 1913, before the successful passage of a similar measure in California. Governor Ernest Lister obediently smothered the Washington bill at Woodrow Wilson's request.[154] Conversely, it has been argued that Hiram Johnson, after quashing two similar previous bills, pushed for the Alien Land Law in 1912 and 1913 largely to spite his rival Wilson and even deliberately left sufficient loopholes to neuter its effective enforcement.[155]

California may have successfully passed Anti-Alien Land Laws before its northern neighbors, but as with San Francisco's racially motivated quarantining of 1900, sometimes the state's commercial interests intervened to prevent measures they viewed as harmful to their business opportunities. For example, a contemporary commentator noted that while "some states have passed laws prohibiting aliens from [a few types of] fishing, Oregon [in 1913] and Washington [in 1915] prohibit aliens from engaging in nearly every kind of fishing."[156] California passed no such legislation—the state's fish canneries saw it as detrimental to their interests. California's Japanese fishermen, particularly San Pedro's tuna fleet, made huge profits during the Great War. This led to attempts by white fishermen to exclude the Japanese from coastal fishing in 1921. The self-interest of parties is demonstrated by the measure's passage through the State Senate, but its failure in the State Assembly was largely due to the continued dependence of cannery interests on Japanese fishermen.

So, although California is seen as the center of the anti-Japanese movement, there is much to suggest that California politicians saw both the promise and the dangers of supporting such discriminatory legislation. During the San Francisco Schools Crisis, the Japanese Exclusion League cannily linked the threat some 93 Japanese schoolchildren posed to the state's girlhood with the issue of Japanese immigration and the labor market. They managed to convince the *Los Angeles Express* that "nothing less than the hanging of the Japanese by the toes would satisfy some of the anti-Japanese agitators in San Francisco."[157] The mood was seen by many outside observers as the culmination of anti-Japanese pressures which had been building for years. Others saw an even more self-serving, sinister undercurrent in the San Francisco crisis. Theodore Roosevelt sensed that the nativists' anti-Japanese fury may have been motivated more by opportunism than outrage—"I am inclined to think that many [California nativists] do not really wish to secure the exclusion of Japanese laborers, because they feel that to do so would be to take away one of their political assets."[158] This was certainly true of the struggling administration of Mayor Eugene Schmitz. The union backed authority, while devoted to restriction of Japanese under the principle of a limited labor supply, jumped at any diversion from its "impending trial for alleged boodling [corruption]...Schmitz used the School Board and the Exclusion League to shield himself, although unsuccessfully, from the Grand Jury."[159]

The dangers inherent in the California anti-Japanese pressures were also apparent to James Duval Phelan. The overwhelming barrage of protests from commercial interests forced him to retreat from his stance over the stringent quarantining of San Francisco's Asian quarter in 1900.[160] Although Phelan's commitment to the issue can be considered more heartfelt than Hiram Johnson's, his electorate did not necessarily support his views. His attempt to use the racial issue in his 1919 senatorial campaign with the motto "Keep California White"[161] can be seen as contributing to his defeat, just as the 1908 Democratic campaign had floundered with the slogan "Labor's choice Bryan—Japs' choice Taft".[162] By contrast, Portland's Republican Senator Llewellyn Banks "was defeated for re-nomination [in 1922] because he had the courage to lead the [1921] fight against the [Alien Land Bill] on the floor of the [state] senate."[163]

In addition, the Oregon Governor (from 1923 to 1927) Walter M. Pierce gleefully followed the xenophobic tendencies of his Ku Klux Klan "king-makers" who mobilized much of his support, at least over the issue of the Japanese. Protesting the failure of previous Alien Land Bills he stated: "when I became Governor in 1923, however, the [Alien Land] bills were passed in the Oregon legislature, and I took great pleasure in signing it [sic]. I am sorry it has not been strictly enforced."[164] Pierce also signed into law the Oregon House bill 205 "prohibiting the issuance of [trading] licenses to aliens in certain instances" and House Bill 120 ordering county-wide surveys of Asian land-ownership and tenancy.[165] Nonetheless, some Northwestern politicians were not so consistent. Oregon's moderate Republican Governor Ben Olcott, ousted by Walter Pierce in 1923, an astute politician who frequently sought the path of least resistance, was convinced by the Davey Report of the necessity that the "Mongol and the Caucasian must each work out their destiny alone."[166]

Some idea of the prominence of the issue is demonstrated by Olcott's vacillations. His position toward the Asian had changed dramatically since his election in 1916 as Oregon's secretary of state. Then he had been seen as the friend of the Chinese:

> There are about 100 American-born Chinese in this city, and, heretofore, nearly all have come to me for information and suggestions in regards to candidates—and tho [sic] we are but few, yet in the past we have helped elect those who were friendly to us. And you, being one of our friends...we shall be very glad to assist you in your coming campaign.[167]

Four years later, it was Olcott who signed a January 1920 memorandum from both houses in Oregon requesting that the Constitution of the United States be amended so that "children born in the United States...whose parents are not citizens and can not under existing laws acquire citizenship...shall not become citizens by reason of their birth in the United States."[168]

Overall, while the California politicians—other than Phelan, whom it seems developed a genuine feeling, at least from 1919, of the importance of the Japanese issue—can be seen as more opportunist, their Northwestern counterparts can be viewed as more sincerely restrictive. It may have been a California, Senator Samuel Shortridge, who attached the total exclusion ban to the 1924 Immigration Act, but it can still be held that the anti-Japanese pressures in California fell short of similar efforts in the Northwest. Having said this, the majority of organizations, including the largest—the Japanese Exclusion League—are seen by historians and contemporaries as overwhelmingly

California in origin and membership. The Japanese in the Northwest represented the only sizable group against which the racial restrictionists *could* rail. One of the reasons for this maybe that unlike California, the Northwest was more racially homogenous, as demonstrated in Table 4.3.[169]

Table 4.3: Population by Race in California, Oregon and Washington, 1910 and 1920

	Total Population	"White"	Black	Others*	White	Black and others
1910						
California	2,377,549	2,259,672	21,645	96,232	95%	5%
Oregon	672,765	655,090	1,492	16,183	97.3%	2.7%
Washington	1,141,990	1,109,111	6,058	26,821	97.1%	2.9%
1920						
California	3,426,861	3,264,711	38,763	123,387	95.2%	4.8%
Oregon	783,389	769,146	2,144	12,099	98.2%	1.8%
Washington	1,356,621	1,319,777	6,883	29,961	97.2%	2.8%

*Aboriginal Americans, Chinese, Japanese and other Asians.

California's "white"[170] population made up 95 percent of the state's total population in 1910 and 95.2 percent in 1920. The corresponding figures for Oregon were 97.3 percent in 1910 and 98.2 percent in 1920. Washington State had 97.1 percent in 1910 and 97.2 percent in 1920. Although these contrasts are small, they are compounded by the nature of immigration. Taking a median date of 1910, in the "Far West" as a region, the European immigrants were predominantly of Northern and Western European stock, of the "old immigration"—much more so than in the nation as a whole as is shown in Tables 4.4[171] and 4.5.[172]

Also unlike California, the Northwest had no "native" Mexican population and did not import "dangerously" large numbers of Mexican laborers. The Chinese had been excluded. The small black populations remained relatively static both numerically and socially, largely invisible or ignored in urban areas.[173] There was no large influx of Latin Americans. The Southern and Eastern Europeans could, to a point, find security and acceptance, at least within the area's relatively isolated communities, by their anti-Japanese stance. They were "white", eligible for citizenship and thus presumably forced to assume American values and assimilate. They were largely employed in the "wage earners' frontier" and although competing for labor they did not in general seek land. They did not represent, in spite of what Albert Johnson claimed, the threat that they were seen to pose on the East Coast.

In the Northwest, even in the wake of the political paranoia and xenophobic tendencies unleashed by wartime One-Hundred Percentism, Europeans in general were seen as "settlers" rather than "colonists". They may not have been seen as desirable by many nativists, but the Northwestern press did not portray a threat of colonization by undesirable Europeans. They could not point to American territories which had been overrun by Poles, Russians or Italians in the way that Hawaii had been by Japanese. For nativists claimed that in Hawaii

> There are nearly as many Japanese as Americans. There are four times as many Chinese. If the racial barrier is to be lowered, sooner or later we will have to admit Chinese also. Then there will happen to America—to California immediately and the rest of the nation within a generation—what has already happened to Hawaii. [174]

Table 4.4: Population by National Origin in the United States and Far West, 1910

National Origin	In U.S.	In Far West*	Percent In U.S.	Percent in Far West*
All Immigrants	13,515,886	1,011,518	14.7	20.3
Scandinavian	1,380,413	190,339	1.5	3.8
Great Britain	1,221,283	125,540	1.3	2.5
Canada	1,204,717	116,887	1.3	2.3
Ireland	1,352,251	80,601	1.5	1.6
Germany	2,501,333	139,278	2.7	2.8
Switzerland	124,848	24,594	0.1	0.5
France	117,418	22,514	0.1	0.1
Total Old Immigration	7,902,263	699,753	8.5	14
Austria-Hungary	1,670,581	53,188	1.8	1
Russia	1,602,782	35,995	1.7	0.7
Portugal	59,360	22,732	0.1	0.5
Italy	1,343,125	93,730	1.5	1.9
Greece	101,282	20,448	0.1	0.4
Mexico	221,915	34,171	0.2	0.6
Total New Immigrant "Whites"	4,999,046	260,264	5.4	4.5

*The Far West is represented by California, Washington State, Oregon, Montana, Idaho and Nevada.

No matter how much the pressures for Japanese exclusion in the Northwest were motivated by local concerns, it would be facile to view the Northwestern nativists as operating independently of the rest of the nation, if only because the area's restrictionists needed to convince the national government of the issue's importance. Making the area a less attractive proposition to Japanese could fall within the remit of state government. Banning Japanese immigration was a federal issue. Western politicians realized that, as with Chinese exclusion, the

Japanese question needed to be presented as a national problem. Also by linking the Japanese with other undesirable immigrants, they hoped that any restrictive measures designed essentially to exclude Europeans would have riders to include Japanese among the undesirable groups. As early as 1911 this linkage was seen as essential:

> Whereas during the year ending June 30th, 1910, Government statistics show that more than 1,000,000 aliens in the United States, of which more than 600,000 came from Southern and Eastern Europe and western Asia, the most undesirable emigrants known....[T]he effect of this alien deluge is to depress the wages and destroy the employment of thousands of American workmen. It is resolved by the house and senate of the State of Washington, that the Congress of the United States be requested to pass such restrictive legislation as will put a stop to the enormous influx of the most undesirable foreigners...[and] each Senator and Congressman from the State of Washington [should endeavor]...to secure the passage of such restrictive legislation.[175]

Often the language of the restrictionists indicated this, for example, informing the United States Senate of the passage of the 1921 Washington State Anti-Alien Land Law, Washington State Senate President William J. Coyle claimed "the overwhelming sentiment of the people of this State regard[s the] increasing numbers of Japanese and their hold on our soil as a grave national menace."[176]

The quest for a commonality of interest resulted in a curious alliance of the interests of Park Avenue and Hood River, a coalition of such unlikely characters as Madison Grant and Walter Pierce. Perhaps this pragmatic symbiosis of interests inherent between the patrician theories of Anglo-Saxon supremacist Eastern restrictionists and the Western land-labor, anti-Japanese confederation is best demonstrated in Albert Johnson's appointment to the presidency of the Eugenics Research Association in 1923. Inasmuch as the California experience provided the model for agitation, it was to the East Coast that the Western restrictionists looked for statistical models and "scientific" justification. The theories of race suicide and the evolution of a hierarchy of race re-enforced the anti-Japanese literature of the Northwest:

> Our people have learned racial lessons in a dangerous school. We have dealt with two inferior darker races, but never with an equal one. We have dealt unjustly with the Negro and he submits. We have dealt unjustly with the Indian and he is dead. If we have many Japanese we will not know how to deal otherwise than unjustly with them, and very properly they will not submit. The only real safety is in separation. Nature erects

> a barrier which man will only overpass at his peril....[It] is resolved that one side of the Pacific shall be the white man's side and the other side is the brown man's frontier. Only so is our race, our civilization, or the peace of the world secure.[177]

Table 4.5: Population by National Origin in Oregon and Washington, 1910.

National Origin	Oregon Foreign Born	Washington Foreign Born (Approx.)	Total Foreign Born Oregon Population	Total Foreign Born Washington Population
Total Population	672,765	1,141,990	672,765 (100%)	1,141,990 (100%)
All Foreign-born	103,001 (100%)	241,197 (100%)	15.3%	21%
Scandinavian	24,891 (24%)	77,000 (32%)	3.6%	6.7%
Great Britain	12,000 (11.6%)	30,000 (12.4%)	1.7%	2.6%
Canada	12,000 (11.6%)	40,000 (16.6%)	1.7%	3.5%
Ireland	4,995 (4.8%)	10,000 (4.1%)	0.7%	0.8%
Germany	17,957 (17.4%)	30,000 (12.4%)	2.7%	2.6%
Switzerland	3,853 (3.7%)	3,466 (1.4%)	0.57%	0.3%
France	1,159 (1.12%)	2,500 (1%)	0.1%	0.2%
Total Old Immigration*	76,855 (74.6%)	192,966 (80%)	11.4%	16.8%
Austria-Hungary	6,401 (6.2%)	13,000 (5.3%)	0.9%	1.1%
Russia	5,321 (5.1%)	10,961 (4.5%)	0.7%	0.95%
Italy	5,535 (5.3%)	13,000 (5.3%)	0.8%	1.1%
Greece	3,555 (3.4%)	4,177 (1.7%)	0.5%	0.36%
Total New Immigrant "Whites"*	20,812 (20.2%)	41,138 (16.8%)	2.9%	3.51%
Japanese	3,148 (3%)	12,929 (5.3%)	0.46%	1.1%

*These figures excluded Portuguese, Belgians, Bulgarians, Turks, Syrians and Mexicans who composed small minorities in both States. Poles at this stage were included in Austria-Hungary and Russia's totals. The Dutch were included in Scandinavia's total.

The majority of the influential texts on the issue acknowledged the importance of appealing to their Eastern audience. For instance Harry Alvin Millis, Montaville Flowers and Valentine Stuart McClatchy all pressed the legitimacy of the racial threat posed by Japanese immigration to the nation as a whole. The idea that the Japanese threatened American workers throughout the continent was re-enforced by their being linked with the undesirable Europeans in their shared ability to live on low incomes.[178] Even when the antirestrictionists Sydney Gulick and Karl Kawakami defended the Japanese as industrious, honest and assimilable, they demonstrated their beliefs by favorable comparisons with Southern and Eastern Europeans.[179] To the restrictionists, Japanese were imbued with the unassimilable qualities of the undesirable Europeans, they could never fit into American society, for as one nativist explained "a Jap's a Jap...the melting pot never warms to him".[180]

In essence, it was their own successes which alienated the Japanese. Unlike the Pole, the Southern Italian or Greek, the Japanese were only rarely attacked for dishonesty, criminality or stupidity. "They [the Asians] had, no doubt, many an unsavory habit, bred unwholesome squalor in the crowded quarters in which they most abounded in the western seaports...but it was their skill, their knack at succeeding and driving duller rivals out rather than their alien habits, that made them feared and hated."[181] It was their ability in agriculture and trade which led to the Japanese being attributed even greater avarice and business acumen than that ascribed to Jews. As a contemporary Japanese resident of Seattle, Mrs Shinowara, recalled, "One day Mary [Shinowara] came home from school and said that her algebra teacher had made the statement in class that if you gave a Jew five cents he would spend two cents and keep three, but if you gave a Jap five cents he would make twenty five cents out of it." [182] The ability, competition and challenge of the Japanese in commerce meant that, compared with the Eastern commercial interests' support for open immigration, the support for continued Japanese immigration was rather muted.

Nevertheless, there was support for the Japanese in the urban areas, particularly those cities where trade Asia was traditional. Unlike earlier opposition to Chinese where the main centers were urban—as demonstrated by the San Francisco, Tacoma, Seattle and Portland movements—the movement for Japanese exclusion in the Northwest was fundamentally rural. The issue emerged from land tenure and was based on the concentration of Japanese on and "colonization" by Japanese of the limited fertile land. The Japanese still received some support in these areas, particularly among those who wished to continue the lucrative rental agreements or wanted to achieve the best prices for land sales. However, the general tenor was one of opposition: "The mass of Oregon people, like those of California and Washington, will support anti-Japanese land legislation with the peculiarly savage joy which from the dawn of time has animated racial conflict."[183]

In urban areas, the situation was different. Although there was considerable opposition to Japanese traders, domestic servants and laborers, there was also commercial support for the lucrative trade with Asia. In Oregon, the old conflict of Portland's commercial interests struggling with the Salem "populists", which underlay much of Oregon's early history, smoldered beneath the issue of anti-Japanese discrimination. Although the pressures underlying calls for Japanese exclusion were similar in all three states of the Pacific Seaboard, it is perhaps Oregon in which the issue most polarized the population. Portland's conservative business community saw no advantage in persecuting the Japanese and set themselves against the intensifying nativist sentiments of the population at large. As the *Oregon Voter* eloquently reported the "commercial patriotism…of representatives of the Portland Chamber of Commerce…jiu jitsiued [sic] the American Legion boys"[184] and defeated two attempts at introducing Land Laws. Portland's commercial interests staunchly fought other anti-Japanese legislation denying that the Japanese posed a racial threat and holding that any discrimination would result in a loss of trade:

> The Portland trade with Japan is now about $69,000,000 a year….According to the Bureau of Labor Statistics, the Japanese of Oregon population increased in two years only 67, and the acreage owned decreased 77 acres. This does not indicate that there is a crisis approaching which will subvert the character of the population of Oregon. The Japanese government sincerely recognizes that it must not force its people where they are not welcome. The 1920 census shows that one-half of one percent of the population is Japanese. A serious menace does not exist….To the action of the previous legislature in not passing hostile legislation can be attributed in part, not solely necessarily, the present friendly attitude of the largest Japanese interests.[185]

There was sound commercial sense in this stance. Portland feared the loss of trade, not only from the West Coast as a region, but also to other areas of the coast—to San Francisco, or Seattle. Oregonians had good reason to worry. For example, as early as 1911, three times as much flour was being exported from Puget Sound as from the Columbia River ports—and 90 percent of this was going to Asia. Equally, Seattle's commercial interests were by no means complacent, they realized the increasing importance of the city's position as the "Portal to the Orient". In 1904, Asia received 74 percent of Seattle's exports and supplied 23 percent of her imports. By 1920, it took 80 percent of the city's exports and supplied 88 percent of her imports.[186] The region's commercial interests gave dire warnings of the consequences of anti-Japanese legislation. For example, in a reversal of the argument that failure to implement Alien Land legislation would lead to Oregon becoming a "Mecca" for dispossessed Japanese, members of Seattle's business community, opposed to restrictionist measures, claimed that the persecution of Japanese would lead to the evaporation, or relocation, of Japanese trade:

> In California, there arose, as there is now in Washington, a vociferous demand that the Japanese must be driven out. Japan did not respond as one government against another, *but the Japanese commercial interests withdrew in large part their favor from the port of San Francisco. Seattle was chosen as the American terminus of the great Japanese steamship lines* [most important the Nippon Yusen Kaisha and the Osaka

> Shosen Kaisha] *and it is a simple truth that Seattle has become a world port because the Japanese in large measure made it such...*
>
> Is there not a lesson in San Francisco's experience for Seattle, for Puget Sound, for the entire state of Washington? Vancouver to the north and Portland to the south loom out of the fog as possible successors of Seattle, just as Seattle was the successor of San Francisco.[187]

All the same, both states passed Alien Land Laws. To restrictionists these arguments were seen as ignoring the dangerous issues which underlay Japanese immigration. Trade was secondary. One restrictionist claimed America would have been better off if it had never started to trade with Japan: "Gentlemen, there are other considerations in this matter than dollars and cents. All I have heard is the almighty dollar. I wish Commodore Perry had stayed at home and minded his own business."[188]

Nativists not only saw the Japanese trading links as inherently damaging to America they felt that American diplomats in their efforts to mollify the Asians conceded unwarranted international standing to Japan. The "high" status of Japan was enshrined as an on-going policy in Washington D.C. throughout the period with John Hay's, somewhat hollow, announcement in March 1900 of an "Open Door" policy agreement. This effectively ranked Japan with other, "white", colonial powers—Russia, France, Britain, Italy and Germany—in Asia. Further, Theodore Roosevelt's mediation at the 1905 New Hampshire Russian/Japanese peace negotiations seemed to support the "crushing terms" imposed on a "European power", Russia, in Asia. To nativists, this appeasement strategy by America was re-enforced with the recognition of Japan's "rights" in China and Korea which both Elihu Root in 1905 and William Taft in 1908, which were effectively traded to prevent Japanese intervention in the Philippines. To many nativists, it appeared that the military and commercial consequences of insulting Japanese sensibilities were of more consequence to Washington D.C. than the imminent danger of the disappearance of the white race on the West Coast.

These "spheres of influence" agreements accorded Japan an inflated international status, which allowed it to continue its expansionist militarist goals in Asia with the tacit agreement of America.[189] In the post-war environment as heightened xenophobia and racial thinking informed the revivified anti-Japanese movement the consequences of this expansion applied equally to mainland America: "Shall this country of ours be held for our white descendants, or shall it be turned over to the Japanese, that they may rule over those descendants as they rule Korea today?" [190] Nativists felt that Washington's interest in retaining amicable relations with Tokyo had allowed the Japanese to illustrate their intention of over-running white America with highly fertile "picture brides", in deliberate circumvention of the "Gentlemen's Agreement":

> My investigations convince me that beyond doubt the Japanese government has loyally lived up to both the spirit and the letter of the Gentlemen's Agreement but that agreement ought to be supplemented by a "Ladies Agreement" because ...the Gentlemen's Agreement is being offset by the numerous picture brides going from Japan to Japanese laborers in America....And besides they bear many more children than do the wives of their American neighbors, thus constantly reminding them of the increasing proportion of Japanese to Americans in Hawaii.[191]

The anti-Japanese lobby also held that the Japanese sought to utilize trade agreements to circumvent legislation designed to protect "native" industry. The 1911 replacement of the 1894 Treaty of Commerce and Navigation, while placating restrictionists by codifying the Gentlemen's Agreement's compromise on immigration, also guaranteed the rights of Japanese within the United States:

> The citizens or subjects of each of the High Contracting Parties shall have liberty to enter, travel, and reside in the territories of the other to carry on trade, wholesale and retail, to own or lease and to employ agents of their choice, to lease land for residential and commercial purposes, and generally do anything incident to or necessary for trade upon the same terms as native citizens or subjects, and submitting themselves to the laws and regulations there established. [192]

It was this section that formed the basis for contention over the constitutional status of the Alien Land Laws, "the Japanese government on behalf of her nationals, claims the right of land-ownership under the most favoured nation clause in her [1911] treaty with the United States."[193] However, the nativist stance was upheld in the Supreme Court when the Washington Alien Land Act was found neither to breach the 1911 Treaty,[194] nor the Fourteenth Amendment[195].

To hard-line Northwestern restrictionists such niceties seemed irrelevant. The issue was more clear-cut—Japan should not be at liberty to dictate America's immigration policy, regardless of any treaty obligations between the two countries. In 1916, Washington's Senator Miles Poindexter claimed that the security of America depended as much on the exclusion of undesirable immigrants—including Japanese—as it did on the military or tariffs.[196] By 1922, Albert Johnson had had enough of the attitude of the American government:

> [I agree with] the distinguished Senator from Massachusetts [Henry Cabot Lodge], who stated over and over again at the recent Limitation of Arms Conference [the Washington Naval

> Conference] that the regulation of immigration is a matter of our own concern, regardless of treaties; that it is *our* matter.[197]

These sentiments fed through to the area's representatives and editors. It could be argued that the region felt Japanese restriction was an idea whose time had come. Unlike similar pressures in California, the Northwest's nativists felt that their objections to Japanese immigration had been sub-sumed to the war effort. This increased the vehemence of the movement when anti-Japanese agitation re-emerged in Oregon. It coincided with the post-war nativist backlash and the growth of organizations dedicated to "American" ideals. Arguably, this created additional political power with which to legislate those ideals. Since the foundation of both States, the racial issue had been of primary importance—be it slavery, coolie labor or Asian land tenure. Northwestern nativism had a long history in a short timespan. The region's nativists saw their task as simple, to ensure that the Northwest "shall be peopled with Americans who will make it what it deserves to be, a white man's paradise."[198]

NOTES

[1] See Margo J. Anderson, *The American Census: A Social History* (New Haven, Connecticut, 1988) pp.84-85.
[2] Figures taken from Richard C. Berner, *Seattle 1900-1920: From Boomtown, Urban Turbulence to Restoration* (Seattle, 1991) pp.31, 33 & 34.
[3] Figures taken from the *Thirteenth Census of the United States*, table IV p.18 cited in Robert E. Wynne, *Reaction to the Chinese in the Pacific Northwest and British Columbia 1850-1910* (PhD Thesis, University of Washington, 1964) p. 492.
[4] John B. Slater (ed.), *Proceedings of Stevens County Pioneer Association* (Colville, 1904) p.49.
[5] *Walla Walla Statesman* March 15, 1867.
[6] For the Tacoma expulsions see George Dudley Lawson, "The Tacoma Method" *The Overland Monthly* VII (39)(March, 1886) 234-239, United States Department of the Interior, *Report of the Governor of Washington Territory to Secretary of the Interior 1884* (Washington, D.C., 1885) pp.614-615, United States Department of the Interior, *Report of the Governor of Washington Territory to Secretary of the Interior 1886* (Washington, D.C., 1887) appendix pp.872-873 and H., "Sequel to the Tacoma Riots" *Overland Monthly and Out West Magazine* 7:39 (March, 1886) 239-240. For the Seattle expulsions see George Kinnear, *Anti-Chinese Riots at Seattle, Washington, February 8th 1886* (Seattle, 1911) and the Seattle *Post Intelligencer* October 1885 through to February 1886. For general information on the anti-Chinese movement in the Northwest in the period see Malcolm Clark, "The Bigot Disclosed: Ninety Years of Nativism" *Oregon Historical Quarterly* 75 (June, 1974) 119-131, and Wynne, op.cit.

[7] Andrew Gyory, *Closing the Gate:Race, Politics and the Chinese Exclusion Act* (Chapel Hill, North Carolina, 1998) p.4.
[8] "Interview with Jasper Howe, Carpenter and Resident of Lake Stevens [Washington]" cited in the William C. Smith Papers, Series A&B (University of Oregon, Eugene) Microfilm, Reel 2.
[9] Editorial *New York Times* September 3, 1865.
[10] George E. Chamberlain to G.H. Thomas June 20, 1904 cited in the George Chamberlain Papers, The Oregon Historical Society.
[11] For example Lancaster Pollard, "The Pacific Northwest: A Regional Study" *Oregon Historical Quarterly* 52 (December, 1951) 211-232; Janet W. Bryant, *The Ku Klux Klan and the Compulsory School Bill of 1922* (MA Thesis, Reed College, 1970) p.24; and Lawrence Goodwyn, *The Populist Moment; A Short History of the Agrarian Revolt in America* (Oxford, 1978) pp.80-85.
[12] See Charles H. Carey, *The Oregon Constitution and Proceedings and Debates of the Constitutional Convention of 1857* (Salem, 1926) pp.318-320.
[13] Article 1, Section 35 of the 1857 Constitution of the Sate of Oregon cited in *The Journal of the Constitutional Convention of the State of Oregon* (Salem, 1882) pp.104-195.
[14] The figures for Oregon's black population in relation to total population are1860—0.24 percent, 1890—0.37 percent and 1920—0.27 percent. Figures taken, and extrapolated, from analysis of United States (decennial) census data cited at Inter-university Consortium for Political and Social Research, *Historical, Demographic, Economic, and Social Data: The United States, 1790-1970* [Computer file]. (Ann Arbor) cited at http://icg.Harvard.edu/census.
[15] Figures extrapolated from *Thirteenth Census of the United States, Taken in the Year 1910, Volume III, Population* (Washington, D.C., 1913), Inter-university Consortium for Political and Social Research, op.cit. and Wynne, op.cit. pp.3-4.
[16] In his analysis of the "Western World's" perception of the Japanese, Rotem Kowner, claims that the view of the Chinese and Japanese see-sawed as each of the two countries slipped in and out of "favour" with the Western world. From the period of initial contact right up until the end of the Second World War, this had the effect of modifying the status of the Japanese from "honorary" whites to mongrelized Chinese. See Rotem Kowner, "Lighter Than Yellow, But Not Enough: Western Discourse on The Japanese 'Race', 1854-1904" *The Historical Journal* 43:1 (2000) 113-115.
[17] Figures extrapolated from the *Thirteenth Census of the United States,* op.cit. and Kiyo Sue Inui, *The Unsolved Problem of the Pacific; A Study of International Contacts, Especially in Frontier Communities, with Special Emphasis on California and An Analytical Study of the Johnson Report to the House of Representatives* (Tokyo, 1925) pp.69-70.
[18] Figures taken from Harry Alvin Millis, *The Japanese Problem in the United States: An Investigation for the Commission on Relations with Japan Appointed by The Federal Council of the Churches of Christ in America* (New York, 1915) p.25.

[19] Figures taken from The Immigration Commission, *Statistical Review of Immigration, 1819-1910 and Distribution of Immigrants 1850-1900* Vol. 3 (Washington, D.C., 1911) pp.291-292.
[20] Figures taken from Calvin F. Schmid and Wayne W. McVey, *Growth and Distribution of Minority Races in Seattle Washington* (Seattle, 1964) p.14.
[21] San Francisco *Morning Call* May 29, 1892.
[22] Figures taken from and extrapolated from the United States Immigration Commission, *Reports; Japanese and Other Immigrant Races in the Pacific Coast and Rocky Mountain States* Vol.23 (Washington, D.C., 1911) pp.5-8, R.D. McKenzie, "The Oriental Finds a Job", *Survey Graphic* 9 (May, 1926) 153 and Millis op.cit. pp.3-5 & 32.
[23] Figures taken from Matthew Frye Jacobson, *Barbarian Virtues: The United States Encounters Foreign Peoples at Home and Abroad 1876-1917* (New York, 2000) p.81.
[24] Edward A. Ross, *The Changing Chinese* (New York, 1912) p.47.
[25]Immigration Commission, *Reports* Vol.23, op.cit. p.47.
[26] Figures taken from Millis, op.cit. p. 38.
[27] "Interview with AR ("Dog Face") Johnson, Mill Superintendant [sic]" Ernest Dolge, Inc. Tacoma, Washington p.4 cited William C. Smith Papers, Series A&B, (University of Oregon, Eugene) Microfilm, Reel 3.
[28]See Max Stern,"The Oriental in the Alaskan Salmon Industry" *The Daily News* (no place, no date) cited in William C. Smith Papers, op.cit. Reel 1 and Jack Masson and Donald Guimary, "Asian Labor Contractors in the Alaskan Canned Salmon Industry: 1880-1937" *Labor History* 22 (1981) 377-397.
[29]The Immigration Commission, Vol. 25, op.cit. p.390.
[30] See Lee F. Pendergrass, "The Formation of a Municipal Reform Movement: The Municipal League of Seattle" *Pacific Northwest Quarterly* 66 (January, 1975) 63-66.
[31] "Interview with Mr Holmes, Mill Foreman", St Paul and Tacoma Lumber Co., Tacoma, Washington, 1924, cited William C. Smith Papers, op.cit. Reel 3. For an upward reappraisal of the earning potential of Japanese laborers see Yuzio Murayama, *The Economic History of Japanese Immigration to the Pacific Northwest, 1890-1920* (PhD Thesis, University of Washington, 1982).
[32] "Interview with AR" cited William C. Smith Papers, op.cit. Reel 3.
[33] *Congressional Record*, 44th Congress, 2nd Session, p.2005.
[34] Seattle *Union Record* November 3, 1900.
[35] See Berner, op.cit. p.172 and the *Union Record* May 1, 8 ,15 and 26 and July 3, 1915.
[36] See "Interview with Mr Mitchell, Lake Stevens Druggist", 1924, cited William C. Smith Papers, op.cit. Reel 3.
[37] American Federation of Labor, *Convention Proceedings, 1901* p.22 cited in Carlos Schwantes, *Radical Heritage: Labor, Socialism and Reform in Washington and British Columbia 1885-1917* (Moscow, Idaho, 1994) p.157.
[38] *Seattle Union Record* January 20, 1906.

[39] Figures taken from Roger Daniels, *The Politics of Prejudice; The Anti-Japanese Movement in California and the Struggle for Japanese Exclusion* (Berkeley, 1977) pp.28-29.
[40]See *Organized Labor* (San Francisco) May 7, 1905 cited Wynne, op.cit. p.335.
[41] Louis B. Schwellenbach, "American Legion Point of View Regarding the Japanese" (Seattle, 1924) cited William C. Smith Papers, op.cit. Reel 2.
[42] "Interview with man working at the slip" Grays Harbor Commercial Co, Cosmopolis, Washington cited William C. Smith Papers, op.cit. Reel 3.
[43] Cited in Philip Foner (ed.), *Jack London American Rebel—A Collection of His Social Writing* (New York, 1947) p.59. Jack London was anti-Asian in general, but particularly anti-Korean, largely because of his experiences of seeing shipwrecked English sailors flogged in the streets of Korean towns. For his own account of his hostility to Asians see Jack London, *The Yellow Peril* (New York, 1904).
[44] Part of an editorial "Silly Race Prejudice" in the *Industrial Worker* April 22, 1909.
[45] "The United Mine Workers in Convention at Denver", *The Miners Magazine* July 18, 1907 cited in Philip S. Foner and Daniel Rosenberg (eds.), *Racism, Dissent and Asian Americans from 1850 to the Present: A Documentary History* (Westport, Connecticut, 1993) p.185.
[46] *Seattle Times* May 28, 1914.
[47] J.H. Walsh, "Japanese and Chinese Exclusion or Industrial Organization, Which?" *Industrial Union Bulletin*, April 11, 1908 cited in Foner and Rosenberg, *Racism* op.cit. p.190.
[48] See Robert L. Tyler in his *Rebels of the Woods: The IWW in the Pacific Northwest* (Eugene, 1967) p.196 claims that Howard Scott, an engineer who considered himself an IWW policy maker, "argued that realistic revolutionaries should even agitate for restriction of immigration and Asian exclusion, since the more scarce, productive and skilled the labor force the more rapid and severe would be the economic crisis [induced by the revolution]." He claims this was published in *One Big Union Monthly* (October, 1920) pp.6-10. Examination of this issue reveals no such argument, nor does the following issue, the year before or the year after. The argument is realistic, and probable, but the evidence is elusive.
[49] "Grays Harbor Commercial Co. Interview with Mr Hinton, City Editor of the *Aberdeen World* cited William C. Smith Papers, op.cit. Reel 3.
[50] Julian Hawthorne (ed.), *History of Washington, The Evergreen State* (New York, 1893) cited in Lorraine Barker Hildebrand, *Straw Hats, Sandals and Steel: The Chinese in Washington State* (Tacoma, 1977) p. 25.
[51] *The Hood River News* September 10, 1919.
[52] For details of the Chick Gin case see Alan M. Kraut, *Silent Travellers* (Baltimore, 1995) pp.83-104.
[53] James D. Phelan in the San Francisco *Chronicle,* May 8, 1900.

[54] For analysis of the Nihomachi district, see S. Frank Minamoto, *Social Solidarity Among Japanese in Seattle* (Seattle, 1939) pp.57-130; Katherine J. Lentz, *Japanese American Relations in Seattle* (MA Thesis, University of Washington, Seattle, 1924); Katherine Dally Woolston, *The Japanese Standard of Living in Seattle* (MA Thesis, University of Washington, 1927); and David A. Takami, *Divided Destiny: A History of Japanese Americans in Seattle* (Seattle, 1998) pp. 25-31.
[55] Figures taken from Immigration Commission, *Reports* Vol.23, op.cit. p.100. By way of comparison San Francisco had 545, Los Angeles 473 and Sacramento 209.
[56] David Starr Jordan in *Maxwell's Talisman* (September, 1905) cited Samuel P. Hays, *Conservation and the Gospel of Efficiency: The Progressive Conservation Movement, 1890-1920* (Pittsburgh, 1959) p.144.
[57]Figures taken from Immigration Commission, *Reports* Vol.23, op.cit. For an analysis of these figures see Millis, op.cit. pp.50-78.
[58] Ibid.p.71.
[59] For example see Nellie Virginia Roe, *The Italian Immigrant in Seattle* (MA Thesis, University of Washington, 1915) pp.41-42.
[60] See the editorial in the Seattle *Trade Register* September 5, 1914.
[61] Millis, op.cit. p.71.
[62] See *Seattle Star* August 12, 1921.
[63] Erastus Brainerd in the *Seattle Post-Intelligencer* cited in Murray Morgan, *Skid Row: An Informal Portrait of Seattle* (New York, 1960) p.171.
[64] See Norman H. Clark, *Mill Town: A Social History of Everett* (Seattle, 1970) pp.99-101.
[65] Greeley cited in George Anthony Peffer, *If They Don't Bring Their Women Here: Chinese Female Immigration Before Exclusion* (Urbana, Illinois, 1999) p. 101. For an account of the threat of erotic appeal of the Asian see Robert G. Lee, *Orientals: Asian Americans in Popular Culture* (Philadelphia, 1999) pp.87-91 and 113-117.
[66] For an analysis of the Japanese "white slave trade" see Yujio Ichioka, "Ameyuki-san: Japanese Prostitutes in Nineteenth Century America" *Amerasian Journal* 4.1 (1977) 1-21.
[67] Chinda Sutemi, Japanese Consul, San Francisco June 13, 1891cited in Yuji Ichioka, *Issei, The World of the First Generation Japanese Immigrants 1885-1924* (New York, 1988) p.39.
[68] See ibid. pp.36-37.
[69] For a highly glossed account of one woman's experience in a Seattle brothel see Tomoko Yamakazi, *The Story of Yamada Waka: From Prostitute to Feminist Pioneer* (New York, 1985).
[70] For the British position see Jenny Clegg, *Fu Manchu and the "Yellow Peril": The Making of a Racist Myth* (Stoke on Trent, 1994). For the American position see, Huping Ling, *Surviving on Gold Mountain: A History of Chinese American Women and Their Lives* (New York, 1998) pp.43-60.

[71] *Oregon Voter* February 17, 1923.
[72] See Ralph Bushnell Potts, *Seattle Heritage* (Seattle, 1955) pp. 79-83
[73] Quotes taken from "Interview with Williamson, Federal Narcotics Agent" William C. Smith Papers, op.cit. Reel 4.
[74] Figures taken from Frank Julian Warne, *The Immigrant Invasion* (New York, 1913) p.137.
[75] Compiled from data extrapolated from Inui, op.cit. pp.69-70.
[76] A.A. Sargent, "The Wyoming Anti-Chinese Riot" *Overland Monthly* 4 (November, 1885) 510
[77] The Japanese-Canadian educationalist Sato Tsutau in 1932 cited in Ichioka (1988), op.cit. p.197.
[78] Figures taken from Immigration Commission, *Reports* Vol. 25, op.cit. p.922. See also Roland L. DeLorme, "The United States Bureau of Customs and Smuggling on Puget Sound, 1851-1913" *Prologue : The Journal of the National Archives* 5:2 (1973) 77-88.
[79] Evolving out of the San Francisco Greater Japanese Association which was formed in 1891 and the Japanese Deliberative Council of America of 1905, the Associations worked on a three-tier system which devolved responsibility for Japanese Communities down from consular to Association to local levels. The first "true" Association was formed in San Francisco in 1908. This was followed by "autonomous" Associations in Portland in 1911 and Seattle in 1913. By 1923 the Seattle Association had 15 locals; Oregon 10; San Francisco 40 and Los Angeles 21. See Yuji Ichioka, "Japanese Associations and the Japanese Government: A Special Relationship, 1909-1926" *Pacific Historical Review* 46:3 (August 1977) 409-38.
[80] *Oregon Voter* November 1, 1919 p.172.
[81] Immigration Commission, *Reports* Vol. 23 op.cit. p.170
[82] Figures taken from Raymond Leslie Buell, "Some Legal Aspects of the Japanese Question" *American Journal of International Law* 17 (1923) 34.
[83] See David B. Ralston, *Importing the European Army: The Introduction of European Military Techniques and Institutions into the Extra-European World, 1600-1914* (Chicago, 1990) pp.168-170.
[84] Joseph Timmons to the House Immigration Committee, July, 1921 cited in Valentine Stuart McClatchy, *Japanese Immigration and Colonization: A brief Prepared for Consideration of the State Department* (Sacramento, 1921) p.65.
[85] Lothrop Stoddard, *The Rising Tide of Color Against White World-Supremacy* (New York, 1920) p.240.
[86] See Putnam Weale, *The Conflict of Color* (London, 1910).
[87] E. Sax Rohmer, *The Insidious Dr Fu Manchu* cited in Clegg, op.cit. p.2.
[88] HG Wells, *War in the Air* (London, 1908) predicted a war in which the struggle of the United States, Britain and France with Germany is submerged under a Japanese/Chinese alliance which attacks all whites indiscriminately.
[89] For a discussion of Lea and Sun's relations see Eugene Anschel, *Homer Lea, Sun Yat-sen and the Chinese Revolution* (New York, 1984).

[90] See Izumi Hirobe, *Japanese Pride, American Prejudice: Modifying the Exclusion Clause of the 1924 Immigration Act* (Stanford, California, 2001) p.3.
[91] San Francisco *Examiner* December 20, 1906.
[92] San Francisco *Examiner* November 3, 1907.
[93] For details see Edward S. Miller, *War Plan Orange: The US Strategy to Defeat Japan, 1897-1945* (Annapolis, 1991) pp.19-30.
[94] See United States Senate Documents, *Brewing and the Liquor Interests and German and Bolshevik Propaganda* 66th Congress, 1st Session, Document 62, Volume 2, p.1426. For an account of German wartime propaganda see Niel M. Johnson, *George Sylvester Viereck: German-American Propagandist* (Urbana, Illinois, 1959) pp.19-57.
[95] Cleveland *Plain Dealer* May 11, 1913.
[96] The Cordova *Alaskan* January 28, 1914 cited in the *Washingtonian* February 21, 1914.
[97] See Hew Strachan, *The First World War, Volume I: To Arms* (Oxford, 2001) pp.455-465.
[98] See Stephen G. Craft, "Angling for an Invitation to Paris: China's Entry into the First World War" *The International History Review* 16 (1994) 1-24.
[99] See *San Francisco Chronicle* October 8, 1919 and Gary Mead, *Doughboys: America and the First World War* (London, 2000) pp.387-388.
[100] Valentine Stuart McClatchy, *The Germany of Asia: Japan's Policy in the Far East* (Sacramento, 1919) p.5.
[101] "Relying upon the Confidence you have been good enough to show me at all times, I have stated or rather repeated all this to you very candidly and in a most friendly spirit, for I realize, as I believe you do, the grave consequences which the enactment of the measure retaining that particular provision [Japanese exclusion] would inevitably bring upon the otherwise happy and mutually advantageous relations between our two countries." Ambassador Mesanao Hanihara to Secretary of State Charles Evans Hughes, April 10, 1924 cited in Inui, op.cit. p.535
[102] A farmer talking to the California Land Settlement Board cited in Elwood Mead, "The Japanese Land Problem of California" *The Annals of the American Academy* 93 (January, 1921) 52.
[103] See Stoddard, op.cit.
[104]Cited in Valentine Stuart McClatchy (1921) op.cit. p.47.
[105] Miss Frances Hewitt, in the *Northman* [of Portland, Oregon] June 10, 1920 cited in ibid. p.87.
[106] Frank Davey, *Report on the Japanese Situation in Oregon, Investigated for Governor Ben W. Olcott, August 1920* (Salem, 1920) pp.8 &15.
[107] A California farmer addressing the initial meeting of the Asiatic Exclusion League, 1905, cited in Eliot Mears, *Resident Orientals on the American Pacific Coast* (New York, 1927) p.146. Perhaps given Theodore Roosevelt's exhortations to American womanhood, this Imperial policy was arguably more plausible in America than it may have been elsewhere.

[108] See Yuji Ichioka, "Amerika Nadeshiko: Japanese Immigrant Women in the United States, 1900-1924"*Pacific Historical Review* 48:2 (May, 1980) 339-357.
[109] *Sacramento Bee* May 1, 1913.
[110] Immigration Commission *Reports* Vol.24, op.cit. p.918. Of 11 Italian farmers, 1 had been a farmer, 4 had farmed for their fathers and 2 had been farm hands in Italy. Of 31 Scandinavian and German farmers, 4 had been farmers, 3 had farmed for their fathers and 8 had been farm hands. See ibid. pp. 918-919.
[111] *Journal of the Senate of the State of California, 1905* (Sacramento, 1905) pp. 1164-65
[112] Figures taken from Ichioka (1988), op.cit. pp.150-151, and Montaville Flowers, *The Japanese Conquest of American Opinion* (New York,1917) p.11.
[113] Millis, op.cit. p. 94.
[114] For example in 1920 in the Gresham area of Oregon the Japanese produced 50 percent of the raspberries, 30 to 40 percent of the loganberries, 90 percent of the strawberries and 60 percent of the vegetables. Davey op.cit. p.12.
[115] Karl K. Kawakami, *The Real Japanese Question* (New York,1921) p.267.
[116] Figures taken and extrapolated from the Seattle Japanese Association, 1921 cited in ibid. p.268.
[117] The 1889 Washington State Constitution prohibited aliens who had not declared an intention to naturalize from purchasing land within the state. Since the Japanese could not naturalize, they could not own land.
[118] *Oregonian* November 26, 1911.
[119]Of the 42,775,040 acres of Washington State 6,573,548 were under cultivation in 1921; in Oregon of the 61,188,280 acres some 11,685,000 were under cultivation. Figures cited in *Oregon Voter* July 9, 1921 p.23.
[120] Portland *Telegram* October 25th 1919.
[121] See Donald Teruo Hata and Nadine Hata, "George Shima: The Potato King of California." *The Journal of the West* Vol. 25:1 (January, 1986) 55-63, Linda Tamura, *The Hood River Issei: An Oral History of Japanese Settlers in Oregon's Hood River Valley* (Urbana, Illinois, 1993) p.91 and Majorie R. Stearns, *The History of the Japanese People in Oregon* (unpublished PhD Thesis, University of Oregon, Eugene, 1937) pp. 27-29.
[122] Figures taken from Immigration Commission *Reports* Vol.24, op.cit. p.301 and Kawakami op.cit. p.268.
[123] Figures taken from Immigration Commission, *Reports* Vol. 24, op.cit. p. 299 and Davey, op.cit. p.14.
[124] Editorial of the *Hood River Glacier* in 1912, reproduced in the same paper September 11, 1919.
[125] The *New York World* cited in the *Hood River News* February 21, 1917.
[126] The California land law was struck down by the California Supreme Court's decision in the Tetsubumi Yano case in 1922 on the grounds that it denied rights guaranteed under the Fourteenth Amendment. The more subtly designed Washington law was upheld in the 1924 Fujimoto case. The Oregon law was not successfully challenged until 1933 in the Yoshida case. For details see The

Walter Pierce Papers at the University of Oregon, Eugene, Box 33, File 15, and "The Japanese Problem in Oregon" *The Oregon Law Review* 24 (1945) 212-213.
[127] See Thomas N. Swale, "American Legion and Oriental" cited in William C. Smith Papers, op.cit. Reel 3.
[128] Davey, op.cit. p.6.
[129] *Journal of the Senate of the State of California, 1905* op.cit. pp. 1164-65.
[130] The articles of the Hood River Anti-Asiatic Association written on a card to be carried by all members, cited Davey, op.cit. p.7.
[131] See John Higham, *Strangers in the Land: Patterns of American Nativism 1860-1925* (rev.ed. New Brunswick, 1994) pp.264-300.
[132] Louis B. Schwellenbach [State Commander of the American Legion in Washington, 1922-23], "American Legion Point of View Regarding the Japanese" cited in the William C. Smith Papers, op.cit. Reel 3.
[133] The Grand Dragon of South Carolina giving a statement on immigration in 1924 cited in Michael LeMay and Eliot Robert Barkan (eds.), *US Immigration and Naturalization Laws and Issues: A Documentary History* (Westport, Connecticut, 1999) pp.142-143.
[134] *Terrace et al. vs. Thompson, Attorney General of the State of Washington* District Court of Washington, July 25, 1921 cited in Buell, op.cit. 42.
[135] Davey, op.cit. p.6.
[136] Table compiled from data in Inui, op.cit. p.88.
[137] *Hood River Glacier* September 11, 1919.
[138] See Davey, op.cit. p.14.
[139] For example the Washington Alien Land Law of 1921 tied up many of the loopholes of California's 1913 Act—particularly the use of land companies, guardianship, rental through "Caucasians" and trusts—

> SECTION 1(a)—"Alien" does not include an alien who has in good faith declared his intention to become a citizen of the United States, but does include all other aliens and all corporations and other organized groups of persons a majority of whole capital stock is owned or controlled by aliens or a majority of whose members are aliens...(c) "Land" also includes any share or interest in a corporation or other organized group of persons teemed an alien in this Act which has title to land either heretofore or hereafter acquired; ...
> SECTION 2. An alien shall not own land or take land or hold title thereto. No person shall take or hold land or title to land for an alien...Land hereafter conveyed to or for the use of aliens in violation of the Constitution or of this Act shall thereby be forfeited to and become the property of the state.
> SECTION 3. An alien is not qualified to be trusted under a will, executor; administrator or guardian, if any part of the

> estate is land; provided, an alien now lawfully Acting in any such capacity may continue for not more than two years.

The remaining loopholes were covered by 1923 amendments which stated that

> SECTION 2a. If an owner of land knowingly convey to or create in an alien, an estate or interest herein less than his own, the state, instead of taking he lesser estate or interest, may take its value in money out of the greater estate, and such value may be determined and be charged upon and recovered out of the greater estate in an equitable action....
> SECTION 2b. If a minor child of an alien hold title to land either heretofore or hereafter acquired, it shall be presumed that he holds in trust for the alien.

cited Inui, op.cit. pp.445- 450.

[140] See census analysis in Robert Higgs, "Landless By Law: Japanese Immigrants in California Agriculture to 1941" *Journal of Economic History* 38 (1978) 222.

[141] See *Hood River News* April 6 &27, 1923 and Lauren Kessler, *Stubborn Twig: Three Generations in the Life of a Japanese Family* (New York,1993) pp.80-82.

[142] Figures taken from Warren M. Engstrand, "Japanese Agriculture on the Pacific Coast" *Journal of Land and Public Utility Economics* 21 (November, 1945) 355.

[143] Takao Ozawa versus the United States cited in Inui, op.cit. pp.556-557.

[144] Thomas N. Swale, "The Report of the National Oriental Committee of the American Legion; Resolutions Unanimously Adopted at the Fifth Annual Convention of the American Legion at San Francisco California, October 15-19, 1923."pp.1 and 25, cited in the William C. Smith Papers, op.cit. Reel 3.

[145] The main organizations being the American Legion, War Veterans, Sons and Daughters of the Golden West, California State Federation of Women's Clubs, California State Federation of Labor, Los Angeles County Anti-Asian League and Japanese Exclusion League of Washington

[146] *Congressional Record* volume 61, April 4, 1921 pp.182 and 520.

[147] *Congressional Record* volume 62, June the 27th 1922 p.9540

[148] The amended bill (HR 1621) was submitted to the House on February 15, see *Congressional Record* volume 64, February 9, 10 and 15, 1923 pp.3380, 3444 & 3735.

[149] *Congressional Record* volume 64, February 19, 1923, pp.3931-32.

[150] Albert Johnson, "Some Reminiscences" in the Grays Harbor *Washingtonian* June 17, 1934.

[151] "Eatonville Lumber Co, Interview with Mr Galbraith Jnr." cited in the William C. Smith Papers, op.cit. Reel 4.

[152] Albert Johnson in the *Congressional Record* Volume 62, May 5, 1922 p.13699.
[153] *Oregon Voter* January 27, 1923 p.37.
[154] See Paolo E. Colletta, " "The Most Thankless Task" Bryan and the California Alien Land Legislation" *Pacific Historical Review* 36 (1967) 163-164.
[155] See Roger Daniels, op.cit. pp.54-64.
[156] Buell, op.cit. 48.
[157] The *Los Angeles Express* (no date) cited in Raymond Leslie Buell, "The Development of Anti-Japanese Agitation in the United States" *The Political Science Quarterly* 37 (December, 1922) 638.
[158] Theodore Roosevelt to Governor Gillett March 9, 1907, cited in Earl Pomeroy, *The Pacific Slope: A History of California, Oregon, Washington, Utah and Nevada* (New York, 1965) p.274.
[159] Buell, (1922), op.cit. 637-638.
[160] See Kraut, op.cit. pp.83-104.
[161] Cited Daniels, op.cit. p.57.
[162] *Fresno Republican* October 29, 1908.
[163] *Oregon Voter* November 18, 1922, 244.
[164] W. Pierce, *Autobiography* (no place, no date) pp. 123-124, cited in Walter Pierce papers, op.cit. Box 75, file 6. For details of the two previous attempts at passing Anti-Alien Land legislation see *Oregon Voter* November 18, 1922, 16-20.
[165] See *Oregon Voter* February 3, 1923, 170 and *Oregon Voter* February 17, 1923, 234.
[166] State of Oregon, *Message of Ben W. Olcott, Governor of Oregon, To the Thirty-First Legislative Assembly* (Salem, 1921) p.18.
[167] Seid Back, attorney, Portland to Olcott, April 30, 1916, cited in the Ben W. Olcott papers, Collection AX 81 University of Oregon, Eugene, Scrapbooks, Vol. 1 p.58
[168] *Congressional Record* volume 59, January 31, 1920, p. 2297.
[169] Figures extrapolated from Inter-university Consortium for Political and Social Research, op.cit.
[170] For the purposes of the United States decennial census "white" was taken to include all populations other than Aboriginal Americans, Asians and blacks. Thus the California "white" population included large numbers of "indigenous" and migratory Latin and Central Americans. Although the figures for these populations are unavailable some 33,444 are recorded as "white persons born in Mexico" see ibid.
[171] Table Compiled from *Thirteenth Census of the United States,* op.cit.
[172] Table compiled from data from ibid., and Leslie W. Koepplin, *A Relationship of Reform; Immigrants and Progressives in the Far West* (New York, 1990) pp.95-97.
[173] This assessment would be disputed by historians of race relations in the region, but for the purposes of immigration control it largely holds true. See

Quintard Taylor, *The Forging of a Black Community: Seattle's Central District from 1870 through the Civil Rights Era* (Seattle, 1994) pp.106-135, and Elizabeth McLagan, *A Peculiar Paradise: A History of Blacks in Oregon, 1788-1944* (Portland, 1980) pp.129-157.

[174] *Oregon Voter* January 22, 1921 p.54. "What we are fighting for on this Coast is that California and Oregon and Washington shall not become what the territory of Hawaii now is...The example of Hawaii should be sufficient to assure the early passage of an exclusion Act." San Francisco *Chronicle* November 11, 1906. For an analysis of the Hawaiian model as a threat to the West Coast see McClatchy (1921), op.cit. pp.29-33, and Kawakami, op.cit. pp.1-45.

[175] A memorial from Washington State January 19, 1911 cited in the *Congressional Record* 63rd Congress, 3rd Session p.2117.

[176] *Congressional Record* volume 61, 7 March 1921, p.11.

[177] Chester C. Rowell cited in the *Oregon Voter* January 22, 1921 p.54.

[178] See the United States Immigration Commission, *Reports* Vol.23 op.cit. pp.137-138.

[179] For example, see Sydney Lewis Gulick, *American Democracy and Asiatic Citizenship* (New York, 1918) p.121.

[180] The Prineville *Central Oregonian* January 22, 1922 cited in Barbara Yasui, "The Nikei in Oregon, 1834-1940" *Oregon Historical Quarterly* LXXVI (1975) 246.

[181] Thomas Woodrow Wilson, *A History of the American People*, Vol. V (New York, 1902) pp.213-214.

[182] "Interview with Mrs Tiro Shinowara, A Teacher in a Japanese Language School, Seattle" cited in William C. Smith Papers, Reel 2.

[183] *Oregon Voter* November 18, 1922 p.19.

[184] *Oregon Voter* January 27, 1923 p.37.

[185] W.D.B. Dodson, secretary of the Portland Chamber of Commerce to the Oregon House Judiciary Committee cited in ibid.

[186] Figures taken from Berner, op.cit. pp.165-166 & 182.

[187] The Seattle *Business Chronicle* cited in the *Oregon Voter* September 6, 1919 pp.3-4.

[188] "Mr" Holbrook for the "Portland Association of Building Owners" cited in the *Hood River News* February 2, 1923.

[189] For a nativist analysis of the Japan's Asian expansion and America's duties to prevent it see McClatchy (1920) op.cit.

[190] *The Sacramento Bee*, July 29, 1919.

[191] Charles H. Sherril to the American-Japan Society in Tokyo cited in the *Hood River News* January 16, 1920. In fact Tokyo halted the issuing of passports to "Piture Brides" on March 1, 1920. For a history of the picture brides see Yuji Ichioka, "Amerika Nadeshiko: Japanese Immigrant Women in the United States, 1900-1924"*Pacific Historical Review* 48:2 (May, 1980) 339-357.

[192] Article 1, The 1911 Commerce and Navigation Treaty cited in Inui, op.cit. p.160.
[193] *Hood River News* September 10, 1919.
[194]*Terrace vs. Thompson* "But the land laws of the Pacific Coast States do not deprive aliens ineligible to citizenship of real property they had before the legislation went into force. These laws contain no provisions which actually deprive them of their property. They simply prohibit them from acquiring real property in the future..." Buell, (1923) op.cit. 39.
[195] "A State may classify with reference to the evil to be prevented, and...if the class discriminated against is or reasonably might be considered to define those from whom the evil is mainly to be feared, it properly may be picked out." Justice Oliver Wendell Holmes citing the 1909 decision upholding the Pennsylvania prohibition on aliens hunting in *Terrace vs. Thompson* cited in ibid. p.41.
[196] See *Congressional Record* 53, p.117922.
[197] Albert Johnson in the *Congressional Record* Volume 62, May 5, 1922, p.13699.
[198] *Hood River News* September 10, 1919.

5

CONCLUSION

While the Northwest undoubtedly had its own approach to the immigration debate, it is apparent that the majority of figures used by Congress' exclusionists in the arguments leading to the passage of the 1924 Immigration Act were culled from East Coast sources and dealt with East Coast cities and largely concentrated on European immigrants arriving on the East Coast. Similarly, it can be argued that neither Walter Pierce, Ole Hanson or Fred Gifford—for example—demonstrated any great commitment to the cause of immigration restriction, rather they utilized the fervor of a populist issue to gain or consolidate power. Equally, given the pervasiveness of the restrictionist argument across the nation, it may be possible to elevate the position of, say, Texas, Wyoming or Arizona to one of greater significance in the immigration debate. In each of those states there had been notorious examples of violent anti-immigrant sentiment. Wyoming miners had initiated a murderous trend against the Chinese in the 1880's. Arizona had seen the unprecedented brutality meted out to suspected radicals at Bisbee in 1917. Fed in some measure by its Southern racial phobias, the 1920s Texan Klan could spread an anti-immigrant, anti-Jewish, anti-Catholic message to rallies that attracted up to 75,000 spectators—a figure never reached by the Oregon Klan, even in its heyday.

The Northwest was by no means alone in its hostility to any of the immigrant groups it opposed. Other regions may have shown more violent reactions earlier and even sustained such levels of animosity for longer, but there are few regions where all these pressures came together with such

concerted pressure group in the nation's legislature. In large measure this was the result of the work of one man. If the region has one claimant to the dubious honor of a high-ranking place in the pantheon of persistent nativism, along side Denis Kearney, Henry Cabot Lodge or Tom Watson, it must be given to Albert Johnson. Johnson was re-elected on his anti-Japanese, anti-radical, anti-Slavic—*anti-immigrant*—plank for over 20 years, only losing his seat in the 1932 Democrat landslide. He spent much of his early congressional career alienated from his fellow Republicans as a result of his monomania. His outspoken hostility continued during the Americanization drive of the Great War—although from a distance, as he stood down to serve in France. But the region continued to re-elect him.

Johnson did not manufacture the anti-radical sentiment which gained him great acclaim with residents of Grays Harbor in 1912 when he took on the local IWW leaders in public debate. Neither did he need to exaggerate the threat that many of Washington's laborers and farmers felt from Asian immigration. But this is not to suggest that Johnson's long political career was the result of an opportunistic opposition to an immediate threat—as was to be the case for San Francisco's mayor Phelan or even Seattle's mayor Hanson. To his supporters it was the considered search for a long-term solution to an escalating danger. If the numbers of alien immigrants arriving directly in the Northwest were not as significant in some regions of the area as they were in the metropolitan areas of the Atlantic Coast in some ways this merely served to increase the animus to aliens. Hostility to outsiders is easy within regions that have a high degree of homogeneity. It is also easier if the outsider is in the abstract, or a faceless member of a group. As one observer of the region's nativists has observed, anti-alien sentiment was "not always directed against individual aliens, Roman Catholics, Jews or Negroes, but [more often, against]...the abstract, almost incomprehensible, symbol of the stereotypes."[1]

Johnson was not only interested in the local, he was interested in the national position. He saw the two as essentially interwoven. He and his constituents realized that a localized response to the alien threat merely postponed the problem, as with the IWW expulsions or alien land legislation, and that each postponement increased the threat inherent in a continued open-door immigration policy. Added to this, the "tribal" divisions of post-war America were re-enforced in the Northwest by the rapid pace of change in the region. Over a period of the preceding 30 years the optimism of the region's "booster era" had given way to a feeling of threatened, and all too finite, resources. During that same period threats to the coherence of American forms of government emerged—external as with the Japanese and Roman Catholics, or internal as with the IWW and socialists. The IWW free speech fights, the struggle for the public schools, the Japanese "invasion" of the Hood River, the Seattle General Strike—these were all manifestations of the nebulous alien threat. Washington and Oregon could inform the nation of dangers of open immigration with the certainty of experience.

If the nation's editors seemed obsessed with these issues—as even a superficial glance at contemporary newspapers, magazines and journals would show—this must been seen as in some measure due to the work of Northwestern restrictionists. Rather than seeing their position as the result of the ubiquitous debate over immigration restriction, it is perhaps more realistic to see it as a cause. Regional personalities, especially Johnson, kept the debate in the headlines, making statements, predictions and proclamations that illustrated the gravity of the threat posed by unchecked immigration to American values and American life. He saw the culmination of his life's work in the 1924 Act, which bore his name. There can be little doubt that he expressed a prevalent mood when he proudly crowed that the Act was America's "second declaration of independence".

NOTE

[1] Eckard V. Toy, *The Ku Klux Klan in Oregon: Its Character and Program* (MA Thesis, University of Oregon, Eugene, 1959) p.17.

SELECTED BIBLIOGRAPHY

ARCHIVES AND MANUSCRIPT COLLECTIONS

Archives of the Roman Catholic Archdiocese of Seattle
Ben W. Olcott Papers, University of Oregon, Eugene
George Chamberlain Papers, The Oregon Historical Society, Portland
Jesuit Oregon Province Archives, Gonzaga University, Spokane
Jewish Historical Society of Oregon, Portland
Ku Klux Klan Records, The Oregon Historical Society, Portland
The Oregon State Archives, Salem
The Walter Pierce Papers, University of Oregon, Eugene
William C. Smith Papers, Series A&B, University of Oregon, Eugene

PRIMARY SOURCES

George M. Allen, *Irrigated Lands of Washington State* (Olympia, 1910).

Nels Anderson, *Hobo: The Sociology of the Homeless Man* (Chicago, 1922).

Jesse Applegate, "Umpqua Agriculture, 1851" *Oregon Historical Quarterly* 32 (June, 1931). 135-144.

Lyman Beecher, *A Plea for the West* (Cincinnati, 1835).

Alexander M. Bing, *War Time Strikes and Their Adjustment* (New York, 1921).

Agnes Foster Buchanan, "The West and the Hindu Invasion" *Overland Monthly* 51:4 (April, 1908). 303-308.

Raymond Leslie Buell, "The Development of Anti-Japanese Agitation in the United States" *The Political Science Quarterly* 37 (December, 1922). 605-683.

Raymond Leslie Buell, "The Development of the Anti-Japanese Agitation in the United States II" *Political Science Quarterly* 38 (1923). 57-81.

Raymond Leslie Buell, "Some Legal Aspects of the Japanese Question" *American Journal of International Law* 17 (1923). 29-49.

A. B. Cain, *The Oregon School Fight* (Portland, 1924).

Ralph Chaplin, *The Centralia Conspiracy* (Seattle, 1920).
Kate Halladay Claghorn, *The Immigrant's Day in Court* (New York, 1923).
Jane Perry Clark, *Deportations of Aliens from the United States to Europe* (New York, 1931).
Blair Coan, *The Red Web* (Boston, 1925).
Frank Davey, *Report on the Japanese Situation in Oregon, Investigated for Governor Ben W Olcott, August 1920* (Salem, 1920).
Lem A. Dever, *Confessions of an Imperial Klansman* (Portland, 1924).
George Estes, *The Old Cedar School* (Portland, 1922).
Joseph Ettor, "The IWW versus the AF of L" *The New Review* 2 (May, 1914). 278–283.
Hiram Wesley Evans, "The Klan's Fight for Americanism" *The North American Review* 223 (March, 1926) 33-63.
Henry Pratt Fairchild, *Immigration: A World Movement and its Significance* (New York, 1913).
Montaville Flowers, *The Japanese Conquest of American Opinion* (New York, 1917).
Elizabeth Gurley Flynn, *Rebel Girl: An Autobiography, My First Life (1906-1926).* (rev.ed. New York, 1973).
Henry Ford and W.J. Cameron, *The International Jew, The World's Foremost Problem* (Dearborn, Michigan, 1922).
William Z. Foster, *Pages from a Worker's Life* (New York, 1939).
Francis Galton, *Hereditary Genius* (London, 1887).
Roy L. Garis, *Immigration Restriction: A Study of the Opposition to and Regulation of Immigration into the United States* (New York, 1927).
Samuel Gompers, *Seventy Years of Life and Labor* (New York, 1925).
J.W. Guinan, *My American Creed* (Detroit, 1923).
Sydney Lewis Gulick, *American Democracy and Asiatic Citizenship* (New York, 1918).
Prescott F. Hall, *Immigration and Its Effects Upon the United States* (New York, 1907).
Ole Hanson, *Americanism versus Bolshevism* (New York, 1920).
Fred W Haslewood, "Barbarous Spokane" *International Socialist Review* 10 (February 1910). 705-713.
William D. Haywood, *Bill Haywood's Book: The Autobiography of William D Haywood* (New York, 1929).
Burton Jesse Hendrick, *The Jews in America* (New York, 1922).
Emerson Hough, *The Web: A Revelation of Patriotism, The Story of the American Protective League* (Chicago, 1919).
Isaac A. Hourwich, *Immigration and Labor: The Economic Aspects of European Immigration to the United States* (New York, 1912).
Cloice R. Howd, *Industrial Relations in the West Coast Lumber Industry* U.S. Dept of Labor, Bureau of Labor Statistics, Bulletin No. 349 (Washington, D.C., 1924).

Immigration Commission, *Statistical Review of Immigration, 1819-1910—Distribution of Immigrants 1850-1900* Vol.3 (Washington, D.C., 1911).

Immigration Commission, *Reports: Immigrants in Industries, Japanese and Other Immigrant Races in the Pacific Coast and Rocky Mountain States* Vol.23 (Washington, D.C., 1911).

Immigration Commission, *Reports: Immigrants in Industries, Japanese and Other Immigrant Races in the Pacific Coast and Rocky Mountain States* Vol.24 (Washington, D.C., 1911).

Immigration Commission, *Reports: Immigrants in Industries, Japanese and Other Immigrant Races in the Pacific Coast and Rocky Mountain States* Vol.25 (Washington, D.C., 1911).

Immigration Commission, *Reports: Immigration and Crime* Vol. 36 (Washington, D.C., 1911).

Kiyo Sue Inui, *The Unsolved Problem of the Pacific; A Study of International Contacts, Especially in Frontier Communities, with Special Emphasis on California and An Analytical Study of the Johnson Report to the House of Representatives* (Tokyo, 1925).

Albert Johnson, *The People of the United States* (Pamphlet, Washington, D.C., 1921).

David Starr Jordan, *The Human Harvest* (Boston, 1907).

Karl K. Kawakami, *The Real Japanese Question* (New York,1921).

Rudyard Kipling, *From Sea to Sea and other Sketches: Letters of Travel* Vol.II (rev.ed. London, 1924).

Robert S. Lynd & Helen Merrel Lynd, *Middletown: A Study in Modern American Culture* (New York, 1929).

Valentine Stuart McClatchy, *The Germany of Asia: Japan's Policy in the Far East* (Sacramento, 1919).

Valentine Stuart McClatchy, *Japanese Immigration and Colonization: A Brief Prepared for Consideration of the State Department* (Sacramento, 1921).

Elwood Mead, "The Japanese Land Problem of California" *The Annals of the American Academy* 93 (January, 1921). 51-55.

Eliot Mears, *Resident Orientals on the American Pacific Coast* (New York, 1927).

Harry Alvin Millis, *The Japanese Problem in the United States: An Investigation for the Commission on Relations with Japan Appointed by The Federal Council Of the Churches of Christ in America* (New York, 1915).

Edwin O'Hara, *A Pioneer Catholic History of Oregon* (Portland, 1911).

Oregon State Immigration Commission, *The State of Oregon: Its Resources and Opportunities* (Salem, 1914).

Constantine M. Panunzio, *The Deportation Cases of 1919-1920* (New York, 1921).

Carleton H. Parker, *The Casual Laborer and Other Essays* (New York, 1920).

Cornelia S. Parker, *An American Idyll: The Life of Carleton H Parker* (Boston, 1919).

Louis F. Post, *The Deportations Delirium of 1920* (Chicago, 1923).
Waldo Roberts, "The Ku Kluxing of Oregon" *Outlook* March 14, 1923 490-491.
Edward Alsworth Ross, *The Old World in the New; The Significance of Past and Present Immigration to the American People* (New York, 1914).
Edward Alsworth Ross, *The Changing Chinese* (New York, 1912).
James Rowan, *The IWW in the Lumber Industry* (Seattle, 1920).
Aaron A. Sargent, "The Wyoming Anti-Chinese Riot" *Overland Monthly* 4 (November, 1885). 510
Antonio Stella, *Some Aspects of Italian Immigration to the United States* (New York, 1924).
Lothrop Stoddard, *The Rising Tide of Color Against White World-Supremacy* (New York, 1920).
Anna Louise Strong, *The Seattle General Strike* (Seattle, 1919).
W.J.H. Traynor "Policy and Power of the APA" *North American Review* 475 (June, 1896). 658-667
Frederick Jackson Turner, *The Frontier in American History* (New York, 1958).
United States Department of Commerce, Bureau of the Census, *Religious Bodies:1926 Volume I, Summary and Detailed Tables* (Washington, D.C., 1930).
Frank Julian Warne, *The Immigrant Invasion* (New York, 1913).
Washington State Bureau of Statistics and Immigration, *Official Report of the State Immigration Conference Held March 27th and 28th 1914* (Olympia, 1914).
Putnam Weale, *The Conflict of Colour* (London, 1910).
Dudley S. Wooten, *Remember Oregon* (Denver, 1923).

SECONDARY SOURCES

Books

Carl Abbot, *Portland: Planning, Politics and Growth in a Twentieth Century City* (Lincoln, Nebraska, 1983).
Aaron I. Abell, *American Catholicism and Social Action* (Garden City, 1960).
Barbara Allen, *Homesteading the High Desert* (Logan, Utah, 1987).
James B. Allen, *The Company Town in the American West* (Norman, Oklahoma, 1966).
Margo J. Anderson, *The American Census: A Social History* (New Haven, Connecticut, 1988).
Eugene Anschel, *Homer Lea, Sun Yat-sen and the Chinese Revolution* (New York, 1984).
Hubert H. Bancroft, *History of Washington, Idaho and Montana* (San Francisco, 1887).
Charles P. Barth, *Hobo Trail to Nowhere* (Philadelphia, 1969).

Richard C. Berner, *Seattle 1900-1920: Boomtown, Urban Turbulence to Restoration* (Seattle, 1991).

Ray Allen Billington, *The Protestant Crusade, 1800-1860: A Study of the Origins of American Nativism* (New York, 1938).

Archie Binns, *The Timber Beast* (New York, 1944).

Brian Booth (ed.), *Wildmen, Wobblies and Whistle Punks: Stewart Holbrook's Lowbrow Northwest* (Corvallis, Oregon, 1992).

William A. Bowen, *The Willamette Valley: Settlement on the Oregon Frontier* (Seattle, 1978).

John Braeman et al.(eds.), *Change and Continuity in Twentieth Century America: The 1920's* (Columbus, Ohio, 1968).

Paul W. Brissenden, *The IWW* (New York, 1957).

Mary E. Brown, *Shapers of the Great Debate on Immigration, A Biographical Dictionary* (Westport, Connecticut, 1999).

David M. Buerge and Junius Rochester, *Roots and Branches: The Religious Heritage of Washington State* (Seattle, 1988).

Paul Buhle and Dan Georgakas, *The Immigrant Left in the United States* (New York, 1996).

Dietrich G. Buss, *Henry Villard: A Study of Transatlantic Investment and Interests, 1870-1895* (New York, 1978).

Norman H. Clark, Mill Town: A Social History of Everett (Seattle, 1970).

Roger Daniels, *The Politics of Prejudice; The Anti-Japanese Movement in California and the Struggle for Japanese Exclusion* (Berkeley, 1977).

Humphrey J. Desmond *The APA Movement* (Washington, D.C., 1912).

Elizabeth Dilling, *The Red Network: A "Who's Who" and Handbook of Radicalism for Patriots* (Kenilworth, Illinois, 1934).

Gordon B. Dodds, *The American Northwest, A History of Oregon and Washington* (Arlington Heights, Illinois, 1986).

Lynn Dumenil, *The Modern Temper: American Culture and Society in the 1920's* (New York, 1995).

Pam Epstein, *The American Protective Association* (New York, 1999).

Stephen Fender (ed). *American and European National Identities* (Keele, 1996).

Robert E. Ficken, *The Forested Land, A History of Lumbering in Western Washington* (Seattle, 1987).

Paul A. Fisher, *Behind the Lodge Door: Church, State and Freemasonry in America* (Rockford, Illinois, 1989).

Philip S. Foner and Daniel Rosenberg (eds.)., *Racism, Dissent and Asian Americans from 1850 to the Present: A Documentary History* (Westport, Connecticut, 1993).

Nancy Gentile Ford, *Americans All! Foreign-born Soldiers in World War I* (College Station, Texas, 2001).

Dana Frank, *Purchasing Power: Consumer Organising, Gender and the Seattle Labor Movement* (Cambridge, 1994).

Robert L. Friedheim, *The Seattle General Strike* (Seattle, 1964).

George W. Fuller, *A History of the Pacific Northwest; With Special Emphasis on the Inland Empire* (New York, 1931).

Lawrence Goodwyn, *The Populist Moment: A Short History of the Agrarian Revolt in America* (Oxford, 1978).

Salvatore J. La Gumina, *Wop! A Documentary History of Anti-Italian Discrimination* (New York, 1973).

Andrew Gyory, *Closing the Gate: Race, Politics and the Chinese Exclusion Act* (Chapel Hill, North Carolina, 1998).

James A. Halseth and Bruce A. Glasrud (eds.), *The Northwest Mosaic: Minority Conflicts in Pacific Northwest History* (Boulder, Colorado, 1977).

Oscar Handlin, *The Uprooted* (rev.ed. New York, 1990).

Steven W. Harmon, *The St Josephs-Blatt, 1896-1919* (New York, 1989).

Lowell S. Hawley & Ralph Bushnell Potts, *Counsel for the Damned: A Biography of George Francis Vanderveer* (Philadelphia, 1953).

Samuel P. Hays, *Conservation and the Gospel of Efficiency: The Progressive Conservation Movement, 1890-1920* (Pittsburgh, 1959).

John Higham, *Strangers in the Land: Patterns of American Nativism, 1860-1925* (rev.ed. New Brunswick, New Jersey, 1994).

Lorraine Barker Hildebrand, *Straw Hats, Sandals and Steel: The Chinese in Washington State* (Tacoma, 1977).

Izumi Hirobe, *Japanese Pride, American Prejudice: Modifying the Exclusion Clause of the 1924 Immigration Act* (Stanford, California, 2001).

Eric Hobsbawm, *The Age of Empire 1875-1914* (London, 1988).

David A. Horowitz, *Inside the Klavern; The Secret History of a Ku Klux Klan of the 1920's* (Carbondale, Illinois, 1999).

Yuji Ichioka, *The Issei: The World of the First Generation Japanese Immigrants, 1885-1924* (New York, 1988).

Matthew Frye Jacobson, *Barbarian Virtues: The United States Encounters Foreign Peoples at Home and Abroad 1876-1917* (New York, 2000).

Matthew Frye Jacobson, *Whiteness of a Different Color: European Immigrants and the Alchemy of Race* (Cambridge, Massachusetts, 1998).

Vernon H. Jensen *Lumber and Labor* (New York, 1945).

Dorothy Johansen and Charles M. Gates, *Empire of the Columbia: A History of the Pacific Northwest* (New York, 1957).

Niel M. Johnson, *George Sylvester Viereck: German-American Propagandist* (Urbana, 1959).

Maldwyn Jones, *American Immigration* (rev. ed. Chicago, 1992).

Lauren Kessler, *Stubborn Twig: Three Generations in the Life of a Japanese Family* (New York, 1993).

Donald W. Kinzer, *An Episode in Anti-Catholicism: The American Protective Association* (Seattle, 1964).

Ira Kipnis, *The American Socialist Movement 1897-1912* (New York, 1952).

Leslie W. Koepplin, *A Relationship of Reform: Immigrants and Progressives in the Far West* (New York, 1990).

William L. Lang, *Centennial West: Essays on the Northern Tier States* (Seattle, 1991).

Lawrence H. Larsen, *The Urban West at the End of the Frontier* (Lawrence, Kansas, 1978).

Shawn Lay (ed.), *The Invisible Empire in the West: Towards a New Appraisal of the Ku Klux Klan of the 1920's* (Urbana, 1992).

Michael LeMay and Eliot Robert Barkan (eds.), *US Immigration and Naturalization Laws and Issues: A Documentary History* (Westport, Connecticut, 1999).

Peter J. Lewty, *Across the Columbia Plain: Railroad Expansion in the Interior Northwest* (Pullman, 1995).

Charles Pierce Le Warne, *Utopias on Puget Sound 1885-1915* (rev.ed. Seattle, 1995).

Richard M. Linkh, *American Catholicism and European Immigrants (1900-1924).* (New York, 1975).

E. Kimball MacColl, *The Growth of a City: Power and Politics in Portland Oregon, 1915-1950* (Portland, 1979).

Carey McWilliams, *Ill Fares the Land: Migrants and Migratory Labor in the United States* (Boston, 1942).

Gary Mead, *Doughboys: America and the First World War* (London, 2000).

Donald William Meinig, *The Shaping of America: A Geographical Perspective on 500 Years of History. Volume 3: Transcontinental America 1850-1915* (New Haven, 1998).

Sally M. Miller, *The Immigrant Radical* (New York, 1974).

S. Frank Minamoto, *Social solidarity among Japanese in Seattle* (Seattle, 1939).

Gwendolyn Mink, *Old Labor and the New Immigrants* (Ithaca, 1986).

Murray Morgan, *Puget's Sound: A Narrative of Early Tacoma and the Southern Sound* (Seattle, 1979).

Gerald B. Nelson, *Seattle: The Life and Times of an American City* (New York, 1977).

Julius J. Nodel, *The Ties Between* (Portland, 1959).

Walter Nugent, *The Tolerant Populists: Kansas Populism and Nativism* (Chicago, 1963).

Walter Nugent, *Crossings: The Great Trans-Atlantic Migrations, 1870-1914* (Bloomington, Indiana, 1995).

Harvey O'Connor, *Revolution in Seattle* (New York, 1964).

Earl Pomeroy, *The Pacific Slope: A History of California, Oregon, Washington, Idaho, Utah and Nevada* (New York, 1965).

Ralph Bushnell Potts, *Seattle Heritage* (Seattle, 1955).

William Preston, *Aliens and Dissenters: Federal Suppression of Radicals, 1903-1933* (Chicago, 1963).

Janet E. Rasmussen, *New Land, New Lives: Scandinavian Immigrants to the Pacific Northwest* (Seattle, 1993).

William G. Robbins, *Colony and Empire: The Capitalist Transformation of the American West* (Lawrence, Kansas, 1994).

William G. Robbins, *Landscapes of Promise: The Oregon Story, 1800-1940* (Seattle, 1997).

Harriet and Fred Rochlin, *Pioneer Jews: A New Life in the Far West* (Boston, 1984).

Robert A. Rockaway, *Words of the Uprooted: Jewish Immigration in Early 20th Century America* (Ithaca, 1998).

Lawrence J. Saalfeld, *Forces of Prejudice in Oregon, 1920-1925* (Portland, 1984).

Calvin F. Schmid and Wayne W. McVey, *Growth and Distribution of Minority Races in Seattle Washington* (Seattle, 1964).

Wilfred P. Schoenberg, *A History of the Catholic Church in the Pacific Northwest 1743 to 1983* (Washington, D.C., 1987).

Wilfred P. Schoenberg, *Defender of the Faith: The 123-Year History of the Catholic Sentinel Newspaper of Portland, Oregon* (Portland, 1993).

Carlos A. Schwantes, *The Pacific Northwest: An Interpretive History* (Lincoln, Nebraska, 1989).

Carlos A. Schwantes, *Radical Heritage: Labor, Socialism and Reform in Washington and British Columbia 1885-1917* (Moscow, Idaho, 1979).

Carlos A. Schwantes, *Hard Traveling: A Portrait of Work Life in the New Northwest* (Lincoln, Nebraska, 1994).

Carlos A. Schwantes and G. Thomas Edward (eds)., *Experiences in a Promised Land: Essays in Pacific Northwest History* (Seattle, 1986).

James W. Scott et al, *Historical Atlas of Washington* (Norman, Oklahoma, 1988).

Michael Selzer and Herbert Gold (eds.), *Kike!* (New York, 1972).

Charles A. Siegel, *West Coast Opinion and Propaganda and the Japanese Exclusion Act of 1924* (Pullman, Washington, 1949).

Dale E. Soden, *The Reverend Mark A Matthews: An Activist in the Progressive Era* (Seattle, 2001).

Gerald Sorin, *The Prophetic Minority: American Jewish Immigrant Radicals, 1880-1920* (Bloomington, Indiana, 1985).

Hew Strachan, *The First World War, Volume I: To Arms* (Oxford, 2001).

David A Takami, *Divided Destiny: A History of Japanese Americans in Seattle* (Seattle, 1998).

Linda Tamura, *The Hood River Issei: An Oral History of Japanese Settlers in Oregon's Hood River Valley* (Urbana, Illinois, 1993).

Matthea Thorseth, *The Color of Ripening* (Seattle, 1949).

William Toll, *The Making of an Ethnic Middle Class: Portland Jewry over Four Generations* (New York, 1982).

George S. Turnbull, *An Oregon Crusader* (Portland, 1955).

Robert L. Tyler, *The Rebels of the Woods: The IWW in the Pacific Northwest* (Eugene, Oregon, 1967).

Marilyn P. Watkins, *Rural Democracy: Family Matters and Politics in Western Washington, 1890-1925* (Ithaca, New York, 1995).

Richard White, *It's Your Misfortune and None of My Own: A New History of the American West* (Norman, Oklahoma, 1991).

Richard White, *Land Use, Environment and Social Change: The Shaping of Island County, Washington* (rev. ed. Seattle, 1992).

Donald E. Winters, *The Soul of the Wobblies: The IWW, Religion and American Culture in the Progressive Era, 1905-1917* (Westport , Connecticut, 1985).

Gregory R. Woirol, *In the Floating Army: FC Mills on Itinerant Life in California, 1914* (Urbana, 1992).

Donald Worster, *Under Western Skies; Nature and History in the American West* (Oxford, 1992).

Tomoko Yamakazi, *The Story of Yamada Waka: From Prostitute to Feminist Pioneer* (Tokyo, 1985).

Journal and Periodical Articles

William G Bean, "An Aspect of Know-Nothingism—The Immigrant and Slavery" *South Atlantic Quarterly* 23 (1924) 328-329.

Arthur J. Brown, "The Promotion of Emigration to Washington 1854-1909" *Pacific Northwest Quarterly* 36 (January, 1945) 3-17.

Glen J. Broyles, "The Spokane Free-Speech Fight, 1909-1910: A Study in IWW Tactics" *Labor History* 19 (Spring 1978) 238-252.

Malcolm Clark, "The Bigot Disclosed: Ninety Years of Nativism" *Oregon Historical Quarterly* 75 (June, 1974) 109-191.

Stanley Coben, "A Study in Nativism: The American Red Scare of 1919-1920" *The Political Science Quarterly* 79 (March, 1964) 52-75.

Paolo E. Colletta, "The Most Thankless Task" Bryan and the Californian Alien Land Legislation" *Pacific Historical Review* 36 (1967) 163-187.

Stephen G. Craft, "Angling for an Invitation to Paris: China's Entry into the First World War" *The International History Review* 16 (1994) 1-24.

Roland L. DeLorme, "The United States Bureau of Customs and Smuggling on Puget Sound, 1851-1913" *Prologue: The Journal of the National Archives* 5:2 (1973) 77-88.

Philip J. Dreyfus, "The IWW and the Limits of Inter-ethnic Organizing: Reds, Whites and Greeks in Grays Harbor, Washington, 1912" *Labor History* 38:4 (1997) 450-463.

Madeline Duntley, "Japanese and Filipino Together: The Trans-ethnic Vision of Our Lady Queen of Martyrs Parish [Seattle]" *US Catholic Historian* 18:1 (Winter, 2000) 74-98.

Ellen Eisenberg, "Beyond San Francisco: The Failure of Anti-Zionism in Portland, Oregon" *American Jewish History* (September, 1998) 313-315.

Ellen Eisenberg, "Transplanted to the Rose City: The Creation of East European Community in Portland, Oregon" *Journal of American Ethnic History* 19: 3 (Spring, 2000) 82-97.

Warren M. Engstrand, "Japanese Agriculture on the Pacific Coast" *Journal of Land and Public Utility Economics* 21 (November, 1945) 355.

Dana Frank,-"Race Relations and the Seattle Labor Movement, 1915-1929" *Pacific Northwest Quarterly* 85 (Winter, 1994).

Robert L. Friedheim, "The Seattle General Strike of 1919" *Pacific Northwest Quarterly* 52 (July, 1961) 81-98.

Charles M. Gates, "A Historical Sketch of the Economic Development of Washington since Statehood" *Pacific Northwest Quarterly* 39 (July, 1948) 214-232.

Susan-Mary Grant, "For God and Country: Why Men Joined Up for the American Civil War" *History Today* 50: 7 (July, 2000). 20-27

Robert Handy, "The American Religious Depression, 1925-1935" *Church History* 29 (March, 1960) 3-26.

Donald Teruo Hata and Nadine Hata, "George Shima: "The Potato King of California." *The Journal of the West* 25: 1 (January, 1986). 55-63

James B. Hedges, "Promotion of Immigration to the Pacific Northwest by the Railroads" *Mississippi Valley History Review* 15 (September, 1928) 183-203.

Robert Higgs, "Landless By Law: Japanese Immigrants in California Agriculture to 1941" *Journal of Economic History* 38 (1978) 205-225.

Alfred J. Hillier, "Albert Johnson, Congressman" *The Pacific Northwest Quarterly* 36: 3 (July, 1945) 193-212.

Craig Holstine, "The Ku Klux Klan in Whitman County in the 1920's" *Bunchgrass Historian* 9: 3 (Fall, 1981) 15-24.

Yuji Ichioka, "Ameyuki-san: Japanese Prostitutes in Nineteenth Century America" *Amerasian Journal* 4: 1 (1977) 1-21.

Yuji Ichioka, "Amerika Nadeshiko: Japanese Immigrant Women in the United States, 1900-1924" *Pacific Historical Review* 48: 2 (May, 1980) 339-357.

Yuji Ichioka, "Japanese Associations and the Japanese Government: A Special Relationship, 1909-1926" *Pacific Historical Review* 46: 3 (August,1977) 409-38.

Jules Alexander Karlin, "The Anti-Chinese Outbreaks in Seattle, 1885-1886" *Pacific Northwest Quarterly* 39: 3 (1948) 103-130.

Rotem Kowner, "Lighter Than Yellow, But Not Enough": Western Discourse on The Japanese "Race", 1854-1904"*The Historical Journal* 43: 1 (2000) 103-131.

Bruce Levine, "Conservatism, Nativism and Slavery: Thomas R Whitney and the Origins of the Know-Nothing Party" *The Journal of American History* 88: 2 (2001) 455-489.

Terje I. Lieren "Ole and the Reds: The Americanism of Seattle Mayor Ole Hanson" *Norwegian American Studies* 30 (1985) 75-95.

Norbert MacDonald, "Population Growth and Change in Seattle and Vancouver, 1880-1960" *Pacific Historical Review* 39 (1970) 297-321.

Jack Masson and Donald Guimary, "Asian Labor Contractors in the Alaskan Canned Salmon Industry: 1880-1937" *Labor History* 22 (1981). 377-397.

Paul G. Merriam, "The Other Portland: A Statistical Note on Foreign-Born, 1860-1910" *Oregon Historical Quarterly* 80 (1979) 258-268.

Paul G. Merriam, "Urban Elite in the Far West: Portland, Oregon, 1870-1890" *Arizona and the West* 18 (1976).

Patrick W. O'Bannon, "Technological Change in the Pacific Coast Canned Salmon Industry, 1900-1925: A Case Study" *Agricultural History* 56:1 (1982). 151-166.

Lee F. Pendergrass, "The Formation of a Municipal Reform Movement: The Municipal League of Seattle" *Pacific Northwest Quarterly* 66 (January, 1975) 63-66.

Hayes Perkins, "Here and There: An Itinerant Worker in the Pacific Northwest, 1898" *Oregon Historical Quarterly* 102:3 (2001) 352-376.

Lancaster Pollard, "The Pacific Northwest: A Regional Study" *Oregon Historical Quarterly* 52 (December, 1951) 211-232.

Richard A. Rajala, "Bill and the Boss: Protest, Technological Change and the Transformation of the West Coast Logging Camp 1890-1930" *Journal of Forest History* 33 (1989) 168-179.

Richard D. Scheuerman, "From Wagon Trails to Iron Rails: Russian German Immigration to the Pacific Northwest" *Journal of the American Society of Germans from Russia* 2: 2 (1979) 37-50.

Carlos A. Schwantes, "Perceptions of Violence on the Wageworkers Frontier: An American-Canadian Comparison" *Pacific Northwest Quarterly* 77 (1986) 52-71.

Carlos A. Schwantes, "Leftward Tilt on the Pacific Slope: Indigenous Unionism and the Struggle Against AFL Hegemony in the State of Washington" *Pacific Northwest Quarterly* 70 (1979) 24-33.

Zosa Szajkowski, "The Attitude of American Jews to East European Jewish Immigrants 1881-1893" *Publications of the American Jewish Historical Society* 40 (March, 1951) 222-240.

William Toll, "Fraternalism and Community on the Urban Frontier: The Jews of Portland—A Case Study" *Pacific Historical Review* 47 (1978) 369-403.

Robert L. Tyler, "The IWW and the West" *American Quarterly* 12 (Summer, 1960) 174-187.

Herman C. Voeltz, "Coxey's Army in Oregon, 1894" *Oregon Historical Quarterly* 65 (1964) 263-295.

Alan M. Wakstein, "The Origins of the Open Shop Movement, 1919-1920" *Journal of American History* 51: 4 (1964) 460-475.

Karyl Winn, "The Seattle Jewish Community: A Photographic Essay" *Pacific Northwest Quarterly* 70 (1979) 69-74.

Barbara Yasui, "The Nikei in Oregon, 1834-1940" *Oregon Historical Quarterly* 76 (1975) 225-257.

Jonathan Zimmerman, "Each Race Could Have Its Heroes Sung": Ethnicity and the History Wars of the 1920's" *Journal of American History* 87:1 (June, 2000) 92-111.

NEWSPAPERS AND MAGAZINES

Aberdeen *Daily World*
Age of Steel
American Legion Weekly
Cleveland Plain Dealer
Fresno Republican
New York World
Northwest Magazine
Oregonian
Oregon Spectator
Oregon Voter
Outlook
Overland Monthly
The *Portland Telegram*
Sacramento Bee
San Francisco *Chronicle*
San Francisco *Examiner*
San Francisco *Morning Call*
Saturday Evening Post
Seattle Post-Intelligencer
Seattle Times
Seattle *Trade Register*
Seattle *Union Record*
Seattle *Star*
Solidarity (IWW).
The *Silverton Journal*
Spokane Spokesman Review
Spokane Chronicle
Survey
Tacoma Ledger
Tacoma News Tribune
Walla Walla Statesman
Washingtonian (Grays Harbor).
Washington Post
Washington Standard
Watcher on the Tower
World's Work

UNPUBLISHED WORKS AND THESES

Janet W. Bryant, *The Ku Klux Klan and the Compulsory School Bill of 1922* (MA Thesis, Reed College, 1970).

Katherine J. Lentz, *Japanese American Relations in Seattle* (MA Thesis, University of Washington, Seattle, 1924).

Henry Beardsell Leonard, *The Open Gates; The Protest Against the Movement to Restrict European Immigration, 1896-1924.* (PhD Thesis, Northwestern University, 1967).

Eugene Kimbark MacColl, "Eight Unique Contributions to Oregon Public Life", A Talk to Oregon Jewish Museum Group, July 23, 1992. Typescript Oregon Historical Society, MSS 2440.

Elizabeth King McKeown, *War and Welfare: A Study of American Catholic Leadership* (PhD Dissertation, University of Chicago, 1972).

C. Seigfried Mickelson, *"Promotional Activities of the Northern Pacific's Land and Immigration Departments"* (Master's Thesis, University of Minnesota, 1940).

Yuzio Murayama, *"The Economic History of Japanese Immigration to the Pacific Northwest, 1890-1920"* (PhD Thesis, University of Washington, 1982).

Lawrence Rakestraw, *A History of Forest Conservation in the Pacific Northwest, 1891-1913* (PhD Thesis, University of Washington, Seattle, 1955).

Edward Roddy, *The Catholic Newspaper Press and the Quest for Social Justice 1912-1920* (PhD Thesis, Georgetown, 1961).

Nellie Virginia Roe, *The Italian Immigrant in Seattle* (MA Thesis, University of Washington, 1915).

C. Easton Rothwell, *The Ku Klux Klan in the State of Oregon* (BA Thesis, Reed College, Oregon, 1924).

Majorie R. Stearns, *The History of the Japanese People in Oregon* (unpublished PhD Thesis, University of Oregon, Eugene, 1937).

James Henry Taylor, *The Restriction of European Immigration, 1890-1924* (PhD Thesis, Berkeley, 1933).

Sister Mary Evangeline Thomas, *Nativism in the Old Northwest, 1850-1860* (PhD Thesis, Catholic University of America, Washington, D.C., 1936).

Alex Toth, *American Catholicism and Immigration* (MA Thesis, Portland State University, 1973).

Eckard V. Toy, *The Ku Klux Klan in Oregon: Its Character and Program* (MA Thesis, University of Oregon, Eugene, 1959).

Katherine Dally Woolston, *The Japanese Standard of Living in Seattle* (MA Thesis, University of Washington, 1927).

Robert E. Wynne, Reaction to the Chinese in the Pacific Northwest and British Columbia 1850-1910 (PhD Thesis, University of Washington, 1964).

INDEX

About the Author

KRISTOFER ALLERFELDT is an independent scholar.

CONTENTS

LIST OF TABLES

LIST OF FIGURES

PREFACE

In the early 1960s it seemed possible that the period of first aid treatment of the built environment was coming to an end and that its renewal and extension at satisfactory standards might soon begin. At that time, when attention generally was focusing on longer-term planning and development, the National Institute decided that, if financial support could be found, they would launch a major study of the problems of urban renewal and development.

More general research into Britain's longer-term prospects indicated not only that this sector would be likely to call for a very significant share of future national resources, but that there was little information on which could be based even very approximate estimates of the size of this share and its impact on the rest of the economy.

It was clear that, to interpret and use such data as could be collected, the research team would need to include specialists other than economists; but the approach adopted would be essentially the economist's approach. It would be concerned with the national problem rather than with specifically local problems. It would seek to quantify the problem in a way which could hope to clarify the social issues and choices before society.

The Nuffield Foundation recognized the importance of the problem and the level of work that would be necessary and very generously made a substantial grant available to the Institute for a three-year period, October 1963 to September 1966. I was appointed to lead the study, initially on secondment from the Building Research Station. This volume contains the first part of the results.

It contains an introduction to the nature of the project and the concepts which have been developed, a section on population projections and a section on housing. The measurement of need for urban facilities is based on projections of the age and sex structure of the population for each region at each quinquennial date over the period of study, 1964–2004. The section on population projections provides a discussion of the range of assumptions made for birth rates and rates of migration and gives the detailed results. The section on housing first discusses the methods used and assumptions made in deriving housing need from the population projections; the estimates of need are then compared with estimates of the supply and conditions of housing current at each quinquennial date. The costs of construction and the land needed for additional construction and for maintaining and improving the stock are estimated on the basis of an analysis of current costs and conditions. The feasibility of various housing programmes is subsequently considered in relation to the size and development of the construction industries and to their ability to produce the required real resources. The financial and administrative constraints imposed by present arrangements are also discussed.

A second volume is in preparation on the other classes of urban facilities, for example, buildings for commercial, industrial and social purposes, roads and public utilities. This again involves a study of the way needs are likely to arise, as well as of the existing stock of facilities and the costs of increasing, improving and maintaining the stock. Finally, the needs for the various types of facilities will be synthesized into settlements and regional developments and related to existing land uses and facilities. The feasibility of the various programmes of development, in relation to economic, financial and social factors, will be discussed.

It is hoped that these volumes will be of interest and value not only to people in central and local government and to economists, but to town planners, architects, surveyors, and many others who take a professional or a citizen's interest in the future of urban Britain.

In a national study which deals with a stretch of forty years ahead and with all aspects of the built environment, there is necessarily a degree of abstraction in the approach—and a corresponding degree of roughness or approximation in the calculations—which will be familiar to economists (for whose purposes a rough sketch of the long-term possibilities can be a valuable and worthy tool), but may dismay town planners, architects and others whose sights are customarily fixed on the particularity of the situations with which they deal professionally. How can a study built on costing units at a certain standard and forecasting population be any guide to a whole world composed of complex local particularities, each unique? How can a study which treats finance as an afterthought be realistic?

It is hoped that the Introduction will reduce some of these doubts. Readers who are not economists may find it advantageous to proceed from the Introduction to the last two chapters of summarized results and conclusions before embarking on the detailed accounts of research procedures and intermediate results.

I am most grateful to the Nuffield Foundation for financing the study. I should also like to express my gratitude to Mr C. T. Saunders (then Director of the Institute) and to Mrs A. K. Jackson (Secretary of the Institute) for their work in formulating the project and for the encouragement and help which they, and the present Director, Mr G. D. N. Worswick, have always given me. My thanks are particularly due to the consultants, Mr D. Rigby Childs, and Messrs D. B. Connal and J. G. Green of Daniel Connal and Partners, for their work in developing a method for costing the upgrading of housing and for all the advice they gave during the early stages of developing the project; also to Mr K. H. Allmark of the School of Architecture, Kingston upon Hull, Mr R. F. Lane of the Brixton School of Building, Mr R. Lee of the College of Estate Management, London, and Mr N. F. Watson of the Bartlett School of Architecture, University College London, for the help they and students at their colleges gave with the field studies of the condition of the stock of houses. Finally, I should like to acknowledge my gratitude to the many central and local government officials, members of firms and other research workers who have provided information and ideas.

The first person to join me on this project was Mrs Y. Ray. She has carried out work of every kind, but particularly the organization of the field studies and the use of this and other data to build up the cost estimates. Mr W. S. Grigson joined the team in May 1964; he was largely responsible for preparing the population projections and estimating the housing needs generated by them. Mrs M. Thomas and Miss S. Fineberg were responsible for extracting and collating the data from field studies and other sources; Mr S. Petch assisted with the measurement of productivity and building resources, and Mrs M. G. Hill and Miss D. Jolly have undertaken the computation. The Hollerith and computer work was carried out by Mr J. P. Mandeville, of the Scientific Computing Service Ltd. The index was compiled by Mrs A. Rowlatt.

P. A. STONE

NATIONAL INSTITUTE OF ECONOMIC
AND SOCIAL RESEARCH

October 1967

CONVENTIONS AND SYMBOLS

Years

Single years, including fiscal years, are indicated by a stroke between two dates, e.g. 1963/4. Where a hyphen is used between two dates this indicates an average or the full period, e.g. two years for 1963–4.

Symbols

.. not available or not applicable

— negligible

References

The numbers in brackets in the text, e.g. (94), refer to items in the list of references on pp. 400–3. Footnotes at the bottom of pages are used almost entirely for information which became available after the first draft of the book was completed.

CHAPTER I

INTRODUCTION

THE BACKGROUND TO THE STUDY

The quality of life in an urban society is powerfully influenced by the volume and quality of the built environment, that is by buildings, roads and other civil engineering works, and the way these are related to one another in settlements. Britain has a very aged stock of buildings, particularly dwellings, many of which are neither physically fit nor capable of meeting the economic and social needs of today. Many people live in overcrowded and insanitary conditions, without modern amenities for washing and heating. Many dwellings are badly located and mixed with decaying industry and derelict land. A great number of industrial, commercial and social buildings are obsolete, have congested sites and are no longer suitably situated in relation to other buildings to form efficient settlement patterns. Many roads are quite inadequate to handle the traffic wishing to use them, and parking space at the place of origin and destination is insufficient. Increasing distances between places of employment and places of residence add to the need for transport. Population is expected to grow rapidly and, even without any rise in standards, this would greatly increase the need for buildings and works of all kinds.

Demands are voiced on all sides for more buildings, roads and works, for higher standards and for speedier redevelopment. Moreover, it is generally assumed that the standard of living will continue to rise and that additional development will be needed to keep the built environment in line with rising incomes and expectations. There is no general consensus on suitable standards or the timing of improvements in standards, on the priorities, nor about the locations and forms of future development. However, any solution will necessitate a very large allocation of national resources to the built environment. About an eighth of the gross national product of Great Britain is currently used for its maintenance, renewal and extension.

The resources available in future for urban development will depend on the rate at which the national product increases and on the competing demands for other public and private purposes; for example, for defence, for welfare services such as education, and for capital and consumer goods. There is, too, the problem of devising the right kind of financial and administrative machinery for shifting resources into the appropriate sectors of the economy.

Except in the very short run, there is, of course, no absolute limit to the resources which can be made available for the maintenance and extension of the built environment: there is no specific sum which represents 'what the nation can afford'. It is a matter of social choice and national housekeeping—a question of priorities in achieving objectives and of finding the right balance between expenditures of different kinds, so that each yields equally good value for money. On one hand, expenditure on and returns from the built environment should be compared with those for other quite different uses; and, on the other, there is a need to make similar comparisons between the various sectors of the built environment. If national resources are to be used efficiently to meet the needs and wishes of the community, decisions about the standards at which to aim, the rate at which general advance towards them should be achieved and the most suitable forms for their attainment should be discussed and taken in the light of the maximum knowledge of the consequences of the alternatives available.

THE NEED FOR LONG-TERM THINKING

The creation of the built environment is a long-term process and, even on a local scale, is often reckoned in decades. It may take two years to design and build a single house. The creation of a small development may take five to ten years and a small town fifteen to twenty years. Once buildings and works have been constructed they are likely to remain for many generations. Development policy is essentially long-term and planning decisions need to be related to expected requirements several decades ahead. For example, planning would need to start now if it were required to halve the age of our present stock of housing and to eliminate bad housing and overcrowding by the end of the century; even so, the attainment of this aim might seriously modify the extent to which it would be possible to rebuild town centres and to provide for a three to fourfold increase in the use of cars. Again, if the increase in the population expected in the next few decades is not to add to the expansion of the conurbations, new towns and planned town expansions will need to be started on an adequate scale without delay. Such development is likely to last half a century or more and, having been built over a period of years, is not likely to be demolished simultaneously. Urban form should be chosen with a view to its suitability for many decades ahead, during which period only minor conversion work may be possible: economic adaptability is, therefore, a highly important quality, given that all the circumstances of economic and domestic life decades or generations ahead cannot be forecast. Predictions can be made, however, of limits within which the main aspects of future needs are likely to lie. The limits will widen the further ahead predictions are carried. While it would be unwise to make detailed plans for a long period ahead, it would be equally unwise to determine short-term plans without taking account of long-term objectives.

Short-term and long-term plans differ in nature. The former are intended to be implemented and must take account of physical, financial and administrative circumstances which cannot be significantly altered in the short run; while the latter are statements of objectives which appear desirable in terms of present knowledge and practicable in relation to the period considered. Many circumstances which must be taken as given in the short run could be changed to secure long-run objectives. Periodically, the long-term plans need revision in the light of new requirements and information.

In the case of the built environment the period for long-term planning needs to be long enough to allow the environment to be substantially rebuilt, yet short enough to limit the errors of prediction in relation to the central values. The period of forty years has been chosen independently by a number of bodies and seems to provide a reasonable compromise between the two requirements. Because creating the built environment takes so long, because buildings and works last so long, and are adaptable, this is a much longer period than it would be sensible to consider in looking at the future provision of most goods and services.

THE AIM AND APPROACH OF THIS STUDY

This study is not a long-term plan but it is an exercise designed to assist in the formulation of long-term plans. It sets out to estimate the cost to the nation of attaining explicit objectives over the whole area of the built environment, over a long period. It offers not one particular set of estimates but a range of possible costs, which reflect alternative possible rates of growth and changes in distribution of the population (factors of major importance which cannot be precisely forecast and might be influenced to some extent by policy), the standards proposed and the rates at which the whole built environment might be raised to these standards. Of course, it has been impossible to cover all conceivable variations, but a basis is provided for developing further estimates covering other alternatives which may, now or later, seem desirable and realistic. This range of estimates is shown in time profile, at quinquennial intervals, over the forty-year period.

The exercise might be thought of as an attempt to furnish a national shop window, in which various recognizable collections of desirable provisions are displayed, with alternative subscription rates shown on the price tags, relating to the longer or shorter periods over which the provisions are to be delivered.

Rational decision as to which collection of 'built environment' provisions to select, and at what subscription rate, would be easier if there was information available on how much could be subscribed altogether, and if there were other shop windows displaying the costs (in terms of national resources) and subscription rates for desirable collections of provisions connected with all other types of consumption, including health and welfare services and education, as well as other consumer goods and services. The best that can be done to assist selection within the compass of this study is to set the range of built-environment costs against estimates of future national income and relevant output. The time profile of costs on varied assumptions can be set against forecasts of the rise in national income over the period; and the resources the various programmes would consume can be set against estimates of probable or feasible output of the industries concerned (taking into account likely increases in productivity), and of competing demands for this output.

The scale of the study ruled out a self-contained cost/benefit approach. The problems of measuring the approximate costs of creating and maintaining the built environment are largely technical: some objective measure is always possible. In contrast, values assigned to the environment can often only be subjective and their measurement is problematical. Because many urban facilities and amenities are provided free or at a nominal charge, no market prices are available to measure their value to the community. The values provided by urban facilities can sometimes be measured individually, but this is generally only possible where the amenities can be replaced by some other facility which has a market price. This method is useful, however, where a comparison of the costs and benefits of alternative solutions to a local planning problem is required.

From the comments already made on the difference between long and short-term considerations and because of the very limited extent to which there is anything approaching a market, it will be clear that any attempt to project demand over the next forty years would have been foolish. Demand cannot be measured in the absence of a market, and it is conditioned by a host of circumstances (including supply!) which, though they may be relatively stable in the short run, can all change in the longer run. Indeed the achievement of chosen long-term objectives is likely to involve, and depend on, changing many of these circumstances.

In the short run, demand for, or provision of, housing and other amenities of the built environment is affected by a complex of administrative, institutional and financial arrangements and circumstances, and by fiscal policy, including details of the tax code. All these are factors which, with due care for repercussions, could be changed over time. The particular arrangements are not inevitable in the longer run. Far from it being unrealistic to leave such factors out of account initially in considering what objectives are possible for the nation, it would be distorting to bring them in until a later stage when, having estimated what seems physically possible, it is important to see what changes in the present administrative and financial set-up would be required to achieve or facilitate the maximum progress; and how safely and speedily such changes could be effected.

The limitations on objectives imposed by the size and age distribution of the population over the years, and by physical or real (as opposed to 'money') resources are of a different kind. Government policy, or national will, could in the long run have some influence on some of the resources concerned, for example on manpower, including trained brainpower, and productivity increase—though just what effect particular policies would have is problematical—and none on others, such as national land area and other natural resources.

In this study costs are measured in terms of physical resources. The relation between possible objectives and the more malleable financial and administrative framework is discussed in chapter 15.

The cost estimates are based on 'requirements' or 'needs' which are directly derived from the various stated assumptions as to size and distribution of population, improved standards and the timing of their application. The words 'need' and 'requirement' are used hereafter in this sense, without quotation marks to warn the reader that they imply no value judgement.

An element of value judgement inevitably enters into the selection of standards for costing. The term 'standard' is used to cover specification of size and form of units, as well as quantity and quality of fixtures, fittings and finishes, and, when appropriate, the rate of provision per head. Wherever possible the effect on cost of varying the standard within a range is given. Selection of the level of standards for costing has been guided generally by good modern practice. This may strike the reader as unambitious and unimaginative until the consequences and costs of raising all parts of urban Britain to these levels by the end of the century, while accommodating the growth of population forecast, have been appreciated. If no parts of urban Britain today fell below the best standards of general provision in the late 1920s, the present urban scene and life would be very different.

In fixing standards it had to be borne in mind that the best is often the enemy of the good. If standards are set too high in one sector of the economy, other sectors will suffer unduly; and if high standards are adopted too early for the built environment there may be insufficient resources to provide facilities at that level, except for a minority, for years to come. If, on the other hand, standards are set too low, their subsequent rise will result in early obsolescence and resources will be wasted in modification or rebuilding.

It is true that over the next forty years there may be dramatic changes in the nation's way of life. For example, the use of machinery will almost certainly increase markedly in every sphere; the growth of automation may increase the industrial space requirements per worker by reducing the number of manual operations per unit of output; improvements in oral and visual communications and the possibilities of linked computers may reduce the need for large congregations of work people (and school children?) and so reduce the need for large concentrated urban areas; transport in cities might be 'de-personalized'; with increasing leisure more space may be required in and around the home and in other parts of town and country; increasing demand for cleanliness, warmth, light and freedom from noise may increase the use of power and lead to considerable changes in standards of insulation.

Historically, such changes in the pattern of life have not been matched by equally dramatic changes in the majority of buildings and works. New constructions will no doubt incorporate some new features as the century goes by, and some modifications along the new lines will be made to old constructions. It is not possible here and now to specify and cost these without a crystal ball.

ESTIMATING COSTS, GIVEN POPULATION AND STANDARDS

In order to assess the size of the construction programme necessary to achieve any particular standard, the available stock of urban facilities must be set against the estimated needs. Unfortunately, apart from the limited information on housing in the Census of Population, it was found that very little information exists on the volume, condition or potential of existing urban facilities. As a consequence extensive field studies of the built environment were necessary, to collect sample data on the present stock and assess the rate at which it is likely to require renewing and improving.

Finally, information was required on the costs of development and on land needs. Some cost studies already existed for the main technical solutions for housing and for the earlier type of new town. Data were also available for individual buildings and for small areas of development. The costs of other forms of development, and land requirements, had to be assessed partly on the basis of published case studies and partly on the basis of model studies. It was necessary from the beginning of the study to accept a time datum point to which all reference and costing could be related; this was taken as the end of March 1964.

Produced resources were measured in 1964 money values and land in acres. The impact on the economy was also measured in terms of labour and materials, and allowance made for possible changes in the levels of productivity in the construction and other industries.

THE REGIONS

It was considered necessary to develop this national study on regional lines for two reasons. First, current urban conditions are known to vary regionally, and the patterns of economic activity and migration are likely to continue to favour certain regions unless positive steps are taken to encourage a different regional pattern. The volume of construction work required per head of existing and additional population will tend to vary from one region to another, so that the resources required nationally may differ according to the pattern of migration. Secondly, the greater the aggregate of population, the greater the chance of a purely statistical matching between needs and the present stock of facilities whereby surpluses in some areas offset deficiencies in others. Hence there is a danger that estimates derived from national aggregates would be too small. Facilities available in Scotland could not meet needs arising in the South East. Theoretically, needs and stocks should be matched for localities small enough for the location of facilities within them to be immaterial. Such refinement was not practicable but a regional analysis should meet a large part of the problem.

For these purposes regions were needed which could be regarded as independent and self-contained both now and over the period of the study. They had

Fig. 1.1. Boundaries of regions used in this study

to be extensive enough to contain all local migratory movements and to have a well defined hierarchy of growth points. They had to have physical, economic and social characteristics which would make them easily identifiable entities. At the same time the regions needed to be drawn so as to facilitate the re-arrangement of published regional statistics. For this reason regions were chosen which, as far as possible, followed established county boundaries and established statistical regions. For statistical purposes the past was more important than the future, especially as future borough, county and regional boundaries were all under discussion at the time when the regional boundaries had to be fixed. The official Standard Regions and the regional boundaries used by other bodies, such as planning authorities, railway, hospital, gas, electricity and water boards, were all examined, but none had outstanding merits for the purpose of this study. The regions finally chosen are illustrated in fig. 1.1. The regions used for this study had already been defined, and a considerable amount of statistical analysis completed, before the Government announced the structure of the development regions. Comparison with the development regions is generally possible by grouping pairs of regions.

The regions 'Scotland', 'North' and 'Midlands', used in this study are identical with the Standard Regions. 'North West' is similar to the Standard Region 'North Western' except for the inclusion of the county of Flint and the exclusion of the north west part of Derbyshire. Flint was included because of the possibility of further expansion along the Dee estuary. The sector of Derbyshire was excluded to avoid splitting the county of Derbyshire. The exclusion makes only a 1 per cent difference to the population of the North West.

The Standard Regions tend to divide central and eastern England along east and west lines, which results in regions that are industrial in the west and rural in the east. A north and south division has been used for the purpose of this study in order to produce regions which are more homogeneous. The 'Pennines' has been taken to cover the industrial axis from the West Riding down to the Nottingham-Derby area. The 'East' is centred on the agricultural and moorland areas from the East Riding down to the Fens.

The industrial south of Wales has been linked with the Bristol area to form the 'West', on the assumption that the Bristol-Swansea axis will be a major growth zone on completion of the motorway links. The remaining area of Wales, except for Flint, is taken as 'North and Central Wales'. The 'South West' consists of Devon, Cornwall and Dorset (except Poole municipal borough).

The counties of Northampton and Leicester and the Soke of Peterborough, having both agricultural and industrial activities, do not easily fit into any regional pattern. They have been grouped into 'Central' and, in considering future developments, this region might possibly be linked to the Pennines, the Midlands or the South East. The last is a large region including the Southampton area, the south coast and much of the M1 and M4 areas, with boundaries following the existing county boundaries, except in the extreme west where Poole is so closely related to the Bournemouth area that it is included. The agricultural counties of Norfolk, Cambridge, and Huntingdon and the Isle of Ely were not included in the East because of their proximity to the South East, but it is not thought likely that the South East will ever extend a strong influence as far as this, and so they were grouped into the small independent 'East Anglia'. The South East and East Anglia combined correspond to the same area as the Standard Regions 'Southern', 'London and South Eastern' and 'Eastern'.

THE TIME DATUM AND NEW DATA

Clearly any study of this type takes a long time to complete and publish. Both the situation under study and data about it change as the study progresses. It is not possible to revise the whole basis of the estimates as the situation changes and new sources of data become available. All that is possible is to test results already obtained against new information. Generally the estimates appear to stand such tests. Reference has been made in footnotes to all the more important results which have been published since the material in the chapters was written.

PART 1

THE PROJECTION OF FUTURE POPULATION

CHAPTER 2

THE NATIONAL POPULATION PROJECTIONS

The prediction of future population inevitably lies at the base of all estimates of urban needs. It was, therefore, necessary to prepare projections of the future population before estimates could be made of housing needs. The age and sex structure of the future population was needed to provide reliable estimates for buildings such as schools or hospitals which cater for particular age and sex groups. The marital structure and the way the population would be grouped into households was also required for the estimation of housing need and for items such as cars which are related more closely to household numbers than to people.

In order to cover the range of possible conditions, alternative projections were necessary. Three alternative assumptions were made for birth rates, and projections were prepared for each quinquennium over the forty-year period. Since the study is a regional one, projections were also required for each of the twelve regions and, again to cover the range of possibilities, for each of three alternative patterns of internal migration. With this amount of calculation it was obviously essential to simplify wherever possible, bearing in mind that the projections were not the main purpose of the study.

Three factors influence the growth of population: the number of deaths, or more appositely the number of people who survive; the number of births, which is largely a function of marriage and fertility rates; and the net gain or loss from external migration.

CURRENT TRENDS IN DEATH RATES

Death rates have been falling relatively steadily for a great many years, not only in industrialized western countries but throughout the world. In this country the fall has been greatest at young ages (table 2.1). Over the last forty years the death rates for children have been cut to a fifth or less, but the improvement gets progressively smaller as age increases. Although in every age group female death rates have declined more than male, taking all ages together the position is reversed, because so many more women than men die at the advanced ages where the decline has only been slight.

However, for projecting the future population it is not the number of deaths which matters so much as the number of people who survive. In these terms the trend looks somewhat different, because death rates at young ages are already so low that even quite dramatic changes make very little difference to the number surviving. Over the past forty years the reduction in the female death rate at ages 5–9 was from 2·8 to 0·3, nearly 90 per cent (table 2.1). But the improvement in the equivalent survival rate was only from 997·2 to 999·7, a gain of 0·3 per cent. In fact, only for the first four years of life, and for females between the ages of 65 and 84, did the survival rates rise by more than 1 per cent. Population projections are therefore relatively insensitive to further reductions in the death rate, particularly at young ages.

Table 2.1. *Changes in United Kingdom death rates* [a]

	Males			Females		
	Deaths per 1000		1961 death rate as % of 1920–2	Deaths per 1000		1961 death rate as % of 1920–2
Age	1920–2	1961		1920–2	1961	
0–4	33·4	6·3	*19*	26·9	4·9	*18*
5–9	2·9	0·5	*17*	2·8	0·3	*11*
10–14	1·8	0·4	*22*	1·9	0·3	*16*
15–19	2·9	0·9	*31*	2·8	0·4	*14*
20–24	3·9	1·1	*28*	3·4	0·5	*15*
25–34	4·5	1·2	*27*	4·1	0·7	*17*
35–44	6·9	2·5	*36*	5·6	1·8	*32*
45–54	11·9	7·4	*62*	9·3	4·6	*49*
55–64	25·3	22·4	*89*	19·2	11·0	*57*
65–74	57·8	54·8	*95*	45·6	31·6	*69*
75–84	131·8	124·8	*95*	111·5	88·5	*79*
85+	259·1	255·7	*99*	232·4	228·5	*98*
All ages	13·5	12·5	*93*	11·9	11·4	*96*

SOURCE: *Annual Abstract of Statistics, 1962* (1), table 35.

[a] Death rates are not published separately for Great Britain.

Nevertheless there is every reason to hope that the downward trend of death rates will continue. The very fact that it is possible to use the word ‘hope’ in this connexion is one of the main reasons. Deaths differ from either births or migration in that, while it is universally accepted that the prolongation of life is good, there is no such unanimity about optimum family size or about migration.

In the official projection, the Registrars General for Scotland and for England and Wales have assumed that, at ages under forty, death rates will decline to less than half those experienced in recent years, but that, at ages over forty, the decline will be progressively smaller until it ceases at ages over ninety. This follows the pattern of past trends (table 2.1) but represents a considerably smaller fall than occurred over the past forty years. However, even if there were to be no further fall whatsoever it would not alter the projected population by more than 1·5 million after forty years.[1]

[1] In 1967, when projecting population for 1966–2006, the Registrar General made only minor modifications to the assumed rates of mortality; see *Registrar General's Quarterly Return for England and Wales* (2).

EXTERNAL MIGRATION

Unfortunately no such simple trends exist for external migration. This is hardly surprising because the item which is relevant to future population growth, the net gain to or loss from Great Britain, is the residual balance of a complex pattern of flows to and from Northern Ireland, the Commonwealth and foreign countries. Indeed the trend of external migration is so erratic that it is virtually impossible to make an estimate for a period as long as forty years.

Table 2.2. *United Kingdom net balance of external migration*

Thousands

Year	Migration balance [a]
1953	−74
1954	−32
1955	−10
1956	−17
1957	−72
1958	+45
1959	+44
1960	+82
1961	+170
1962	+136
1963	+10

SOURCE: *Overseas Migration Board Statistics:1963* (3), table 7.

[a] Migration balance is immigration minus emigration.

A change of over 100,000 in the net balance for the United Kingdom has occurred twice in the last ten years (table 2.2). There is no reason to believe that if figures for Great Britain were available they would show any greater stability.

Now that the Commonwealth Immigrants Act is in force it is unlikely that net immigration will again rise to the high levels of the early 1960s, and it might swing back to net emigration.[1] Apart from this, however, there is little that can be said with any certainty and the assumption made by the Registrars General in 1964, that there will be a net gain of 30,000 annually to Great Britain, which is as reasonable as any other, has been adopted in this study.

BIRTH RATES

With births, as with external migration, there is considerable doubt about the causes of current trends and the course of future changes. The number of births per thousand population appears to have reached a peak of about 35 in the

[1] Since 1963 there has been a net loss of population by migration from the United Kingdom; the estimated figures are 60,000 (1964), 75,000 (1965) and 83,000 (1966), see *Registrar General's Quarterly Returns for England and Wales* (various issues), H.M.S.O., London.

1870s; it then fell strongly for the next sixty years to 15 per thousand in the 1930s (fig. 2.1). An upward trend may then have started but the war intervened before it became clearly apparent. The upheavals of the war and early postwar years resulted in violent fluctuations of the birth rate, which made it extremely difficult to decide whether there had been any change from the long-standing downward trend. When the early 1950s saw a resumption of this downward tendency the most probable future course was a continuing fall. But in 1956 a rise began which has taken the birth rate for England and Wales from its low point of 14·9 in the middle of 1955 to 18·5 in the middle of 1964 (4).[1] Apart from the postwar surge this figure was last recorded in the 1920s. The question now to be answered is whether the upward trend during the decade to 1964 represents the beginning of a fundamental break with the history of the last hundred years or merely a temporary divergence. Analysis of the change in marriage and fertility rates, which together determine the flow of births, may help to throw some light on the question (5).

MARRIAGE RATES

Over 90 per cent of children are born to women married once only. The illegitimate birth rate, the divorce and remarriage rates and the fertility rate of remarried women are therefore of only minor significance. The two important factors are the rate at which spinsters get married and their fertility rates in the years following marriage. Between them they determine the proportion of women who marry, the age at which they marry, the speed at which families are built up and their ultimate size.

Table 2.3. *Spinsters' marriage rates, England and Wales*

Age	Marriage rates per 1000 single women		Percentage increases 1931–61
	1931	1961	
15–19	17·1	60·8	*262*
20–24	106·8	271·7	*154*
25–29	119·1	179·4	*61*
30–34	57·2	88·7	*55*
35–44	21·3	32·2	*51*
45–54	7·9	10·5	*33*
55+	2·2	2·3	*5*

SOURCE: *Registrar General's Statistical Review of England and Wales, 1961* (6).

After a long period when they were nearly stationary, spinsters' marriage rates at all ages started rising in 1932, though for the 15–19 age group the rise

[1] Since 1964 the rate has again declined and is currently (1967) over 5 per cent below the 1964 figure, see *Registrar General's Quarterly Return for England and Wales* (2).

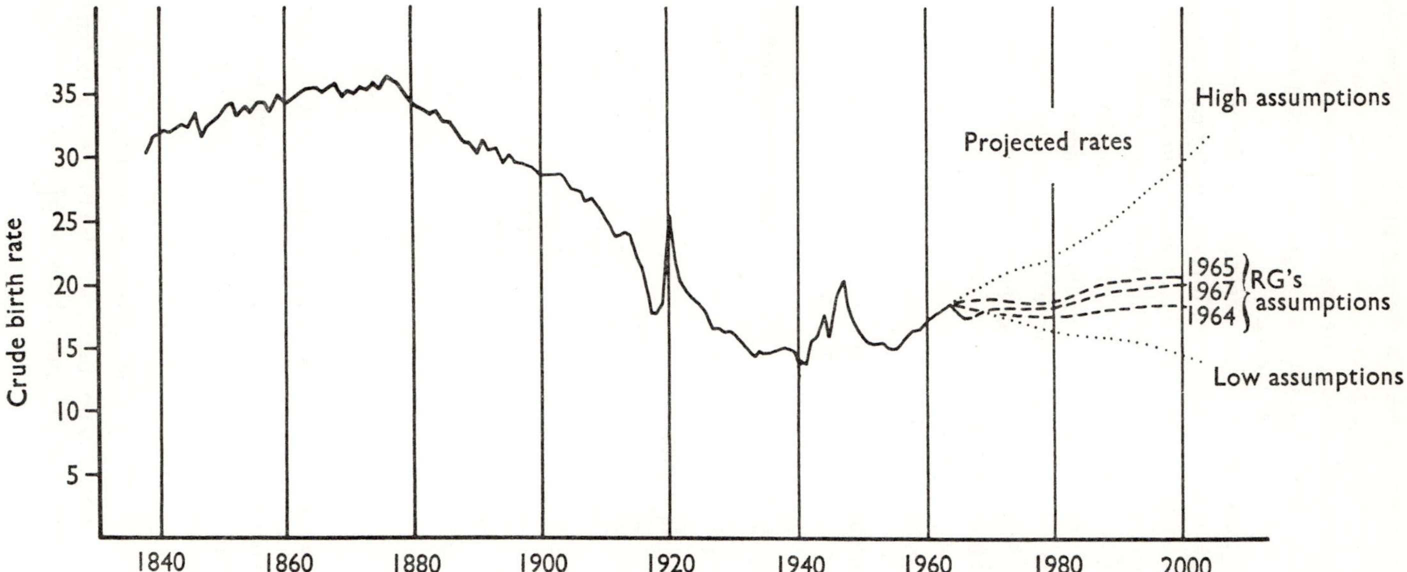

SOURCES: Mitchell and Deane, *Abstract of British Historical Statistics* (7); Registrar General's projections calculated from ***Registrar General's** Quarterly Return for England and Wales*, and from *Economic Trends* (8); high and low projections, NIESR estimates.

Fig. 2.1. Live births per 1000 population, England and Wales, 1838–2004

had started somewhat earlier. Here too the war produced violent fluctuations but, with the exception of the age group 25–9, where the postwar rise has been much slower than before, the prewar rise has been resumed. It is particularly important to notice that the rise has been much greater at young ages (table 2.3); Scottish data would show a similar change.

This rise at young ages has far larger consequences for population growth than would an equivalent rise at older ages. It results in a greater increase in the proportion of women who are married, because at young ages the marriage rates apply to a large number of single women, whereas at older ages the number of single women 'at risk' is much reduced. An increase in the marriage rates of the two age groups under twenty-five would make more difference to the proportion of women married within the fertile age bracket than an increase of a similar order in the rates of all five age groups over twenty-five (table 2.4). Moreover, the greatest difference occurs in just those young age groups where fertility after marriage is highest: women married under twenty end up with families three times as large as those who marry between thirty and thirty-five.

Table 2.4. *Illustration of the effect of higher marriage rates, England and Wales, 1961*

Per thousand

	Actual		20% higher marriage rates: for those under 25		20% higher marriage rates: for those over 25	
Age	Spinsters' marriage rates	Numbers in age group who have married	Spinsters' marriage rates	Numbers in age group who have married	Spinsters' marriage rates	Numbers in age group who have married
15–19	61	65	73	83	61	65
20–24	272	602	327	691	272	602
25–29	179	893	179	921	215	898
30–34	89	943	89	957	107	950
35–39	41	958	41	967	49	964
40–44	23	963	23	972	28	970
45–49	14	966	14	975	17	974

SOURCE: *Registrar General's Statistical Review of England and Wales, 1961* (9).

This upward tendency of all marriage rates since the 1930s has resulted in a reduction in the average age of marriage and a substantial increase in the proportion of women married.

FERTILITY RATES AND FAMILY SIZE

The increase in marriage rates is not the only cause of the rise in the birth rate since 1956. Indeed it accounts for only about a third of it. The remaining

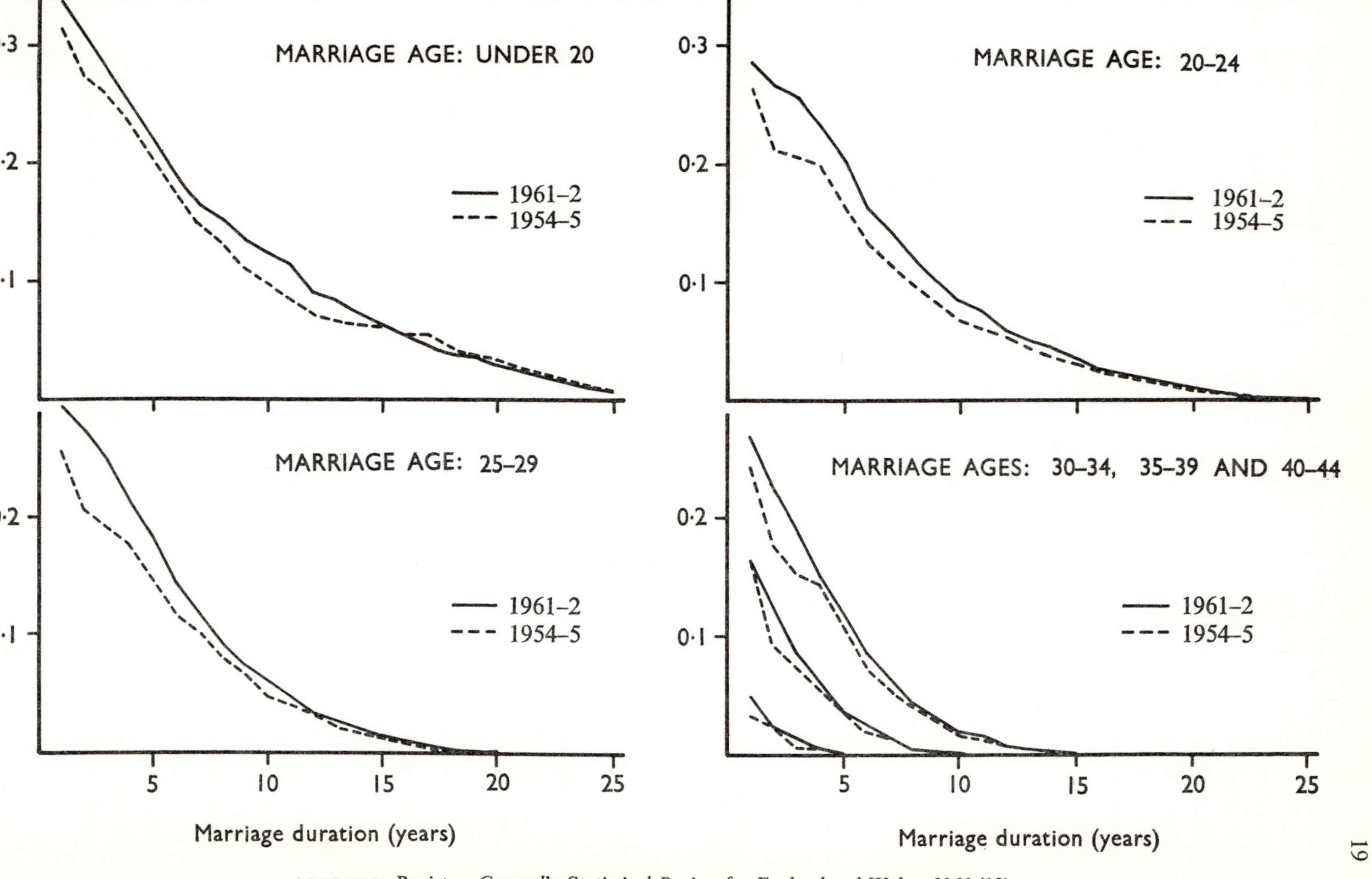

SOURCES: *Registrar General's Statistical Review for England and Wales, 1961* (10).

Fig. 2.2. Fertility rates by age and duration of marriage, England and Wales

two-thirds is the result of the higher fertility rates of married women. Unlike the rise in marriage rates, the fertility increase is not heavily concentrated at the younger ages (table 2.5). The first four age groups, which together account for 88 per cent of all births, all show a similar increase.

Fertility is highest in the first few years of marriage and then declines quite rapidly (fig. 2.2). The increased fertilities shown for the middle age groups (table 2.5) do not indicate any change in this pattern. Those who married young in the 1940s have not tended to have more children later on in married life: on the contrary the trend has been for couples to start building their families sooner than before, and the reason why the increases extend to the older ages is because

Table 2.5. *Increase in age specific birth rates, England and Wales, 1955–63*

	Legitimate births per 1000 married women		
Age	1955	1962	Percentage increase
15–19	391·5	464·6	*18·7*
20–24	248·9	283·6	*13·9*
25–29	171·8	205·9	*19·8*
30–34	94·8	111·8	*17·9*
35–39	49·4	50·9	*3·0*
40–44	13·8	14·2	*2·9*
45+	0·9	0·9	*0*

SOURCE: *Registrar General's Statistical Review of England and Wales, 1955* and *1963* (11).

this trend applies to all marriages, even where the bride is thirty or over. At least, this was the trend until recently, but in the last few years fertility rates have also started to rise at marriage durations between ten and fifteen years (fig. 2.2). In other words the marriages of the late 1940s and early 1950s are now having more children after ten years of marriage than those of the war and early postwar years.

The higher initial fertilities of the marriages of recent years may represent merely the bringing forward in time of children who would otherwise have been born a few years later, or they may represent a trend towards larger families. Both result in more births now and both have some permanent effect on the future birth rate. However, if it is the timing of families which is changing rather than their ultimate size, the long-term effect is much less. This kind of uncertainty makes it very difficult to forecast future fertilities.

For this reason it is difficult to estimate the mean ultimate family size of current marriages or even of ten-year-old marriages. Only for the marriages of the early 1930s, where even the youngest bride is now over forty-five, are families definitely completed. However, since only 3·5 per cent of children are born after fifteen years of marriage, it is possible to foresee the probable completed family size of marriages up to 1950.

The trend of mean completed family size has been very similar to that of the crude birth rate (fig. 2.1). Completed family size fell rapidly from over six children for the marriages of the 1860s to four for those at the beginning of the century and levelled out at just over two for those of 1930. It probably stayed at this level for ten years but, barring a catastrophic fall in fertilities late in marriage, it is now rising. If future fertilities stayed at the 1961–2 level, they would give an average of two and a half children in each completed family (12).

THE ASSUMPTIONS OF THE REGISTRARS GENERAL

The latest projection of the Registrars General at the start of this study was the one published in April 1964 based on the population at mid-1963. All subsequent references to the assumptions and figures of the Registrars General refer to this particular projection except where otherwise stated.

The flow of future births which is assumed in this projection is clearly stated, but not, unfortunately, the precise marriage and fertility assumptions which underlie this number of births. All that is known is that the age of women at marriage is assumed to fall 'at a gradually declining rate' and that 'for women married at any given age a modest increase' in completed family size is assumed (13).

For the projection published in 1965, based on a considerably higher birth rate than that of the preceding year (fig. 2.1), we know, for the first time, the actual marriage and fertility rates assumed. Together they produce a completed family size of 2·75 in 1984 with a slow increase thereafter (8).[1]

THE NEED FOR ALTERNATIVE ASSUMPTIONS

It will be obvious from what has already been said that the assumptions on future births, migration and deaths used by the Registrars General in preparing the official projection are not the only ones that could reasonably be made. On births, at least, there are several other estimates that could be put forward, bearing in mind the lack of knowledge about causes. Since the birth rate started to rise, the Registrar General for England and Wales has made substantial upward revisions to his future birth rate assumptions in eight out of ten years. Therefore, although the official projection, which is widely used and is based on the fullest information available, should clearly be taken as the principal basis for forecasting future need, it is also necessary to consider the consequences of adopting different assumptions. Because of the need for simplicity, because there is really no basis for forecasting future external migration and because changes in birth rates have more effect than changes in migration on the age composition

[1] In the light of more recent evidence on fertility the ultimate family size for the mid-1966 based projection has been slightly reduced. The gain assumed from migration has also been slightly reduced in making the last projections, see *Registrar General's Quarterly Return for England and Wales*, 1st quarter 1967 (2).

of the population, it was decided to evaluate the consequences of two different birth rates, one above and one below that assumed by the Registrars General. Before considering these, however, it should be mentioned that different external migration assumptions can have a considerable effect on the size of the population. If external migration differed permanently by 100,000 from the net annual gain of 30,000 assumed by the Registrars General, then the migrants themselves and their subsequent natural increase would alter the population after forty years by over 5 million.

HIGHER BIRTH RATE ASSUMPTIONS

There are several reasons why a higher birth rate seems possible. Marriage rates are still rising and it is hard to see why this rise should now cease: part of the explanation of the increase at the all important young ages may lie in the continuing growth of hire purchase and mortgage facilities which allow the early setting-up of separate households: stepping up the house-building rate would remove another obstacle to early marriage: moreover, if the widely accepted aim of faster national economic growth is achieved, the economic barriers to early marriage will be further reduced. The trend of fertility rates is also upwards, so that the assumptions of the Registrars General represent a break with present trends, relying on a conjectural fall in fertilities later in marriage to offset the present high fertilities at short marriage durations. However, the trend of the last few years has been for fertilities to rise at longer durations also; in contrast to the nineteenth century, there now appears to be a positive association between economic prosperity and high fertility which suggests that faster national growth may accelerate the fertility rise. A continued build up of the immigrant population, even if the net migration balance were small, would increase fertilities still further.

Subtle social and psychological changes are probably behind the recent rise, in addition to the more obvious factors mentioned above. Enough has been said, however, to show that a further increase in the birth rate is quite possible. In choosing a high birth rate assumption the aim was to pick on the maximum probable increase, not the increase considered most likely. It was obviously sensible to avoid extreme assumptions but at the same time desirable to adopt ones which would demarcate a range within which events might well fall. For marriage rates, it was felt that the rise which has now been running for over thirty years could well continue: the rates adopted for 2004 were therefore above those of 1962, the latest year available at the time, by four-thirds of the amount by which the 1962 rates exceeded those of 1931. On fertility it was felt that the rates of rise in recent years could not continue, but that an upward trend was perfectly possible: the rates adopted for 2004 were therefore 40 per cent up on those of 1962, which represents a rate of increase less than half that of recent years and considerably slower than the rate of fall in the nineteenth century.

Table 2.6. *Great Britain, projected total population at 31 March, low birth rate assumptions*

Thousands

Age	1964		1969		1974		1979		1984		1989		1994		1999		2004	
	M	F	M	F	M	F	M	F	M	F	M	F	M	F	M	F	M	F
0–4	2261	2145	2471	2342	2526	2394	2491	2360	2407	2280	2377	2247	2384	2260	2368	2237	2289	2163
5–9	1970	1870	2254	2141	2466	2341	2521	2394	2486	2357	2407	2276	2375	2244	2381	2257	2363	2235
10–14	1960	1862	1970	1870	2252	2141	2464	2339	2522	2393	2486	2359	2404	2277	2373	2244	2381	2258
15–19	2099	2007	1961	1866	1969	1874	2256	2145	2465	2343	2523	2399	2490	2363	2406	2282	2377	2249
20–24	1720	1678	2108	2027	1970	1886	1979	1894	2265	2162	2475	2363	2533	2416	2499	2381	2418	2301
25–29	1687	1605	1729	1694	2115	2042	1979	1901	1990	1909	2275	2179	2485	2379	2545	2435	2511	2398
30–34	1696	1630	1694	1613	1736	1702	2121	2049	1986	1909	1998	1918	2282	2188	2494	2387	2552	2443
35–39	1739	1717	1693	1629	1692	1613	1736	1702	2120	2049	1987	1909	2000	1918	2284	2190	2494	2390
40–44	1829	1850	1726	1706	1682	1620	1683	1605	1727	1695	2110	2041	1979	1906	1992	1916	2275	2187
45–49	1637	1701	1797	1829	1698	1688	1658	1606	1660	1592	1703	1684	2085	2029	1956	1894	1972	1904
50–54	1737	1821	1583	1666	1745	1796	1648	1659	1614	1582	1618	1571	1665	1661	2038	2002	1916	1870
55–59	1608	1740	1631	1763	1490	1617	1649	1747	1564	1618	1534	1544	1543	1536	1590	1628	1955	1965
60–64	1292	1557	1444	1651	1471	1680	1350	1544	1503	1672	1431	1554	1409	1484	1423	1481	1473	1572
65–69	944	1327	1090	1427	1229	1521	1257	1554	1158	1432	1301	1560	1244	1451	1233	1392	1252	1394
70–74	671	1069	725	1146	845	1237	959	1327	988	1362	916	1259	1042	1384	1000	1290	1000	1243
75+	758	1470	780	1587	836	1720	955	1875	1103	2044	1200	2170	1198	2162	1283	2248	1317	2246
Total	25608	27049	26656	27957	27722	28872	28706	29701	29558	30399	30341	31033	31118	31658	31865	32264	32545	32818
0–14	6191	5877	6695	6353	7244	6876	7476	7093	7415	7030	7270	6882	7163	6781	7122	6738	7033	6656
Working age [a]	17988	18633	18456	18871	18797	19039	19316	19406	20052	19963	20955	20722	21715	21331	22460	21988	23195	22673

SOURCE: NIESR estimates.

[a] Working age is taken to be 15–69 for both males and females.

Table 2.7. *Great Britain, projected total population at 31 March, Registrars General's birth rate assumptions*

Thousands

Age	1964		1969		1974		1979		1984		1989		1994		1999		2004	
	M	F	M	F	M	F	M	F	M	F	M	F	M	F	M	F	M	F
0–4	2261	2145	2471	2342	2526	2394	2577	2443	2656	2516	2854	2699	3071	2910	3221	3044	3301	3120
5–9	1970	1870	2254	2141	2466	2341	2521	2394	2572	2440	2656	2512	2852	2696	3068	2907	3216	3042
10–14	1960	1862	1970	1870	2252	2141	2464	2339	2522	2393	2572	2442	2653	2513	2850	2696	3068	2908
15–19	2099	2007	1961	1866	1969	1874	2256	2145	2465	2343	2523	2399	2576	2446	2655	2518	2854	2701
20–24	1720	1678	2108	2027	1970	1886	1979	1894	2265	2162	2475	2363	2533	2416	2585	2464	2667	2537
25–29	1687	1605	1729	1694	2115	2042	1979	1901	1990	1909	2275	2179	2485	2379	2545	2435	2597	2481
30–34	1696	1630	1694	1613	1736	1702	2121	2049	1986	1909	1998	1918	2282	2188	2494	2387	2552	2443
35–39	1739	1717	1693	1629	1692	1613	1736	1702	2120	2049	1987	1909	2000	1918	2284	2190	2494	2390
40–44	1829	1850	1726	1706	1682	1620	1683	1605	1727	1695	2110	2041	1979	1906	1992	1916	2275	2187
45–49	1637	1701	1797	1829	1698	1688	1658	1606	1660	1592	1703	1684	2085	2029	1956	1894	1972	1904
50–54	1737	1821	1583	1666	1745	1796	1648	1659	1614	1582	1618	1571	1665	1661	2038	2002	1916	1870
55–59	1608	1740	1631	1763	1490	1617	1649	1747	1564	1618	1534	1544	1543	1536	1590	1628	1955	1965
60–64	1292	1557	1444	1651	1471	1680	1350	1544	1503	1672	1431	1554	1409	1484	1423	1481	1473	1572
65–69	944	1327	1090	1427	1229	1521	1257	1554	1158	1432	1301	1560	1244	1451	1233	1392	1252	1394
70–74	671	1069	725	1146	845	1237	959	1327	988	1362	916	1259	1042	1384	1000	1290	1000	1243
75+	758	1470	780	1587	836	1720	955	1875	1103	2044	1200	2170	1198	2162	1283	2248	1317	2246
Total	25608	27049	26656	27957	27722	28872	28792	29784	29893	30718	31153	31804	32617	33079	34217	34492	35909	36003
0–14	6191	5877	6695	6353	7244	6876	7562	7176	7750	7349	8082	7653	8576	8119	9139	8647	9585	9070
Working age [a]	17988	18633	18456	18871	18797	19039	19316	19406	20052	19963	20955	20722	21801	21414	22795	22307	24007	23444

SOURCE: Based on a projection supplied by the Government Actuary.

[a] Working age is taken to be 15–69 for both males and females.

Table 2.8. *Great Britain, projected total population at 31 March, high birth rate assumptions*

Thousands

Age	1964		1969		1974		1979		1984		1989		1994		1999		2004	
	M	F	M	F	M	F	M	F	M	F	M	F	M	F	M	F	M	F
0–4	2261	2145	2495	2365	2730	2589	3019	2864	3271	3101	3656	3458	4132	3916	4786	4525	5552	5248
5–9	1970	1870	2254	2141	2490	2364	2725	2589	3014	2861	3271	3097	3654	3455	4129	3913	4782	4523
10–14	1960	1862	1970	1870	2252	2141	2488	2362	2726	2588	3014	2863	3268	3098	3652	3455	4129	3914
15–19	2099	2007	1961	1866	1969	1874	2256	2145	2489	2366	2727	2594	3018	2867	3270	3103	3656	3460
20–24	1720	1678	2108	2027	1970	1886	1979	1894	2265	2162	2499	2386	2737	2611	3027	2885	3282	3122
25–29	1687	1605	1729	1694	2115	2042	1979	1901	1990	1909	2275	2179	2509	2402	2749	2630	3039	2902
30–34	1696	1630	1694	1613	1736	1702	2121	2049	1986	1909	1998	1918	2282	2188	2518	2410	2756	2638
35–39	1739	1717	1693	1629	1692	1613	1736	1702	2120	2049	1987	1909	2000	1918	2284	2190	2518	2413
40–44	1829	1850	1726	1706	1682	1620	1683	1605	1727	1695	2110	2041	1979	1906	1992	1916	2275	2187
45–49	1637	1701	1797	1829	1698	1688	1658	1606	1660	1592	1703	1684	2085	2029	1956	1894	1972	1904
50–54	1737	1821	1583	1666	1745	1796	1648	1659	1614	1582	1618	1571	1665	1661	2038	2002	1916	1870
55–59	1608	1740	1631	1763	1490	1617	1649	1747	1564	1618	1534	1544	1543	1536	1590	1628	1955	1965
60–64	1292	1557	1444	1651	1471	1680	1350	1544	1503	1672	1431	1554	1409	1484	1423	1481	1473	1572
65–69	944	1327	1090	1427	1229	1521	1257	1554	1158	1432	1301	1560	1244	1451	1233	1392	1252	1394
70–74	671	1069	725	1146	845	1237	959	1327	988	1362	916	1259	1042	1384	1000	1290	1000	1243
75+	758	1470	780	1587	836	1720	955	1875	1103	2044	1200	2170	1198	2162	1283	2248	1317	2246
Total	25608	27049	26680	27980	27950	29090	29462	30423	31178	31942	33240	33787	35765	36068	38930	38962	42874	42601
0–14	6191	5877	6719	6376	7472	7094	8232	7815	9011	8550	9941	9418	11054	10469	12567	11893	14463	13685
Working age [a]	17988	18633	18456	18871	18797	19039	19316	19406	20076	19986	21183	20940	22471	22053	24080	23531	26094	25427

SOURCE: NIESR estimates.

[a] Working age is taken to be 15–69 for both males and females.

THE CONSEQUENCES OF HIGHER BIRTH RATE ASSUMPTIONS

This particular set of marriage and fertility rate assumptions was used for all calculations but a similar population would result if the fertility rate rise turned out to be greater and the marriage rate rise smaller than assumed, or vice versa. The technique used was first to calculate the number of women by age of marriage and duration of marriage at the end of the century. Secondly, use was made of the 1962 fertilities to derive age specific birth rates for married women; adjustments were made for illegitimate births to provide age specific birth rates for all women. These rates were increased by 40 per cent and the rates at intervening years interpolated linearly. Finally, the interpolated rates were used to build up the population at each date. The population projections on the basis of the three sets of assumptions are given in tables 2.6, 2.7 and 2.8.

On the high assumptions the total population would have risen by 62 per cent to over 85 million by the end of the forty-year period. This rise would accelerate from 3·8 per cent in the first five years to 6·2 per cent in the 1984–9 period and 9·7 per cent in the last five years. Only the population under the age of forty differs from that projected by the Registrars General, so the population of pensionable age is unaffected and the population of working age is increased only gradually from 1980 onwards, finally reaching a level about 9 per cent above the official projection (table 2.9). The pre-school age group shows the greatest rise, being finally 68 per cent higher than the official projection and nearly two and a half times the present population of pre-school age. The effect of these changes is to reduce the ratio of the population of working age to the remainder from 2·3:1 at present down to 1·5:1 in 2004. The official projection also involves some fall in this ratio, but only to 1·9:1 in 2004.

Table 2.9. *Age structures of the high and low birth rate assumptions as percentages of the Registrars General's assumptions*

Percentages

	High assumptions				Low assumptions			
	Age 0–4	Age 0–14	Working age	Total population	Age 0–4	Age 0–14	Working age	Total population
1964	100	100	100	100	100	100	100	100
1969	101	100·4	100	100·1	100	100	100	100
1974	108·1	103·2	100	100·8	100	100	100	100
1979	117·1	108·9	100	102·2	96·6	98·9	100	99·7
1984	123·2	116·3	100·1	104·1	90·6	95·7	100	98·9
1989	128·1	123·0	101·1	106·5	83·3	89·9	100	97·5
1994	134·5	128·9	103·0	109·3	77·6	83·5	99·6	95·6
1999	148·6	137·5	105·6	113·4	73·5	77·9	98·5	92·5
2004	168·2	150·9	108·6	118·9	69·3	73·4	96·7	90·9

SOURCE: NIESR estimates.

On the high assumptions, the marriage rates would be at very high levels by the end of the period (table 2.10), reducing the average age of first marriages by two full years.

Table 2.10. *Alternative marriage rates*

Age	1962 actual		2004 High assumptions		2004 Low assumptions	
	Average marriage rates of spinsters per 1000	Spinsters as percentages of all women	Average marriage rates of spinsters per 1000	Spinsters as percentages of all women	Average marriage rates of spinsters per 1000	Spinsters as percentages of all women
15–19	58	*93*	127	*87*	44	*95*
20–24	267	*40*	491	*16*	200	*46*
25–29	179	*14*	259	*3*	134	*18*
30–34	90	*9*	130	*2*	68	*10*
35–39	43	*8*	57	*2*	32	*7*
40–44	24	*9*	35	*1*	18	*6*

SOURCES: *Registrar General's Statistical Review of England and Wales, 1962* (14); NIESR estimates.

Age specific fertility rates would rise most at young ages owing to this downward shift in marriage age (table 2.11) and, if fertilities then stayed constant, the mean completed family size of marriages in 2004 would be about four.

Table 2.11. *Alternative age specific fertility rates*

Per thousand

Age	1962 actual	2004 High assumptions: With higher marriage rates only	2004 High assumptions: With higher marriage and fertility rates	2004 Low assumptions: With lower marriage rates only	2004 Low assumptions: With lower marriage and fertility rates
15–20	39	59	83	29	23
20–24	179	233	326	147	118
25–29	182	177	248	168	134
30–34	105	91	127	94	75
35–39	48	41	57	45	36
40–44	14	12	17	13	10
45–49	1	1	1	1	1

SOURCES: 1962 figures from *Registrar General's Statistical Review of England and Wales, 1962* (15); NIESR estimates.

LOWER BIRTH RATE ASSUMPTIONS

It can also be argued, however, that lower birth rates than those assumed by the Registrars General are quite likely. The hitherto insurmountable difficulties of achieving rapid economic growth, the probability of a rising student population and the possibility of widely used, effective contraception resulting in fewer reluctant marriages, could all lead to lower marriage rates, particularly at young ages. Fertility rates may also be reduced as oral contraceptives become convenient and widespread; the present fertility rise may consist wholly of children brought forward in time, perhaps to allow the wife to work again sooner, and may have no permanent effect on completed family size: alternatively, it may be partly due to the high level of immigration in recent years. In the United States, where the birth rate has followed virtually the same course as here, the trend is now downwards.

In choosing a set of lower assumptions the aim was again to set a reasonable limit to the possible variation from the official assumptions. It was assumed that marriage rates might fall to three-quarters of their present level. This would take them back to the rates of the 1930s for ages over twenty-five, but only to the rates of the early postwar years for ages under twenty-five, for which it was felt that part of the recent rise is probably permanent. Fertility rates were assumed to fall by 20 per cent over the period, as it was not considered likely that any fall would be as great as the possible rise. This would return them to the levels of the early 1950s.

THE CONSEQUENCES OF LOWER BIRTH RATE ASSUMPTIONS

While only one set of low assumptions was used as a basis of projection, a similar population projection would have resulted from many other combinations of lower marriage and fertility rates. The same technique was used to build up this lower projection as for the higher alternative. The results show that the variations from the official projection are considerably less than in the case of the high projection and do not start until after 1974 (tables 2.6, 2.7 and 2.8). This is because the official projection itself assumes an initial fall in the birth rate. By the year 2004, however, the differences from the official projection amount to 9 per cent for the total population, 3 per cent for that of working age and 30 per cent for that under five. The ratio of working-age population to the remainder falls at first, but then rises to 2.4:1 at the end of the period.

The changes in marriage and fertility rates are generally the opposite of those under the high assumptions, and the number of births actually starts to decrease after 1974. The mean completed family size for marriages of 2004 would be just above two, equivalent to the lowest level so far recorded.

COMPARISONS BETWEEN THE PROJECTIONS

The difference between the upper and lower projections builds up to a considerable amount: at about 85 and 65 million respectively, the difference in the total population is some 30 per cent after forty years, although it is only 5 per cent after twenty years (fig. 2.3). In terms of the increase in population compared with 1964[1], the differences are also very large: an increase of 32·8 million on the high assumptions but only 12·7 million on the low. The lower limit diverges from the official current projection later in the period than the

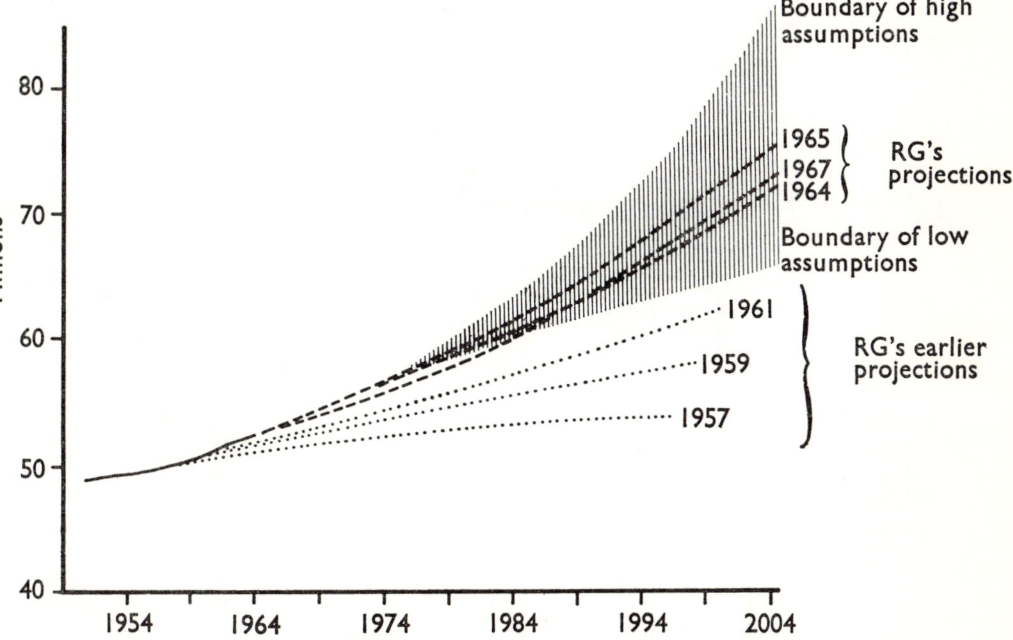

SOURCES: *Registrar General's Quarterly Return for England and Wales* and *for Scotland;* NIESR estimates.

Fig. 2.3. Population growth in Great Britain, 1951–2004

upper limit, because the Registrars General have assumed that there will be an initial fall in fertility. At the end of the period the upper limit suggested diverges from the official 1964 projection by about the same amount as that projection differs from the official projection published in 1957. But in the light of recent experience, the assumed balance of net inward migration of 30,000 a year could vary by 100,000 either way depending on economic conditions, population growth and government policy here and abroad. Variations of this order could reduce the projection of the Registrars General to 67 million or increase it to 75 million.

[1] The Registrars General's projections are usually known by the year of publication, although based on population in the middle of the preceding year. The mid-1964 projection published in 1965 was raised considerably above the mid-1963 projection in the light of the new evidence, but the mid-1966 projection was lower and closer to that published in 1964, see fig. 2.3.

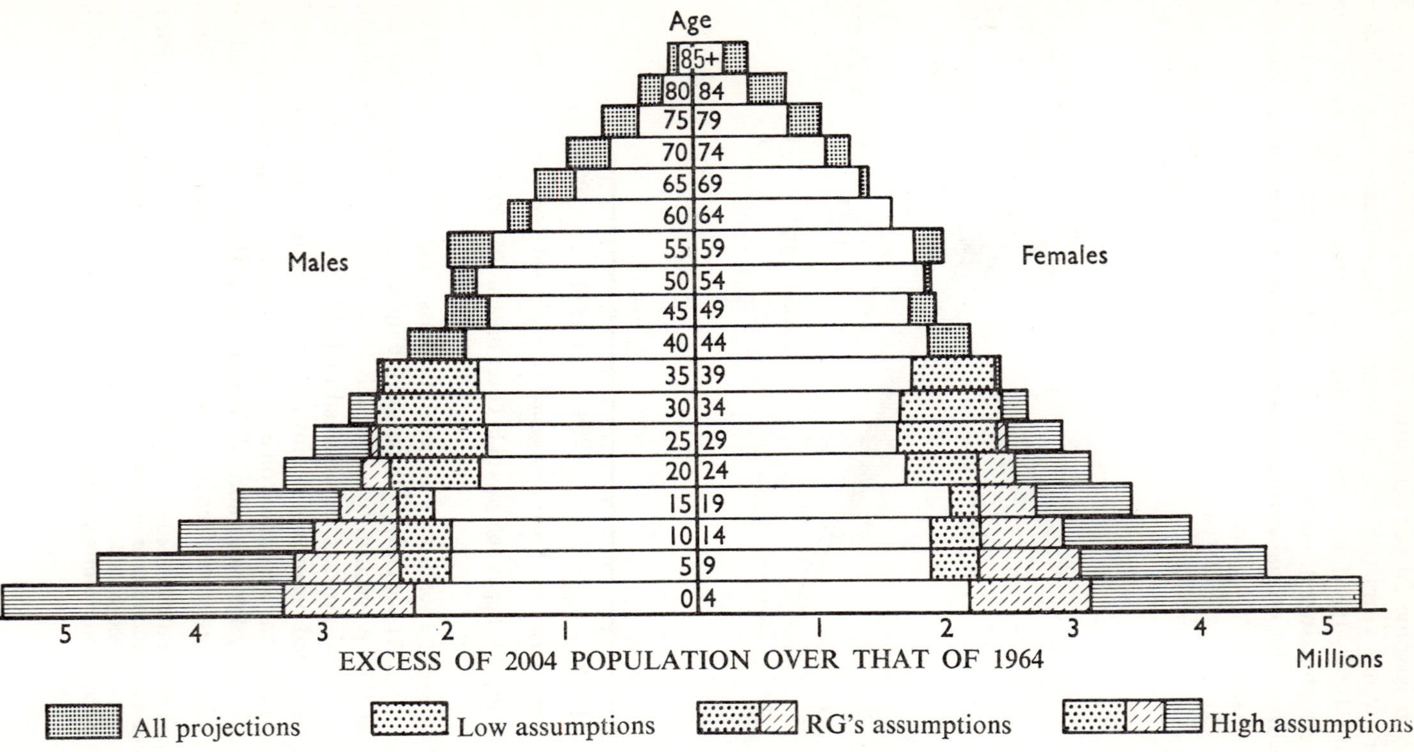

SOURCES: *Registrar General's Quarterly Return for England and Wales* and *for Scotland;* NIESR estimates.

Fig. 2.4. Population of Great Britain: 2004 and 1964 compared

Clearly the projected numbers of people over forty years of age are not affected, as the same age specific rates of death have been used in all the projections. The lower birth rate assumptions have the effect of levelling out the proportions of population in the under-forty age groups, while the higher birth rate assumptions have the effect of greatly extending the relative sizes of the younger age groups (fig. 2.4).

CHAPTER 3

THE REGIONAL POPULATION PROJECTIONS

The discussion so far has been in terms of Great Britain as a whole, but it is also necessary to consider the regional distribution of the population. National population growth is very largely the result of the excess of births over deaths: on the assumptions used by the Registrars General, growth from natural increase is ten times as great as growth from net external migration. On the regional level, however, both internal and external migration are operative and are as important as natural increase. When preparing regional projections it is therefore essential to give considerable attention to future migration levels. Before discussing this, however, there are other significant differences between national and regional populations which affect future growth and should be taken into account.

REGIONAL DIFFERENCES

The population of each region has a slightly different age structure. These differences have a large effect on the projected populations: the older the population structure, the greater the deaths and the fewer the births and hence the smaller the natural increase. So it was essential to take account of existing differences in the age structure of each region. Estimates of the present regional age structures were built up from the 1961 census data and from the more up-to-date information which was available for the Standard Regions (16). It will be evident that while the age structure differences between the most diverse regions do not at first appear to be large, they result in very different natural increase rates (table 3.1).

Inter-regional variations in death rates will not have a great effect on the size of the future population, for the same reasons that limit the effect of temporal changes in national death rates. Moreover, with the long-standing tendency towards greater equality between urban and rural mortality (17), it seems probable that inter-regional differences are declining. For the future, it seems quite possible that this trend will continue. The improvement of the urban environment which is the subject of this whole study will tend to reduce still further the inequalities between regions. For this reason it was decided to ignore inter-regional death rate differences and to use national rates throughout. Even if there were no further reduction in these differences the most anomalous region would not be more than 2 per cent in error after forty years.

The differences in regional birth rates are rather smaller, but have a greater effect on future population. The present position is still the classic one with the lower birth rates in the more prosperous areas. But these differences are currently declining (table 3.2). Now that the previous association between prosperity and low birth rates appears to have gone into reverse, the differences built up in earlier years are being eroded. The present differences may therefore be expected to decline still further.

It is, of course, possible that the trend will continue until the present position is reversed and birth rates in the more prosperous regions are above those

Table 3.1. *Maximum differences in regional age structure*

		Scotland	South West	Scotland as a proportion of South West
		per thousand		%
Distribution for age-groups:	0–4	92	73	*126*
	5–9	83	68	*122*
	10–14	80	70	*114*
	15–19	80	74	*108*
	20–24	65	58	*112*
	25–29	62	55	*113*
	30–34	62	59	*105*
	35–39	64	56	*114*
	40–44	66	63	*105*
	45–49	60	62	*97*
	50–54	65	70	*93*
	55–59	61	70	*87*
	60–64	53	63	*84*
	65–69	40	55	*73*
	70–74	30	43	*70*
	75+	37	61	*61*
Births at 1962 national rates		18·7	16·5	*113*
Deaths at 1962 national rates		10·9	15·1	*72*
Natural increase		7·8	1·4	*557*

SOURCES: *Registrar General's Statistical Review of England and Wales, 1962*; *Registrar General's Statistical Review of Scotland, 1962.*

elsewhere. The Registrars General assume, however, that nationally the increase in birth rates will not continue, despite the probability of rising prosperity. It is also one of the premises of this study that there will be greater equality between regions. It was therefore assumed that the present regional differences would disappear. To have assumed otherwise would have required three separate projections of the birth rate to be made for each region, consistent with the differing levels of prosperity implied by the alternative internal migration patterns adopted. This amount of work could not be justified in view of the rather spurious accuracy such projections would have had. The use of one national rate for all regions could lead to errors of up to 5 per cent in the most anomalous regions after forty years if there were no further reduction in regional differences. All regional projections were therefore developed from the local age structures using national birth and death rates.

Table 3.2. *Relationship between local adjusted birth rate and national birth rate*[a]

Percentages

Standard Region	1955	1956	1957	1958	1959	1960	1961	1962
Northern	112	110	111	111	109	105	102	100
East and West Ridings	101	103	102	101	100	99	100	100
North Western	103	104	104	102	104	102	103	103
North Midland	103	102	102	102	103	102	100	101
Midland	100	100	101	101	99	100	101	100
Eastern	105	104	103	104	103	101	98	98
London and South Eastern	89	88	88	89	90	90	91	92
Southern	107	105	105	105	105	105	103	102
South Western	102	101	101	101	100	100	97	98
Wales I	100	101	101	100	98	98	98	95
Wales II	103	102	99	101	101	102	99	98
Standard deviation	*5·8*	*5·4*	*5·5*	*5·2*	*4·7*	*3·9*	*3·3*	*3·2*

SOURCES: As table 3.1.

[a] The adjustment to local birth rates removes the effect of differences in age structure and the number of women in psychiatric hospitals.

Some idea of the influence which the age structure of the region has upon natural increase is given by assuming that the net gain from external migration would be evenly distributed between the regions. It will be seen that the percentage natural increase on the official assumptions is about three-quarters more in some regions than in others and that the relative differences in the percentage increases are greatest for the low birth rate assumptions (table 3.3).

Table 3.3. *Regional population growth, 1964–2004, as percentages of 1964 population*

	Low assumptions	Registrars General's assumptions	High assumptions
Scotland	31	45	72
North	30	43	70
North West	24	36	62
Pennines	24	37	62
Central	24	37	62
East	26	39	65
North & Central Wales	18	30	54
West	24	36	62
South West	14	26	50
Midlands	29	41	68
East Anglia	21	33	58
South East	21	33	58

SOURCE: NIESR estimates.

INTERNAL MIGRATION[1]

In practice both internal and external migration operate together to produce changes of the same order of magnitude as those from natural increase. It is therefore necessary to consider inter-regional migration in some detail.

Three major tendencies can be identified in recent migration: a net outward movement from the congested centres of conurbations and large cities, a continuation of rural depopulation, and losses from northern and peripheral regions. The first is in many ways the most important. It involves more people than either of the other two and, because it has been a movement of residence without any comparable movement of employment, it is one of the main causes of traffic congestion. It has virtually no direct effect on regional population totals, however, because the continued dependence on the old employment centre ensures that the movement remains within the city region (18). Its indirect effects may be considerable because the living space vacated in the city is partly taken up by newcomers from other regions.

This outward movement from city centres also obscures the second tendency,

[1] Since this section was written additional information has become available. The pattern of regional migration in England and Wales has changed over the last fifteen years: the rate at which the three northern economic planning regions and Wales have been losing population has fallen and the rate of gain has risen most for East Anglia and the South West, as will be seen from the following table of net migration in England and Wales:

Percentages

Economic planning region	1951–6	1956–61	1961–6
Northern	−1·5	−0·9	−1·1
Yorkshire & Humberside	−1·0	−1·3	−0·1
North West	−0·9	−0·9	−0·2
Wales	−1·0	−0·8	+0·2
East Midlands	+0·4	+1·2	+1·4
West Midlands	−0·1	+1·2	+1·2
East Anglia	+0·1	+2·0	+4·0
South West	+0·4	+2·7	+3·1
South East	+0·7	+2·1	+1·0

SOURCE: *Registrar General's Quarterly Return for England and Wales* (19).

More detailed figures for 1961–6 indicate that, whereas the northern regions have been losing population both to other parts of England and Wales and elsewhere, mainly abroad; Wales and the South West have gained from England and Wales but lost to abroad; and the East Midlands and East Anglia have gained from abroad and lost to other parts of England and Wales. Scotland continues to lose population on a substantial scale both to England and Wales and abroad.

During the period 1961–6 there has been no net migration within England and Wales to the South East or West Midlands; increases resulting from migration have arrived from outside sources. Most external migration has gone initially to these two regions, affecting their rate of gain. Most overseas migration to the South East has, in fact, gone to Greater London, which, however, lost population heavily to the rest of the region.

rural depopulation. Many of the districts in which the commuters settle are still classed as rural districts for administrative purposes. Consequently the 1961 Census shows that the rural districts as a whole experienced a net gain from migration of 5 per cent in the preceding decade. This overall figure conceals a pattern of losses in the sparsely inhabited areas and considerable gains in those districts already well populated, which are generally those within city regions. The long-standing tendency for genuinely rural areas to lose population seems therefore to be continuing (20). At the same time many country areas are changing from a rural economic base to direct dependence on remote city employment.

The third aspect of recent migration trends is the gain by the south and midland regions accompanied by losses from the urban north and Scotland. This is a more recent tendency than rural depopulation but one which, because it has become more marked in recent years, is currently the cause of much concern. It is too vast a subject for detailed discussion here and, like the rising birth rate, one which is only partly understood. Differential rates of employment growth are one of the underlying causes, and until recently the whole emphasis of government policy was on providing more employment in the less prosperous areas (21). This is not, however, the complete answer (22), and it is now officially recognized that new roads, better housing and modernization of the infrastructure generally are essential if morale is to be improved in the areas of emigration (23).

FUTURE MIGRATION

The proper distribution of the population in the years ahead has become the subject of wide concern. As the excess of births over deaths is not generally regarded as a proper field for public action, the controversy centres around future internal migration. The net balance is only the end product of much larger flows and counterflows and, unlike international movement, both ends of every flow are within the jurisdiction of the government. It is argued that the government should therefore be able to influence the net gains and losses. However, in most regions there is not as yet any official policy on future migration, though statements have been made on central Scotland and the North East and, with less finality, on the South East.[1]

It was therefore felt that the consequences of alternative patterns of internal migration should be explored, bearing in mind that, at the regional level, migration is as important as natural increase. In the discussion of these alternatives which follows it is assumed that internal migration is superimposed on an even distribution of net external migration. This may be an unrealistic assumption, but it is the only one which can be made until more information is available, from the 1961 Census and other sources, about the origin and destination of

[1] Since this section was written regional policy has been further developed and the incentives to industry developing in the northern and peripheral regions have been greatly strengthened.

external migrants.[1] Since the scale of external migration is not expected to be large the demographic characteristics of internal and external migrants have been assumed to be similar.

Pattern one

The first pattern adopted is based on the continuation of population losses from Scotland and the northern regions, and of gains to the Midlands and the South East. It assumes that the net migration will remain unchanged throughout the period, giving the gains and losses shown in table 3.4 for every five-year period.

Table 3.4. *Migration pattern one*

	Thousands Net migration after every 5 years
Scotland	−150·0
North	−43·5
North West	−62·5
Pennines	−28·5
Central	+26·4
East	−1·7
North & Central Wales	−9·8
West	+22·7
South West	+11·5
Midlands	+32·4
East Anglia	+3·0
South East	+200·0

SOURCE: NIESR estimates.

This pattern can be used as a standard against which the advantages or disadvantages of adopting new policies can be measured. At the same time it is obviously a pattern which could easily occur. It is possible, for example, that the present efforts to cut back the southward movement might succeed only in halting the acceleration which is taking place. Indeed, *The South East Study, 1961–1981* (18) argues that, despite the policy of cutting back the losses from Scotland and the North East, migration to the South East would be a third higher than that assumed here. It would be perfectly feasible, therefore, for actual migration changes to be on a much greater scale than those shown in pattern one.

Pattern two

The second pattern assumes that the losses from the four northern regions will continue as at present, giving the same figures as in pattern one. In the Midlands and the South, however, it assumes that the present pattern of losses from rural

[1] The information available still indicates only where external immigrants first settle.

areas and gains in urban areas will be reversed. In other words the net effect of the southward flow of population would be diverted from the congested conurbations into the more spacious countryside between city regions. In practice it is likely that many of the newcomers from the North would still make for the major urban centres. This gain would then be offset by a large increase in the amount and distance of the outward movement from these centres.

In the rural reception areas this pattern would require a large number of new and expanded towns. It is unlikely that the new country dwellers would take to rural life so, although rural depopulation would be halted, it would be more by a growing urbanization in rural areas than by a genuine revival of rural life. The new communities would, however, differ from those now forming in the countryside within city regions, because the distance from the cities would preclude commuting. In the south of England, for example, the regions which show increased migration under pattern two are East Anglia and the South West, while the South East region shows reduced migration compared to pattern one (table 3.5). The distances envisaged for the outward movement are therefore considerable. The proposed new town in central Wales or the Town and Country Planning Association's proposal for an East Anglian Development Corporation (24) are examples of the type of scheme that would be necessary, though on a very much larger scale.

Under pattern two (table 3.5) migration in the first five years is the same as at present, the same as in pattern one. Thereafter it is steadily altered, except for the northern regions, to reach the levels shown for the 1999–2004 period. The four southern and midland regions where the density is lowest, North and Central Wales, the South West, the East and East Anglia, all show a pronounced swing towards immigration. Indeed, in the last period these four rural regions together would have to absorb as much immigration as the vastly larger Midland and South East regions are now taking. Unless there is a change of this magnitude, however, it would not be possible to halt the inflow to the urban South. As it is, immigration to the southern regions would continue until nearly the end of the century.

Pattern three

Whereas the emphasis in pattern two was mainly on dispersal to relieve congestion (25), it is also quite possible that, with urban renewal taking place on a vast scale, the amount of dispersal will decrease. This possibility is covered by the third pattern. It assumes that Scotland and the north of England will revive, with the present losses from these regions being eliminated by about 1985, after which mounting annual gains develop. In the South and Midlands the rural regions would show increased losses and the urban regions would mirror the North, with the present gains changing to substantial losses by the end of the period.

Pattern three has the advantage that the contrast between urban and rural areas is more strongly maintained than in pattern two. This would be particularly

Table 3.5. *Migration pattern two*

	Persons per acre [a] 1964	Net migration in five-yearly periods (thousands)								Persons per acre [a] 2004
		1964–9	1969–74	1974–9	1979–84	1984–9	1989–94	1994–9	1999–2004	
Northern										
Scotland	*0·27*	−150·0	−150·0	−150·0	−150·0	−150.0	−150·0	−150·0	−150·0	*0·30*
North	*0·69*	−43·5	−43·5	−43·5	−43·5	−43·5	−43·5	−43·5	−43·5	*0·88*
North West	*3·33*	−62·5	−62·5	−62·5	−62·5	−62·5	−62·5	−62·5	−62·5	*4·18*
Pennines	*1·85*	−28·5	−28·5	−28·5	−28·5	−28·5	−28·5	−28·5	−28·5	*2·42*
Total		−284·5	−284·5	−284·5	−284·5	−284·5	−284·5	−284·5	−284·5	
Southern rural										
East	*0·52*	−1·7	+4·5	+10·8	+17·0	+23·3	+29·5	+35·8	+42·0	*0·80*
North & Central Wales	*0·20*	−9·8	−0·9	+8·0	+16·8	+25·7	+34·6	+43·5	+52·3	*0·32*
East Anglia	*0·45*	+3·0	+13·4	+23·8	+34·2	+44·6	+55·0	+65·3	+75·8	*0·79*
South West	*0·45*	+11·5	+19·1	+26·8	+34·4	+42·0	+49·7	+57·4	+64·9	*0·69*
West	*0·86*	+22·7	+32·5	+42·0	+51·8	+61·4	+71·1	+80·8	+90·4	*1·30*
Total		+25·7	+68·6	+111·4	+154·2	+197·0	+239·9	+282·8	+325·4	
Southern urban										
Midlands	*1·51*	+32·4	+26·0	+19·8	+13·5	+7·2	+0·9	−5·3	−11·6	*2·19*
Central	*1·03*	+26·4	+22·0	+17·8	+13·4	+9·1	+4·7	+0·4	−3·9	*1·54*
South East	*2·22*	+200·0	+167·9	+135·5	+103·4	+71·2	+39·0	+6·6	−25·4	*3·11*
Total		+258·8	+215·9	+173·1	+130·3	+87·5	+44·6	+1·7	−40·9	

SOURCE: NIESR estimates.

[a] Persons per acre relates to all land and inland water.

valuable in the South where the contrast is less marked geographically. Valuable as this would be for the city dwellers, it would bring little benefit to the rural areas. With the reversal of migration from the North and a massive programme of urban renewal, the amount of overspill from the conurbations would be much reduced and rural areas would very probably show large migration losses.

The figures show that pattern three represents a more marked revival of the North than any official policy at present assumes (table 3.6). Whereas the White Papers on central Scotland and the North East aim no higher than cutting back the present losses, pattern three envisages large-scale migration to the North from 1985 onwards. Changes on this scale are essential if the losses suffered by the North in the first half of the period are to be fully offset in the second half. To go further than this and attempt to achieve a net migration gain in the North over the period as a whole would require migration levels by the end of the period which it would be difficult for the northern regions to absorb (see figs. 3.1 and 3.2). Migration losses from the South would also have to be heavier, with the risk of producing the same problems as now afflict the North.

CHARACTERISTICS OF THE MIGRANTS

The effects of the three alternative patterns of internal migration which have been adopted, will depend on the characteristics of the migrants.[1]

Any assumptions about the age, sex and marital composition of the net migration balance are even more arbitrary than those about the amount of net migration. This is because, even if each migration flow were regular in itself, it would need only a slight variation in the strength of different flows to produce a drastic alteration in the net balance. A new table recently published by the Registrar General, Appendix C to the *Registrar General's Quarterly Return for England and Wales*, illustrates the point. It shows that, while the total movement into and out of England and Wales consisted of 51 per cent males and 49 per cent females, when the outward movement is deducted from the inward movement the net balance consists of 93 per cent males and 7 per cent females: or again, there was a net inward movement of both single and married women from the rest of the United Kingdom and a net outward movement of both categories to the rest of the world, but taken together they give an inward movement of single women and an outward movement of married women. Trying to estimate the composition of the net migration balance is therefore rather like trying to say whether the number of green vans in a town centre is going up or down while traffic of all descriptions is continually entering and leaving on numerous roads.

Nevertheless an estimate has to be made because it profoundly affects the consequences of migration. At least it can be said that, while any projection

[1] It will be seen from the additional information given in previous footnotes about the current levels of migration that the recent trends are not unlike those assumed in pattern two.

Table 3.6. *Migration pattern three*

	Persons per acre [a] 1964	Net migration in five-yearly periods (thousands)								Persons per acre [a] 2004
		1964–9	1969–74	1974–9	1979–84	1984–9	1989–94	1994–9	1999–2004	
Northern										
Scotland	*0·27*	−150·0	−112·5	−75·0	−37·5	—	+37·5	+75·0	+112·5	*0·36*
North	*0·69*	−43·5	−22·2	−0·9	+20·3	+41·6	+62·8	+84·1	+105·4	*1·03*
North West	*3·33*	−62·5	−42·1	−21·8	−1·4	+18·9	+39·3	+59·7	+80·1	*4·54*
Pennines	*1·85*	−28·5	−15·0	−1·5	+12·1	+25·7	+39·2	+52·7	+66·2	*2·58*
Total		−284·5	−191·8	−99·2	−6·5	+86·2	+178·8	+271·5	+364·2	
Southern rural										
East	*0·52*	−1·7	−2·6	−3·4	−4·3	−5·2	−6·1	−6·9	−7·8	*0·70*
North & Central Wales	*0·20*	−9·8	−10·9	−11·9	−13·0	−14·1	−15·2	−16·2	−17·3	*0·21*
East Anglia	*0·45*	+3·0	−0·8	−4·7	−8·5	−12·3	−16·1	−20·0	−23·8	*0·55*
South West	*0·45*	+11·5	+3·5	−4·5	−12·5	−20·5	−28·5	−36·5	−44·5	*0·51*
West	*0·86*	+22·7	+15·3	+7·9	+0·5	−6·9	−14·3	−21·7	−29·1	*1·17*
Total		+25·7	+4·5	−16·6	−37·8	−59·0	−80·2	−101·3	−122·5	
Southern urban										
Midlands	*1·51*	+32·4	+23·3	+14·1	+5·0	−4·2	−13·3	−22·5	−31·6	*2·15*
Central	*1·03*	+26·4	+20·6	+14·9	+9·1	+3·4	−2·3	−8·1	−13·9	*1·49*
South East	*2·22*	+200·0	+143·4	+86·8	+30·2	−26·4	−83·0	−139·6	−196·2	*3·00*
Total		+258·8	+187·3	+115·8	+44·3	−27·2	−98·6	−170·2	−241·7	

SOURCE: NIESR estimates.

[a] Persons per acre relates to all land and inland water.

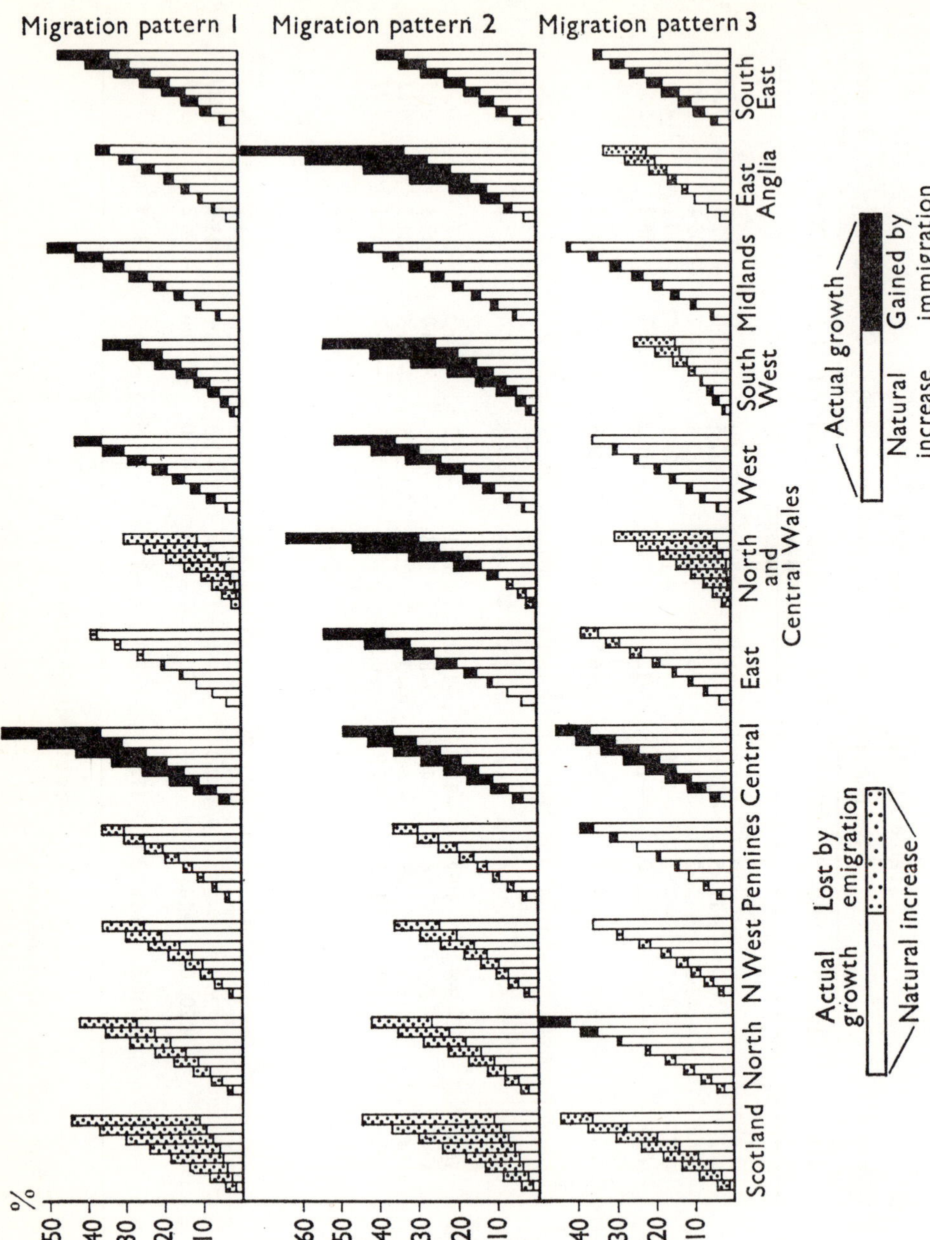

Note: The eight columns for each region refer to the periods: 1964–9, 1969–74, 1974–9, 1979–84, 1984–9, 1989–94 1994–9, 1999–2004.

SOURCE: NIESR estimates.

Fig. 3.1. The contribution of net migration to cumulative population growth

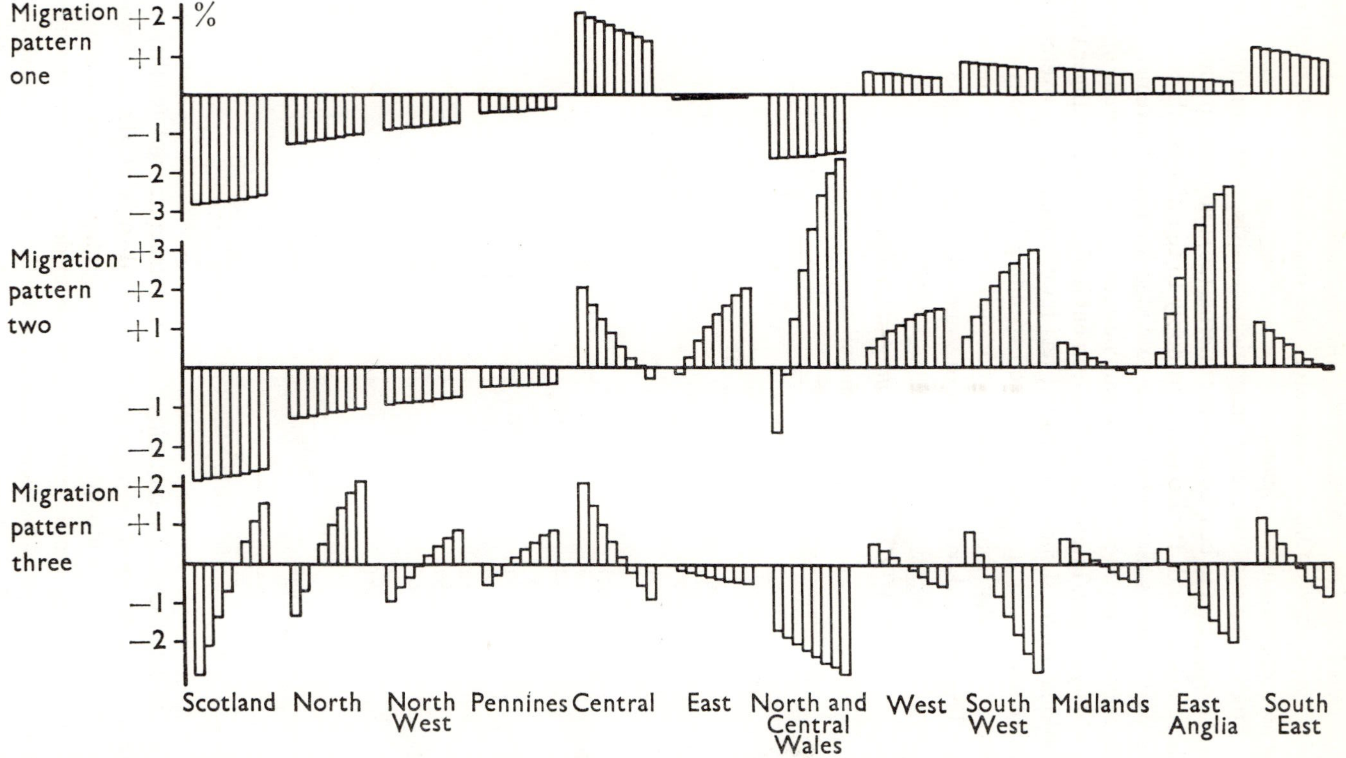

Note: The eight columns for each region refer to the periods: 1964–9, 1969–74, 1974–9, 1979–84, 1984–9, 1989–94, 1994–9, 1999–2004.

SOURCE: NIESR estimates.

Fig. 3.2. Net migration in each quinquennium as a percentage of population

assumptions selected may be widely astray, the characteristic which has the greatest effect, age composition, is fortunately the one about which most is known and which appears most regular.

Numerous studies have shown that migration consists predominantly of young adults. This appears to be true both for internal (26) and international (27) movement, here and abroad. It also seems to apply to the nineteenth century, and to net as well as gross movements. The peak age for male movement lies in the 15–24 age group who after a decade would be aged 25–34; the female movement is somewhat younger. Inter-regional movement is likely to be younger than either international or local movement, as it has fewer obstacles to overcome than the former and is less influenced by the expanding housing needs of the latter. The age and sex distribution that was adopted for all internal migration (table 3.7) can be compared with that found in some other studies (fig. 3.3).

Table 3.7. *Age composition of net migration*

Age	Net migration after five years, per 1000	
	Males	Females
0–4	30	30
5–9	20	18
10–14	10	26
15–19	40	100
20–24	130	120
25–29	95	60
30–34	50	35
35–39	30	23
40–44	20	16
45–49	14	12
50–54	11	10
55–59	10	10
60–64	10	10
65–69	10	10
70–74	10	10
75+	10	10
Total	500	500

SOURCE: NIESR estimates.

Far less is known about the mortality, marital structure and fertility of migrants. Here again, however, some assumptions had to be made, so it was assumed that the age specific mortality of the net migration balance would be the same as for the rest of the population. There is evidence that more single women migrate than married women, at least over the distance involved in inter-regional migration (28). Though they may subsequently marry, there

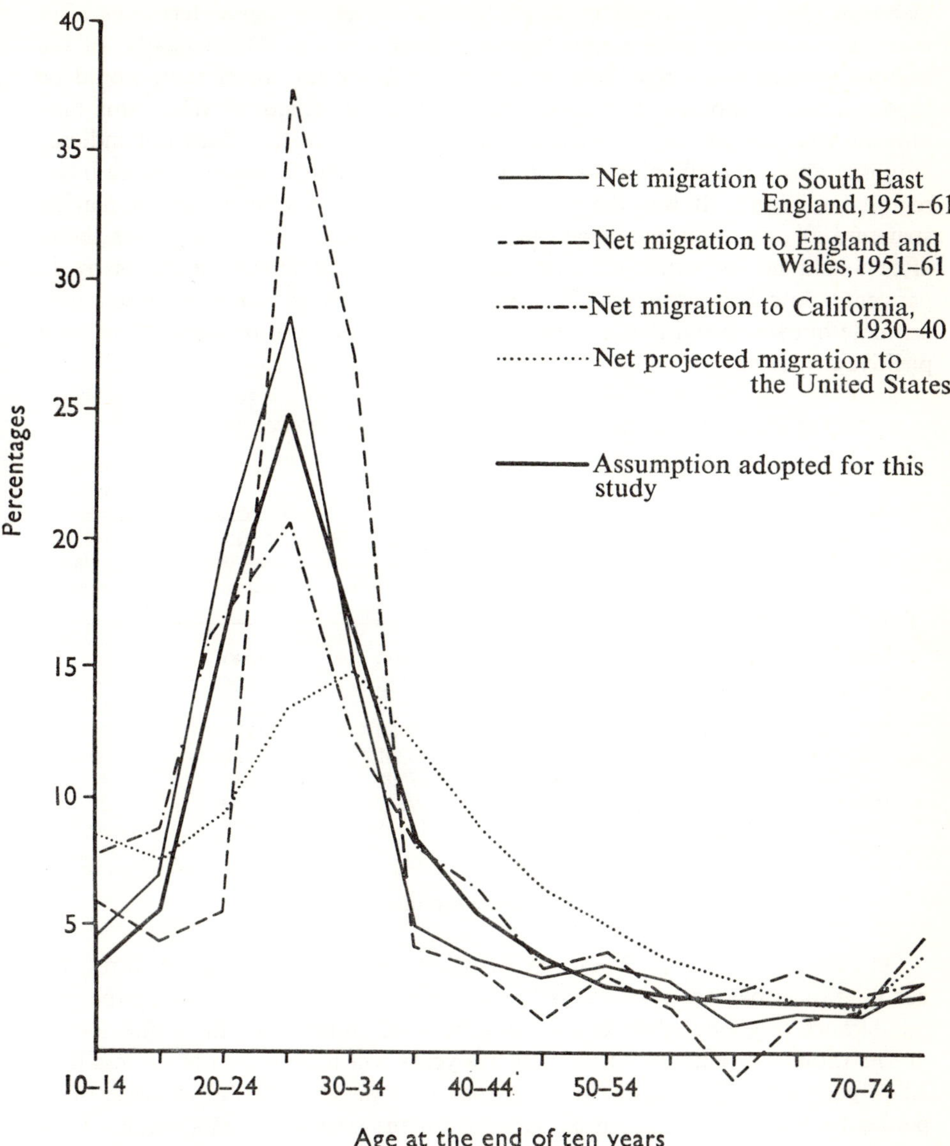

SOURCES: British figures calculated from census reports and vital statistics; United States figures from Siegel, Zitter and Akers, *Projections of the Population of the United States by Age and Sex, 1964–85 with extension to 2010.* (27); Californian figures from *The Population of California* (29).

Fig. 3.3. Age distribution of net male migration over a decade

would be some permanent reduction in fertility due to the postponement of marriage (30), which might or might not be offset by higher fertilities after marriage. However, in the new towns around London, where nearly all the married women are recent migrants, birth rates are no higher than would be expected for a population of that age and marital structure. While this may indicate that the fertility of married migrants is normal, it does not indicate anything about the effect of the high proportion of single women among inter-regional migrants. It was therefore assumed that the joint effects of marital structure at migration, marriage rates after migration and fertility rates thereafter would be to reduce the age specific fertility of female migrants by 10 per cent below that of the rest of the population. This may well be a conservative estimate but it was felt that a greater reduction should not be assumed without positive evidence.

Table 3.8. *The growth of migration per 1000 in each five years*

	Accumulated migration	Accumulated natural increases resulting from migration	Total accumulated changes from migration	Increases in each five-year period	Natural increases as percentages of accumulated changes
1964–9	1000	0	1000	1000	*0*
1969–74	2000	126	2126	1126	*6*
1974–9	3000	384	3384	1258	*11*
1979–84	4000	760	4760	1376	*16*
1984–9	5000	1261	6261	1501	*20*
1989–94	6000	1898	7898	1637	*24*
1994–9	7000	2647	9647	1749	*27*
1999–2004	8000	3455	11455	1808	*30*

SOURCE: NIESR estimates.

On these assumptions about age structure, birth rates and death rates, the net migration balance shows a very rapid natural increase. Owing to the preponderance of young adult females and the small number of old people, a total of one thousand migrants in the first five years will have grown to no less than 1,800 people by the end of the forty-year period. This natural increase of 80 per cent compares with about 33 per cent for the population as a whole on the official assumptions.

The result is that, when migration is taking place at a constant rate, as assumed for each region under pattern one for example, the joint effect of this migration and the subsequent natural increase grows at an accelerating rate (table 3.8). For this reason it is necessary for the present levels of migration to be more than reversed by the end of the period if the net effect over forty years is to be zero.

Table 3.9. *Net change from migration,*[a] *North West region, migration pattern three*

Thousands

Age	1969		1974		1979		1984		1989		1994		1999		2004	
	M	F	M	F	M	F	M	F	M	F	M	F	M	F	M	F
0–4	−1·9	−1·9	−6·0	−5·8	−8·8	−8·4	−9·7	−9·2	−9·2	−8·7	−7·4	−7·0	−3·3	−3·1	+2·8	+2·7
5–9	−1·3	−1·1	−2·7	−2·6	−6·5	−6·2	−8·8	−8·4	−9·3	−8·9	−8·5	−8·0	−6·2	−5·9	−1·7	−1·6
10–14	−0·6	−1·6	−1·7	−2·2	−2·9	−3·2	−6·5	−6·2	−8·6	−7·9	−8·9	−7·8	−7·8	−6·4	−5·4	−3·8
15–19	−2·5	−6·3	−2·3	−5·8	−2·5	−4·4	−3·0	−3·3	−5·7	−4·3	−7·1	−4·0	−6·6	−1·9	−4·7	+1·6
20–24	−8·1	−7·6	−8·0	−11·4	−5·1	−8·5	−2·7	−4·6	−0·5	−1·1	−0·6	+0·4	+0·7	+3·1	+3·8	+7·7
25–29	−5·9	−3·8	−12·2	−10·1	−10·1	−12·8	−5·3	−8·7	−0·9	−3·5	+3·2	+1·3	+5·0	+4·0	+8·3	+8·0
30–34	−3·1	−2·2	−8·1	−5·2	−13·3	−10·9	−10·2	−12·9	−4·4	−8·0	+1·0	−2·1	+6·2	+3·4	+9·1	+6·8
35–39	−1·9	−1·4	−4·4	−3·2	−8·7	−5·7	−13·3	−10·9	−9·6	−12·4	−3·2	−7·1	+2·8	−0·8	+8·6	+5·2
40–44	−1·3	−1·0	−2·7	−2·1	−4·8	−3·5	−8·7	−5·7	−12·9	−10·6	−8·8	−11·8	−2·0	−6·2	+4·4	+0·5
45–49	−0·9	−0·8	−1·8	−1·5	−3·0	−2·3	−4·7	−3·5	−8·3	−5·5	−12·2	−10·0	−7·9	−11·0	−0·9	−5·2
50–54	−0·7	−0·6	−1·3	−1·2	−2·0	−1·7	−2·9	−2·3	−4·4	−3·2	−7·7	−5·0	−11·2	−9·3	−6·8	−10·1
55–59	−0·6	−0·6	−1·1	−1·0	−1·5	−1·3	−1·9	−1·7	−2·6	−2·1	−3·8	−2·8	−6·8	−4·3	−10·0	−8·3
60–64	−0·6	−0·6	−1·0	−1·0	−1·2	−1·2	−1·3	−1·3	−1·6	−1·4	−2·0	−1·6	−2·9	−2·1	−5·5	−3·4
65–69	−0·6	−0·6	−1·0	−1·0	−1·1	−1·2	−1·0	−1·1	−1·0	−1·0	−1·0	−0·9	−1·1	−0·9	−1·8	−1·2
70–74	−0·6	−0·6	−0·9	−1·0	−1·0	−1·1	−0·8	−1·0	−0·6	−0·8	−0·4	−0·5	−0·2	−0·2	−0·1	—
75+	−0·6	−0·6	−1·1	−1·2	−1·3	−1·6	−1·3	−1·7	−1·0	−1·6	−0·5	−1·1	+0·1	−0·4	+0·7	+0·4
Total	−31·2	−31·3	−56·3	−56·3	−73·8	−74·0	−82·1	−82·5	−80·6	−81·0	−67·9	−68·0	−41·2	−42·0	+0·8	−0·7

SOURCE: NIESR estimates.

[a] Accumulated effects.

The case of the North West region under pattern three can be taken as an example (table 3.9). Migration starts at −62,500 in 1964–9 (table 3.6), passes zero in 1982 and reaches 80,100 by the end of the period. Although there is a net gain of 70,200 migrants over the period this is fully offset by the natural increases lost with the early emigrants: the net effect after forty years is therefore negligible, although individual age groups are altered.

THE EFFECT OF ALTERNATIVE MIGRATION PATTERNS

The influence of the natural increase in each migration pattern makes it difficult to see at a glance what the effect of the alternatives will be. The cumulative effect of the three patterns is therefore shown in tables 3.10, 3.11 and 3.12.

Pattern one would give a steady acceleration in the influence of migration in every region, with just under 60 per cent of the final total occurring in the second twenty years. Scotland and the South East region would show the largest absolute losses and gains, though in proportion to population the gain in the small Central region would be greater than that in the South East.

The second pattern shows the same losses in the North. In southern rural regions, however, there would be a very rapid build up of migration in the second half of the period, more than three-quarters of the total gain being in these years. This would produce some very large rates of gain, particularly in East Anglia and North and Central Wales. In the southern urban regions, on the other hand, the growth of migration would fall off in the later years, though a sizeable total would still be reached in the South East.

Pattern three assumes that, after forty years, there would be no overall effect of migration in Scotland and the northern regions. By 1984 there would be a loss of a full three-quarters of a million people, however; and a northward flow of over a third of a million in the last five years would be necessary to offset the effect of early losses (table 3.6). In the South the rural regions would show a loss of nearly half a million people, almost all of which would occur in the second half of the period. The urban regions would show a modest gain, though they too would reach far higher levels at an intermediate date. In general the totals of net migration by regions in pattern three are smaller by 2004 than on either of the other alternatives.

REGIONAL POPULATIONS

The addition of these three migration patterns to the three regional projections prepared on the assumption of no internal migration gives nine alternatives for each region (appendix 3). All the population projections are of home population[1] for the period mid-year 1963 to mid-year 2003, as this was the basis on which the projections were originally made. For the purposes of this study the figures were then modified to run from 31 March 1964 by applying a constant

[1] That is people actually in the country, excluding Forces serving abroad.

Table 3.10. *The effects of migration pattern one*[a]

Thousands

	1969	1974	1979	1984	1989	1994	1999	2004
Northern								
Scotland	−150·0	−319·3	−507·6	−714·2	−939·1	−1184·8	−1447·0	−1719·0
North	−43·5	−92·5	−147·0	−206·9	−272·3	−343·6	−419·3	−498·0
North West	−62·5	−132·7	−211·5	−297·4	−391·2	−493·6	−603·1	−716·0
Pennines	−28·5	−60·7	−96·3	−135·5	−178·1	−225·2	−275·2	−326·0
Total	−284·5	−605·2	−962·4	−1354·0	−1780·7	−2247·2	−2744·6	−3259·0
Southern rural								
East	−1·7	−3·4	−5·7	−8·0	−10·8	−13·4	−16·4	−19·8
North & Central Wales	−9·8	−20·9	−33·2	−46·4	−61·4	−77·3	−94·8	−112·5
East Anglia	+3·0	+6·7	+10·1	+14·2	+18·7	+23·9	+28·9	+34·3
South West	+11·5	+24·4	+39·0	+54·9	+71·9	+90·5	+110·5	+131·7
West	+22·7	+48·1	+76·8	+107·8	+142·1	+179·6	+219·1	+259·8
Total	+25·7	+54·9	+87·0	+122·5	+160·5	+203·3	+247·3	+293·5
Southern urban								
Midlands	+32·4	+68·9	+109·4	+154·0	+202·9	+255·8	+312·9	+371·1
Central	+26·4	+56·0	+89·3	+125·7	+165·2	+208·4	+254·5	+302·4
South East	+200·0	+425·4	+676·7	+951·8	+1252·5	+1579·7	+1929·9	+2292·0
Total	+258·8	+550·3	+875·4	+1231·5	+1620·6	+2043·9	+2497·3	+2965·5

SOURCE: NIESR estimates.

[a] Accumulated total effects of migration and the natural increase of migration.

Table 3.11. *The effects of migration pattern two*[a]

Thousands

	1969	1974	1979	1984	1989	1994	1999	2004
Northern								
Scotland	−150·0	−319·3	−507·6	−714·2	−939·1	−1184·8	−1447·0	−1719·0
North	−43·5	−92·5	−147·0	−206·9	−272·3	−343·6	−419·3	−498·0
North West	−62·5	−132·7	−211·5	−297·4	−391·2	−493·6	−603·1	−716·0
Pennines	−28·5	−60·7	−96·3	−135·5	−178·1	−225·2	−275·2	−326·0
Total	−284·5	−605·2	−962·4	−1354·0	−1780·7	−2247·2	−2744·6	−3259·0
Southern rural								
East	−1·7	+2·4	+13·1	+32·5	+59·6	+96·0	+143·0	+200·0
North & Central Wales	−9·8	−11·7	−5·3	+11·0	+38·8	+78·4	+131·8	+200·0
East Anglia	+3·0	+17·3	+42·7	+81·8	+135·9	+206·0	+293·9	+400·0
South West	+11·5	+32·1	+63·1	+104·5	+158·1	+224·8	+305·7	+400·0
West	+22·7	+57·7	+106·9	+171·0	+251·1	+349·3	+465·8	+600·0
Total	+25·7	+97·8	+220·5	+400·8	+643·5	+954·5	+1340·2	+1800·0
Southern urban								
Midlands	+32·4	+62·7	+89·8	+113·3	+131·8	+145·2	+152·0	+150·0
Central	+26·4	+51·6	+75·7	+97·7	+116·5	+132·7	+144·2	+150·0
South East	+200·0	+393·1	+576·4	+742·2	+888·9	+1014·8	+1108·2	+1159·0
Total	+258·8	+507·4	+741·9	+953·2	+1137·2	+1292·7	+1404·4	+1459·0

SOURCE: NIESR estimates.

[a] Accumulated total effects of migration and the natural increase of migration.

Table 3.12. *The effects of migration pattern three*[a]

Thousands

	1969	1974	1979	1984	1989	1994	1999	2004
Northern								
Scotland	−150·0	−281·4	−390·4	−470·5	−516·8	−526·6	−490·5	−400·0
North	−43·5	−71·2	−80·5	−68·8	−32·5	+29·8	+122·9	+250·0
North West	−62·5	−112·5	−147·8	−164·6	−161·7	−135·9	−83·2	—
Pennines	−28·5	−46·9	−54·1	−47·5	−26·1	+12·3	+70·5	+150·0
Total	−284·5	−512·0	−672·8	−751·4	−737·1	−620·4	−380·3	—
Southern rural								
East	−1·7	−4·3	−8·6	−13·6	−20·6	−28·6	−38·7	−50·0
North & Central Wales	−9·8	−21·8	−36·7	−53·8	−73·6	−96·4	−121·9	−150·0
East Anglia	+3·0	+2·3	−1·6	−10·6	−24·1	−43·4	−68·4	−100·0
South West	+11·5	+16·3	+13·9	+2·9	−18·3	−49·6	−93·5	−150·0
West	+22·7	+40·8	+53·6	+60·0	+59·0	+49·2	+30·6	—
Total	+25·7	+33·3	+20·6	−15·1	−77·6	−168·8	−291·9	−450·0
Southern urban								
Midlands	+32·4	+59·8	+81·1	+94·8	+99·8	+95·6	+79·6	+50·0
Central	+26·4	+50·1	+71·4	+88·2	+100·8	+107·6	+107·6	+100·0
South East	+200·0	+368·8	+499·7	+583·5	+614·1	+586·0	+485·0	+300·0
Total	+258·8	+478·7	+652·2	+766·5	+814·7	+789·2	+672·2	+450·0

SOURCE: NIESR estimates.

[a] Accumulated total effects of migration and the natural increase of migration.

Table 3.13. *Population increases by regions, 1964–2004*

Percentages

	Low birth rate assumptions			Registrars General's assumptions			High birth rate assumptions		
	Migration pattern 1	Migration pattern 2	Migration pattern 3	Migration pattern 1	Migration pattern 2	Migration pattern 3	Migration pattern 1	Migration pattern 2	Migration pattern 3
Northern									
Scotland	−1·9	−1·9	23·4	11·4	11·4	36·7	38·9	38·9	64·3
North	14·2	14·2	36·9	27·3	27·3	50·0	54·3	54·3	77·0
North West	13·0	13·0	23·6	25·5	25·5	36·1	51·3	51·3	62·0
Pennines	18·0	18·0	26·6	30·4	30·4	39·0	56·1	56·1	64·8
Total	10·8	10·8	26·4	23·6	23·6	39·2	50·0	50·0	65·7
Southern rural									
East	24·4	41·1	22·1	37·1	53·7	34·8	63·3	79·9	61·0
North & Central Wales	−0·6	51·7	−6·9	11·2	63·5	5·0	35·6	88·0	29·4
East Anglia	24·7	63·3	10·6	36·7	75·3	22·5	61·6	100·2	47·4
South West	23·6	42·5	3·7	35·0	54·0	15·2	58·7	77·6	38·8
West	30·2	38·7	23·7	42·6	51·1	36·1	68·1	76·6	61·6
Total	25·3	43·5	16·3	37·5	55·7	28·4	62·6	80·8	53·6
Southern urban									
Midlands	35·9	31·4	29·4	48·8	44·3	42·2	75·4	70·8	68·8
Central	49·8	36·9	32·6	62·2	49·3	45·0	87·9	75·0	70·7
South East	34·5	27·9	22·8	46·5	39·9	34·9	71·5	64·9	59·9
Total	35·6	29·1	24·7	47·8	41·3	37·0	73·1	66·7	62·3

SOURCE: NIESR estimates.

Table 3.14. *Population increases by regions, 1964-2004*

Thousands

	Low birth rate assumptions			Registrars General's assumptions			High birth rate assumptions		
	Migration pattern 1	Migration pattern 2	Migration pattern 3	Migration pattern 3	Migration pattern 2	Migration pattern 3	Migration pattern 1	Migration pattern 2	Migration pattern 3
Northern									
Scotland	−102·6	−102·6	1219·0	594·4	594·4	1916·0	2031·1	2031·1	3352·8
North	468·3	468·3	1217·6	899·2	899·2	1648·5	1790·9	1790·9	2540·1
North West	873·4	873·4	1590·6	1716·8	1716·8	2434·1	3459·6	3459·6	4176·8
Pennines	997·1	997·1	1473·7	1685·9	1685·9	2162·6	3111·0	3111·0	3587·7
Total	2236·2	2236·2	5500·9	4896·3	4896·3	8161·2	10392·6	10392·6	13657·4
Southern rural									
East	325·1	547·0	294·4	493·8	715·7	463·1	842·7	1064·6	812·0
North & Central Wales	−3·4	310·3	−41·0	67·6	381·3	30·0	214·2	527·9	176·6
East Anglia	235·3	603·3	99·7	350·0	718·1	214·5	587·1	955·2	451·5
South West	337·0	607·8	53·1	500·2	771·0	216·4	838·4	1109·2	554·6
West	1221·0	1565·1	957·5	1721·5	2065·6	1494·5	2755·2	3099·3	2491·7
Total	2115·0	3633·5	1363·7	3133·1	4651·7	2418·5	5237·6	6756·2	4486·4
Southern urban									
Midlands	1770·9	1548·6	1447·5	2402·0	2179·7	2078·6	3709·5	3487·2	3386·1
Central	596·0	441·5	390·3	744·7	585·1	538·9	1052·2	897·6	846·4
South East	5974·6	4828·8	3960·3	8064·5	6918·6	6050·2	12392·8	11246·9	10378·5
Total	8341·5	6818·9	5798·1	11211·2	9683·4	8667·7	17154·5	15631·7	14611·0

SOURCE: NIESR estimates.

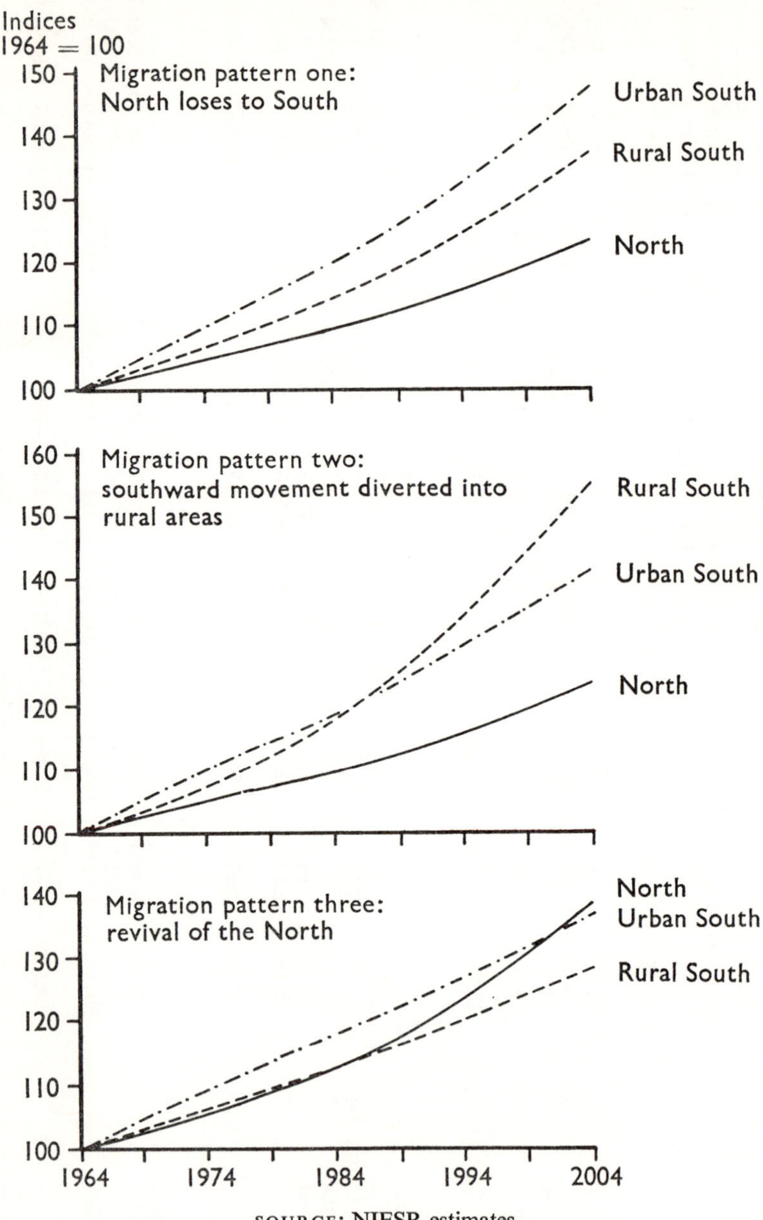

SOURCE: NIESR estimates.

Fig. 3.4. Future population growth in three divisions of Britain: effect of alternative patterns of migration

multiplier to each regional projection. For this reason the percentage increases shown in table 3.13 are unaltered whichever period is considered.

Out of a possible 108 alternative projections, 104 show an increase (table 3.14). Only if the birth rate fell would there be any regions which did not increase their population. With a rising birth rate some regional populations might almost double in size. For comparison, the present rate of growth in Britain would, if continued, give an increase of some 33 per cent in forty years. Some acceleration is forecast, however, so that the projected growth on the official assumptions is 37 per cent.

All the regional projections also show an accelerating rate of growth on the official and the high assumptions, despite a rapid build up of migration loss in some cases. On the low assumptions the general picture is of a declining rate of growth, though migration to the southern rural regions under pattern two is sufficient to offset this and give accelerating growth.

The effect of the different birth rate assumptions is usually rather greater than the effect of the alternative migration patterns. This is particularly marked in the southern urban regions, but does not apply to Wales, East Anglia and the South West.

When the regional projected populations are broken down into age groups (appendix 3) these changes are more marked. At ages under forty where both sets of alternatives operate, the effect of different birth rates is much the greater. At the extremes, the number of children under fifteen can either be trebled or reduced to 80 per cent by the end of the period. At ages over sixty the range is much smaller, varying from plus 40 per cent to minus 10 per cent.

SUMMARY OF REGIONAL CHANGES

On the basis of migration pattern one, Scotland would lose 1·7 million people by migration over the forty-year period and the northern regions 1·5 million; this population would be gained by the South and Midlands, 2·3 million by the South East. As a result, by the end of the period the population of the urban South would have increased by 50 per cent and of the North by only 25 per cent (fig. 3.4).

Under migration pattern two, the losses from Scotland and the northern regions would be the same, but only just over a million would be gained by the South East, the balance being spread over the rural South, which would increase its population by 55 per cent, and the urban South by 40 per cent.

Under migration pattern three, Scotland would lose only 400,000 people by migration, which would be offset by a balancing gain in the northern regions; there would be small losses from the rural regions and balancing gains by the urban regions of the South; the South East would gain only 300,000. As a result the urban South and the North would each increase their population by 40 per cent and the rural South by 30 per cent.

While, under each of the three migration patterns, one or two regions show a decline of population over the period, generally the migration losses are far less than the natural increase. The rate of natural increase implied by the 1964 projection of the Registrars General is such that each of the three groups of regions is likely to obtain at least 20 per cent more population whichever pattern of internal migration is assumed. The result of reversing the present migration trend would be to even out the percentage gains.

PART 2

THE ESTIMATION OF HOUSING NEEDS AND COSTS

CHAPTER 4

THE HOUSING STUDIES

It will be helpful to have a general picture of the range of studies covered in this volume of the book, and of the way they are related, before considering each individually. Their relationship can perhaps best be appreciated visually (fig. 4.1).

As explained earlier, projections of the natural growth of population were first prepared for each region and these were combined with patterns of internal migration to provide regional projections. These figures were then used as a basis for estimating the household formation in each region, and these were used in turn as a basis for calculating the numbers of dwellings of each size required at each quinquennial date for each regional programme.

The second stage was to adjust the housing data given in the 1961 Census for changes resulting from constructions, demolitions and alterations between the census date and March 1964. The results were analysed to provide size distributions of dwellings in each region and the proportion without the basic census services. Census data, available from 1801 to 1961, and data from other sources were analysed to enable the regional distributions to be divided into age groups. Field studies were carried out to find the relationship between age, size and census services of dwellings, and their condition and other amenities. These relationships were then applied to enable the regional distributions to be further broken down by condition and amenity. The resulting classifications were used to estimate the rates at which the housing stocks would be demolished.

The third stage was to compare regionally, at each quinquennial date, the estimates of dwellings required for each size with the corresponding figures for the stocks. The differences represented the needs for additional dwellings. Studies were made of the construction costs of dwellings, garages, roads and public utilities, and of densities of dwellings. Estimates were developed of the costs and of the way they were affected by size, standards, form of development and region. These figures were applied to the numbers of dwellings required to obtain the total costs. The effect of form on land use was studied, and also the density of development of dwellings to be demolished. These figures were applied to the estimates of constructions and demolitions to obtain estimates of land use.

The fourth stage was to estimate the costs of improving the stock of dwellings and their environment prior to replacement. Studies were made of the costs of making good arrears of maintenance, of adding missing services, of building garages and improving housing environments. The costs were related to the size, age, standard, conditions and future life of the dwellings. The returns from expenditure on improvement were compared with the returns from expenditure on new dwellings. The costs of improving the stock were then estimated, for that part of the stock for which improvement was worthwhile, by applying the costs

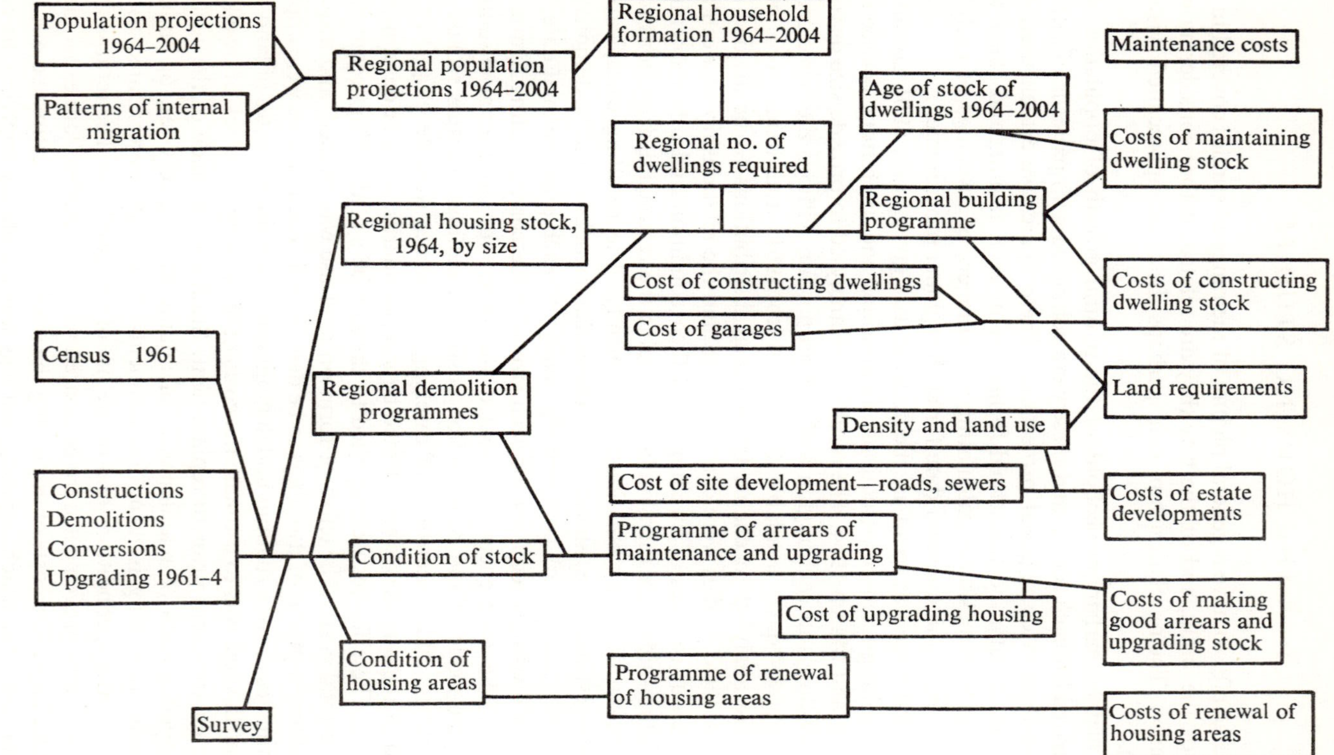

Fig. 4.1. Network diagram of the programme used to estimate housing costs

to the stocks in relation to their measured attributes and their lives as determined by the demolition programmes.

The fifth stage was to calculate the costs of maintenance. Studies of maintenance indicated a relationship between maintenance costs and age. The age of the stock at each quinquennial date was obtained by adjusting the age distribution in 1964 for constructions and demolitions. The total maintenance costs were then obtained by applying the age-related costs to the age distributions of the stocks.

Finally, the various types of costs were summed to provide estimates of the resources required for the alternative programmes. These were analysed in relation to the resources required for other forms of urban development, the probable capacity of the construction industry and the availability of finance.

In this part of the book a description is given of the basic processes of projecting household formation, estimating housing space standards, densities, construction and maintenance costs and estimating the size and condition of the stock. This information is used to examine the economics of different types of housing and housing improvement.

CHAPTER 5

HOUSEHOLDS AND DWELLINGS

The first use made of the figures from the regional population projections (chapter 3) was to obtain estimates of household sizes, which were in turn used as a basis for estimating the needs for dwellings of various sizes. The household calculations were made in the usual way by applying headship rates to selected age and marital groups. The dwellings needed were then derived from the households, using the 1961 Census relationship of dwellings to households modified by the elimination of overcrowding and under-occupation.

MARITAL STRUCTURE

Married men and older women are more likely to be the heads of households than single or young people. For this reason it is essential to classify the population by age and marital condition before estimating the number of separate households that are expected to be formed.

A breakdown by age and sex was already available in the population projections, which also embody alternative assumptions about future female marriage rates. It only remained, therefore, to convert the marriage rate assumptions, which state the proportion of spinsters who will marry each year, into assumptions as to the proportion of women single, married, widowed and divorced at each age and to make compatible assumptions for the male population. The proportion of single women was calculated first, for the three alternative marriage rate assumptions. The proportion of women widowed and divorced was not varied but was based on the present ratios (14) and on two forecasts made for 1980 (31) (32), all of which were similar: the proportion married could then be found for each alternative. The same division of assumed future marriage rates into single, married, widowed and divorced was carried out for the male population, subject to the condition that the number of married men in the population should be equal to the number of married women. This required the proportion of married men to be raised by 1 or 2 per cent.

HEADSHIP RATES

Once the population is divided into age, sex and marital groups, the number of separate households likely to be formed from each group can be found by multiplying by the appropriate headship rate, that is by the percentage of each age/marital group who are heads of households.

The only firm information on British headship rates is that given by the 1951 Census (table 5.1). The age grouping used there has been used in most subsequent studies and is used in this study. However, the 1951 Census figures are over fourteen years old so, with 1961 Census figures due shortly, it was a most unfortunate moment at which to have to make long-term forecasts.[1]

With no British data prior to the 1951 Census and no current information, there is very little that can be established about the present trends in headship rates. The 1951 Census ventured that headship rates 'may well have been very similar in 1931 and 1951' (33), and American studies have suggested a similar stability over much longer periods. It might well be expected, however, that the headship rates in Britain would be higher in 1961 than in the depression of the early 1930s, and than in 1951 when the acute postwar shortage of housing had not been overcome. The total number of households recorded in the 1961 Census shows that there must have been some rise in headship rates since 1951, but the precise changes are a matter of speculation (table 5.1).

Table 5.1. *Headship rates*

Percentages

Age	Age and marital status	1951	1961 (estimates)	Rates used in this study	Forecasts 1980	Forecasts 1990
15–39	Married males	79	89	95	98	98
	Unmarried, both sexes	4	4	14	6	13
40–59	Married males	96	97	98	98	98
	Single males	27	30	34	27	35
	Widowed and divorced males	68	70	74	68	75
	Single females	29	32	36	29	37
	Widowed and divorced females	78	79	80	78	81
60+	Married males	97	98	98	98	98
	Single males	39	44	49	39	50
	Widowed and divorced males	64	66	69	64	70
	Single females	47	51	57	47	58
	Widowed and divorced females	68	70	74	68	75

SOURCES: 1951 headship rates from *Census 1951* (33); 1961 headship rates and 1990 forecasts based on figures prepared by Miss D. C. Paige (32); 1980 forecast from Needleman, 'A Long-Term View of Housing' (31).

The headship rates used in this study are higher than those independently estimated for 1961 (32), particularly for the age groups 15–39. This reflects the probability that increasing prosperity, earlier marriage and the elimination of the housing shortage will combine to raise the number of separate households that are formed, particularly by young married couples. Strictly speaking the

[1] Headship rates based on the 1961 Census have not so far been published (January 1968).

rates adopted should have been varied over time and between the different marriage rates assumed in the population projections. In view of the weakness of the base from which the headship rates had to be forecast, this would not have led to any real increase in accuracy.

The total number of households is very sensitive to changes in headship rates. The effect of assuming headship rates slightly higher than those estimated for 1961 has been to add nearly 2 million households to the total for 2004, about 8 per cent. Of course the higher the headship rates the smaller the average size of the household. The headship rates assumed for this study would give an average household size of 2·84 persons in 1963 and 2·97 persons in 2004, as against an average household size based on the estimated 1961 headship rates of 3·06 persons in 1963 and 3·20 persons in 2004, taking the population forecasts of the Registrars General.[1]

Some authorities expect household fission to proceed much further and have suggested that, in future, average households might contain only 2·5 or even 2·2 persons. Since the rates of household formation which have been assumed for married males, and to a lesser extent widowed and divorced people, are very high and most unmarried people are very young, significant changes in household formation depend on marked increases in the rate at which young people form households. Some idea of the relationship between household size and headship rates can be obtained by examining a mid-period position. For example, in terms of the 1973 population as forecast by the Registrars General the headship rates used in this study would give an average household size of 2·87. To obtain an average size of 2·5 persons it would be necessary to assume, not only that most married men and widowed and divorced people formed their own households, but that over a quarter of unmarried people of 15–25 (well over half of whom would be under twenty) and over half of those aged 25–40 would form their own separate households (table 5.2). An average size of household of 2·2 persons would imply that over half the unmarried people of 15–25 would form separate households and virtually all those over twenty-five. Such rates of household formation would appear to be unlikely; although with growing affluence there may be an increasing tendency for young people to move away from home and share a group dwelling. For lack of any firm evidence of such a tendency, a trend of this kind is not allowed for in this study.

HOUSEHOLD SIZE

The number of households having been calculated by applying headship rates to the projected population, it remains to distribute them between categories of household size. The headship rates and size distributions assumed must be compatible in that they combine to give the total population less those in institutions.

[1] The actual size of households in Great Britain in 1961 was 3·16.

Table 5.2. *Household size and headship rates, Great Britain, 1973*

	RG's population assumptions	NIESR assumptions[a]		Variation 1[b]		Variation 2[c]	
		Headship rates	No. of households	Headship rates	No. of households	Headship rates	No. of households
	000s	%	*000s*	%	*000s*	%	*000s*
Married males							
15–39	5127	*95*	4871	*99*	5076	*99*	5076
40–59	5864	*98*	5747	*99*	5805	*99*	5805
60+	3339	*98*	3272	*99*	3306	*99*	3306
Single males							
15–24	3195	*10*[d]	320	*25*	799	*61*	1949
25–39	947	*24*[d]	227	*50*	473	*95*	900
40–59	506	*34*	172	*60*	304	*95*	481
60+	295	*49*	145	*70*	207	*95*	280
Single females							
15–24	2456	*10*[d]	246	*30*	737	*52*	1277
25–39	357	*26*[d]	93	*55*	196	*95*	339
40–59	476	*36*	171	*65*	309	*95*	452
60+	803	*57*	458	*75*	602	*95*	763
Widowed or divorced males							
15–24	2	*50*[d]	1	*90*	2	*95*	2
25–39	51	*74*[d]	38	*95*	48	*95*	48
40–59	209	*74*	155	*95*	199	*95*	199
60+	722	*69*	498	*90*	650	*95*	686
Widowed or divorced females							
15–24	6	*80*[d]	5	*90*	5	*95*	6
25–39	81	*80*[d]	65	*95*	77	*95*	77
40–59	601	*80*	481	*95*	571	*95*	571
60+	2605	*74*	1928	*90*	2345	*95*	2475
Total all ages	54249		18893		21711		24692

SOURCE: NIESR estimates.

[a] Average household size 2·87 persons.
[b] Average household size 2·50 persons.
[c] Average household size 2·20 persons.
[d] Fitted figures.

With household size, as with headship rates, there is a lack of recent information and forecasts had to be based on out-of-date census material. The higher future headship rates adopted imply that most households will in future consist of family units, and that composite households where two or more married couples live together will be unusual. The size distribution adopted for each headship category was therefore based on the size distribution of family units in 1951 (table 5.3). It will be seen that households headed by married men and,

Table 5.3. *Household size distribution by headship categories, 1951*

Age and marital status of head		Average size of household	Size of household by number of persons							
			1	2	3	4	5	6	7+	All
		Persons	*Percentages*							
15–39	Married males	*3·5*	1	21	33	28	11	4	2	100
	Unmarried, both sexes	*1·9*	50	26	14	6	3	1	0	100
40–59	Married males	*3·4*	2	29	30	21	9	5	4	100
	Single males	*1·7*	51	32	12	4	1	0	0	100
	Widowed and divorced males	*2·1*	42	30	15	7	3	2	1	100
	Single females	*1·4*	69	24	6	1	0	0	0	100
	Widowed and divorced females	*2·1*	43	31	14	6	3	2	1	100
60+	Married males	*2·5*	3	61	23	8	3	1	1	100
	Single males	*1·6*	58	32	8	1	1	0	0	100
	Widowed and divorced males	*1·8*	48	34	12	4	1	1	0	100
	Single females	*1·4*	69	24	6	1	0	0	0	100
	Widowed and divorced females	*1·7*	54	31	11	3	1	0	0	100

SOURCES: *Census 1951, England and Wales* and *Scotland*

to a lesser extent, by widowed and divorced persons are larger than those headed by single people.

Because of these differences the overall size distribution, taking all headship categories together, changes with the changing age composition and marital structure. For example, on the high marriage rate assumptions the number of married men and women is increased at the expense of the single, thereby increasing the average household size. Also, because marriage and fertility rates have been assumed to increase together, higher completed family sizes are associated with higher marriage rates, and hence the households of married, widowed and divorced heads are increased in size. It was therefore necessary to modify progressively the assumed household size distribution of these headship classes for use with the high and low birth rate assumptions. The headship rates and household size distribution always combine to give the total population in private households. This was checked, using throughout the 1961 proportion of 96·6 per cent of the total population in private households.

On the regional level the full process of calculating households from marital structure, headship rates and size distribution would have been too cumbersome and of doubtful validity. Regional age structures were therefore grouped into five categories, giving males and females aged 15–39, males aged 40–59, females aged 40–59, males aged 60 plus and females aged 60 plus: these age groups were then converted directly into households by size using national marital structure and headship rates.

On these assumptions, the greatest difference in household size distribution arises from the alternative birth rate assumptions (table 5.4). The differences build up gradually over the forty-year period, until at the year 2004 the high assumptions give an average household size of 3·2 persons and the low assumptions 2·8 persons.

Table 5.4. *Household size distribution, 1964–2004*

Percentages

Persons per household	1964	1969	1974	1979	1984	1989	1994	1999	2004
				Low birth rate assumptions					
1	16	16	15	15	15	14	14	13	13
2	32	32	32	31	31	33	34	35	36
3	25	24	24	25	25	25	27	27	28
4	16	16	17	17	17	16	14	14	13
5	6	7	7	7	7	7	6	6	5
6	3	3	3	3	3	3	3	3	3
7+	2	2	2	2	2	2	2	2	2
				Registrars General's birth rate assumptions					
1	16	16	15	15	14	14	13	13	13
2	32	32	31	31	31	31	31	31	30
3	25	24	25	25	25	25	26	26	26
4	16	16	17	17	18	18	18	18	18
5	6	7	7	7	7	7	7	7	8
6	3	3	3	3	3	3	3	3	3
7+	2	2	2	2	2	2	2	2	2
				High birth rate assumptions					
1	16	16	15	14	14	13	12	12	11
2	32	32	31	31	30	30	29	27	26
3	25	25	25	25	24	23	24	24	24
4	16	16	17	17	18	18	19	20	20
5	6	6	7	8	9	10	10	11	12
6	3	3	3	3	3	4	4	4	5
7+	2	2	2	2	2	2	2	2	2

SOURCE: NIESR estimates.

These figures are all based on the higher headship rates assumed, and the differences therefore arise entirely from demographic changes. The adoption of these higher headship rates, implying the splitting up of composite households, itself leads to a considerable increase in the number of small households (table 5.5) and reduces the present average household size by about 10 per cent.

Table 5.5. *Household size distribution, differences in Great Britain, 1961–4*

Percentages

Persons per household	1961	1964 [a]	Differences
1	13·5	16·1	+2·6
2	29·6	31·8	+2·2
3	22·8	24·8	+2·0
4	18·3	16·1	−2·2
5	9·0	6·4	−2·6
6	3·9	2·8	−1·1
7+	2·9	2·0	−0·9
All households	100·0	100·0	—

SOURCES: 1961 figures from *Census 1961*, *England and Wales* and *Scotland* (34); 1964 figures, NIESR estimates.

[a] High headship rates.

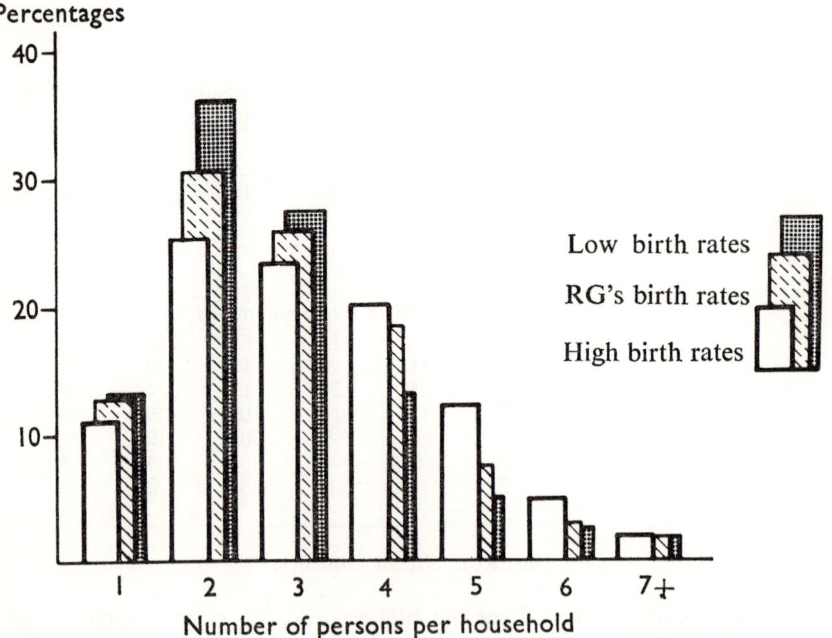

SOURCES: *Registrar General's Quarterly Return for England and Wales* and *for Scotland;* NIESR estimates.

Fig. 5.1. Projected size distribution of households in Great Britain, 2004

By the end of the forty-year period average household size would have changed from 3·06 to 2·97 on the assumptions accepted by the Registrars General, to 3·22 on the high birth rate assumptions and to 2·78 on the low assumptions. The effect of the higher headship rates alone would be to reduce the average household size from 3·06 in 1961 to 2·84 in 2004. Whichever set of population assumptions is accepted, two person households are the most common, followed by three and four person households (fig. 5.1). The proportion of small households declines with increases in the assumed marriage and birth rates: on the low assumptions 77 per cent of all households consist of three persons or less, on the assumptions of the Registrars General the figure is 69 per cent and on the high assumptions it is 61 per cent.

In comparison with these possible national changes the differences between regions, which arise on the methodology followed solely from differences in regional age structure, are on a more modest scale and are likely to decline over the period (table 5.6).

Table 5.6. *Household size distribution, regional differences*

Percentages

Persons per household	1964			2004		
	Midlands	South West	Difference	Midlands	South West	Difference
1	15·2	17·2	+2·0	12·6	13·0	+0·4
2	31·1	33·2	+2·1	30·5	30·9	+0·4
3	25·2	24·0	−1·2	25·8	25·6	−0·2
4	16·6	14·9	−1·7	18·5	18·1	−0·4
5	6·8	6·1	−0·7	7·6	7·4	−0·2
6	3·0	2·7	−0·3	3·0	3·0	0
7+	2·1	1·9	−0·2	2·0	2·0	0
All households	100·0	100·0	0	100·0	100·0	0

SOURCE: NIESR estimates.

THE RELATIONSHIP BETWEEN HOUSEHOLDS AND DWELLINGS

The next step was to assess the sizes of dwellings needed by the households. Size was defined by the number of habitable rooms,[1] so as to ensure comparability with the figures for the present stock obtained from the Census—the best source of information. Other definitions which could be used are the number of bedrooms or the total floor area; in neither case is there any comparable information about the size of dwellings already built nor, as a guide to future need, about the way in which households occupy them.

It was also decided to base the estimate of housing need on the census figures

[1] For the definition of habitable rooms see chapter 6, p. 79 n. 2.

rather than on a set of assumptions relating household size to dwelling size. There are several reasons for this. Most previous attempts at setting standards of dwelling-need have been more or less elaborate modifications of the assumption that there should be one habitable room for each person in the household. This ratio itself is little more than a numerical convenience, which bears no special functional relationship to the way rooms are used. It is true that some sixty years ago the number of rooms and the number of people in the country were approximately equal, but since then the amount of space has grown until there are now three rooms for every two people. Moreover, even when the two overall totals were similar, less than 20 per cent of the population actually lived in households with one person per room; the great majority lived, and still do live, at a wide range of higher and lower densities.

The modifications which have been suggested to the one person per room standard (31) (35) (36) have usually put forward a lower overall density of occupation and have not insisted on every household conforming to this one density figure. However, the range of densities which they allow for is still far smaller than that which actually exists (fig. 5.2). Households live in an extraordinary diversity of economic, social and personal circumstances which cannot be matched by any simple set of arbitrary assumptions. How far, for example, is the assumption that, 'half the households of each size require a room per person and one spare, and half two spare rooms' (31), able to meet the variations in personal circumstances?

On this basis a married couple with three children would require six or seven rooms, whereas it is perfectly possible that two living rooms and three bedrooms would provide all the accommodation they need. Nor, on the other hand, would it cover the case of the married couple whose children have all married and left the household, who would be allocated three or four rooms, but who might require a house with six or seven rooms to allow for weekend visiting.

Furthermore, as the circumstances of each household are constantly changing, a restricted range of permissible densities would necessitate a higher level of mobility than now exists, with a consequent increase in the number of dwellings standing vacant at one time. It is far more expensive to provide extra dwellings for vacancies than it is to provide larger dwellings in the first place. The additional cost of one extra room is only about a twelfth of the cost of a typical three bedroom dwelling; therefore, for the cost of every dwelling which has to be added to the pool of vacancies, it would be possible to provide an additional room in each of twelve new dwellings. Moreover this extra space would be in use, not vacant.

The application of 'fitting standards', relating rooms and persons, which aim to secure an intensive use of rooms, inevitably leads to a level of provision which is below that of the average household today. Larger dwellings represent an increase in the standard of living. Only when they are larger than the occupiers want can space be said to be wasted and the use of the dwellings uneconomic.

The same difficulty, with greater force, makes it impossible to use official standards of space requirements. These are normally the minimum standards for households as they exist at that time. Households tend to move when they grow,

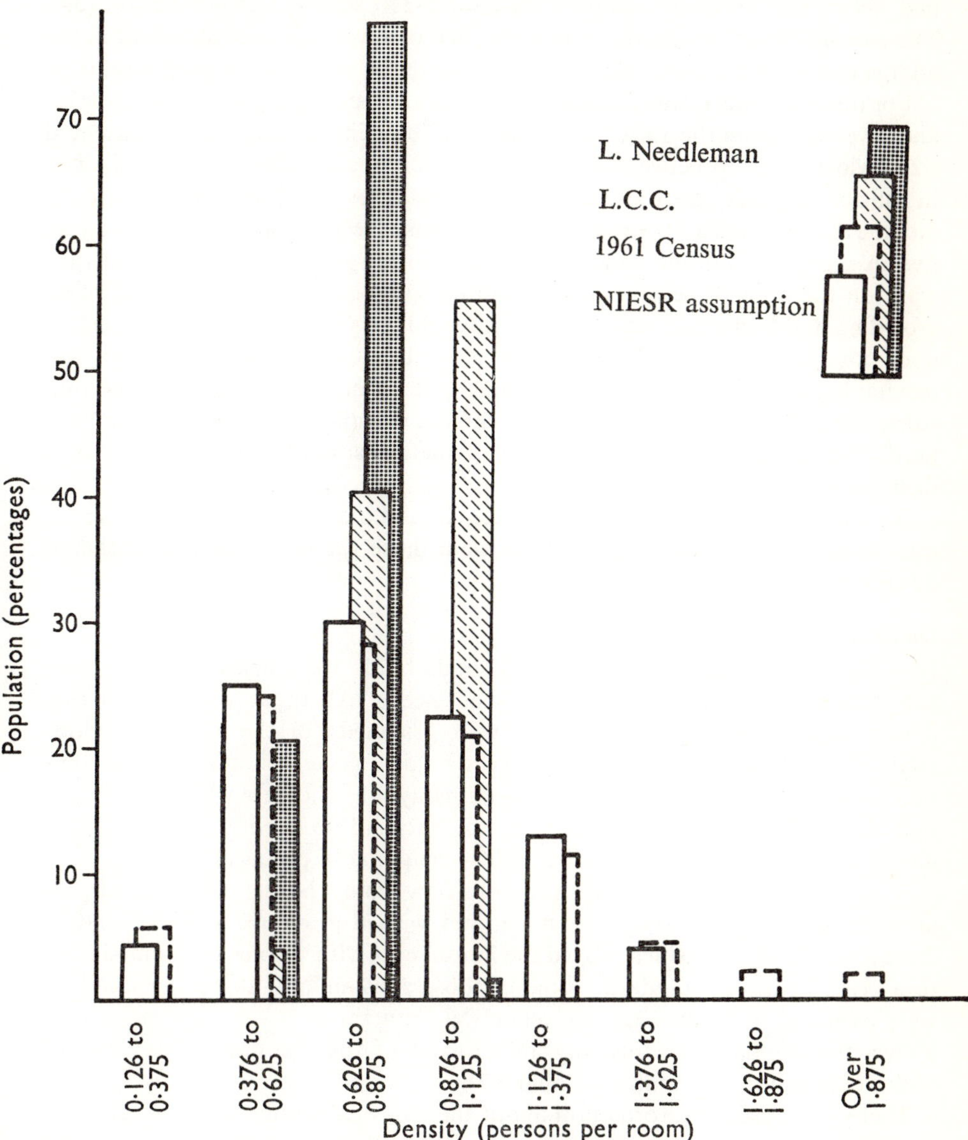

SOURCES: Needleman, 'A Long-Term View of Housing' (31); L.C.C., *The Planning of a New Town* (37); *Census 1961* (34); NIESR estimates.

Fig. 5.2. Distribution of population by residential density

but not when they decline, so that the existing provision is usually above official standards. While the Parker Morris Report recommends minimum standards of less than 250 square feet per person (38), in 1960 the average person already had about half as much again as this, some 370 square feet per person (39). The use of official standards to find the size of dwellings needed would imply a large excess of medium and large dwellings and a shortage of small dwellings.

For these reasons it was decided to develop a relationship between households and dwellings from the 1961 Census figures. These indicate how each household size divides itself up between dwellings of different sizes (34). The figures allow in full for the wide range of personal circumstances which exist in real life. In fact the allowance is a little too full, for the Census records uncritically those who live in slums on the one hand and those who have far more space than they want on the other. The range had therefore to be curtailed by removing overcrowding and under-occupation. Even after this has been done the relationship does not provide an ideal measure of need, because present households will inevitably have adapted themselves to fit the stock of houses available, and that stock will reflect past needs, or the convenience of builders, as well as the present needs. Nevertheless it gives the best available measure of need, one that has a firm foundation in reality.

As the basic assumption is that each household will, in future, have its own dwelling, the census figures used were those for households in unshared dwellings.

Under-occupation

In a survey on housing in 1960 (39), households were asked whether their accommodation was big enough for their needs. All those who replied that it was larger than they really needed were assumed, for the purposes of this study, to be under-occupying. This gives a fairly generous estimate of under-occupation, because there may have been many householders who would agree that they had surplus accommodation, but who had no intention of reducing it and cannot therefore be said to be under-occupying in practical terms.

It was necessary to estimate not only how many households had surplus accommodation but also by how much they wished to reduce it. This could be done from the figures which related the households with surplus accommodation to a given bedroom standard: some of those substantially above the standard were assumed to want a greater reduction than those at, or only marginally above, the standard. In this way an estimate of the amount and severity of under-occupation was built up (table 5.7).

There is no precise information about the size of the households which have surplus accommodation or about the size of dwellings in which they live. It had therefore to be assumed that under-occupation would be concentrated among the small households and, within these, among the larger dwellings. Even at the lowest occupancies, however, where one person may occupy fifteen rooms, it is

Table 5.7. *Under-occupation, England and Wales, 1961*

Reduction in accommodation required	Percentages of all households
One room less	6·55
Two rooms less	2·42
Three rooms less	0·78
Four rooms less	0·17
Five rooms less	0·04

SOURCE: Gray and Russell, *The Housing Situation in 1960* (39).

unlikely that every single case represents unwanted accommodation. No existing occupancy category was therefore eliminated entirely.

The effect of these assumptions is to increase the overall intensity of occupation by about 3 per cent from 0·68 persons per room to 0·70. For one person households the increase is nearer 12 per cent. It also reduces the need for all dwellings of five or more rooms, the largest category falling by 25 per cent, and increases the need for dwellings of two or four rooms by about 13 per cent (table 5.8).[1]

Overcrowding

As well as removing under-occupation it is necessary to modify the other end of the density range where overcrowding occurs. For this purpose the legal definition of overcrowding, which discounts children less than one year old and counts children aged one but under ten as a half, is both too involved and too low for this study. It is set at a level of rather more than two persons per room. This was the level at which legal action was considered necessary even in 1935, so it is obviously too low a standard against which to measure for the next forty years.

At the other extreme, however, a minimum standard as high as one person per room would be too severe. It is possible to think of many cases where four people, a widow and three young children for example, could live quite adequately in three rooms. With larger households the position is easier still. In fact, one person in five was living at a density of more than one person per room in 1961 (34).

The overcrowding standard adopted was therefore 1·5 persons per room. An allowance was made for the effect of redistributing households living at greater densities than this among the larger dwellings.

[1] Over the period 1961–6 about 1·2 million dwellings were added to the stock against an increase in population of about 1·9 million. As a result the number of persons per dwelling fell by about 1 per cent. The average number of persons per room also appears to have fallen, perhaps by rather over 5 per cent.

Table 5.8. *Distribution of non-sharing households between dwelling sizes, Great Britain, 1961*

Dwelling size in rooms	Percentage distribution of households							Occupancy rates	
	1 person	2 persons	3 persons	4 persons	5 persons	6 persons	7+ persons	Persons per room	Persons per dwelling
	Before removal of under-occupation								
1	5	1	1	0	0	0	0	1·76	1·76
2	16	7	3	2	2	1	1	1·03	2·06
3	18	15	13	10	7	6	4	0·88	2·64
4	28	30	30	25	22	21	20	0·74	2·96
5	22	31	36	42	44	43	41	0·67	3·35
6	8	11	12	14	15	16	18	0·57	3·42
7	2	3	3	4	5	6	7	0·52	3·64
8+	1	2	2	3	5	7	9	0·43	3·86
All dwellings	100	100	100	100	100	100	100		3·11
Persons per room	*0·26*	*0·46*	*0·65*	*0·83*	*0·99*	*1·15*	*1·44*	*0·68*	
Rooms per household	*3·85*	*4·39*	*4·61*	*4·83*	*5·04*	*5·21*	*5·30*		
	After removal of under-occupation								
1	5	1	1	0	0	0	0	1·76	1·76
2	21	7	3	2	2	1	1	0·97	1·94
3	28	16	13	10	7	6	4	0·83	2·49
4	25	43	30	26	22	21	20	0·71	2·85
5	14	23	39	43	44	43	41	0·71	3·53
6	5	7	11	14	16	16	18	0·61	3·67
7	1	2	2	3	5	6	7	0·57	3·97
8+	1	1	1	2	4	7	9	0·47	4·34
All dwellings	100	100	100	100	100	100	100		3·11
Persons per room	*0·29*	*0·48*	*0·66*	*0·84*	*1·00*	*1·15*	*1·44*	*0·70*	
Rooms per household	*3·44*	*4·15*	*4·55*	*4·78*	*5·02*	*5·21*	*5·30*		
	After removal of under-occupation and overcrowding								
1	5	0	0	0	0	0	0	1·00	1·00
2	21	7	3	0	0	0	0	0·82	1·64
3	28	17	13	10	0	0	0	0·75	2·26
4	25	43	30	26	24	23	0	0·70	2·78
5	14	23	39	44	49	46	31	0·70	3·50
6	5	7	11	15	17	18	33	0·64	3·85
7	1	2	2	3	5	6	16	0·64	4·45
8+	1	1	2	2	5	7	20	0·54	4·99
All dwellings	100	100	100	100	100	100	100		3·11
Persons per room	*0·29*	*0·48*	*0·66*	*0·82*	*0·96*	*1·11*	*1·18*	*0·69*	
Rooms per household	*3·44*	*4·18*	*4·56*	*4·85*	*5·23*	*5·39*	*6·63*		

SOURCES: *Census 1961;* NIESR estimates.

Compared to the relationship after the removal of under-occupation, this modification reduces the density of occupation of the larger households substantially and takes the overall figures down to 0·69 persons per room (table 5.8). The need for dwellings of four rooms or less is reduced.

The joint effect of removing under-occupation and overcrowding is not great as far as the overall occupancy figure is concerned. The occupancy of small households is raised and that of large ones reduced, giving a smaller contrast between the two. The effect on the size of dwellings needed is quite modest because the removal of under-occupation releases large dwellings and absorbs small ones, while the removal of overcrowding does the opposite. The number of one room dwellings needed is nearly halved, but all other changes are around 10 per cent or less.

Table 5.9. *Size of dwellings and occupancy, 1961*

Habitable rooms per dwelling	Average number of persons per dwelling	
	Before modification	After modification
1	1·76	1·00
2	2·06	1·64
3	2·64	2·26
4	2·96	2·78
5	3·35	3·50
6	3·42	3·85
7	3·64	4·45
8+	3·86	4·99

SOURCES: as table 5.8.

The modified relationship between households and dwellings still preserves two generalizations which were applicable to the original figures: as household size increases the space available to each household and the intensity of occupation both rise; as dwelling size increases the number of persons per dwelling rises but the intensity of occupation falls. However, this fall is much less marked than before modification, with the result that there is a far closer correspondence than previously between dwelling size and the number of persons per dwelling (table 5.9).

THE EFFECT OF DIFFERENT RELATIONSHIPS BETWEEN HOUSEHOLDS AND DWELLINGS

The various alternative relationships between households and dwellings which have been discussed do not, in fact, give as great a difference in the overall occupancy rate as a glance at fig. 5.2 might suggest. The rate given by the modified census relationship which was finally adopted is about 0·70 persons per room, varying slightly from one date to another and from one set of population assumptions to another. The relationships suggested elsewhere give overall figures that are either the same (31), or about 20 per cent greater at about 0·86 persons per room (36). These figures compare with occupancy rates of 0·59, 0·83 and 0·64 for those who, at the time of the 1961 Census, were respectively owner-occupiers, local authority tenants, and tenants of unfurnished accommodation.

When the size distribution of dwellings needed is considered, the relationships which put forward a limited range of densities of occupation produce a greater proportion of large and small dwellings and a smaller proportion of medium-size dwellings than the modified census relationship used in this study. However, as the main purpose of this study is not to describe the physical form of future building but to estimate its cost, this difference is not of crucial importance. The extra cost of additional large dwellings would be offset by the reduced cost of additional small dwellings. Furthermore, the cost of dwellings does not vary in direct proportion to their size: in fact an eight room dwelling costs less than twice as much as a dwelling with only one room (chapter 7). For these reasons it is possible for widely differing dwelling-size distributions to give similar costs. If the extreme standard of one person per room had been used, for example, the reduction in the space available to each person would have been about 40 per cent, but the saving in the cost of construction would have been only 15 per cent.

CONSEQUENCES OF THE HOUSEHOLD AND DWELLING DISTRIBUTIONS ADOPTED

The relationship used to determine the size of dwellings needed (table 5.8) shows that the most common need is for four or five room dwellings. Because all

Table 5.10. *Dwelling size distribution for Great Britain, 2004*

Percentages

No. of rooms	Low birth rate	RG's birth rate	High birth rate
1	0·6	0·6	0·6
2	6·1	5·6	4·8
3	14·8	13·9	12·6
4	32·6	31·6	30·4
5	31·2	32·6	34·5
6	10·1	10·7	11·5
7	2·6	2·8	3·1
8+	2·0	2·2	2·5
All dwellings	100·0	100·0	100·0
Average no. of habitable rooms	*4·41*	*4·47*	*4·56*

SOURCE: NIESR estimates.

households from two to six persons show their strongest need in these same sizes, there is less variation in the sizes of dwellings needed than in the sizes of households. The greatest variation still arises from alternative birth rate assumptions, with present regional differences as the next most important factor. By 2004 the size differences in the national housing stock needed have reached their maximum level of about 3 per cent (table 5.10).

By the end of the forty-year period the average size of dwelling would have changed from 4·41 to 4·47 habitable rooms on the assumptions accepted by the Registrars General, to 4·56 on the high population assumptions, and would remain at 4·41 on the low population assumptions. It will be seen that the size of dwellings required is not greatly affected by the population assumptions (fig. 5.3). The need will be mainly for dwellings of four and five habitable

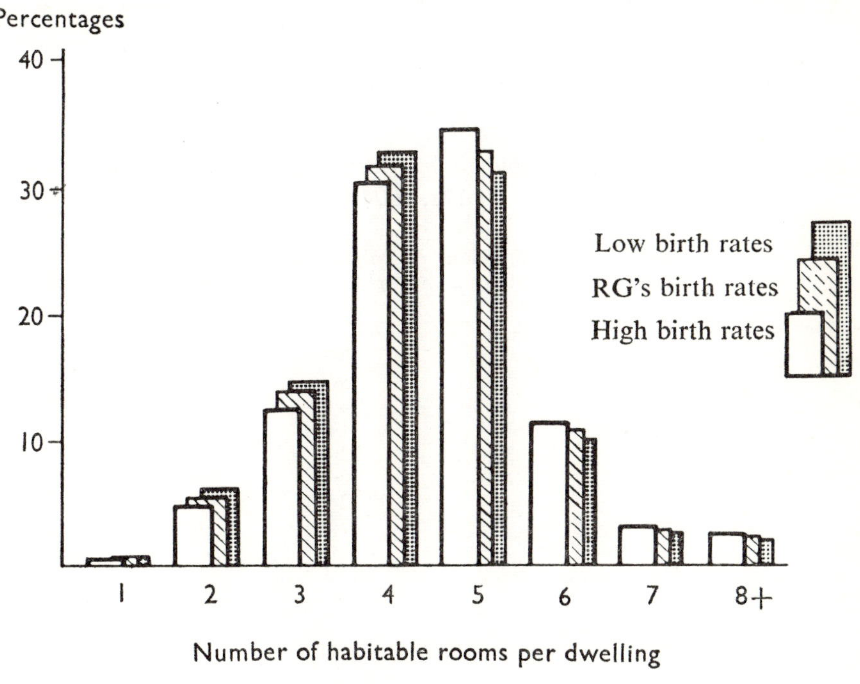

SOURCES: as fig. 5.1.

Fig. 5.3. Projected size distribution of dwellings in Great Britain, 2004

rooms, about 65 per cent being required in these sizes. Only 20 per cent of dwellings will be needed with less than three habitable rooms or more than six.

The regional variations in household size (table 5.6) are carried through into dwelling-size differences (table 5.11). Migrational variations are given in table 5.12. These details of the total stock of dwellings are of less importance, however,

Table 5.11. *Dwelling size distribution, regional differences*

Percentages

No. of rooms	1964			2004		
	Midlands	South West	Difference	Midlands	South West	Difference
1	0·8	0·9	+0·1	0·6	0·7	+0·1
2	6·1	6·6	+0·5	5·5	5·6	+0·1
3	14·5	15·1	+0·6	13·9	14·0	+0·1
4	31·5	31·9	+0·4	31·5	31·6	+0·1
5	31·7	30·8	−0·9	32·7	32·5	−0·2
6	10·5	10·1	−0·4	10·8	10·7	−0·1
7	2·7	2·6	−0·1	2·8	2·7	−0·1
8+	2·2	2·0	−0·2	2·2	2·2	0
All dwellings	100·0	100·0	0	100·0	100·0	0

SOURCE: NIESR estimates.

Table 5.12. *Dwelling size distribution, migration differences, North and Central Wales, 2004*

Percentages

No. of rooms	Migration pattern 2	Migration pattern 3	Differences
1	0·6	0·7	+0·1
2	5·4	5·7	+0·3
3	13·7	14·0	+0·3
4	31·3	31·6	+0·3
5	33·0	32·4	−0·6
6	10·9	10·7	−0·2
7	2·8	2·7	−0·1
8+	2·3	2·2	−0·1
All dwellings	100·0	100·0	0

SOURCE: NIESR estimates.

than those of the net additions which have to be made if the required total stock is to be achieved. Because there is already a substantial stock of dwellings standing whose characteristics can only be altered in minor ways, a relatively small variation in the total stock required can entail a very large variation in the net addition required. This raises the question of demolitions as well as the demographic changes already discussed. This point will be more fully discussed in chapter 11.

CHAPTER 6

THE PRESENT STOCK OF HOUSING

The net need for new dwellings can be obtained by setting the housing stock against the gross need. The size of the stock of dwellings was therefore required for each region at each quinquennial date classified by size of dwelling measured in terms of the number of habitable rooms. The last complete count of dwellings available when the estimates were needed was that made in the course of the Census for 1961. These figures had to be adjusted for the demolitions, new constructions and conversions which had taken place between the census date and the starting point of the study, 31 March 1964. Because many of the dwellings in the stock are obsolete and in a poor condition, estimates were needed of the rate at which they would be replaced and of the improvement and conversion work that would be necessary to make them suitable for future use.

The physical condition of dwellings and the facilities within them were expected to be closely associated with their age and size. Maintenance costs are also associated with these factors. It was therefore essential to classify the stock of dwellings in each region by age as well as by size.

SIZE AND TYPE OF DWELLING AND PROVISION OF SERVICES ON 31 MARCH 1964

A dwelling is defined as a building or part of a building which provides structurally separate living quarters. Broadly this means that there is direct private access to the dwelling from the street or from a public staircase or landing. The Census (34) divides dwellings into permanent and non-permanent,[1] and classifies them by the number of habitable rooms (one to seven, eight or nine, and ten and over),[2] and by the category of building in which the dwelling is contained: houses with one dwelling, mixed buildings with one dwelling (probably mainly shops with living accommodation), and buildings with more than one dwelling (flatted accommodation). For this last class, information is available on the distribution of dwellings by the number of dwellings per building, but not by the actual size of the dwelling. The size distribution of permanent dwellings in 1961 was computed for each region from the county volumes of the Census.

[1] A non-permanent dwelling is a dwelling in a mobile structure such as a caravan, boat, etc.

[2] A habitable room is a bedroom or a living room, or a kitchen in which meals are regularly taken; bathrooms, working kitchens and halls are excluded. Habitable rooms are hereafter referred to simply as rooms, and dwelling size may be taken to mean the number of rooms. This definition was changed for the Sample Census of 1966 and as a result comparisons are difficult. The definitions of accommodation units and of rooms used in Woolf, *The Housing Survey in England and Wales, 1964* (40), and Cullingworth, *Scottish Housing in 1965* (41), also differ to some extent from those used in the 1961 Census.

The number of dwellings built or demolished between April 1961 and March 1964 is available for each local authority area from the appendices to the *Housing Returns* (42). There is no direct information on the size and type of these dwellings, but information is available for England and Wales, and for Scotland, on the number of bedrooms in each dwelling constructed. Regionally, the new constructions were taken as following this national pattern, on the assumption that the number of habitable rooms is related to the number of bedrooms. For regional demolitions each category was reduced in proportion to the number of dwellings in the stock in 1961.

Information on conversions is only available nationally (42). Grants were given for fewer than two dwellings in every 1000 between the years 1961 and 1964. A great deal of work on estimates of conversions is not therefore justifiable. Data were obtained from the Ministry of Housing and Local Government for sample areas (appendix 5) and the figures were weighted by the mid-1961 population figures to give estimates for each region.

As only the total number of conversions was known, it was assumed that each conversion of a dwelling of six to nine rooms provided two dwellings with three rooms each, while dwellings with ten or more rooms provided three dwellings of three rooms.

It is difficult to split flatted dwellings because of the problems of access, and so it was assumed that all the dwellings converted were houses and that they had at least six rooms, since the larger the dwelling the more likely it is to be sub-divided.

After these adjustments for changes since the Census, the figures indicated that there were about 16·8 million dwellings in Britain on 31 March 1964.[1] Of these, some 14 million are houses and the balance flats, about a seventh of which are in buildings which were only partly residential (tables 6.1–6.4). Just under a third of the flats are in Scotland and well over a third in the South East. As would be expected, there is a heavy concentration of dwellings in the medium-size range. About 60 per cent of the dwellings have four or five rooms, and 87 per cent have between three and six rooms. Less than 2 per cent of the dwellings have only one or more than nine rooms. The distribution by size varies with the type of dwelling. The most common size for houses is five rooms, closely followed by the four room group. For mixed buildings the order is reversed. The most common size for flats is three rooms, but the two and four room groups together contain as many dwellings, with roughly equal numbers in each group. The regional pattern for all types of dwellings shows that the most numerous size group is five rooms, except in Scotland where it is three rooms and the North where it is four rooms. However, the numerical superiority

[1] This figure is about 400,000 lower than an official estimate would suggest (*Housing Statistics, Great Britain* (43)), but the official estimates for April 1966 are about 600,000 higher than the indications from the Sample Census, 1966.

Table 6.1. *Numbers of dwellings by size and region, 31 March 1964*

	Rooms per dwelling									Total
	1	2	3	4	5	6	7	8–9	10+	
Scotland	51,455	328,712	606,286	435,260	143,839	51,077	26,803	24,260	10,043	1,677,735
North	3,755	69,698	199,708	340,589	311,649	79,569	27,520	18,290	6,246	1,057,024
North West	7,564	64,470	178,933	785,656	792,102	259,518	70,751	40,783	12,175	2,211,952
Pennines	6,430	80,332	216,188	551,154	747,468	167,718	40,483	24,393	7,047	1,841,213
Central	1,040	9,428	33,518	93,743	182,210	54,807	11,678	7,008	2,414	395,846
East	1,262	12,699	41,271	124,403	174,592	51,145	15,985	9,922	3,358	434,637
North & Central Wales	609	6,358	18,167	56,791	60,096	34,742	14,138	11,618	4,717	207,236
West	4,010	31,862	100,772	276,744	474,873	249,884	65,239	35,906	12,133	1,251,423
South West	1,475	13,619	48,865	122,586	153,229	73,183	27,489	22,912	8,782	472,140
Midlands	5,595	43,824	152,277	415,372	645,870	174,270	40,941	25,079	8,994	1,512,222
East Anglia	1,130	8,873	27,121	83,377	123,362	46,568	13,224	10,034	4,064	317,753
South East	65,504	241,504	717,468	1,290,081	1,869,108	780,810	224,034	172,833	67,914	5,429,256
Great Britain	149,829	911,379	2,340,574	4,575,756	5,678,398	2,023,291	578,285	403,038	147,887	16,808,437

SOURCE: NIESR estimates.

Table 6.2. *Numbers of houses by size and region, 31 March 1964*

	Rooms per dwelling									Total
	1	2	3	4	5	6	7	8–9	10+	
Scotland	6,274	72,832	282,209	294,116	114,378	42,331	23,964	22,349	9,380	867,833
North	919	47,965	165,314	318,993	302,468	75,978	26,014	17,288	5,796	960,735
North West	1,268	32,260	123,265	734,960	763,996	249,599	67,335	38,404	11,193	2,022,280
Pennines	2,535	61,234	182,328	522,108	728,726	160,770	38,023	22,700	6,399	1,724,823
Central	178	5,218	25,527	87,276	177,790	52,754	10,967	6,494	2,200	368,404
East	356	7,726	33,125	117,365	169,017	48,654	14,908	9,194	3,066	403,411
North & Central Wales	143	4,665	14,349	52,907	57,443	32,893	13,182	10,741	4,319	190,642
West	617	14.621	63,475	246,211	455,834	240,078	61,232	32,838	10,884	1,125,790
South West	344	6,507	31,020	109,027	145,515	69,138	25,551	21,298	8,083	416,483
Midlands	1,673	24,212	110,377	382,792	626,760	167,468	38,403	23,221	8,133	1,383,039
East Anglia	398	5,341	19,215	78,712	119,500	44,437	12,151	9,156	3,722	292,632
South East	5,780	56,850	320,191	1,005,323	1,744,630	733,740	207,379	160,085	62,055	4,296,033
Great Britain	20,485	339,431	1,370,395	3,949,790	5,406,057	1,917,840	539,109	373,768	135,230	14,052,105

SOURCE: NIESR estimates.

Table 6.3. *Numbers of flatted dwellings by size and region, 31 March 1964*

	Rooms per dwelling									Total
	1	2	3	4	5	6	7	8–9	10+	
Scotland	44,763	253,677	320,147	137,192	26,928	7,247	2,129	1,326	438	793,847
North	2,756	20,957	31,283	15,678	3,992	1,028	396	232	146	76,468
North West	6,044	29,543	41,136	28,065	11,717	2,719	816	562	216	120,818
Pennines	3,745	17,647	27,833	13,762	5,037	1,212	421	306	148	70,111
Central	821	3,854	6,536	3,062	1,078	314	110	97	56	15,928
East	859	4,607	6,656	3,414	1,378	351	149	115	68	17,597
North & Central Wales	444	1,556	3,359	2,627	1,092	458	169	167	92	9,964
West	3,234	16,177	33,417	20,556	7,800	2,735	1,102	984	494	86,499
South West	1,074	6,717	16,569	10,069	3,855	1,350	505	443	257	40,839
Midlands	3,721	17,940	34,613	18,366	6,736	1,330	554	454	319	84,033
East Anglia	707	3,340	7,371	2,766	1,435	407	173	176	104	16,479
South East	58,875	178,320	374,599	238,545	87,322	27,039	8,800	6,763	3,543	983,806
Great Britain	127,043	554,335	903,519	494,102	158,370	46,190	15,324	11,625	5,881	2,316,389

SOURCE: NIESR estimates.

Table 6.4. *Numbers of mixed-use buildings by size and region, 31 March 1964*

	Rooms per dwelling									Total
	1	2	3	4	5	6	7	8–9	10+	
Scotland	418	2,203	3,930	3,952	2,533	1,499	710	585	225	16,055
North	80	776	3,111	5,918	5,189	2,563	1,110	770	304	19,821
North West	252	2,667	14,532	22,631	16,389	7,200	2,600	1,817	766	68,854
Pennines	150	1,451	6,027	15,284	13,705	5,736	2,039	1,387	500	46,279
Central	41	356	1,455	3,405	3,342	1,739	601	417	158	11,514
East	47	366	1,490	3,624	4,197	2,140	928	613	224	13,629
North & Central Wales	22	137	459	1,257	1,561	1,391	787	710	306	6,630
West	159	1,064	3,880	9,977	11,239	7,071	2,905	2,084	755	39,134
South West	57	395	1,276	3,490	3,859	2,695	1,433	1,171	442	14,818
Midlands	201	1,672	7,287	14,214	12,374	5,472	1,984	1,404	542	45,150
East Anglia	25	192	535	1,899	2,427	1,724	900	702	238	8,642
South East	849	6,334	22,678	46,213	37,156	20,031	7,855	5,985	2,316	149,417
Great Britain	2,301	17,613	66,660	131,864	113,971	59,261	23,852	17,645	6,776	439,943

SOURCE: NIESR estimates.

of the five room group over the four room group is marginal in the North West and North and Central Wales, and slight in the Pennines.[1]

The major differences lie between Scotland and the rest of Britain. For Scotland the proportion of dwellings with three rooms or less is about 59 per cent and that for dwellings with five rooms or more about 16 per cent; the proportions for the rest of Britain are more or less reversed. In terms of the number of rooms per dwelling, Scotland compares with France and certain poorer countries of Europe, while the rest of Britain compares with Switzerland, the Netherlands and Belgium and with the United States (44).

Basic engineering services, such as hot and cold water supplies, sanitary and bathing facilities and heating and lighting systems are not found in all dwellings. The Census gives information on households which share or lack piped cold water, piped hot water, a fixed bath and a water closet. A service is counted as lacking if it is not within or attached to the building containing the dwelling. The size of dwellings sharing or lacking services is known only for dwellings occupied by one household. It was assumed that one household in three could be given sole use of a shared service. The proportion of dwellings occupied by one household which would then be without services was applied to all dwellings. It appeared from studies of non-permanent dwellings that about 83 per cent lack hot and cold water, and that few contain water closets or fixed baths (45), (46). This number was therefore subtracted from the total number of dwellings without services, except where this would have resulted in the small dwellings showing a better provision of services than the average for all sizes; in such cases the average proportion was taken. These assumptions are not of great importance, since the numbers and proportions of non-permanent dwellings are only significant in the relatively small one room class (table 6.5).

Changes in the census services between April 1961 and March 1964 can be calculated from the returns for standard and discretionary grants; it was assumed that there were no appreciable additions to services which were not grant aided. Information in terms of the services affected is available for standard grants, but for discretionary grants only the number of grants was available, without any information on the amount of the individual grants or the services affected. Details were available from a few local authorities and these suggested that the census services affected might be assumed to be similar for standard and discretionary grants. It was also assumed that the dwellings demolished between 1961 and 1964 would be those most deficient in services.

The picture which emerges shows a considerable improvement over the situation in 1961. By March 1964 less than 1 per cent of dwellings were without

[1] These differences may indicate regional differences in the attitude to meals in the kitchen and in the size of the kitchen, as well as differences in the number of bedrooms and living rooms. Such evidence as is available suggests that, nationally, defining kitchens in which main meals are eaten as habitable rooms may increase the number of habitable rooms by as much as 13 per cent over estimates based on bedrooms and living rooms other than kitchens.

Table 6.5. *Numbers and proportions of non-permanent dwellings, 1961*

	1 room		2–3 rooms		4 rooms+		Total	
	000s	*%[a]*	*000s*	*%[a]*	*000s*	*%[a]*	*000s*	*%[a]*
Scotland	1·5	*3·0*	2·4	*0·3*	0·1	—	4·0	*0·2*
North	1·4	*36·0*	1·0	*0·4*	0·1	—	2·5	*0·2*
North West	2·6	*34·0*	1·5	*0·8*	0·2	—	4·3	*0·2*
Pennines	2·8	*36·0*	1·6	*0·6*	0·2	—	4·6	*0·3*
Central	1·3	*68·0*	0·9	*2·6*	0·2	*0·1*	2·4	*0·6*
East	1·6	*67·0*	1·5	*3·3*	0·2	*0·1*	3·3	*0·1*
North & Central Wales	0·7	*63·0*	0·3	*1·4*	0·1	*0·1*	1·1	*0·5*
West	5·6	*70·0*	3·8	*3·6*	0·4	—	9·8	*0·8*
South West	3·1	*73·0*	2·2	*4·2*	0·3	*0·1*	5·6	*1·2*
Midlands	5·6	*60·0*	3·0	*1·8*	0·3	—	8·9	*0·6*
East Anglia	1·8	*71·0*	1·5	*5·4*	0·1	—	3·4	*1·1*
South East	20·0	*25·0*	12·2	*1·4*	1·1	—	33·3	*0·6*
Great Britain	48·0	*26·5*	31·9	*1·1*	3·3	—	83·2	*0·5*

SOURCE: *Census 1961* (34).

[a] Proportion of non-permanent dwellings in all dwellings of that size.

a cold water system, but nearly 5 per cent were without a water closet, about a sixth lacked a hot water system, and an even larger proportion was without a fixed bath (table 6.6). The smaller the dwelling the more marked is the absence of services. Dwellings with only one or two rooms are more than twice as deficient

Table 6.6. *Dwellings without census services, 31 March 1964*

Percentages

	Habitable rooms									Total
	1	2	3	4	5	6	7	8–9	10+	
Houses only										
No cold water	6·15	4·03	1·04	1·05	0·21	0·28	0·34	0·34	0·27	0·65
No hot water	41·42	34·20	16·75	21·16	11·98	11·84	11·48	6·51	6·53	15·37
No fixed bath	45·21	42·10	20·04	25·22	12·19	13·66	13·26	4·43	4·58	17·35
No W.C.	23·55	16·43	5·79	7·14	1·98	2·00	2·01	1·64	1·67	4·17
All dwellings										
No cold water	3·56	2·69	0·93	1·01	0·21	0·28	0·34	0·34	0·27	0·71
No hot water	39·11	37·47	15·83	21·92	11·95	11·82	11·50	6·51	6·54	16·62
No fixed bath	45·56	45·47	18·42	24·56	12·13	13·63	13·26	4·45	4·59	18·47
No W.C.	24·33	17·81	5·09	6·90	1·96	2·00	2·01	1·64	1·68	4·80

SOURCE: NIESR estimates.

as those with three and four rooms. These latter dwellings are twice as deficient as dwellings with five, six or seven rooms, which are in turn twice as deficient as larger dwellings. The proportion of small dwellings with no provision of services is high, more because they never had the services than because they have been converted from larger dwellings.

Table 6.7. *Regional differences in the incidence of census services, 31 March 1964*

Percentages

	Dwellings without			
	Cold water	Hot water	Fixed bath	W.C.
Scotland	0·1	17·9	23·8	8·6
North	0·5	15·1	17·9	1·4
North West	0·1	12·6	20·3	2·0
Pennines	—	12·7	17·7	8·4
Central	0·5	23·9	19·0	4·6
East	2·7	21·2	22·4	8·0
North & Central Wales	8·0	26·0	31·0	17·8
West	0·9	18·6	19·9	5·7
South West	3·4	17·6	18·5	8·4
Midlands	0·7	20·2	19·4	5·2
East Anglia	7·9	27·9	25·7	14·6
South East	0·3	16·0	14·6	2·3
Great Britain	0·7	16·6	18·5	4·8

SOURCE: NIESR estimates.

The lack of census services varies from one region to another (table 6.7). As would be expected, piped cold water is most often lacking in regions with extensive rural areas, such as North and Central Wales and East Anglia, and, to a lesser extent, the South West and the East. In other regions less than 1 per cent of dwellings are without cold water. Since the other services are water based, it is not surprising that regions deficient in cold water supply also suffer from a serious lack of other services. North and Central Wales and East Anglia are consistently the regions with the greatest deficiency of services, the East also is poor in this sense, while Scotland and the South West are seriously deficient in some services.

THE AGE OF DWELLINGS

Direct information on the numbers of dwellings built and demolished is only available for recent periods. Reliable figures of new construction are available for England and Wales, and for Scotland, from 1919 onwards. Information on demolitions is only available consistently from 1956, although some information is available for earlier periods. Censuses of population, which include information on the housing stock, have been carried out every ten years since 1801, with the exception of 1941. Some estimates of population are available for earlier years. Inevitably, the definition of a unit of housing and the rigour with which the definitions have been applied have changed from time to time, but the census data provide the only evidence of the numbers of dwellings available in the past. The census data give information on the stock of dwellings; to obtain the distribution of dwellings by age it is necessary to estimate the dates of construction.

The number of dwellings constructed in each decade is the difference in the stock at two consecutive Censuses, together with the number of dwellings demolished during that period. Since no information is available on the number of demolitions, the number can only be inferred. The simplest assumption is that the oldest housing is demolished first. Given a duration of life, the number demolished then equals the number erected that many years earlier. There is no direct evidence on the duration, but an estimate can be made by comparing the consequences of assumed rates of construction and demolition with census figures and known construction figures for more recent periods. In order to estimate new construction over a sufficiently long period, the dwelling stock had to be calculated for the century prior to 1801. This was based on estimates of population (7), on the assumption that the average number of persons per dwelling was the same as in 1801. It was assumed that dwellings were built at a steady rate before 1701. The new constructions, assuming dwelling life spans of 100, 120, 140 and 150 years, were then calculated and compared with the actual construction figures for the period 1921 to 1961. A duration of 150 years gave very close agreement and was, therefore, adopted. This method was used to obtain regional figures, with the additional assumption that the distributions of dwellings between regions did not change from 1701 to 1801. Some adjustment was required to bring the resulting figures into agreement with the actual construction figures, which were known regionally from 1934 onwards, and with the size distribution in each region for 1964. While some data were available on size and type of dwelling from census returns from 1891, satisfactory data have not been available until recently.

The reliability of the indications given by the figures in these tables depends on the reliability of the census figures and on the validity of the assumptions made. In fact housing is not demolished strictly in accordance with its age. The best housing from earlier periods continues to be used because it is worth adapting to meet contemporary requirements. Moreover, war damage affected houses of all ages, although probably a disproportionate number were old. The age distributions, therefore, tend to underestimate the actual ages of the dwellings. Similarly the use of indications of dwelling size from a later period has probably distorted the size distribution upwards for the first half of the nineteenth century. Such bias must be allowed for in any use of the figures. For the purpose of this study the figures are used as an indication of amenity for estimating renewals and the possible bias discussed is not important.

It was found that about 27 per cent of the dwellings in Great Britain were built in each of the three periods selected, pre-1881, 1921–41 and 1941–64, and that about 18 per cent were built in the period 1881–1921. These figures agree quite well with earlier estimates based on census data, when allowance is made for the differences in the basis and date of the estimate. The figures obtained from the survey suggested that the stock of dwellings was a little younger (table 6.8). It is, however, very difficult to date dwellings on the basis of their appearance.[1]

Table 6.8. *Distribution of dwellings by dates of construction*

Percentages

NIESR estimates [a]			White Paper [b]	Social Survey [c]		Allen Report [d]	
Great Britain			England & Wales			England	Scotland
Pre–1881	27	Pre–1880	26	19			
1881–1920	18	1880–1918	21	29			
Pre–1921	45	Pre–1919	47	48	Pre–1915	43	36
1921–40	27	1919–44	30	30	1915–39	31	29
Post–1940	28	1945–60	23	22	1940–63	26	35

[a] At 31 March 1964.
[b] *Housing in England and Wales* (47).
[c] Gray and Russell, *The Housing Situation in 1960* (39).
[d] *Report of the Committee of Inquiry into the Impact of Rates on Households* (48).

Only a few countries in Europe have as large a proportion of pre-1921 dwellings as Great Britain; these are mainly countries which also became industrialized in the nineteenth century (44). Similarly, those countries with a large proportion of postwar dwellings are those which have developed more recently. The exception is the United States, which has a lower proportion of pre-1921 dwellings and a higher proportion of postwar dwellings.

The average age of dwellings on 31 March 1964 was about fifty-six years. The average varied regionally from fifty years in the South East to seventy-nine years in North and Central Wales, the ages being higher in regions that had large rural areas (table 6.9). There has been a considerable amount of building in all regions since 1941, in practice mainly since 1945. In Britain as a whole, 28 per cent of dwellings have been built in the last twenty years; even in North

[1] Different estimates have been obtained in subsequent surveys, for example those carried out by Government Social Survey in 1964 (40) and the Scottish Development Department in 1965 (41), but they are not significantly different from those given above.

Table 6.9. *Regional age distribution of dwellings, 31 March 1964*

	Proportion of dwellings built				Average age of stock
	Pre–1881	Pre–1921	Pre–1941	Post–1941	
	Percentages				*Years*
Scotland	33	51	69	31	*59*
North	25	45	70	30	*52*
North West	31	49	76	24	*58*
Pennines	27	46	74	26	*55*
Central	23	40	67	33	*51*
East	31	48	73	27	*60*
North & Central Wales	48	59	78	22	*79*
West	30	51	72	28	*61*
South West	37	53	75	25	*69*
Midlands	24	38	69	31	*51*
East Anglia	36	48	71	29	*66*
South East	21	40	72	28	*50*
Great Britain	27	45	72	28	*56*

SOURCE: NIESR estimates.

and Central Wales 22 per cent of dwellings have been built in this period. As would be expected, the average age of dwellings is lowest in the growth areas. In the South East, Midlands and Central regions 60 per cent of the dwellings have been built since 1921; the proportion falls below 50 per cent only in Scotland, North and Central Wales, the South West and the West, which, with the exception of Scotland, are all rural areas.

The proportion of dwellings which have been constructed of medium size (three to five rooms) has tended to rise over the years. Before 1921 about two-thirds of the dwellings constructed were of medium size, and since that time the proportion has been about 80 per cent. Since 1941 there has been a marked increase in the proportion of dwellings of three rooms.

About a half of the smallest and largest dwellings surviving in 1964 were built before 1881 (table 6.10). While a quarter of the smaller size (one to two rooms) have been built since 1941, only a small proportion of the larger sizes (six rooms and over) have been built during that period.

The size of dwellings constructed since 1921 has depended to a large extent on the number of dwellings built for private owners as compared with public authorities. The average size of the former is usually larger than that of the latter. As a consequence of the growing proportion of public authority housing since 1941, the average size of dwellings in the stock for 1941 to 1961 is lower than for any other period (table 6.10).

Table 6.10. *Dwellings in Great Britain by size and age group, 31 March 1964*

Age	Percentage distribution							Average rooms per dwelling
	1–2 rms.	3 rms.	4 rms.	5 rms.	6 rms.	7+ rms.	All dwellings	
Pre–1881	49	24	29	18	27	40	27	*4·465*
1881–1921	19	20	18	14	24	26	18	*4·616*
1921–41	6	19	27	36	28	26	27	*4·775*
Post–1941	26	37	26	32	21	8	28	*4·326*
Total	100	100	100	100	100	100	100	*4·539*

SOURCE: NIESR estimates.

THE PHYSICAL CONDITION OF DWELLINGS

While the census data can be used to provide information on the size of dwellings, on the absence of certain services and on age, no information can be obtained from this source on the standard and physical condition of dwellings, nor on the presence or absence of other facilities. This information is essential for costing. In order to obtain it, field studies were undertaken (appendix 6).

It was not possible to make a completely random selection of survey districts because of the cost. However, it was expected that most of the factors under consideration would be broadly related to age and census condition,[1] information which had already been compiled nationally and regionally from the census statistics. This expectation was borne out by earlier field work studies and by the analysis of the total sample results (table 6.11). It will be seen that physical condition[2] rises very significantly as the census condition rises and as age falls. Whereas only about 14 per cent of the pre-1881 dwellings which lack all census services fall into the 'good' and 'fair' classes, 95 per cent of the post-1940 dwellings which had all census services were in these classes. In fact, none of the pre-1921 dwellings which lacked all census services or census services other than cold water were in 'good' condition. Similarly, the proportion graded 'very poor' were all within the pre-1921 group and were short of at least one of the census services.

Some corroborative evidence for the data in this table is available in *The Housing Situation in 1960* (39), based on a sample survey and returns from local authorities. Because of differences in concept and categorization no exact

[1] Census condition signifies the possession of some or all of the four census services—cold water, hot water, fixed bath, W.C.

[2] The physical condition classes used in the NIESR survey were: good, fair, fair–poor, poor and very poor (appendix 6).

comparisons could be made; the closest approach to parity occurs in the category representing all dwellings, and here the discrepancy was found to be well within the estimated margin of error arising from the residual differences. In two further instances (all census services available; lacking all census services except cold water) the two sets of data were found to be in broad agreement—in the former case, indeed, the discrepancy was almost negligible. For the two remaining categories, any realistic comparison between the two studies was found to be impossible.

Table 6.11. *Physical condition, age and census condition, 31 March 1964*

Percentages

Census condition	Physical condition	Age: Pre-1881	1881–1920	1921–40	Post-1940	All ages
Lacking all census services	Good	— }14	— }47			— }23
	Fair	14	47			23
	Fair-poor	2	11			4
	Poor	21	21			21
	Very poor	63	21			52
Lacking all census services except cold water	Good	— }33	— }55			— }48
	Fair	33	55			48
	Fair-poor	11	11			11
	Poor	45	17			26
	Very poor	11	17			15
Lacking hot water and/or fixed bath	Good	15 }65	16 }76	30 }81		16 }72
	Fair	50	60	51		56
	Fair-poor	10	12	11		11
	Poor	16	11	8		13
	Very poor	9	1	—		4
All census services available	Good	24 }82	30 }86	57 }92	77 }95	48 }89
	Fair	58	56	35	18	41
	Fair-poor	12	11	7	4	9
	Poor	6	3	1	1	2
	Very poor	—	—	—	—	—
All dwellings	Good	18 }67	25 }82	56 }92	76 }95	40 }84
	Fair	49	57	36	19	44
	Fair-poor	10	11	7	4	9
	Poor	13	6	1	1	5
	Very poor	10	1	—	—	2

SOURCE: NIESR sample (unweighted), see appendix 6.

Even a sample of 3,500 dwellings is not sufficient to provide regional sub-samples large enough to measure significant differences between regions within each age and census condition of dwelling. The sample data were therefore grouped into North and South. The differences between North and South within the sub-classes were not very large, nor consistent, and it was concluded that the major differences in physical condition between regions resulted from the different proportions of dwellings in each age and census condition group, rather than from differences in physical conditions within these groups.

Unfortunately it was not possible to apply proportions of both census condition and age-based physical condition to the population of housing at the same time, since the joint distribution of age and physical condition was not available for the housing population. The application of national proportions by physical condition within census condition groups and within age groups produced results which could not be reconciled. The former method was preferred, partly because the proportions by census condition in the housing population were known with a higher degree of certainty, and partly because census condition can be determined with precision during fieldwork, whereas age cannot. The application of physical condition/census condition properties helps to remove any bias resulting from limited field studies. The effect of introducing the weighting was to reduce the importance of 'good' and 'fair' dwellings and to increase that of 'poor' dwellings. The proportion of dwellings classified as 'fair-poor' and 'very poor' was not significantly changed (table 6.12).

Table 6.12. *National condition of dwellings, 31 March 1964*

Percentages

Condition	Sample	Weighted national estimate
Good: excellent state of repair	40	35
Fair: structurally sound, in need of minor repairs	44	41
Fair–poor: structurally sound, in need of moderate repairs	9	9
Poor: some structural defects, in need of extensive repairs	5	13
Very poor	2	2

SOURCE: NIESR estimates.

It appeared that about 85 per cent of the dwellings in Great Britain were structurally sound including only 9 per cent that needed more than minor repairs (table 6.12). However, there were about 2 per cent apparently so defective that they needed to be rebuilt and 13 per cent needing extensive repairs. Thus about 340,000 dwellings, out of a total stock of 16·8 million dwellings in March 1964, were suitable only for demolition. Allowing for demolition and closures, this would suggest that in 1961 there were about 560,000 dwellings which were in very poor condition, compared with the Ministry of Housing's estimate (February 1961) of 600,000 in England and Wales (47).[1]

There appears to be little difference in the proportion of structurally sound dwellings in the mainly urban regions, the range lying between 84·3 and 85·5 per cent (table 6.13). There is a greater range among the mainly rural regions: North and Central Wales and East Anglia showing rather low percentages.

Table 6.13. *Regional condition of dwellings, 31 March 1964*

Percentages

	Structurally sound dwellings		Very poor dwellings
	Good	All	
Scotland	33·5	84·3	2·4
North	35·3	85·3	1·4
North West	34·8	85·4	1·3
Pennines	35·0	84·5	2·1
Central	33·7	84·6	2·0
East	33·7	83·3	3·2
North & Central Wales	30·6	79·2	7·0
West	34·6	84·4	2·2
South West	34·5	83·0	3·4
Midlands	34·5	84·6	2·0
East Anglia	31·1	79·4	6·8
South East	35·8	85·5	1·2
Great Britain	34·8	84·7	1·9

SOURCE: NIESR sample, see appendix 6.

The regional differences in the percentage of 'very poor' dwellings are much greater: in the mainly rural regions it is over twice as high as in the urban regions, North and Central Wales and East Anglia again having particularly high figures. The condition of dwellings in some of the mainly urban regions appears much better than might have been expected. This may be partly because most published figures relate to statutory unfit dwellings, and because general impressions of housing conditions tend to be based more on a visual impression

[1] The official estimate of unfit dwellings was given in 1965 (49) as about a million, the number already identified as slums. The definition of a slum is based on the absence of services as well as on physical condition. The identification of slums is carried out locally, and both physical and social standards will vary. The criteria applied in this study for classifying dwellings are purely physical. A distinction must be drawn between physical condition and economic potential. The proportion of dwellings in a given condition to be demolished over a given period depends on the balance between need and supply, the capacity of the construction industry and the value of resources to be used in improving existing dwellings (chapters 8 and 9). A better return for the resources used may be obtained from rehabilitating a dwelling in a poor condition and lacking basic services than from demolition and rebuilding.

obtained from the environment than on the dwellings themselves.[1] Moreover, it may be that greater progress has been made in clearing unfit housing from the large settlements in urban regions than from the smaller ones in the rural regions.

Physical condition is a measure of neglect, and does not give any information on the standard to which the dwelling was originally built. Standard relates to the size of rooms, room height, the amount of facilities and their quality and the standard of finish. High standard dwellings tend to be more flexible than low standard dwellings: because they were built to meet high standards they are

[1] The statutory definition of unfitness is based on a mixture of specifications some of which relate to condition and some to standard. Estimates of expected life are frequently recorded on the basis that no repairs or improvements are carried out. Such information provides no clear guide as to the potential of the stock, although it is probable that such figures reflect condition. It will be noticed that, while the various official surveys differ in the proportions classified as unsatisfactory, there is general agreement that about a seventh of the existing stock of dwellings needs urgent attention.

Percentages

	England and Wales 1964[a]	Scotland 1965[b]	England and Wales 1966[c]	Great Britain 1964[d]
Unfit	4	4	12	2 Very poor
Less than 15 years' life	8	13	28[e] (both rows)	13 Poor
15 but less than 30 years' life	17	12		9 Fair–poor
Over 30 years life	71	71	60[f]	76 Fair–good

[a] Woolf, *The Housing Survey in England and Wales, 1964* (40).
[b] Cullingworth, *Scottish Housing in 1965* (41).
[c] 'House Condition Surveys', *Housing Statistics, Great Britain*, No. 10, 1968.
[d] Table 6.12, p. 93.
[e] Needing more than minor repairs. [f] Remainder.

The various official surveys also give some support for the regional differences in condition which were found. The percentage of unfit dwellings in rural districts is 13·3 as against 11·3 in urban areas, and generally there are fewer unfit dwellings in the South East.

It is difficult to explain why the estimated proportion of unfit dwellings should be so high in the official North West and in Yorkshire and Humberside. An unfit dwelling is one deemed not reasonably suitable for occupation because of damp and defects in the standard of repairs, stability, natural light, ventilation, drainage and other water services, and facilities for food preparation and storage. While the instances of dampness would tend to be high in the North West and in West Yorkshire this does not explain all the difference. It would seem that either more stringent standards are being applied in those regions than elsewhere, or that dwellings in those regions are particularly inadequate in one or more of the requirements considered. The test of unfitness is essentially negative and substantially different results would be obtained if an unfit dwelling were taken as one not economically worth improving.

Judgment of the relative condition of the housing stock depends on the basis of comparison. Conditions in the North would appear much worse in relation to those in the South of England than in relation to conditions in Great Britain as a whole. It is possible that, superficially, the condition of the stock in the North appears to be worse than it is.

more likely to meet present and future standards than a dwelling which was built to satisfy past minimum standards. The cost of maintaining higher standard dwellings will also tend to be greater than for other dwellings because of the greater space and facilities. It was, therefore, necessary to try to establish the standards of dwellings.

While it is fairly easy to distinguish substandard and high cost dwellings from other grades, it is difficult to draw a line between low cost and medium cost dwellings. The survey indicated that 3 per cent of the dwellings were substandard—many of these will also be in very poor physical condition—and 5 per cent were high standard: these figures applied to survey areas both in the North and in the South. While the proportion of low and medium cost dwellings taken together was the same in both sets of areas, the ratio of low to medium cost dwellings varied from 62:38 in the south to 75:25 in the north. Because of the difficulties of distinguishing between low and medium cost dwellings and of the resulting uncertainty about the proportions, and because there seemed to be no strong reasons for expecting the standard at which a dwelling was built to be associated with age and census condition, there existed no valid basis for estimating the proportions of dwellings of different standards either nationally or regionally.

Table 6.14. *Quality of dwellings, 31 March 1964*

Percentages

High standard	5
Medium standard	27
Low standard	65
Substandard	3

SOURCE: NIESR sample.

About 70 per cent of the sample of housing appeared to be low cost standard or below, and 30 per cent of a higher standard (table 6.14). If the weights used for the costs of making good arrears of maintenance (table 8.2) are applied to these percentages the result would suggest that the average standard of the stock is nearly 15 per cent above the standard of dwellings classified as low cost standard. In fact, the weights used for costing arrears of maintenance are probably higher than the weights applicable to the costs of new construction and as a result overestimate the lack of standard in the stock. The percentage to allow for extra quality is probably closer to the corresponding percentage for current construction, which appears to be around 10 per cent (chapter 7).

Information was also collected during the field survey about certain services not covered by the Census. This information was then combined with that from the Census, to which it was closely related (table 6.15). The water closet was

Table 6.15. *Provision of services, Great Britain and the U.S.A.*

Percentages

	Great Britain, 1964	USA, 1960
Dwellings without a cold water supply	0·7	7·1
Dwellings with a cold water supply	99·3	92·9
Dwellings without a W.C.	4·8	10·3
Dwellings with an external W.C. only	13·4	3·0
Dwellings with an internal W.C.	81·8	86·7
Dwellings without a hot water supply	16·6	12·8
Dwellings with a hot water supply	83·4	87·2
Dwellings without a fixed bath	18·5	14·8
Dwellings with a fixed bath but no bathroom	3·6	85·2[a]
Dwellings with a fixed bath in a bathroom	77·9	

SOURCES: British figures, NIESR estimates; US figures, *Statistical Abstract of the United States: 1966*, U.S. Bureau of the Census, Washington, D.C., 1966.

[a] Exclusive use of bathtub or shower.

external in about 14 per cent of the dwellings with this service,[1] and about 4 per cent of the dwellings with fixed baths were without bathrooms. Most dwellings appeared to have access to mains services. Over 99 per cent of the dwellings surveyed had both a water and an electricity supply: this might be higher than the national average, since the survey did not include an adequate proportion of rural dwellings. The provision of services in British housing compares not unfavourably with the standards in Europe and the United States.

THE PROVISION OF GARAGES

Information was collected during the field inquiries on the provision of private garages and on spaces in private gardens or yards which could be used for a garage. The proportion of dwellings without a garage or a garage space fell as their age fell; the proportion where the space had already been used increased as their age fell. There was a sharp break in provision between dwellings built before and after 1920 (table 6.16). The proportion of houses of all ages without a garage or a space was about 63 per cent; it was about 68 per cent for dwellings in mixed buildings and about 75 per cent for flats. The differences between North and South revealed by the sample were inconsistent and no firm conclusions could be drawn.

[1] This figure and figures in table 6.14 appear to agree closely, where comparable, with those obtained in the Sample Census 1966.

Table 6.16. *Provision of garages and spaces for garages, 31 March 1964*

Percentages

	With garage	Without garage but with space	Without garage or space
Sample results			
Pre-1881	8	8	84
1881–1920	12	8	80
1921–40	32	21	47
Post-1940	37	20	43
Weighted national estimate [a]			
All dwellings	23	14	63

SOURCE: NIESR estimates.

[a] The proportions given for each age group were weighted by the number of dwellings in each age group in each region to give a weighted national estimate.

THE CONDITION OF THE RESIDENTIAL ENVIRONMENT

A part of the amenity of housing is derived from the locality in which it is situated. The amenity of an area is related to such factors as the condition of roads and services, the availability of open space, the quality of landscaping, the disposition of the buildings, noise, and the amount of traffic. There appears to be no published information for Britain on the condition of the environment in residential areas and data were collected by field studies.

Most dwellings were found to have main services, although the supply of these is probably not quite so complete as the survey suggested, since the rural areas were under represented. In most housing areas the estate roads are made up and footpaths paved. Unmade roads were found predominantly in high class residential areas, mainly in areas developed between the wars. Nationally it did not appear to be an important problem.

The field work teams were asked to assess the amenity of the street in which the dwellings were situated as 'good', 'fair' or 'poor'. The northern samples had a higher proportion graded 'good' than the South, and a higher proportion graded 'poor'. While this remained broadly true for each of the four age groups, the proportions varied; the proportion of 'good' was much the same in the North and the South for the 1881–1921 and the post-1941 age groups, and the proportion of 'poor' was much the same in the 1921–41 and the post-1941 groups. The grading is inevitably very subjective and the differences between North and South may be largely a result of differences between field workers' standards. The relationship between the grades and age was reasonably consistent in the South but not in the North. The relationship for the country as a whole was also reasonably consistent (table 6.17).

Table 6.17. *Condition of environment and age of dwellings, 31 March 1964*

Percentages

	Grading of residential environment		
	Good	Fair	Poor
Sample results			
Pre–1881	23	51	26
1881–1920	27	55	18
1921–40	62	34	4
Post–1940	73	23	4
Weighted national estimate [a]			
All dwellings	48	39	13

SOURCE: NIESR estimates.

[a] The proportions given for each age group were weighted by the number of dwellings in each age group in each region to give a weighted national estimate.

RATEABLE VALUE INDICATORS

Rateable values are related to rents and should, therefore, provide a general indicator of the amenities of dwellings. They have often been used for this purpose. However, rents and rateable values vary from one part of the country to another for properties which are similar in size, quality and situation. Before rateable values can be used as an indicator of residential amenities, some allowance must be made for the differences in rating levels from one area to another. Rating levels are affected both by region and by size of town. A study of the rateable values of similar local authority housing has indicated that rateable values are 50 per cent higher in the larger towns than in the smaller (appendix 7). Outside the South East there is a range of values of two to one over the eleven regions. In the South East outside London, rateable values are over twice as high as in some regions and in metropolitan London three times as high. These relationships can be used to standardize actual rateable values by removing the influence of region, size and type of local authority. The resulting distributions reflect regional differences in the size of dwellings as well as in their amenities. The effect of dwelling size can be removed by using factors based on the rateable values for different sizes of dwelling. An allowance for size has the greatest significance for Scotland, for which the average size of dwelling is so much lower than elsewhere (table 6.18). The result for the South West seems to be quite inexplicable, although, of course, this is a region with a high postwar rate of dwelling construction, and one within which a high proportion of construction was private.

While on average the number of habitable rooms per dwelling is not greatly different between the North and the rest of Great Britain, the proportion of small dwellings is substantially lower in the North than in Great Britain as a whole. This is partly because of the smallness of dwellings in Scotland, and partly because the ratio of flats is small in the North and flats are usually smaller than houses. The ratio of missing services declines as the number of habitable rooms per dwelling increases. Hence the proportion of dwellings of a medium size with inadequate services is greater in the North than the average figures imply. Since the measures of a physical condition are based on the association between physical condition and the incidence of services, the level of condition will also tend to be marginally worse than implied by averages. Thus the indications from the standardized rateable value figures may be more representative of the relative quality of dwellings in the North than those given earlier.

Table 6.18. *Indices of rateable values for 1963/4 before and after standardization*

	Average rateable values	Rateable values standardized for region and rating differences	Rateable values standardized for region, rating differences and size of dwelling
Scotland	59	90	106
North	90	96	101
North West	102	92	92
Pennines	84	90	91
Central	111	99	96
East	87	94	91
North & Central Wales	74	94	91
West	100	106	101
South West	118	121	118
Midlands	106	102	101
East Anglia	95	96	92
South East	174	120	120
Great Britain	100	100	100

SOURCE: Appendix 7.

REGIONAL DIFFERENCES IN HOUSING QUALITY

It is of interest to compare the various measures of the quality of housing which are given in table 6.19.

Nearly all the indicators show that conditions are worst in North and Central Wales, while other mainly rural regions also have poor housing conditions. Generally the South East has the highest quality housing, followed by the North and the Midlands. The corrected rateable value indices are only in broad agreement with the other indicators. The disagreements appear more likely to be the result of inadequacies in the corrected rateable values than in the physical indicators.

Table 6.19. *Regional quality of housing, 31 March 1964*

	Average age of dwelling	Average size of dwelling	No cold water	No hot water	No fixed bath	No W.C.	Rateable value index [a]
	Years	*Rooms*		*Percentages*			
North & Central Wales	79	5·1	8	26	31	18	91
South West	69	5·0	3	18	19	8	118
East Anglia	66	4·9	8	28	26	15	92
West	61	5·0	1	19	20	6	101
East	60	4·7	3	21	22	8	91
Scotland	59	3·5	—	18	24	9	106
North West	58	4·7	—	13	20	2	92
Pennines	55	4·5	—	13	18	8	91
North	52	4·3	1	15	18	1	101
Central	51	4·8	1	24	19	5	96
Midlands	51	4·7	1	20	19	5	101
South East	50	4·7	—	16	15	2	120
Great Britain	56	4·6	1	17	19	5	100

SOURCE: NIESR estimates.

[a] As in last column of table 6.18.

CHAPTER 7

THE DENSITY AND COSTS OF NEW HOUSING DEVELOPMENT

DENSITIES OF NEW DWELLINGS

The costs of dwellings, and of the roads and services that support them, depend to a large extent on the density of development. While the concept of density is not difficult to understand, there are so many measures of density and so many variations in their meaning that considerable confusion exists in all discussions of residential densities.

Briefly, density is usually specified as net, gross or town density. Net residential density relates to the net housing area and includes the land occupied by the housing sites, by the estate roads and by any incidental open space in the housing area. The gross residential density relates to the land in the net housing area together with the land used for local shopping, primary schools, other local institutes and local open space. Town density obviously relates to all the land within the urban boundaries of the town. In this sector discussion is limited to net residential density.

Net residential density is normally expressed in one of four ways: dwellings, habitable rooms, bedspaces, or persons per acre. Each method has its own advantages and disadvantages. Dwellings per acre is a useful measure for assessing the requirement for roads and services, but it takes no account of capacity. Habitable rooms per acre[1] cannot easily be related to roads and services, but this measure gives a better measure of capacity than dwellings per acre. Bedspaces per acre provides the best measure of capacity. Persons per acre reflects not only capacity, but also the way the dwellings are occupied, and is useful for measuring the need for other services, for example schools and shopping.

A recent study of public authority housing (50) showed that the relationships

Table 7.1. *Relationship between dwellings, habitable rooms and bedspaces for public authority housing, 1963*

Type of housing	Habitable rooms per dwelling	Bedspaces per habitable room
Houses	4·1	1·0
Low flats	3·1	1·1
High flats	2·6	1·1

SOURCE: *A Survey of Local Authority Housing Schemes in Great Britain* (50).

[1] It is unusual to count kitchens in the number of habitable rooms when considering new housing, but a kitchen is counted for census purposes if main meals are taken there. Bathrooms, W.C.s, halls and landings are not usually counted as habitable rooms.

between dwellings and habitable rooms varied with the type of housing (table 7.1). While the average ratios of bedspaces to habitable rooms were very similar for all types of housing, the variations between schemes ranged from 0·7 to 1·4 bedspaces per room. No similar information was available for private housing, but other sources of information suggested that the figures for new private houses were similar to those for public authority housing (51).

A clear division must be made between dwellings with private gardens and those without; the amenities provided by the two types are distinct.

For dwellings with private gardens, mostly houses, density is mainly determined by the size of the garden. The number of storeys makes little difference, except at the highest possible densities. The effect on the densities when the size of the garden is changed can be seen in relation to a simplified housing layout (table 7.2). If two storey housing is used, it is not possible to obtain densities much higher than twenty-eight dwellings per acre with normal layouts because of the limitation of daylight requirements. At this density the houses could hardly contain more than four habitable rooms, so that the net residential density would be about 112 habitable rooms per acre. However, such a density is not compatible with an adequate provision of incidental open space, an attractive layout, or garages. The provision of garaging space for each dwelling is difficult when the densities exceed about fifteen dwellings per acre. Nevertheless, with careful planning and small private open spaces, garaging on a one-to-one

Table 7.2. *Plot sizes and densities for houses with private gardens*

Width of plot	Length of back garden	Depth of house	Length of front garden	Area of back garden	Area of plot	Area for roads and paths	Total area per dwelling	Dwellings per acre
Feet				*Square feet*				
16	35	25	20	560	1280	275	1555	*28·0*
18	40	25	20	720	1530	311	1841	*23·7*
20	50	25	20	1000	1900	350	2250	*19·4*
24	66	25	20	1584	2664	432	3096	*14·1*
30	90	25	25	2700	4200	556	4756	*9·2*
40	120	25	25	4800	6800	768	7568	*5·8*
50	150	25	30	7500	10250	1000	11250	*3·9*
60	180	25	30	10800	14100	1241	15341	*2·8*

SOURCE: Stone, *Housing, Town Development, Land and Costs* (52).

Note: In calculating the figures given in this table it has been assumed that the paths and carriageway will be 30 feet wide and that the houses will be laid out in parallel roads with side roads every 440 yards.

basis is possible up to densities of about twenty dwellings per acre. In practice, the densities achieved with houses are considerably lower than the maximum suggested as possible. Contours, old watercourses, trees and other obstructions, and small, irregular shaped sites tend to make it difficult to achieve densities as high as those theoretically possible.

A recent survey (50) gave the median density of public authority houses as fifty habitable rooms per acre, about thirteen houses per acre. A study of private housing (53), which was based mainly on houses, suggested a figure of eleven dwellings per acre. Since private houses contain on average about four habitable rooms (51), this would suggest a density of about forty-four habitable rooms per acre. In 1963–4 there were nearly three times as many houses built by private agencies as by public authorities, so it would appear that, on average, houses are built at about forty-six habitable rooms or 11·5 dwellings per acre.

The difference in the average densities at which public authority and private houses appear to be developed is a reflection of the relative proportions of low and high density houses in the two programmes. Whereas only about a third of public authority houses are developed at a density of less than forty habitable rooms per acre (ten dwellings per acre or less), about half of private houses are developed at this density (table 7.3). For very low density development of less than twenty habitable rooms per acre (five or less dwellings per acre), there is an even greater difference, the proportion being about four times as great for private as for public authority houses. For high density houses the position is reversed; the public authority's proportion of houses at a density of eighty or more habitable rooms per acre being about three times that for private houses.

Table 7.3. *Densities of public authority and private houses, 1960–2*

Habitable rooms per acre	0–19	20–39	40–59	60–79	80+	
Dwellings per acre (approx. equivalent)	0–5	5–10	10–15	15–20	20+	All densities
			Percentages			
Public authority	4	25	34	23	14	100
Private	16	34	38	7	5	100

SOURCES: Stone, 'The Prices of Sites for Residential Building', *The Property Developer* (53); unpublished data from the Building Research Station.

It is difficult to interpret the meaning of these differences. In some areas, densities are held down for private housing by planning authorities in order to maintain an existing type of amenity. But it is in the interest of landowners, whether or not they are developers, to push up densities since this leads to higher land prices (53). If densities of private houses are lower than those of public authority houses, even though there are pressures to raise densities, this would seem to argue that the demand is for lower density development. The evidence from abroad is that space standards increase as the standard of living rises (54).

For dwellings without private gardens the first limitation on density is imposed by daylight requirements. The increases in maximum density in terms of dwellings, rooms, or bedspaces as the number of storeys is increased is by no means proportional, since the higher the buildings the farther apart they

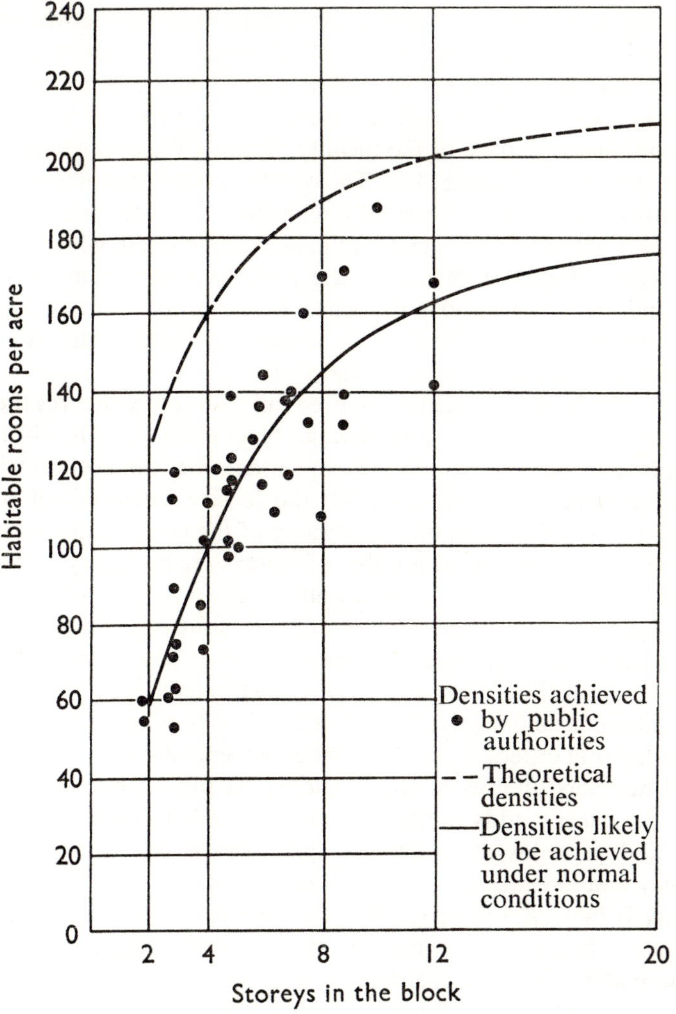

SOURCE: NIESR estimates.

Fig. 7.1. Density and number of storeys in flatted blocks

must be sited in order to provide sufficient daylight for an adequate part of the day. For example, the effect of increasing the number of storeys arranged in parallel blocks (street formation) from two to twenty is only to double, approximately, the number of rooms per acre (fig. 7.1). In theory, much greater densities can be achieved by the use of broken cruciform layouts, by reducing the size of rooms, or by making the blocks sufficiently deep to enable dwellings to be placed either side of a central corridor or back to back. Greater densities can also be achieved by utilizing special features of the site, such as changes in level and proximity to open space, or by constructing buildings between the blocks for which daylight and sunlight are of little importance. It is possible to achieve densities of 200 to 300 rooms per acre without going above ten storeys in favourable circumstances (55). However, the erection of a very tall building on one site pre-empts the sky space of the locality, limiting the opportunities to build similar high blocks on adjacent plots. The very high densities sometimes achieved in this country are a result of special circumstances which cannot be repeated over large areas of a city. The high densities achieved abroad, which are generally quoted in terms of persons per acre, are partly a result of an acceptance of different standards of amenity, in particular low levels of floor space per person (56). For countries nearer the equator, where the angle of the sun is higher, high densities can be achieved more easily.

In practice, the densities actually achieved fall short of the figures theoretically possible even on the assumption of parallel blocks (fig. 7.1). It will be noticed that some planners have achieved much higher densities than others without any increase in the number of storeys. Usually the density is determined on the basis of planning policy rather than on the capacity of the site, and the architect then decides what type of block and number of storeys are necessary to achieve that density, and the type of environment and visual impact which are required. As will be shown later, the greater the number of storeys, the higher the costs of construction, but such additional costs are more or less offset to the housing authority by the subsidies from the central government (52).

There has been little incentive to exploit the density potentials possible on the basis of daylighting criteria from different arrangements of blocks with varying shapes and numbers of storeys. But, while increasing the number of storeys in relation to the density adds to the real costs, it tends to make it easier to plan the estate and provides more ground space per habitable room for roads, parking, play and amenity space, and other purposes.

As density is increased in relation to the number of storeys the space about buildings per habitable room falls. At the theoretical densities (fig. 7.1) the average space about buildings per habitable room is about 200 square feet (52). At the average dwelling size for high density housing of 2·6 habitable rooms, there would be only just over 500 square feet of space about buildings for each dwelling. Roads and paths are likely to occupy 100 to 150 square feet per dwelling and about 250 square feet is needed for access and standing space for a car (52): so that, if provision is made for one car per dwelling, with half a space for visitors' cars, the space about buildings per dwelling for play space, planting, and other amenities is on average less than the size of a small room. Hence it is not surprising to find that densities fall considerably short of those theoretically possible (fig. 7.1). Higher blocks, with a greater number of storeys, often need to be used in order to increase the space about buildings rather than to increase the densities. Even so, without destroying other amenities, it is often only possible to provide adequate space for cars by using multi-level car parking (38). It would appear that daylight criteria no longer provide a useful indicator of acceptable densities.

Public authorities appear to be obtaining about 80 habitable rooms per acre (26 dwellings at 3·1 habitable rooms per dwelling) with low flatted blocks (two to four storeys) and about 138 habitable rooms per acre (53 dwellings at 2·6 habitable rooms per dwelling) with high flats (50). However, the provision of parking appears to be far below the level considered necessary in this study, in the longer term.

It seems clear that the densities likely to be achieved in future by the use of

Table 7.4. *Densities and number of storeys in flatted blocks of local authority housing*

Storeys	Habitable rooms per acre	Dwellings per acre		Bedspaces per acre [c]
		(1) [a]	(2) [b]	
2	58	19	22	64
3	80	26	31	88
4	99	32	38	109
5	115	37	44	127
6	128	41	49	141
7	138	45	53	152
8	146	47	56	161
9	152	49	58	167
10	156	50	60	172
11	160	52	62	176
12	163	53	63	179
13	166	54	64	182
14	168	54	65	185
15	170	55	66	187
20	176	57	68	194

SOURCE: NIESR estimates.

[a] Taking 3.1 habitable rooms per dwelling
[b] Taking 2.6 habitable rooms per dwelling
[c] Taking 1.1 bedspaces per habitable room
} see table 7.1

5

flatted blocks will probably not be better than the average of past achievements (fig. 7.1) and (table 7.4), and, that if 100 per cent garaging is to be provided, it will be necessary at least for high density development to use multi-level garaging and to make some use of the lower floors for car parking.

Fig. 7.1 relates broadly to schemes developed during the period 1956–60. A comparison between the densities reported over the period 1960–3 (50) and the average number of storeys of development over this period would suggest that density in relation to the number of storeys has fallen for high flatted developments. In that sector the average number of storeys appears to be about thirteen (table 7.5), to produce a density of 138 habitable rooms per acre, whereas earlier this density was being achieved with about seven storeys. The difference is, no doubt, a result of providing more space about buildings, in particular more space for parking.

Public authorities appear to be building at about 68 habitable rooms per acre,[1] while private housing is developed at about 44 habitable rooms per acre. Combining the information for public and private housing indicates current densities of about 17·4 dwellings, 59 habitable rooms and 60 bedspaces per acre (table 7.5).

Table 7.5. *Current densities of development*

Type of development	Habitable rooms [a] per dwelling	Habitable rooms [a] per acre	Habitable dwellings per acre	Percentages being built of each type
Houses	4·0	46	11·5	*74*
Low flats, 2, 3 and 4 storeys (average 3 storeys)	3·1	80	26·0	*18*
High flats 5 storeys and over (average 13 storeys)	2·6	138	53·0	*8*
All types	3·7	59	17·4	*100*

SOURCE: NIESR estimates.

[a] Bedrooms and reception rooms only.

Densities vary with the size of town; generally the larger the town the higher the densities, and in conurbations densities decline with the distance from the centre (50) (53). Generally flats are used in the central areas and houses at the periphery. The densities in terms of persons per acre depend on the number of bedspaces provided, that is on capacity, and on the rate at which they are occupied.

[1] Subsequent information confirms that densities are still of the same order despite a falling proportion of houses and a rising proportion of flats, particularly high flats (see *Housing Statistics, Great Britain* (57)).

DENSITIES IN THE FUTURE

It seems unlikely that density in relation to the type of dwelling will rise; in fact it is perhaps more likely to fall as space standards rise. Moreover, more space about buildings is likely to be needed for garaging and other facilities. Additional space about buildings would simplify the provision of further facilities which may be required in the future and reduce the risk of housing areas becoming obsolete, as have the more densely planned areas of the past. Any future increase in overall density appears more likely to be achieved by building greater proportions of flats, particularly high flats, than by increasing the densities for each

Table 7.6. *Combinations of types of housing, and density*

	Habitable rooms per acre					Overall housing density
	0–19	20–39	40–59	60–79	80+	
	Percentages					*Habitable rooms per acre*
Houses only						
Combination (1)	50	50	..	..	..	*20*
(2)	25	75	..	..	..	*25*
(3)	25	50	25	..	..	*30*
(4)	25	40	35	..	..	*32*
(5)	20	40	30	10	..	*36*
(6)	15	35	35	15	..	*40*
(7)	15	30	35	15	5	*43*
(8)	10	30	40	15	5	*45*
(9)	10	30	35	20	5	*46*

	Houses only, combined as above						Habitable rooms per acre in Low flats [a]		High flats [b]			
	(1)	(3)	(5)	(6)	(7)	(9)	70	80	100	120	138	
	Percentages											
Houses and flats	95	..	..	..	..	..	5	..	..	..	..	*23*
	..	90	..	..	..	..	10	..	..	..	..	*34*
	..	..	90	..	..	..	10	..	..	..	..	*39*
	..	..	..	90	..	..	10	..	..	..	..	*43*
	..	..	..	..	80	..	15	..	5	..	..	*50*
	..	..	..	..	75	..	20	..	..	5	..	*52*
	..	..	..	..	..	74	..	18	..	..	8	*59*
	..	..	..	..	..	50	..	40	..	..	10	*69*
	..	..	..	..	..	50	..	20	..	..	30	*80*
	..	..	..	..	..	40	..	10	..	..	50	*95*

SOURCE: NIESR estimates.

[a] 3 and 4 storeys.

[b] 5 storeys and over (average 13 storeys).

type of housing. However a larger proportion of households may require houses at the lower levels of density, and the densities of flatted blocks in relation to the number of storeys may fall to provide more space about buildings.

Some idea of the level of densities which could be obtained, and the composition of the types of housing needed to provide them, can be given by combining the various types of housing in different proportions (table 7.6).

A large range of combinations has been examined giving a fourfold density range (table 7.6). The combinations of types and densities of housing giving the lowest and highest densities are extremely unlikely in this country, but it is of interest to examine the way density affects land requirements and costs over a wide range. The effect on land use can be seen in table 7.7. At lower densities it is possible to provide a large proportion of dwellings in the form of houses. To secure high densities it is necessary to provide a large proportion of dwellings in high flats built close together. Since all the bedspaces will not be regularly used, the land required for 1,000 persons will be substantially greater than that required for 1,000 bedspaces.

Table 7.7. *Types of housing, density and land use*

Housing form [a]	Density of each type	Overall density		Land required for 1000 habitable rooms	Land required for 1000 bedspaces
Percentages	*Habitable rms/acre*	*Habitable rms/acre*	*Bedspaces/acre*	*Acres*	*Acres*
90 : 10 : 0	36 : 70 : 0	39	40	25·6	25·0
80 : 15 : 5	43 : 70 : 100	50	51	20·0	19·6
74 : 18 : 8	46 : 80 : 138	59	62	16·9	16·1
50 : 40 : 10	46 : 80 : 138	69	73	14·5	13·7
50 : 20 : 30	46 : 80 : 138	80	86	12·5	11·6
40 : 10 : 50	46 : 80 : 138	95	103	10·5	9·7

SOURCE: NIESR estimates.

[a] Percentages of houses: low flats: high flats.

THE SIZE OF DWELLINGS

The size of a dwelling depends on the number of rooms or persons to be housed, and on the standards of space to be provided. In Britain as a whole about 60 per cent of dwellings are of four or five habitable rooms, and nearly 90 per cent have from three to six habitable rooms. The sizes required in the future will depend on the size of the additional households to be housed.

The Parker Morris Committee (38) suggested floor space standards for public housing which varied with the number of people to be housed and with the number of floors on which the space was provided. The net floor areas, including space for storage, derived from their figures are shown in table 7.8.

Table 7.8. *Parker Morris standards*

Bedspaces	Equivalent nos. of		Net floor space including storage		
	Bedrooms	Habitable rooms	On 1 floor	On 2 floors	On 3 floors
				Square feet	
1	1	1	350	—	—
2	1	2	500	—	—
3	2	3	650	—	—
4	2–3	3–4	775	825	—
5	3	5	875	925	1050
6	3–4	5–6	950	1025	1100

SOURCE: *Homes for Today and Tomorrow* (38).

Note: The extra space where the accommodation is on more than one floor is to provide for the additional circulation space. Accommodation on three floors is not often provided but is normally in the form of houses.

TENDER PRICES

The tender prices for public authority housing are summarized by the relevant government departments for England and Wales and for Scotland. While only very limited information is published (58),[1] summaries are prepared monthly and are available on a confidential basis. The range of data available has varied from time to time and, for England and Wales, increased considerably in January 1964. The range of data available for Scotland is much more limited than for England and Wales. In addition, information is available from previous studies of public authority housing price data (52), (59), (60), (61), (62). No similar source of price data is available for private housing, and an inquiry among the larger house-builders was made, but little satisfactory data could be obtained.

Individual tender prices for public authority housing differ considerably: large price differences arise from differences in design, in marketing conditions and in contractor efficiency; they also vary with time and place. The differences tend to be so great that even the means of quite large groups often vary

[1] This situation has now changed with the production of *Housing Statistics, Great Britain*, published by H.M. Stationery Office for the Ministry of Housing and Local Government since 1966.

substantially. It is clear, therefore, that the indications of price level given by monthly and even quarterly groups of tenders can be very misleading. In fact, such price levels represent no more than the prices which were accepted at the places and times, and for the dwellings, for which tenders were received. If the dwellings for which tenders were received had been of different design in different places, or if they had interested different contractors, the price levels would, no doubt, have been different. The prices required for this study are those which would have been applicable on a regional scale; the tender price data represent no more than sample results from which estimates of the pattern of prices can be deduced.

For the range of sizes of dwellings with which the study is concerned, the dwellings covered by the tender price data provided much the same range of services and facilities. As a result, the price of a dwelling does not change proportionately to changes in the floor area, and the greater the floor area the lower the price per square foot. For example, tender prices per square foot, for one and two storey public authority housing, are about 30 shillings (60 per cent) lower for dwellings of 1,175 square feet than for those of 350 square feet (table 7.9).

Table 7.9. *Tender prices for public authority bungalows, houses and two storey flats in England and Wales (outside London)*

Type of dwelling	Bed-spaces	Bed-rooms	Habit-able rooms	Net floor area	Price [a]	Price per square foot
				Sq. ft.	£	£
Flats or bungalows	1	1	1	350	1351	3·86
	2	1	2	500	1557	3·11
	3	2	3	650	1803	2·77
	4	2–3	3–4	775	2005	2·59
Houses or maisonettes	4	2–3	3–4	825	2083	2·52
Flats or bungalows	5	3	5	875	2159	2·47
Houses or maisonettes	5	3	5	925	2243	2·42
Flats or bungalows	6	3–4	5–6	950	2292	2·41
Houses or maisonettes	6	3–4	5–6	1025	2447	2·39
Houses (3 storeys)	6	3–4	5–6	1100	2621	2·38
Flats or bungalows	7	4–5	6–7	1025	2447	2·39
Houses or maisonettes	7	4–5	6–7	1100	2621	2·38
Flats or bungalows	8	5–6	7–8	1100	2621	2·38
Houses or maisonettes	8	5–6	7–8	1175	2777	2·36

SOURCE: NIESR estimates based on material supplied by the Ministry of Housing and Local Government.

[a] The tender price includes the dwelling itself and storage space, whether or not included within the main structure, and external works within the curtilage of the dwelling and its private space. It does not include any allowance for garages, roads and services, or for land. The price is estimated at 31 March 1964.

Comparisons of the prices of dwelling must, therefore, be made on the basis of common floor areas.[1]

As will be shown later, prices in the London area are very much higher than in other areas of England and Wales. The difference is greater than the total difference between the other regions. Moreover, the numbers and types of dwellings built appear to vary more, month by month, in the London area than elsewhere in England and Wales. For these reasons, prices for England and Wales outside London will be used as the basis of comparison.

The price base for the purpose of this study is the end of March 1964.[2] Prices for one particular month may be unrepresentative and price data have been analysed over a period long enough to provide an adequate amount of data.

PRICES OF ONE AND TWO STOREY PUBLIC AUTHORITY DWELLINGS

Since the various sizes of one and two storey dwellings provide broadly comparable facilities, the differences in price per square foot are mainly a result of differences in floor area. The formula relating price per square foot to floor area only applies over a small range of areas and becomes less reliable as the range extends. Therefore initially, each type and size group of dwelling was considered separately and mean prices were established from price data for the first six months of 1964 by the use of the formula for each group. These were plotted against the average floor areas and a smooth curve was drawn through the points (fig. 7.2). The prices appropriate for the Parker Morris (38) floor area recommendations are given in table 7.9. There appeared to be no important differences in the prices of houses and flats of two storeys with similar floor areas, or between houses and bungalows of similar floor areas.

An earlier study of the tender prices of two storey dwellings indicated that up to mid-1957 prices were 20 to 25 per cent higher in the London region than in the rest of England and Wales (52). This disparity in prices appears to have increased. An analysis of the tender prices for public authority two storey, three bedroom houses, adjusted to a standard floor area of 900 square feet, over

[1] A regression analysis of the tender prices of a large group of two and three bedroom public authority dwellings (63) gave the following relationship between the price per square foot for different sizes of dwelling:

$$y_a = y_o[1{\cdot}5-(\tfrac{1}{2}\cdot x_a)/x_o]$$

where y_a is the price per square foot for required area 'a'
y_o is the price per square foot for given area 'o'
x_a is the required area 'a'
and x_o is the given area 'o'.

This relationship appears to hold good both for houses and blocks of flats. It would not, of course, hold good for large differences between x_a and x_o.

[2] By the latter part of 1967, tender prices of dwellings appeared to have increased about 25 per cent over those for March 1964. This is about twice the rate of increase of building prices generally and no doubt reflects the growing extent to which Parker Morris standards are now accepted.

the period from the beginning of 1962 to the first quarter of 1964, indicates that prices were about 30 per cent higher in the London region than in other regions of England and Wales.[1] Part of the difference in prices between the London region and the rest of England and Wales can be accounted for by the higher rates of earnings of building workers in London, although the difference in hourly earnings is less than 10 per cent. In 1948–50, labour productivity was found to be about 10 per cent lower in London than in the rest of England and

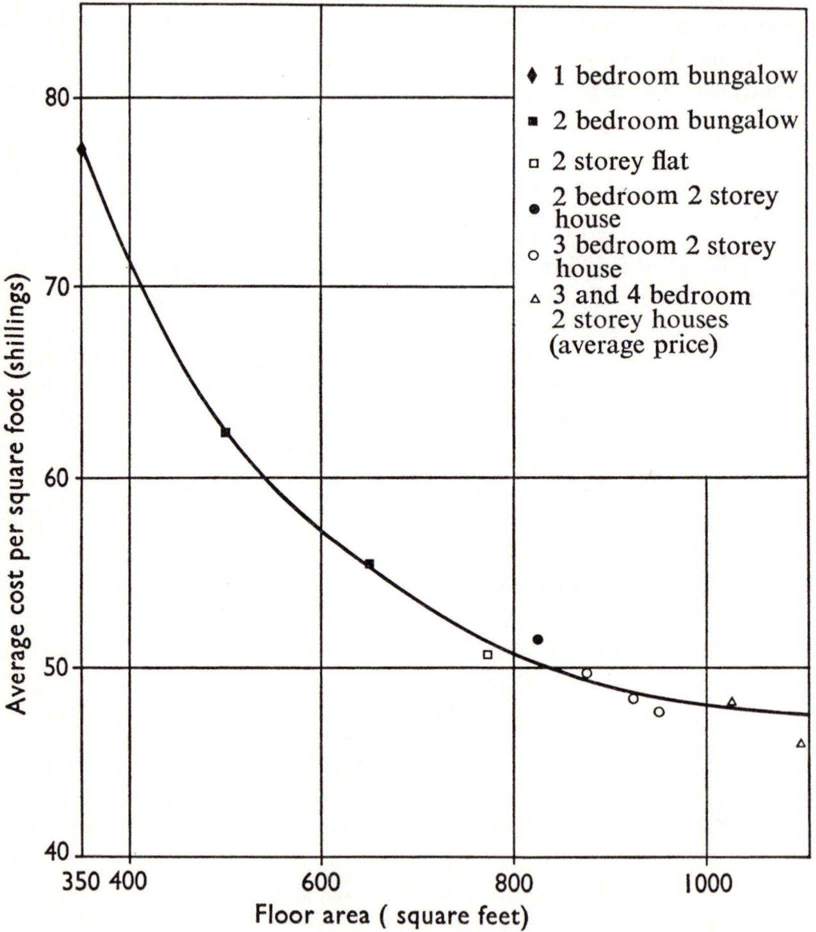

SOURCES: Unpublished data supplied by the Ministry of Housing and Local Government; NIESR estimates.

Fig. 7.2. Tender prices of local authority dwellings, January–June 1964, England (excluding London)

[1] Recent figures indicate that the situation has persisted, see *Housing Statistics, Great Britain*, H.M.S.O.

Wales (64). Even if this were still true the combined effect of higher earnings and lower labour productivity would only account for about half the higher prices in the London region. Such indications as are available do not suggest that the difference in material prices would be anything like sufficient to account for the balance: part of this may be the result of design differences, and the additional costs of substructure and site works where development takes place on recently disturbed land and land containing old service connexions rather than on virgin land. The ratio of prices for substructures and external services in London compared with elsewhere for two storey, three bedroom houses are over twice as great as for the superstructures. Over the first half of 1964 the difference in the tender prices accounted for by the extra costs of substructures and external services, as compared with superstructures, was 230 per cent. Thus it would appear that, of the 30 per cent increase in price in the London area, 24 per cent may be the result of higher general price levels and 6 per cent the extra costs of building substructures and external services in made-up ground. This latter element of price will eventually be important elsewhere as existing areas are redeveloped. An allowance for the extra costs of using redevelopment land is calculated later in chapter 12.

While the price levels for the other regions in England and Wales do not differ from the average by as much as the price level for the London region, there is, nevertheless, a spread of price levels of nearly 10 per cent on either side of the average (table 7.10). The actual percentage differences for the different regions have fluctuated from one quarter to another, but over the nine quarters

Table 7.10. *The regional relationship between tender prices for two and three storey public authority dwellings in England and Wales* [a]

Standard Region	Price indices
Northern	91
East and West Ridings	97
North Western	104
North Midland	92
Midland	100
Eastern	99
South Eastern	105
Southern	108
South Western	105
Wales	99
England and Wales, excluding London	100

SOURCE: as table 7.9.

[a] Tender prices over the period 1962 to first quarter 1964 for two storey, three bedroom houses and three storey, two bedroom flats.

from the beginning of 1962 (the period for which suitable data are available) there has been no discernible trend in the movement of the percentages. Over this period the ordering of the regions, in terms of price level, has remained consistent. This is true for both two storey, three bedroom houses and three storey, two bedroom flats; in each case the analysis was based on tender prices per square foot for similar floor areas. Subsequent analysis of similar data for 1964 and later years has confirmed these results. Analysis of measured rates taken from successful tenders over this period produces a regional pattern similar to that obtained from analysing the tender prices. Since the effect of design differences should not be reflected in the rates for units of similar work, it is reasonable to conclude that regional differences in price levels stem mainly from differences in regional efficiency, the costs of labour and materials, and long-term differences in supply and demand.

Unfortunately, price data for public authority housing in Scotland are not available on the same scale or in the same form as for England and Wales. The comparison between prices for Scotland and the rest of Britain must, therefore, be more tentative than between different regions in England and Wales. It would appear, however, that over the comparable period of 1962 and 1963 tender prices in Scotland have been about 20 per cent higher than in the rest of Britain outside London, for dwellings of the same size.[1] This difference is perhaps not surprising. In some respects the specifications of dwellings in Scotland are higher than in England and Wales, partly for climatic reasons. Moreover, a large proportion of housing in Scotland is still contracted under the trades contracting system, which theoretically, and probably in practice, is less efficient than the main contractor system used in England and Wales. Again, building materials are short in Scotland; many basic materials have to be imported from England or from the Continent, and hence tend to be more expensive than in England.

It is also of interest to consider whether building prices in new towns are different from building prices in existing towns. The amount of construction in new towns greatly exceeds the capacity of local builders; construction firms from other parts of the country carry out a great deal of the work, for which they bring in outside labour, involving extra costs for travelling or billeting. Against such factors, which tend to raise costs, can be set the scale and repetitive nature of the designs and the freedom from the congestion of the existing urban areas. The amount of price data available for a comparison between the tender prices of public authority dwellings in new towns and in existing towns is rather limited and the comparisons are not very consistent. It would appear, however, that tender prices are a little higher in new towns than in existing towns, perhaps of the order of about 3 per cent. Of course, it will be appreciated that most of the new towns are now well established with their own labour forces; prices

[1] Again published data now available suggest that this situation is unchanged, see *Housing Statistics, Great Britain*, H.M.S.O.

may be higher only in the early stages when labour must be brought into the town from other areas.

A growing number of public authority dwellings are now being system built. In 1964 about 18 per cent of public authority dwellings were built in this way in England and Wales, and the proportion has since increased. Hence it is of some importance to consider what effect this change is likely to have on prices. Information has only been available recently: during the first three quarters of 1965 tender prices of system built houses in England and Wales were about 3 per cent more than those of traditional houses, and it is understood that the difference was less than in 1964 (65).[1] Increases of this order will not greatly influence the figures for average costs, even if the proportion of proprietary system built housing increases considerably. There appear, therefore, to be no grounds for altering the base date figures already given.

PRICES OF THREE AND FOUR STOREY DWELLINGS

In the main, three and four storey housing is in the form of flats and maisonettes. This type is transitional between two storey housing and multi-storey blocks of five storeys and above. Three and four storey housing is normally similar in construction to two storey housing with masonry, load-bearing, external or cross walls. Lifts are not generally provided and usually no special problems of access arise.

Greater difficulties arise in determining the average price levels for three and four storey dwellings than for two storey dwellings. This is partly because fewer such dwellings are built and have been built, and hence there are far fewer price data on which to base estimates; and partly because the prices are more variable since there is less experience in design and erection, and more opportunity for different design solutions. The relationships between the tender prices of public authority two, three and four storey blocks tend to vary considerably from month to month according to the nature of the dwellings for which tenders are made. Relationships can therefore be established only by examining trends over a fairly long period. The results of a statistical analysis of tender price data referred to previously suggested that the comparative price levels (per square foot, for dwellings of the same size) for two, three and four storey housing could be taken at that time, 1957–9, as 100, 120 and 136, respectively (52). The results from theoretical design studies were in close agreement (61) (62). Since then the price gaps appear to have narrowed, and factors of 100, 112 and 122 would be more appropriate.

The difference in price levels for this type of housing between London and the rest of England and Wales appears to be less than for two storey housing, being 20 rather than 30 per cent more for London. The regional price differences

[1] While the extra price of system built (industrialized) houses fluctuates from quarter to quarter, it appears to average about the figure given above, see *Housing Statistics, Great Britain* (66).

outside London appear to be much the same for both two and three storey buildings, and in fact the figures given in table 7.10 are based on the indications from both series. Such information as there is does not appear to conflict with the expectation that similar, if slightly less variable, relationships apply for four storey buildings. Similar information on tender prices could not be obtained for Scotland and it will be assumed that the prices of three and four storey blocks for Scotland as compared with England and Wales (outside London) are a little lower than for two storey blocks. New towns have little experience of building three and four storey blocks, or of building higher blocks. Again the amount of price data available for proprietary system building is small, although it does appear that this form of building is a little more expensive than other forms (65), but not by enough to make a significant difference to the price levels.

PRICES OF DWELLINGS IN HIGH MULTI-STOREY BLOCKS

While the use of high blocks for housing is growing (although it is almost entirely confined to the public sector), still less than a tenth of all dwellings are provided in blocks of five storeys or more and hence the number of schemes of each height available for analysis is very small. Moreover, because of the lack of experience in design and construction and the great range of solutions possible with flatted blocks, prices are very variable and it is extremely difficult to determine the pattern.

The results of a study (52) of the tender prices of blocks with different numbers of storeys indicated that the pattern of prices for blocks of from two to twelve storeys varied considerably as between inner and outer London and the rest of England and Wales. Whereas in inner London twelve storey blocks were 58 per cent more expensive than two storey blocks, the extra cost was 85 per cent for outer London and 110 per cent elsewhere. However, this was not because high blocks were more expensive outside London than in London—in fact there was little difference—but because the prices of low blocks were so much less outside London. While the overall tender prices per square foot were much the same for high blocks whether in London or outside, a separate analysis for the trades showed a divergence between price ratios for trades where the specifications were likely to be similar and those where important differences in specification were possible. For trades for which specification differences were likely to be small, the regional price pattern had the same direction as for the lower blocks, although the percentage differences were smaller. For other trades the prices were lowest for inner London. Thus it appeared that the regional price pattern existed, although percentage difference declined, as the number of storeys increased, but that the pattern was masked by the higher costs of the design solutions actually used outside London. Moreover, the trades showing the regional price pattern were those likely to be sub-let to local firms, while those not showing the pattern were principally basic trades carried out by the main contractors, who were largely national firms.

For these reasons it was expected that the prices outside London for high blocks would fall as designers acquired experience more in line with the designers of the blocks in London, and as provincial firms gained experience in constructing high blocks. It was, therefore, suggested (52) that the relationship between prices per square foot with increasing storeys outside London would be more like outer London relationships, that is about half way between the relationships for inner London and those for towns outside London. Furthermore, design studies by the Ministry of Housing and Local Government (61) and by the Cost Research Panel of the Royal Institution of Chartered Surveyors (62) produced relative price relationships for blocks of three storeys and above very similar to those established statistically.

It is clear that the expectation of a fall in the proportional extra costs of building high blocks outside London has, in fact, been realized. While price levels have risen considerably since 1957, the percentage increases in tender price per square foot with increases in the number of storeys have become progressively

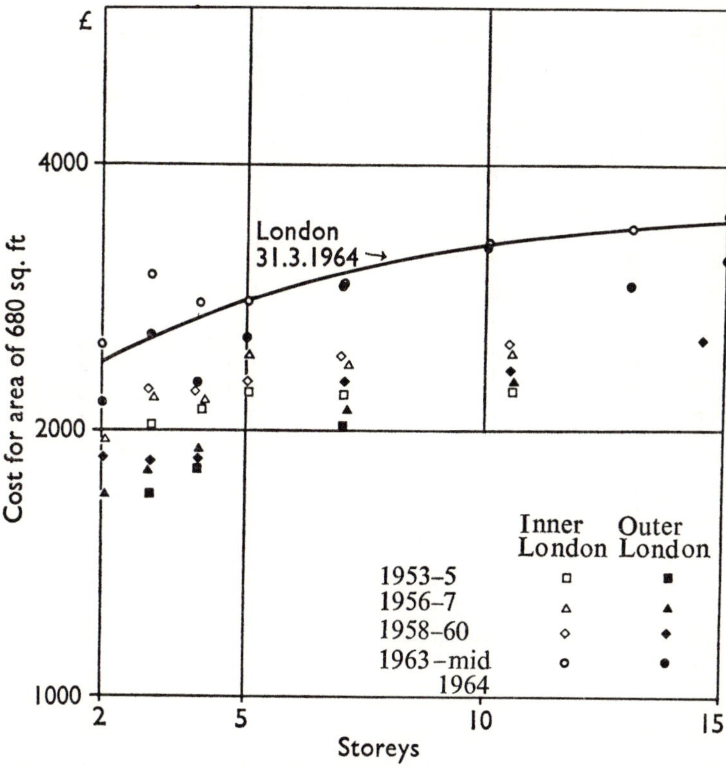

SOURCES: Unpublished data supplied by the Ministry of Housing and Local Government; NIESR estimates.

Fig. 7.3. Costs per dwelling and number of storeys in flatted blocks, London

less with the years (figs. 7.3 and 7.4). At the same time the percentage increases have tended to become greater in inner London and, to a lesser extent, outer London. It would appear that in London tender prices have risen faster for high blocks than for low blocks. As a result the difference in price levels between London and outside London has widened, although it is still not as great as for two storey housing. It would appear that the regional differences found between the prices of three and four storey housing have gradually declined, while the differences for blocks of eight storeys and above were about 10 per cent (table 7.11).

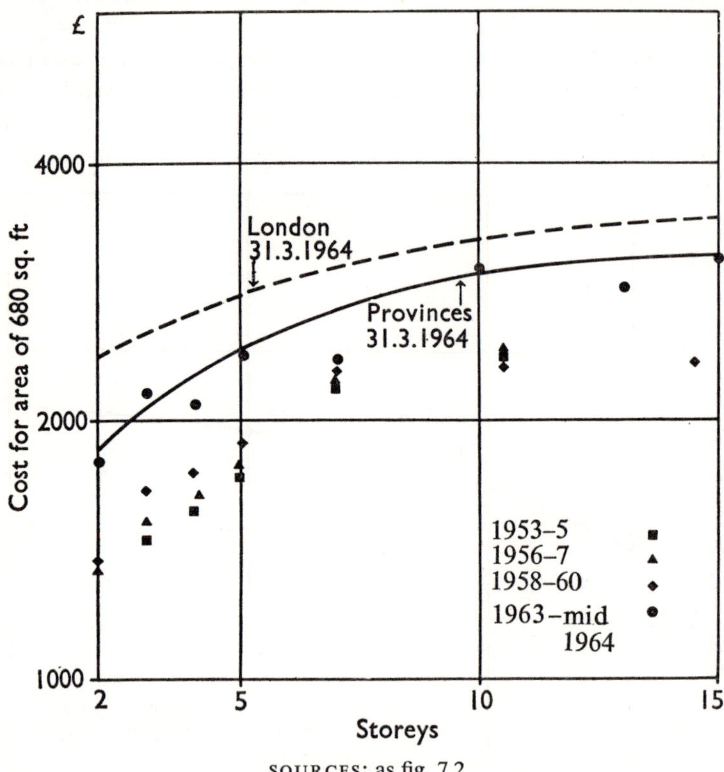

SOURCES: as fig. 7.2.

Fig. 7.4. Costs per dwelling and number of storeys in flatted blocks, provinces

In view of the scarcity and irregular nature of current price data for high blocks, the estimates need to be based on the indications from all the available data. It will be seen from figs. 7.3 and 7.4 that the trends have a similar shape for each of the periods for which data are available. For the London area the trends have become a little steeper and, for outside London, a little flatter, over the years. The figures which appear to apply at the base date show the expected fall in the difference between prices in London and outside. In fact, a crude average for flats in blocks of five storeys and above, as compared with houses and bungalows, for England and Wales for the first nine months of 1965, indicates that the former cost about 80 per cent more than the latter (65). While this figure does not necessarily indicate any increase in price of high flats, it does suggest that their price is not falling relatively to that of houses.[1]

Table 7.11. *Price levels of flatted blocks by number of storeys, 31 March 1964*

Storeys	Prices for flats of 680 square feet				London as a percentage of provinces
	London		Provinces		
	£	%	£	%	%
1–2	2395	100	1842	100	130
3	2539	106	2063	112	123
4	2682	112	2247	122	119
5	2802	117	2413	131	116
6	2922	122	2560	139	114
7	3018	126	2689	146	112
8	3090	129	2800	152	
9	3161	132	2892	157	
10	3233	135	2966	161	
11	3305	138	3021	164	110 (8–15)
12	3353	140	3058	166	
13	3401	142	3095	168	
14	3425	143	3113	169	
15	3449	144	3131	170	

SOURCE: as table 7.9.

The number of schemes with high blocks built outside London is too small to provide useful indications of the price levels in the separate regions. Clearly, the regional differences found between the prices for two and three storey blocks cannot be applied automatically to the high multi-storey blocks. It would seem that because high blocks are in general constructed by national contractors, who often use system building, the normal regional price differences are reduced. This probably accounts for the smaller price differences between London and elsewhere for high blocks as compared with houses and low flats. It seems reasonable to assume that the price differences outside London will be smaller for high flats in the same way as between London and the provinces. This assumption is reflected in the prices of flats, the regional differences for which fall progressively as the number of storeys increases (table 7.12).

[1] This is confirmed by analysis of more recent data, see *Housing Statistics, Great Britain* (66).

The amount of price data available for high blocks is too limited for comparisons of the prices of proprietary system built blocks with the prices of other blocks. Crude averages for the first nine months of 1965 indicate some saving from system building (65), but in this field there is not the same clear cut division between system and traditional building, and it seems unlikely that changes in the types of construction will be sufficient to have any significant effect on the relative price levels in the near future.

Table 7.12. *Regional price indices for housing, 31 March 1964*

Percentages

Storeys:	2	3	4	5	6	7	8+
England & Wales (excluding London)	100	100	100	100	100	100	100
London	130	123	119	116	114	112	110
Scotland	120	115	113	110	109	108	107
North	91	91	93	94	95	96	97
East and Pennines	95	95	96	97	97	98	98
North West and West	104	104	103	102	102	101	101
East Anglia and N. & C. Wales	99	99	99	100	100	100	100
Central and Midlands	100	100	100	100	100	100	100
South West and South East	105	105	104	103	103	102	102

SOURCE: as table 7.9.

FUTURE PRICE LEVELS

Since costs are measured in this study in real terms, no allowance is required for inflationary rises in price. It is expected that real costs of construction will fall in the future because of increases in productivity. This will be examined later. In this chapter it is only necessary to consider to what extent real costs might be changed as a result of changes in the price relationship by size, by number of storeys and by region.

The price relationship by size of dwelling is largely governed by the materials and labour needed to construct dwellings of given floor areas. Generally, prices per square foot fall as the size increases because the area of enclosing walls falls in relation to the floor area. This fall in price would be reduced if the number of rooms increased more than in proportion to size, or if the services provided in each dwelling increased irrespective of size. There is, as yet, no evidence of either of these tendencies and hence no basis for modifying the differences in price established at the base date.

While there has been some reasonable fall in the differences in the prices of flatted blocks of different numbers of storeys over the past ten years (figs. 7.3 and 7.4), there is no evidence that this movement is continuing. Such evidence as is available would suggest that the fall in the differential price arose from increased experience in the design and construction of high blocks relative to low ones. In the absence of the development of some revolutionary new method the effect of increased experience is likely to decline.

It has been suggested that in the long run the regional price differences are largely a result of differences in the costs of labour and materials, and in efficiency. No evidence is available on which to determine the relative strength of each factor or its future effect. The effects do appear, however, to have persisted over a fairly long period.

Since the price differentials under discussion appear to be firmly based and there is no evidence to indicate the way they might change, their use throughout the period can only be accepted.

HOUSING STANDARDS

The prices analysed for the purpose of establishing price levels at the base date relate to the types of dwellings actually built over the last few years. Little information is available on the extent to which the dwellings built in the last year or two satisfy the standards put forward in the Parker Morris Report (38), but opinion suggests that only a minority of public authority dwellings were built to these standards. Data on floor areas indicate average areas below Parker Morris standards; some large authorities, for example the London County Council, did not adopt these standards until mid-1964. Less than a third of the local authorities submitting rateable value data (appendix 8) could provide examples of dwellings built to Parker Morris standards. By the latter half of 1964 it would appear that over two-thirds of the dwellings built by public authorities had incorporated some of the improved standards. About half had the improved standard for space-heating, nearly a half the standard for kitchen fittings and electric sockets, and about an eighth for wash-basins and a second water closet (49).

About half the additional cost of raising standards to the Parker Morris level is a result of increases in floor area. Since the prices derived earlier have been related to Parker Morris floor areas, this aspect is covered. An analysis of the costs given in the Parker Morris Report, with an allowance for price rises since, suggests that an extra 5 per cent should be added to the prices derived earlier to cover the additional facilities recommended in that report. The 5 per cent would cover the addition of such items as better heating, kitchen fittings and bedroom cupboards, and more socket outlets. While it is said that the costs in the report were underestimated, the effect of this would be more or less offset by the inclusion in the base figures of some of the improved standards. The prices given earlier, together with the addition of 5 per cent, will, therefore, be taken as the prices of basic housing as at the base date.

While much of private housing is at or near this basic standard, some is both larger and better equipped. Most of this housing is built for sale and a large part of it is purchased by mortgage. The only finance house known to provide information on prices and specifications of dwellings being purchased is the Co-operative Permanent Building Society. An analysis of their data for April 1963, which was made specially available, throws some light on the standards of the housing now being built. The prices given include the land and development, and garages, so that it is necessary to make some allowance for this in order to obtain a picture of the standards of new housing now being purchased.

The price data were analysed by region and by floor area. Regional price indices were calculated for the main size groups based on the regional means for each group. The different sets of indices showed fair consistency and were averaged to provide a regional index. The cumulative regional distributions of prices were then graphed and their price scales adjusted on the basis of the index to give distributions at national prices. A deduction was made for the cost of land. This was taken at the median price of residential land, £5,000 an acre (53). Densities were assumed to range from fifteen dwellings an acre for dwellings under £2,000 to four dwellings an acre for dwellings over £6,000; the average density of eleven dwellings an acre (55) being equated with the £3,000–£3,500 group. The distribution was then used to determine the proportion of dwellings at various price levels above the public authority standard.

It was found that 57 per cent of the privately built dwellings were at about public authority standards as judged by prices, 11 per cent were 25 per cent better, 29 per cent 50 per cent better, and 3 per cent about 100 per cent better.

As far as is known, the prices of new dwellings financed through the Co-operative Permanent Building Society are not radically different from those financed in other ways: if any bias exists it is likely that the lower price ranges are overweighted, but in the absence of other evidence the Society's figures must be accepted. Using them as a basis and assuming that about 50 per cent of dwellings are public authority, the following distribution is obtained of the standards of dwellings now being erected (table 7.13).

Table 7.13. *Distribution of dwellings by standards*

Percentages

Local authority standard	79
25 per cent higher	6
50 per cent higher	14
100 per cent higher	1

SOURCE: NIESR estimates.

A study of the data for private enterprise housing indicated that the higher quality houses have a combination of greater floor areas, better heating, fittings and finishes, and greater garage provision. An analysis of the prices of dwellings built by contractors for sale showed the way the prices rose as the floor area was increased and the facilities improved. It also provided some indication that the differences in prices found among the regions in the Midlands and South for public authority house building apply also to private house building.

If it is assumed that dwellings of a better standard than public authority dwellings are built in about the present proportions, the cost of housing at the basic level will be raised by a factor of 10 per cent.

The standards of all housing tend to rise over time. The floor areas of low cost housing in this country have increased annually by perhaps half a square foot per head over the last 120 years (67). The rate of increase has not been uniform and is a result of increases in space for circulation, storage and bathrooms rather than in the net living area. It thus reflects the rise in the provision of services and other facilities. Standards in low cost housing have tended to rise markedly after each world war, and subsequently to settle at a slightly lower level (68). The standards in private housing are less satisfactorily documented, but clearly have improved. In the last decade the proportion of dwellings with multiple washing and toilet facilities and with full house heating has increased rapidly: average standards appear likely to continue to rise for these reasons alone in the next few decades.

The evidence for comparing standards of British housing with those of other western countries is limited and contradictory. Data are only available for low cost housing. These indicate that the ratio for British low cost housing between average annual earnings and cost is low compared with other countries, whereas floor areas are higher in Britain than elsewhere (table 7.14). It is, however, impossible to distinguish between the effect of relative levels of productivity and standards.

In recent years, Britain has been spending a rather lower proportion of its gross national product on gross capital formation for housing than most other European countries, although a little more than the United States (69). The Scandinavian countries appear to spend a quarter to a third more than Britain, and Belgium, France and Italy rather over two-thirds more. However, these figures do not necessarily indicate either higher standards now or the intention to increase standards rapidly in the future. A greater proportion of gross national product might be spent on housing for a number of other reasons: for instance, low standards in the current stock; an inadequate supply of dwellings; a rapidly increasing population; or a low level of productivity in house construction. As indicated in chapter 6, while the stock of British housing is older than that of countries which have advanced technically more recently than Britain, British dwellings compare very favourably in size and quite well in the provision of services; British housing also has one of the lowest ratios of persons per room.

The extent to which housing standards are likely to rise will depend partly on rises in national product in relation to population and on its distribution, and partly on the propensity to devote income to housing as distinct from other consumer goods and services and from capital accumulation. The latter will depend on relative prices, on the availability and need for goods and services of various types, and on the machinery and climate of opinion for the acquisition of housing facilities. Over the period 1953–63, household expenditure on housing increased only about three-quarters as much as expenditure on goods and services in general, and the proportion appeared to be falling (70). But the propensity to consume housing may rise as the desire for household durables and cars is satisfied. Such a tendency could be strengthened by government financial and fiscal policy, and by raising statutory minimum standards.

Table 7.14. *Low cost housing 1955–7: construction costs per dwelling expressed in average earnings for a year (man-years); and average floor areas*

	Construction costs	Floor area
	Man–years	*Sq. ft*
United Kingdom	2·7	970
Austria	4·3	590
Belgium	4·8	660–930
Denmark	3·6	750
Finland	4·0	540–590
France	4·9	600
Ireland	3·8	810
Italy	4·9	860
Netherlands	3·8	620
Norway	3·4	750
Sweden	3·4	650–750
Switzerland	4·0	430
U.S.A.	2·6	..
West Germany	3·7	610

SOURCE: *Financing of Housing in Europe* (71).

If expenditure on housing increased at about three-quarters the rate of increase in national output per head, as over the past decade, a 3 per cent annual increase in national output per head would imply an increase in housing expenditure per household of 2·25 per cent a year. At a constant rate over forty years, expenditure at the end would be nearly two and a half times the level today. An increase at 1·75 per cent per annum would have the effect of doubling expenditure, while an annual increase of 2·75 per cent would have the effect of trebling it by the end of the period. The effect of percentage increases in standards can readily be calculated once the total cost has been obtained at base year standards.

While it is impossible to know how such increases in expenditure might change the standards of housing, some idea can be obtained by examining the additional facilities provided in housing of above average cost. Some examples of the additions to and changes in specification of a low cost dwelling, each of which could be obtained by adding about 5 per cent to the basic price, are set out below (table 7.15). It will be seen, for example, that for an additional 25 per cent

Table 7.15. *Additional facilities for a low cost dwelling which could be provided for additional expenditure of about 5 per cent each*

Size and type

1. Additional floor space of 6 to 7 per cent.
2. Semi-detached instead of terrace.
3. Detached instead of semi-detached.
4. Spacious balcony or small sun room.

Services

5. Whole-house heating instead of partial heating.
6. Additional toilet room with W.C. and basin.
7. Shower closet.
8. Central vacuum cleaning.
9. Water borne waste disposal.

Insulation

10. High standard of thermal insulation.
11. Improved standard of sound insulation.

Internal fittings and finishings

12. Oak instead of deal internal and external doors.
13. Oak instead of deal staircase.
14. Polished hardwood floors instead of thermoplastic tile and deal.
15. Generous use of wall tiling, plastic or hardwood panels.
16. Large amount of built-in cupboards.

External features

17. Good quality facing bricks instead of flettons on external walls or high class dry finish.
18. Screen walls around garden instead of chain link fencing.

SOURCE: NIESR estimates.

Note: These facilities have been priced in relation to the standard low cost 2 and 3 bedroom dwelling in the form of houses or low flatted blocks.

on expenditure the dwelling could be 6 to 7 per cent larger, semi-detached, have whole-house heating, an additional toilet room and a high standard of thermal insulation. For an additional 50 per cent the dwelling might have features in addition to the above consisting of yet a further addition of space, a shower closet, polished hardwood floors, oak or other hardwood doors and either an oak staircase or a generous use of wall tiling and other high class finishes to the walls. For an expenditure of 75 per cent over that of a low cost house, a detached house with an extra 25 per cent of floor space could be provided, together with, for example, whole-house heating, an additional toilet room, a shower closet, improved thermal and sound insulation, and a high standard of finishes to walls, with hardwood doors, staircases and floors. A doubling of expenditure could be used to obtain further increases in floor area, extra equipment, and better finishes.

COSTS OF PARKING AND GARAGING IN HOUSING AREAS

The provisions of spaces for cars, even on a basis of one and a half to a dwelling, presents no real difficulty at densities up to about fifteen dwellings per acre. Usually there will be space to accommodate a garage, either beside or as part of each individual house, or at the rear of the garden when access can be provided from service cul-de-sacs. Treatment of this type is probably possible up to a density of about twenty dwellings per acre, although the problem becomes more difficult as the density increases and it may be necessary to provide grouped rather than separate garages on the individual plots. Grouped garages can be provided for about £150 a car, garages on individual plots for about £225 and hard-standing for about £40. These are prices applicable outside London and include an allowance for price changes since the figures given in the Parker Morris Report (38) were estimated. In the light of these figures it seems reasonable to take an average price of £200 per dwelling for garaging for low cost housing. The corresponding figure is probably around £250 for middle price housing, for which the garages would mainly be on the individual plots, and around £350 for high price housing, for which a large proportion of double garages would be required.

The problem of providing parking and garaging for medium and high density housing is more complex. As indicated earlier, parking for even one car per dwelling would occupy nearly half the space about buildings. This is generally considered unacceptable. The Parker Morris Committee suggested that not more than 10 per cent of this space should be used for parking: it was felt that open parking up to this limit would not unduly reduce the other amenities of the estate. The rest of the cars would need to be accommodated in multi-level or decked garages, or on the lower floors of the flatted blocks. If densities were to be maintained, it would be necessary to build higher flatted blocks in order to make additional space about buildings available for the garages and to offset the accommodation lost as a result of using the lower floors of the flatted blocks for garaging.

Various ways of providing the garage and parking space at the rate of one car per dwelling were examined and costed. It was found that, for densities of between 100 and 160 habitable rooms per acre, the cost for garaging and for building higher to maintain densities would be £250–£270 a dwelling. Just over a third of this sum would be the extra costs of the dwellings themselves. This figure was based on the assumption that a third of the cars would be parked on open hard-standing. If garages were needed for these cars to protect them from the weather, to provide additional private storage and work places, or to improve the appearance of the estate, the extra costs of decking over the hard-standing would have the effect of raising costs by an average of £100 a dwelling. The figures are based on a dwelling size of 3·77 habitable rooms per dwelling which would generate about twenty-seven cars per 100 habitable rooms (38). The average size of dwellings in high density housing is 2·6 habitable rooms per dwelling which would generate about thirty-eight cars per 100 habitable rooms. The costs of garaging for such dwellings would be greater, although not proportionately, since sites with smaller dwellings would already contain blocks with a greater number of storeys. Costs will tend to be lower for dwellings of a larger size. Rough calculations on these lines suggest that for a density of 140 habitable rooms per acre, at 2·6 habitable rooms per dwelling, that is fifty-four dwellings and fifty-four cars per acre, the cost per dwelling would be at the upper end of the £250–£300 range.

The figures given below are based on figures suggested by the Parker Morris Committee with an increase of one-eighth to allow for price changes since 1961 (table 7.16).

Table 7.16. *Extra costs per dwelling for car accommodation on estates of medium and high density, March 1964*

£s

Habitable rooms	Open hard-standing on 10 per cent of space about buildings [a]	All garaging under cover
2	340	370
3	320	
4	300	
5	280	
6	270	

SOURCE: NIESR estimates.

[a] Assumes 200 square feet per habitable room of space about buildings, which, at a density of 138 habitable rooms per acre, allows space for 10 cars. The price per dwelling for putting cars under cover naturally falls as the number of dwellings rises.

Some provision must normally be made for visitors' cars. The rate usually suggested is half a car per dwelling. Where garages are provided on individual plots, as they often are with houses, visitors' cars can be left on the garage approach. Thus, special provision is not normally necessary for low density housing. On medium and high density estates the garaging is usually grouped and is not sited close to the individual dwellings. In such cases provision for visitors' cars and even temporary parking for occupants' cars is usually necessary. This might add about £25 a dwelling.

It would, therefore, appear that about £200 per dwelling should be added to the cost of each house to allow for providing a garage and parking for visitors. For flatted developments the addition would appear to be about £300: the balance is the cost of using blocks with a greater number of storeys and this is already reflected in the relationship between the number of storeys and the density. The additional 10 per cent for higher cost housing can be applied to the figures for garaging to allow for the incidence of better class accommodation.

Since there was close agreement between the regional differences in price for two and three storey housing, and for a cross-section of prices for units of measured work, the regional price index based on two and three storey housing is used for obtaining the regional prices for garaging (table 7.12, column 1).

COSTS OF SITE CLEARANCE, ROADS AND SERVICES

The various phases of site preparation are usually contracted separately from each other, and from the construction of the buildings. Where there is a large amount of demolition work, as there is in the case of redevelopment, this also is usually the subject of a separate contract. Other contracts are let for levelling, constructing roads and sewers, and for landscaping. Usually the public utility services undertake the installation of their networks, often by direct labour but sometimes by contract.

In most cases housing development takes place either on land formerly used mainly for housing, or on virgin land. Local authorities were asked to state the costs of demolition in relation to the amount of building on the site and about twenty authorities supplied data of this type. The range of costs per dwelling demolished was quite narrow and averaged about £20. The cost figures related mainly to two storey and three storey dwellings of brick. These types of dwelling are easy to demolish, and the resulting rubble has a value as hardcore. Some figures obtained for the costs of demolishing stone tenement buildings were rather higher.

An analysis of a sample of town plans suggested that on average pre-1881 housing was developed at about twenty-eight dwellings per acre, housing built over the period of 1881–1920 at a density of about twenty dwellings per acre, and housing built over the period 1921–40 at about thirteen dwellings per acre. At £20 a dwelling, the cost of site clearance would be £560, £400, and £260 an acre respectively. The density figures can also be used as a basis for estimating the rate at which land will be realized as a result of demolition.

Generally, contracts for developing sites for residential areas are let as a whole, and a single contract is made for general site clearance, levelling, the construction of estate roads and sewers, footpaths, hard-standing, street lighting and often landscaping. At this stage no separation is usually made between the costs of developing the land intended for housing and land for other purposes in the housing area, such as shops, schools and open space. The costs applicable to land for housing can only, therefore, be estimated statistically by regressing costs per acre against the acreages and densities of the different types of uses.

Cost and land-use data were obtained from local and new town authorities in respect of sites recently developed by them. Adequate similar data could not be obtained from private developers. A previous study of this type (52) had indicated that costs and densities were related logarithmically and these data were analysed in a similar way. The two sets of results compared favourably, but it was found that the level of costs had risen since 1957 by more than might have been expected from the change in building prices. This difference in price level may have arisen because the general building indices have increased less than the prices for this type of work. It appears more likely, however, that standards have risen; probably there is now a greater provision of footpaths, lighting and hard-standing. The use of Radburn type layouts normally necessitates a greater provision of such facilities than traditional layouts. It was found that on average costs are about 50 per cent higher for redevelopment sites than for virgin sites.

The public utility undertakings do not normally appear to record costs and development data for individual sites. In the absence of suitable survey data, figures from the earlier study (52) were brought up to date on the basis of data from examples and average price movements. The costs of the public utility services were added to the other costs for site development (table 7.17). These figures were adjusted for regional price differences (table 7.12, column 1).

Table 7.17. *Costs of site development, roads and services on virgin land, March 1964*

Dwellings per acre	4	6	8	10	12	14	16	18	20	22	24
Costs per dwelling (£)	708	589	508	446	397	356	323	295	272	253	238

Dwellings per acre	26	28	30	32	34	36	38	40	42	44	46
Costs per dwelling (£)	226	216	208	199	192	185	179	173	167	161	155

SOURCE: NIESR estimates.

COSTS OF LAND

Land is not a produced commodity. The community possesses a set of sites; no resources are used in the mere transfer of the sites from one group of users to another, and hence the price of sites is not a real cost. Of course, if the use of a site is changed, costs are incurred in two ways. First, costs arise as a result of the development of the site itself; these are the development costs already considered. Secondly, costs arise as a result of the change in use of the site. The goods or services formerly obtained from the site are lost and the costs of providing them elsewhere must be considered. On the other hand, the produce obtained from the site in its new use has a value. This is either an addition to the national income or takes the place of a product formerly obtained elsewhere, the costs of production of which are now saved. Thus the real costs of taking a piece of land from one use to another is not the market price but the resultant net cost of developing it and the consequential balance between benefits and costs which results.

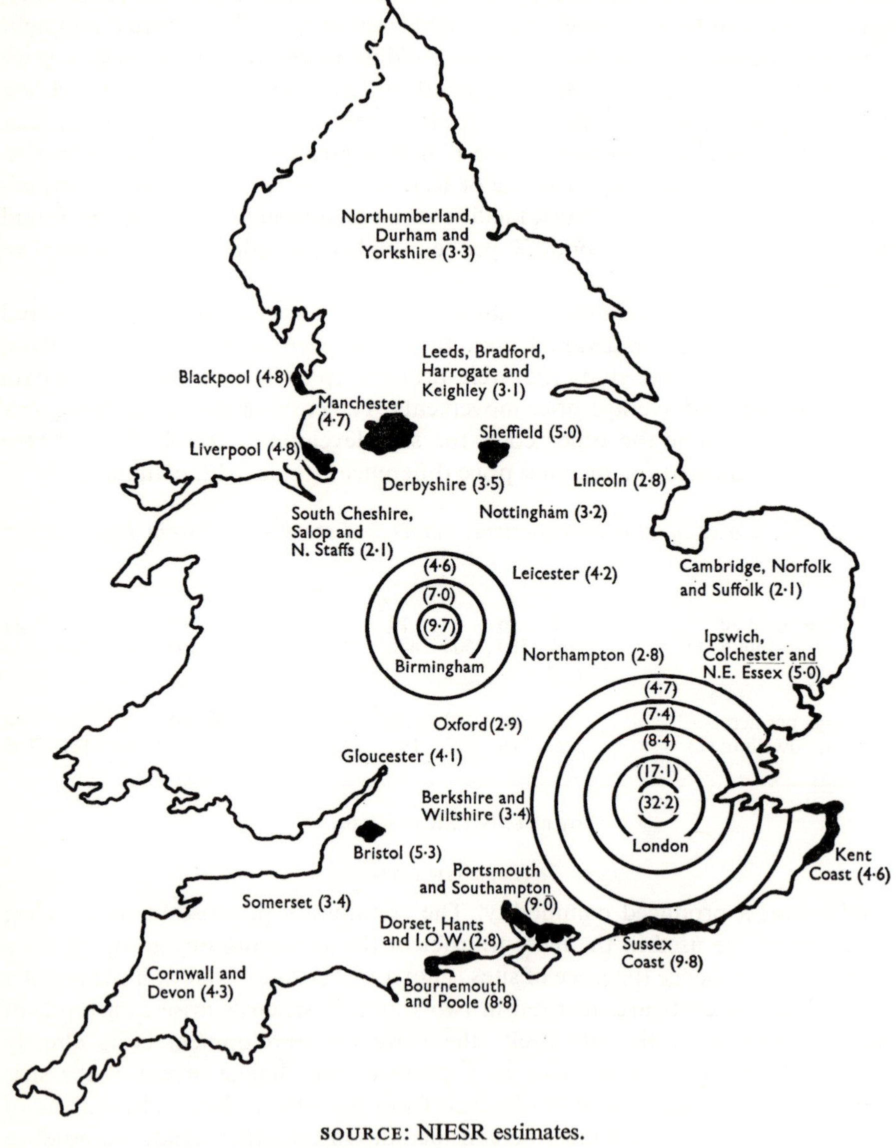

SOURCE: NIESR estimates.

Notes: Prices in £ thousands shown in brackets.
Circles round London and Birmingham at ten mile intervals.

Fig. 7.5. Prices of residential land per acre, England, 1960–4

But while the price of land is not relevant when considering real costs, it is relevant to financial costs. The price of land is an important determinant of the way it is developed and used, and some knowledge of land prices will be necessary when discussing land policy.

The only source of published data which appears to be available for land prices is the results of auctions of land which are published in the *Estates Gazette* each week. An analysis of these indicated that site prices varied according to the region, the distance from the centre of the region and the density of development (72). The overall regional picture which emerged for site prices per acre was of a plateau of prices covering the country, with peaks in the London and Birmingham regions and along the south coast, and perhaps minor peaks for the largest cities (fig. 7.5). The relationship between price per acre and distance from the centre of the region was exponential, while the relationship between price per acre and density was linear. These relationships[1] could only be established for London and Birmingham, as these were the only regions with dominant centres and adequate data. Prices have been increasing at about 10 per cent per annum over the period 1960–4 and so prices at the end of March 1964 were about 15 per cent higher than shown in the figure.

[1] Equation for the London region

$$y = \frac{1000}{3}(23+4x)\,e^{-z/28}$$

Equation for the Birmingham region

$$y = \frac{1000}{5}(30+4x)\,e^{-z/21}$$

where y is price per acre,
z is distance from the regional centre in miles,
and x is density in dwellings per acre.

CHAPTER 8

THE COSTS OF IMPROVING AND MAINTAINING EXISTING HOUSING

UNIT COSTS OF RESTORING AND UPGRADING DWELLINGS

A schedule of the costs of making good arrears of maintenance, and of adding missing services and providing bathrooms, was necessary as a basis for estimating the costs of upgrading the existing stock of dwellings. The required schedule of costs was compiled in a form matching the classification of the stock of dwelling by age, size, standard and condition.

Two methods of approach were considered. After some investigation a sample survey of improvement work and its costs was rejected because of the difficulties of obtaining a sufficiently large and representative selection of costs over the required range of dwellings. Moreover, it would have been difficult to determine the standard to which the dwellings were raised and the extension of life obtained as a result of the recorded expenditure. Instead a model approach was used, and this was supported by evidence collected from local authorities and other bodies which had carried out work of this nature.

The model approach[1] consisted of costing the work necessary to meet standard requirements compatible with the standards associated with current new housing (chapter 7). The basis of the costing was prices in force at the end of March 1964 for contracts of conversion and maintenance of a fairly large size to be carried out in the home counties. Detailed costing was undertaken for a skeleton of specification points and intermediate points were found by differencing. For example, all skeleton points over the range of dwelling sizes were taken at two, five and eight roomed dwellings (table 8.1). Separate figures were prepared for houses, flats and dwellings in mixed buildings. Similarly skeleton points were selected for different ages, standards and conditions of dwellings. Costs were prepared for work needed on dwellings with a range of life expectations. The effect on the costs of upgrading of such factors as floor area, number of storeys in the building and degree of detachment was also studied.

The separate sets of costs were analysed to establish the central tendencies and the relationships between the various main factors and the costs of upgrading (fig. 8.1). The levels of costs were compared with data obtained from local authorities and other sources. Finally, a schedule of cost factors was prepared, based on the results of the analysis.

The central point of the cost relationships between the arrears of regular attention, maintenance, replacements and repairs can be conveniently taken as the costs for a standard low cost dwelling, sixty years old with five habitable rooms, which has been allowed to fall into a state of marked disrepair, although

[1] This was devised and worked out by consultants.

Table 8.1. *Composition of costs of arrears of maintenance and repairs*[a]

£s

		Habitable rooms		
		2	5	8
Regular attention				
Internal	Painting or equivalent	45	80	110
	Washers for taps etc.	3	3	3
External	Painting etc.	30	50	120
	Cleaning gutters and gulleys	2	2	5
	Total	80	135	238
Repairs and replacements				
Internal	Floors	18	25	35
	Worm infection etc.	20	25	30
	Sanitary fittings and piping	45	60	60
	Electrical installation	55	75	115
	Gas installation	5	5	5
	Fireplaces	34	34	60
	Sundries	5	6	10
	Built-in equipment	5	5	5
External	Roof	70	70	90
	Brickwork	10	20	40
	Lintels	5	20	35
	Damp	20	20	20
	Facings	15	25	40
	Windows	20	50	85
	Rainwater gutters etc.	15	25	40
	Drains	15	15	15
	Frost damage	20	25	25
	Sundries	8	10	15
	Total	385	515	725
TOTAL		465	650	963

SOURCE: Consultants' estimates.

[a] Low cost dwelling, fair–poor condition, aged 60 years, expected future life 40 years, price level for home counties, March 1964.

structurally reasonably sound. The cost of making good such a dwelling, to give it a future life of about forty years, adjusted to average prices in Britain outside London, has been estimated to be about £650. There do not appear to be any substantial or consistent differences between the different types of dwellings, in the costs of making good arrears. Costs for this work in detached, semi-detached or terraced dwellings do not vary by more than 5 per cent. The effect of the number of storeys, the slope of the site, floor area and other similar factors also appears to be small. The results are not surprising, since differences in these factors mainly affect the structure, the repair costs of which form only a small

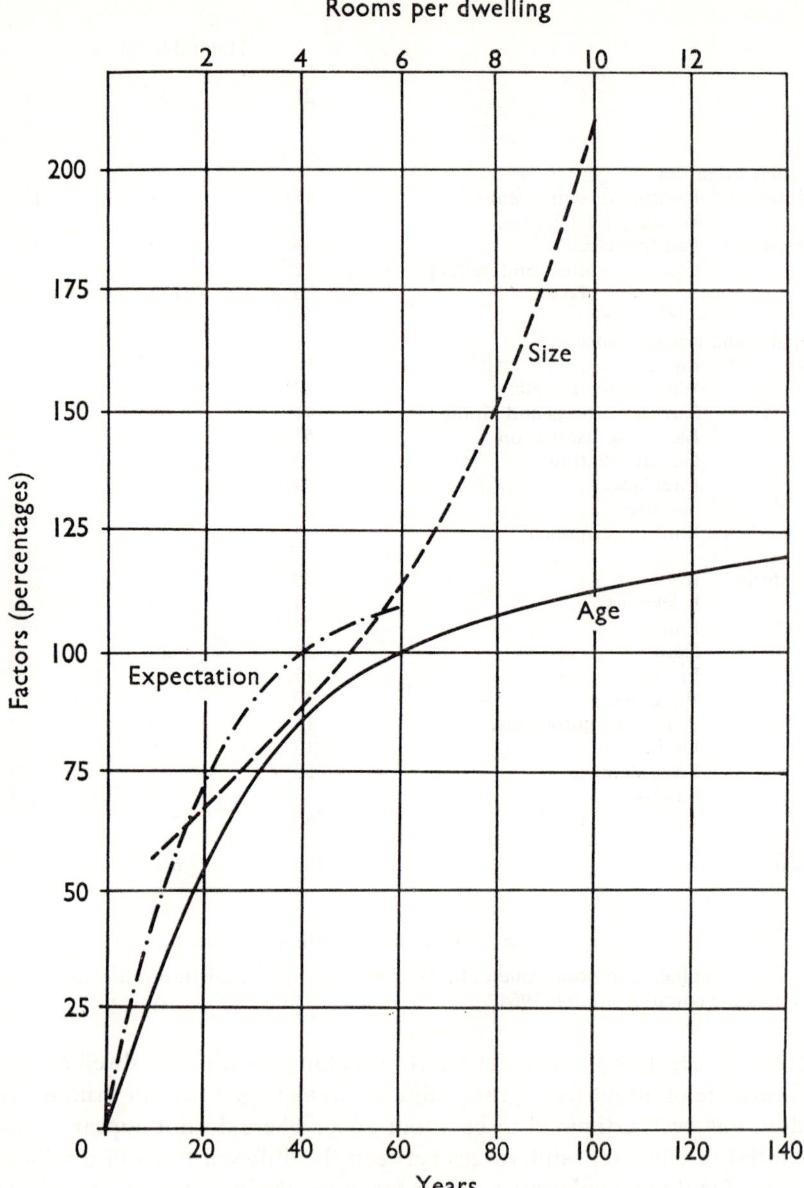

SOURCE: NIESR and consultants' estimates.

Note: Factors are those given in table 8.2.

Fig. 8.1. Variational factors for age, life expectation and size of dwelling

part of the total cost under consideration. Nevertheless, errors which might have been introduced by such differences have been minimized by setting the cost at levels for representative dwellings. The major factors affecting the costs of making good arrears are the standard of the dwelling, the condition, the age, the size and the future expectation of life. The factors for adjusting the average cost are given in table 8.2 and fig. 8.1, and some examples of the effect of combining the information in table 8.2 with fig. 8.1 are shown in table 8.3.

Table 8.2. *Costs of making good arrears of maintenance (renewals, repairs and decorations)*

Adjustment for condition

Condition	Factor
Good	20
Fair	50
Fair–poor	100
Poor	160
Very poor	225

Adjustment for standard

Standard	Factor
Substandard	75
Low cost	100
Medium cost	140
High cost	200

Adjustment for size

Habitable rooms	Factor
1	57
2	67
3	77
4	88
5	100
6	114
7	131
8	152
9	178
10	210

Adjustment for age

Years	Factor
0	0
10	30
20	54
30	72
40	85
50	94
60	100
70	104
80	107
90	110
100	113
110	115
120	117

Adjustment for future life

Years	Factor
5	23
10	43
15	59
20	72
25	82
30	90
35	96
40	100
45	103
50	105
55	107
60	109

SOURCE: NIESR and consultants' estimates.

Note: Base cost for a dwelling of 5 habitable rooms, fair–poor condition, low cost standard, 60 years old, to give a future life of 40 years is £650.

An allowance for the costs of renewing the water and power services has already been made in the costs of arrears. The additional costs for providing services in dwellings without them are given below (table 8.4).

The cost of creating bathrooms varies with the type and condition of the

Table 8.3. *Average costs per dwelling of making good arrears of maintenance*

£s

Habitable rooms		2			5			8		
Expected life		15 years	20 years	40 years	15 years	20 years	40 years	15 years	20 years	40 years
	Age									
Low cost										
Poor	*40*	349	426	592	522	636	884	793	967	1344
	60	411	502	697	614	749	1040	933	1138	1581
	100	465	567	787	693	846	1175	1054	1286	1786
Fair–poor	*40*	218	267	370	326	398	553	495	605	840
	60	257	314	436	384	468	650	583	711	988
	100	290	354	492	433	529	735	659	804	1116
Fair	*40*	109	133	185	163	199	276	248	302	420
	60	128	157	218	192	234	325	291	356	494
	100	145	177	246	217	264	367	329	402	558
Good	*40*	44	53	74	65	80	111	99	121	168
	60	51	63	87	77	94	130	117	142	198
	100	58	71	98	87	106	147	132	161	223
Medium cost										
Poor	*40*	489	597	829	730	891	1238	1110	1354	1881
	60	576	702	976	859	1048	1456	1306	1593	2213
	100	650	794	1102	971	1185	1645	1475	1801	2501
Fair–poor	*40*	306	373	518	456	557	774	694	847	1176
	60	360	439	610	537	655	910	816	996	1383
	100	406	496	689	607	740	1028	922	1125	1563
Fair	*40*	153	187	259	228	278	387	347	423	588
	60	180	219	305	268	328	455	408	498	692
	100	203	248	344	303	370	514	461	563	782
Good	*40*	61	75	104	91	111	155	139	169	235
	60	72	88	122	107	131	182	163	199	277
	100	81	99	138	121	148	206	184	225	313

SOURCES: Table 8.2; fig. 8.1.

dwelling and with the solution adopted. A bathroom can be created within the existing dwelling by using an existing room or by partitioning off existing space. Alternatively, where no space is available, a bathroom can be built on the rear or on the side of a dwelling (table 8.5). Where insufficient space is available for a bathroom, a shower closet can usually be provided and the basin fitted into a bedroom or with the water closet. This would cost about the same as providing a bath and basin within the existing space.

Table 8.4. *Costs of adding services to dwellings*

	£s per dwelling
Cold water services	45
Hot water services	40
Bath and basin	60
W.C.	40

SOURCE: Consultants' estimates.

Note: These costs are additional to the costs for arrears of maintenance.

Table 8.5. *Costs of builders' work in creating bathrooms*

	£s
Within existing dwelling	50
By back addition	200

SOURCE: Consultants' estimates.

Very little information has been published on the costs of making good arrears of maintenance and of adding missing services. Some information was obtained from public authorities who have undertaken this work, but because of the problems which led to the rejection of the survey technique it was not possible to make a formal statistical analysis. The case studies tended, however, to indicate figures in line with those given in tables 8.2–8.5. Comparisons with figures produced by other research workers have also indicated that the figures given here are of the right order.

COSTS OF CONVERTING DWELLINGS

The distribution of dwellings in terms of size tends, in many areas, to be less than optimum and some large dwellings are converted into a number of smaller ones, while small ones are paired to provide larger dwellings: in this way the excess of very small and very large dwellings is reduced and the stock in the medium-size ranges is increased. The volume of conversion of this type is not very large: over the last few years less than 0·05 per cent of dwellings a year have been dealt with in this way. Since both the subdivision and amalgamation of dwellings usually involves extensive movement of services, making good and redecoration, it is generally more economic to convert dwellings in need of substantial maintenance and improvement than dwellings already in a good condition.

Again, little information was available as to the appropriate level of costs.

Price data were collected from a number of authorities. These suggested that the size of the converted dwellings had a more important effect on costs than the size of the dwellings in their original form. The costs of conversion, including the addition of services and formation of bathrooms, appeared to be about £400, £560, £600 and £640 for the creation of a dwelling of one, two, three and four habitable rooms respectively. The costs of making good arrears of maintenance would be additional to these figures.

COSTS OF UPGRADING RESIDENTIAL AREAS

To improve the environment of the housing areas it may often be necessary to change the road patterns so as to eliminate through traffic, limit the speed of estate traffic, improve safety, reduce noise and provide adequate parking. In some cases it may be necessary to replace and add to the sewers to meet the increasing load of sewage arising from the expected increase in the use of water. Often it may be necessary to improve the appearance of the housing areas and the value of the incidental open space by removing derelict buildings and hoardings, by renewing street furniture and by landscaping. There are some grounds for believing that upgrading can be accomplished without the demolition of satisfactory dwelling units. While there may be losses of dwelling units in order to provide space for main roads, general open space and schools, it seems unlikely that in the near future satisfactory dwellings would be demolished in order to provide incidental amenity space. The areas in which the need for environmental improvement is the greatest will be areas of redevelopment and, generally, these will be areas in which a large number of demolitions is most likely. In the better areas, densities will generally be lower and the need for amenity space less pressing.

The public utility district distribution networks are usually as old as the dwellings and some will need replacement. The upgrading of dwellings will add to the load on the services for fuel and water, and some additional pipes and cables may be necessary.

Very little of such upgrading has ever been carried out and such figures as could be obtained were not very conclusive. A study was made of area-upgrading on the basis of a sample of 1/2500 plans. While the results showed considerable variability, they were in broad agreement with the figures obtained from local authority schemes. The costs appear to be quite low because of the limited nature of improvements feasible without demolishing sound dwellings. The figures used for costing were related to the condition of the dwellings in the following way:

	£
Poor	110
Poor-fair	70
Fair	42·5
Good	17·5

COSTS OF PROVIDING GARAGES IN EXISTING HOUSING AREAS

The problem of garaging for private cars is one which is already creating difficulties. In many areas the roads are congested at nights with parked cars belonging to the residents. The proportion of households with cars is expected to continue increasing, and by the end of the period considered in this study there may be between 0·9 and 1·8 cars per household. It has been recommended (Parker Morris Report) that new development should be planned to provide space for one car per dwelling with additional parking space for visitors' cars at one car per two dwellings (38). This would seem to be an adequate standard at which to aim, at least for low cost standard housing, in which it is reasonable to expect that car ownership rates will be a little less than average. Parking spaces for visitors' cars will help to provide night parking space for multi-car households.

Cars could probably be manufactured to withstand permanent outside parking, and this might be more economical than providing garages. However, the presence of large numbers of parked cars spoils the amenity of an area. Moreover, open parking areas provide no facilities for car maintenance, general workshop facilities, or storage of tools and spares, and no protection for cars against vandalism. Generally, therefore, it is considered preferable to provide garaging for most cars and to provide this as near to the dwellings as possible (38).

Studies of the costs of providing garages (chapter 7) indicated that permanent single garages built on the ground as single storey structures cost about £200 per car. Garages provided as part of a multi-storey structure with garaging at two levels, or with garaging on the ground floor and some other use above, cost about £300 per car. It is assumed here that single storey garages will be provided wherever there is space, otherwise multi-storey garages will be required, and that sufficient land for grouped garages can be found from the space already available, or as a result of programmed demolitions or environmental improvement schemes.

ANNUAL COSTS OF MAINTAINING HOUSING

The annual cost of maintaining the housing stock is an important item in the national costs of housing. Over the life of a dwelling the necessary expenditure on maintenance—repairs, renewals and decoration—is commensurable, at constant prices, with the amount originally spent on its construction. In the past, maintenance has been neglected; hence the high incidence of housing in a poor condition. One of the basic tenets of this study is that the housing stock should at all times be maintained in good condition. Dwellings should be kept weather-tight, components and equipment not functioning properly should be repaired or renewed and the dwellings should be kept in a good state of decoration. It is not a part of the maintenance function to provide additional equipment, or to provide renewals merely because fashion has changed. This is a problem of changing standards which will be dealt with separately. However, where renewal is necessary because the component or equipment has ceased to function properly, the replacement is usually the contemporary style and standard.

Since, particularly in the private sector, maintenance is not carried out to an adequate standard, average annual national expenditure on maintenance provides little guide to the level of expenditure needed to cover adequate maintenance. A better guide is provided by the annual expenditure incurred for maintenance by local housing authorities. Generally they maintain an adequate standard for repairs and renewals, although not for decoration, particularly internal decoration.

The annual expenditure per dwelling on repairs and renewals varies regionally, partly because of differences in practice and partly because of differences in regional prices. It is not possible to determine the size of each effect, but the regional differences in the average annual expenditure on decorations are so large that it would appear that it is decoration policy rather than unit price differences which are mainly responsible for the different levels of expenditure (table 8.6). As in other fields, expenditure in London is far higher than elsewhere, particularly for decorations, for which London authorities appear to accept far greater responsibility than authorities outside the capital.

Table 8.6. *Average annual expenditure on maintenance per dwelling by local housing authorities, 1959*

Percentages

	Decorations		Repairs and renewals	
	Prewar dwellings	Postwar dwellings	Prewar dwellings	Postwar dwellings
North	68	70	94	88
Midlands	94	102	104	109
South	138	127	102	104
England (excluding London)	100	100	100	100
London	240	249	121	126

SOURCE: Clapp, 'Cost Comparisons in Housing Maintenance', *Local Government Finance* (73).

The expenditure on repairs and renewals increases with the age of the dwelling in accordance with the following formula, which has been devised from the above source (73):

$$y = £3{\cdot}8 + x \,.\, £0{\cdot}305,$$

where y is the annual expenditure per dwelling of age x and x is the age in years.

This relationship is based on 1959 price levels. Between that date and March 1964 net output per man in new construction has risen about 40 per cent, whereas there has been little rise in output per man in repair and maintenance work (74). It is not, therefore, surprising to find that the costs of maintenance work rose about 31 per cent over this period. The formula corrected for price changes is therefore:

$$y = £5{\cdot}0 + x \,.\, £0{\cdot}4.$$

These figures are averages for England and Wales as a whole. Without London they might be 5 per cent less, but it may well be that in some regions the level of maintenance is not as high as it should be. While London prices are probably higher than elsewhere, they certainly are not as high as the relative expenditure on decorations (two and a half times as much). This regional difference in the expenditure on decorations must be largely a result of policy. In fact it is known that many authorities, especially in the North, decorate internally only on a change of tenancy. Probably not even the authorities in London decorate to a satisfactory standard. The figures of expenditure on decorations found for London will, therefore, be taken as applying to a full service of decoration, that is assuming that none of the decoration is left to the tenants. The additional expenditure resulting from higher prices will be assumed to offset any shortfall in the decorative standard. While it is not thought that the costs of decoration vary very much with age, the costs for this sector will be based on prewar dwellings, which at the date of analysis would have been on average about thirty years old. The appropriate expenditure per dwelling for London in 1959–60 was £11·45. Allowing for price changes to March 1964, the figure would be £15.

This would suggest that for a dwelling of average age, say, thirty years the maintenance costs would be £17 a year for repairs and renewals, and £15 for decorations; and further, that more is now being spent on decoration than in the early 1950s (52).

The evidence, on which the formula given above for the age effect was based, did not, naturally, contain any evidence for dwellings over forty years old. But the observations all lie so close to the line of fit that it seems reasonable to assume the relationship with age would apply to dwellings much older than forty years. If the formula were applied over the whole age range of dwellings being studied, the following results would be obtained (table 8.7).

It seems unlikely that expenditure would go on rising at the rate indicated. On the other hand, the excess of the total for the last forty years over what it would be at the average rate for the first sixty years is, at £800, only around the costs for a renewal. The properties to which these annual maintenance costs are applied will have been costed for renewal to a good condition, and it seems unlikely that the costs will rise in the way the extension of the trend would indicate. It is, therefore, assumed that the rate at which the cost of the variable element of repairs and renewals increases will decline, the costs being taken as constant, at £50 in all, from age 100 onwards. On this basis the total annual maintenance costs would increase as shown in table 8.7 to age forty, when the figure would be £34, and subsequent figures would be £38, £41, £44, £47, £48, £49, and £50 from age 100 onwards. Since the maintenance costs are to be applied to dwellings of average age, any errors in extrapolating the costs for high ages will be substantially reduced. The evidence for non-traditional forms of construction is naturally very limited. Such evidence as there is (73) suggests that maintenance costs of non-traditional constructions might be higher than for traditional, but not by a significant amount.

Table 8.7. *Annual costs of maintaining an average local authority dwelling*

Age of dwelling	Expenditure on			£s
	Repairs	Renewals	Decorations	Total expenditure
Years				
0–10	5	2	15	22
10–20	5	6	15	26
20–30	5	10	15	30
30–40	5	14	15	34
40–50	5	18	15	38
50–60	5	22	15	42
60–70	5	26	15	46
70–80	5	30	15	50
80–90	5	34	15	54
90–100	5	38	15	58

SOURCE: NIESR estimates.

The average size of local authority houses at present is about 4·6 habitable rooms and these levels of costs can, therefore, be related to a dwelling of that size. It is probably reasonable to apply the percentage adjustments for making good arrears of maintenance (table 8.2) to adjust for the size of dwelling.

It was suggested earlier that the costs for improvements to above-standard housing would be broadly proportional to their construction cost relationship and this relationship will probably hold good for maintenance costs. In the absence of information on the maintenance costs of private housing, the costs are taken at the level for local authority housing, but 10 per cent is added over all housing to allow for better quality housing (chapter 7).

In a previous study (52) it was found that the maintenance costs for low blocks of flats, two to four storeys, were 13 per cent higher than for housing and that the corresponding figure for high blocks was 39 per cent.

Maintenance costs will also arise for the estate roads and for incidental open space. Some of this expenditure is clearly related to the work of the construction industry, while some may be handled by other departments of the local authority.

In an earlier study (52) it was estimated that estate roads cost about £800 a year per mile for maintenance, lighting, cleaning and verge cutting. Since the date at which this estimate was made prices have risen about 40 per cent. These figures would suggest about six shillings per nominal yard of frontage, of which about half might be for work done by the construction industry. On the basis of a density of say fourteen dwellings per acre, this gives a figure of £1 a dwelling for estate services carried out by the construction industry which is too small for the effects of density to be important.

MAINTENANCE AND HOUSEHOLDERS

Some maintenance work is carried out by the householders rather than by the construction industry. Such work makes no demands on the contracting side of the industry, but still creates demands on the manufacturing side. The percentages of contractors' costs of repairs and renewals, and of decorations which are represented by materials, labour and overheads are probably about 30, 50 and 20, and 20, 60 and 20 respectively. There is no information on the extent to which householders carry out maintenance work or the extent to which they may do so in the future. More leisure might lead to a greater readiness to do such work and to a larger number of people taking courses in the appropriate skills. On the other hand, higher incomes and a greater ability to afford to pay for maintenance might lead to householders preferring to put the work out to contractors.

The most likely work for a householder to do himself is decoration, particularly internal decoration, perhaps two-thirds of the total, and repairs. Renewal work, and, to a lesser extent, repair work, generally involves rather special skills and tools. A third of the heads of households are likely to be over sixty and two-fifths of these may be female. The balance will be predominantly married males. Perhaps a quarter of households are unlikely to carry out any appreciable amount of maintenance. Since many of the balance may be disinclined to do this work themselves, it may be, at best, that half of the households would do repair and internal decoration work. For various reasons the households occupying local authority and, to a lesser extent, other rented housing are less likely to do maintenance work than owner-occupiers. Most local authorities redecorate on a change of tenancy and other householders are likely to engage contractors for decoration work at least occasionally. The proportion of external decoration carried out by householders is likely to be less than for internal decoration. External decoration for flatted blocks and for local authority and other group-owned housing is unlikely to be undertaken on the basis of an individual dwelling. Many tenants bear no responsibility for external decoration and this type of work is likely to be carried out by the contracting industry. Over the period under consideration, perhaps two-thirds of dwellings will fall into these categories. Moreover, because external decoration is on a much larger scale than internal decoration and requires more equipment, fewer householders are inclined to tackle it. It would, therefore, appear that, perhaps, only a third of internal decoration and repairs and renewals, and a sixth of external decoration, is likely to be carried out by householders.

On the basis of the estimates given above, it would appear that, at most, the contracting side of the industry might be relieved of about a quarter of potential maintenance work, but of this about a fifth would represent materials which would still need to be produced. However, the work carried out by local authorities is mainly the type which needs to be executed professionally. The allowance for decoration, £15 a year, is clearly the cost of only minimal work; it is probably not much more than sufficient for external decoration. It therefore seems likely that a large proportion of the maintenance work carried out by householders will be to meet standards above those provided by local authorities and that householders' work will not make much contribution to the work which is covered by the cost estimates given in this chapter.

REGIONAL COSTS

An attempt was made to collect information on the regional pattern of prices for maintenance work. Unfortunately only about forty authorities returned the information required; moreover the returns made were not always complete and there was considerable doubt as to the uniformity of the quotations of measured work prices. Several regions were unrepresented. The figures indicated regional price variations of the same scale as shown by the indices based on housing construction, but the direction of the trends was often contrary to all the other evidence. In view of the uncertainty about the figures, there was no option other than to assume that relative regional maintenance prices were the same as the relative regional prices for house construction (table 7.12, column 1).

CHAPTER 9

THE COSTS OF DWELLINGS

FACTORS AFFECTING THE COST OF HOUSING

Before examining the total costs of the various housing programmes which have been analysed, it is of interest to examine some of the factors which affect housing costs. The major factors affecting the costs of the dwellings themselves are the size, standard, and form of the dwelling, and the region within which it is built. The form of housing affects the form of garaging and its cost, and the costs of developing the housing estate. Form also affects, through density, the amount of land required and hence its cost. Size, standard and form jointly affect the cost of maintaining the dwellings and of providing the estate services. However, it is the annual costs rather than the capital costs which mainly concern the householder. Usually housing is either purchased through a mortgage or rented. The annual cost of a dwelling depends, of course, not only on the capital outlay but also on the life and the rate of interest. Public housing authorities receive subsidies from the central government which considerably reduce the annual costs of housing which need to be covered by rents. These subsidies are dependent partly upon the form of the housing and partly on its purpose. Owner-occupiers purchasing through mortgage arrangements obtain a rebate of income tax in respect of the interest paid. Owner-occupiers not paying sufficient income tax to be able to enjoy this benefit are now eligible for a special subsidy. Both owner-occupiers and the tenants of public authority dwellings also enjoy some benefit from repaying loans in cash sums rather than in real values, a benefit which can be substantial during periods of inflation.

SIZE AND COSTS

As indicated in chapter 7, the price per square foot of dwellings falls with increases in size. The cost per square foot of a dwelling of 500 square feet is only just over 80 per cent of the cost per square foot of a dwelling of 350 square feet (table 9.1). The cost per square foot of a dwelling of 1,175 square feet is about 60 per cent of the cost per square foot of a dwelling of 350 square feet.

Because the price of dwellings rises less than proportionately to increases in size, it is not very costly to increase the amount of floor area per dwelling. For example, an additional 50 to 100 square feet could be added to a medium-size dwelling for less than thirty shillings per square foot. Floor space standards have been rising for at least the last 100 years (67) and are expected to increase with increasing affluence (54). The provision of generous floor space is probably the cheapest way of reducing the risks of early obsolescence, while it also simplifies adaptation. The cost of housing large households is much less per

Table 9.1. *Costs per square foot for one and two storey dwellings* [a]

Floor area of dwelling	Price per sq. ft.	
Sq. ft.	£	%
350	4·05	*100*
500	3·27	*81*
650	2·91	*72*
925	2·54	*63*
1175	2·48	*61*

SOURCE: NIESR estimates.

[a] Estimated price of public authority dwellings (Parker Morris standards) at March 1964 for England and Wales excluding London.

head than the cost of housing small ones. The cost per bedspace in an eight bedspace house (1,175 square feet) is only about a quarter of the cost in a one bedspace house (350 square feet) even before allowance is made for development and land (table 9.2). A similar scale of costs applies in the case of dwellings in flatted blocks.

Table 9.2. *Costs per dwelling and per bedspace for houses of different sizes* [a]

Bedspaces per dwelling	Cost per dwelling		Cost per bedspace	
	£	%	£	%
1	1419	*100*	1419	*100*
2	1635	*115*	818	*58*
3	1893	*133*	631	*44*
5	2355	*166*	471	*33*
8	2916	*205*	364	*26*

SOURCE: NIESR estimates.

[a] Estimated price of public authority dwellings (Parker Morris standards) at March 1964 for England and Wales, excluding London.

As a consequence of the above relationships, the economic rents of small dwellings in relation to the number of bedspaces are substantially higher than those of large dwellings. For example, five bedspace dwellings only cost about a quarter more than three bedspace dwellings. However, they provide room for a growing household without the need to change dwellings and allow the smaller household additional living space for the occupants and their guests. A stock based on typical five bedspace dwellings provides the flexibility to meet a growth of household size and reduces the need to accept overcrowding or to increase the size of the stock. Another consequence of the size-cost relationships is the difficulty of providing small dwellings at rents sufficiently low to attract households declining in size away from larger dwellings so as to release them for larger households.

STANDARDS AND COSTS

Increasing the floor area in relation to the number of bedspaces in the household is only one way of increasing standards. They can also be raised by providing additional and better equipment and fittings, better finishes, more built-in storage and by improving access, circulation and external space, including, for example, garaging, stores, boundary screens and landscaping. The costs given in the tables relate to the standards recommended by the Parker Morris Committee. Where dwellings are built to this standard they cost 10–15 per cent more than dwellings built to the previous standard (75). As indicated in chapter 7, it is quite easy to raise standards and double the cost of a dwelling providing the same number of bedspaces without being extravagant in the specifications.

Improving standards not only increases costs of construction but frequently increases running costs. Additional floor space used to obtain greater spaciousness in the same number of rooms usually has little effect on maintenance or other running costs, but these costs rise, of course, when the extra space is provided in the form of additional rooms. Additional fittings usually add to the maintenance costs for their renewal, repair and cleaning. Additional services also add to the maintenance costs in this way, and add to the consumption and cost of fuel. Often in flatted blocks additional staff are required for operating and servicing lifts and heating installations. Finishes which are self-cleaning, or at least permanently decorated, will have lower maintenance than those needing frequent decoration, but their physical life may not be very long, or early replacement may be necessary as a result of a change in tastes.

FORM AND COSTS

There would appear to be little difference in the costs of houses and bungalows of the same size and standard. While the cheapest form of housing is terraced, semi-detached dwellings are probably only about 5 per cent more expensive and detached dwellings about 10 per cent more expensive. The additional cost of building houses to three storeys is probably quite small. Once the block is divided horizontally into one or more flats or maisonettes prices tend to rise, mainly because of the provision of concrete floors and the concrete staircases which are a necessary safety precaution in case of fire.

The relationship of prices between flatted blocks and houses varies with the region in which construction takes place. The variation stems more from regional differences in the cost of houses than in the cost of flatted blocks (table 9.3). Thus the price differentials of flatted blocks built in London are less than those built in the provinces and are less again for those regions with the highest price for houses. Whereas the price of equivalent dwellings in fifteen storey blocks in London is about 44 per cent greater than for two storey houses, on average the price of equivalent dwellings in fifteen storey blocks in the provinces is 70 per cent greater than for houses. The price differentials are greatest for regions such as the North for which the price of constructing houses is the lowest.

Table 9.3. *Construction prices for dwellings of four bedspaces* [a]

£s

Storeys	London	Scotland	North	East, Pennines	North West, West	East Anglia, N. & C. Wales	Central, Midlands	South West, South East
1–2	2737	2526	1916	2000	2189	2084	2105	2210
3	2905	2715	2147	2231	2442	2337	2358	2484
4	3073	2905	2379	2463	2652	2547	2568	2673
5	3200	3031	2589	2673	2821	2758	2758	2842
6	3347	3200	2779	2842	2989	2926	2926	3010
7	3452	3410	2947	3010	3094	3073	3073	3136
8	3536	3431	3094	3136	3242	3200	3200	3263
9	3621	3536	3200	3242	3347	3347	3305	3368
10	3705	3621	3284	3326	3431	3431	3389	3452
13	3894	3789	3431	3473	3579	3579	3536	3600
15	3936	3831	3473	3515	3621	3621	3579	3642

SOURCE: NIESR estimates.

[a] Public authority, Parker Morris standard, 775 square feet, March 1964.

GARAGES AND COSTS

While it is not difficult to provide garaging on the basis of one garage per dwelling where development takes the form of low density housing, the problem becomes much more difficult where development takes the form of high density flatted blocks. The difficulty is twofold: the housing of a vehicle, whether on a parking space or in a garage, takes up a large proportion of the space about buildings associated with each dwelling, and it becomes difficult to fit the rest of the land use in the remaining space; secondly, large areas of parking and of lock-up garages are generally thought to reduce the amenity of an area. The normal solution in high density developments is to place the garages on the ground floor of the blocks and to deck over the lock-up garages so that the space can be used for some amenity purpose. Using the lower floors of flatted blocks for garaging increases the height of the flatted blocks, and hence their cost. The height of the flatted blocks is often increased in order to obtain necessary additional space about the buildings; this, too, adds to their costs. Garages provided under the flatted blocks and under decking, or as multi-storey garages, are more expensive than the normal lock-up individual garages, and increase the cost per garage from about £200 to £300, including parking for visitors.

ESTATE DEVELOPMENT AND COSTS

The costs of site development for roads, sewers, and other public utility services fall with density. Whereas at a density of four dwellings per acre the cost of development per dwelling is about £700, this falls to about £150 at densities of forty-eight dwellings per acre (table 9.4). The costs fall rapidly as the density is increased from low to moderate levels, but then fall more slowly as density goes on increasing. For example, whereas the cost at a density of sixteen dwellings per acre is less than half the cost of four dwellings per acre, doubling the density to thirty-two dwellings per acre reduces the costs by only about a further 40 per cent. The saving in the costs of development as density increases is small compared with the additional costs of providing blocks of additional storeys to secure the densities.

Table 9.4. *Costs of development of roads, sewers and other public utility services*[a]

Dwellings per acre	Cost per dwelling
	£
4	708
10	446
16	323
22	253
34	192
48	149

SOURCE: NIESR estimates.

[a] England and Wales (excluding London), March 1964.

LAND PRICES

The prices of sites with planning consent for residential development vary little from one part of Great Britain to another, except for the conurbations of London and Birmingham and the south coast (fig. 9.1). The prices for these areas form dominant peaks in an otherwise flattish plateau. The greater the density at which housing is developed, the less land is required per dwelling. The saving in land costs is, however, less than proportionate to the saving in land, since the price of residential sites per acre and density are related. A study of the prices of residential sites has indicated that the relationship between the

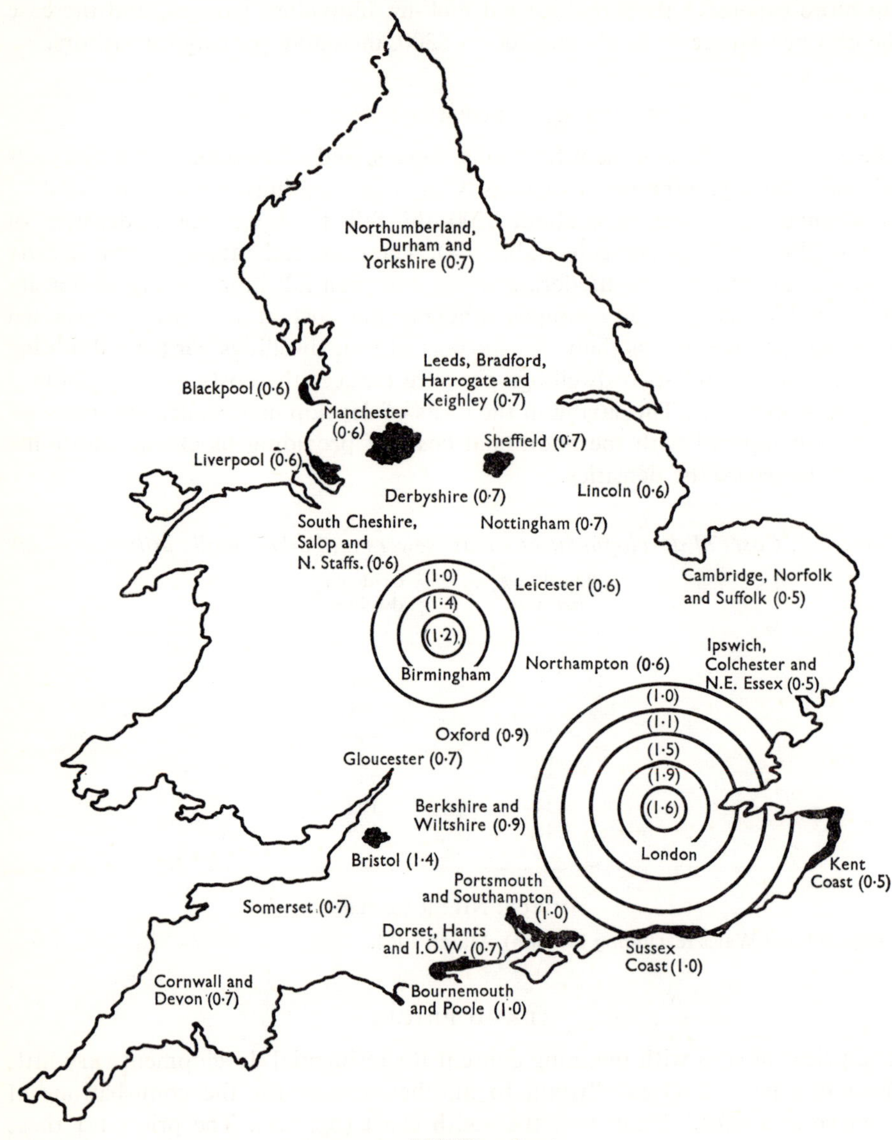

SOURCE: NIESR estimates.

Notes: Prices in £ thousands shown in brackets.
Circles round London and Birmingham at ten mile intervals.

Fig. 9.1. Prices of land per dwelling (plot), England, 1960–4

price of land per dwelling and density is hyperbolic (72). For example, the prices of land per dwelling in London and Birmingham fall by about half when densities increase from five to forty dwellings per acre (table 9.5).

Table 9.5. *Prices of residential land per dwelling in relation to density*[a]

Dwellings per acre	Comparative prices per dwelling	
	London	Birmingham
	%	%
5	100	100
10	73	70
15	64	60
20	60	55
30	56	50
40	53	48

SOURCE: NIESR estimates.

[a] Assuming constant distance from the centre of the region.

Another determinant of the price of residential land is the distance from the centre of the region. The study of the prices of residential land (72), has indicated that the price of land falls exponentially as the distance increases, so that for example, in Birmingham the price of land fifteen miles from the centre of the region is only half what it would be in the centre of the region (table 9.6).

Table 9.6. *Prices of residential land in relation to distances from the regional centre*

Distance from the centre	Price of land in	
	London region	Birmingham region
Miles	%	%
1	100	100
5	87	83
10	73	65
15	61	51
20	51	41
40	25	—

SOURCE: NIESR estimates.

MAINTENANCE COSTS

The costs of maintenance are not proportionate to the size of the dwelling, because a large part of them, particularly in older dwellings, represents the costs of repairing and renewing the services and other fittings, the quantity of which is not greatly affected by the size of the dwelling; nor are the costs of maintenance much affected by the spaciousness of the dwelling. The costs of external decoration are largely related to the number of doors and window frames and thus are not affected by the size of the rooms; similarly the costs of internal decoration depend more on the number of window frames and doors, and on cutting in at corners or between walls and ceiling, than on the area. Maintenance costs are, however, affected by the form of the dwelling. Dwellings in flatted blocks of two to four storeys cost about 13 per cent more to maintain than dwellings in the form of houses and bungalows, while maintaining dwellings in high blocks of flats costs about 39 per cent more. The additional costs arise mainly because of the cost of maintaining lifts and public space within and about the buildings.

Maintenance costs rise with age, increasing by a factor of about 2½ over the life of the building (table 9.7).

Table 9.7. *Annual costs of maintaining an average local authority dwelling*[a]

Age of dwelling	Total cost of maintenance
Years	£
0	20
25	30
50	40
75	50

SOURCE: NIESR estimates.

[a] England and Wales (excluding London), March 1964.

However, while maintenance costs rise with age, they do not rise sufficiently to make it worthwhile to replace the dwellings before their physical life is complete. The annual equivalent maintenance charge increases only slightly with increases in the expected life of a dwelling. Whereas the annual equivalent maintenance cost for a dwelling with a life of ten years would be about £23, it would be only about £25 for a dwelling with a life of thirty years, and £28 for a dwelling with a life of sixty years. Thus, other things being equal, the reduction in equivalent maintenance costs from building dwellings for a shorter life would be quite small.

The costs of the maintenance and servicing of estate roads are related to the length of the road. At present these costs work out at about six shillings per nominal yard of frontage, so that while the annual cost per dwelling for maintaining, lighting and cleaning roads falls with density, the decrease is small.

DURABILITY AND THE RATE OF INTEREST

The relation between the capital costs of development and the annual costs of a dwelling depends on its durability and the rate of interest to be paid on the capital. As the expected life of a building falls, the annual equivalent of its development cost rises. The increase in the annual equivalent cost rises only slowly at first as the expected life is reduced; the difference in the equivalent annual cost at 5 per cent interest between an expected life of forty years and 100 years is only about one sixth. As the expected life is further reduced, the increase in the annual equivalent cost increases more rapidly; for a life of twenty years it is 60 per cent greater than for a life of 100 years; and for a life of ten years 160 per cent greater (table 9.8). The lower the rate of interest, the greater the increase in the equivalent annual cost as the life is reduced.

Table 9.8. *Annual equivalent of £100 of initial cost*

£s

Life in years	Rate of interest 3%	5%	7%
100	3·2	5·0	7·0
60	3·6	5·3	7·1
40	4·3	5·8	7·5
20	6·7	8·0	9·4
10	11·7	13·0	14·2

It will be seen that the reductions in the annual equivalent maintenance costs as the expectation of life is shortened are smaller than the increases in the annual equivalents of the initial cost (table 9.9). Assuming 5 per cent interest,

Table 9.9. *Annual equivalent costs of construction and maintenance*[a]

£s

Life in years	Annual equivalent of £3,000 [a]	Annual equivalent of maintenance cost	Total net rent
60	159	28	187
40	174	26	200
30	195	25	220
20	240	24	264
10	390	23	413

SOURCE: NIESR estimates.

[a] Typical cost of four person dwelling with land and development, but without garage, and assuming a 5 per cent rate of interest, England and Wales (excluding London), March 1964.

shortening the expectation of life from sixty to twenty years has the effect of raising total annual costs by 40 per cent. The annual costs can only be held constant when the life expectation is shortened if the capital costs can be reduced. If the rent is to be held at £187, the capital cost would need to be reduced from £3,000 to about £2,030. A site might cost about £500. If the life of the dwelling were only twenty years instead of sixty, the site would be available for another use that much earlier, and its capitalized cost would be reduced to about £330. Site works would cost about £300 and would be unlikely to be any less because the expected life of the dwelling was lower. About £700 of the costs of construction would consist of components brought in, such as sanitary ware, heating appliances, joinery items, pipes, and electrical and gas fittings. These would be no cheaper because the expected life was shorter. Thus there remains about £1,500 for the structure and finishings of a house with a life of sixty years, and this would need to be reduced to about £700 in order that the rent of a house with a life of twenty years should be no greater than that for a house of a similar standard with a life of sixty years (76). At present there would appear to be no form of construction which would enable costs to be reduced in this way. Neither the postwar temporary bungalows nor the current large mobile houses show any saving in cost over standard long-life dwellings of the same floor area, although they are less durable. It is difficult to see how annual housing costs can be reduced by shortening expected lives unless standards are substantially reduced.

DENSITY AND TOTAL COSTS OF DEVELOPMENT

The total comparative real costs of housing in high blocks as compared with housing on the ground (one and two storey dwellings) are not quite as great as are the comparative costs of constructing the dwellings themselves (table 9.10). Nevertheless, for areas outside London and Scotland it would cost about half as much again to house a group of people in fifteen storey blocks as in two storey housing. The percentage difference would be a little less in London and Scotland, where the cost of two storey dwellings is substantially more than in most other areas. The smaller the dwelling the greater the difference in the absolute costs for each bedspace provided.

The greater the number of storeys used the less land is required for each person housed. However, the real costs of providing and maintaining dwellings rise more rapidly than the requirement for land falls; hence the real costs per acre of land saved rise with increases in the number of storeys. The cost per acre of land saved also increases as the size of the dwelling falls. The land saved by developing four bedspace dwellings in four storey blocks, instead of in two storey blocks, costs about £21,500 per acre (table 9.11). The cost per acre of land saved is over twice as much if fifteen storey blocks are used. If two bedspace dwellings are developed in this way to save land, the costs are about twice as

Table 9.10. *Comparative initial cost equivalents in real terms of housing (10,000 bedspaces)*[a]

£ millions

	Number of storeys			
	2	4	10	15
Dwelling	5·47	6·42	8·47	8·95
Garage	0·50	0·75	0·75	0·75
Site development [b]	0·81	0·58	0·46	0·43
Total initial costs	6·78	7·75	9·68	10·13
Capitalized maintenance and management costs [c]	1·80	2·04	2·75	2·75
Total equivalent initial costs	8·58	9·79	12·43	12·88

SOURCE: NIESR estimates.

[a] Dwellings of 4 bedspaces each at Parker Morris standards, England and Wales (excluding London), prices at March 1964.

[b] Estate roads, sewers and public utility services, and development on virgin sites.

[c] Costs capitalized at 5 per cent over 60 years.

great as for four bedspace dwellings. In the long run the land saved is farmland, typically worth about £200 an acre in 1964. Clearly, building high is an extravagant way of saving land.

Table 9.11. *Costs of saving land by high density development*

	4 bedspace dwellings		Cost per acre of land saved	
Storeys	Land	Cost per 10,000 bedspaces	4 bedspace dwellings	2 bedspace dwellings
	Acres	*£mns*	*£000s*	*£000s*
2	156	8·58	—	—
4	100	9·79	21·5	44·4
10	69	12·43	44·4	..
15	64	12·88	46·7	..

SOURCE: NIESR estimates.

Note: Parker Morris standards, England and Wales, excluding London, prices at March 1964.

The saving of agricultural land is not the only, or usually the primary, reason for using high blocks. Frequently the use of high density development is advocated as a means of housing more people nearer the centre of the city and nearer their work. If people are to be provided with all the urban facilities normally considered necessary in the same locality as their housing, space must be made available for local shopping, schools and recreational facilities. This, of course, increases the amount of land required and hence reduces the number of people who can be housed near the centre. The amount of land required per person housed is, for these reasons, more than doubled at high densities, but only increased by between a half and two-thirds at low densities. As a result a fourfold increase in net densities only achieves a trebling of gross densities. When allowance is made for land for other town purposes a fourfold increase in net densities tends only to increase town densities by about a half.

The alternative to rehousing at higher densities in the centre of existing cities is to develop the housing at the periphery of the city or to overspill some of the people to other towns where space is available. At current fitting standards (chapter 5) fifty-five to sixty more people could be housed on an acre of land if high flatted blocks were used instead of two storey housing. The additional equivalent annual costs for constructing and servicing the dwellings per 10,000 rooms developed would be about £230,000. This is in terms of March 1964 prices when passenger fares per mile were about threepence. The difference in costs would therefore be equivalent to about 364,000 miles of travelling a week. Thus accommodation, together with travelling costs, would equal the costs of living in the centre of the city if each person housed at the periphery had to travel just over ten miles a day. In practice only about half or less of the people housed at the periphery would make daily journeys, and so there would be sufficient saving to cover the cost of over twenty miles a day of travelling, or to provide five shillings an hour to cover travelling time as well as the cost of travelling ten miles a day. More sophisticated methods of examining the comparative costs of central and peripheral development have been described elsewhere (77). Overspill to other towns also usually uses fewer resources than building high in the city of origin, even when allowance is made for new town construction and the disturbance and cost of moving industry (52).

High density development is also undertaken in order to obtain the urban values which this form of development provides. In such cases these values are enjoyed by all the people housed in this way, and to some extent by other citizens. The additional costs should, therefore, be spread over all the inhabitants of the estate, not just the extra people who can be housed by using high density as against low density development. The additional annual equivalent cost of developing four bedspace dwellings in fifteen storey as compared with two storey housing is £32·5 per person. The annual value of the difference in amenities between the two forms of housing should, therefore, be at or above this figure.

HOUSING COSTS TO DEVELOPERS AND USERS

While, from the point of view of the community, the price of the site does not represent a real cost of development, the price of the site is a real cost to the developer and to the user of the housing. Housing development costs are not reduced as much as might be expected by an increase in densities because site prices per acre rise with density (table 9.12). Site prices also rise with increasing proximity to the centre, so that the more central the site the greater the savings in site costs resulting from raising densities. It will be seen (table 9.13) that total development and site costs of high and low density developments are not likely to break even except for very high site prices.[1] These are most likely to occur in the centre of large conurbations. Even under these conditions the housing is,

Table 9.12. *Cost per acre for land, estimated prices at March 1964*

£ thousands

	Miles from centre	Dwellings per acre 5	10	15	20	25	30	35	40
London	10–20	17·3	25·4	33·4	41·5	49·5	57·6	65·6	73·7
	20–30	10·9	16·0	21·0	26·2	31·2	36·3	41·3	46·4
	30–40	9·6	14·1	18·5	23·0	27·5	32·0	36·4	40·9
	40–50	7·3	10·7	14·1	17·5	20·9	24·3	27·7	31·1
Birmingham	0–10	12·6	17·6	22·7	27·7	32·8	37·8	42·8	47·9
	10–20	9·3	13·0	16·7	20·5	24·2	27·9	31·6	35·3
	20–30	6·1	8·5	11·1	13·4	15·9	18·3	20·7	23·2

SOURCE: NIESR estimates.

Table 9.13. *Total cost of development per dwelling*[a]

£ thousands

	Miles from centre	Storeys 2	4	10	15
London	10–20	5·65	5·73	6·17	6·40
	20–30	4·84	5·01	5·50	5·71
	30–40	4·65	4·87	5·36	5·58
	40–50	4·40	4·60	5·11	5·32
Birmingham	0–10	4·15	4·41	5·07	5·23
	10–20	3·74	4·07	4·76	4·93
	20–30	3·40	3·55	4·46	4·63
Equivalent density (dwellings per acre)		*16*	*25*	*36*	*39*

SOURCE: NIESR estimates.

[a] Four bedspaces at Parker Morris standards, March 1964 prices: including costs of roads, land, site development, public utilities, dwelling and garage.

[1] The inclusion of the cost of all public utility services raises the cost per dwelling slightly above the financial cost but has little effect on cost comparisons.

of course, much more expensive than lower density development further from the centre. The difference in the prices of sites of similar densities does not appear to be closely related to travelling costs. For example, in Birmingham site prices fall between £30 and £35 a mile. This is equivalent to less than £2 a mile in annual costs, less than twopence a day, and would clearly fall far short of the cost of a double journey.

The total cost of land and development is affected less by variations in dwelling size than is the initial cost of constructing the dwelling. Garage costs are, of course, not affected by the size of the dwelling. Whereas the construction costs

9.14. *The effect of size, height and locality on the capital costs of housing*[a]

	Storeys	Bedspaces per dwelling	Distance from centre: 0–10 miles	Distance from centre: 10–20 miles
			£000s	*£000s*
London	1–2	2		4·52
		3		5·06
		4		5·65
		5		6·00
	4	2		4·72
		3		5·29
		4		5·73
		5		6·23
	10	2		..
		3		5·71
		4		6·17
		5		6·71
Birmingham	1–2	2	3·25	2·94
		3	3·70	3·36
		4	4·15	3·74
		5	4·38	3·99
	4	2	3·58	3·29
		3	4·02	3·71
		4	4·41	4·07
		5	4·82	4·47
	10	2	..	..
		3	4·64	4·35
		4	5·07	4·76
		5	5·55	5·24

SOURCE: NIESR estimates.

[a] Capital cost includes roads, land, site development, public utilities, dwelling and garage; Parker Morris standards, March 1964 prices.

of dwellings providing four bedspaces are about a third as much again as for those providing two, the total capital costs are only about a quarter as much again (table 9.14). This relationship strengthens the arguments given earlier for the use of dwellings large enough to provide flexibility. It will be seen that, because

Table 9.15. *Comparative annual costs of housing*[a] *related to the type of finance available*

£s

	3 bedspace dwellings			5 bedspace dwellings		
	1–2 storeys	4 storeys	10 storeys	1–2 storeys	4 storeys	10 storeys
Public authority[b]						
Interest at 6¾% p.a.						
London	312	327	359	371	391	430
Birmingham	218	240	284	260	291	344
Interest at 4% p.a.						
London	211	220	232	246	261	278
Birmingham	159	172	191	186	205	229
Owner-occupied[c]						
Interest at 7% p.a.						
London	444	469	511	520	545	592
Birmingham	299	331	390	350	392	462
Interest at 4½% p.a.						
London	346	367	401	404	424	463
Birmingham	234	260	306	273	306	360
Privately rented[d]						
London	607	635	685	720	748	805
Birmingham	403	445	522	479	536	629

SOURCE: NIESR estimates.

[a] Parker Morris standards, March 1964 prices, site 10–20 miles from centre of London or Birmingham.

[b] Loan repayable over 60 years, figures include subsidies payable by central government: basic subsidy £24 with 6¾% interest, nil with 4% interest; subsidy for high flats; subsidy for expensive sites.

[c] 100 per cent mortgage repayable over 30 years at 7% and 4½% (i.e. less 2½% special tax allowance).

[d] Return of 12% on capital: 80% borrowed at 7% p.a.; 1½% allowance for maintenance, management, voids, debts, insurance; provision for sinking fund over 40 years at 2½%.

the costs of constructing houses is higher in London than in Birmingham, the cost differential between houses and high blocks is much less in London. The total extra capital costs of developing high blocks are naturally a little less when use is made of more expensive land near the centre.

The annual costs depend not only on the capital costs but also on the rate of interest at which the loan is serviced, the period of loan and the subsidies or tax reliefs obtained. Public housing authorities currently pay about $6\frac{3}{4}$ per cent and service the loans over sixty years. In 1964 they received basic subsidies related to the type of housing, subsidies for multi-storey flatted construction and subsidies for expensive sites. Such subsidies tend to favour the use of expensive sites, tall blocks and small dwellings (table 9.15). The 1967 Housing Subsidies Act substituted for the basic subsidies a new form of subsidy, which in effect reduces the rate of interest actually paid to 4 per cent (appendix 13). Owner-occupiers normally purchase with the aid of a mortgage. Usually the longest period of loan is about thirty years and often the purchaser is required to provide 10 to 15 per cent of the purchase money from some other source; sometimes this can be borrowed through special arrangements. Where tax is paid at the full current rate the net cost is reduced to about $4\frac{1}{2}$ per cent (gross rate $7\frac{1}{8}$ per cent). A scheme which in effect subsidizes borrowers not paying tax at the to full rate, and brings them on to a nearly equal footing with those who do, has now been introduced by the Government. Such subsidies, however, do not change the relative costs of different types and forms of housing. The use of tall blocks only begins to be justifiable on very expensive land; in such cases total costs are usually too high for most people to meet. Absolute costs are, of course, greater for rented property where the financial risks are greater, where there are no subsidies, and where tax is payable on the money required to repay the loan.

PART 3

NATIONAL AND REGIONAL HOUSING NEEDS, COSTS AND LAND

CHAPTER 10

THE DEVELOPMENT OF THE HOUSING MODEL

Part 2 of this book has provided a description of the way estimates of household formation, space standards, densities and various types of costs have been prepared. Part 3 is concerned with their use in estimating the need for dwellings, and with cost and land requirements.

THE TOTAL REQUIREMENTS FOR HOUSING

The method of estimating household formation and the fitting of households to dwellings have already been described in chapter 5. Estimates were prepared separately for each of the three population projections and for each of the three migration patterns of the dwellings required by size to match the households expected in each region. The estimates were prepared for each quinquennium over the period 1964–2004.

THE EXISTING STOCK AND DEMOLITION POLICY

While the lives of some dwellings are determined by the poor quality of their construction and the lives of others are shortened as a result of inadequate maintenance, by and large the physical life of a well maintained dwelling is indefinite. Only about 2 per cent of the stock of dwellings were found to be in very poor condition, structurally unsound and substandard, and these will, it has been assumed, be demolished and replaced within the period 1964–9.

While a great deal of the housing built in the eighteenth and nineteenth centuries was very inadequate by contemporary standards, the evils arising from such housing were not publicly recognized until the 1840s. Since that time local and national statutes have set minimum standards in respect of the supply of pure water, sewerage, the provision of water closets, daylight and ventilation, and the occupation rates for rooms. Model dwellings and, later, local authority housing established standards of space and amenity. Dr Hole has shown that the overall floor space per person has risen by about half a square foot every year over the last 120 years (67). The extra space has generally been required for the provision of a bathroom, storage and circulation, although there has also been a slight increase in net living space. These improvements are reflected in the way the proportion of dwellings without census services declines as the age of the dwellings falls.

There are, therefore, grounds for believing in a strong association between the facilities and amenities provided by a dwelling and its age. Of course, facilities have been added and amenities improved as standards have risen. Such changes can go a long way towards keeping the standards of existing dwellings in step with the standards provided by new dwellings. Better class housing was usually well built, with generous provision of space, daylight and ventilation, and it has been worthwhile to modernize it, adding services and other facilities in accordance with modern standards. The better class housing of all ages is, therefore, likely to meet current standards, certainly over the period under study. This group of housing includes housing likely to be retained because of historical interest or aesthetic merit. About 5 per cent of dwellings were estimated to fall into this category; few of them were in the older age groups.

The improvement of standards by the replacement of dwellings was approached through the dates of construction. The number of dwellings constructed during or before the early nineteenth century and still surviving is small, the number gradually increasing as their date of construction approaches the present day. As the size and productivity of the construction industry increases, the number likely to be replaced will rise. It is assumed that only substandard dwellings and those in a very poor physical condition will be replaced during the first quinquennium, but that in subsequent quinquennia demolitions will proceed according to age.

The demolition programmes studied were built up as follows:

(1) All dwellings classified as in a very poor condition and substandard have been regarded as unfit and it has been assumed they will be demolished in the period 1964–9.

(2) Other dwellings (those of high standard being excluded) it is assumed will be demolished in accordance with their age, the stock being demolished during the second to eighth quinquennia in the order in which the dwellings were erected.

The percentages to be demolished in each quinquennium are:

Period	Percentages
1969–74	8
1974–9	9
1979–84	11
1984–9	13
1989–94	16
1994–9	19
1999–2004	24
1969–2004	100

These percentages were applied to three alternative programmes:

(A) pre-1881 dwellings
(B) pre-1921 dwellings
(C) pre-1941 dwellings.

The percentages to be demolished in each period were determined so as to reduce the average age of dwellings at an accelerating rate over the forty-year period. For convenience the same rates were set for each of the three programmes for clearance. Because the number of dwellings to be cleared under programme A is so much less than under the others, the date before which the average age starts to decline consistently is delayed until the 1980s.

THE PROGRAMMES OF CONSTRUCTION

The numbers and sizes of dwellings to be constructed under each programme were found by deducting the stock from the total number required at each date to satisfy household formation and fitting standards. The stock of dwellings was adjusted at each date for demolitions and constructions over the previous quinquennium. This gave twenty-seven programmes of construction for each of the twelve regions.

These programmes were then costed separately for the dwellings and works within their curtilage, for garages and for site clearance, roads, development and public utility services. Initially, costs and land requirements were calculated on the basis of a density of fifty-nine habitable rooms per acre, the proportions of houses, low flats and high flats being taken as 74:18:8 (table 7.7). The costs of the dwellings and works within the curtilages were obtained from the basic costs of public authority dwellings (table 7.9). It was assumed that dwellings for less than four persons were flats or bungalows. Larger dwellings were assumed to be distributed as follows:

Storeys	Type of dwelling	Persons per dwelling	
		4	5 or more
		%	%
1–2	flats	5	5
	maisonettes	95	95
3–4	flats	90	80
	maisonettes	10	20
5 and over	flats	80	70
	maisonettes	20	30

An addition of 15 per cent was made to the cost of all dwellings, 5 per cent to cover rises in facilities over those covered in the base costs and 10 per cent to cover a proportion of better quality dwellings (chapter 7). The costs were further adjusted to allow for the number of storeys and regional differences. The regional indices for the South East and London were weighted together according to the number of dwellings likely to be built in these regions (tables 7.11 and 7.12). Garages were costed at £200 where they were to be built in association with houses and £300 where they were to be built in association with flats. Again 10 per cent was added for the proportion of better class dwellings to cover the provision of additional garage spaces. An allowance was made for regional differences in costs (table 7.12, column 1). Site clearance, roads, development and public utility services were costed on the basis of density in dwellings per acre (table 7.17). The density was obtained for each quinquennial group by dividing the average density (fifty-nine rooms per acre) by the average number of rooms per dwelling, obtained by dividing the total number of rooms by the total number of dwellings. Again an allowance was made for regional differences in costs (table 7·12 column 1).[1]

A large part of future housing development will take place on land to be cleared under the programmes of demolition. The use of this land gives rise to costs in addition to those of developing housing on virgin land. Demolition costs vary with the existing densities of development. The costs of site clearance, development, and roads and sewers are about 50 per cent greater on redeveloped sites than on virgin sites. Under-building and external services probably average about £100 a dwelling more for redeveloped than for virgin land. An allowance for these costs was made on the basis of the average density of development, 17·4 dwellings per acre, equivalent to the basic density of fifty-nine rooms per acre. The addition of these three figures gave the extra costs arising from clearing and developing existing housing land of £7,050, £6,890 and £6,750 per acre for pre-1881 housing, 1881–1920 housing and 1921–40 housing respectively. An allowance was made for regional differences in costs (table 7.12, column 1).

THE PROGRAMMES FOR IMPROVING THE STOCK OF HOUSING

As will have been appreciated from chapter 6, many of the dwellings in the existing stock are in an unsatisfactory physical condition, lack the basic census services as well as many other standard facilities and amenities such as garages, and exist in a poor residential environment. While some of these dwellings, particularly the older ones, can never be the equal of dwellings built to current standards, many will continue to be occupied for a period of years before their place in the demolition programmes is reached. They will not meet acceptable minimum standards during this period unless arrears of maintenance are made good, minimum services incorporated and some improvement made to the residential environment. The provision of garaging may also be required.

The estimated costs of restoration and upgrading are heavy (chapter 8) and this work will be uneconomic if the number of years of life available to a dwelling is small. The annual equivalent cost of restoration and upgrading should be no greater than the equivalent cost of a new dwelling providing similar facilities.

[1] A set of percentage adjustments was calculated for estimating the effect of levels of density above and below the level used in the basic calculations. The percentage adjustments were obtained by costing for 1,000 habitable rooms at a range of densities on the basis of various combinations of houses, low flats and high flats when developed at various densities (table 7.7).

Strictly, allowance should be made for differences in future maintenance costs, but the costs of renewals will not be as great in relation to age for dwellings which have been restored and upgraded at the beginning of the period considered as for dwellings regularly maintained (table 8.7). How large this effect will be is not known, but some allowance for it is necessary in deciding on the identity of dwellings to be costed for various types of restoration and upgrading. In considering the equivalents between new and existing housing, allowance must be made for the size of the dwelling and for the period during which it is available. An index of equivalents can be obtained by relating annuity values for various lives (table 10.1).

Table 10.1. *Percentages of new cost equivalent at various lives*

Expected future life	Equivalent of new cost
Years	%
5	22
10	38
15	52
20	62
25	70
30	77
35	82
40	86

Note: Interest taken at 5% p.a.

If these factors are applied to the costs of new dwellings, they set the maximum amounts which are worthwhile spending on improving dwellings with expected lives shorter than those expected for new dwellings. These factors have been

Table 10.2. *Amounts economically worth spending to improve existing dwellings*

£s

Expected future life	Size of dwelling in habitable rooms							
	1	2	3	4	5	6	7	8+
Years								
5	420	480	550	620	660	710	760	840
10	730	830	940	1060	1140	1230	1310	1460
15	1000	1130	1290	1450	1560	1680	1790	2000
20	1190	1350	1540	1730	1860	2000	2130	2380
25	1350	1520	1740	1960	2100	2260	2400	2690
30	1480	1680	1910	2150	2310	2480	2640	2950
35	1580	1780	2030	2290	2460	2650	2820	3150
40	1650	1870	2130	2410	2580	2770	2950	3300

SOURCE: NIESR estimates.

applied to the national costs of dwellings themselves at densities of fifty-nine habitable rooms per acre (chapter 7), together with garages, for the range of dwelling size (table 10.2).

It will be seen from a study of table 10.3 that these sums exceed the costs of making good arrears of maintenance but are not sufficient in all cases to cover the addition of missing services.

The older the dwellings, the worse their condition and the shorter their expectation of life, the smaller the programme of improvements which is

Table 10.3. *Average costs of upgrading a low cost dwelling and its environment, March 1964*

£s

Condition and age of dwelling	Type of improvement [a]	Habitable rooms	Expected life: 5 years	10 years	20 years	40 years
Poor condition, 100 years old	(1)	2	181	339	567	787
	(2)		566	724	952	1172
	(3)		676	834	1062	1282
	(4)		926	1084	1312	1532
	(1)	5	270	506	846	1175
	(2)		655	891	1156	1485
	(3)		765	1001	1266	1595
	(4)		1015	1251	1516	1845
	(1)	8	411	769	1286	1786
	(2)		796	1154	1558	2058
	(3)		906	1264	1668	2168
	(4)		1156	1514	1918	2418
Fair–poor condition, 40 years old	(1)	2	85	160	267	370
	(2)		470	545	652	755
	(3)		540	615	722	825
	(4)		790	865	972	1075
	(1)	5	127	238	398	553
	(2)		512	623	708	863
	(3)		582	693	778	933
	(4)		832	943	1028	1183
	(1)	8	193	362	605	840
	(2)		578	747	877	1112
	(3)		648	817	947	1182
	(4)		898	1067	1197	1432

SOURCE: NIESR estimates.

[a] (1) = arrears of maintenance,
(2) = (1)+missing services and bathroom provision,
(3) = (2)+environmental improvement,
(4) = (3)+garage provision.

economically justifiable. The most difficult case is dwellings in poor condition, of 100 years of age or more, with an expectation of life of only five years. The most that can be justified for such dwellings of between two and five habitable rooms is making good arrears of maintenance (table 10.3). However, the larger the dwelling the larger the programme of improvement economically justifiable. It would be justifiable to add missing services in the case of such a dwelling with eight habitable rooms even if it was in poor condition and over 100 years of age. The costs and economic levels of expenditure for higher standard houses are proportional, and hence the same breakeven points would apply.

The normal policy is to deal with all the housing on an estate in the same way and this is usually most convenient from an administrative point of view. Except for unfit dwellings, the dwellings on an estate are best cleared together, so that the area can be comprehensively redeveloped, and this is the normal practice. Generally, dwellings in a group are of a common age and standard, but conditions will vary with owner and occupier. More improvement might be economically justified for dwellings in a better condition but this would not always be a feasible policy. For convenience the level of improvement to be costed is based on the oldest group of dwellings classified as in a poor condition. Dwellings classified as in a very poor condition have been assumed to be unfit and ready for demolition: the cost of improving such dwellings would be uneconomic. The following programmes of improvement have therefore been applied:[1]

(A) 5–10 years of expected life:

Arrears of maintenance, together with the addition of the missing services, except that a shower would be provided instead of a bath.

(B) 10–20 years of expected life:

Arrears of maintenance, together with the addition of missing services, a bathroom and improvement of the environment.

[1] The effect of the policy followed is to cost a minimum rather than a maximum standard of housing. No allowance is made for improving dwellings with an expected life of less than five years. All dwellings with an expectation of at least five years are assumed to be improved as necessary to a proper standard of repair and to have a full complement of services. For dwellings with an expected life of ten years or over the environment would also be improved, and garages would also be provided where the expected life was twenty years or more. Thus, except for marginal cases, the equivalent annual cost of improvement would be less, generally much less (since the criterion is based on the worst dwelling), than the equivalent cost of a new dwelling. Of course, the amenities offered by the improved dwelling would usually, although not always, be less than for a new dwelling. In the case of the worst dwellings they would be unfit if not improved and hence valueless except for the site, the value of which has been excluded from the calculations. The annual value (rent) of a dwelling in a free market in which supply and demand balanced would reflect the amenity provided by the dwelling. Thus, broadly, the value of an improved or an unimproved dwelling relative to that of a new one would reflect the difference in amenity levels, and the undertaking of improvement work would be justified by an increase in annual value comparable to the cost of improvement. Hence in a market in which rents were not dominated by scarcity, or in which fair rents in this sense were enforced (a situation now being approached), rents would reflect the condition and standard of dwelling, and the improvement of dwellings would be justified financially, as well as from the point of view of the economic use of resources.

(C) 20 years or more of expected life:

As for (B) above, together with a garage.

THE COSTING OF ARREARS OF MAINTENANCE

In order to apply the costs of making good arrears of maintenance (table 8.2) to the basic stock of dwellings, it is necessary to know the distribution of dwellings by age, life expectancy, size, standard and physical condition. These proportions of dwellings by age and size can be calculated from the national data (chapter 6), while the proportions by life expectancy can be calculated from the demolition programmes. As there were no national data on physical condition, the information available from the survey was related to the distribution of the dwellings through its relationship with census condition and age. Census condition can be related to the population figures only through size. The distribution of dwellings by standard was also taken from the survey, but this was applied directly to all the dwellings, as there were no strong reasons for expecting any association with age or census condition. In building up estimates of the costs of improvement work, the various estimates were related in the order of the reliability of the associations which had been established.

The starting point for estimating the arrears of maintenance costs was the calculation of weighted cost indices for physical condition, standard, age and expectation of life. These were calculated as follows:

1. The cost indices (I) appropriate to each physical condition were weighted by the proportion of dwellings (P) in each physical condition for each of the census condition categories. The proportions were taken from the sample. (A zero value was given to the cost for very poor condition, since such dwellings were regarded as unfit and were programmed for immediate demolition.) This process gave four weighted indices for $C = 1$ to 4, of the form

$$\sum_{c=1}^{c=5} I_c \,.\, P_{cC_i}$$

where c refers to the physical condition category and C_i to the census condition category.

2. The cost indices appropriate to each standard were weighted by the proportion of dwellings in each standard category; the proportions being taken from the sample. (A zero value was given to the cost of the substandard, since such dwellings were programmed for immediate demolition.) This gave an index of the form

$$\sum_{s=1}^{s=4} I_s \,.\, P_s$$

where s refers to the standard.

3. The cost indices appropriate to each decennial age group were weighted by the proportion of dwellings in each age group for each region; the proportions

were those prepared earlier from an analysis of census and other data (chapter 6). This gave twelve regional weighted indices for $R = 1$ to 12, of the form

$$\sum_{a=1}^{a=16} I_a \, . \, P_{aR_j}$$

where a refers to age group, R_j to the region.

4. The cost indices appropriate to each expectation of life, taken in quinquennial groups, were weighted by the proportion of dwellings expected to survive for that period according to the three demolition programmes. This gave three demolition programme weighted indices for $D = 1$ to 3, of the form

$$\sum_{e=1}^{e=9} I_e \, . \, P_{eD_k}$$

where e refers to expectation of life group, D_k to demolition programme.

The next step was to apply the weighted physical condition cost indices to the numbers of dwellings (N) in each regional census condition/size group. The products were summed over each size group. These were subsequently weighted by the cost indices for size and summed. This gave weighted, physical condition/size cost indices for each region, $R = 1$ to 12, of the form

$$\sum_{g=1}^{g=10} \left[I_g \, . \sum_{i=1}^{i=4} \left(N_{igj} \sum_{c=1}^{c=5} I_c \, . \, P_{cC_i} \right) \right]$$

where g refers to the size group.

The total cost for each region and for each demolition programme was now obtained by multiplying the above expression by the appropriate values of the remaining three indices derived above and by the basic cost of arrears of maintenance, £650. The estimate for region j and demolition programme k was thus:

$$£650. \sum_{g=1}^{g=10} \left[I_g \sum_{i=1}^{i=4} \left(N_{igj} \sum_{c=1}^{c=5} I_c \, . \, P_{cC_i} \right) \right] \sum_{s=1}^{s=4} I_s \, . \, P_s \sum_{a=1}^{a=16} I_a \, . \, P_{aR_j} \sum_{e=1}^{e=9} I_e \, . \, P_{eD_k}$$

These expressions were then adjusted according to the regional price indices (table 7.12, column 1). The indices for the costs of arrears of maintenance were those derived earlier (table 8.2).

THE COSTING OF THE PROVISION OF MISSING SERVICES

The number of dwellings lacking census services (cold water, hot water, water closet and fixed bath) were estimated for each region from the Census and other data (chapter 6). Since there is a strong association between census condition (based on the absence of census services) and physical condition, it was assumed that the dwellings which were in such a poor condition that they would be replaced by 1969 would be those most lacking the census services. The number of dwellings in each region without each service was therefore reduced by the number of dwellings to be replaced over the period 1964–9. The additions of services to the remaining dwellings were then costed (table 8.4). It was assumed that water closets and baths would be installed even where they existed, if the water closet was outside the dwelling and if the bath was in a room other than a bathroom (chapter 6). For dwellings with a life of less than ten years it was assumed that a closet and basin would be provided, rather than a bathroom with a bath and basin. It was also assumed that back additions would be necessary in the case of all one and two room dwellings, for three-quarters of three room dwellings and for two-thirds of four room dwellings, half five room dwellings and a quarter of larger dwellings. These costs were adjusted according to the regional price indices (table 7.12, column 1).

THE COSTING OF THE UPGRADING OF RESIDENTIAL AREAS

It was not possible to relate the demolition programmes directly to the condition of residential areas. In order to eliminate the dwellings programmed for demolition in the first ten years from the numbers falling into different categories of condition of residential area, it would have been necessary to have based the estimates on the association between condition of the area and condition of the dwellings. The condition of dwellings was known with more certainty than the condition of the residential areas. Moreover, the costs of upgrading areas could not be very precise. It was, therefore, thought preferable to cost directly in terms of the condition of the dwellings (chapter 8). The costs were adjusted for regional prices as before (table 7.12, column 1).

THE COSTING OF THE PROVISION OF GARAGES

The distribution of dwellings with and without garages, and without garage spaces, was known for each age group of dwellings for each region. The numbers of dwellings programmed for demolition during the first twenty years in each age group were similarly known. Since no association had been established between the condition of a dwelling and garage provision, the numbers of dwellings lacking a garage and the numbers lacking a garage space were reduced in proportion to the numbers of dwellings programmed to be demolished in the first twenty years. The numbers of dwellings lacking a garage were then costed (chapter 8) and the usual adjustment was made for regional prices (table 7.12, column 1).

THE COSTING OF REGULAR MAINTENANCE

Since maintenance costs are closely related to age, the first step in estimating the costs of regular maintenance was to compute the age distribution of the stock of dwellings at the mid-point of each quinquennial period. The method was to adjust the estimated age distributions at the end of the previous quinquennium for demolitions and new constructions. Adjustment to the maintenance costs for the sizes of the dwellings proved to be unnecessary, because the average size of the stock was found to be very close to the average size of the 1964 stock and to the size on which the maintenance costs were based. This was because the reduction in the proportion of small dwellings was largely offset by the reduction in the proportion of large dwellings. The numbers of dwellings in each age group at each quinquennium were costed (table 8.7) and adjustments were made for regional price differences (table 7.12, column 1).

CHAPTER 11

HOUSING REQUIREMENTS

THE LONG-TERM NEED FOR DWELLINGS

The need for housing depends on a number of factors, of which population changes, household formation, vacancies, second dwellings and the rates of demolition are the most important. On the basis of the fitting standards taken for this study and assuming population growth on the basis of the projections of the Registrars General, the number of households by 2004 would be about 23·4 million. There would be either 22·7 or 25·6 million households if the lower or higher birth rates were assumed. There is only a small difference in the number of dwellings required for the low assumption as compared with that of the Registrars General because, as a result of differences in the composition of the population at 2004, the difference in population is reflected in the size of households rather than in their number. The total number of households is very sensitive to changes in headship rates and the effect of making some allowance for an increase in headship rates has been to increase the number of households by about 8 per cent (chapter 5).

Dwellings are vacant for some part of their lives, partly because of the period which elapses between one occupier departing and the next arriving, and partly because the occupiers may be temporarily away from home. On the night of the 1961 Census, 3·9 per cent of the dwellings in Great Britain were unoccupied (the 1951 figure was about 2·5 per cent, and the 1931 one about 2·9 per cent). Of the vacancies in 1961 over half, 2·2 per cent of all dwellings, were without an occupier and 1·7 per cent of all dwellings were temporarily unoccupied.

About 8 per cent of households move each year; a true vacancy rate of 2·2 per cent implies an average gap between one occupier departing and the next arriving of fourteen weeks. A period of this length is most unlikely under the conditions of housing shortage in 1961. It would seem that many of the dwellings recorded as vacant in this sense were either closed and awaiting demolition, or unfinished. In the early 1960s, local authorities were closing dwellings at the rate of about 0·5 per cent of the stock each year; there must also have been some private closures. New constructions were then running at the rate of about 2 per cent of the stock each year. The assumption that about 1 per cent of dwellings are vacant but available for occupation, giving a six and a half week turnover period, seems to be compatible with these figures.

Some of the households normally occupying the 1·7 per cent of dwellings temporarily vacant would have been staying with other households, and would be counted for purposes of this study as households requiring a dwelling. Others would have been counted as residents of hotels and other residential institutions and included in the assessment of that type of accommodation. Others again would have been staying in temporary dwellings and counted as needing a permanent dwelling. Some may have been abroad and missed the census count. The balance are likely to have been at a second dwelling. This number must be quite small, perhaps not more than a half per cent.

In the long run, greater affluence and leisure is likely to stimulate household movement and the desire for second homes. The latter development is the more important. It is reported that in Sweden one in eight families already have summer cottages (78). The trend towards second homes is growing in other Scandinavian countries also and in America. Many of these second homes are not dwellings of permanent construction. In Britain, use is made of caravans and boats, and otherwise obsolete cottages in rural and coastal towns are also used for second homes. The lengthening of the weekend might result in the second home being located at the place of work, rather than the place of leisure. This might provide further life for dwellings becoming obsolete for permanent occupation. The trend towards second homes might, therefore, lead more to improving existing housing and retarding demolitions than to additional construction of new dwellings. In either case, there would be some addition to the load on the construction industry. If, by 2004, 10 per cent of the households formed by married males required second homes, an additional 1·8 million dwellings would be needed on the Registrars General's population assumptions. If two-thirds were obtained from reductions in demolitions and from temporary dwellings, 0·6 million would involve additional construction. After allowing for vacancies during changes in occupation, the additional need might be about a million dwellings.

The information available on the need for dwellings to provide a pool of vacancies and second homes cannot be nearly as precise as that which can be derived from population information about the formation of households and their size. Little is known about the size of households who might require second homes, or for that matter about households who might wish to share or use temporary dwellings. Since in this study the effect of the scale of requirements is

Table 11.1. *Dwellings needed, 1964–2004*

Millions

	Birth rate assumption		
	Low	RG's	High
Stock required at 2004	22·7	23·4	25·6
Stock at 1964	16·8	16·8	16·8
Number of additional dwellings to be constructed,[a] 1964–2004	6·1	6·8	9·0

SOURCE: NIESR estimates.

[a] This includes an allowance for conversions but makes no allowance for demolitions.

more important than the actual number of dwellings, it appears better to accept the numbers and sizes of dwellings based on population and demolition rates as bench marks. The introduction of arbitrary requirements for vacancies and second homes at this stage would only reduce the precision of the specification and costs, and complicate the interpretation of the results.

On this basis about 24 million dwellings would be required in 2004, a few more or less if the population increased faster or slower than generally expected (table 11.1). Since there were about 16·8 million permanent dwellings in 1964, about 7 million additional dwellings would be needed over the forty-year period.

REGIONAL REQUIREMENTS AND THE EFFECT OF MIGRATION

The number of dwellings required for each region depends on the strength of the factors discussed above and in particular on the population assumptions. The regional population varies not only with the birth rates but also with the inter-regional patterns of migration. The migration patterns represent a reasonable range of possibilities rather than a forecast, since the object is to test the effect of regional migration on needs for urban facilities. The effect on the number of additional dwellings is far greater than the effect on the size of the total stock estimated to be necessary in 2004. The relative differences in the number of new additional dwellings needed to meet the requirements of a region arising from given birth and migration rates will be reduced by the addition of the number of dwellings needed to replace the older part of the stock. There is little interest in comparing one region with another, since the large absolute variations in numbers merely reflect the range in the sizes of region. The differences in numbers required within a region are important, since they reflect the extent to which the load of work is likely to vary with the migration pattern. These differences, however, are better discussed in terms of costs, since costs provide a weighted comparison of needs.

It is of interest that the national totals of numbers of dwellings required under different migration patterns vary little: only by about a tenth of one per cent. There are two reasons for this: first, losses of population by migration are never so great as to exceed natural increase; secondly, except in Scotland, there is no surplus of dwellings, even of particular sizes. The net result is that, within the limits of the migration rates assumed, all dwellings are utilized except in Scotland, and no reduction in the number of constructions can be obtained by changing the rates of migration. It is not, of course, possible within the terms of the model to measure the effects of the rate of migration on individual settlements. These are likely to be uneven and the populations of some settlements might decline more rapidly than the population of a region as a whole. In fact, the population of some settlements might decline while the population of the region as a whole was increasing: this would be likely to occur with or without the effect of migration. In this sense, the estimate of the need for dwellings produced in this study must be minimal. The scale of any such underestimate would not normally be large. Generally only dwellings of the lowest standard would become vacant and these would be absorbed in the demolition programme. Often, especially in the case of rural depopulation, the vacant dwellings would be used as second homes. Moreover, generally industry will be developed and expanded where there is a pool of labour, that is where the homes are. Thus, while within a given region migration is likely to add to the number of dwellings which would need to be constructed, it seems likely that, in the long run, the effect on national constructions would be small, since the effect of the migration would be absorbed through changes in demolition and in the way households were fitted to dwellings.

THE REPLACEMENT OF THE EXISTING STOCK OF DWELLINGS

It has been assumed that dwellings which are both substandard and in a very poor condition, and which would not be worth repairing and improving, would be given priority and replaced during the first quinquennium. There are about 344,000 dwellings in this category. Many other dwellings are in poor condition and lack services now considered essential. While arrears of maintenance can be made good and services installed—and allowance for the costs has been made—the older dwellings will still tend to be badly planned: the floor spaces will be small, and lighting and access inadequate. These standards tend to be associated with the date of construction. Three possible assumptions for demolition and replacement have therefore been explored (chapter 10). These assume demolition and replacement of all except the higher standard dwellings built prior to 1881, 1921 and 1941 respectively. It has been assumed that demolitions would be programmed in relation to age, so that average age would gradually fall. This would result in the number of demolitions increasing each quinquennium. Since the capacity of the construction industry is expected to grow at a compound rate, such programming would have the advantage of increasing demand broadly in step with probable increases in supply. The application of these assumptions would achieve the following results by 2004:

Programme A demolish 4·6 million dwellings—most dwellings over 123 years old in 2004.

Programme B demolish 7·4 million dwellings—most dwellings over 83 years old in 2004.

Programme C demolish 11·5 million dwellings—most dwellings over 63 years old in 2004.

It will be seen that the number of dwellings which would have to be constructed to meet the needs for additional population, for raising household fitting standards, and for replacements, ranges between 10·7 million and 20·5 million (table 11.2). The effect of the replacement assumptions which have been considered could be greater than the effect of even extreme changes in population (fig. 11.1). The changes in the number of new dwellings likely to be required as a result of changes in household formation or vacancy rates are small compared with the combined effect of the assumptions concerning population and replacement. The number of dwellings which are likely to be built is subject to the constraint imposed by the capacity of the industry, and the willingness of the community, individually and collectively, to finance house building in preference to other forms of built environment or other expenditure. For reasons which will be explained more fully later, it seems unlikely that the number of dwellings to be constructed would much exceed the limits considered in this study. A higher rate of household formation, or a greater demand for second dwellings, would probably be matched by extending the life of existing dwellings. The

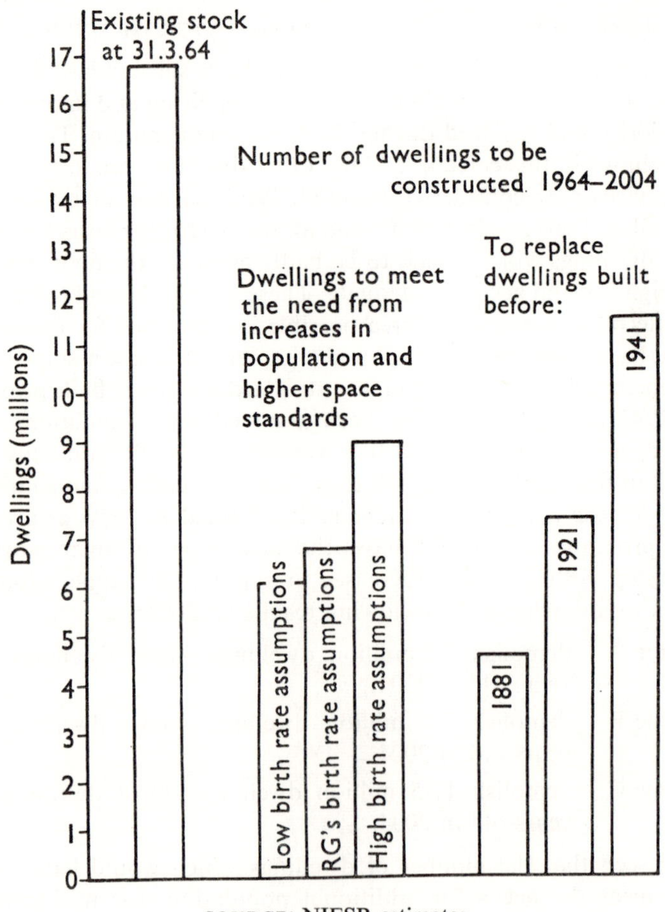

SOURCE: NIESR estimates.

Fig. 11.1. The stock of dwellings and constructions, Great Britain

effect of other assumptions on the numbers of dwellings required can be studied by relating the number estimated as necessary to the cost consequences of a similar number computed on different assumptions.

THE TIMING OF CONSTRUCTION

While on average it would be necessary to build between a quarter and half million dwellings a year to meet the alternative levels of requirement (table 11.2), in the short run the number built may depend more on supply factors than on demand. Nevertheless, the number needs to be related to the likely level of requirements, and some reasonable set of assumptions is needed to establish a basis of estimate and to examine the implications of likely short-term changes in housing needs. In this study it has been assumed that the stock should match the number of households, and that the rate of replacement should increase as the capacity of the house-building industry increases so as to reduce the average age of the stock at an increasing rate. Initially, it has also been assumed that there is a strong demand from households and potential households for a dwelling of their own and that, given the availability of dwellings, household fission would increase by 1969 to the level assumed in this study (chapter 5).

Table 11.2. *Estimated construction requirements for dwellings in Great Britain, 1964–2004*

Millions

Demolition programme	Birth rate assumption		
	Low	RG's	High
A	10·7	11·4	13·6
B	13·5	14·2	16·4
C	17·5	18·3	20·5

SOURCE: NIESR estimates.

On these assumptions an additional 1·8 million dwellings would be required by 1969 (table 11.3). This is nearly three times as many as would be required in the following quinquennium and more than would be required in any other quinquennia during the period 1964–2004. The addition of the number required for replacements increases the total to be constructed during the first quinquennium to just over two million and, by adding to the future quinquennial requirements, does something to reduce the differences in the scale of requirements between the quinquennia over the period (fig. 11.2).

The numbers of dwellings to be constructed each quinquennium under the various sets of assumptions are set out in table 11.4. The fall between the first two quinquennia followed by steady increases is a common feature. Until the

Table 11.3. *Quinquennial construction requirements for dwellings*

Thousands

	Replacements for demolition programmes			Additional dwellings required by birth rate assumptions		
	A	B	C	Low	RG's	High
1964–9	340	340	340	1770	1770	1820
1969–74	350	570	900	550	570	670
1974–9	390	640	1010	520	560	670
1979–84	480	790	1240	570	610	790
1984–9	550	910	1450	690	760	900
1989–94	680	1120	1780	620	750	1090
1994–9	800	1340	2110	680	800	1370
1999–2004	1020	1700	2680	660	950	1670
1964–2004	4610	7410	11510	6060	6770	8980

SOURCE: NIESR estimates.

Note: These figures are approximate and are based on the number of conversions associated with demolition programme A, see p. 191 n.

factors of supply have been examined it is not possible to decide whether the number of constructions in the first quinquennium is too high, and a stock somewhat short in relation to ideal requirements should be accepted, or whether it would be possible and sensible to sustain a much higher output subsequently

Table 11.4. *Number of dwellings to be constructed in Great Britain*

Thousands

	1964–9	1969–74	1974–9	1979–84	1984–9	1989–94	1994–9	1999–2004	1964–2004
Demolition programme A									
Low birth rate	2109	900	907	1049	1242	1299	1480	1687	10673
RG's birth rate	2109	919	948	1092	1308	1429	1602	1979	11386
High birth rate	2163	1013	1057	1274	1451	1762	2178	2695	13593
Demolition programme B									
Low birth rate	2104	1119	1154	1353	1606	1745	2011	2358	13450
RG's birth rate	2104	1138	1195	1395	1671	1877	2132	2649	14161
High birth rate	2158	1232	1304	1577	1814	2210	2708	3366	16369
Demolition programme C									
Low birth rate	2100	1443	1519	1800	2139	2402	2790	3342	17535
RG's birth rate	2100	1461	1560	1842	2205	2533	2912	3634	18247
High birth rate	2154	1555	1669	2024	2348	2866	3488	4350	20454

SOURCE: NIESR estimates.

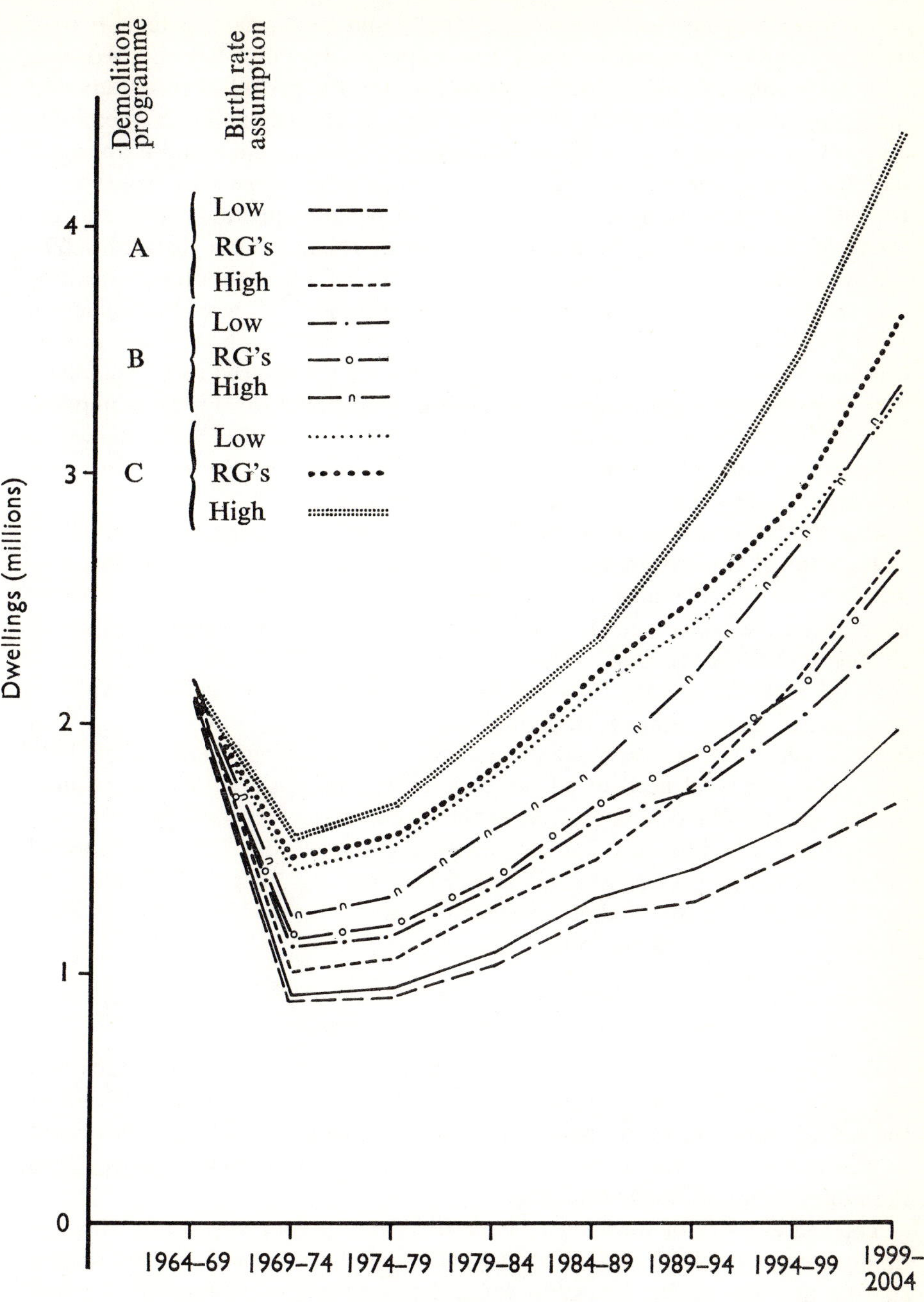

SOURCE: NIESR estimates.

Fig. 11.2. Dwellings to be constructed in Great Britain, 1964–2004

and replace existing stock both more rapidly and to a greater extent. It is of interest to note the extent to which the output of dwellings has changed, and with it the implications for future output, during the period of this study and the preparation of the book for publication. At the beginning of the study, output was running at 1·5 million dwellings per quinquennium and it appeared that the size of the stock would remain below requirements for some time. By 1967 the output was running at 2 million per quinquennium (42) and the target of nearly half a million dwellings a year, originally put forward in *The National Plan* (79), was still retained. There appeared little doubt that something very near the requirement suggested for 1964–9 (table 11.4) would be achieved. Thus the figures for the first quinquennium are no longer in much doubt: it is changes in figures for subsequent quinquennia which need to be examined. Such consideration will be held over until later (chapter 16). First the implications of various possible programmes of construction need to be examined in relation to both the supply and demand conditions. In the meantime, the programmes set out above will be used as a basis of study.

The number of dwellings required does not change in a regular manner from one quinquennium to another (fig. 11.2). The effects of the demolition programmes are greater than those of household formation and, except at the beginning of the period, can readily be manipulated to provide programmes which change in the way required.

At the regional level the total dwelling need and the rate of building required is, of course, more variable. In regions such as North and Central Wales which have an old housing stock, the demolition of all dwellings built before 1941 only raises the total need to 50 per cent above that required if demolition is limited to pre-1881 dwellings. Where the dwelling stock is younger, as in the South East, this difference rises to nearly 70 per cent. The effect of regional differences in the present amount of sharing and migration are considerable, and could result in the total requirements for some regions being twice as great on some assumptions as on others.

THE SIZE OF DWELLINGS

A third of the dwellings in the stock for Great Britain at 31 March 1964 had five rooms; nearly as many had four rooms (table 11.5). Nearly 90 per cent of the stock had between three and six rooms. Since many of the three to six room dwellings are of recent origin, a smaller proportion will need to be replaced than of smaller and larger dwellings.

The average size of dwelling to be built does not vary much after the first quinquennium (table 11.6). During that period allowance is made for eliminating sharing and for raising headship rates. Consequently, the number of small dwellings required is very large and the average size is low. After 1969 the average size of dwelling to be built returns to just under five rooms per dwelling, although it maintains this size to the end of the period only when the high birth rate is assumed. With the official assumptions and the low birth rate, the average size required falls to around 4·5 rooms per dwelling.

Nationally, the size distribution of dwellings needed in 2004, on the basis of the assumed changes in population, fitting standards and household formation

Table 11.5. *Number of dwellings at 31 March 1964*

	Rooms						Total dwellings
	1–2	3	4	5	6	7+	
	Percentages						
Scotland	23	36	26	8	3	4	1,677,735
North	7	19	32	29	8	5	1,057,024
North West	3	8	35	36	12	6	2,211,952
Pennines	5	12	30	40	9	4	1,841,213
Central	3	8	24	46	14	5	395,846
East	3	9	29	40	12	7	434,637
North & Central Wales	3	9	27	29	17	15	207,236
West	3	8	22	38	20	9	1,251,423
South West	3	10	26	32	16	13	472,140
Midlands	3	10	27	43	12	5	1,512,222
East Anglia	3	8	26	39	15	9	317,753
South East	6	13	24	34	14	9	5,429,256
Great Britain	6	14	27	34	12	7	16,808,437

SOURCE: NIESR estimates.

Table 11.6. *Average size of dwellings to be built*

Rooms

	1964–9	1969–74	1974–9	1979–84	1984–9	1989–94	1994–9	1999–2004
Demolition programme A								
Low birth rate	3·5	4·8	4·9	4·6	4·4	4·4	4·4	4·4
RG's birth rate	3·5	4·8	4·8	4·7	4·6	4·7	4·6	4·6
High birth rate	3·5	4·8	4·9	5·0	4·7	4·8	4·8	4·8
Demolition programme B								
Low birth rate	3·5	4·8	4·9	4·7	4·5	4·5	4·5	4·5
RG's birth rate	3·5	4·8	4·8	4·8	4·6	4·7	4·7	4·6
High birth rate	3·5	4·8	4·9	4·9	4·7	4·8	4·8	4·8
Demolition programme C								
Low birth rate	3·5	4·8	4·9	4·7	4·6	4·6	4·6	4·6
RG's birth rate	3·5	4·8	4·8	4·8	4·7	4·7	4·7	4·7
High birth rate	3·5	4·9	4·9	4·9	4·7	4·7	4·8	4·8

SOURCE: NIESR estimates.

is similar to that of the stock in 1964 (table 11.7). The proportions are not much affected by the assumptions for birth rates; the proportion of larger dwellings is naturally a little greater the higher the birth rate.

Table 11.7. *Size of dwellings in Great Britain, 1964 and 2004*

	Rooms per dwelling							
	1–2	3	4	5	6	7+	All sizes	Total dwellings
	%	%	%	%	%	%	%	*mns*
1964	6	14	27	34	12	7	100	*16·8*
2004								
Low birth rate	7	14	30	32	11	6	100	*22·7*
RG's birth rate	6	13	29	34	12	6	100	*23·4*
High birth rate	5	12	28	35	13	7	100	*25·6*

SOURCE: NIESR estimates.

The past and expected rises in the rates of household formation are proportionately greater for small households than for large households. This trend, which creates a need for proportionately more small dwellings, particularly those of one and two rooms, is most marked during the early years of the period 1964–2004. As the rates of household formation level off and rising birth rates increase household size, the proportionate requirement for larger sizes of dwellings increases. The effect on the sizes of the dwellings to be constructed is obviously greater than on the sizes in the stock. The increases in the sizes of dwellings to be constructed are paralleled by the effects of demolitions (fig. 11.3), since the oldest and poorest housing tends to be the smallest and largest in terms of number of rooms. As a result, the proportion of small dwellings to be constructed is greater during the period 1964–84 than the proportion in the stock, but the proportion falls again in the period 1984–2004 (table 11.8). The proportion of larger dwellings required rises in the second period because of the rise in household size. Again, the alternative birth rate assumptions make little difference.

The regional picture is again more varied. The size distribution of the current stock in most regions was very similar to that for Great Britain as a whole (table 11.5). The North and South East, however, had a higher proportion of small dwellings, while the South West, and North and Central Wales had a higher proportion of large dwellings. The high proportion of small dwellings in the South East probably reflected the extent to which the larger dwellings have been sub-divided. The most notable area of departure from the national average was Scotland, where a third of the dwellings had three rooms and 85 per cent between one and four rooms.

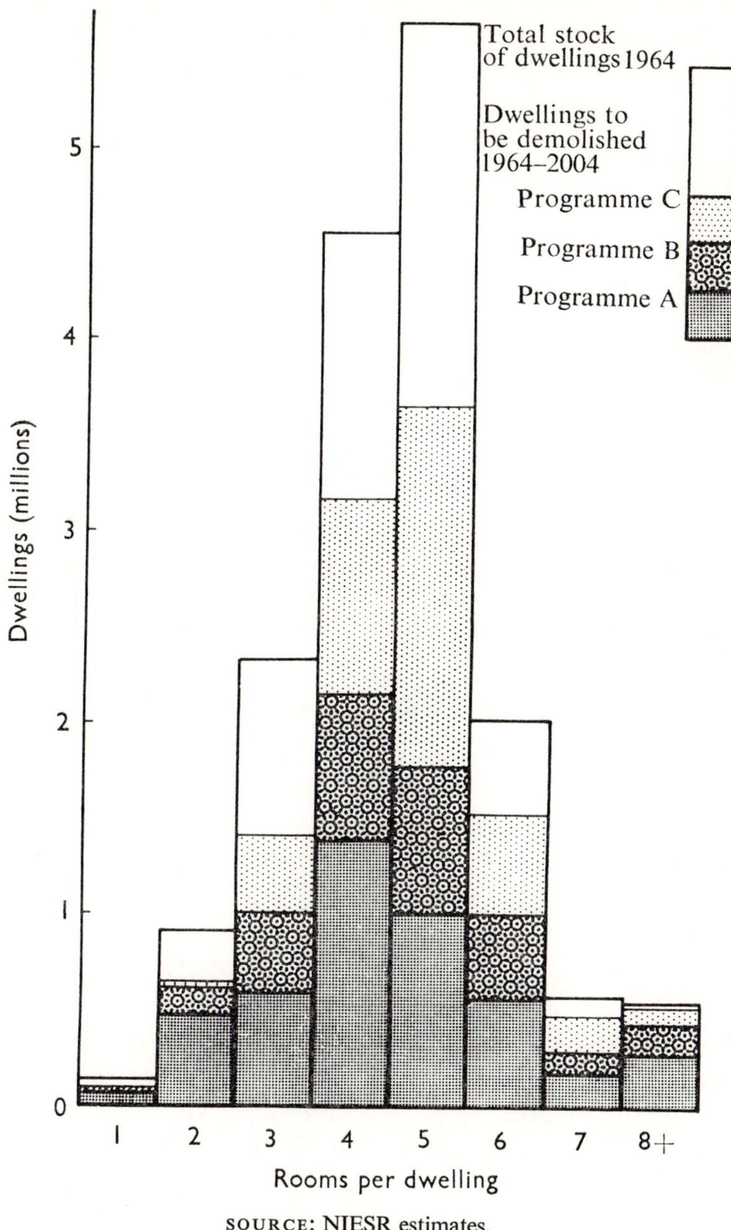

SOURCE: NIESR estimates.

Fig. 11.3. Demolitions and present stock of dwellings, Great Britain

Table 11.8. *Size of dwellings to be constructed in Great Britain, 1964–2004*

Percentages

	Rooms per dwelling						
	1–2	3	4	5	6	7+	All sizes
Low birth rate							
1964–84	13	19	29	23	11	5	100
1984–2004	9	15	35	24	10	7	100
Registrars General's birth rate							
1964–84	13	18	29	24	11	5	100
1984–2004	7	12	31	30	12	8	100
High birth rate							
1964–84	11	17	28	26	12	6	100
1984–2004	5	9	28	35	14	9	100

SOURCE: NIESR estimates.

The size distribution of households expected in 2004 and the required size distribution of dwellings, differ little from one region to another (table 11.9). The size distribution of dwellings needed in 2004 is not much affected by differences in assumptions about birth and marriage rates, or by different internal migration rates.

Table 11.9. *Regional differences in size of dwellings, 2004*

Percentages

	Rooms per dwelling						
	1–2	3	4	5	6	7+	All sizes
Scotland	6	14	32	32	11	5	100
North	5	16	30	33	11	5	100
North West	6	10	32	35	11	6	100
Pennines	6	12	28	38	11	5	100
Central	6	13	24	40	12	5	100
East	6	13	27	37	11	6	100
North & Central Wales	6	12	24	28	16	14	100
West	6	14	23	34	16	7	100
South West	6	14	25	31	14	10	100
Midlands	6	14	28	36	11	5	100
East Anglia	6	14	24	35	13	8	100
South East	6	14	29	32	12	7	100
Great Britain	6	13	29	34	12	6	100

SOURCE: NIESR estimates.

Note: Registrars General's birth rate assumption; migration pattern 1.

Some idea of the regional variability can be obtained by examining the size distribution over the periods 1964–84 and 1984–2004 (table 11.10). The size groups vary by as much as 36 per cent between one region and another. Scotland shows the greatest variability, but the other regions each show a distinctive pattern in the size of dwellings required. Many regions, particularly Scotland and North and Central Wales, require a radically different balance of sizes in the second period from that required in the first period. This is largely a result

Table 11.10. *Regional differences in size of dwellings to be constructed over the periods 1964–84 and 1984–2004*

Percentages

	Rooms per dwelling						
	1–2	3	4	5	6	7+	All Sizes
1964–84							
Great Britain	13	18	29	24	11	5	100
Scotland	0	0	16	51	27	6	100
North	5	11	21	36	22	5	100
North West	22	18	26	24	6	4	100
Pennines	16	17	21	22	16	8	100
Central	17	24	19	25	10	5	100
East	17	25	21	23	9	5	100
N. & C. Wales	24	26	9	15	11	15	100
West	16	29	21	20	9	5	100
South West	20	28	16	19	8	9	100
Midlands	14	23	29	19	10	5	100
East Anglia	19	27	17	21	10	6	100
South East	11	18	43	17	7	4	100
1984–2004							
Great Britain	7	12	31	30	12	8	100
Scotland	32	23	18	14	6	7	100
North	9	19	34	22	9	7	100
North East	3	6	42	34	8	7	100
Pennines	5	11	34	34	11	5	100
Central	4	10	29	36	15	6	100
East	3	8	34	32	14	9	100
N. & C. Wales	2	6	28	26	16	22	100
West	3	8	26	36	17	10	100
South West	3	10	28	32	13	14	100
Midlands	4	11	31	32	16	6	100
East Anglia	2	9	31	31	16	11	100
South East	7	14	29	29	13	8	100

SOURCE: NIESR estimates.

Note: Registrars General's birth rate assumption; migration pattern 1; demolition programme A.

of the age-size distribution in the current stock. Further details of the size of dwellings required is provided in appendix 9.

THE SIZE PROBLEM FOR DWELLINGS IN SCOTLAND

In estimating the size of the dwellings it was assumed that each household would be able to have its own. At the same time it was assumed that households which were overcrowded and households with unwanted space would ideally prefer dwellings with the same space standards as other households. On these assumptions there would be a surplus of dwellings of certain sizes. In practice, additional dwellings would not be built if dwellings of an adequate size were already available. In all regions other than Scotland there was a shortage of small dwellings during the first period, 1964–9, which was balanced by a surplus of larger dwellings. Some households would, therefore, continue for a time to occupy dwellings which were a little too large for them. By adopting a programme of concentrating on smaller dwellings in the early years, it would be possible to provide a slight permanent improvement in the way households were matched to dwellings, without increasing the overall size of the programme.

Because of the large proportion of small dwellings in Scotland, it would not be possible to match household size to dwelling size there in the same way as in other regions. If this were tried, there would be a surplus of over half a million small dwellings, but a shortage of nearly 700,000 medium and large dwellings. This figure does not allow for the incidence of vacancies. Over the five years to 1967 less than 180,000 dwellings were built in Scotland, although the rate has been increasing. It would not be possible to build over 700,000 dwellings in five years and it is unlikely that over half a million dwellings would be demolished because of their size.

Although Scottish dwellings are small compared with those in other regions of Great Britain, 3·5 as against 4·6 habitable rooms per dwelling, household sizes are much the same. Moreover, Scottish dwellings are more in line with the size of dwellings in many other European countries. Only the Netherlands, Belgium and Switzerland have dwellings which, on average, are as large or larger than those in Great Britain. A group of countries—Denmark, Ireland, Spain, Norway and West Germany—have at least four rooms, but most other European countries have dwellings at least as small as those in Scotland (44). It may be that the current size distribution is more suitable for the Scottish way of living, or perhaps it is simply a result of historical forces and an attempt to keep rents low. All the evidence quoted earlier suggests that space standards rise with increases in affluence. It would seem unlikely that the Scots will be prepared to accept indefinitely dwellings which offer substantially lower space standards than elsewhere in Great Britain, particularly if other standards reach national levels. They might, however, be prepared to wait longer to secure the higher national space standards.

In the past most dwellings built in Scotland were constructed of stone. For this reason, and because of the nature of the climate, the structures tend to be massive. Moreover, a large proportion of dwellings were built as tenements. Nearly half the dwellings in Scotland in 1964 were flats, whereas, in Great Britain as a whole, only one seventh of the stock were flats (chapter 6). These features clearly add to the difficulties of combining small dwellings and of converting them to larger dwellings. It is probably not practical to combine one room dwellings to form larger dwellings, but it should be possible to combine some pairs of two and three room dwellings to form dwellings of four and five rooms.

Substantial increases in the volume of housing work and large scale demolition could be avoided if the period for reaching space standards comparable to the rest of Great Britain were taken as twenty years. Over 200,000 of the required number of four and five room dwellings could probably be provided by combining and converting two and three room dwellings.[1]

If this policy were followed, about half of the three room and a third of the one and two room dwellings would need to be converted—only about a seventh of this group are one room dwellings. These proportions should not be so great as to create difficulties in finding suitable dwellings for conversion. During the period up to 1984 new construction could be concentrated on dwellings of four rooms and above (table 11.10). The smallest dwellings also tend to be the oldest and poorest, and the demolitions during the period 1984–2004 could continue to concentrate heavily on dwellings with three rooms or less. Since, however, the need and supply of dwellings by size would be in balance by 1984, demolitions subsequent to 1984 would need to be replaced. While the number of small dwellings constructed in this period would exceed those of four rooms and above (table 11.10), few additional small dwellings would be created as a result.

The surplus of small dwellings would be less the greater the population, whether this arose from higher birth rates or a smaller rate of migration from the region. The effect of such changes would be less during the first twenty years when the surplus of small dwellings arose. Where the surplus was smaller fewer dwellings would need conversion, which would result in a saving in costs. This problem of conversions would not arise in other regions, since there would be no surplus of dwellings of any size.

It is difficult to compare the sizes of dwellings required under the various programmes examined with the sizes actually being erected, because the information is available in terms of the number of bedrooms only for England and Wales. In 1964 about 12 per cent of dwellings had one bedroom, 31 per cent

[1] As it was difficult to select intermediate levels for achieving this standard, it was assumed that conversions took place at a steady rate over the twenty years. The net result of the conversion policy for Scotland was to alter slightly the total number of dwellings to be built for the increases in population on a given birth rate assumption according to the demolition assumption selected.

two bedrooms, 54 per cent three bedrooms, and 3 per cent four or more bedrooms (42). Equating these figures, as far as is possible, with the percentages given on a different basis (table 11.7), would suggest that the percentage of small dwellings being constructed is perhaps rather high. On the other hand, about five times the proportion of dwellings now being built with four bedrooms would appear to be required over the next two decades.

Regional figures for the size of dwellings being built at present are not available except for Scotland, and there, only for public authority dwellings, although these account for over three-quarters of constructions. In 1964, nearly a quarter of the dwellings completed were of two rooms or less, half had three rooms and most of the balance four rooms (42). By 2004, there is likely to be little difference between the size of dwellings required for Scotland and for Great Britain as a whole (table 11.8). As the problem for Scotland is one of an excess of small dwellings and a shortage of large dwellings, it appears mistaken to build a large proportion of small dwellings, since this only increases the lack of balance between the size of dwellings and the size of households.

HIGHER SPACE STANDARDS

It could be argued that the space standard provided is too low. In terms of rooms, the standard adopted is the standard now enjoyed by the majority of the population who live in unshared dwellings and who are neither overcrowded nor have a genuine excess of space. This standard provides on average about 4·5 habitable rooms per household (table 11.11). It is of interest to consider how dwelling sizes would be changed if more space were provided and to what extent it is practicable to provide extra space. If it is assumed that the standard is to be raised to 5.5 habitable rooms per household by giving each household one extra room, the following increases would be needed (table 11.11).

Table 11.11. *The size of dwellings: the effect of one extra room*

Persons per household	Rooms per household as fitted	One extra room	Percentage increases
1	3·4	4·4	*30*
2	4·2	5·2	*24*
3	4·6	5·6	*22*
4	4·9	5·9	*21*
5	5·2	6·2	*19*
6	5·4	6·4	*18*
7+	6·6	7·6	*15*
All households	4·5	5·5	*22*

SOURCE: NIESR estimates.

The size distribution of the present stock limits the extent to which extra space can be provided unless the number of demolitions is increased; with a higher rate of demolition more space could be provided. The limitation on the provision of extra space without increasing further the rate of demolitions varies with region. In most regions virtually all the households could be provided with extra space on the scale specified. However, it would not be possible to provide with more space anywhere near all the households in the four northern regions, or in the South East, if demolitions were at the rate of the first programme. If demolitions were at the rate of the second programme, provision would fall seriously short only for Scotland. Inevitably, the larger the area for which the housing problem is considered, the better the apparent results. In terms of the first programme of demolitions, 94 per cent of households could apparently be provided with extra space by 2004. This figure drops to 85 per cent if the programme is worked out separately for each region. The percentage would be even less if it was worked out in terms of smaller areas.

In every region the exact timing of the provision of the extra room for each household depends on the age of the stock, the rate of growth and the extent of present sharing. Broadly speaking, a start must be made now if most households are to get one extra room by the end of forty years. Over Britain as a whole just under half the households can be given the extra space in the first period, when most of the household fission is occurring, after which only a few per cent can be added in each period.

HOUSING PROGRAMMES AND THE AGE OF THE STOCK

The average age of the stock of dwellings at March 1964 was fifty-six, the average year of construction being 1908. The age falls as more dwellings are added to the stock to provide additional accommodation and replacements; the larger the programme of demolition and the higher the assumed birth rate, the more rapidly the average age of the stock falls. By the end of the period, 2004, the stock of dwellings, on the birth rate assumed by the Registrars General, will have average construction dates of 1958, 1969 and 1979 under the three demolition programmes (table 11.12). While the difference between the demolition programmes is equivalent to a reduction in the average age of twenty years, the effect of the changes in the assumptions about the birth rate alters the average by only two and four years.

The average age in 2004, on the assumption of demolition programme A, varies between forty-three and forty-seven years, having improved over the forty-year period from an average of fifty-six years. On the assumptions of demolition programme B, the average age range is reduced to thirty-three to thirty-six years; and on demolition programme C, to twenty-four to twenty-six years. The proportion of dwellings over sixty-four years old is reduced to about 32 per cent, 21 per cent and 3 per cent respectively (table 11.13).

Table 11.12. *Average year of construction of dwellings in Great Britain*

	1964	1969	1974	1979	1984	1989	1994	1999	2004
Demolition programme A									
Low birth rate	1908	1915	1919	1923	1928	1934	1941	1948	1957
RG's birth rate	1908	1915	1919	1923	1928	1934	1941	1949	1958
High birth rate	1908	1915	1919	1924	1929	1935	1943	1951	1961
Demolition programme B									
Low birth rate	1908	1915	1920	1926	1934	1942	1951	1959	1968
RG's birth rate	1908	1915	1921	1927	1934	1942	1952	1960	1969
High birth rate	1908	1915	1921	1927	1935	1943	1953	1961	1971
Demolition programme C									
Low birth rate	1908	1915	1923	1931	1942	1952	1961	1969	1978
RG's birth rate	1908	1915	1923	1931	1942	1952	1961	1970	1979
High birth rate	1908	1915	1923	1932	1942	1953	1962	1971	1980

SOURCE: NIESR estimates.

Table 11.13. *Age structure of stock of dwellings in Great Britain, 2004*

Percentages

	Date of construction					
	Pre–1881	1881–1920	1921–40	1941–64 [a]	1964–84	1984–2004
Demolition programme A						
Low birth rate	—	13	20	21	21	25
RG's birth rate	—	12	20	20	21	27
High birth rate	—	11	18	18	21	32
Demolition programme B						
Low birth rate	—	1	20	21	24	34
RG's birth rate	—	1	20	20	24	35
High birth rate	—	1	18	18	24	39
Demolition programme C						
Low birth rate	—	1	2	21	29	47
RG's birth rate	—	1	2	20	29	48
High birth rate	—	1	2	18	28	51

SOURCE: NIESR estimates.

[a] For practical purposes 1946–64.

There would be some falling off in the programme of constructions after 2004, unless the rates of renewing the stock were changed by that date, although the higher the birth rate assumptions the less the number of constructions would fall. The smaller the demolition programme adopted over the period 1964–2004, the greater the likelihood that the average age would be further reduced after

Average year of construction of stock by region, 2004

Demolition programme	Birth rate assumption	Migration pattern	Scotland	North	North West	Pennines	Central	East	North & Central Wales	West	South West	Midlands	East Anglia	South East
A	Low	1	1962	1954	1955	1956	1961	1959	1962	1960	1962	1959	1964	1955
		2	1962	1954	1955	1956	1960	1962	1972	1964	1964	1959	1969	1955
		3	1967	1960	1958	1958	1958	1959	1961	1958	1956	1958	1959	1953
	RG's	1	1962	1956	1957	1958	1963	1961	1963	1962	1963	1961	1964	1957
		2	1962	1956	1957	1958	1960	1962	1973	1964	1965	1960	1969	1955
		3	1967	1960	1958	1959	1960	1958	1962	1959	1957	1959	1961	1955
	High	1	1964	1959	1959	1959	1965	1963	1965	1964	1964	1963	1967	1961
		2	1964	1959	1959	1959	1963	1967	1974	1964	1968	1963	1971	1959
		3	1969	1964	1961	1961	1962	1963	1964	1964	1960	1963	1964	1958
B	Low	1	1971	1966	1968	1967	1969	1968	1968	1970	1971	1968	1968	1967
		2	1971	1966	1968	1967	1968	1971	1975	1971	1974	1967	1973	1966
		3	1974	1971	1970	1968	1967	1968	1968	1970	1968	1966	1965	1965
	RG's	1	1971	1968	1969	1968	1970	1969	1968	1972	1971	1967	1969	1968
		2	1971	1968	1969	1968	1969	1971	1976	1974	1974	1967	1974	1966
		3	1975	1971	1970	1969	1969	1969	1968	1970	1969	1967	1967	1966
	High	1	1974	1971	1971	1970	1971	1972	1972	1974	1974	1970	1972	1971
		2	1974	1971	1971	1970	1969	1973	1977	1974	1975	1969	1975	1968
		3	1977	1972	1973	1971	1969	1971	1970	1973	1970	1968	1968	1967
C	Low	1	1979	1977	1978	1978	1978	1977	1978	1978	1978	1972	1978	1978
		2	1979	1977	1978	1978	1977	1978	1981	1978	1979	1972	1980	1978
		3	1981	1979	1979	1980	1978	1977	1974	1978	1975	1972	1974	1977
	RG's	1	1979	1977	1978	1979	1979	1978	1978	1978	1978	1972	1977	1978
		2	1979	1977	1978	1979	1978	1978	1982	1979	1979	1972	1981	1978
		3	1981	1979	1980	1980	1978	1977	1977	1977	1977	1972	1974	1977
	High	1	1981	1979	1981	1981	1980	1980	1978	1979	1979	1974	1979	1979
		2	1981	1979	1981	1981	1978	1980	1982	1981	1980	1973	1982	1979
		3	1982	1981	1983	1981	1978	1980	1977	1978	1977	1973	1977	1978

SOURCE: NIESR estimates.

2004 and the less important the likely change in the construction programme after that date. Clearly, in practice, the programmes would be under constant adjustment in relation to other construction requirements, to the labour force and to the general economic situation.

The average age of the stock in 2004 varies between regions and within regions in relation to the migration patterns, as well as with the birth rate assumptions, with the demolition patterns, and with the age structure in 1964 (table 11.14). Since each of the alternatives studied is affected by the additions of dwellings to meet increasing needs and to replace dwellings demolished, the average age of the stock falls in all cases and the differences in average age narrow. In 1964, the regions with the greatest and least average age were North and Central Wales and the South East; by 2004, the region with the newest stock of dwellings would be Scotland, North and Central Wales, the South West, the West or East Anglia, whereas that with the oldest stock would be the Midlands, the South East or the North according to the various assumptions. Scotland would have the newest age structure of any region because of the large programme of construction that would be necessary if the size of the dwellings in relation to the size of the households were to be increased to the size elsewhere in Britain. The larger the demolition programme, the greater the reduction in age and the greater the uniformity in age structure:[1] increases in population have a similar effect on age structure.

[1] This is because the assumption has been made that the rates of demolition will increase at a compound rate. It is the rates of demolition rather than increases to the stock of dwellings that mainly affect the average age of the stock. The average age falls only slowly, particularly when the volume of demolition is low. Substantial reductions in average age do not occur until towards the end of the period of forty years.

CHAPTER 12

HOUSING COSTS

COSTS OF NEW CONSTRUCTION

The costs[1] of constructing housing set out in the programmes considered in chapter 10 are of four types. The largest element of cost relates to dwellings themselves and accounts for about 77 per cent, while about 12 per cent consists of the costs of site development, roads, sewers and public utility services (table 12.1). Demolition and large scale site clearance of existing developed areas account for about 3 per cent and the remaining 8 per cent is the cost of garages (table 12.1). The costs of demolishing existing dwellings and of clearing their sites vary with the demolition programme but are not affected by predicted population. Site development is more costly on a redeveloped site than on virgin land; under-building is also more expensive. An allowance for these costs has been made in respect of the acreage of land made available for redevelopment as a result of demolition.

Table 12.1. *Cost components for new housing, Great Britain, 1964–2004*

£ millions, 1964 prices

Type of cost	Low birth rate, demolition programme A	Registrars General's birth rate, demolition programme A	B	C	High birth rate, demolition programme A
Dwellings	28765	31074	38855	50429	37696
Site development, roads, sewers, public utilities; Demolition, clearance, additional redevelopment costs for cleared land	5299	5665	7822	11707	6671
Garages	2800	2988	3697	4741	3567
Total costs	36864	39727	50374	66877	47934

SOURCE: NIESR estimates.

The total construction costs as defined above for new housing for Great Britain over the period 1964–2004 have been estimated to range between about £37,000 million and £75,000 million (table 12.2). Sufficient dwellings to meet the needs of the population predicted on the basis of the birth rate assumptions of the Registrars General, and to allow for an increase in household formation and improved space standards, about 7 million dwellings in all, would probably

[1] All costs in this chapter are calculated on the various assumptions set out in chapters 7 and 8, and are at 1964 prices.

cost approximately £24,000 million, while the costs of replacing all but the best of the pre-1881 dwellings and for clearing and redeveloping their sites would be approximately £16,000 million, making a total of about £40,000 million for this combined programme (table 12.2). About 700,000 dwellings fewer would be needed for the low birth rate assumptions, and about 2·2 million more if the high birth rate assumptions proved correct. The total costs of construction would be reduced by about £2,900 million or increased by £8,200 million.

Table 12.2. *Total construction costs of new dwellings in Great Britain, 1964–2004*

£ millions, 1964 prices

Demolition programme	Birth rate assumption		
	Low	RG's	High
A	36864	39727	47934
B	47512	50374	58580
C	64014	66877	75084

SOURCE: NIESR estimates.

The national effect of different migration patterns is small because population in a region rarely falls; there is no surplus of dwellings, except in Scotland. The difference in the national costs of alternative migration patterns, therefore, mainly reflects differences in regional prices and these in themselves are not large. The total differences are generally about a tenth of one per cent. The number of dwellings to be constructed and the costs would be much more affected by the acceptance of higher rates of demolition than by changes in birth rates or in migration patterns. If replacement were extended to include all but the best 1881–1921 dwellings, construction costs would be increased by about £10,600 million, an increase of about 27 per cent over the cost for pre-1881 replacements, assuming a 2004 population of 72 million. In addition, the replacement of all but the best of 1921–41 dwellings would add about £27,200 million to the costs, about 68 per cent more (fig. 12.1).

The costs of housing development depend on the size of the dwellings as well as on their numbers, so that changes in costs are not quite proportional to changes in the number of dwellings required. The demolition and clearance costs, and the costs of redeveloping cleared sites, depend partly on the number of dwellings cleared and partly on the area of land involved. The densities at which the 1881–1921 dwellings were developed were lower than the densities of the pre-1881 dwellings, and the densities of the 1921–41 dwellings were substantially lower than the 1881–1921 densities. Hence the demolition and clearance costs associated with dwellings to be replaced are lower for the more recently built dwellings. In contrast the development costs are higher, since more development takes

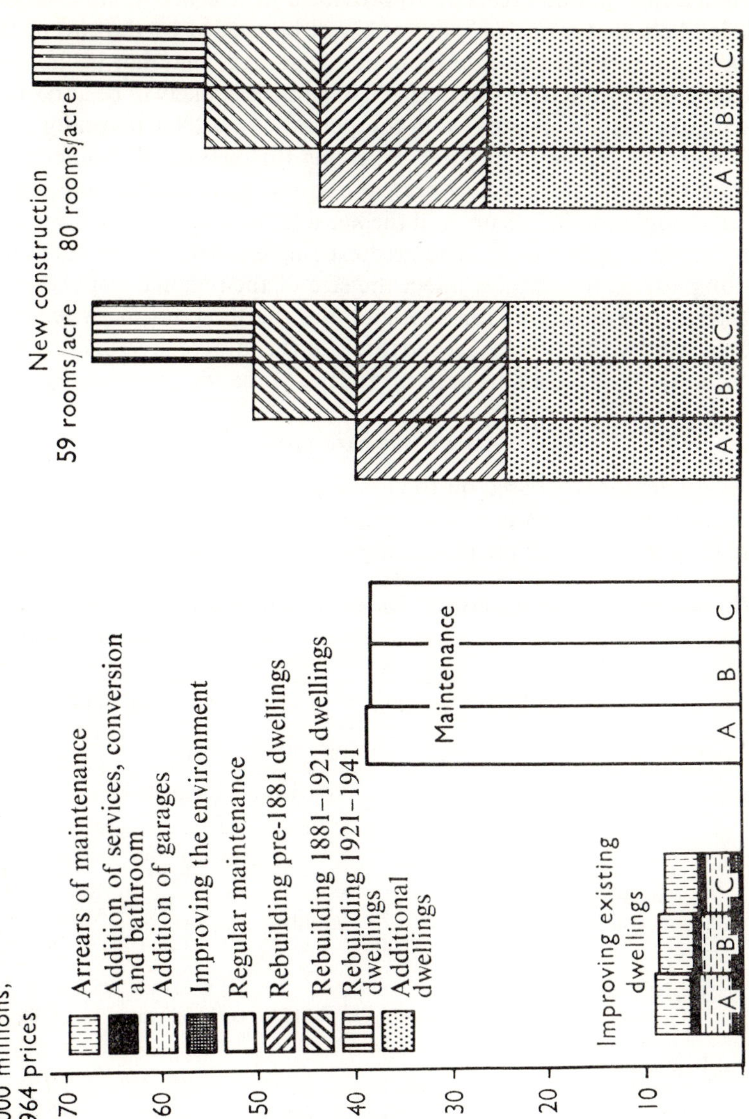

SOURCE: NIESR estimates.

Notes: Based on the Registrar General's birth rate assumptions; A, B, C indicate demolition programmes.

Fig. 12.1. Total cost of housing

place on previously developed land. Nevertheless, the errors from estimating the costs for other rates of demolition by proportional adjustment will not be too great. While it may not be necessary to provide a garage with every dwelling at present, it is likely that a one-for-one ratio will be needed by the end of the period, in 2004. Thus, while the rate of building garages may lag behind the building of dwellings, in the long run the total of garages is likely to be as costed.

The construction costs estimated over the period 1964–2004 naturally vary considerably from one region to another, reflecting the considerable differences in the sizes of the regions, the effect of present age and sex structure and migration on the way population builds up, and the age and condition of the dwellings in the existing stock (appendix 10). The greatest single differences are between those migration patterns which most affect the size of the regional populations: migration patterns two and three for Scotland and the three northern regions, pattern two compared with patterns one and three for the rural regions of the South and Midlands; and, of course, all the patterns for the Midlands and South East.

URBAN FORM AND CONSTRUCTION COSTS

The costs of construction are based on the assumption that the dwellings would be developed in the urban form of today, with about three-quarters of the total as houses and only 8 per cent of the flats in high blocks. Flatted blocks are more

Table 12.3. *Housing form and construction costs, Great Britain, 1964–2004*

£ millions, 1964 prices

		Housing form [a]				
		90:10:0	74:18:8	50:40:10	50:20:30	40:10:50
Demolition programme	Birth rate assumption	Net housing density (rooms per acre)				
		39	59	69	80	95
A	Low	36294	36864	37568	40306	43029
	Registrars General's	39111	39727	40485	43444	46389
	High	47187	47934	48856	52444	56017
B	Registrars General's	49604	50374	51326	55025	58705
C	Registrars General's	65878	66877	68116	72918	77692
	High	73954	75084	76485	81921	87323
Percentage costs		*98*	*100*	*102*	*109*	*116*

SOURCE: NIESR estimates.

[a] Percentages of houses and bungalows: low flats: high flats.

expensive than houses and bungalows; their costs rise with the number of storeys in a block and it is this rather than the resulting density which mainly determines costs. Savings of about £600 million, about 2 per cent, might be made if in future housing were based on 90 per cent houses and 10 per cent flats in low blocks (table 12.3). The costs might be increased by 9 per cent if the percentage of houses was reduced to 50 per cent and 30 per cent of the flats were in high blocks. If the resources and finance for new housing development were limited, the number of units of new housing which could be made available would be substantially greater if the less expensive housing forms were used. The land implications will be considered later.

QUINQUENNIAL COSTS OF NEW CONSTRUCTION

Because of the current shortage of dwellings to meet the requirements arising from existing and potential household formation, more dwellings are required during the first quinquennium than during subsequent quinquennia (chapter 10). The costs of new construction naturally follow this pattern (table 12.4).

Table 12.4. *Total costs*[a] *of new construction, 1964–2004*

£ millions, 1964 prices

	1964–9 [b]	1969–74	1974–9	1979–84	1984–9	1989–94	1994–9	1999–2004	1964–2004
Demolition programme A									
Low birth rate	6596	3253	3295	3763	4305	4541	5187	5924	36864
RG's birth rate	6595	3322	3438	3938	4613	5089	5715	7017	39727
High birth rate	6763	3662	3869	4648	5185	6325	7827	9655	47934
Demolition programme B									
Low birth rate	6577	4078	4221	4902	5660	6221	7260	8593	47512
RG's birth rate	6576	4147	4365	5077	5968	6768	7787	9686	50374
High birth rate	6744	4486	4796	5785	6541	8005	9899	12324	58580
Demolition programme C									
Low birth rate	6559	5299	5607	6594	7721	8841	10546	12847	64014
RG's birth rate	6559	5369	5750	6769	8027	9388	11074	13941	66877
High birth rate	6727	5709	6180	7477	8601	10626	13185	16579	75084

SOURCE: NIESR estimates.

[a] Costs of erection of dwelling, garage and total estate development.

[b] The slight differences in the total costs during the first quinquennium between the different demolition programmes is due to the adjustments made to the programme for Scotland (see p. 191 n.).

A smoother pattern of construction costs would be obtained either if the potential need for dwellings was made good over a longer period of time or if the rate of replacing existing dwellings was increased. Changes could also be effected if dwellings were initially constructed without garages and if standards were to increase over time. Clearly such possibilities cannot be usefully considered until the potential output of the construction industry has been examined (chapters 14 and 16).

COSTS OF ARREARS OF MAINTENANCE AND UPGRADING

It was argued earlier that, although so much of the existing stock of housing falls short of acceptable standards, much of it is likely to remain in use for most of the century, so that the improvement of the existing stock is in itself an important social objective. Subsequent analysis indicated that adequate improvement was economically worthwhile for a large proportion of the existing stock which is currently below acceptable standards, even though much of it is expected to be replaced during the next forty years. The policy implications are that the relevant question to ask about a dwelling in relation to its environment ought to be, 'Is it economically worthwhile to improve it?' and not, 'Should it be condemned?'

The costs of making good the arrears of maintenance and of upgrading the dwellings are not greatly affected by the differences in the three assumed rates of demolition since these do not have a great effect on the number of dwellings likely to have moderate expectations of life. It is worthwhile to make good arrears and to provide services as long as the expectation of life is five to ten years. If a dwelling has an expected life of ten to fifteen years it is worthwhile to undertake the structural work necessary to provide a bathroom and to improve the environment. Where dwellings have an expected life of twenty years it is worthwhile to provide garages. The difference in costs of maintenance and upgrading between demolition assumptions A and B is only about 5 per cent; the difference in costs between assumptions B and C is a little more (table 12.5). Conversions are only anticipated on a large scale in Scotland, where nearly a

Table 12.5. *Costs of upgrading housing areas in Great Britain, 1964*

£ millions, 1964 prices

	Demolition programme		
	A	B	C
Arrears of maintenance, renewal and decoration	3880	3677	3447
Addition of services and bathrooms	911	894	877
Addition of garages	3366	3144	2820
Improvement of the environment	763	750	732
Total	8920	8465	7876
Cost of conversions	72	69	64

SOURCE: NIESR estimates.

third of the dwellings are too small to meet Britain's space standards. The estimated costs of making good the arrears of maintenance and upgrading the dwellings appear to be in line with the results from official surveys in which such costs have been estimated.

The major elements of cost arise in respect of the arrears of maintenance and the addition of garages. The former accounts for over two-fifths of the costs and the latter just under two-fifths. The addition of services and bathrooms accounts for just over one-tenth of the total cost, while improvement of the environment accounts for a little less than one-tenth. About two-fifths of the costs of making good arrears arises from the pre-1881 dwellings, which are generally in the poorest condition and are the most expensive to bring to a reasonable standard. The proportion of cost arising for the 1881–1921 dwellings is about a quarter. About half the cost of services arises from the structural work necessary to form bathrooms (table 12.6). About a quarter of the cost of this group is for the provision of baths and showers, about an eighth for the provision of water closets and most of the balance is for hot water systems. Again the major part of the cost of improving the environment arises from the older and poorer dwellings.

Table 12.6. *Costs of providing missing services, 1964*

£ millions, 1964 prices

	Demolition programme		
	A	B	C
Cold water	—	—	—
Hot water	106	107	104
First W.C.	23	23	24
Internal W.C.	94	95	95
Shower	38	64	103
Fixed bath	155	142	126
Replacement of bath not in a bathroom	38	38	38
Structure of bathroom	457	425	387
Total	911	894	877

SOURCE: NIESR estimates.

The regional differences in the upgrading costs reflect mainly the relative sizes of the regions (appendix table A10.3). The internal relationships within each region between the demolition programmes and the various types of costs reflect the regional differences in age, condition and facility patterns. Generally, the younger and the better the quality of the regional stock of housing, the smaller the size of the demolition programme and the greater the reduction in the costs of upgrading if the more stringent demolition programmes are assumed. Thus the upgrading costs associated with the three demolition programmes are closest for North and Central Wales, with the oldest and poorest stock, and furthest apart for the South East, with the youngest and highest quality housing.

The upgrading costs represent about 10 per cent of the total costs of the housing programmes (fig. 12.1). The proportion is clearly too large to be carried out within a period of five years and would need to be spread over several quinquennia. In practice this is likely to happen. The most urgent part of the programme is that for dealing with the arrears of maintenance of the structurally unsound dwellings, and with the installation of the missing services and the addition of bathrooms. Generally the unsound dwellings would also be dwellings with most missing services. This part of the programme would cost just over 25 per cent of the entire programme of upgrading, that is about £2,500 million, and could probably be completed in the next five to ten years. If dealing with the arrears of maintenance of the unsound dwellings is delayed too long many of these dwellings are likely to be in such a poor state that improvement would no longer be economic; as a result replacement would be necessary, which would reduce the costs of attending to the arrears of maintenance but add a greater figure to the costs of new construction. The arrears of maintenance for dwellings in a better condition could be spread over a somewhat longer period, as could work for improving the environment. The addition of garages is in any case a long-term programme: they are only expected to be required gradually over the forty-year period as the ownership of cars spreads.

Since no allowance is made for providing garages for dwellings with a life of less than twenty years, the cost of garages arises mainly for the younger and better dwellings, which have a reasonable expectation of life (table 12.7). The

Table 12.7. *Costs of providing garages, 1964*

	Demolition programme A		Demolition programme B		Demolition programme C	
	£ millions, 1964 prices	*%*	*£ millions, 1964 prices*	*%*	*£ millions, 1964 prices*	*%*
For dwellings with a life of						
20–25 years	155	*4*	257	*8*	400	*14*
25–30 years	190	*6*	315	*10*	460	*16*
30–35 years	226	*7*	363	*11*	461	*16*
35–40 years	289	*9*	458	*15*	537	*19*
40 or more	2505	*74*	1751	*56*	962	*35*
Total	3365	*100*	3144	*100*	2820	*100*

SOURCE: NIESR estimates.

greater the delay in providing garages the fewer will ultimately be worth providing with the dwellings now in the stock, since advancing age will reduce the number of dwellings with an expectation of life long enough to justify the provision of a garage. While the provision of a garage is more likely to be made in relation to a dwelling with a long life than one with a short life, the incidence of car ownership is not likely to be closely related to the expectation of the life of the dwelling occupied by the car owner.

COSTS OF REGULAR MAINTENANCE

If standards are to be kept up, full maintenance must be provided for all dwellings. Maintenance costs are related to age, and hence they would be lower, other things being equal, with a greater rate of demolition. They would also fall, in terms of costs per dwelling, the faster population rose, since the proportion of newer dwellings would be increased. In this case, however, the overall costs would rise, since the stock of dwellings would be increased. In fact, neither the rate at which population increases, nor the rate of demolition, has much effect until the later years of the period under consideration. Hence there are only small differences between the total maintenance costs over the period (table 12.8): the difference over the range of birth and demolition rates is about

Table 12.8. *Costs of regular maintenance in Great Britain, 1964–2004*

£ millions, 1964 prices

Demolition programme	Birth rate assumption		
	Low	RG's	High
A	38303	38388	39356
B	37972	38107	38866
C	37699	38022	38775

SOURCE: NIESR estimates.

Note: Regional costs of maintenance are given in appendix 10.

4 per cent. The maintenance costs for the present stock are about twice as high as the value of maintenance work currently carried out for housing by the construction industry. This is mainly a reflection of the extent to which dwellings are currently under-maintained (see also chapter 16), and hence the large cost of the arrears of maintenance: eight to nine times current annual expenditure on housing maintenance. It is also partly a reflection of the extent to which householders do their own maintenance work, particularly decorating, although only about a quarter of such work is likely to be carried out by householders (chapter 8).

OVERALL COSTS OF HOUSING

Since neither the costs of upgrading and improvement, nor those of regular maintenance, vary as much as the costs of new construction, total housing costs also vary less than those of new construction. Total housing costs lie between £84 and £122 thousand million (table 12.9). The alternative scales of demolition have a greater effect on total costs than the alternative population projections.

Table 12.9. *Total housing costs, 1964–2004*

£ millions, 1964 prices

Demolition programme	Birth rate assumption		
	Low	RG's	High
A	84159	87107	96283
B	94018	97016	105981
C	109654	112839	121801

SOURCE: NIESR estimates.

Demolition programme B adds £10 thousand million, about 11 per cent, while demolition programme C adds a further £16 thousand million, about 18 per cent. In contrast, the low birth rate assumptions only reduce costs by £3 thousand million, about 3 per cent, as compared with the birth rate assumptions of the Registrars General, while the high birth rate assumptions raise costs by £9 thousand million, about 10 to 11 per cent.

Whereas for the smallest housing programme the costs of new construction are about equal to the maintenance costs, so that the value of upgrading and maintenance work exceeds the costs of new work, the costs of new work are nearly twice those of maintenance work for the largest housing programme (table 12.10). Generally, on the basis of the birth rate assumptions of the Registrars General, the cost of new work varies only slightly from the costs of upgrading and maintenance (fig. 12.1): only if the highest demolition programme is followed is the cost of new work substantially greater than the costs of upgrading and maintenance work. These relationships between new work and what is broadly maintenance work are, of course, rather different from the present position. Currently, for housing, new work is about twice as great by value as the maintenance work carried out by the construction industry. The addition of the value of maintenance work carried out by the householder is unlikely to change this ratio substantially. The cost of conversion work is negligible and has been added to the cost of upgrading.

The effect on the total costs of other levels of housing requirements, arising, for example, from greater or less household formation, from higher or lower

Table 12.10. *The main elements within total housing costs over the period 1964–2004*

£ thousand millions, 1964 prices

	New construction						Maintenance and adaption			
	Dwellings	Estate development	Demolition and clearance	Sub-total, dwellings only	Garages	Total	Up-grading	Regular maintenance	Total	Total housing costs
Demolition programme A										
Low birth rate	29	4	1	*34*	3	37	9	38	47	84
RG's birth rate	31	5	1	*37*	3	40	9	38	47	87
High birth rate	38	5	1	*44*	4	48	9	39	48	96
Demolition programme B										
Low birth rate	36	5	2	*43*	4	47	9	38	47	94
RG's birth rate	39	5	2	*46*	4	50	9	38	47	97
High birth rate	45	7	2	*54*	4	58	9	39	48	106
Demolition programme C										
Low birth rate	48	7	4	*59*	5	64	8	38	46	110
RG's birth rate	50	8	4	*62*	5	67	8	38	46	113
High birth rate	57	9	4	*70*	5	75	8	39	47	122

SOURCE: NIESR estimates.

space standards, or from additional requirements for a second house, can readily be calculated approximately by combining the estimates of the effect on the stock required (chapter 11) with the figures given in this chapter and in chapter 10.

Clearly the phasing of the housing work is of importance. There is, however, little value in considering the phasing of the programme in isolation from the expected growth in output of housing work. They will be considered jointly in a later chapter (chapter 16).

STANDARDS AND COSTS

Housing standards and housing costs are closely related. The costs given in this study have been based on current best standards, in the case of new housing interpreted as Parker Morris recommendations for low cost housing (38), with an addition to allow for the current proportions of housing at a standard better than low cost. The interpretation in the case of existing housing is that dwellings should be in a good state of repair and decoration, and should be provided with all the recognized basic services; that the housing environment should be orderly, adequately maintained and attractive; and that garages should be available. Even so, many dwellings, because of their form and layout, will inevitably be below Parker Morris recommendations in many respects. This is likely to be true particularly of the older dwellings. Three rates of demolition and replacement have therefore been specified. As a result some dwellings appear to have an expectation of life too short to justify, economically, the expenditure necessary to ensure a good standard of repair, full services and improvements to the environment. The proportion of dwellings fully maintained at the Parker Morris level and the proportion with nearly equivalent services will increase rapidly as the period studied progresses. A quarter of the total dwellings would at least satisfy Parker Morris recommendations by 1984 on the assumptions of the Registrars General for birth rates and demolition programme A; the corresponding date would be 1979 on demolition programme C (table 12.11) By the end of the period about half of the total dwellings would satisfy this standard with demolition programme A and about three-quarters with demolition programme C. The rate of demolition would not greatly affect the date by which all dwellings will be in an adequate state of repair, and have full services and an adequate housing environment.

Two broad questions can be raised about the standards assumed: first about their current level, and secondly about future levels. The higher the current standard is set for new dwellings, the more expenditure can be justified on the dwellings in the existing stock. This higher expenditure could be used either to raise the standard for improvement, or to increase the number of dwellings to be improved to the standards already set. In either case the total costs of housing would be increased. Similarly, lower standards for new dwellings would reduce the amount worth spending on existing dwellings. Changes in the rate of demolition and replacement will have less effect on the cost of upgrading than on the cost of replacement. Since existing dwellings cannot normally provide the same standards as new dwellings, such standards can only be spread widely if a high rate of replacement is accepted.

Table 12.11. *Housing standards in Great Britain: proportion at Parker Morris standard*

Percentages

	Demolition programme		
	A	B	C
1969	11·4	11·4	11·4
1974	15·9	17·0	18·7
1979	20·5	22·7	26·2
1984	25·2	29·0	34·6
1989	30·6	34·0	44·0
1994	36·1	43·4	54·0
1999	42·0	51·3	65·2
2004	48·7	60·6	78·1

SOURCE: NIESR estimates.

Note: Registrars General's birth rate assumptions.

In practice the acceptable level of standards is likely to rise over time. For every rise in the standards of new housing, and hence in costs, there will be an increase in the level of expenditure justified for improving existing housing. The costs of regular maintenance are likely to change broadly in proportion to the costs of new construction, partly because maintenance will become more expensive, and partly because the maintenance of existing housing will include work to raise standards in step with the higher standards of new housing. Estimates of the effect of increased standards on costs can, therefore, be based on the assumption that all costs of housing will be raised by a given percentage.

While it is likely that standards of housing will increase broadly in step with general standards of living, it is difficult to predict whether the rate of increase will be above or below average. Past experience is little guide because the propensity to consume housing could change in the future; this will be discussed more fully in chapter 15. It is equally difficult to predict at what rate the standards of living are likely to rise. The effect of a rise in housing standards depends on the way in which the necessary housing work is phased over the forty-year period. The amount of work to be done in the final quinquennium would be increased by nearly 50 per cent if standards rose by 1 per cent a year; a 2 per cent rate of increase would more than double the amount of work in the final quinquennium; while a 3 per cent rate would more than treble it. The effect on the total programme would depend on the way the total work was phased. If the programme of development tended to increase steadily over the period, the total amount of work would be increased at about half the rate of increase in the final period. The greater the rate of increase in the programme of development, the greater would be the average effect of rises in standards. While higher rates of birth and demolition would not have a large effect on the rate of increase, they would raise the overall rate of increase in work load, since their effect is felt mainly in the later quinquennia.

CHAPTER 13

LAND REQUIREMENTS AND AVAILABILITY

LAND REQUIREMENTS FOR NEW HOUSING

If the development of housing were to continue at the present densities, and with the present proportional distribution of types of dwellings,[1] about half a million acres of land would be required to provide dwellings for the additional households resulting from household fission and population growth (table 13.1). This figure is based on the assumptions about birth rates accepted by the Registrars General; if the higher birth rate assumptions were fulfilled, an additional 200,000 acres would be required; if birth rates fell in accordance with the lower assumption, the land requirement would be about 70,000 acres less.

LAND REQUIREMENTS AND REDEVELOPMENT

In fact the needs for land are likely to be rather more complicated. The total programmes for housing include the replacement of housing which is obsolete or not worth repairing. While the replacement of dwellings creates a demand for additional land, their demolition naturally releases land suitable for development. The densities at which the dwellings to be replaced were originally developed vary from those currently used for new development. Whereas current densities average about 17·4 dwellings per acre, the average prior to 1881 was probably about 28 dwellings per acre. Hence the land cleared is likely to be sufficient to replace only about two-thirds of the dwellings, and the balance adds to the total of land required (table 13.1).

Later, housing was developed at lower densities which probably averaged about 20 dwellings per acre during the period 1881–1921. Between 1921 and 1941 densities were about 13 dwellings per acre, and so redevelopment of these dwellings provides rather more land than is required to replace the dwellings at current densities. If the surplus is available at the right times and in the right places, it will reduce the total net need for housing land or for land for other urban purposes. The higher the densities of further development and the younger the dwellings included in the replacement programme, the lower the net land requirements. Of course, since the war, densities have risen again and

[1] 74 per cent of houses and bungalows at an average density of 13 dwellings, 46 bedrooms and reception rooms per acre; 18 per cent of dwellings in 3 and 4 storey flatted blocks at an average density of 80 bedrooms and reception rooms per acre; and 8 per cent of dwellings in high flatted blocks, averaging 13 storeys, at an average density of 138 bedrooms and reception rooms per acre. In estimating the areas of land required, an allowance has been made for the difference between the census definition of rooms and the definition used by planners (chapter 6). Since the number of rooms required has been estimated on the basis of the census definition, the densities quoted in this chapter have been multiplied by 1·13 to allow for the incidence of kitchens in which meals are taken. Densities will, however, be discussed on the basis of the better understood, planning definition of bedrooms and reception rooms.

the proportional saving from the use of such land for redevelopment is likely to show a decline over the use of land developed between the wars.

It is clear that the rate of redevelopment will not have much effect on land requirements. These depend largely on the rate at which the population increases and on the density of development; and the lower the rate the more generous it will be possible to be with land for urban development.

Table 13.1. *Land requirements for housing development, 1964–2004*

Thousand acres

	Birth rate assumption								
	Low			RG's			High		
Demolition programme	A	B	C	A	B	C	A	B	C
Gross land for replacement housing	300	500	800	300	500	800	300	500	800
Land available from demolitions	170	310	620	170	310	620	170	310	620
Land for housing needs of additional household formation [a]		400			470			650	
Net land required for all housing	530	590	580	600	660	650	780	840	830

SOURCE: NIESR estimates.

[a] These figures are approximate, slightly different results can be obtained according to how the average density is calculated.

NET LAND REQUIREMENTS OVER TIME

The pattern of land requirements over time depends on the pattern of household formation, the densities at which the additional dwellings are developed and the rates at which dwellings are to be replaced. Each of the programmes investigated would require nearly 100,000 acres of additional land for housing during the first quinquennium (table 13.2). The amount of additional land which would be required during the next quinquennium would drop sharply as the result of the fall in household formation; land requirements would then tend to rise in subsequent quinquennia, but this would depend on the balance between the effects of changes in the number of households and the land released by the replacement of obsolete housing. The increase in land made available by redevelopment offsets the need for land arising from household formation. The lower the age of the stock being replaced, the less land required. The area of land required actually falls in the later quinquennia for programmes in which a large number of 1921–41 dwellings is being replaced. This reduction is offset in the case of programmes based on the highest population increases. As explained earlier, the scale of constructing dwellings in the eight quinquennia may differ substantially from the figures given for the programmes under analysis (table 13.2).

Table 13.2. *Net land requirements in Great Britain, 1964–2004*

Thousand acres

	Birth rate assumption	Demolition programme A	B	C
1964–9	Low	96·8	96·4	96·1
	RG's	96·7	96·3	96·0
	High	99·6	99·2	98·9
1969–74	Low	53·2	61·0	73·0
	RG's	54·3	62·2	74·4
	High	61·7	69·6	81·6
1974–9	Low	51·8	60·8	74·5
	RG's	54·6	63·7	77·2
	High	64·9	74·2	87·6
1979–84	Low	56·0	67·1	83·9
	RG's	60·4	71·5	88·3
	High	77·0	88·3	104·9
1984–9	Low	62·4	75·4	87·5
	RG's	70·7	83·8	95·7
	High	84·8	97·6	109·9
1989–94	Low	62·1	76·5	78·7
	RG's	76·2	90·6	92·6
	High	103·7	118·2	120·1
1994–9	Low	70·0	74·3	52·8
	RG's	83·6	87·9	66·4
	High	130·1	134·6	112·9
1999–2004	Low	75·1	74·3	30·0
	RG's	99·9	99·2	55·0
	High	158·3	157·6	113·4
Total, 1964–2004	Low	527·4	585·8	576·5
	RG's	596·4	655·2	645·6
	High	780·1	839·3	829·3

SOURCE: NIESR estimates.

REGIONAL LAND REQUIREMENTS

Since the effect of the demolition programmes on land requirements is much less than the effects of the birth rate assumptions, it is convenient to summarize the regional land requirements according to population, birth rates and migration rates rather than by demolition programmes; full details are given in appendix 11. The comparison of land requirements between regions is not itself of much interest since this largely reflects the size of the regions as defined for the purposes of the study. The differences within each region according to the birth rate and migration assumptions are of more interest. For many regions these indicate differences of more than a factor of two.

LAND REQUIREMENTS AND DENSITY

The demand for additional land for housing can be reduced either by developing each type of housing at a greater density, or by using a greater proportion of flatted blocks, or by a combination of these methods. While the potential range of densities for each type of housing is large (chapter 7), it seems unlikely that the densities will rise much above current levels. It is already difficult to provide all the facilities and amenities required, and if the densities are raised further, standards will fall and it will become much more difficult to adapt the environment to meet future needs. A lack of adaptability is likely to lower future standards rather than lead to early obsolescence because, as this study shows, it is unlikely that sufficient resources will be available to allow postwar dwellings

Table 13.3. *The effect of density on net land requirements, 1964–2004*

Thousand acres

	Housing form [a]					
	90:10:0	80:15:5	74:18:8	50:40:10	50:20:30	40:10:50
	Average density of development (rooms per acre)					
	39	50	59	69	80	95
Demolition programme A						
Low birth rate	884·3	652·7	527·4	426·5	344·7	263·7
RG's birth rate	988·7	734·1	596·4	485·5	395·6	306·5
High birth rate	1266·6	950·9	780·1	642·6	531·1	420·6
Demolition programme B						
Low birth rate	1044·8	746·9	585·8	456·1	350·9	246·6
RG's birth rate	1149·8	828·8	655·2	515·4	402·0	289·7
High birth rate	1428·3	1046·0	839·3	672·9	537·8	404·1
Demolition programme C						
Low birth rate	1189·0	791·5	576·5	403·4	263·0	123·9
RG's birth rate	1293·5	873·0	645·6	462·5	314·0	166·8
High birth rate	1571·4	1089·8	829·3	619·6	449·4	280·9

SOURCE: NIESR estimates.

[a] Percentages of houses and bungalows: low flats: high flats.

to be rebuilt before the end of the century. If higher standards coupled with higher densities are required, it is more likely that they will be obtained by increasing the proportion of dwellings in flatted blocks. The costs of saving land in this way are extremely high in relation to the value of the land which is saved (chapters 7, 9 and 12).

The net amount of land required does not fall in inverse proportion to changes in density because the volume of land contributed by the clearance of existing housing is not affected by the density of new development. The net amount of land required for housing could be reduced by about a quarter if the percentage of rooms provided in houses and bungalows were reduced from the present figure to about 50 per cent, with 10 per cent in high flatted blocks; and about halved if the percentage of houses and bungalows were reduced to 40, with 50 per cent of the balance provided in high flatted blocks (table 13.3). At this latter density, if families with children were housed on the ground, most other people would have to be housed in flats above ground level. On the other hand, if 90 per cent of rooms were provided in houses and bungalows and the balance in low flatted blocks, the net area of land required would be increased by nearly 75 per cent. If this policy were followed, the total additional land required for all urban purposes would be increased by about 50 per cent.

THE AVAILABILITY OF LAND

It would appear that about 7 per cent of the land in Great Britain is used for broadly urban purposes (80), and, of this, about 40 per cent is used for residential purposes (52). Altogether there are about 56 million acres of land in Great Britain, so that on the basis of the above figures about 1·6 million acres are used for housing. The additional land required for housing has been predicted as between about 0·5 and 0·8 million acres, that is between a third and a half of the area already used for this purpose.

The land needed for housing in the period 1964–2004 represents about 1 per cent of the area of Great Britain. A further 1·5 to 2·0 per cent is likely to be needed for other urban purposes. It seems unlikely that much urban development will take place on land used for rough grazing, as ungrazed deer forests, or for afforestation or other non-agricultural purposes, since the greater part of such land is unsuitable for building. Most urban development is likely to take place on arable and permanent grassland, of which the total area is at present about 29 million acres. Between 1·7 and 2·8 per cent of this would be required for residential development, possibly 5 per cent for all urban purposes.

The long-run trend in agricultural output per acre has been strongly on the increase for three reasons: improved methods of husbandry, better use of the land available (a reduction of waste land and land improvements), and the use of a higher proportion of land for the most valuable types of production. Thus, although average yields rose only 1 or 2 per cent a year over the last decade, and the rise from 1965–75 is estimated at 1·28 per cent a year (81), the value of net output rose by 3¾ per cent compound on the basis of a slightly reduced acreage.

Even a 1·28 per cent annual improvement in yield per acre would be sufficient to make good, within the first two years, the farm produce lost through taking, from agriculture, the land required for housing over the period 1964–2004, and the loss from taking land for all urban purposes within four years. Over forty years the output of farm produce on the remaining land would be 43 per cent more than in 1964. At the current rate of consumption of home grown food this would be sufficient to provide for over 76 million people, which is a population substantially larger than that projected on the basis of assumptions accepted by the Registrars General. Food consumption tends to rise with increases in real incomes. One estimate (82) suggests a rise in food consumption at a rate, over the next decade, of nearly a third of the rise in real incomes, although such a rate of increase is unlikely to be sustained over a period as long as forty years. More home grown food might also be needed to save imports. Increases by value would be likely to be more important than increases by volume: over the last decade, increases by value have been three times as great as increases by volume. The impact of these factors on the need for home grown food over the next four decades is uncertain, but the loss of land likely to be sustained by agriculture from urban development probably will have no more than a marginal effect.

These estimates relate to the total area of arable and permanent grass. In the past some of the best agricultural land has been taken for development. Such land produces about three times as much per acre as average land (82) and yields appear to be rising faster on the better land. It is, therefore, of importance to steer development, as far as possible, away from the better land if substantial increases in home produced food are required. The poorer the land, the less the yield and the less important are losses to urban development—rough grazing land has yields of only a tenth of average land. However, the average value of arable and permanent grass farmland in 1964 was probably only about £200 an acre. This would have been equivalent to about £15 a dwelling at average densities; a sum which would normally be quite inadequate to meet the additional costs of under-building and drainage likely to be necessary on land which is not reasonably flat and well drained. Good farmland is usually also the best building land; resources might be better used in developing on good rather than poor farmland and by replacing the produce lost in some other way.

In fact, there appears to be a good spread of land of all qualities in most regions.[1] The amounts of land that would be required for housing and, as far as can be seen, for all development are small compared with the amounts of

[1] As there was no current information on the regional distribution of agricultural land according to quality, the percentage distribution of land according to quality derived from the land utilization survey carried out in the period 1938–42 (83) has been used to estimate current acreages.

suitable land which are probably available in the regions. In most regions the amount of poor quality permanent grass is greater than the amount of land likely to be required for housing over the next forty years. The major exception is the Midlands, which appears to have little poor quality or even medium quality permanent grass in relation to the area of land likely to be necessary. In practice, of course, the poorer land will not always be located where development is required and some use of better land is inevitable. The lower the ratio of poor quality land to land required for development, the more likely it is that good quality land will be used. From this point of view, development should be steered away from the Midlands and other regions where this is the case.

PART 4

RESOURCES AND FINANCE FOR HOUSING

CHAPTER 14

THE OUTPUT OF THE CONSTRUCTION INDUSTRY

OUTPUT OF BUILDING WORK AND THE SUPPLY OF HOUSING

Three economic tests can be applied to housing and other development policies: tests of the availability of resources, of the availability of finance, and of value for money. A test of the first type has already been applied to land (in the previous chapter), and tests of value for money were applied to the types and forms of housing (chapter 9) and to housing improvement (chapter 10).

In order to apply tests of the availability of building resources to the housing programmes under consideration, it is necessary first to estimate the volume of work of which the industry might be capable and the conditions likely to be necessary for such levels of output to be achieved. Before this can be assessed it is necessary to have some understanding of the nature of the industry, of the way it functions, of changes taking place in it and in the form of its work, and of recent trends in applying innovations and in productivity, scale and costs.

THE ORGANIZATION OF THE CONSTRUCTION INDUSTRY[1]

Housing is one of the major products of the construction industry. Some building organizations specialize exclusively in housing, although most also carry out other types of work. The construction of housing cannot be sensibly examined except as a part of the activities of the construction industry as a whole. Hence it is necessary at this stage to anticipate information that will be needed in the second volume of this book.

The construction industry has three sectors; planning and design, and related professions; materials production; and contracting organizations, which are concerned with assembly. A large part of housing, and most other building and civil engineering is 'bespoke' work. It is planned and designed to meet the requirements of particular clients, either individuals or—more likely today—groups. In such cases the buildings and works are designed and planned by one group of organizations, the materials and components are produced by another group and erected by a third. Many houses and other single buildings are provided 'off the peg', the client purchasing a complete building as it stands or choosing from a catalogue subject only to minor variations. In such cases the design group, whether or not a part of the contractor's organization, prepares designs for the contractor rather than for the client. Even in the case of 'off the peg' building, materials and components are mainly purchased on the market from producers who manufacture for stock and general demand, rather than for the particular demand of a contractor. Some contractors producing 'off the peg' buildings

[1] The information in this chapter will be found in greater detail in the author's book *Building Economy: Design, Production and Organization* (84).

manufacture or purchase purpose-made components to facilitate the construction of their buildings.

For 'bespoke' building the client usually engages, on a fee basis, an architect who, in consultation with engineers, planners and surveyors, prepares plans and designs to meet the client's requirements. Construction organizations subsequently contract to carry out the erection work at a price which covers materials, labour and overheads, and provides for a profit which varies with their success. Often much of the work is sub-let to other contracting organizations. Labour and materials are purchased on the market. This process is modified for 'off the peg' and package building but the same functions are still performed. Design and construction in these cases form part of the same contract. Basic materials and most components are still obtained from the market.

The output of the construction industry depends on the size of the work forces and on the productivity of the three sectors of the industry. The producers of materials and components are financially of the same order of importance as the contractors, but are members of a number of separate industries, some of which are not identifiable as part of the construction industry. The professional side is of relatively less importance in terms of the value of work; its work is valued at about a fifth of that of the contracting side, but it determines the consumption of both labour and materials.

THE CONSTRUCTION PROCESS AND FUTURE CHANGE

It is difficult to classify construction in a comprehensive and uniform way because technical and organizational factors are difficult to separate. Most types of construction are described as traditional; the innovations of this century are generally described as non-traditional, or as industrialized or system building. None of these names clearly defines a type of construction. Broadly, traditional building embraces all those methods of construction in which materials and components are purchased from the market and assembled on the site into buildings and works designed to the requirements of individual clients or expected clients. System building usually implies construction by the assembly of specially manufactured or prefabricated units, or formwork or profiles to produce buildings to standard designs. However, it can imply simply a rational and systematic approach to the building process. Both forms of construction, traditional and system building, can be industrialized. Whether or not this adjective applies depends on whether the design and production have been integrated to provide a related programme of construction.

Traditional building is simply the form of building normal for the time and place. Its current form depends on the materials and labour available, on technical knowledge, on the economy in which construction take place and on the resources of the client. Innovations in building are largely a response to changes in the economy and in technical knowledge. The use of materials found on the site declines when transport is sufficiently well organized to enable processed materials to be produced in bulk and brought from distant places, and when the occupiers of the building are fully employed elsewhere. As the price of labour rises so does the use of highly processed materials, management skills and machinery. Hand decorated materials such as carved wood, stone and decorative plasterwork give way to decoration by the use of colour and texture.

As the price of labour has increased and technical knowledge has grown, the preparation of materials and components has become more and more the province of specialists. Prices fall as the manufacturers obtain the economies of specialization, scale and mechanization. The scale of construction work is so great that manufacturers of all kinds of products naturally seek an outlet for them in this field. In this way steel has to some extent replaced timber, asbestos cement products have partly replaced galvanized iron sheets, concrete products have partly replaced clay products, and plastic products have partly replaced timber and metal ones. At the same time the degree of prefabrication has been increasing. Joinery *in situ* has been almost completely replaced by prefabricated windows, doors, staircases and cupboards, often manufactured in some material other than timber. Brick and concrete construction *in situ* has been partly replaced by precast concrete products, while ready-mixed concrete is now used for much of the remainder. The extent to which such substitution occurs depends on the degree of standardization of dimensions, connexions and performance. The greater the area of agreement on standards, the more it is economic to mass produce standard components for stock. In the field of government building, particularly housing, standard dimensions and performance standards are gradually being accepted.

Because construction, particularly building construction, is largely an assembly industry, the scope for using mechanical plant is less than in manufacturing, where mass production is normal. Mechanical plant is mainly used for three types of construction process: earth moving, and mixing and handling materials.

Mechanical plant probably has its greatest economic potential in earth movement. Mechanical excavating, levelling and shovelling are rapidly becoming almost universal even on small sites.

While mechanical mixing of materials is almost universal, the economic advantages are far less than with earth movement. Because of the limitations imposed by succeeding operations, the full potential of the machine can rarely be obtained. Moreover, whereas earth moving plant can be used intensively and then withdrawn for use elsewhere, mixing plant is required intermittently over long periods. Often it is more economic to use ready-mixed materials. Ready-mixed concrete is particularly economic where the concrete can be placed directly in position by the mixer truck. Its use has increased rapidly in the last decade.

The weight of materials to be handled is considerable—a traditional house contains about 150 tons of materials, much of which is handled more than once. Many types of horizontal and vertical handling aids are now used. Since 1950, the tower crane has increasingly become the universal aid for handling materials in building work on any scale. Again, however, the economic advantages are small, because succeeding operations limit the extent to which the machine's capacity can be used. Mechanical hand tools are also increasingly used, but again it is difficult to organize their continuous use and hence to use them economically.

The potential value of mechanical plant in construction work itself is surprisingly small, particularly in building construction. For example, perhaps only about a third in all of the work on a traditional house is capable of being mechanized; this is equivalent to about 10 per cent of the costs. Since plant itself has a cost, it would appear to be necessary to reduce man-hours by perhaps a half to two-thirds (which is unlikely) to save 3 to 4 per cent of the costs of a house by this method.

The low potential value of mechanical plant in construction arises from the limited number of operations capable of mechanization and the low proportion of the capacity of a machine which can be utilized. Most plant is only used 50 per cent of the potential time and probably only to 50 per cent capacity. Capacity is lost because contractors tend to maintain an excessive and unnecessarily diverse stock of plant, because of the seasonal nature of construction and the intermittent nature of site work, and because potential output is wasted as a result of limitations imposed by succeeding operations. A greater use of hired plant, less specialization by size and type, and better site planning would be likely to increase plant use and reduce costs.

The ownership of plant is not the only aspect of the vertical integration of contracting organizations which tends to lead to diseconomies. It is doubtful whether it is economic for contracting organizations to own material processing plants. Large-scale forward purchasing and storage of materials is not necessarily economic. Available evidence on systems of accounting and costing throws doubt on whether many contracting organizations have an adequate knowledge of the returns obtained from capital used to finance such trading activities.

While more pooling of plant and less specialization by type and size would increase plant utilization rates, it would not lead to the utilization of more potential capacity. This can only be achieved by rationalizing, or industrializing, the construction process. Normal practice, particularly in the construction of traditional housing, has been to allow the various trade gangs to work their way through the construction process with a minimum of planning or organization. At the extreme, site management has been concerned with little more than setting the order of houses to be constructed, ordering materials and subcontractors, and supervising to ensure that the operatives provided adequate quality and quantity. More planning has been necessary for civil engineering work. It is now generally recognized that organization is as at least as important as, and perhaps more important than, labour supervision. As much can be lost in non-productive and idle time resulting from bad organization as from the lack of operative effort. The increasing use of large, expensive items of mechanical plant has directed attention to the importance of site organization.

The development of systems analysis and critical path techniques has provided powerful methods for analysing construction programmes. Efforts to reduce idle time, and to combine operations so as to eliminate preparation and clearing up time, often lead to prefabrication and off-site work, and to innovations in building materials and components. So far construction techniques developed in this way appear to have been more successful than those originating from a desire to exploit new materials and techniques for their own sake.

These aspects of industrialization have led to others. Tighter construction schedules necessitate reliable delivery of materials and plant, and an assured supply of labour. Some variation in the times taken to carry out operations is inevitable, but it can be reduced by protecting work and workers from the weather and bad light, by using methods for the rapid curing of wet work and by the substitution of materials and prefabricated units which can be built in dry. However, the tighter the schedule of operations, the greater the risks and costs of departures from the programme.

Clearly, pre-planning will be most successful when all the design detail is known before the work on the site is planned. The design and programming of construction work should proceed together, since slight modifications in the design may enable large savings to be achieved in construction costs. These are only possible if the design team has the technical knowledge to prepare the programme, if the design team and contractor work together, or if the contractor provides the design as well as carrying out the erection. This raises problems of contracting procedure which will be considered later.

At first sight it often appears surprising that the use of industrialized factory methods does not result in substantial economies in building construction, but the scale of the differences between the normal manufactured article and a building can be overlooked. As compared with most manufactured goods, buildings are large, heavy, bulky and cheap in relation to their size. Because of their size, weight and comparatively low price, they are difficult and costly to transport even sectionally. Hence, and because of the need to tailor them to their site and to attach them to site services, the advantages of building on the site are considerable. Moreover, building is an assembly industry and therefore less easy to mechanize than manufacturing industries. Because of the size of a unit of building, the variety of purposes and clients' needs, and because of site limitations, a large variety of buildings is required. The construction industry can thus be more sensibly compared with shipbuilding or aircraft construction than with manufacturing.

Over half of the cost of new construction is represented by the cost of materials. For the most part these are processed by large-scale manufacturers. Well over half of this expenditure represents fittings, equipment and finishing materials, which frequently are not affected by the form of construction. Labour represents only about a third of the cost of new construction; the remainder is overheads and profits.

Traditional structural materials are cheap in relation to their bulk and weight, particularly in Great Britain. Dimensional accuracy and freedom from distortion during curing are not of great importance for construction *in situ*, although the tolerances for prefabricated factory-made units are clearly much narrower. Dimensional accuracy and freedom from distortion usually necessitate the use of more expensive materials and greater care in manufacture. Costs tend to be further increased when components are produced specially for a system, since it is difficult to ensure production at capacity level.

The costs of the structural materials are about two-thirds greater than those of structural labour. Rises in material costs have therefore to be offset by disproportionately larger reductions in labour costs. Frequently such savings have proved to be small because only part of an operation is eliminated; often the more difficult part, as well as the preparation and clearing up work, remain. When, as often happens, special plant is needed to handle the prefabricated units, the overheads tend to be increased.

The cost relations in Great Britain are less favourable to factory production than in most other countries. Traditional building is based on the brick. Burnt clay is dimensionally not a very accurate material; it only provides rather small building units and does not lend itself to factory prefabrication. It is, however, very cheap compared with the basic materials available in many other countries. Further, the differential advantage in wage rates of skilled as against unskilled workers is smaller in Great Britain than in most other countries,[1] so that there is less point in using techniques which replace skilled work by unskilled work. Moreover, while in Great Britain labour costs of site workers are generally a little less than those of factory workers, in many countries they are more, often substantially more. As a result there is little advantage, in Great Britain, in transferring work away from the site.

It seems clear that it is by no means easy to develop systems of factory built construction which are more economic of resources than traditional forms of construction. For example, in spite of the hundreds of systems which have been developed in the last fifty years, especially for housing, none appears, at best, other than marginally cheaper than traditional forms. Nevertheless, improvements in productivity have occurred, for the factory built systems are probably at least as competitive today as in the past, and so have at least equalled improvements in the productivity of the construction industry as a whole. The challenge and the development of innovations in the non-traditional sector undoubtedly stimulate the industry as a whole and may constitute the principal gain from that sector. It is possible that innovations in organization have been more important as a basis of improved productivity in the non-traditional sector than innovations

[1] The differential has fallen since 1900 from about 50 per cent to about 15 per cent.

in the use of materials. It would appear that the factory based systems flourish mainly when the traditional sector is disorganized, as after the two world wars, or when they receive strong government support, as in the Eastern European countries, in France and recently in Great Britain.

It is difficult not to conclude that, short of a revolution in the development of materials and prefabrication, improvements in productivity in construction will depend on general progress in the development and implementation of innovations in all aspects of the industry. Progress will need to be made in the standardization and coordination of dimensions, connexions and the performance standards of materials and components. Acceptance of such innovations should lead to reduced material costs, a greater degree of prefabrication, and a reduction in design and assembly time. Designers will need to obtain a better general understanding of the problems of construction, and be able to design in relation to the construction problems posed by the design, as well as in relation to the long-term performance and use of the building. Constructors will need to improve their costing techniques and their planning of contracts and subsequent site management. Contractual methods will need to be accepted which provide the spur to efficiency provided by competitive tendering without sacrificing the benefits of integrated design and production. Given these fundamental conditions, the best choice between construction *in situ*, site casting, prefabricated units and factory production, between different materials and between different mechanical methods, will be found in relation to the building need and the capabilities of the contractor.

THE CONSTRUCTION OF DWELLINGS

Most of the comments made in the previous section apply at least equally to housing construction as to other types of building. Dwellings are built on a substantially greater scale than any other type of building and are more uniform in their specification; it is not, therefore, surprising to find that system building has been applied more intensively and for a longer period to housing than to other building forms. However, economic success has been limited.

While many extravagant claims have been made for the economy of system built dwellings, the limited evidence available suggests that, over the last five decades, system building has at best broken even, and generally has been more expensive, than traditional construction. In the 1950s system built dwellings were about 3 per cent more expensive than others. Currently the position is probably about the same. On the basis of tender price averages for 1964–5 for dwellings of equal size, system built low rise dwellings were about 109 per cent, medium rise dwellings 106 per cent and high rise dwellings 97 per cent of other prices. There does not appear to be any evidence of subsequent changes. Such limited evidence as there is would indicate that the position on the Continent is similar.

In fact, few of the systems employed make much use of new materials or of factory prefabrication techniques. In 1965 about a half of the system built dwellings approved in Great Britain were based on *in situ* concrete, a quarter on factory precast concrete, and only a tenth on factory prefabrication. Until that year the vast majority of system built dwellings were either Wimpey 'No Fines' or Laing 'Easiform'. These two systems accounted for three-quarters of system built dwellings in 1964. Both are based on *in situ* concrete and depend for their success on the quality of the site organization. Both systems have a long history; the former was developed in 1946 and the latter just after the First World War.

Factory production was used to a much greater extent for the temporary bungalows built in the late 1940s and is used for the temporary houses and mobile homes of today. Generally their price per square foot is higher than for permanent dwellings of the same size, even when allowance is made for the cost of the additional fittings and equipment which they normally contain. Moreover, they are generally far less durable and more expensive to maintain.

It is notable that even in the United States, where the traditional form of construction, timber load-bearing panel construction, lends itself to factory prefabrication, its use is very limited (85). There, the methods of construction range from contractors who purchase the raw materials and assemble on the site, to those who purchase, from a home manufacturer, a complete package of pre-cut timber and prefabricated units ready for assembly. In 1964, home manufacturers and building merchants produced only 22 per cent of the total output of houses.

The difficulty in achieving economy by the use of factory prefabrication and other non-traditional forms of building lies in the small proportion of the costs of a dwelling in which economies can be achieved in this way. This can be illustrated by examining the way costs are incurred in a typical low cost (about £4,000) house. Land might cost about £1,000, a garage £200, and road and site works £400, leaving £2,400 for the works within the curtilage other than the garage. Of this sum about £1,300 would be the cost of materials, of which only about £600 would be basic structural materials. Labour costs are likely to be about £700, of which about £350 represents the costs of work to the structure above ground. The balance represents the cost of work to foundations, site works within the curtilage, the installation of fittings and equipment, and finishings. As a result, economies from changing the form of structure are largely limited to the structure itself and to the services in the walls and floors. These represent only about a quarter of the total costs. Moreover, in order to prefabricate and save on labour, it is necessary to use precision materials which are more expensive than traditional materials. However, even traditional materials account for about two-thirds of the costs.

CONTRACTING ARRANGEMENTS

The traditional division between designer, contractor and the manufacturer of materials clearly creates a number of problems, especially if, as argued earlier, account needs to be taken of the method of erection and the materials available in the design process. The training of the designer would become very long if he needed an expert understanding of construction techniques. Moreover, practical expertise in construction problems and a knowledge of programming and organizing site operations is difficult to obtain without regular participation in site management. A possible solution would be to engage a construction engineer to serve as a consultant with the design team. While the most economic method of construction depends to some extent on the experience and equipment of the contractor, this is probably less important than the integration of construction and design knowledge at the design stage.

The current solution, the joint appointment of a contractor and design team, creates difficulties in testing the competitiveness of the construction contract. At the stage of appointment no design exists to provide an adequate basis of tendering, even on a management fee basis. Any fee agreed can only be crudely based and is unlikely to provide an incentive to design or construction efficiency. As long as only a minority of contracts are let in that way, the contract for construction can be compared with market prices, but this safeguard would be lost if joint appointments became universal.

Similar difficulties arise where the contractor provides the design, either in the course of a package deal or as a standard building. The package deal type of contract provides a comprehensive service to a client who requires a building designed to meet his needs without having to engage consultants and a contractor. A package deal or turnkey type of contract certainly saves the client time and trouble, but he probably pays as much or more for the combined service as he would for separate services. There appears to be no evidence that design and production are any better coordinated in a package deal contract than under normal conditions. Where no special specifications are required, a suitable building may be found either among those being erected or about to be erected speculatively, or from the catalogues of system builders. Again, comparison of prices is difficult unless competitive bids are obtained, and clearly, competitive bidding for design and construction is even more wasteful of resources than bidding for construction alone.

While some form of competitive bidding appears necessary, at least over a part of the field, in order to provide a basis of comparison and a stimulus to efficiency, under present conditions it has only limited value in promoting efficient construction. Costing to an acceptable level of accuracy cannot be achieved without first preparing a programme. Contractors claim that tenders cannot be based on a programme because the time allowed for tendering is too short, because sufficient detail is rarely available and because they cannot afford the cost of preparing a programme when they need to place a number of tenders to obtain one contract. In the absence of programme based costing, tender prices are said to be too insensitive to encourage economic design. Contractors tend to add contingent allowances to cover the uncertainties. There is a danger that the resulting margin will discourage efficiency.

The problems of price fixing are in part a reflection of the number of clients and of the number of individual designs. There is a tendency for even large clients, such as large local authorities, nationalized industries and government departments, to design each building individually. Both design time and planning and tendering time could be reduced if the design for each building type was progressively modified until an optimum was reached. This would facilitate serial contracting with only an occasional reference to the market. The growth of building-client consortia and the likely reduction in the number of housing authorities should facilitate this type of development.

The system builder approaches this problem from the supply side by finding individual clients prepared to purchase from a limited range of designs. The repetition of the same design makes it worthwhile to put more time into the study of the planning and erection process. By combining design, manufacture and erection within one organization many problems are solved. In particular the design can be related to production and erection convenience. It is, of course, not necessary, and not necessarily desirable, that the building organization should substitute specially made components for those purchased from the market, since this may result in a loss of the economies of scale.

System building need imply no more than an organization which is prepared to erect buildings to a standard range of designs. Economy can be obtained from a method of building developed scientifically in relation to the design. The method will imply an orderly form of construction which enables the best use to be made of plant and labour so as to minimize costs. The more sophisticated the method, the less flexible the organization will tend to be and the more necessary it will be to set up a marketing organization to ensure an adequate regular flow of orders.

Clearly, however, there is little point in restricting the designs which the organization is prepared to build and accepting the market limitations involved unless the resulting economies are large enough. The possible savings arise almost entirely from the way the work is organized and hardly at all from the scale of erection. While economies of scale can be obtained, these tend to be exhausted very rapidly; generally the number of man-hours per dwelling is much the same whether the batch to be constructed is 30 or 300 (86). The more efficient the organization the smaller tend to be the savings in man-hours by increasing the size of the batch. This is also true for the production of building components, although in this field economies of scale continue to larger batch sizes than for building erection (87).

PRODUCTIVITY AND OUTPUT OF CONSTRUCTION WORK

It is clear from the above analysis that the construction industry is in a state of evolution both in organization and in method. The rate at which innovations are adopted tends to be rather slow, which perhaps is inevitable in a sector of the economy so long established. Unless there is an unexpected revolution in the concept of buildings and their form of production, increases in efficiency will tend to depend on the acceptance and adoption of innovations by existing organizations. The range of efficiency is naturally very wide. For example, the range of man-hours required to construct a traditional house is still, it is believed, threefold. At the current rate of evolution the innovations already known are unlikely to be fully absorbed for many years. Thus it is, perhaps, not too optimistic to expect a steady rate of evolution to continue over the period covered by this study.

In order to evaluate numerically the probable increase in productivity, it is necessary to evaluate past changes in productivity. It is difficult to obtain reliable indicators of productivity but it would appear that over the last seven or eight years (to 1965) output per man of new work rose by 3·0 to 3·5 per cent a year, and of repair and maintenance work by 1·0 to 1·5 per cent a year. These figures appear to be of the right order in relation to movements in the prices of labour, materials and new construction (appendix 12).

However, the hours worked per operative appear to have risen. In 1950 they were 47·6 per week and rose to a peak of 49·4 in 1956; they rose to a new peak in 1960 and have since fluctuated at a high level. Clearly, this increase in hours has made some contribution to the growth in the level of productivity, possibly about a quarter per cent a year, but it is unlikely to go any further. Moreover, if hours worked per week drop, other things being equal, output per man-year is likely to drop proportionately.

The proportion of clerical, administrative and technical staff has increased over the last few years. While some of these workers may be employed in selling, the majority are likely to be concerned with management and processing the data necessary to achieve higher productivity. An allowance for the increase in these workers reduces the increase in output per worker in the industry for new work to about a half per cent below that of operatives.

PRODUCTIVITY AND REAL COSTS IN THE FUTURE

The unexhausted potential of innovations in the construction industry and the wide range of efficiency suggest that the industry should be able to improve productivity as rapidly as in the last decade for a long period ahead. No doubt other possibilities for increasing productivity will arise in the future. There must, however, be some limit. Continuous rises in productivity, even at moderate rates, for a period as long as forty years would yield substantial reductions in the man-hours required. A 3 per cent rate of improvement amounts to a 70 per cent reduction in man-hours by the end of the period, while a 5 per cent rate of improvement would amount to an 86 per cent reduction. It is difficult to contemplate a sevenfold increase in output per hour in construction work. While such increases might easily occur on the site, they would be of only limited value if the savings were made at the expense of additional labour in off-site factories, or in the factories of the producers of building materials and components.

Output per man-year is more important than output per man-hour. The rate of increase in output per man-year could be considerably reduced by a fall in hours worked per week and by lengthening holidays. If the average weekly hours worked fell to forty and two or three more days' holiday were granted, there would be a reduction of a sixth in annual working time. A thirty-two hour working week and another five or six days' holiday would reduce annual working time by a third. While the fall in output might not be proportional, if it were it would have the effect of reducing a gross increase in productivity of 3 per cent to about 2½ per cent in the first case and to about 2 per cent in the second.

The increase in the productivity of work in the maintenance and conversion sector has been small in the past, possibly not more than 1½ per cent a year. It is possible that this rate might be improved in the future. The use of sheet and film surfaces might reduce the need for labour for painting and decoration. The spread of prefabricated and standardized components, and their design as replaceable units, might result in less labour in renewal work.

If productivity in the maintenance and renewal sector continues to improve slowly compared with improvements in the new work sector, labour requirements per unit of work will fall much faster in the new work sector than in the maintenance sector. Since the amount of labour at present levels of productivity in new work is expected to be less than in the other sector, much more labour will eventually be needed in the maintenance and renewal sector than in the new work sector.

Of course, the costs per unit of work in the two sectors will not widen as much as the man-hour requirements, since changes in costs of materials and components will affect both sectors. About 54 per cent of the costs of new work consists of materials. The materials content of maintenance and renewal work is only about 28 per cent. If past trends continued the real prices of new work would remain about the same, while the real prices of maintenance work would rise about 1½ to 2¼ per cent per annum.

In view of the uncertainty about future levels of productivity, it is not possible to estimate any one rate of improvement as most likely. Programmes of development and replacement will, therefore, be assessed in terms of a range of levels. For new work the range would appear to lie between 2 and 4½ per cent, while for maintenance and renewal work the range will be taken as between 0 and 2 per cent.

DESIGN WORK AND ADMINISTRATION

If the design and administrative sides of the industry are to be able to handle the increased loads of work likely to be forthcoming, they too will need either to increase their productivity or to recruit at a faster rate.

Design time can be reduced partly by rationalization and partly by greater repetition. Rationalization could include a greater use of codification of such design information as standard solutions and standard detailing, and a greater use of computer and other techniques for drawing, specification, measuring quantities and preparing bills. Much more design information could be made available if research were organized in this field. Such research should also help to reduce the use of resources in the construction and servicing of buildings. Attention would need to be paid to the problems of erection and to the resources required to service buildings and developments over their lives, as well as to their appearance, convenience and structure. The productivity of design work would also be increased if a limited range of standardized and coordinated building components were accepted. While site differences will always necessitate some special features in each building, it is unnecessary to design each building individually. Monotony is not an inevitable consequence of repetition, and individual design does not necessarily lead to a more attractive townscape or to greater convenience. Much design time could be saved by developing existing or standard designs, removing weaknesses or adapting to different requirements, instead of preparing a new design on each occasion. Such developments in design procedure will be all the more necessary because of the need to give more attention than in the past to providing designs and development plans which minimize costs in relation to values over the life of the building or development.

Innovations are being adopted, but perhaps not rapidly enough to ensure the rate of increase in productivity likely to be necessary. It is very difficult to measure increases in productivity in design work. Such information as is available suggests that the rate of increase has been less than in contracting (appendix 12).

Similar streamlining of procedures will be necessary in building and development administration. There is need both to economize in manpower and to reduce the time taken to reach decisions. There would appear to be two ways of achieving these aims; by making a greater use of fiscal and financial machinery, and by delegating physical controls to one body in each area.

All too frequently methods of taxation, of making grants and subsidies and of providing loans operate in a contrary direction to the ends dictated by the best interests of the community. The actions stimulated by fiscal and financial policy subsequently need to be curbed by physical controls. For example, housing subsidies and rate deficiency grants encourage high rather than low density housing and the development of new housing rather than the improvement of existing housing, and grants for highway development encourage roads rather than tracked transport systems. The phasing of grants often encourages development in one field uncoordinated with the needs and priorities of development in other fields. Planning and other administrative machinery is often inadequate to correct such tendencies.

The administration of planning and other physical controls is operated by many different departments of central and local government; often uncoordinated and sometimes in direct conflict. For example, industrial policy often encourages industry in areas for which planning policy requires a substantial overspill of population. Delegation of powers to one body in each area should result in a consistent application of policy decisions, reduce the time taken to obtain the necessary consents, and save manpower both in applying the controls and in applying for consent. The time and manpower involved in obtaining land for development could also probably be reduced if greater foresight were shown—and in some cases if cash settlements were more generous. It is likely that the additional costs of delay, administration and legal work are often greater than would be the additional costs of an immediately acceptable offer. Some of the administrative changes under discussion may result in rises in administrative productivity.

Generally the redevelopment of existing areas is more time consuming than development of new areas, both in development planning and in legal and administrative work. Similarly, small schemes tend to be relatively more time consuming than large ones. While it is likely that the amount of redevelopment work will increase relatively to new work, the schemes of both are likely to rise in size and to this extent productivity may increase.

CHAPTER 15

THE AVAILABILITY OF FINANCE FOR HOUSING

HOUSING NEEDS AND HOUSING DEMAND

The amount of new housing construction, improvement and maintenance work depends not only on the ability of the construction industry to carry out the work but also on effective demand. The demand arises partly from owners ordering new dwellings or maintaining and adapting existing dwellings, partly from developers and investors building and improving housing for letting or sale, and partly from the government and its agencies increasing the stock of their dwellings and improving those already in their possession. The demand from these various sources depends in turn on people's preference for housing as against other goods and services, on people's willingness to invest their savings in housing finance, and on the extent to which public authorities are prepared to borrow to finance housing and to raise money through taxation to subsidize it.

This study has been concerned with housing needs rather than with demand. It does not follow that the kind of programmes which emerge from a study of need would occur spontaneously as a result of the working of the market in its present form. The purpose of the present chapter is to examine how far the existing market structure is likely to result in the housing programmes which appear necessary and to what extent the market would appear to need modification. It will be necessary to examine, at least briefly, the nature of the housing market and the way different types of market organization affect the real costs of housing to the user.

THE CHANGING MARKET FOR HOUSING

Before the First World War, nine-tenths of dwellings were rented from private owners and the balance were occupied by their owners (88). House property was considered a sound investment. During that war the rents of the majority of dwellings were controlled by the government and most have been held below market rates ever since. Investors expect a return on their capital comparable, in relation to the risks, to that obtained from other forms of investment. As controlled rents have not been adequate to provide comparable returns, this source of finance for the provision of housing has tended to dry up, and the quality of the privately held stock has been allowed to deteriorate. Private finance for house purchase has been available through building societies and other financial institutions, and generally the rate of return has been sufficient to ensure an adequate supply of finance for people able to afford purchase under these conditions. Thus, owner-occupation has grown rapidly. Meanwhile, public authorities, who originally entered the housing market to meet the needs of the poorest people, have expanded their activities to fill the gap left by the withdrawal of private capital for financing property to let. As a result of ageing and of sales, the number of privately let dwellings has halved and now only represents about a fifth of the total stock (49). The number of owner-occupied dwellings has increased eightfold and now stands at about eight million. Public authorities have provided about five million dwellings, about 30 per cent of the stock. Perhaps surprisingly, about 5 per cent of dwellings are still occupied by virtue of employment.

PRIVATE HOUSING FOR RENT

Rent control was first imposed in 1915. By 1920, when the real value of the rents was less than half their prewar value, an Act was introduced which allowed them to be increased by 40 per cent. The rents of about four million dwellings were still pegged at this level in 1939, when rents were once again frozen (88). The 1957 Act allowed some increase in rents and decontrolled some dwellings. The median rent in England and Wales in private rented unfurnished dwellings was still only £54 in 1964–5, varying from £38 in the northern regions to £77 in East Anglia and the South East (49). Rents were even lower in Scotland, over a quarter being less than £13 a year and over 60 per cent less than £26, the average rent (41). An economic rent at that time for a three bedroom dwelling of Parker Morris standards would have been nearly £500 even outside London; the corresponding rent for a two bedroom dwelling would have been over £400 (table 9.15). Thus, even in England and Wales, the median rent represented only about a tenth of the economic rent of a dwelling at good current standards. It is true that most rented dwellings would have been substantially below current standards, but the shortfall would not be of that order. There is little doubt that rent control has resulted in rents much below the economic level. In many cases the rents are inadequate to cover the costs of regular maintenance. While investors can obtain an adequate return from new investments in housing already rented, since their prices reflect the rents obtained, the returns which can be obtained by investment in new housing for rent are quite inadequate.

At first sight an economic rent of £480 a year on a dwelling costing £4,000 seems to be very high. However, although the tenant would be paying annually 12 per cent on the capital cost, a landlord paying tax and interest at the normal current rates and amortizing by means of a sinking fund might only be getting a return of about 5 per cent net on the money he had invested in the dwelling. This is little more than he could obtain from a building society under comparable conditions, although the risks, in the light of past government rent policy, would be far greater.

The relationship between the rent and the net return depends on the way tax is calculated, on its rate, on the rates of interest, on the proportion of capital borrowed and on the period of amortization. Under current arrangements interest paid on loans, actual expenditure for repairs, maintenance, management and insurance may be deducted from the rent revenue before tax is calculated. Sinking funds, other amortization and reserve funds for maintenance must be met from net income. The shorter the period of amortization the greater the importance of the way tax is calculated. Where the period of amortization is short, for example fifteen years, the net return at normal current rates of taxation would be 5 to 6 per cent greater if the cost of amortization could be deducted as an expense for tax purposes (89). For a longer period of amortization, thirty to forty years, the difference would be only 1 or 2 per cent. Clearly the higher the rate of interest and the greater the rate of taxation, the larger the proportion of capital the landlord has to provide from his own resources; and the shorter the period of amortization, the more important is the method of calculating tax and the more difficult it is to obtain an adequate return on the investment without charging rents at a high proportion of the capital expended. Cheaper forms of depreciation could be used but only by accepting further risks. Of course, small investors paying low rates of tax would obtain higher net rates of return, but so would they on other forms of investment. In practice, the allowance for maintenance would be too great during the early years and too little in later years. The money put away to reserve would also be subject to tax.

It can be argued that, at the end of the period of depreciation, the investor still retains the dwelling. However, by that time, if not before, the value may have dropped if substantial sums have not been spent to bring the dwelling up to acceptable standards. In either case the net value remaining from the initial investment at the end of the period of depreciation is much reduced; its discounted value at the time of the investment decision is hence so small that usually it can be ignored. The eventual cost of improving the dwelling is, of course, treated as capital for tax purposes.

The main reason (apart from lack of confidence engendered by rent control legislation) why neither private landlords nor housing associations make much contribution to the supply of housing to let is clear: as long as depreciation and reserves for maintenance must be met from net revenue after tax, the rents necessary to provide a reasonable return in relation to other investments need to be much higher than the economic rents that could be charged by public authorities, or the equivalent costs to owner-occupiers (table 9.15). Other forms of property investment are taxed in the same way, but commercial and industrial organizations can charge rent as a business expense and the effective cost to the occupier is about halved.

Since improvement costs are also treated as capital and must be depreciated out of net revenue, high gross rates of return are necessary. Although the gross permissible increase in rent for money spent by the landlord on improvements is 12½ per cent, the net returns are very low. Even if the improvement cost is depreciated over twenty-five years, the net return is only about 4½ per cent; generally it would be even less, since maintenance and renewal costs in respect of the improvements would increase over a period as long as this. The shorter the life over which the expenditure can be recovered, the lower the rate of return.

The grant aid for improving a dwelling is of direct assistance to the tenant since it does not contribute to the rent increase, but for the same reason it is of no monetary advantage to the landlord. The rent of an improved dwelling must not exceed the rent of the dwelling before improvement by more than 12½ per cent of that part of the approved expense which is borne by the landlord. The rent can be greater than this in the case of dwellings not subject to a controlled tenancy (90). The landlord may, of course, incur expenses for 'ordinary' repairs for which he can obtain neither a grant nor any increase in rent.

There seems to be little doubt that, because of the way regulations on improvements operate, property companies and housing associations cannot obtain an economic return on money used for these purposes. In many cases the returns would be too small to meet the cost of borrowing the money, even for charitable bodies and individuals with little or no tax liability. Many landlords are people with little capital or income, and many lack either the will or knowledge necessary to undertake the improvement of their property. Some local authorities discourage applications for improvement grants because they hope to redevelop rather than improve areas of poor housing. Moreover, many of the tenants in dwellings which need improving are poor and old—in Deeplish, a twilight area in Lancashire, there was twice the national proportion of pensioners, and a third of the households had incomes of under £10 a week compared with a fifth in the country as a whole (91). Thus the tenants are often not able, even if willing, to meet the extra rent and extra rates which result from improvements.

PUBLIC HOUSING FOR RENT

Public authorities, mainly local authorities, began to build for letting on a substantial scale in the 1920s. In each of the first three decades 600,000 to 700,000 dwellings were built; and nearly 1·9 million in the 1950s. The rate of production has fallen since then but is now being increased again.

Nearly all public authority housing is subsidized.[1] The amount of subsidy per dwelling and the form in which it has been paid has varied considerably over this period. Since the Second World War the amount paid by the Exchequer in housing subsidies has increased fivefold (49).

The amount of Exchequer subsidy in relation to the debt charges to be met depends on the phasing of the development in relation to subsidy policy and construction costs. Authorities with a substantial proportion of dwellings built at periods of comparatively low costs, and high subsidies relative to costs, obtain

[1] During the 1920s nearly half of private house building was also subsidized. While subsidies were still available for private housing during the 1930s, few of the dwellings built then satisfied the requirements.

much more assistance from the Exchequer subsidies than other authorities. For county boroughs in England and Wales the amount of subsidy per £1 of debt charges in 1962/3 varied from 3*s.* 2*d.* to 7*s.* 3*d.*, and for metropolitan boroughs from 4*s.* to 12*s.* 1*d.* Some local authorities also subsidize their dwellings from the rates. The corresponding figures for rate subsidies varied from a credit of 1*s.* 8*d.* to a deficit of 6*s.* 5*d.* for county boroughs, and from deficits of 1*d.* to 10*s.* 11*d.* for metropolitan boroughs (92). A substantial stock of dwellings built in earlier periods also results in low average debt charges. Hence, the average amount of net debt charges per dwelling to be included in the rent varies considerably from one authority to another, without any relationship to need, or much relationship to the standard of dwelling.

In order to try to reduce these financial differences between authorities a new system was introduced into the Housing Act 1961 (appendix 13). Under this Act the level of the subsidy was related to the balance in the housing account of each authority between expenditure and potential revenue (measured in terms of gross value). Special subsidies were also provided in the Housing Subsidies Act 1967 where there was a special need which could only be satisfied at the expense of an unreasonable burden on the rates.

Housing subsidies have usually been related to the number of dwellings, and not to their size, and so have tended to encourage the construction of smaller dwellings. In a similar way the payment of additional subsidies for dwellings in high blocks and on expensive land has tended to encourage these forms of development rather than the more economical two storey housing or low flats.

A large proportion of local authority revenue, particularly for the poorer authorities, is received from the Exchequer by way of general grants and rate deficiency grants (the name of these special grants changes from time to time). Not only do these not increase as a direct consequence of development expenditure, but, in the case of rate deficiency grants, improvement to the urban areas tends to reduce the grant. Both general and rate deficiency grants are related to the population under the local authority and decline with losses of population. Frequently the saving in costs from population loss is far less than the corresponding loss from rates and from the general and rate deficiency grants. For this reason local authorities try to prevent the loss of population. It is often worthwhile for a local authority to develop at very high densities and on very expensive land, rather than house population more economically on land within the boundaries of another authority.

Not only is there little relationship between the financial assistance received from the Exchequer and the needs of local authorities, but there is little relationship between the allocation of this assistance by a local authority and the needs of its residents. Local authority dwellings are usually allocated in terms of the need for a dwelling and a local residence qualification, rather than in terms of financial need. While the inadequacy of existing accommodation has relevance when a household is first rehoused, its relevance declines as time passes, the family grows up and its income changes. However, since income is usually not taken into account, even at the time of initial allocations, the need for a rent subsidy varies even at that stage. Rents and incomes can be brought into line, within a local authority area, by pooling the subsidies and allocating them as grants towards the economic rent to those households with proven need. A large number of authorities have, however, made no attempt to introduce a differential rent rebate scheme of any form. Such schemes would not remove the anomalies between local authorities; only a nationally operated system could achieve this. But not even a national system confined to public authority housing would remove the anomalies between public and private rented housing. While the private rented dwellings have rents only about 70 per cent as great as public authority dwellings, most of the former were built before 1919 and most of the latter after that date (39). Moreover, the standard of fitness and facilities provided in private sector dwellings is much less than in the public sector. The median income of households in private rented dwellings is about a sixth less than that of households in public rented dwellings (49).

HOUSING FOR SALE

Generally, the market for dwellings for sale is a competitive one in which prices broadly reflect the supply and demand for dwellings of the available size, quality and location, although the overall level of prices is likely to be influenced by the availability of alternative subsidized or rent controlled dwellings. The amount of housing which can be built for sale is limited by the availability both of land for which planning permission can be obtained and of finance. It is not clear if there is a universal shortage of land for which planning permission can be obtained for housing development, but there is certainly a shortage in some areas, particularly in and around the conurbations in the South East and the Midlands. Periodic limitations on the amount of capital available for financing mortgages stem from the inability of building societies and other mortgage financing institutions to attract funds in competition with other forms of saving. The shortage can usually be corrected by offering more attractive rates of interest. On the other hand, the number of households able and willing to buy houses is limited, partly by poverty, partly by a reluctance to use their income in this way, and partly because the financial arrangements involved in borrowing for house purchase are often particularly onerous.

Finance houses advancing money for house purchase naturally wish to safeguard themselves against losses. This they do in two ways: first by lending only a portion of the value of the dwelling, usually 80 to 90 per cent; and secondly by limiting the period of the loan, not only to one considerably shorter than the likely life of the dwelling, but also often considerably shorter than the expected, earning life remaining to the borrower. As a result, the borrower needs to raise a substantial amount of money to meet that part of the purchase price not covered by the loan. The need to meet part of the capital cost from the borrower's own resources is particularly difficult for someone purchasing a dwelling for the first time. Moreover, the burden of the annual repayment is usually greatest during the first years, when incomes tend to be at their lowest and outgoings at their highest.[1] The burden tends to fall as the borrower's income rises with increases in age and experience, and with inflation. For example, with an average annual rate of inflation of many incomes of about 3 per cent, a mortgage payment which initially represents 25 per cent of an income would represent only half this proportion by the end of twenty-five years. The number of potential purchasers of housing could therefore be increased considerably if mortgage payments could be related more closely to the probable incomes of the borrowers over the period of repayment. Such arrangements as loans for the whole of the purchase price, repayment periods extended over the working life of the purchaser, payments limited to interest in the early years, and tax or tax-equivalent rebates on interest, all tend to bring payments and income into a better relationship. It is likely that once housing users become accustomed to a certain standard of housing they would be prepared to increase their expenditure on housing, even at the cost of other goods and services, in order to retain that standard. Some form of short-term subsidy is, therefore, more likely to stimulate the demand for housing of an increased standard than one spread over a long period. In the case of the usual type of building society mortgage with equal payments of capital and interest, rebates on interest have this type of effect.

Clearly the longer the period of a loan, the greater the proportion of the value which is lent and the more slowly the capital is repaid, the greater is the lender's risk from default. Nationally, however, the risks would be small, and could easily be covered by some form of insurance. It might be difficult under present arrangements to satisfy a demand for considerably more finance for house purchase without an increase in the rate of interest to stimulate more savings, and to attract savings from other types of investment. In so far as new arrangements shifted purchasing power from consumer durables, the savings formerly providing credit for these might then become available to lend for housing.

Since the difficulty in obtaining money for house purchase is particularly great for the first dwelling purchased, special schemes to attract young people might be worth considering. A capital grant related to savings might be offered to people entering a savings scheme related to subsequent house purchase. This might tap pre-marriage affluence, and both stimulate saving and funds available for house purchase and ease the burden of house purchase on marriage.

While a rise in the rate of interest would increase the payments which the borrower would need to make, the real costs of borrowing have in the past been small as a result of inflation. The price of even the cheapest dwellings has

[1] While the size of the annual repayment declines with the length of the repayment period, the rate at which it falls declines rapidly as the period is increased.

been rising at 5 or 6 per cent per year for some time (93). With tax rebates, or subsidies in lieu, equivalent to about 3 per cent, even a rate of interest of 7 or 8 per cent involves little or no real cost to the house purchaser.

The owner-occupier has more incentive than the tenant to maintain his dwelling in good condition, since failure to do this is likely to be reflected in the price the property will eventually fetch, as well as in the value enjoyed throughout occupation. The government improvement grants are very favourable to owner-occupiers, enabling them to obtain improvements often at no more than half their cost. Difficulties arise both where the cost of arrears of maintenance (not allowable for grants) is high, and where the owner does not possess, and perhaps cannot borrow, the capital required. Owner-occupied housing also carries difficulties on transfer as compared with rented houses: the cost of selling one house and purchasing another, in terms of agent's and solicitor's fees and legal duties, can be substantial. It is doubtful, however, whether owner-occupiers are any less mobile than households occupying rented dwellings. Households occupying dwellings with rents below the economic level cannot easily arrange an exchange with another household in a similar situation.

THE COST OF HOUSING TO OCCUPIERS

The cost of housing to the occupiers is met through mortgage payments, through the sacrifice of interest which might otherwise be earned on the money tied up in a dwelling, and through payments for maintenance and other servicing costs, or alternatively through rents. Since local authority revenue is largely raised in the form of rates, broadly proportional to the size and quality of the dwelling and the value of its site, rates are regarded as part, and a sizeable part, of the costs of a dwelling. Most occupiers see their housing costs as an annual expenditure, the capital being provided either by private investors through mortgage loans, or in the form of property for rent, or publicly through the provision of rented accommodation.

The annual costs of housing represent over a tenth of consumers' expenditure, and nearly a sixth if the costs of fuel and light are included. Generally the poorest households cannot afford to meet the economic costs of a minimum standard of housing. In the absence of housing either at subsidized rents or rents held below the market level by government controls, they could afford only substandard accommodation. Such housing frequently offers the lowest value for money. It is for these reasons that governments initially intervene in the workings of the market. However, there is no absolute minimum standard. The acceptable standard is a matter of judgment. Clearly, the higher it is fixed, the more households there are likely to need special treatment.

Housing competes with other consumer goods and services, so that the higher the level of preferences for other goods and services the less the income likely to be available for housing. Thus, even households with incomes judged adequate may not feel able to afford the economic cost of housing of a minimum standard. It can be argued that in this situation there is no case for government intervention to improve the standard of housing, since the household has an adequate income to secure at least the minimum standard but prefers to spend its money on other goods and services. This argument, however, is not valid if there are external diseconomies of consumption: that is if substandard housing and overcrowding affect adversely other people besides those living in the overcrowded dwellings. In this case the community may wish to enforce minimum standards. In fact this has been normal practice for many years in most western countries. The higher these minimum standards are set, the more households will need to change their demand schedules for other goods and services unless the government is prepared to intervene in the market on their behalf.

However, the effect of government intervention in the housing market in the past has not been altogether satisfactory. It has not ensured either an adequate number of dwellings or dwellings of an adequate standard, and it has not prevented the deterioration of a substantial part of the existing stock. Neither the control of rents nor the subsidizing of dwellings has been altogether successful in helping those most in need. Moreover, government policy has created the need for a substantial amount of public borrowing which has tended to increase financial difficulties. It appears likely that considerable changes in public policy and private attitudes will be necessary if a more economic housing solution is to be obtained, and if the standard of housing is to be raised in accordance with the alternatives suggested in this study. Before such changes can be considered it is necessary to examine how the cost of housing is affected by factors which can be subject to government influence.

THE EFFECT OF TAXATION AND SUBSIDIES ON HOUSING COSTS

While the costs of constructing and maintaining housing are affected in various ways by the incidence of taxation on the factors of production (materials, components and labour), the only tax levied directly on housing is local rates. These form a substantial proportion of housing costs: one third in England and Wales and a half in Scotland (48). Since, moreover, they are related directly to the amenity offered by the housing, they tend to be a disincentive to improving housing standards. In the past, this form of taxation has been favoured as being broadly related to capacity to pay and unavoidable without leaving the district. The tax is, however, unrelated to the services provided by the local authority or to the authority's needs and no longer bears much relationship to the capacity to pay. Its virtues have now largely disappeared, partly because a substantial proportion of local authority revenue is now provided by the Exchequer and partly because, with the growth in the ownership of other consumer goods and the consumption of services, the dwelling no longer provides a very good indicator of taxable capacity.

Until recently owner-occupiers were required to pay income tax on the imputed value of their dwelling under Schedule A. The logic of this was that the ownership of the dwelling provided an element of income, which would have otherwise been obtained by investing the capital value of the dwelling and would then have been subject to tax. The property tax thus did something to put owner-occupiers and those renting housing on an equal footing. It would be equally logical to impute an income from other durable goods, many of which can already be rented as an alternative to purchase. The property tax naturally had the same kind of disincentive effect on housing quality as local rates.

The incidence of tax must, of course, be considered as a whole. While tax might appear to bear heavily on housing, it might be even greater on other consumer expenditure. But this was certainly not true in 1963, when taxation on housing was about 50 per cent greater than on other goods (94).

There would appear to be considerable confusion about the effect of personal taxation (income and surtax) on housing costs. It is seen that taxpayers can apparently reduce their tax bill by borrowing capital to purchase housing and, that the higher the marginal rate of taxation, the more tax saved. This is frequently described as a subsidy to housing although it involves no actual transfer of money from one group of people to another. The confusion arises from looking at one part of the tax process in isolation from the rest.

Personal taxation is not a satisfactory medium for changing the incidence of housing costs because the effect depends to such a large extent on the rate of tax which is paid. The strength of this objection would be less in the case of depreciation allowances to the owners of housing for rent, since most would pay tax at about the same rate, and the action of the market would tend to reduce rents in a uniform way.

Owner-occupiers can be given direct subsidies, as they are by the Option Mortgage Scheme. By insisting that the option must be selected for the whole period of the mortgage, the government has limited the subsidy not only to those with very low incomes but also to those with no great expectation of any substantial improvement in earning capacity. Even so, the value of the subsidy is less than that provided for public authority housing (appendix 13).

Whereas taxation and the Option Mortgage Scheme relate to individual households, Exchequer housing subsidies are paid to housing authorities and bear no direct relationship to the needs of individual households. The incidence on households depends on the balance of dwellings built at different periods by the authority, the authority's rate contribution and its method of fixing rents. In addition, all households can obtain assistance from the National Assistance Board (now the Supplementary Benefits Commission). These benefits are, of course, related to need.

The Exchequer also provides improvement grants to aid owners of both public and private housing. As explained earlier, these are of considerable financial value to owner-occupiers and to public authorities, but of little value to owners of rented housing. The maximum amount of these grants has not been increased for some years and their value is now relatively less than subsidies on new dwellings.

THE EFFECT OF INFLATION ON HOUSING COSTS

The effect of inflation is to reduce the real cost of interest paid on loans or lost on money which, if not used for purchasing real assets, would have been lent. Such benefits may, however, be offset by the addition of a premium to the pure rate of interest to cover the losses from inflation which would otherwise be suffered by the lender. The gain to the purchaser of housing as a result of inflation may be no greater or less than could have been obtained by the purchase of some other real asset. The exclusion from the capital gains tax of capital gains on the dwelling occupied increases its value to the owner-occupier. Thus while the gains from house purchase for occupation to owners with other real assets are uncertain, most other owner-occupiers will obtain some gains as the result of inflation.

Rents are usually difficult to increase and tend to lag behind falls in the value of money. In so far as probable future inflation is not anticipated in fixing rents, occupiers of rented housing tend to obtain some benefit from inflation at the expense of the owners. In the case of public authority housing, rents depend on the authority's outgoings. Since the interest and repayment charges for dwellings already constructed do not rise as the value of money falls, the tenants as a body tend to gain as a result of inflation.

INCOMES AND HOUSING COST

Another factor which affects the standard of housing bought is, of course, the relation between incomes and housing costs.

Some idea of the proportion of households which could afford adequate housing can be obtained by comparing household incomes with the economic costs of dwellings. For example, just over 30 per cent of households would need to spend more than 30 per cent of the income of the head of the household to meet the annual economic costs of a Parker Morris standard, five bedspace house, even with allowance for the current level of Exchequer subsidies (fig. 15.1A). About 60 per cent would have to spend over 30 per cent of the income of the head of the household with a thirty-year mortgage under an Option Mortgage Scheme contract. A doubling of the period of repayment to sixty years would reduce annual costs by about a sixth, and hence substantially reduce the proportion of households who would need to spend 30 per cent or more of the income of the head of the household. The proportion would increase as the rate of interest rose and the period of loan was shortened, but would fall where it was possible to offset tax savings.

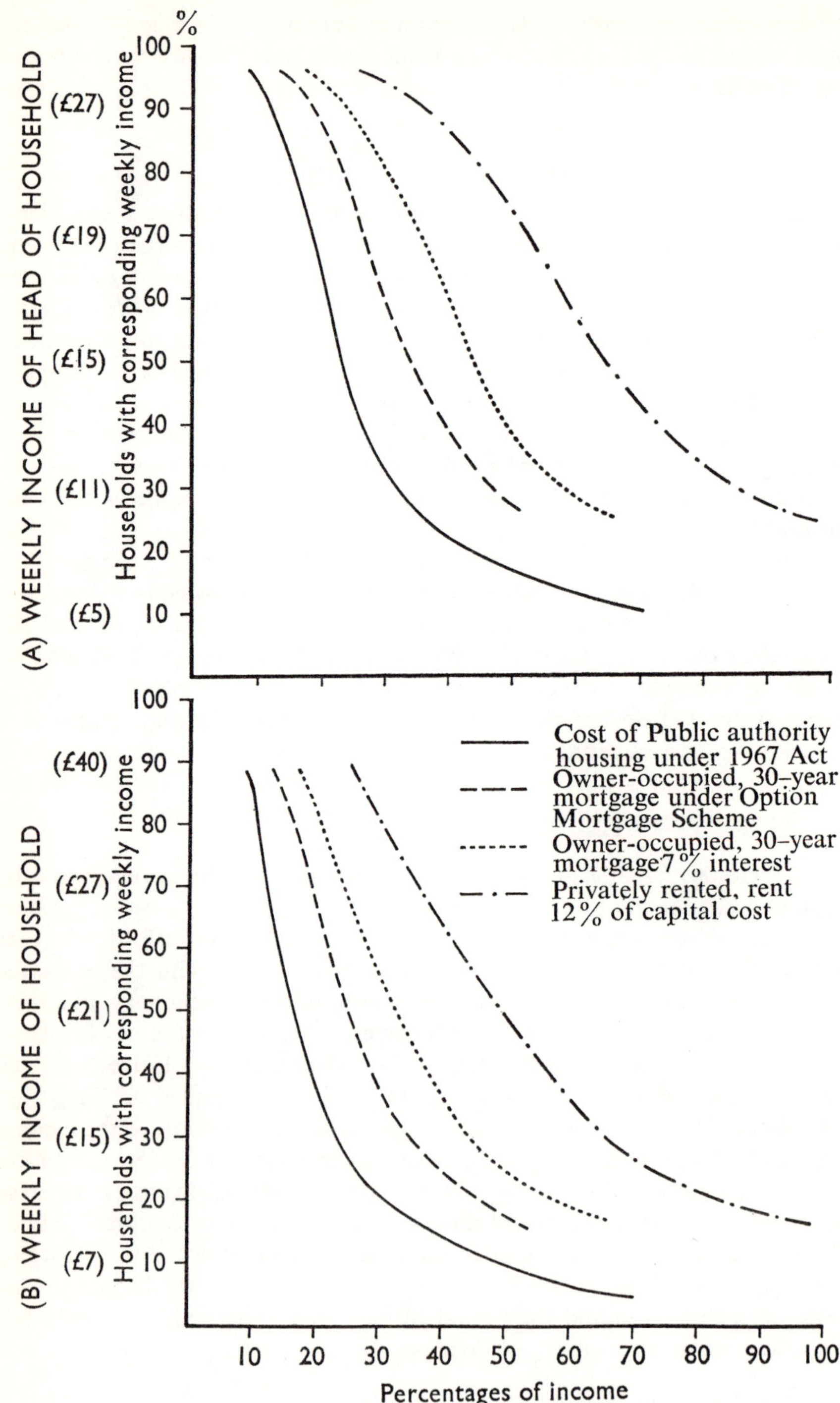

SOURCES: *Family Expenditure Survey, 1964* (71); NIESR estimates.

Fig. 15.1. Annual economic cost of a five bedspace Parker Morris house as a percentage of income

If total household income is taken into account the proportion of households needing to spend 30 per cent or more of income on housing naturally falls (fig. 15.1B). There would still be 20 per cent of households needing to spend at least 30 per cent of total income on housing, even if it were subsidized local authority housing. On this basis, nearly two-thirds of households earn sufficient to cover the purchase of a dwelling without exceeding an outlay of 30 per cent of household income on the basis of the Option Mortgage Scheme and a thirty-year period of repayment. There would still, however, be only 20 per cent who would need to spend less than 30 per cent of income to meet a 12 per cent rent.

Of course, every household does not require a five bedspace dwelling; a few require a larger dwelling, while many would find a smaller one satisfactory. For example, in 1964 practically all households with a household income of less than £5 a week consisted of one person, this group constituting two-thirds of households with combined incomes of less than £10 a week, with the balance almost all two person households. About three-quarters of households with a total weekly income of less than £15 were also in these two classes. The weekly cost for housing would be about 25 per cent less for a two bedspace dwelling than for a five bedspace dwelling; a one bedspace dwelling would be a little cheaper still. Thus, probably not more than about 10 per cent of households have total incomes less than three and a third times the annual cost of an appropriate dwelling.

The figure of 30 per cent of income has been taken only as a convenient level for comparison. In present circumstances it would be a very high proportion; currently rent is, on average, only equivalent to about 12 per cent of the income of the head of the household and 8 per cent of household income (49). Only households with a high level of income would be expected to devote as much as 30 per cent to housing. The basic cost of living cannot be reduced in proportion to income, and hence the lower the income the less of it can be spared for housing. The proportion which would be acceptable for housing expenditure depends not only on the level of income, but also on what expenditure is deemed essential; this in turn depends on the real costs of various types of goods and services, and these will change over time. It is likely that the real costs of housing will rise in relation to the real costs of other goods, and hence that the proportion of income spent on housing will rise (chapter 14).

The relationship between the proportion of households and the percentage of income they need to spend to meet the economic costs of a standard Parker Morris, five bedspace house is very sensitive to the level of income. For example, if 20 per cent of households needed to spend more than 30 per cent of income to cover the cost of a subsidized local authority house, nearly 40 per cent of households would need to spend over 20 per cent of income. Similarly, the percentage in the case of a dwelling purchased under the Option Mortgage Scheme would be increased from about a third to two-thirds.

It is clear that unless real income rose substantially there would be an appreciable proportion of households with incomes insufficient to meet the costs of minimum standard housing even with the aid of subsidies at the current level. It follows that there would not be sufficient effective demand for housing of the standard costed in this study.

SUBSIDIES AND MINIMUM STANDARD HOUSING

In fact the actual rents now paid are substantially lower than the economic rents considered above (fig. 15.1). The rents of privately let dwellings are about equal to gross value, those of public dwellings are about 10 per cent less (49). The gross value information (appendix 7) suggested that gross values of postwar public authority housing were about half the economic rents, that is the rents necessary on a replacement basis. If these relationships apply generally, they imply that the revenue from rented housing is nearly £700 million less than would be necessary to cover its replacement. About £100 million of the shortfall consists of subsidies from the Exchequer and rate funds; about £325 million represents the shortfall between the housing authorities' loan charges and the current replacement costs of the real capital. The shortfall between rent revenue and replacement costs for private rented housing is probably about £250 million. These figures ignore the effect of taxation. On the one hand, the owners of rented property are paying tax on money that should be set aside to replace their capital, while on the other, people buying dwellings through loans not offset by other investment are thereby saving tax, although probably at a lower rate than owners of rented housing are paying. The two effects may offset each other. Private purchasers also repay loans in a depreciated currency: at a 3 per cent rate of depreciation this would be worth about £200 million, perhaps half of which may be offset by higher interest rates. Thus the extent to which the economic costs of housing are not borne by the users may be of the order of £800 million a year out of a total of about £3,000 million. If this money were to be applied to help the poorer households, while other households paid full economic rents, none would need to spend more than about an eighth of their household income on rents.

The replacement of the worst of the present stock and the improvement of the rest, together with adequate regular maintenance, would probably raise the annual economic costs by about two-thirds. If no household were to be required to pay more than 30 per cent of its income on rent, housing grants to the poorer households of about £700 million a year would be required; about £1,000 million would be required if the limit was 25 per cent, and about £1,300 million if it was 20 per cent. If public authority housing were let at economic replacement rents, there would be a surplus, in which is included current housing subsidies, of about £425 million (1964). If economic rents and interest rates were paid, the yield from taxes would be greater than today and would provide a basis for paying additional housing grants. In fact, housing subsidies have been increasing at more than £10 million a year for some years and will probably increase even more in 1968 as a result of the 1967 Act. Since the replacement and improvement of the existing stock of housing is likely to take many years, the surplus on the public housing account mentioned above could easily be as much as £700 million a year by the time the work was completed, enough to limit the percentage of household income on rent to a maximum of 30. A doubling of the rate at which housing subsidies are increasing would enable the maximum proportion of household income spent on rent to be limited to 25 per cent. Clearly the cost would fall if real incomes rose.

Thus, at present levels of income, many households might be reluctant to spend a sufficient proportion of their incomes on housing to secure the minimum standard considered in this study. The proportional costs of housing would fall as real income levels rose: if real incomes rose at 3 per cent a year they would double in 24 years' time. In these circumstances the maximum proportion of household income to be spent on housing need not be more than about an eighth, even if housing grants absorbed only the present proportion of national income devoted directly and indirectly to subsidizing public housing. It would then be sufficient to follow the logic of the fair rents policy and allow rents to rise gradually to economic levels both in the public and private sectors. The public housing authorities could be empowered to use the surplus on their housing accounts to finance housing grants to households in need whatever the type of housing occupied. Exchequer subsidies could be reorganized and supplemented to subsidize those authorities whose surpluses on housing were insufficient to meet grants needed in their areas. The additional cost could be met largely from additional tax revenue arising from higher payments for private housing and from savings in supplementary benefits on the ending of supplements for rents. The economic rents for privately owned dwellings would not need to be higher than for publicly owned ones if depreciation could be set off against income for tax purposes. In view of past government interventions in the housing market it is, perhaps, doubtful if much new private money would be put into housing for letting without some government assurances about future conditions.

In the past, the idea of housing grants to households has been rejected because of the fear that they might lead to higher prices for accommodation or to lower wages. This risk would be much smaller if they were introduced when the supply and demand for housing were broadly in balance. Moreover, since the grant would depend on personal circumstances at any particular time, there would be no easily identifiable class of recipient.

Since grants towards rents are already paid by the Supplementary Benefits Commission and the need for them arises simply as one part of general poverty, it might be thought easier to include the payment of housing grants in supplementary benefits and make the Commission responsible for such payments.

However, if rents were allowed to rise to economic levels there would be considerable surpluses in most public authority housing accounts. It might be more difficult to transfer such surpluses to the Exchequer than to arrange for local authorities to distribute them to households in need in their area.

THE LEVEL OF HOUSING STANDARDS AND ITS SUPPORT

While such measures could prevent hardship arising from a housing standard fixed higher than the poorest households could afford, and presumably would ensure that those households receiving benefits secured dwellings at the minimum standard, such measures do not ensure that other households have housing at or above the minimum standard. Up to a point, standards can be enforced by means of regulations, but their drafting and enforcement become difficult as standards increase. In the long run standards will rise only as the values attributed to housing rise and comparative costs fall.

The values attributed to housing may rise as appetites for other goods and services are satiated and, perhaps, as increasing leisure leaves more time to be spent at home. The more society tends to become family orientated, the more value is likely to be placed on the amenity provided by the dwelling. This tendency could be encouraged, if required, by propaganda and, perhaps more usefully, by ensuring a high standard of amenity within the housing areas. If the environment of dwellings is well maintained and free from disfigurement and dirt, householders will be encouraged to maintain a high standard of internal environment.

Housing costs could be lowered in comparison with other costs partly by tax concessions and grants, and partly by taxing other goods and services. As suggested earlier, comparative housing costs could be considerably reduced by transferring local taxation from rating to taxes on other goods and services. Personal tax allowances are too dependent on the occupier's income to provide a reliable incentive towards increased expenditure on housing. Nevertheless, the ability to offset interest on loans against income provides an incentive to house purchase, since it is comparatively the most valuable at the time of the first purchase of housing, when the incentive is likely to have its greatest effect. In a market in which supply and demand are in balance, housing costs are also likely to fall if taxes on the factors of production and on land are lowered, if subsidies are provided or if interest rates are lowered. Grants for the improvement of dwellings are also likely to have this effect.

Owner-occupation would be encouraged if annual costs were lower, loans more freely available, and administrative and legal procedures simpler. Annual costs could be reduced by spreading repayments over longer periods and by reducing legal charges. Legal work and costs could be reduced by a simple system of property registration through a central organization. A large proportion of dwellings are mortgaged to building societies and other mortgage institutions: if they were to set up a clearing arrangement with access to each other's papers the legal and other formalities could be greatly reduced. Similarly, the introduction of sellers to buyers could be operated simply and cheaply through a computer-based register of those with dwellings to sell and those wishing to purchase. If a professional report was available on the condition and value of each property offered, and a simple system of property registration was available, further professional assistance might not be necessary.

Of course, if real incomes rose, more money would be likely to be spent on housing and the standards of housing would rise. Under these circumstances the standards acceptable as minimum today might cease to be considered adequate. There would once again be the problem of financing an adequate minimum standard of housing for the poorer households. There would appear to be no final solution other than large subsidies or raising the relative level of the real incomes of the poorer part of the population.

THE ORGANIZATION OF HOUSING

The form of organization for housing depends to a large extent on the way housing is financed. If local authorities performed their housing welfare functions through the payment of housing grants, they would not necessarily need to provide rented housing. A small stock of dwellings for socially difficult households might be all that was necessary. There would be no need for housing for rent to be supplied exclusively by the commercial sector; housing associations of many types could be developed. Different types of organization competing in the same market would help to set high standards of quality and efficiency. While the formation of larger local authorities would remove some of the technical objections to local authorities as large-scale owners of housing, it still might be preferable, if a large publicly controlled sector was required, to institute some other form of organization less involved in politics and able to obtain capital from the market.

The problem of handling existing areas of housing is different from that of additions to the stock, and more complex. Given that steps were taken to ensure that households had adequate means to obtain housing of an acceptable standard, and that there was no shortage of housing, dwellings of an inadequate standard could be closed under building and health regulations. Such closures would tend to be spread widely over a housing area, and often it would be many years before substantially all the dwellings had been closed. Large areas of housing would tend to become blighted for long periods as decay gradually spread. In order to obtain an area large enough to develop successfully, it may often be necessary to include in the purchase some sound property, thus tending to raise the cost of land above the cost of virgin land at the periphery of the town. Unless the area of redevelopment is adjacent to an area with a good infrastructure, the prices which can be commanded after redevelopment will be low.

Thus, except in fashionable areas, there will be little incentive to redevelop areas of decaying housing until the decay of dwellings is far advanced. Socially this is clearly undesirable.

One method of approaching this problem would be to restrict the land available for housing development to the point at which site prices rose, so that it became worthwhile to purchase areas of old housing for redevelopment before decay had proceeded very far. Most areas of old housing are developed at high densities, and unless decay were widespread the price of virgin sites would need to be very high before it became worthwhile to redevelop old areas. In many cases the price of obtaining old housing areas, even 50 per cent derelict, would be double the current price of virgin sites. Such a policy, however, would result in an uneven spread of windfall gains and, even if these were taxed away, would still introduce distortions into the market and considerably increase the cost of housing.

Another method would be to provide grants or subsidies to cover the additional costs of acquiring land with some sound property. This is already the practice, in effect, in the case of local authority development. It has been suggested that the Land Commission might purchase such areas and sell them to developers at a competitive price, using the surpluses made on other transactions to finance this procedure. It would appear, however, that it will be many years before the Land Commission has sufficient funds to finance land transactions of this type on the scale required.

At an earlier stage in the cycle of a housing area many dwellings are economically worth repairing and upgrading. It was shown in an earlier chapter that even dwellings with considerable physical deterioration, and with a serious lack of basic services, are worth improving where there can be a moderate expectation of life.

The present system of improvement grants provides a substantial incentive to owner-occupiers to improve their dwellings, providing that the expectation of the life of the dwelling is reasonable, that the dwelling has been adequately maintained, that they can afford their share of the cost and that they are able to handle the problems arising in claiming a grant, in ordering the building work and in obtaining loans. Landlords cannot afford to improve, even with grants, unless either the expected life is very long, or they can depreciate their part of the expenditure against rents for tax purposes and obtain a rent return on money spent on necessary repairs. Again, for small landlords management and finance create problems. Tenants are not always willing to meet additional rents even where substantial improvements are provided; many could not afford the additional rents.

An adequate expectation of life depends on the policy for the housing area. The demand for dwellings in the area will only be sustained long enough to justify the expenditure on improvements if improvement is on a large scale, and if the environment and the local infra-structure is maintained at a reasonable standard. While owners of large blocks of housing may undertake improvement to the environment, improvement of the environment and infra-structure is in the main the responsibility of the local authority. As a first step, improvement might be stimulated if the local authority declared that the area would not be subject to a clearance order for a given number of years and that it was prepared to improve the environment. The provision of housing grants would enable more owner-occupiers to afford improvements to their property and enable more tenants to meet the rents of improved property. The problems of organizing grants, building work and finance, which create difficulties for many owners, could be overcome by building and other organizations providing these services for a fee. There is at least one contractor who undertakes all the organization and provides the finance for an inclusive charge payable monthly over a period of a year or two. Rather longer periods of repayment are necessary in many cases.

If many unimproved dwellings remain, and if improvements are not made to the environment and the infra-structure, the benefits from improvement of individual dwellings will be limited, the rate of decay of the area may not be arrested, and total clearance may occur before the cost of improvements has been recovered. Usually the original development was fairly uniform and the different types of houses in an area are few. Large potential economies are likely to be possible if all the dwellings and environment are improved in a single operation.

Improvement on a universal basis is usually difficult to achieve except on the basis of universal ownership. Some owners always tend to stay outside a voluntary scheme. Again, without some reserve powers, it is unlikely that a private developer, a housing association or even a local authority could unify the ownership of a sufficiently large block of property to obtain a viable improvement scheme. Given unified control and satisfactory financial arrangements, the form of organization is less material. A voluntary housing association, especially if closely associated with the owners and occupiers, might be able to carry out improvement with less friction than a public body. Moreover, it might be able to raise private finance and thus reduce the commitments of the public sector.

Housing improvement cannot be regarded as a once-only operation. Standards would fall if adequate maintenance were not provided. Even so, a point in time will usually arrive when the amenities provided by the housing will fall below the general level of requirement. The higher the minimum standard is pushed by regulation and housing grants, the more rapidly an area will become obsolete. If grants of public money are provided for housing improvement, especially when these are generous, an opportunity is provided for making terminal arrangements with the owners, so that when the area is economically ripe for redevelopment there will be no financial or legal hindrances to acquisition for this purpose. In the absence of such an arrangement the cycle of gradual and uneven decay might only start again in two or three decades' time. One consequence of the right to purchase leaseholds will be to increase the problems of dealing with areas of decaying housing.

Clearly it is necessary to consider not only the loss of potentially satisfactory dwellings if improvement is not undertaken, but the social miseries of living in an area of decay. An area of housing is only likely to be voluntarily renewed if the demand for accommodation in the area is sufficient to raise the price of potential sites by enough to offset the costs of purchasing the existing property and redeveloping. This is not likely to occur in areas from which population is migrating in large numbers. The higher the existing density, the greater are likely to be the costs of acquisition, but this may be associated with a higher than average level of demand. If people are not to live in decaying housing areas, these must either be purchased and redeveloped long before the entire stock becomes unfit, or improved so that satisfactory conditions can be provided until the area is ripe for demolition. The second solution will be preferable financially as well as in terms of resources.

It is not part of the purpose of this study to determine housing policy; rather it is to analyse the housing situation as a part of the need and supply of built environment. Unless some radical changes are made in the financial and fiscal policies relating to housing, it is most unlikely that even the minimum programmes analysed in this study will take place. While large numbers of public authority dwellings might be built if sufficient subsidies are made available, the decay of existing housing will not be arrested and the sum total of satisfactory dwellings may be less than it might have been had other policies been followed.

PART 5

HOUSING POLICIES

CHAPTER 16

PROGRAMMES AND PRIORITIES

NEW HOUSING

On the basis of the fitting standards provisionally accepted for study (chapter 5), it appeared that about 1,200,000 additional dwellings would be necessary during the first quinquennium to meet current shortfalls, and these have been added to about 600,000 dwellings expected to be needed to meet a rise in households due to an increase in population (chapter 11). Also an additional 340,000 dwellings would be needed in that quinquennium (chapter 6) to replace dwellings which were not worth repairing and improving. On this basis the total requirement during the first quinquennium amounted to about 2,100,000 dwellings. The estimates of new dwellings required in each of the three subsequent quinquennia amount to about 600,000 for additional households, and about 400,000 on average for replacements (chapter 11). It was not expected that fitting standards would increase as fast as these figures imply. A balance would therefore be available for vacancies and second dwellings.

These figures vary in a number of ways from those put forward by the Government White Paper (95) in 1965. The White Paper accepted initially a lower standard of fitting than that assumed in chapter 5, and assumed that household formation rates would rise more slowly. The two sets of assumptions produce similar results by 1979 (table 16.1). On the other hand, the estimate given in the White Paper of unfit dwellings not worth improving is much higher than that put forward in this study. It is not made clear how rapidly these are to be replaced, nor to what extent they are to be improved in the meantime. It would seem possible that about 400,000 dwellings might be completed in 1967/8. If the target of about 500,000 a year by 1970 were achieved, the output in 1968/9 might be about 450,000, giving about 2 million dwellings over the five years 1964–9. This would be nearly enough to meet the assumptions in this study, and, in terms of the White Paper, would give a reserve of 1,100,000 towards the shortage of 700,000 and the unfit dwellings estimated by the government at between 1 and 3 million (table 16.1). If 500,000 dwellings a year were built in subsequent years up to 1979, there would be 3 million excess dwellings on our assumptions and about 609,000 in excess of the maximum requirements given in the White Paper.[1] About a third of the additional 3 million dwellings over the requirements assumed here could be used if the object was to replace

[1] Recent estimates suggest that at the end of 1966 there were 16,043,000 dwellings in England and Wales (49) as against 15,457,000 households (96). This would give a surplus of nearly 600,000 dwellings, more if temporary dwellings were included, nearly 4 per cent of the stock for vacancies and second homes. The growth in households in the three subsequent quinquennia has been estimated at 651,000, 485,000 and 467,000 respectively (96). Thus, even after allowing for Scotland, 750,000 additional dwellings per quinquennium appears a generous figure. By the end of the period, 1981, the surplus of dwellings over households might be over a million.

the majority of pre-1941 rather than pre-1881 dwellings by the end of the period in 2004 (table 11.3).

Table 16.1. *Comparison of dwellings to be built in Great Britain, 1964–79*

Thousands

	Additional dwellings		Replacement dwellings		Total requirements		Possible
	NIESR	Government	NIESR	Government	NIESR	Government	output [a]
1964–9	1770	750	340	150	2110	900	2000
		+700 [b]		+1000–3000 [c]		+1700–3700	
		up to 1450		1150–3150		2600–4600	
1964–74	2340	1500	690	300	3030	1800	4500
		+700 [b]		+1000–3000 [c]		+1700–3700	
		up to 2200		1300–3300		3500–5500	
1964–79	2900	2250	1080	450	3980	2700	7000
		+700 [b]		+1000–3000 [c]		+1700–3700	
		up to 2950		1450–3450		4400–6400	

SOURCES: NIESR figures, table 11.3, p. 179; Government figures, *Housing Programme 1965 to 1970* (95).

[a] Progress April 1964 to March 1967, 1,050,000 (estimate); 400,000 in 1967/8; 450,000 in 1968/9; 500,000 a year thereafter.

[b] To overcome shortages.

[c] Range for replacement of unfit dwellings.

The difference between the figures in this study and those in the Government White Paper arises mainly from the priority given in the former to improving fitting standards as compared with the replacement of existing dwellings. As a result the stock of dwellings would grow much more rapidly in relation to construction on the basis of our assumptions than on those of the White Paper (table 16.2). The stock on the basis of our assumptions would, of course, be a little older than that on the basis of the government figures and, unless properly repaired and improved, it would be of a lower average standard.

The White Paper does not go beyond the suggestion of a figure of half a million dwellings a year by 1970, although there is a hint that a larger figure would subsequently be necessary. About 300,000 dwellings a year were constructed in Great Britain over the decade up to 1963. Output was then increased about 25 per cent to nearly 375,000 in 1964. Despite the target of half a million dwellings by 1970, output rose only marginally in 1965 and 1966. The number of dwellings started was also lower in 1965 and 1966, but rose steeply in 1967. However, it is unlikely that output could be pushed higher than 400,000 in the year 1967/8. On the basis of past experience it might, therefore, be possible to achieve 450,000 dwellings in 1968/9, and perhaps 500,000 in 1969/70 if sufficient resources were diverted from other work. Clearly the number could be absorbed either in increasing the stock of dwellings or in replacing the oldest and poorest of the existing stock.

Table 16.2. *Comparison of constructions and additions to stock of dwellings in Great Britain, 1964–79*

Thousands

	NIESR		Government	
	Construction	Addition to stock	Construction	Addition to stock
1964–9	2110	1770	2600–4600	750–1450
1964–74	3030	2340	3500–5500	1500–2200
1964–79	3980	2900	4400–6400	2250–2950

SOURCES: as table 16.1.

Similarly the White Paper (95) does not indicate over what period the replacement is expected to take place of the identified slums and the further 2 million dwellings thought not worth repairing. Presumably it would be hoped to replace them by about 1980. This would be possible if the target rate of half a million dwellings were maintained over that period. If this rate of building was achieved, 7 million dwellings would be built in the fifteen years 1964–79.

On the basis of the assumptions of the Registrars General, the estimate for additional dwellings over the period 1964–2004 is 6·77 million (table 11.3). The estimate of replacements to cover all but the best 5 per cent of pre-1881 dwellings, and dwellings unfit and not worth repairing (demolition programme A), is 4·61 million.[1] Thus the need over the twenty-five years 1979–2004 would be 4·38 million, an average of 175,200 dwellings a year. If the target for replacement by 2004 was taken to be pre-1921 dwellings (demolition programme B), the average construction required per year would be 287,200. Even if the replacement of pre-1941 dwellings (demolition programme C) was taken as the target, the average requirement would be only 451,200 dwellings per year. In fact 500,000 dwellings a year over this period could only be absorbed if birth rates increased substantially above current expectations, which now appears less likely, and if household formation rates, vacancies or second dwellings all increased and coincided with ambitious replacement targets. A combination of

[1] The 30,000 a year, 150,000 per quinquennium, shown in the White Paper and given in table 16.1, is to replace dwellings lost as a result of road and town development. It is likely that these will be, in the main, the older dwellings and hence in the long run would be part of the general replacement.

KEY

Supply, assuming 1,150,000 dwellings at 31.3.67 and—

A 400,000 built 1967/8, 450,000 built 1968/9, 500,000 a year thereafter.
B 400,000 built 1967/8, 450,000 a year thereafter.
C 400,000 a year built from 1.4.67.
D 375,000 a year built from 1.4.67.
E 300,000 a year built from 1.4.67.

Demand to meet:

1 Demographic changes (RG's birth rates).
2 1 and higher fitting standards.
3 2 and demolition programme A.
4 2 and demolition programme B.
5 2 and demolition programme C.

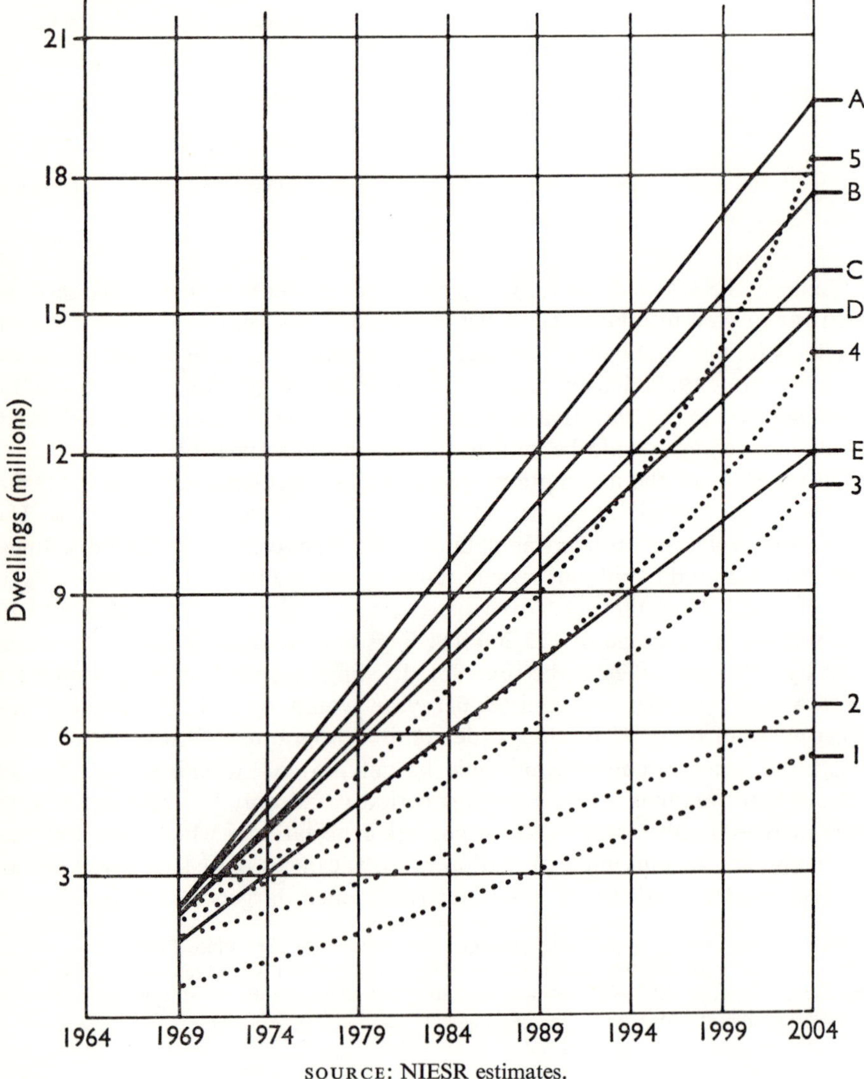

SOURCE: NIESR estimates.

Fig. 16.1. Supply of dwellings and demand for their construction, 1964–2004

these events is unlikely and an annual rate of output of 500,000 dwellings would in all probability need to be reduced sooner or later.

If the number of dwellings produced is likely to be much in excess of need in the long run, this should be considered in framing current policy. An annual output of 300,000 from 1967/8 to 2003/4 would be sufficient to meet the needs expected to arise on the basis of the current birth rate expectations and the need for replacements on demolition programme A, and would provide about three-quarters of a million dwellings to meet the need for vacancies and second dwellings (fig. 16.1). In fact, after about 1972, it would allow a much more rapid replacement of the stock than appeared likely when demolition programme A was determined.

An output of 375,000 dwellings a year from 1967/8 to 2003/4, that is a continuation at the 1964–6 levels of construction, would enable demolition programme B to be completed, again at faster rates than originally assumed, and provide a balance of something over three-quarters of a million dwellings for other purposes—for example, for 3 per cent of dwellings as a pool of vacancies. If output was increased to 450,000 dwellings a year from 1968/9 demolition programme C could almost be achieved.

Thus even ambitious targets could be achieved without raising annual output to half a million dwellings, and a continuation at the 1964–6 rate of output appears likely to produce sufficient dwellings for all purposes. The replacement of pre-1921 dwellings would reduce the average age of the stock to about thirty-five years by 2004. If, however, the rate of construction is not increased, the rate of replacing the stock will increase more slowly than might otherwise be possible. During the first five years it would be possible to provide enough dwellings to meet the expected rise in the number of households and the better fitting standards, and to replace two-fifths of the number of dwellings which in 1964 were estimated to have structural defects and be not worth repairing (table 16.3). During the next five years, 1969–74, the surplus over the dwellings required for additional households would be sufficient to replace all dwellings not worth repairing, and would, in fact, clear three-fifths of the dwellings estimated in 1964 to have some structural failures. Alternatively, the replacements could be considered as a third of pre-1881 dwellings. By the end of the third quinquennium all the dwellings estimated to have structural failures could be cleared and a substantial volume of those dwellings estimated as being in need of minor repairs; the rest could be cleared in the fourth quinquennium. Alternatively 90 per cent of pre-1881 or over a half of pre-1921 dwellings could be cleared by the end of 1984. The programme of replacement set out in the White Paper could be nearly half completed by 1974 and completed by 1984. This might, therefore, be considered a satisfactory rate of replacement if accompanied by improvements to stock. In practice it is unlikely that household formation would increase as fast as this in the early quinquennia, and a surplus would be available for vacancies and second dwellings. In later quinquennia

Table 16.3. *The consequences of stabilizing the output of dwellings in Great Britain*

	NIESR assumptions									Government White Paper		
				Alternative proportions of dwelling replacements								
	Cumulative output from 1964	Needed for additional dwellings[a]	Available for replacement[b]	Pre-1881	Pre-1921	Not worth repairing	With structural defects	All needing more than minor repairs	Needed for additional dwellings	Available for replacement	Proportion of total replacements
Position reached by:	*000s*	*000s*	*000s*	%	%	%	%	%	*000s*	*000s*	%
1969	1900	1770	130	3	2	39	5	3	1450	450	14
1974	3775	2340	1435	32	19	100	57	36	2200	1575	48
1979	5650	2900	2750	60	36	100	100	68	2950	2700	78
1984	7525	3510	4015	88	53	100	100	100	3600	3925	100
1989	9400	4270	5130	100	68	100	100	100	4350	5050	100
2004	15025	6770	8255	100	100	100	100	100	..	..	..

SOURCES: as table 16.1.

[a] On Registrars General's birth rate assumptions.

[b] If not required for vacancies and second dwellings, or higher rates of household formation.

such requirements could be met from a surplus to the requirements for replacement. Of course, in so far as demolitions for road and town development took sound dwellings of a low age, the demolition of other dwellings would need to be postponed.

If faster rates of improvement were required, the rate of building dwellings would need to be raised and subsequently reduced below the current level; if 500,000 a year were built over the period 1969/70 to 1979/80, only 175,000 a year would be necessary for the balance of the period 1964–2004 to achieve the replacement of pre-1881 dwellings, or 287,000 a year to replace pre-1921 dwellings. Thus the decline in construction would be large, and while the sharpness in the rate at which construction was cut back could be reduced by phasing it over a longer period, this would increase the eventual scale of cut-back.

While it is likely that any reduction in labour for house building, notably the less specialized labour, could be readily absorbed in other building, particularly if phased over a long period, it would probably be less easy to switch management, plant, and design and administrative expertise on a large scale without at least a temporary waste of resources. System building based on special formwork, on special precast concrete units, and on prefabricated units, especially where off-site factories are used, tends to be less flexible than the more traditional forms of building, even in its use of manpower, and would be difficult to convert to other uses without a waste of resources. It would seem to be especially important to determine the size and period over which a market for system building is likely to exist.

Again, while such basic materials as cement, sand and gravel are widely used in construction, other materials, for example, bricks and tiles, tend to be used to a large extent in house building only, and other building components are even more specialized in their use. This is particularly true in the case of components manufactured for building systems: often such components cannot be used beyond a narrow range of special designs without expensive modifications to the manufacturing process. Some building components are used in renewal and improvement work, for example, baths and other plumbing and heating components, electrical components, floor and wall finishes, doors, windows and joinery items. Hence, consideration is necessary of the joint demand for building materials and components. Ideally, if the best use is to be made of the existing stock of dwellings both physically and socially, improvement to the stock, and particularly making good the arrears of maintenance and upgrading, should take place over the next decade. If this occurred together with an expansion of new construction, the demand for a much greater volume of certain types of building components for upgrading would occur at the same time as a substantial growth of demand from an increased programme of construction.

The effect of building programmes on the construction industry needs consideration. It is not merely a problem of expansion within the required period, but also of whether demand is likely to be sustained at that level for a sufficient period to justify such a use of resources. If the period of additional demand is likely to be short in relation to the technological life of the plant and management required, the resources cannot be used economically and the supply may not be forthcoming. No useful estimate of demand for building components can be prepared until possible programmes of improvements have been formulated and accepted.

The study of possible programmes of dwelling construction indicates the existence of substantial present needs for dwellings, but future needs are relatively modest in relation to the supply facilities now being created. While, in the short run, further increases in the supply facilities are indicated, it would appear that needs are likely to be substantially less in a few years. The advantage of long-term stability in demand is likely to be considerable, and the best policy at present might be to maintain the current level of output until more is known of the ultimate level of replacement, of future fitting standards, and of future rates of birth.

COSTS OF HOUSE BUILDING

At 1964 prices the cost of new housing on the basis of our assumptions for the period 1964–9 would be about £6,600 million (chapter 12). At the current level of output this amount of new housing would take about six years to complete. It could be completed within the five years only if the real value of output during the last two years of the period was increased by about a half. On average during this period the estimated cost of dwelling, garage and development is about £3,150. Thus construction at the rate of 375,000 dwellings a year would cost about £1,181 million, which is somewhat more than this number of dwellings would have cost at 1964 prices, if constructed at the standards current at that time, that is before the acceptance of Parker Morris standards.

The average dwelling on the assumptions in this study differs from the average dwelling actually being constructed in a number of ways. On the one hand, it costs more because full Parker Morris standards and one garage on average for each dwelling has been assumed. On the other hand, it costs less because it was assumed that a smaller use would be made of high flatted blocks and of public authority housing. It is also likely that, in practice, changes in specification between going to tender and completion raise costs above the tender figure.

It is difficult to be certain about the value of the new housing work which has been carried out. No figures are published of the new housing output of the direct labour departments of local authorities and public boards. Figures are not published separately for the value of roads and public utilities and other housing estate development, and their incidence on other figures is uncertain. There is uncertainty as to the date of contract of the work carried out in particular quarters. The lack of confidence in current indices of price changes is commented upon further in appendix 12. However it would appear that the current annual output of housing as defined for the purposes of this study is worth about £1,100 million at 1964 prices.

A programme of 375,000 dwellings a year at our standards would, therefore, result in an increase in the value of output of about 7 per cent. Currently, only about two-fifths of public authority and two-thirds of private sector dwellings have garages, so that the average total cost per dwelling is about £100 less than it would be if garages were provided on a one to one basis as assumed in this study. At the present ratio of garage provision, about £38 million would be saved on the cost of 375,000 dwellings. Similarly, further reductions could be achieved by building below Parker Morris standards. Currently only about 60 per cent of local authority dwellings built in England and Wales have reached Parker Morris standards for space, and only about a quarter have reached these standards in all respects (49). Parker Morris standards have by no means been fully accepted in the private housing sector. While space standards cannot be easily rectified at a later date, the omission of components or finishes can usually be made good, although at an increased cost. A programme of 375,000 dwellings could, therefore, be provided for £1,100 million a year, the estimated current value of annual output; the balance of expenditure being held over to the future.

A rise in standards is not the only reason for a rise in real costs per dwelling. Costs will also tend to rise if the proportion of dwellings in high blocks is increased, if more use is made of system building, if the proportion of building in the more expensive regions rises, or if an attempt to increase the output of dwellings has an adverse effect on efficiency or on the prices of the factors of production. It appears unlikely that real costs would rise less than 2 per cent a year if Parker Morris standards were to be implemented in the near future. Consequently, even with optimistic assumptions for rises in productivity and the national labour force, the output of dwellings is unlikely to rise more than about 15,000 a year unless labour is transferred, either from other parts of the construction industry, or from other sectors of the economy. To achieve a steady rise in output to 500,000 dwellings a year by 1970 would require (assuming an increase in productivity of 4 per cent) an increase in the labour force for the new housing sector of about 3 to 4 per cent a year. This figure could be lower if the proportion of dwellings built by off-site factory methods (now very small) was substantially raised: in consequence, however, more labour would be used indirectly elsewhere in industry.

In 1963/4 an increase in the output of new housing of about 25 per cent at constant prices was achieved. This was about twice the increase achieved by the construction industry as a whole, and resulted in the proportion of total work in the new housing sector rising from 25 per cent to about 28 per cent. Much of this increase was at the expense of the maintenance sector. While there was some rise in the productivity of the construction industry, a large part of the increase in output was the result of an increase in the labour force. This appeared to be a favourable time for the construction industry to obtain labour, since there was a large pool of unemployed and most other industries were either reducing their labour forces or increasing them only marginally. Clearly, during a period when the national labour force is growing only slowly, the construction industry cannot increase its labour force substantially unless either productivity in other sectors increases substantially, or the community is prepared to reduce its relative consumption of other goods and services in favour of construction goods. Moreover, the amount of labour suitable for transfer to the construction industry is not unlimited.

Given favourable conditions, the labour force on new housing construction could probably be raised about 5 per cent a year for two or three years, but perhaps not for much longer. If the level of construction were to be maintained for some years, other building work and particularly maintenance and improvement work would need to be postponed on a substantial scale unless, of course, a reduction, or at least slower growth, was accepted in other sectors of the economy. The required level of construction could not, however, be achieved unless certain other conditions were satisfied. The output of building materials and components would need to be increased by about 8 per cent a year. While some materials for housing could be obtained by withdrawing supplies from other building sectors, this is not possible for all materials or for many components. It takes much longer to set up additional plant and train labour to produce building materials and components than to train semi-skilled and unskilled labour for building operations, although really skilled building labour for housing can only be obtained rapidly from other building work. A shortage of materials has usually occurred when output has been increased rapidly, and the time to complete construction has lengthened in consequence. Whether this would occur would depend on whether sufficient additional capacity is being developed. The supply of construction plant would be similarly affected. Contractors' engineering and management staff, design, legal and administrative staff cannot be trained in the time scale under consideration. Unless there is currently a large surplus of such people, considerable streamlining of procedures would be necessary, and this in itself takes time.

In the longer run Parker Morris standards are unlikely to be sufficient, and even more than one garage per dwelling on average may be required. As explained earlier in chapter 7, housing standards are a part, and an important part, of the standard of living and tend to rise in step with it. It would seem unlikely, perhaps, that housing standards will rise at a rate less than two-thirds of the rate of rise of general living standards. Unless efforts to improve productivity are very unsuccessful this would probably imply an average rise of about 2 per cent a year, more than doubling standards by the end of the period in 2004.

It is unlikely that increased productivity will be achieved in construction except as part of a wider movement in the levels of productivity in the economy as a whole. Generally, the greatest increases in productivity occur in the newest industries, and the smallest in long established industries such as construction.

It is therefore by no means unlikely that, in the long run, the rise in the standard of housing would absorb a large part of the rise in the productivity in housing work. If this occurred, an additional volume of housing would entail a proportional increase in the labour force. Since the increase in people of working age is unlikely to be more than about $\frac{3}{4}$ per cent a year on average, and the increase in the labour force, particularly males, is likely to be even less, any substantial rise in the volume of housing can only be achieved by withdrawing labour from other activities, unless population increases faster than expected—which would, in turn, increase the demand for housing.

In fact the load on the construction industry for housing would increase slightly more than in proportion to the rise in population. If the high assumption for population was fulfilled, the volume of work would be increased by about 10·5 per cent, given replacement of the pre-1881 dwellings (by less if replacements were at a greater rate), while the working population would increase only about 8·5 per cent. If population increased only in accordance with the low projection, the reduction in working population as compared with the Registrars General's basis would be about proportional to the reduction in the volume of housing work.

COSTS OF IMPROVING AND MAINTAINING THE HOUSING STOCK

It was estimated above that construction at the rate of 375,000 dwellings a year would, on the assumptions given, cost a minimum of £1,100 million. In order to achieve a volume of development at this figure, standards would need to be reduced below current best standards which have been accepted in this study. The saving achieved would be about £80 million a year, about half of which would be for garages. It will be assumed that this work would only be postponed and that it would be put in hand as soon as possible. The postponement does not reduce the load of housing work except in the short run: it creates a backlog of work to be performed in a later period. This work would probably be handled by the maintenance sector.

The maintenance sector deals not only with maintenance and repair work but with alterations, improvements and other small works. Its labour force has remained at much the same level for some years, productivity has increased only slightly, and hence there has been little increase in real output. The labour force declined in 1965 and real output declined absolutely, as well as relatively to the output of the new work sector. Because prices have risen faster in the maintenance sector than in the new work sector, the fall in real output in the former as compared with the latter is faster than is apparent from a comparison of the value of work done at current prices. Currently, output is worth about £350 million at 1964 price levels, which is only about 4 per cent of the estimated cost of repairing and improving dwellings and housing areas, and is less than half the estimated costs of adequate regular maintenance.

Improvement grants have been obtained for over 100,000 dwellings a year (49) and grants of nearly £20 million a year have been paid. Not all improvement work is grant aided. While the grants are financially attractive to owner-occupiers carrying out improvements, a good deal of administrative work is necessary to obtain them. Further, it is understood that some local authorities discourage improvement work, particularly in areas they hope to redevelop. Arrears of maintenance must be made good in order to obtain a grant but have not themselves been eligible for a grant. Thus while grants have been paid to up to 50 per cent of approved work, the total value of improvement work is likely to be more than twice the value of the grants. Further, over 100,000 dwellings which have been declared unfit are made fit each year (49). It is not known to what extent this group are grant aided. There may be considerable overlapping between the two groups. It would appear that something of the order of £60 million is spent each year on improvement work.

If this figure is accepted, the value of regular maintenance work would be about £290 million at 1964 prices. Of this amount probably £90 million represents the maintenance cost of local authority and new town housing, and the balance private housing. On these figures the average expenditure per dwelling is just over £17. Public authorities with the younger part of the stock spend more than this on their dwellings. Even so, they spend only about £6 a year on all decorations. The amounts spent on the renewal and improvement of fittings are also very small. Clearly, little can have been done to maintain a high standard of dwelling. Maintenance has been costed in this study at a rate which gives a figure of about £42 a year (prices for England and Wales excluding London) for a dwelling of average age, fifty-six years old. This, it will be recalled, sets the standard at that adopted by local authorities for repairs and renewals and at the standard of expenditure on decorations at the London local authority level, £15 a year. Obviously this amount is minimal and will be inadequate to support a high standard of maintenance. Even so, on this basis national expenditure would amount to about £850 million a year now, and would rise in the future. It was suggested in chapter 8 that, at most, a quarter of maintenance work might be carried out by the occupier, but that little of this would relate to the work costed in this study. Clearly, a great deal of work is already carried out by occupiers, and since the standards of maintenance costed are modest, it is likely that the aim of most of this is to provide a better standard, so that it would not reduce the load on the construction industry for basic work.

If, in the last three years, £180 million has been spent on improvements, this would reduce the cost of arrears of maintenance, renewals and decorations, and the provision of services and bathrooms, and of conversions, to about £4,700 million. In addition, expenditure of over £3,300 million is required for garages and £760 million for environmental improvement.

A considerable increase in the amount of maintenance work is necessary if arrears are to be made up in time to prevent further deterioration, and if the stock is subsequently to be properly maintained. Some resources might be created by stabilizing the output of new housing work at about the present level, 375,000 dwellings a year. If productivity per man-year continued to rise, the number of operatives on new work could be reduced. Labour thus released, together with new labour coming into the housing industry, could then be utilized for maintenance work. But the increase in the labour force for the maintenance sector obtained in this way is not likely to be very large; initially it might amount to perhaps 17,000 a year. The annual increase would fall in future as the size of the labour force remaining in new construction declined. The labour force in the housing sector is expected to decrease slightly in the near future as the number of people of working age declines (96). Subsequently it will increase, and over the next fifteen years the size of the working population will be affected by changes in activity rates rather than by birth rates, since the persons contributing to the working population are already born.

The increase in the output of maintenance work which might be made available will depend on the relative movements of productivity in the new and maintenance sectors, and on the hours of work. Productivity in the maintenance sector is likely to increase faster in future if the proportion of remedial repair work declines and that of renewal and improvement work rises, and it is likely to be higher if more improvement work can be organized on the basis of large housing areas rather than individual properties. At best, the average annual rate of increase in the real output of maintenance work is unlikely to exceed 10 per cent; it could be less than half this figure.

The provision of additional garages is probably the least urgent work. The most urgent is the arrears of maintenance, renewal and decoration, and with it the addition of missing services and the consequential formation of bathrooms. First priority should probably be given to improving the estimated 2·2 million dwellings needing structural repairs. Even if the £60 million a year already being spent on improvement work, together with the additional volume of maintenance work which could be obtained by holding the output of new work constant, was devoted to dealing with the dwellings needing structural repairs, their repairs and improvement might take about ten to twelve years (fig. 16.2). The work on the 1·5 million dwellings in a slightly better condition might take another two to three years, and so it might be about fourteen years before the dwellings in the poorest condition were made good. There would remain another four years' work on improvements to those dwellings requiring only limited repairs, and work on improving the amenities of other existing dwellings and the housing areas would take a year or two more. The last could, of course, be given greater priority, or it might be necessary to spread it over a longer period to allow more general maintenance work to be carried out.

Thus, on this programme, it would be at least the late 1970s before the poorest dwellings were repaired and improved, and much later before a start could be made on the work of bringing the amenities of the stock as a whole back

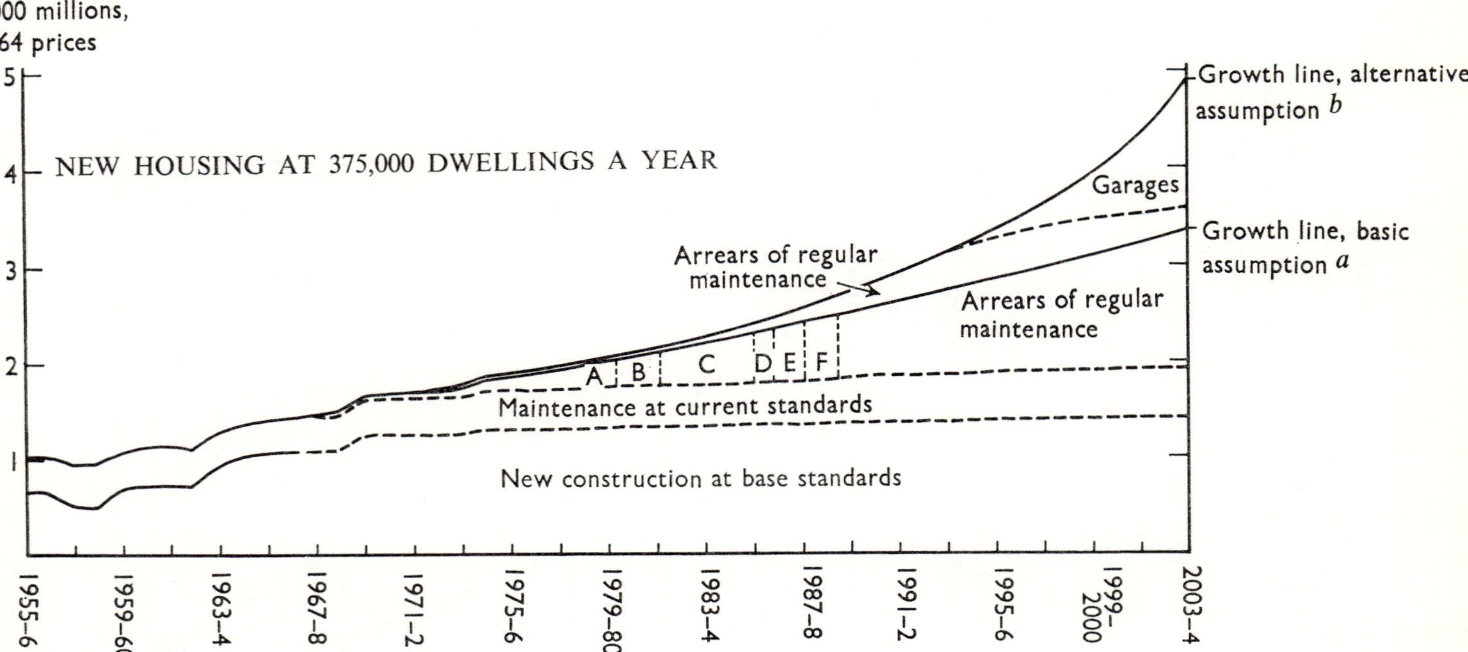
KEY
A Work to dwellings needing structural repair and improvement
B Work to dwellings needing substantial repair and improvement
C } Work to dwelling needing less serious repair and improvement
D }
E Work on improving housing areas
F Deferred work on standards of dwellings built in 1970s
£000 millions,
1964 prices
5
4
3
2
1
NEW HOUSING AT 375,000 DWELLINGS A YEAR
Growth line, alternative assumption b
Garages
Growth line, basic assumption a
Arrears of regular maintenance
Arrears of regular maintenance
A
B
C
D
E
F
Maintenance at current standards
New construction at base standards
1955–6
1959–60
1963–4
1967–8
1971–2
1975–6
1979–80
1983–4
1987–8
1991–2
1995–6
1999–2000
2003–4

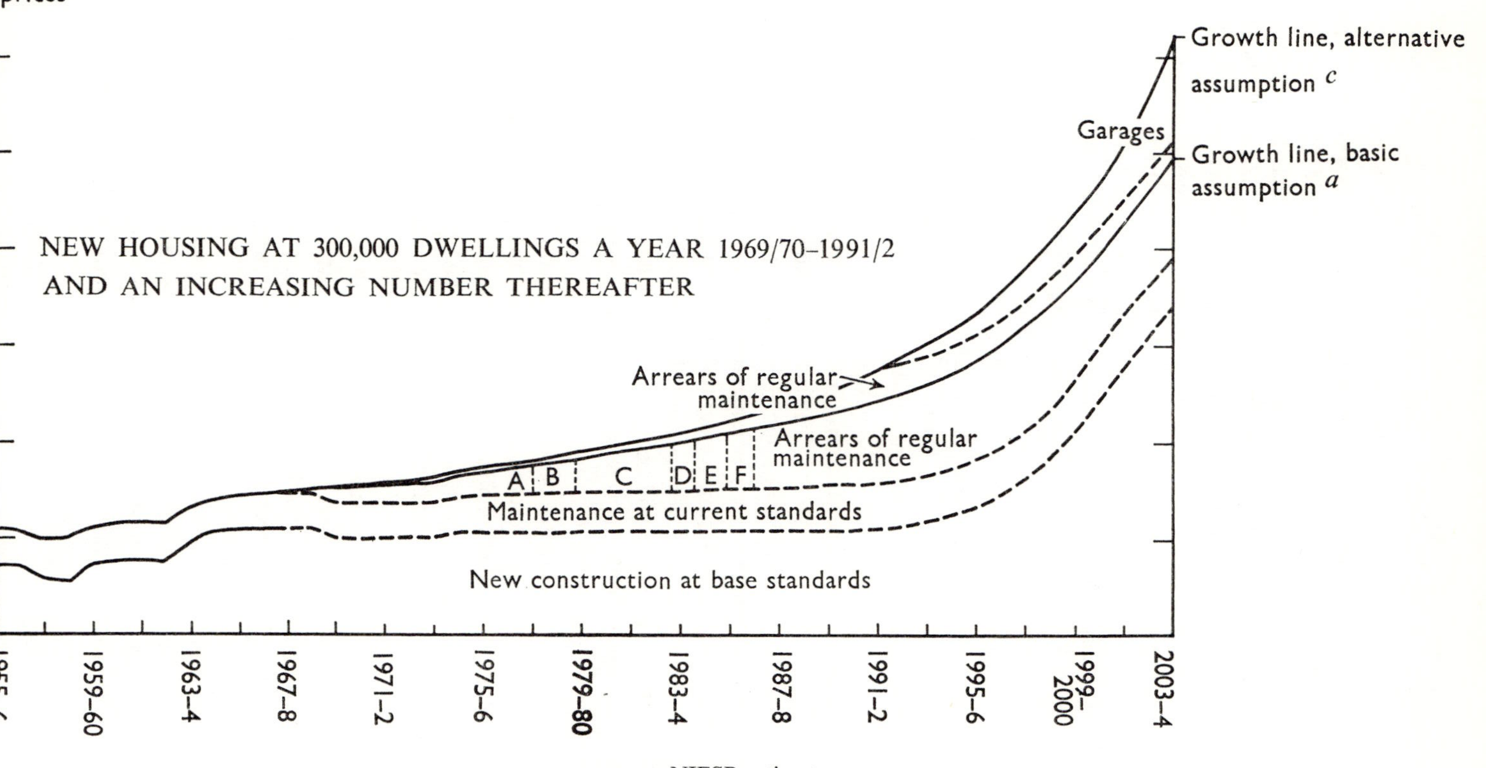

SOURCE: NIESR estimates.

a Assuming current proportion of labour force on housing with annual increase in productivity of 4% on new work and 2% on maintenance

b Assuming labour force on all housing increased initially by 1% and thereafter by $\frac{1}{7}$th of 1% a year

c Assuming labour force on all housing increased initially by 1% and thereafter by $\frac{1}{8}$th of 1% a year

Fig. 16.2. Housing output until 2003/4

to the current equivalent of their standards when they were new. In practice, far less would be achieved for the resources used. The classification of the stock by condition was based on a survey carried out in 1964. Since that date the real volume of maintenance work has declined, and it is probable that some of the dwellings classified as structurally unsound would no longer be economically worth improving. Further dwellings are likely to reach this condition during the decade while they await repair and improvement. If no additional resources are available for the other categories of dwellings for another decade, these too will deteriorate and become more expensive to improve.

Unless more resources than are available on this programme can be devoted to maintenance, the number of dwellings not worth improving will inevitably increase and the stock will deteriorate further. The costs of repairing and improving that part of the stock for which improvement is economically worthwhile will be increased, and the amenity level of the existing stock will fall. In the absence of a detailed study of the condition of the stock it is not possible to indicate with any accuracy the relative size of the changes.

The 2·2 million dwellings classified as needing structural repairs are likely to have large structural cracks, and movement of door and window frames (the frames may be split and largely devoid of paint). Tiles or slates may be missing and gullies and downpipes broken. Water may be entering the building and damaging timber and plasterwork. The worst of these dwellings are likely to have been condemned as unfit, although some may be economically worth repairing and improving if they have a reasonable expectation of life. If, as a result of the delay in repair and improvements, 5 per cent a year deteriorated to a point at which repair and improvement ceased to be economic—a not unlikely event—over 100,000 dwellings would be lost from the stock each year. This may already be occurring. It would represent an annual increase in the number of dwellings needing replacement without delay—an extra third on the rate at which unfit dwellings are currently being closed and demolished (49).

The number of dwellings not now economically worth improving is probably about half a million. The number officially declared unfit is probably twice as large (49); a recent official survey estimated that the number unfit is probably 1·8 million (95). The tests for unfitness are not, of course, economic tests; many dwellings which fail them are economically worth improving. The rigour with which tests are applied varies from one local authority to another. Authorities predisposed to improvement rather than total redevelopment tend to apply them less rigorously and with more imagination than those preferring total redevelopment. Detailed technical studies indicate that many dwellings classified as unfit are worth repair and improvement.

In practice it is unlikely that all the improvement expenditure would be used for the poorest dwellings, and hence unlikely that the dwellings with priority would be improved even as rapidly as indicated above. Consequently, the rate at which dwellings cease to be worth repairing and improving is likely to be greater than indicated. In turn the closure and abandonment rates are likely to increase.

Thus it would appear that, even in the short run, stabilizing output of new dwellings at 375,000 a year, reducing standards temporarily below full Parker Morris levels and stabilizing the proportion of dwellings with garage provision would not provide sufficient resources to raise the standards of the current stock faster than they are naturally declining. Moreover, the rate of improvement of the worst dwellings would be so slow that the rate at which they ceased to be suitable for habitation would probably exceed the rate of replacement in the early years. As a result, not only would the gap between the standards provided by new dwellings and existing dwellings widen, but in the short run the number of habitable rooms would probably decline.

In the long run, the resources assumed to be available would not be sufficient for the programme considered (fig. 16.2). It would not appear to be possible to complete the arrears of regular maintenance, nor to make good the backlog of garages, unless the labour force on housing work was increased more than in proportion to increases in the national labour force. Of course, much of the regular maintenance which was not carried out when it was required might never be carried out at all. While the resources required for structural repairs and preservation tend to increase if the repairs are not attended to, other maintenance —for example, much of renewals and decoration—represents an attempt to keep up standards. Postponement of such work results in a fall in the standards enjoyed (which represents a loss of satisfaction that cannot be made good by subsequent work) as well as in a saving in resources. Thus the increase in labour might not be as great as shown on fig. 16.2. Of course, further resources would be needed in so far as standards rose above those considered right at the base date of the study, 1964.

The scale of additional resources required to provide adequate maintenance and improvement of dwellings is too great to allow a rapid solution. The current shortfall in the amount of regular annual maintenance work, even in terms of the moderate standards accepted, represents about an eighth of the total output of the construction industry. The amount of urgent improvement work is ten times as great. To raise regular maintenance standards to the level suggested, and to clear the urgent improvement work even over a period of ten years, would require an additional annual rate of output of the order of £500 million, in addition to the anticipated increases from improvements in productivity and from the expected long-term natural increase in the labour force. This would imply an increase in the annual output of the construction industry of about an eighth, all of which would need to be devoted to housing maintenance. The increase in the labour force would be proportionally greater, since output per man is substantially lower on maintenance than on new work. Even so, no start would have been made on the backlog of garage provision. If the rate of construction of new dwellings was simultaneously raised to half a million, something in excess of £350 million would be added to the demand on the industry. Of course, in that case there would be sufficient dwellings each year to achieve a substantial reduction in the number of unfit dwellings.

Until the results of the non-residential studies have been completed the likely demands on the industry for this type of work cannot be assessed. Preliminary indications point to large backlogs of work for many types of buildings and works. It is most unlikely that, even if the resources for an expansion of the construction industry of this order could be found, more than a small proportion of the additional output could be used for housing maintenance.

The only alternative source of maintenance resources would appear to lie in a reduction of the output of new dwellings. If output, instead of being stabilized at 375,000 dwellings a year were temporarily reduced to 300,000, about £220 million of building resources a year would be released for maintenance work. A further £20–£30 million could be released by temporarily concentrating on the most economic forms of construction, one and two storey dwellings, and limiting the use of high blocks to situations where very high densities were imperative. A reduction in the number of dwellings constructed could only be implemented gradually and it might be 1969/70 before the number of completions was reduced to 300,000. If the labour thus released from new construction was used for maintenance work, the arrears of maintenance could be undertaken earlier, and an earlier start could be made on raising regular maintenance to an adequate standard (fig. 16.2).

A policy such as this would reduce the number of dwellings which deteriorated beyond the point at which they were not worth repairing and reduce the cost of making good arrears of maintenance. It would enable the stock of old dwellings to be put in a reasonable state of repair at an earlier date and increase the level of satisfactions they provided. Towards the end of the period the labour which became surplus to maintenance needs would be available for increasing the number of dwellings completed. In fact, the total number of dwellings which could be constructed with the identical labour force over the period to 2004 would not be any less, even although the number of constructions in the early years was lowered.

If the expectation that productivity in new work will rise faster than in maintenance work is realized, the greater the priority given to maintenance work in the early years and the greater the weight given to new work in the later years, the greater the total of work which can be achieved in the long run with the same labour force. Given the labour force and the rates of productivity assumed, that is 4 per cent for new work and 2 per cent for maintenance work, reducing new constructions from 375,000 dwellings to 300,000 a year during the early years would, even though the number built in the long run remained unchanged, reduce by about an eighth the extent to which the programme of work exceeded capacity, so that less additional labour would be required (fig. 16.2). If the number of dwellings built during the early years was reduced to 250,000 a year, the excess over capacity would be more than halved. It would only be possible to eliminate the excess of programmed work over capacity if, additionally, the number of dwellings constructed was reduced significantly below an average of 300,000 dwellings a year over the whole period. Since much of the regular maintenance not carried out when it is required will never be done, it appears probable that a programme of about 300,000 dwellings a year on average could be carried out, together with the maintenance work programmed, without increasing the proportion of the national labour force used on housing work.

While, in the short run, a lower rate of constructing new dwellings would result in a lower rate of replacing the existing stock of dwellings, this loss would be compensated for by the restoration of dwellings which might have been lost if the work were delayed further. Thus the total stock of habitable dwellings might be no less, even in the early years, than it would be if a greater proportion of the resources were devoted to new construction, and their general standard and level of amenity would be higher. During the early years the age of the stock would fall more slowly but, by 2004, the age of the stock would be lower, and it would thus be more likely to meet current needs than if a greater number of dwellings had been constructed from the beginning of the period.

Similarly, if sufficient additional labour could be found to sustain a programme of half a million new constructions, it would appear to be more economic to use the labour to increase the rate of dealing with the arrears of maintenance than to increase the rate of new construction.

Of course, the longer improvement work is delayed, the greater its real price will tend to be and the fewer the dwellings there will be which it is economically worthwhile to improve instead of replace. As a result the rate at which dwellings of an acceptable standard could be provided might be reduced.

COSTS OF RAISING THE GENERAL LEVEL OF HOUSING STANDARDS

The convenience of assuming constant general housing standards as a basis for preparing the projections was argued earlier. Up to this point the projections have been based on the assumption that, broadly, Parker Morris standards would be acceptable over the whole period under study. However, housing standards are an integral part of the general standards of living, and both would be expected to rise in step with the general level of productivity. Since there is also likely to be some relationship between increases in productivity in construction and in the economy as a whole, the growth in output expected from increases in productivity in construction will not be available to meet both the need for a greater volume of construction and a rising standard of construction.

Clearly it would be hazardous to try to predict the rate at which the general level of productivity will rise over a period as long as forty years. Usually the greatest increases in productivity occur in the newest industries, particularly in those which are developing from batch to mass production, and in those in which large economies can be obtained from increasing the scale of production. The improvement is, however, usually reduced by the slower rises of productivity in the service industries, where it is more difficult to save labour without reducing the quality of the service. It would seem unlikely that productivity in construction will rise faster than the level for the economy as a whole. Since it is expected (fig. 16.2) that all or more than all of the increase in output derived from increases in productivity in construction, and from an enlargement in the labour force proportional to the increase in the working population, will be absorbed in dealing with a greater volume of work, work arising from an uplift in standards will entail a further increase in the labour force. If, for instance, the increase in housing standards were to keep in step with rises in the general level of productivity and this were at the rate of about 3 per cent, the labour force in construction would need to increase at about this level over and above the rise expected from increases in the population of working age. How far housing standards rose would depend on the extent to which the community was prepared to lower its demand for other goods and services in favour of housing. Even a 2 per cent rise would more than double the proportion of the labour force in housing work over the forty-year period.

Housing already absorbs about a third of the output of the construction industry and could not be expanded to the extent indicated without substantial growth of the industry as a whole unless non-residential construction was substantially curtailed. Preliminary indications are that growth of needs for non-residential development might be on the same scale as for housing, so that there would be no spare capacity to move into the housing sector.

THE CONSEQUENCES FOR LABOUR AND MATERIALS

If the rates of increase in productivity are as great as has been assumed, that is 4 per cent and 2 per cent, the output per man-year would rise over a period of forty years by a factor of nearly 5 in the case of new work and over 2 in the case of maintenance work. The value of annual output per man is already twice as great in new work as in maintenance work, so that, by the end of the period, output in new work per man-year would be nearly five times that in maintenance work. As a result, whereas now there are over a third more workers on new housing work than on housing maintenance, by the end of the period the number on housing maintenance would be several times greater than on new work (fig. 16.3). The greater the number of constructions now rather than later, the greater the eventual proportion on maintenance work. The result of transferring labour from a sector of relatively high productivity to a sector of relatively low productivity with a lower rate of increase would be to depress the average increase in output per man-year. For some of the programmes of work examined, the combined average rise in productivity would be no greater than that expected for maintenance work, but as the comparative level of productivity in

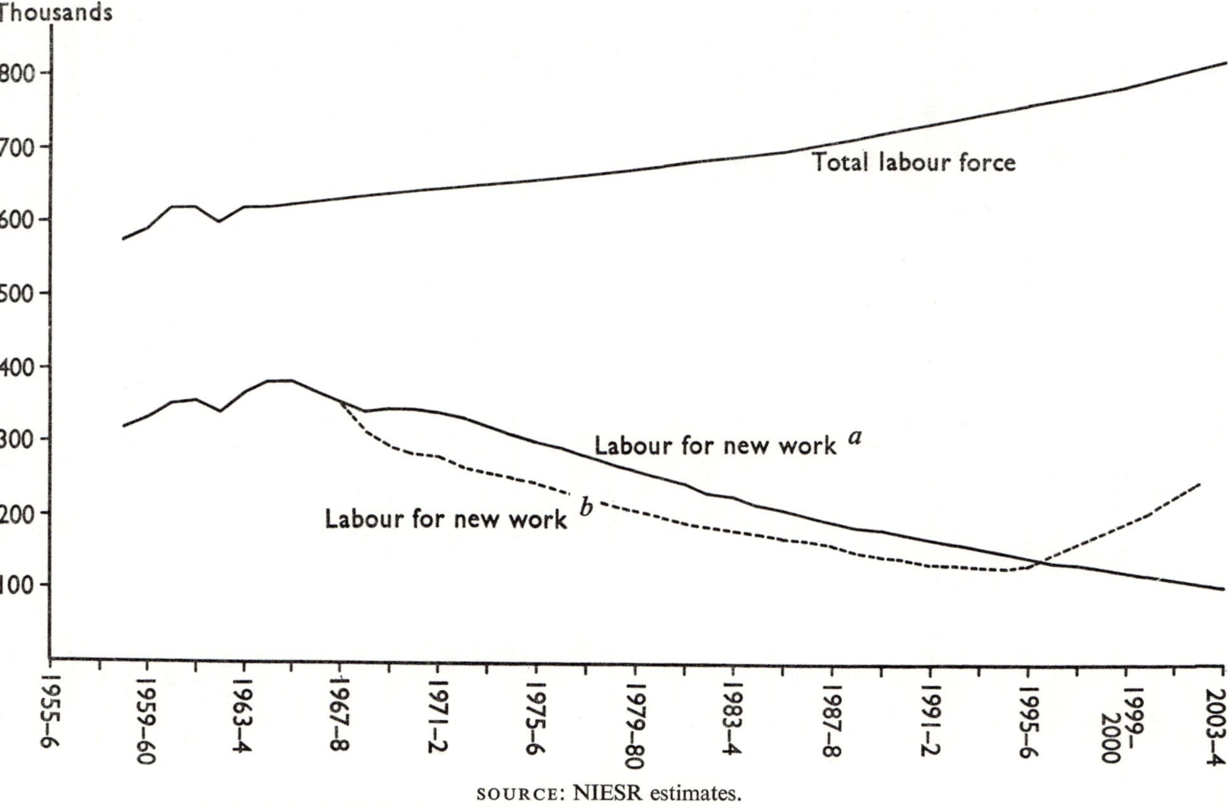

SOURCE: NIESR estimates.

a Assuming 375,000 dwellings a year.
b Assuming 300,000 dwellings a year 1969/70 to 1991/2 and an increasing number thereafter.

Fig. 16.3. Changes in the use of labour for housing work

maintenance fell, the number of dwellings economically worth improving as compared with replacing would fall, shifting the ratios of labour more in favour of new work.

It would appear that much more attention should be given to the organization of maintenance work, and to the development of building techniques and building components which would facilitate maintenance and improvement.

The use of industrialized systems in the future is uncertain, and it is difficult to forecast which ones might be employed. Therefore no direct allowance has been made for the impact of system building on labour requirements. The effect of its use in the past has contributed to the rates of productivity recorded and hence is reflected in the trends in productivity which have been assumed. As explained earlier (chapter 14), most system built dwellings now in use are based on casting *in situ* or on the site, and probably result in only small savings in the labour force of the construction industry. The less frequently used systems based on off-site factory prefabrication, which do save substantial site labour, are generally more expensive than traditional forms of construction. Unless, therefore, their promoters are writing off capital unduly rapidly, or making large profits, their use appears unlikely to save a great deal of labour overall, but rather has the effect of transferring labour requirements from the construction industry to other industries, particularly those manufacturing materials and production equipment. The overall effect on the total resources required would not appear, on present evidence, to be very large.

It was argued in chapter 14 that system building, as it is known today, may only be an interim stage in the industrialization of dwelling construction. The gradual standardization and coordination of building components may make it possible to mass produce a limited range of highly prefabricated, interchangeable building units, which could be assembled on the site to provide an adequate range of dwelling types. Such a development, together with the development and use of management and design techniques and mechanical aids, would lead to a steady improvement in productivity. Part of the load of work would be shifted back to the manufacturers, but the limiting of the range of components and the growth in the size of units would contribute, through the economics of mass production, and through a comparative reduction in handling, stocking and storage, to increases in productivity in this field. Similarly, the availability of prefabricated, interchangeable building units would reduce the time taken to design dwellings, which would probably become more standardized.

In the long run the greater use of prefabricated building units of a size larger than used today would result in some important changes in the types of materials employed. Economy in prefabrication depends to a large extent on the production of building components which are light and easy to handle. While larger units can be prefabricated on the basis of clay and concrete products, they are inevitably expensive to load, transport and assemble, so there is a need for new materials, no more expensive than traditional ones, which can be used to manufacture cheaply building components with the properties of their predecessors, and with greater dimensional precision and the ability to withstand handling and transport. At present neither the basic nor the newer materials possess the desired characteristics. It might, of course, be possible to find new ways of using existing materials to provide components with the required qualities.

In the short period the present range of products is likely to be used, and it is necessary to consider whether the demands which could arise from different programmes of housing work could be met by the materials industries. Clearly if, as seems logical, the output of new dwellings is kept within the range of 300,000 to 375,000 dwellings a year, demands from this source will not rise above present levels. A demand for certain materials would, however, arise from the increase in improvements and regular maintenance work.

The additional volume of basic materials required would be quite small. For example, the programmes of improvements found feasible would not involve building more than about 300,000 bathrooms a year at most. In terms of basic materials this would be equivalent to not more than 30,000 to 40,000 dwellings a year. Other improvement work would generally make a fairly small use of basic materials. Perhaps the total equivalent of improvement work in terms of dwellings might amount to 50,000 dwellings a year. This is only 40 per cent of the additional demand which might be required were the number of dwellings to be raised to 500,000 a year, and only two-thirds of the increase in demand for materials met in the year 1964. In fact of course the demand could only increase gradually, as the increase in productivity in new work released more labour.

The demand for some building components would be far greater. The annual demand for baths and basins, for instance, might be increased by nearly 100 per cent, and there might also be a large percentage increase for W.C. suites, sinks, water heaters and space-heating appliances, although again the demand would build up gradually.

The possibility of meeting such increases in demand depends not only on the scale of increase, but also on the proportion of the output used in the housing sector and on the movements in the demand from other sectors. About three-quarters of bricks, lightweight concrete blocks and roofing tiles appear to be used in housing, and the same is true for such accessories as wall tiles, sarking felt and paper (97). A large proportion of materials such as plasterboard, plaster and carcassing timber also find their chief use in housing. Again much joinery and floor finishes are employed in this sector (97). (The other major outlet for such materials lies in schools; the movement in these two types of buildings therefore needs to be considered jointly.) Clearly, housing is where the great majority of baths are used, and high proportions of other sanitary appliances, but the consumption of electrical wiring and components is not likely to be particularly concentrated on housing, and housing takes only small proportions of structural steel and concrete.

The production of building materials obviously depends largely on the demand, which for some types of materials has fallen over the last decade, although other materials are in high demand and have been produced in substantially greater quantities over this period. For example, the production of aggregate increased about 75 per cent, that of cement by 30 per cent, plaster 95 per cent, plasterboard 47 per cent and concrete roof tiles 40 per cent. Even materials of which the production did not increase over the decade were produced in much large quantities in 1964 than in 1963: the output of some materials increased by over 20 per cent over those two years. Whether or not such substantial increases could be achieved again would depend on the amount of unused capacity which was available and on the speed with which additional capacity could be installed. It would, however, appear unlikely that the programmes examined need be held up by a shortage of materials.

REGIONAL PROBLEMS

It is not proposed to examine in detail the position of housing in each region. It is likely that the feasibility of regional programmes will be more affected by the incidence of non-residential development than national programmes will be and, in the absence of the projections for non-residential development, a full discussion will be postponed until Volume II. The detailed regional projections for housing are, of course, given in the appendices. Discussion in this sector will be limited to major factors likely to affect the feasibility of regional housing policies.

As was pointed out earlier, because the losses of population as a result of regional migration are unlikely to exceed the amount of natural increase, and because, except for Scotland, there is no regional surplus of dwellings of any size, the national total of new constructions required varies little with the regional pattern of migration. It is necessary to consider whether the intra-regional migration would give rise to surpluses of dwellings in some districts and so add to the regionally based estimate of dwellings required. While migration is largely influenced by the availability of employment, it is also influenced by the availability of dwellings. Many people are likely to be discouraged from moving to a new area if suitable accommodation is not at their disposal, and firms are likely to be discouraged from creating additional jobs which can only be filled by migrant labour if accommodation is not available for the workers. At the more local level, people will travel longer distances to work if dwellings are in short supply at the place of work. Moreover, the numbers of dwellings replaced each year are likely to be of a similar order to the numbers of additional dwellings. The rates of replacement in the short period can be adjusted to help meet shortages or remove surpluses. Again, because of the relative size of the national increases, only exceptionally will the movement from a district exceed the natural increase. Thus it seems unlikely that there will be a serious lack of balance in supply and demand for dwellings even within individual districts, or, consequently, that the total new constructions of the districts within a region will substantially exceed the regionally based estimates. How well supply and demand will be in balance at the district level will depend on the rate of natural increase and the rate of migration; the less the latter and the greater the former, the greater the imbalance is likely to be. Unless, however, districts containing a large amount of sound housing are to be cleared and closed, it appears unlikely that the imbalance would be sufficient to affect seriously the regional estimates given in this report.

The possible range of loads of housing work in each region is naturally greater than in Great Britain as a whole. This arises partly because of the possible variation in future population, partly because of the possible scales of migration, partly because of the regional differences in the shortfall of housing stock in relation to need, and partly because of regional differences in the relative size, age and condition of the stock of housing and the resulting effect on rates of replacement and improvement (table 16.4).

Generally the effect of feasible changes in birth rates is similar in all the regions. A fall in birth rates to the extreme low point would reduce the number of dwellings which would need to be built in most regions by about 6 or 7 per cent. In contrast, if birth rates rose to the extreme high point the number required would be increased from about 17 to 25 per cent. Naturally the relative effects increase with time; they are small during the period to 1984 but increase substantially during the following twenty years.

Similarly, the effect of regional migration grows with time and has about four times as great an effect on the number of dwellings to be constructed during the second twenty-year period as during the first period. For the four northern regions both migration patterns one and two imply the same degree of drift to the gain of the southern regions. Migration pattern three represents a reversing of this process and hence an increased need for the construction of dwellings. The effect is naturally greatest for Scotland, which is losing population the most rapidly. Over the whole period this would add 40 per cent to the number of dwellings to be built, more than twice that for any of the other northern regions except the North. The second migration pattern, which assumed that some of the migrants to the South would be diverted away from the South East, Midlands and Central regions, would naturally result in a reduction of the numbers of dwellings needed in these areas, nearly 9 per cent in the case of the South East, giving anything up to a 50 per cent gain to the other regions in the South. The South East would be mainly affected by migration pattern three; the number of new dwellings required would then be about 15 per cent less.

Generally, the effect of the demolition programme would be greater than the effect of either the population growth rate or the migration pattern assumed, although all are quite radical. Nationally, demolition programme B would add about 25 per cent to the number of dwellings to be constructed and demolition

Table 16.4. *Effect of birth rates, migration and replacement on regional construction programmes: annual average of dwellings constructed*

Thousands

		RG's birth rate assumptions, migration pattern 1, demolition programme A	Changes for					
			Other birth rate assumptions		Other migration patterns		Other demolition programmes	
			Low	High	2	3	B	C
Great Britain	1964–84	253·0	−5·0	+22·0	—	—	+38·0	+95·0
	1984–2004	316·0	−31·0	+88·0	—	—	+100·0	+248·0
	Average	285·0	−18·0	+55·0	—	—	+69·0	+171·0
Scotland	1964–84	27·3	−0·5	+2·1	—	+3·4	+2·5	+5·4
	1984–2004	23·8	−3·1	+8·6	—	+16·5	+8·9	+18·5
	Average	25·5	−1·8	+5·4	—	+10·0	+5·7	+12·0
North	1964–84	12·1	−0·4	+1·4	—	+2·1	+2·9	+6·2
	1984–2004	16·9	−2·0	+5·6	—	+9·5	+7·3	+15·9
	Average	14·5	−1·2	+3·5	—	+5·8	+5·1	+11·1
North West	1964–84	23·4	−0·6	+2·7	—	+2·1	+5·3	+13·0
	1984–2004	37·4	−3·9	+11·1	—	+9·0	+13·5	+33·3
	Average	30·4	−2·3	+6·9	—	+5·6	+9·4	+23·2
Pennines	1964–84	21·3	−0·6	+2·2	—	+1·4	+4·3	+11·2
	1984–2004	30·3	−3·2	+9·2	—	+6·0	+11·2	+28·7
	Average	25·8	−1·9	+5·7	—	+3·7	+7·8	+20·0
Central	1964–84	6·8	−0·1	+0·5	−0·5	−0·6	+0·8	+2·2
	1984–2004	9·9	−0·8	+2·1	−2·0	−2·6	+2·2	+5·7
	Average	8·4	−0·5	+1·3	−1·3	−1·6	+1·5	+4·0
East	1964–84	6·2	−0·1	+0·5	+0·7	−0·1	+1·0	+2·4
	1984–2004	8·7	−0·8	+2·3	+2·8	−0·4	+2·5	+6·1
	Average	7·5	−0·5	+1·4	+1·8	−0·3	+1·8	+4·3
North & Central Wales	1964–84	2·0	−0·1	+0·2	+0·9	−0·1	+0·3	+0·8
	1984–2004	3·8	−0·4	+0·9	+3·9	−0·5	+0·7	+1·9
	Average	2·9	−0·3	+0·6	+2·4	−0·3	+0·5	+1·4
West	1964–84	22·8	−0·4	+1·8	+1·0	−0·8	+3·4	+6·6
	1984–2004	28·2	−2·4	+6·9	+4·4	−3·4	+8·7	+17·0
	Average	25·5	−1·4	+4·4	+2·7	−2·1	+6·1	+11·8
South West	1964–84	6·0	−0·2	+0·6	+0·8	−0·8	+0·9	+2·3
	1984–2004	10·6	−0·8	+2·3	+3·5	−3·6	+2·5	+5·8
	Average	8·3	−0·5	+1·5	+2·2	−2·2	+1·7	+4·1
Midlands	1964–84	30·3	−0·5	+2·2	−0·6	−0·9	+2·7	+7·3
	1984–2004	32·3	−3·0	+8·7	−2·8	−4·1	+6·8	+18·7
	Average	31·3	−1·8	+5·5	−1·7	−2·5	+4·8	+13·0
East Anglia	1964–84	4·9	−0·1	+0·4	+1·1	−0·4	+0·5	+1·4
	1984–2004	6·7	−0·6	+1·6	+4·7	−1·8	+1·2	+3·5
	Average	5·8	−0·4	+1·0	+2·9	−1·1	+0·9	+2·5
South East	1964–84	90·6	−1·8	+7·5	−3·3	−5·7	+13·8	+36·4
	1984–2004	107·8	−10·1	+29·3	−14·5	−25·5	+35·5	+93·5
	Average	99·2	−6·0	+18·4	−8·9	−15·6	+24·7	+65·0

SOURCE: NIESR estimates.

programme C, 60 per cent. Because the age and condition of dwellings varies from one region to another, so do the percentage increases. Generally, the percentage increases are higher in the northern regions than in the southern regions: Scotland is somewhat anomalous (chapter 11). In relation to current fitting standards, Scotland has a surplus of small dwellings of about half a million, although a shortage of medium and large dwellings of about 700,000. In the course of getting rid of the surplus of smaller dwellings, the age of the stock under demolition programme A is substantially reduced so leaving less to do under demolition programmes B and C.

Combinations of assumptions which affect construction in the same direction could have a large relative effect on the numbers to be constructed. For example, the number of dwellings required could be more than doubled if there was a high birth rate combined with a favourable level of migration and a high rate of replacement. Generally the largest changes are related to population increases and to rates of demolition, and the latter could have much the larger effect.

The differences in the estimated costs of new constructions at the regional level are even larger, because dwelling sizes as well as the number of dwellings increase with population. The costs of upgrading are only about a fifth of the costs of new construction, and because they are little affected by the demolition programme they tend to stabilize the figures. Again the costs of regular maintenance do not vary much with any of the factors under consideration. Since, for the combinations with the lower levels of costs, the costs of regular maintenance over the period are on the same scale as for new construction, their addition further damps down the differences. Thus the regional differences in overall costs are only about half the scale indicated for the number of dwellings to be constructed.

Because building firms operate outside the regions in which they are registered, the value of work they carry out and the number of operatives they employ do not provide a satisfactory guide to the work carried out in a region. Some guide can be obtained by using estimates of orders, although regional data for orders have only been available for the last two years and do not cover all types of work. Not all the regions used in this book are the same as those now used officially, but a reasonable matching is possible. While too much weight must not be put on the results of the exercise, some indications of regional problems can be obtained.

Even if it is assumed that the standard of dwellings in the future would be no higher than today's best, the resources required, even for a programme of 375,000 dwellings a year, would be greater than the resources used today. On the other hand, if the rate of increase in the productivity of new work was sustained at 4 per cent a year and labour increased in relation to the rise in the national labour force, capacity would be greatly increased. Over the forty-year period, for Great Britain as a whole, capacity for new construction work would be nearly three times as large as that needed for new construction work at today's best standards. The excess capacity would vary from region to region in accordance with changes in regional population, with the age of the stock in the region and with the amount of new house building in the region over the last two years. Increases in regional population would both increase the need for additional dwellings and swell the potential labour force. A comparison of the figures for orders with past completions suggests that the orders provide a reasonable indication of the regional pattern of new housing work. Some regions, such as the North West and Scotland, have relatively low excess capacities because of relatively low rates of construction in the past and relatively old stocks. Even so, capacity for new construction work would exceed the need for it by a factor of two over the forty-year period.

On the other hand, the potential capacity of the housing maintenance sector is less than would be required if the specified standards of improvement and maintenance are to be achieved. Even if excess labour was moved from the new work sector and that labour, as well as the expected proportional gains from an increasing total labour force, were added to the present maintenance labour force, capacity would still appear likely to fall short nationally over the forty years, probably by about 5 per cent. Of course, the labour transferred from new work to maintenance work would achieve less output if, as assumed, productivity increased at a rate of 2 per cent less in maintenance than in new work. The relationship between need and capacity would, of course, vary regionally. The South East and East Anglia are likely to have some excess capacity, while most of the other regions would be short on capacity. Again the greatest shortage of capacity would be in the North West and Scotland, where the relatively poor position in the case of new construction capacity is intensified by a combination of past and current poor standards of maintenance. The capacity of the housing maintenance sector of the North West would be about a third too low to meet needs over the forty-year period. That of Scotland would be about a quarter too low, although actually smaller if the loss of the natural increase of population was stemmed. Generally, the shortage of capacity would be greater for the northern regions than the southern ones.

The comparative shortages of capacity depend on a large number of factors, on some of which there is little reliable information; for example, the relative regional levels of productivity, the rates at which they will vary in the future, and the effect on capacity of changing the relative sizes of regional labour forces. The size of such changes can therefore only be suggested very tentatively. Nationally, on average, an additional 40,000 to 50,000 operatives would appear to be required in the housing sector over and above that expected as a result of natural increase. The South East and East Anglia would be expected to have 25,000 to 30,000 in excess of needs, considerably less if the number of migrants were substantially reduced. This would about balance the expected shortfall in the North West. There would also be considerable shortfalls in the labour available in Scotland and the other northern regions.

The national shortfall in capacity would be eliminated if the output of new dwellings was reduced to about 300,000 in the near future and the capacity released used for advancing the maintenance and improvement work. Towards the end of the period sufficient capacity surplus to maintenance requirements would be available to make good the new dwellings lost. Similarly, the sizes of the shortfalls in the regional labour forces would be reduced, the surplus in the South East and East Anglia would be increased, and the small shortfalls in some other southern regions would be eliminated or converted to small surpluses.

Current best standards are hardly likely to be acceptable for a period as long as that discussed in this study: additional labour will be required to provide building capacity to meet any rise in standards, and such labour needs will be proportionally greater in regions already short of capacity.

HOUSING POLICY AND PROGRAMMES

While there would be little value in attempting to determine a firm housing policy and programmes over a period as long as forty years, it is necessary to appreciate the long-term implications of short-term policies. The important element in a housing policy, however, is not the annual output of new dwellings but the size and quality of the existing stock, and the way this matches demand.

Demand is not independent of the government housing policy but shapes and is shaped by it. While effective demand depends on people's propensity to use their incomes to purchase housing services, it also depends on the extent to which the government is prepared to supplement purchasing power directly through subsidies and indirectly through favourable tax and financial incentives. It is difficult to measure future demand as distinct from need as long as the operation of the market is frustrated by such a complex of financial and fiscal controls as it is today. If the policy of fair rents were followed to its logical conclusion, it would be easier to measure the preferences people are prepared to accord housing among other consumer services. However, if fair rents are to provide this evidence, they must eventually develop into free market rents comparable with the free market prices for house purchase. Socially, the full rigour of the market appears unlikely to be acceptable until, by and large, the supply of housing is sufficient to reduce to an unimportant level the element of scarcity in prices, and until social payments are adjusted to assist those less well-off to obtain housing above a minimum, socially acceptable standard.

Housing policy needs to be comprehensive and coordinated. The development of universal fair rents, the raising of minimum housing standards, the development of universally applicable social payments for housing and other fiscal and financial encouragements to householders and owners, and the growth and improvement of the stock, all need to be related. In the short period, demand and supply need to be kept in balance and, in the long period, the incentives to the growth and improvement of the stock need to be balanced against the growth of demand in relation to the supply price. If the best return is to be obtained on the resources used for housing, it is necessary not only to balance supply and demand but also to produce the supply at the lowest cost. Thus the scale and standard of housing cannot be considered without at the same time considering the form in which it is supplied.

Scale, standard and form depend on the nature of the stock. Since people's relative valuation of housing services will vary, the standards demanded in relation to price will vary over a wide range, even if a minimum standard is set as a matter of policy. The schedules of demand need to be established. It is unlikely that the stock will match the demand schedules as long as so much attention is accorded to the standards of new housing and so little to the standards of the rest of the stock. The first step is to examine how well the standards in the stock match the required standards, and how the two can be brought into harmony.

In the absence of a self-regulating process only a rough indication can be obtained of the extent to which need is likely to be translated into effective demand, and how this would be modified by fiscal, financial and physical changes which can be brought about by government action. The effect of changes in the parameters of demand can be assessed by the use of a model on the lines of that developed in this study. The costs of dwellings, under various assumptions about their finance, could be compared with the amounts households of different types, classes and incomes are likely to be prepared to spend on housing. This would give some indication of the demand schedules which could be applied to the crude rates of household formation to provide estimates of total demand. These estimates could subsequently be evaluated, and the requirements for resources could be compared with the probable potential output to test the feasibility of meeting such levels of demand. Estimates could be revised annually in the light of the latest evidence of the likely values of the parameters. Since the gross annual contribution to the stock of dwellings is small, only about 2 per cent, and the net contribution is likely to be only about half this level, quite small changes in the desirable level of stock could lead to large fluctuations in the annual demand for constructions. Therefore, if large fluctuations in annual output and the wastage of resources which is likely to result are to be avoided, it is necessary to try to regulate output in the light of the long-term trends in demand and to avoid putting too much weight on short-term indicators. The latter are particularly likely to be affected by real and apparent changes in the parameters of demand. The rate at which dwellings are closed can be used to adjust the size of the stock so as to smooth out fluctuations in the annual demand for new dwellings.

New constructions make only a small contribution to raising the standard of the stock. Even at the current rates of construction it would take fifty years to replace the stock. The standard depends far more on maintenance, improvement and conversion than on new constructions. An important element, therefore, in matching the supply of housing to the demand is the use made of the existing stock. A first step is to ascertain the standards currently provided by it, and the costs of improvement and conversion to required standards in relation to expected future lives. On the basis of this information it is possible to determine supply costs and ascertain the most economic way of using the existing stock.

This study should provide sufficiently accurate estimates on which to base the broad lines of policy for the next few years, but will need to be revised in the future as the parameters change. The success of a housing policy depends not only on reaching the best national policies but also on their application at the local level. Models such as that used in this study could be used for estimating the size and specification of the stock required locally. Much of the information required is already held centrally and could easily be applied to local models. The largest gap in the information is knowledge of the size, condition and potential of the local stock.

A simple account of the distribution of unfit dwellings is not very relevant to this problem. An estimate is required of the stock of dwellings in each local area, classified by the cost of carrying out any arrears of maintenance and necessary improvement in relation to their potential amenities and physical life. Such estimates should be based on assessments prepared by professional surveyors on the lines used in the recent survey of housing conditions organized by the Ministry of Housing and Local Government. It is, of course, only necessary for short-run policy to provide detailed assessments for the poorest part of the stock. The expected lives of each block of property can be determined in relation to national replacement programmes, local development programmes for roads, central area and other redevelopment programmes, and the economic potential of the property in relation to repair and improvement. In this way it is possible to estimate nationally the best balance between replacement and repair and improvement, with the best regional distribution of available resources in these various directions, and to indicate the criteria to be applied at the local level.

CHAPTER 17

SUMMARY AND CONCLUSIONS

THE GOVERNMENT AND HOUSING POLICY

The importance of reaching the best answers for the development of housing and other built environment can hardly be over-emphasized. Perhaps no sector of the economy touches the life of the community so closely or in so many ways. More resources are used for urban development than for any other sector of economic activity, apart from the supply of food. A half of the country's fixed capital formation is used for construction; if the costs of improvement and maintenance are added to those for renewal and extension of the urban fabric, the total amounts to about an eighth of the gross national product. This is twice as much as the national expenditure on defence and four times as much as expenditure on education or health. Housing accounts for about a third of the expenditure on construction.

The costs of development can be measured in terms of the implied sacrifices of alternative uses of national resources—for consumer goods and services, education, social services and defence, among others. The rational aim is to try to allocate resources so that the best value for money is obtained. It is equally important to try and obtain the best use of resources within each sector. The best is often the enemy of the good. If standards are set too high in one direction, other needs will suffer to the detriment of the sum of satisfactions.

In contemporary Britain the market provides, for most consumer and producer goods and services, a reasonably adequate mechanism for aligning values and costs, but, for a long time past, the market for housing has ceased to operate in this way.

The amount and form of housing are only partly the result of decisions of the users. They are also affected by a complex of government policies, some of which have little direct connexion with housing as such. The government influences the supply of housing not only through its policies for housing and rent control, but also through decisions on physical planning, regional development, building, transport, education, social services and agriculture, and through its financial and fiscal policies. These policies stem from many different departments of government, both central and local. While it would be naive to expect that the needs of housing policy should be allowed to dictate policy in every other sector, nevertheless there is a need for coordination. The government, as the agent of the community, in deciding housing policy, needs to know the wishes of the community.

In the absence of market guidance, the planners and other national and local administrators have to act as middlemen, and make some guess as to the values the community attaches to housing and the resources it wishes to devote to its provision. In the absence of any attempt to estimate the alternative policies which might be followed and their costs, it is not possible to know to what extent the balance is right between the expenditure on housing and on other sectors.

The object of the study described in this volume has been to provide some understanding of the needs for housing, of the ways needs are likely to change with changes in population and its spatial distribution, and of the effect of the scale, standard and form of housing on national resources. The resources required have been compared with the likely output of the construction industry and with national resources, in order to test the feasibility of meeting needs in various ways and of according them various levels of priority. Although this approach does not provide a direct solution to the optimization of housing provision—this is not possible until more is known about the values the members of the community accord to housing—it does provide an understanding of the constraints within which housing policy must operate.

POPULATION AND THE NEED FOR HOUSING

The starting point for estimating housing needs is the future population, but its projection can never be an exact science. On the basis of the 1964 projections of the Registrars General the 1964 population of Great Britain (between 52 and 53 million) will increase to 72 million by the year 2004. In their projections the Registrars General have assumed that birth rates will remain at much their present levels over this period. While there is general acceptance of the assumptions for mortality and external migration, there is less certainty about birth rates. It is possible that the present upward trend might continue, although this now looks less likely than it did three years ago. On the other hand, birth rates might decline again. If present marriage rates continue to rise in accordance with the 1931–61 trend, and if fertility rates rise by no more than two-thirds of the recent rate, the population in 2004 would be about 85 million. Even so, birth rates at the end of the period would be no higher than in 1890. If, however, marriage and fertility rates were to decline gradually to the levels of 1940, the projected figure would be 65 million by 2004. The effect of the higher assumption is to raise population, as compared with the figure obtained on the basis currently adopted by the Registrars General, by nearly as much as the figure on the Registrars General's current basis exceeds the figure on their 1957 projection. These figures can, perhaps, be taken as the probable boundaries to the projections of the Registrars General.

The spatial distribution of population is affected by the pattern of internal and external migration. At present, Scotland and the northern regions are losing a substantial part of their natural increase, while the regions of the South and Midlands are gaining population from both internal and external sources. The major alternative policies for internal migration would appear to be either to build up the attractions of Scotland and the northern regions so as to stop them losing their natural increases, or to accept these losses and direct migrants to the rural regions of the South and Midlands, away from the South East and urban Midlands. Naturally, the migration trends could be changed only gradually; if Scotland and the northern regions are not to be net losers of population over the forty-year period the flow will need to be reversed not just stopped. While the pattern of internal migration may not have a major effect on the total resources needed for housing, it is likely to have a considerable effect on regional requirements.

The number and size of households was estimated from the population projections on the basis of headship rates. Headship rates have been rising, and allowance was made for rates slightly higher than those recorded in 1961; this increased households and the number of dwellings required by about 8 per cent above the levels that would have been given by the 1961 rates. The basis used gave an average household size in 2004 of 2·97 persons. Some authorities expect household fission to proceed much further, and have suggested future household sizes of 2·5 and even 2·2 persons. Such rates imply not only that practically all married males and about 95 per cent of widowed and divorced males and females would form separate households, but that a third to two-thirds of single people of fifteen years and over would form separate, one person households and require separate dwellings. This seems unlikely both on financial and social grounds. While the number of dwellings would increase in inverse proportion to the household size, costs would increase less than proportionately since dwellings would be smaller.

In fitting households to dwellings it was assumed that, on the one hand, the present degree of overcrowding would not be acceptable, but that on the other, the proportions of dwellings with a large number of rooms would be reduced by rebuilding and conversions so that the degree of under-occupation would also be reduced. The relationship between household size and rooms was therefore determined on the basis of households who were neither overcrowded nor had excess space. On average this implied 0·69 persons per room. While people are often disinclined to move from dwellings too large for them, the combined effects of death and demolition will tend to be considerable over a period as long as forty years.

On this basis about 23·8 million dwellings would be required to house the population of Great Britain projected by the Registrars General over the forty-year period. The probable range of needs on the basis of the lower and upper population projections would be 23·1 to 26·0 million. It was estimated that in March 1964, there were about 16·8 million permanent dwellings in Great Britain, so that the number of additional dwellings required above the present stock would be 7·0 million, 6·3 million and 9·2 million respectively.

THE HOUSING STOCK

At 31 March 1964, the base date for this study, many of the existing stock of dwellings were much below the standards considered appropriate for today.

About 5 per cent lacked a water closet and about 18 per cent had no fixed bath. Something like 15 per cent needed structural repairs and about 50 per cent needed fairly extensive repair and redecoration. About 13 per cent of dwellings existed in a very poor environment, and the environment was unsatisfactory for about half of the dwellings. Less than a quarter had garages and nearly two-thirds had neither a garage nor space for a garage.

While some of the dwellings were not economically worth repairing, most of those falling short in their condition and facilities could be put right. However, even if they were put into a good state of repair and decoration, provided with bathrooms and with adequate sanitary and water services, many would still fall a good deal short of the amenities provided for by Parker Morris standards. A rough measure of this inadequacy in amenities is provided by age. The average age of the stock in 1964 was about fifty-six years. About 27 per cent of the dwellings were built before 1881 and thus are over eighty years old: about 45 per cent were built before 1920; they are over forty years old now and will be over eighty years old by the end of the century.

Some of the old dwellings provide a high level of amenity, but it seems unlikely that more than a very small percentage will provide acceptable homes by the end of the century, even if they are kept in good condition and provided with modern services. The number of dwellings which might need rebuilding would depend on the standards thought appropriate for space, layout, lighting, heating, insulation and external environment. Including unfit dwellings which would not be economically worth repairing, but excluding better quality dwellings, there will remain 4·6 million dwellings, built before 1881, which will be over 123 years old in the year 2004, 2·8 million which will be between 83 and 123 years old and 4·1 million between 63 and 83 years old.

HOUSING CONSTRUCTIONS

Improvements in urban standards imply improvements in the existing stock as well as in newly constructed dwellings. The stock can be improved partly by replacement, and partly by making good arrears of maintenance and by up-grading. If the numbers of dwellings needed to eliminate dwellings either unfit or built before 1881 were added to those required to meet the needs arising from the growth of population to 72 million by 2004, the numbers to be built would be 11·6 million, or 14·4 million and 18·9 million to replace buildings earlier than 1921 and 1941 respectively. The number of dwellings to be constructed is more affected by the rate at which the stock might be replaced than by possible differences in future population.

A separate allowance could be made for vacancies. Currently, true vacancies are estimated to be about 1 per cent of the stock, which at the present rate of moving would give an average vacancy period of about six and a half weeks. In addition to permanent dwellings there is a further half per cent of permanently occupied temporary dwellings, mainly caravans, and 6 per cent of households sharing. It is unlikely that all these households would require permanent dwellings or that all dwellings in the appropriate age groups would be demolished, and it was assumed that as a first approximation an additional special allowance for vacancies was not necessary.

The number of dwellings which would need to be constructed in each region would vary with the migration as well as the population pattern. The national differences between migration patterns are insignificant because the expected regional losses by migration are not likely to exceed the natural increase and because, except in Scotland, there is no surplus of dwellings, even of particular sizes. It is not expected that important surpluses would appear even in local housing areas, because of the scale of population increases and of replacements, and because of the degree to which households migrate to the areas with a surplus of housing and adapt to it.

The dwellings in Scotland, on average, are considerably smaller (3·5 habitable rooms per dwelling) than in the rest of Great Britain (4·6 habitable rooms per dwelling): a difference of the greatest importance with the result that, if national standards of fitting households to dwellings were adopted for Scotland, about half a million (nearly a third) of the present stock of dwellings there would be too small. At current rates of building this number would take fifteen years to erect, and in addition dwellings would be required to replace unfit and obsolete dwellings and to meet the needs of population increases. But, it may be that the size of dwellings in Scotland, which is more in line with continental than British standards, suits the Scottish way of life.

The size of dwellings required at the end of the period 2004 does not differ markedly from the size distribution in 1964 and is not much affected by birth rate assumptions, although the higher these are, the greater the household size and the greater the proportions of the larger sizes of dwelling. The expected increase in the formation of households will naturally lead to a fall in size and to a need for a greater proportion of smaller dwellings. If, as anticipated, this occurs during the first half of the forty-year period, the proportion of small dwellings to be constructed during this period would be markedly increased; the lower the rates of replacement the greater would need to be the proportion of small dwellings. The proportions of dwellings of different sizes required vary considerably from one region to another and with the pattern of migration. Because of the high proportion of small dwellings in the housing stock in Scotland, only large sizes would be needed there during the first half of the period, and a higher proportion than elsewhere would be needed in the latter half. Currently, far too many small dwellings appear to be constructed in Scotland, perpetuating the smallness of dwellings there in relation to the rest of Great Britain.

The average age of stock naturally falls faster the larger the population to be housed and the greater the rate of replacement. If the lowest rate of replacement were achieved, covering only pre-1881 dwellings, the average age at the end of the period, in 2004, would fall from fifty-six years to forty-six years. The effect of high and low levels of births is small. In the first case the average age is reduced by about three years and in the second case it is raised by one year. Increasing the proportion of demolitions reduces the average ages by eleven and twenty-one years respectively.

HOUSING COSTS AND LAND NEEDS

It has been estimated that the costs of constructing some 11·6 million new dwellings to meet the basic standards put forward would be about £40,000 million at 1964 prices over the forty years 1964–2004. This is based on Parker Morris standards plus 10 per cent to allow for a proportion of better quality dwellings. Of these dwellings 4·6 million would be to meet the replacement of dwellings built prior to 1881. The balance would be to meet the needs of the additional population which would be generated if the birth rates assumed by the Registrars General proved to be correct, and to provide additional dwellings to meet increased household formation and space standards. The costs of constructing the dwellings, 10·9 million and 13·8 million, that would be required on the low and high birth rate assumptions respectively, would be about £37,000 and £48,000 million. If the dwellings, other than those which were unfit or of better quality, built prior to 1921 were to be replaced, costs would rise by about £10,000 million; or, if replacement of pre-1941 dwellings were required, the costs would be raised by about £27,000 million, making them £67,000 million in all.

Thus, the effect on costs of raising standards would be greater than the effect of substantially increased birth rates. Whereas the high birth rates would raise costs about a fifth, higher standards in the form of higher rates of replacement would raise costs by about a quarter if dwellings built between 1881 and 1920 were replaced, and by about two-thirds if dwellings built between 1881 and 1940 were replaced. The effect of higher birth rates is to raise household size as well as population, so that the increase in the number of dwellings required is less than proportionate to the rise in population. Increases in the size of dwellings have less effect on costs than increases in numbers, because cost does not rise in proportion to size of dwelling—dwellings for eight persons are only about twice as expensive as those for one person.

These costs of construction are based on the assumptions that the dwellings would be developed in the urban form of today, with about three-quarters of the total as houses and less than 10 per cent as flats in high blocks. Houses are the cheapest form of dwelling; dwellings in three and four storey blocks are at present about 10 per cent more expensive in London and about 17 per cent more in the provinces; dwellings in high blocks are 35 to 45 per cent more expensive in London and 60 to 70 per cent more expensive in the provinces. While the use of high blocks provides a way of achieving higher housing densities, it results in much greater costs. About 80 per cent of the cost of housing construction is for the dwelling itself, about 8 per cent is for garages, and the balance for site clearance and development with roads, services and sewers. Thus, although the last cost, expressed per dwelling, falls when density is increased, its effect in offsetting the rising costs associated with density is small. For example, if the proportion of dwellings in the form of houses were reduced to 50 per cent and 30 per cent of dwellings were in high blocks, the costs of house construction on the basic assumptions of population and replacement would rise from about £40,000 million to about £44,000 million, that is by about a tenth. If the proportion of dwellings in houses were reduced to 40 per cent and dwellings in high blocks were raised to 50 per cent, costs would rise to about £47,000 million; a rise of about a fifth. Some land would, of course, be saved.

As explained above, the basic assumption was that the form of housing would follow present practice. Nationally, a density of about fifty-nine rooms (bedrooms and reception rooms) per acre is being obtained with 74 per cent of dwellings in houses, 18 per cent in low flats and 8 per cent in high flats. On this basis about 471,000 acres are needed to house the extra population expected on the assumptions used by the Registrars General and to provide for higher space standards. If the higher birth rate assumptions were fulfilled about 180,000 acres would be needed in addition; on the lower assumptions about 70,000 acres less would be required. Generally, the dwellings that would be replaced would have been built at higher densities than are generally acceptable today, and some 130,000 acres would be needed for their development. The more recent dwellings would have been built at lower densities than dwellings built earlier, so proportionately less new land will be necessary to replace them. About a further 60,000 acres would be needed to provide for the rebuilding of the pre-1921 dwellings and just a little less for rebuilding pre-1941 dwellings; the inter-war densities being lower than those of today.

If more use were made of flats, particularly flats in high blocks, higher densities could be obtained and less land would be required. For example, if only 50 per cent of dwellings were in houses and 10 per cent were in high flats, the national density could be about sixty-nine rooms per acre, and, if only 50 per cent of dwellings were in houses and 30 per cent were in high flats, the national density would be about eighty rooms per acre. Whereas nearly 600,000 acres would be required at a density of fifty-nine rooms per acre to meet needs on the basis of the birth rate assumptions of the Registrars General, including provision for better space standards and for rebuilding pre-1881 dwellings, at sixty-nine rooms per acre the land needed would fall to about 490,000 acres, and at eighty rooms per acre to 400,000 acres. The cost of saving an acre of land by building to these higher densities would be about £30,000. Most of the land saved would be farmland worth at present some £200 per acre.

Generally, only sites in the central parts of large towns cost as much as £30,000 an acre, so that developers would not find it worthwhile to consider high flatted blocks for most housing sites. However, site prices rise with the density for which planning consent can be obtained, so that the savings in the costs of sites per dwelling from development in this way tend to be very small. The costs per dwelling for this type of development tend to rise steeply with the density secured, and such development is only financially feasible if subsidies are available to offset the additional costs, which is usually the situation for public housing.

Savings may be achieved in other sectors of development as a result of high density development. If such development were carried out on a large scale, towns would be more compact, roads and pipelines would be shorter and travelling less. However, it is difficult to find situations in which the external economies offset the additional housing costs, especially as maintenance and servicing costs tend to rise broadly in step with construction costs.

Naturally, land is required for other development purposes as well as for housing development. It has been estimated that, in all, about 1,600,000 acres of additional land would be required over the forty-year period for urban development in Great Britain, to meet the needs of a population of 72 million in 2004. This is equivalent to nearly 3 per cent of the area of Great Britain or just over 5 per cent of the area of arable and permanent grass—the type of land most likely to be taken, in the final analysis, for development.

The output of the agricultural industry increased in value over the last decade by nearly 4 per cent per annum on the basis of a slightly reduced area. Part of this increase appears to have been the result of a rise in the proportion of the output of more valuable produce; the increase in yields was only between 1 and 2 per cent. It is generally anticipated that productivity will continue to rise. Even if the rate of increase in productivity were only as little as 1¼ per cent a year, the loss of farm produce from taking agricultural land for housing over the period 1964–2004 would be made good in about two years, and the loss of land for all urban purposes in about four years. Over the forty-year period the output of the remaining farmland would increase enough to provide for 76 million people at the current rate of consumption of home grown food.

The best land produces about three times as much as average land. The levels of output would therefore be far less if a disproportionate amount of the best land were taken for development. While it is, therefore, important to avoid the use of the best land as far as possible, the extent to which this can be achieved is limited by the costs of developing on unsuitable sites. Good farmland is also usually land which can be developed economically. Even good farmland is worth only about £15 for a site for a dwelling, a small sum compared with the additional costs likely to arise in developing unsuitable land. In fact there is a good spread of land of all qualities in most regions. While the best land is often in the areas most obviously suitable for development, it should not be too difficult to steer development away from the best land, except perhaps in the Midlands.

The loss of amenity might be more serious than the agricultural loss, particularly if development were concentrated in small areas of Britain, and away from those regions, notably Scotland and the North, where there are large areas of poor hill land which could be used for recreational purposes without much loss of farm output. If large increases of population are housed in regions such as the South East and Midlands, it is likely either that there will be large losses of farm output as a result of taking good land for recreational purposes, or that such amenity land will not be provided on an adequate scale.

It will be seen that the savings in land likely to be secured by developing housing at high densities are not very significant in relation to land needs. There must be considerable doubt whether the high cost of such development and the loss of adaptability in relation to rising standards are worthwhile.

Even if the rates of construction were raised considerably above those of today, it would be many years before all those dwellings with inadequate facilities and poor amenities had been replaced. If no improvement is made to these dwellings many of them are likely to be unfit for habitation long before their turn for replacement arrives. As a result the stock will not rise as rapidly as required. Moreover, the continued use of substandard housing over a long period is unlikely to be acceptable socially. The extent to which it is economically worthwhile to improve this housing depends on the buildings' expectation of life. On the basis that expenditure on improving existing dwellings should give an annual return equal to that from expenditure on new dwellings, about £8,000 to £9,000 million might be worth spending. The expected life of the majority of existing dwellings is so long, whichever rate of replacement is assumed, that the replacement rate assumptions have only a relatively small effect on these costs. About £1,000 million would be saved if the fastest rate of replacement were adopted. The most expensive item would be arrears of maintenance, about £3,500 to £3,900 million; adding services and bathrooms might cost about £880 to £910 million; adding garages at a rate of one per dwelling, where economically worthwhile, might cost about £2,800 to £3,400 million; and improving the environment about £730 to £760 million. The first two items are the most pressing; the addition of garages would be spread over the forty-year period as the rate of car ownership increased.

The costs of maintaining dwellings vary with such factors as size, type and age. Local authority standards have been used for costing; these tend to be minimal in relation to functional need. The effect of building additional dwellings and replacing existing ones is, naturally, to reduce the average age, the major influence being the rate of replacement. The age structure of the stock is, however, only modified slowly by additions and replacements, and the effect on the costs of maintenance over the period as a result of different rates of addition and replacement is small. The total costs of maintenance average about £38,000 million, a little more in the case of the slowest rate of replacement and a little less in the case of the fastest. The costs would, of course, be a little higher if the larger stock of dwellings were provided.

The costs of maintenance are based on the levels of expenditure incurred by local authorities in maintaining their dwellings. These are usually adequate to maintain the fabric and fittings, but provide for only minimum decoration and replacements. The work is usually supplemented by that of the occupiers. Other occupiers also carry out maintenance work, mainly trivial running repairs and decorations. Despite the low standard of maintenance on which the cost estimates are based, they represent a cost per dwelling about twice the current level. This is an indication of the inadequacy with which many dwellings are maintained, a fact which is reflected in the costs of the arrears of maintenance, which represent eight to nine times the current annual expenditure on maintenance work.

THE CAPACITY OF THE CONSTRUCTION INDUSTRY

The future capacity of the construction industry depends on its size and on levels of productivity. The measurement of the productivity of construction work is difficult, but it would appear that, over the last decade, productivity in contracting has risen 3 to 3½ per cent for new work and perhaps not more than 1 to 1½ per cent for maintenance work. The increases in productivity have been obtained by the use of innovations over the whole field of construction; the development of new and improved materials; the prefabrication and the standardization and coordination of building components; the development of new techniques of construction; mechanization; use of improved management techniques; and better design. The potential for improvement in the future appears to be considerable. It takes a long time for innovations to spread right through the industry and it should be possible at least to maintain the present rate of improvement for a long period. As the nature of maintenance work changes, and more attention is given to the improvement of large areas of housing and to renewal as distinct from repair work, there should be an improvement in the productivity of maintenance work, perhaps a doubling of the annual rate of increase. The probable greater use of standardized building designs, based on a limited range of standardized and coordinated components, is likely to reduce the work involved in design and enable this side of the industry to increase its productivity in step with the contracting side. The use of a limited range of standardized components should also assist manufacturers to secure adequate improvements in productivity. Past improvements have, however, been realized in a period when the working week did not shorten. It will be much more difficult to secure similar rates of improvement if working hours decline and holidays increase.

The scale of increase in output per man will appreciate. A 3½ per cent rate of increase implies a doubling of output per man in twenty years. Even a 2 per cent rate of increase would considerably more than double output per man by the end of forty years. These are substantial rates of increase to achieve in the context of a single product.

The construction industry is concerned not only with the output of housing, but also with the construction and maintenance of building and civil engineering work of every kind. Housing accounts for only about a third of the work. Rough preliminary estimates suggest that the total expenditure which may be necessary over the forty year period may, at current prices, amount to between £190,000 and £240,000 million. If the load of work were to increase steadily, it would entail an increase in output of about 1¾ to 2¾ per cent per annum compound over the forty-year period. If the construction industry were to obtain the same proportion of the labour force as it does today, this load of work could be achieved by an increase in productivity of about 1 to 2 per cent. Clearly there must be a considerable degree of uncertainty about these figures. The rate of increase is very sensitive to the current level of output of the construction industry, the rate of change of which has recently been rather uneven. Clearly if past rates of improving productivity continue, it should not be too difficult to meet the load of work implied. However, the proportion of maintenance work is likely to increase substantially, particularly in the case of housing; as a result the average rate at which productivity is likely to increase will be considerably reduced.

All the same, it is unlikely that increased productivity in the construction industry will be achieved except as a part of a wider movement in levels of productivity in the whole economy. Generally, the greatest increases in productivity occur in the newest industries and the least in old industries such as construction. Standards of living to which the built environment contributes tend to rise in step with productivity increases. In so far as increases in the standard of living were reflected in the standards of construction, increases in productivity would not be available to meet the needs arising from an increased population and from making good the existing built environment at current standards. The construction industry would need to obtain the additional output from an addition to its labour force. While it might obtain up to ¾ per cent from the growth of the total national labour force, the other 1 to 2 per cent could only be obtained if other industries were prepared to reduce their present proportions of the labour force sufficiently. On the basis indicated, the construction industry's share of the labour force would have to be increased by about 80 per cent over the forty-year period. Whether or not it would be acceptable to devote to construction as large a proportion of the national output as these figures imply—nearly a quarter instead of the current figure of an eighth—would depend upon what other goods and services the community required and the extent to which the rest of the economy could meet this level of demand from higher efficiency. Most western economies devote a larger proportion of their national output to new construction than does Great Britain, although few by as much as 80 per cent.

While it would appear from preliminary estimates that a half to two-thirds of the construction work arises from the need to renew and improve the existing stock, the increase in the working population is expected to change less than proportionately to changes in the total population. As a result, if the population increased to 85 million by the end of the period the output per head of workers in the construction industry would need to be nearly one-fifth greater than if the population were 72 million. On the other hand, if the population were to rise only to 65 million, an output per head of workers of about an eighth less would be adequate. Generally, the greater the rate of increase in the population, the more difficult it is likely to be to find the resources to provide an adequate built environment.

URBAN DEVELOPMENT, FINANCE AND ADMINISTRATION

While the community might collectively prefer a certain set of urban standards, it might individually be reluctant to finance their provision. The cost of improving urban standards must inevitably be reflected in prices and in taxation. The costs of some forms of urban development appear less onerous than others. The costs of commercial and industrial development are, generally, partly absorbed by improvements in the efficiency of producers and distributors, and partly passed on through the prices of goods and services. Improvements to roads, to public buildings and to the buildings needed for educational and social services are paid for through taxation and rates, and such development costs are far more noticeable. The costs operating privately for housing are probably the most onerous of all, since there is no way for the householder to offset such costs except by sacrificing expenditure on other goods and services. Some private householders are likely to resist meeting the full cost of the redevelopment and upgrading of their housing—a point of considerable importance in the redevelopment of twilight areas.

The demand, as distinct from the need, for housing depends on the extent to which private people are prepared to use their incomes to purchase and rent housing, and to maintain and improve it; on the extent to which they are prepared to save and invest their money in creating a supply of private housing to let; and on the extent to which the government is prepared to borrow the finance for housing, and to arrange taxes and subsidies to favour its consumption. Currently, the incidence of inflation, interest policy, rent controls, taxes, subsidies, grants and local rates is so complex that it is impossible to obtain any clear idea of the values people attach to housing.

The number of householders prepared to purchase housing depends on such factors as the availability of rented property and its costs, on the relationship between the financial costs of housing and incomes, and on the availability of finance and suitable properties. As real incomes rise more householders will be able to finance house purchase. Many potential purchasers are likely to be frustrated, because of the difficulty of finding a part of the purchase money from their own resources and of meeting mortgage payments during the early years.

Under present arrangements, and with continuing inflation, the ratio of mortgage payment to income tends to fall each year, even for people whose income does not increase with age and experience. With a rate of inflation running at 3 per cent, a mortgage payment which initially amounts to 25 per cent of income would represent only half of this proportion by the end of twenty-five years. The number of potential purchasers of housing could be increased considerably if mortgage payments could be related more closely to the income, and perhaps the other outgoings, of the borrower. Such arrangements as loans for the whole of the purchase price, pre-purchase saving schemes, repayment periods extended over the working life of the purchaser, and payments limited to interest in the early years, would tend to bring payments and income into a better relationship. While loans for house purchase arranged on such terms would increase the lender's financial risks for each mortgage, the national risk would be small and could easily be covered by insurance. The effect of setting mortgage interest against income for tax purposes is to reduce the net cost of the mortgage to owner-occupiers who are net borrowers during the early years when it is most needed. The new subsidies in lieu of tax rebates are also at their most valuable during the early years.

An increase in the number of borrowers and proportionately larger loans would increase the amount of finance required, and this might only be obtained if interest rates were increased. Lenders of mortgage funds are very vulnerable to inflationary losses and might require either interest sufficiently above current rates to cover this, or payment guaranteed in real terms: in either case rates would rise. However, if the prices of housing continue to rise at about 5 per cent a year, and if tax rebates, or subsidies in lieu, of about 2 to 3 per cent can be obtained by the less well-off purchaser, his real housing costs would be small even if the rate of interest was 7 to 8 per cent.

While the prices of owner-occupied housing broadly reflect the supply and demand under current conditions, rents bear little relation either to the value of the dwellings or to the ability of the occupiers to pay rents. The rents of public authority dwellings reflect partly the standard of the dwelling, partly the influence of the pattern of interest rates, subsidies and construction prices at the times at which the stock was built up, and partly the authorities' preparedness to subsidize housing from the rates and to operate differential rent schemes. Private rents reflect the complexity of various rent Acts and the way they have affected the rent of dwellings in relation to the date of first letting and their rateable value.

The tenants of local authority dwellings have incomes about a sixth higher than the tenants of private dwellings and pay rents about two-fifths higher. The stock of local authority housing is, of course, much younger and better maintained and equipped than the stock of private rented housing. Because of the effect of rent control and the absence of allowances for depreciating capital expenditure, and because many owners of private rented property are poor, it is generally badly maintained. In the absence of fair rents and depreciation allowances, little new property has been built for renting for about fifty years. A flow of private finance to new property for rent is unlikely unless landlords can feel confidence in being allowed to obtain a fair financial return in future.

While improvement grants provide a considerable incentive to many owner-occupiers to improve their property, in the absence of depreciation allowances they provide little incentive to landlords. The areas of badly maintained and unimproved housing usually also have a poor housing environment and inadequate local facilities and services, and this provides little encouragement to owners to improve their dwellings. Also the future of the areas is often uncertain. Local authorities could give a stimulus to improvement by giving assurances about the future of the areas and by undertaking area improvement. Piecemeal property improvement is not really adequate but, except where there is unified ownership, this inadequacy will be difficult to avoid unless the local authority is prepared to coordinate private efforts and provide additional financial and other help to the poorer owners.

Often the redevelopment of obsolete areas of housing is not economic because some properties are in a much better condition than others, and as a result the costs of acquiring such areas are substantially higher than the costs of virgin sites. Perhaps, in return for the considerable public money which will be involved in the short-term improvement of areas of old housing, agreement can be reached over the eventual basis of valuation, so that when an area becomes ripe for redevelopment on physical grounds the redevelopment will be economically viable.

While, in the absence of a unified market for housing, it is difficult to obtain a measure of the way people value it, many people could not afford market prices even for dwellings of the standard taken as minimum in this study. It has been shown that it would be possible to provide adequate housing grants to households in need if existing housing subsidies were used in this way. Many households, however, would have to spend a greater proportion of income on housing than currently if the minimum standards taken in this study were accepted, and it would be difficult to ensure acceptance by regulation.

There are various ways in which people might be encouraged to spend a greater proportion of their incomes on housing, for example by grants and subsidies, by tax treatment favourable in relation to other consumer goods, and by legal and financial arrangements that would facilitate the purchase of housing services. Such arrangements have already been discussed. Tax arrangements based on personal taxation are uncertain in their incidence, and it seems better to rely on removing taxes from the factors of production of housing (materials, labour, capital and land), and such taxes as local rates which are levied directly on dwellings in accordance with their quality. If tax revenue so lost is levied on other consumer goods and services, this will tend to raise the value for money obtained from housing and people's propensity to spend on it.

The amount of finance and administration involved in improving areas of poor housing and in their subsequent redevelopment is likely to be considerable, and may be beyond the capacity of many local authorities. The reduction in the volume of additional dwellings to be built will leave private financial institutions and property firms with spare capacity of both finance and manpower. Some way of bringing these organizations into housing improvement and redevelopment work, and of coordinating them with local authority activities, seems to be essential. The formation of some kind of housing association may be worth exploring. Associations could take many forms to suit local circumstances, from those of local householders at one extreme to public corporations at the other.

HOUSING PRIORITIES

It would appear that over the period 1964–2004 about seven to eight million additional dwellings will be needed. More would not be required unless population grew much more rapidly than is expected, or unless household formation proceeded much further than appears likely. Nearly a million dwellings have already been provided since 1964; of these only about a third have been required to meet household formation arising from increases in the population of marriageable age; the rest have been available to meet needs arising from household fission. Until the 1980s an annual addition to the housing stocks of about 150,000 dwellings is likely to be adequate to meet all needs. Unless household fission proceeds further, the number required after that will be not much greater, although the population of marriageable age will rise at an increasing rate. On average, less than another 150,000 constructions a year would be sufficient to replace all but the best pre-1881 dwellings and provide a margin of about 30,000 dwellings a year to replace other losses. Another 70,000 a year on average would be sufficient to enable all but the best 1881–1920 dwellings to be replaced. Thus, if the number of replacements is not too ambitious, 300,000 dwellings a year on average is likely to be sufficient. An average of 375,000 dwellings a year will probably be enough to allow for all pre-1921 dwellings to be replaced.

The rate of replacement is most important to decisions on housing targets. At current rates of construction and demolition there would be an adequate supply of dwellings by the early 1970s and continued output at current levels would yield about a quarter of a million of dwellings a year for replacements. This would allow replacement of unsatisfactory dwellings at three times the current rate. There would thus be a marked change in the type of housing programme. It is necessary to consider how this would affect financial requirements. Sites in redevelopment areas are generally more expensive than sites in new areas, and neither private nor public housing developers can usually afford redevelopment without substantial subsidies. New housing rents, even with subsidies, are likely to be several times as large as the rents typical in the areas likely to be redeveloped. Considerably more money will have to be found, either by tenants, or by the government for subsidies and grants, in order to sustain a large programme of redevelopment. Renewal is usually much cheaper. Upgrading to reasonable standards, even of old property in very poor condition, can normally be carried out at a third of the cost of replacement.

However, while financing a programme of replacements of a quarter of a million a year from the early 1970s is likely to be expensive, the amount of money involved would not be large enough to allow the poorer parts of the stock to be replaced rapidly. For example, it would be the late 1970s before all the structurally unsound dwellings had been replaced—even if no other dwellings were replaced in the meantime—and these are usually the dwellings most lacking in the essential services. If they are not improved and repaired they will provide a progressively poorer service. Many may become uninhabitable. Thus not only would the stock of satisfactory dwellings be likely to decline, in spite of new constructions, but the total of useable dwellings might also decline. Thus it would seem sensible both for economic and social reasons to improve the stock as rapidly as possible.

At present only about £60 million worth of improvement work is carried out a year, against a total need of about seventy times as much. The expenditure on regular maintenance is considerably less than half that which would be necessary even if only local authority maintenance standards were applied. If the rate of construction were held at 375,000 a year and there was some slowing down in reaching Parker Morris standards and in providing garages, it would still take until the late 1970s or early 1980s to improve the structurally unsound dwellings. This estimate is on the optimistic side, since it has been assumed that the housing sector would obtain an increase in labour proportionate to the natural increase in population of working age and improve productivity in new work at a rate of 4 per cent per annum and in maintenance work at 2 per cent. Moreover the estimates are based on conditions in 1964 and further deterioration is likely to have taken place since.

If additional resources cannot be made available for repair and improvement work, it would appear worthwhile to reduce the number of constructions. This would reduce the rate of replacements initially, but it would enable a better use to be made of the existing stock of dwellings. Moreover, since the productivity of new work is expected to rise faster than that of maintenance work, total output over the forty-year period would be greater. If output were reduced to 300,000 dwellings a year, the repair and improvement of the worst class of dwelling could be completed three or four years earlier. The rate of dealing with the various classes of work would be progressively increased as time passed and the need for replacing dwellings would be reduced. Before the end of the period in 2004, not only would it be possible to complete the arrears of maintenance and improvements and increase the volume of regular maintenance to an adequate scale, but there would be sufficient surplus capacity to make up all the output of dwellings lost by reducing output earlier. Perhaps, however, 300,000 dwellings a year on average over the period is as much as is likely to be achieved if all the standards of housing rise in step with standards of living. The effect of delaying some of the replacements would be to lower the average age of the stock at the end of the period, making it more likely to meet the demands of the twenty-first century.

While, over the period, all regions have more than sufficient capacity simply to construct the additional dwellings likely to be required, all regions are short of capacity to achieve this and in addition to repair and improve the poorer dwellings and increase regular maintenance to an adequate level. The South East and East Anglia have almost enough capacity, but additional resources will be necessary for other regions, particularly for those such as the North West which have been constructing proportionally fewer new dwellings, as well as providing a particularly poor standard of maintenance.

Unnecessary fluctuations in the load of work on the industry are likely to lead to a loss of efficiency. Most labour can probably be fairly readily transferred from one type of work to another, but the transfer of some types of skilled labour, or management and plant on a large scale, particularly over a short period, is more difficult. Again, while basic materials are widely used in construction, some materials and building components tend to be specialized in their use. This is particularly true of components manufactured for building systems. Further large increases in the number of constructions are therefore better avoided if demand is not to be sustained at that level. The additional materials and components likely to be necessary for even a large programme of improvement and repair work would have a small effect on the materials industries compared with that of a large increase in new constructions.

Clearly, far too little is known about people's propensity to use their incomes to secure housing services. The number of new dwellings will depend on this, and on the amount and form of government assistance. Until these factors are known it is not possible to determine with any precision the number of dwellings that need to be constructed. It is clear, however, that this will depend to a large extent on the demand for replacements. On present evidence it would appear unlikely that any long-term increase over the current rate of construction will be required; a number substantially smaller will probably be adequate. There would appear to be little doubt about the economic and social advantages of repairing and improving the existing stock of dwellings as rapidly as possible. Which dwellings should be improved, and to what extent, depends on their future expectation of life. The expectation depends on the rate of replacement. Given this and an enumeration of the poorest dwellings in terms of the cost of restoring them to good condition, it is possible to determine the level of expenditure on each category which will give the best economic return and hence the best balance in each locality between new constructions and repair and improvement work. The resulting programmes can be updated in the light of progress and of new information as this becomes available.

APPENDIX I

PUBLIC AND PRIVATE BODIES CONSULTED

GOVERNMENT DEPARTMENTS, ETC.

H.M. Treasury
Ministry of Education (now Department of Education and Science)
Government Actuary's Department
Ministry of Housing and Local Government
Inland Revenue Department, Valuation Office
Ministry of Public Building and Works
Scottish Development Department
Ministry of Technology, Building Research Station (now under Ministry of Public Buildings and Works)
Ministry of Transport, Road Research Laboratory
National Economic Development Office

RESEARCH BODIES, UNIVERSITIES, ETC.

Cambridge University, Department of Land Economy
Edinburgh University, School of Architecture
Glasgow University, Department of Social and Economic Research
Imperial College of Science and Technology, London, Department of Transport Engineering
Liverpool University, Department of Architecture
London School of Economics
Manchester University, Department of Planning
Oxford University, Institute for Research in Agricultural Economics
University College, London, Centre for Urban Studies
University of York
Acton Society Trust
Cambridge Estate Management Advisory Service
Chicago Area Transportation Study
Civic Trust
Resources for the Future Inc.
Royal Institute of Chartered Surveyors, Building Cost Information Services

CONTRACTORS

Bryant Homes Ltd
Bunting Estates Ltd
George Calverley & Sons Ltd
Richard Costain Ltd
Davies & Rentowl Ltd

The Laing Housing Co. Ltd
John McLean & Sons Ltd
New Ideal Homesteads Ltd
Page-Johnson Ltd
Taylor Woodrow Industrial Estates Ltd
The Unit Construction Co. Ltd
George Wimpey & Co. Ltd

MISCELLANEOUS

Architectural Association
British Road Federation Ltd
Electricity Council
Gas Council
National House-Builders Registration Council
Messrs O. W. Roskill

LOCAL AUTHORITIES

County Councils

Bedfordshire
Buckinghamshire
Cambridgeshire
Essex
Hertfordshire
Kent
London County Council, including Standing Conference on London Regional Planning
Middlesex
Midlothian
Nottinghamshire
Renfrewshire
Staffordshire
Surrey
East Sussex

Cities, Boroughs etc.

Bedford
Birmingham
Bristol
Cardiff
Coventry
Darlington
Doncaster

Dundee
Edinburgh
Glasgow
Gloucester
Hertford
Kilmarnock
Manchester
Merthyr Tydfil
Middlesbrough
Newcastle upon Tyne
Nottingham
Norwich
Oldham
Portsmouth
Widnes
York

Other Planning Bodies

Town and Country Planning Association

New Town Development Corporations

Basingstoke
Cumbernauld
Livingston
Skelmersdale

REGIONS OF GREAT BRITAIN USED IN THIS STUDY

Scotland

North
- Cumberland
- Westmorland
- Durham
- Northumberland
- Yorkshire, North Riding

North West
- Cheshire
- Lancashire
- Flintshire

Pennines
- Derbyshire
- Nottinghamshire
- Yorkshire, West Riding

Central
- Leicestershire
- Northamptonshire
- Soke of Peterborough

East
- Rutland
- Lincolnshire
- Yorkshire, East Riding

North and Central Wales
- Anglesey
- Caernarvonshire
- Cardiganshire
- Denbighshire
- Merionethshire
- Montgomeryshire
- Pembrokeshire
- Radnorshire

West
- Breconshire
- Carmarthenshire
- Glamorgan
- Gloucestershire
- Monmouthshire
- Somerset
- Wiltshire

South West
- Cornwall
- Devon
- Dorset (except Poole municipal borough)

Midlands
- Herefordshire
- Shropshire
- Staffordshire
- Warwickshire
- Worcestershire

East Anglia
- Cambridgeshire
- Huntingdonshire
- Isle of Ely
- Norfolk

South East
- Bedfordshire
- Berkshire
- Buckinghamshire
- Dorset, Poole municipal borough
- Essex
- Hampshire
- Hertfordshire
- Isle of Wight
- Kent
- London
- Middlesex
- Oxfordshire
- Suffolk
- Surrey
- Sussex

APPENDIX 3

POPULATION BY AGE GROUPS

Table A3.1. *Scotland*

Hundreds

		1968	1973	1978	1983	1988	1993	1998	2003	1963
LOW BIRTH RATE										
Migration pattern 1	M & F 0–14	13803	14131	13886	13378	12569	11686	10886	10082	13310
	M & F 15–39	17182	17330	18001	18613	18883	19186	19012	18123	17330
	M 40–59	6128	5927	5874	5659	5718	5802	6027	6482	6260
	F 40–59	6677	6416	6290	6091	6158	6116	6195	6432	6850
	M 60+	3656	3932	3997	4149	4191	4185	4141	4107	3350
	F 60+	5357	5722	5840	6001	6007	5936	5835	5790	4940
	Total	52803	53458	53888	53891	53526	52911	52096	51016	52040
Migration pattern 2	M & F 0–14	13803	14131	13886	13378	12569	11686	10886	10082	13310
	M & F 15–39	17182	17330	18001	18613	18883	19186	19012	18123	17330
	M 40–59	6128	5927	5874	5659	5718	5802	6027	6482	6260
	F 40–59	6677	6416	6290	6091	6158	6116	6195	6432	6850
	M 60+	3656	3932	3997	4149	4191	4185	4141	4107	3350
	F 60+	5357	5722	5840	6001	6007	5936	5835	5790	4940
	Total	52803	53458	53888	53891	53526	52911	52096	51016	52040
Migration pattern 3	M & F 0–14	13803	14184	14078	13847	13482	13220	13225	13369	13310
	M & F 15–39	17182	17584	18763	20116	21327	22731	23819	24394	17330
	M 40–59	6128	5949	5944	5818	6039	6397	7012	7959	6260
	F 40–59	6677	6435	6349	6223	6411	6580	6990	7672	6850
	M 60+	3656	3948	4041	4235	4332	4399	4450	4546	3350
	F 60+	5357	5736	5885	6091	6159	6167	6167	6257	4940
	Total	52803	53836	55060	56330	57750	59494	61663	64197	52040
REGISTRARS GENERAL'S BIRTH RATE										
Migration pattern 1	M & F 0–14	13803	14131	14064	14074	14252	14611	15063	15363	13310
	M & F 15–39	17182	17330	18001	18613	18883	19363	19704	19793	17330
	M 40–59	6128	5927	5874	5659	5718	5802	6027	6482	6260
	F 40–59	6677	6416	6290	6091	6158	6116	6195	6432	6850
	M 60+	3656	3932	3997	4149	4191	4185	4141	4107	3350
	F 60+	5357	5722	5840	6001	6007	5936	5835	5790	4940
	Total	52803	53458	54066	54587	55209	56013	56965	57967	52040

Migration pattern 2	M & F 0–14	13803	14131	14064	14074	14252	14611	15063	15363	13310
	M & F 15–39	17182	17330	18001	18613	18883	19363	19704	19793	17330
	M 40–59	6128	5927	5874	5659	5718	5802	6027	6482	6260
	F 40–59	6677	6416	6290	6091	6158	6116	6195	6432	6850
	M 60+	3656	3932	3997	4149	4191	4185	4141	4107	3350
	F 60+	5357	5722	5840	6001	6007	5936	5835	5790	4940
	Total	52803	53458	54066	54587	55209	56013	56965	57967	52040
Migration pattern 3	M & F 0–14	13803	14184	14256	14543	15165	16145	17402	18650	13310
	M & F 15–39	17182	17584	18763	20116	21327	22908	24511	26064	17330
	M 40–59	6128	5949	5944	5818	6039	6397	7012	7959	6260
	F 40–59	6677	6435	6349	6223	6411	6580	6990	7672	6850
	M 60+	3656	3948	4041	4235	4332	4399	4450	4546	3350
	F 60+	5357	5736	5885	6091	6159	6167	6167	6257	4940
	Total	52803	53836	55238	57026	59433	62596	66532	71148	52040
HIGH BIRTH RATE										
Migration pattern 1	M & F 0–14	13850	14590	15432	16677	18100	19733	22134	25421	13310
	M & F 15–39	17182	17330	18001	18660	19340	20721	22329	24064	17330
	M 40–59	6128	5927	5874	5659	5718	5802	6027	6482	6260
	F 40–59	6677	6416	6290	6091	6158	6116	6195	6432	6850
	M 60+	3656	3932	3997	4149	4191	4185	4141	4107	3350
	F 60+	5357	5722	5840	6001	6007	5936	5835	5790	4940
	Total	52850	53917	55434	57237	59514	62493	66661	72296	52040
Migration pattern 2	M & F 0–14	13850	14590	15432	16677	18100	19733	22134	25421	13310
	M & F 15–39	17182	17330	18001	18660	19340	20721	22329	24064	17330
	M 40–59	6128	5927	5874	5659	5718	5802	6027	6482	6260
	F 40–59	6677	6416	6290	6091	6158	6116	6195	6432	6850
	M 60+	3656	3932	3997	4149	4191	4185	4141	4107	3350
	F 60+	5357	5722	5840	6001	6007	5936	5835	5790	4940
	Total	52850	53917	55434	57237	59514	62493	66661	72296	52040
Migration pattern 3	M & F 0–14	13850	14643	15624	17146	19013	21267	24473	28708	13310
	M & F 15–39	17182	17584	18763	20163	21784	24266	27136	30335	17330
	M 40–59	6128	5949	5944	5818	6039	6397	7012	7959	6260
	F 40–59	6677	6435	6349	6223	6411	6580	6990	7672	6850
	M 60+	3656	3948	4041	4235	4332	4399	4450	4546	3350
	F 60+	5357	5736	5885	6091	6159	6167	6167	6257	4940
	Total	52850	54295	56606	59676	63738	69076	76228	85477	52040

SOURCE: NIESR estimates.

Table A3.2. *North*

Hundreds

			1968	1973	1978	1983	1988	1993	1998	2003	1963
LOW BIRTH RATE											
Migration pattern 1	M & F	0–14	8436	8883	9037	8957	8661	8319	8018	7689	8103
	M & F	15–39	11526	11785	12325	12841	13041	13434	13709	13595	11213
	M	40–59	4036	3998	4029	4034	4301	4428	4565	4799	4136
	F	40–59	4049	3928	3897	3891	4190	4363	4506	4711	4159
	M	60+	2471	2655	2723	2828	2845	2905	2949	3037	2251
	F	60+	3329	3536	3624	3730	3725	3710	3708	3783	3080
		Total	33847	34785	35635	36281	36763	37159	37455	37614	32942
Migration pattern 2	M & F	0–14	8436	8883	9037	8957	8661	8319	8018	7689	8103
	M & F	15–39	11526	11785	12325	12841	13041	13434	13709	13595	11213
	M	40–59	4036	3998	4029	4034	4301	4428	4565	4799	4136
	F	40–59	4049	3928	3897	3891	4190	4363	4506	4711	4159
	M	60+	2471	2655	2723	2828	2845	2905	2949	3037	2251
	F	60+	3329	3536	3624	3730	3725	3710	3708	3783	3080
		Total	33847	34785	35635	36281	36763	37159	37455	37614	32942
Migration pattern 3	M & F	0–14	8436	8912	9146	9222	9178	9187	9345	9554	8103
	M & F	15–39	11526	11930	12757	13695	14428	15444	16432	17154	11213
	M	40–59	4036	4011	4068	4123	4482	4766	5124	5636	4136
	F	40–59	4049	3938	3931	3965	4334	4626	4957	5413	4159
	M	60+	2471	2663	2748	2877	2927	3027	3124	3286	2251
	F	60+	3329	3544	3650	3781	3812	3843	3896	4048	3080
		Total	33847	34998	36300	37663	39161	40893	42878	45091	32942
REGISTRARS GENERAL'S BIRTH RATE											
Migration pattern 1	M & F	0–14	8436	8883	9148	9390	9708	10139	10606	10951	8103
	M & F	15–39	11526	11785	12325	12841	13041	13545	14138	14633	11213
	M	40–59	4036	3998	4029	4034	4301	4428	4565	4799	4136
	F	40–59	4049	3928	3897	3891	4190	4363	4506	4711	4159
	M	60+	2471	2655	2723	2828	2845	2905	2949	3037	2251
	F	60+	3329	3536	3624	3730	3725	3710	3708	3783	3080
		Total	33847	34785	35746	36714	37810	39090	40472	41914	32942

Migration pattern 2	M & F 0–14	8436	8883	9148	9390	9708	10139	10606	10951	8103
	M & F 15–39	11526	11785	12325	12841	13041	13545	14138	14633	11213
	M 40–59	4036	3998	4029	4034	4301	4428	4565	4799	4136
	F 40–59	4049	3928	3897	3891	4190	4363	4506	4711	4159
	M 60+	2471	2655	2723	2828	2845	2905	2949	3037	2251
	F 60+	3329	3536	3624	3730	3725	3710	3708	3783	3080
	Total	33847	34785	35746	36714	37810	39090	40472	41914	32942
Migration pattern 3	M & F 0–14	8436	8912	9257	9655	10225	11007	11933	12816	8103
	M & F 15–39	11526	11930	12757	13695	14428	15555	16861	18192	11213
	M 40–59	4036	4011	4068	4123	4482	4766	5124	5636	4136
	F 40–59	4049	3938	3931	3965	4334	4626	4957	5413	4159
	M 60+	2471	2663	2748	2877	2927	3027	3124	3286	2251
	F 60+	3329	3544	3650	3781	3812	3843	3896	4048	3080
	Total	33847	34998	36411	38096	40208	42824	45895	49391	32942
HIGH BIRTH RATE										
Migration pattern 1	M & F 0–14	8465	9169	10003	11016	12109	13329	14992	17173	8103
	M & F 15–39	11526	11785	12325	12871	13326	14404	15789	17309	11213
	M 40–59	4036	3998	4029	4034	4301	4428	4565	4799	4136
	F 40–59	4049	3928	3897	3891	4190	4363	4506	4711	4159
	M 60+	2471	2655	2723	2828	2845	2905	2949	3037	2251
	F 60+	3329	3536	3624	3730	3725	3710	3708	3783	3080
	Total	33876	35071	36601	38370	40496	43139	46509	50812	32942
Migration pattern 2	M & F 0–14	8465	9169	10003	11016	12109	13329	14992	17173	8103
	M & F 15–39	11526	11785	12325	12871	13326	14404	15789	17309	11213
	M 40–59	4036	3998	4029	4034	4301	4428	4565	4799	4136
	F 40–59	4049	3928	3897	3891	4190	4363	4506	4711	4159
	M 60+	2471	2655	2723	2828	2845	2905	2949	3037	2251
	F 60+	3329	3536	3624	3730	3725	3710	3708	3783	3080
	Total	33876	35071	36601	38370	40496	43139	46509	50812	32942
Migration pattern 3	M & F 0–14	8465	9198	10112	11281	12626	14197	16319	19038	8103
	M & F 15–39	11526	11930	12757	13725	14713	16414	18512	20868	11213
	M 40–59	4036	4011	4068	4123	4482	4766	5124	5636	4136
	F 40–59	4049	3938	3931	3965	4334	4626	4957	5413	4159
	M 60+	2471	2663	2748	2877	2927	3027	3124	3286	2251
	F 60+	3329	3544	3650	3781	3812	3843	3896	4048	3080
	Total	33876	35284	37266	39752	42894	46873	51932	58289	32942

SOURCE: NIESR estimates.

Table A3.3. *North West*

Hundreds

		1968	1973	1978	1983	1988	1993	1998	2003	1963
LOW BIRTH RATE										
Migration pattern 1	M & F 0–14	16802	17854	18039	17707	17150	16657	16276	15782	15831
	M & F 15–39	21878	22446	23811	25449	26407	27295	27951	27729	21587
	M 40–59	8558	8261	8115	7766	7923	8257	8621	9425	8766
	F 40–59	9052	8555	8265	7936	8231	8535	8850	9427	9406
	M 60+	5172	5611	5791	6026	6073	6019	5962	5883	4635
	F 60+	7747	8198	8321	8512	8429	8194	7961	7870	7165
	Total	69209	70925	72342	73396	74213	74957	75621	76116	67390
Migration pattern 2	M & F 0–14	16802	17854	18039	17707	17150	16657	16276	15782	15831
	M & F 15–39	21878	22446	23811	25449	26407	27295	27951	27729	21587
	M 40–59	8558	8261	8115	7766	7923	8257	8621	9425	8766
	F 40–59	9052	8555	8265	7936	8231	8535	8850	9427	9406
	M 60+	5172	5611	5791	6026	6073	6019	5962	5883	4635
	F 60+	7747	8198	8321	8512	8429	8194	7961	7870	7165
	Total	69209	70925	72342	73396	74213	74957	75621	76116	67390
Migration pattern 3	M & F 0–14	16802	17881	18143	17961	17645	17490	17548	17570	15831
	M & F 15–39	21878	22584	24228	26266	27738	29221	30563	31137	21587
	M 40–59	8558	8272	8151	7853	8097	8581	9156	10227	8766
	F 40–59	9052	8564	8297	8007	8369	8788	9281	10100	9406
	M 60+	5172	5619	5814	6074	6150	6135	6130	6121	4635
	F 60+	7747	8206	8346	8563	8510	8319	8142	8122	7165
	Total	69209	71126	72979	74724	76509	78534	80820	83277	67390
REGISTRARS GENERAL'S BIRTH RATE										
Migration pattern 1	M & F 0–14	16802	17853	18254	18546	19184	20205	21344	22185	15831
	M & F 15–39	21878	22446	23811	25452	26406	27507	28783	29747	21587
	M 40–59	8558	8261	8115	7766	7923	8257	8621	9425	8766
	F 40–59	9052	8555	8265	7936	8231	8535	8850	9427	9406
	M 60+	5172	5611	5791	6026	6073	6019	5962	5883	4635
	F 60+	7747	8198	8321	8512	8429	8194	7961	7870	7165
	Total	69209	70924	72557	74238	76246	78717	81521	84537	67390

[illegible]	[illegible]	[illegible]	[illegible]	[illegible]	[illegible]	[illegible]	[illegible]	[illegible]	[illegible]	[illegible]
pattern 2	M & F 15–39	21878	22446	23811	25452	26406	27507	28783	29747	21587
	M 40–59	8558	8261	8115	7766	7923	8257	8621	9425	8766
	F 40–59	9052	8555	8265	7936	8231	8535	8850	9427	9406
	M 60+	5172	5611	5791	6026	6073	6019	5962	5883	4635
	F 60+	7747	8198	8321	8512	8429	8194	7961	7870	7165
	Total	69209	70924	72557	74238	76246	78717	81521	84537	67390
Migration pattern 3	M & F 0–14	16802	17880	18358	18800	19679	21038	22616	23973	15831
	M & F 15–39	21878	22584	24228	26269	27737	29433	31395	33155	21587
	M 40–59	8558	8272	8151	7853	8097	8581	9156	10227	8766
	F 40–59	9052	8564	8297	8007	8369	8788	9281	10100	9406
	M 60+	5172	5619	5814	6074	6150	6135	6130	6121	4635
	F 60+	7747	8206	8346	8563	8510	8319	8142	8122	7165
	Total	69209	71125	73194	75566	78542	82294	86720	91698	67390
HIGH BIRTH RATE										
Migration pattern 1	M & F 0–14	16861	18421	19921	21700	23843	26421	29935	34395	15831
	M & F 15–39	21878	22446	23811	25506	26970	29173	31984	34936	21587
	M 40–59	8558	8261	8115	7766	7923	8257	8621	9425	8766
	F 40–59	9052	8555	8265	7936	8231	8535	8850	9427	9406
	M 60+	5172	5611	5791	6026	6073	6019	5962	5883	4635
	F 60+	7747	8198	8321	8512	8429	8194	7961	7870	7165
	Total	69268	71492	74224	77446	81469	86599	93313	101936	67390
Migration pattern 2	M & F 0–14	16861	18421	19921	21700	23843	26421	29935	34395	15831
	M & F 15–39	21878	22446	23811	25506	26970	29173	31984	34936	21587
	M 40–59	8558	8261	8115	7766	7923	8257	8621	9425	8766
	F 40–59	9052	8555	8265	7936	8231	8535	8850	9427	9406
	M 60+	5172	5611	5791	6026	6073	6019	5962	5883	4635
	F 60+	7747	8198	8321	8512	8429	8194	7961	7870	7165
	Total	69268	71492	74224	77446	81469	86599	93313	101936	67390
Migration pattern 3	M & F 0–14	16861	18448	20025	21954	24338	27254	31207	36183	15831
	M & F 15–39	21878	22584	24228	26323	28301	31099	34596	38344	21587
	M 40–59	8558	8272	8151	7853	8097	8581	9156	10227	8766
	F 40–59	9052	8564	8297	8007	8369	8788	9281	10100	9406
	M 60+	5172	5619	5814	6074	6150	6135	6130	6121	4635
	F 60+	7747	8206	8346	8563	8510	8319	8142	8122	7165
	Total	69268	71693	74861	78774	83765	90176	98512	109097	67390

SOURCE: NIESR estimates.

Table A3.4. *Pennines*

Hundreds

		1968	1973	1978	1983	1988	1993	1998	2003	1963
LOW BIRTH RATE										
Migration pattern 1	M & F 0–14	13616	14688	15112	14870	14444	14091	13863	13548	12669
	M & F 15–39	18655	19023	19976	21360	22124	23045	23795	23909	18390
	M 40–59	7273	7110	7089	6857	7112	7303	7494	8032	7396
	F 40–59	7348	7019	6856	6693	7032	7290	7536	7942	7544
	M 60+	4295	4710	4883	5118	5189	5225	5247	5225	3834
	F 60+	5995	6434	6615	6832	6837	6725	6613	6632	5501
	Total	57182	58984	60531	61730	62738	63679	64548	65288	55334
Migration pattern 2	M & F 0–14	13616	14688	15112	14870	14444	14091	13863	13548	12669
	M & F 15–39	18655	19023	19976	21360	22124	23045	23795	23909	18390
	M 40–59	7273	7110	7089	6857	7112	7303	7494	8032	7396
	F 40–59	7348	7019	6856	6693	7032	7290	7536	7942	7544
	M 60+	4295	4710	4883	5118	5189	5225	5247	5225	3834
	F 60+	5995	6434	6615	6832	6837	6725	6613	6632	5501
	Total	57182	58984	60531	61730	62738	63679	64548	65288	55334
Migration pattern 3	M & F 0–14	13616	14707	15182	15040	14771	14644	14709	14736	12669
	M & F 15–39	18655	19117	20253	21903	23005	24324	25530	26173	18390
	M 40–59	7273	7118	7112	6915	7227	7517	7850	8565	7396
	F 40–59	7348	7026	6877	6739	7124	7459	7824	8390	7544
	M 60+	4295	4714	4898	5149	5240	5302	5359	5384	3834
	F 60+	5995	6440	6631	6864	6891	6808	6733	6800	5501
	Total	57182	59122	60953	62610	64258	66054	68005	70048	55334
REGISTRARS GENERAL'S BIRTH RATE										
Migration pattern 1	M & F 0–14	13616	14687	15289	15558	16110	16991	18003	18777	12669
	M & F 15–39	18655	19023	19976	21359	22123	23222	24477	25560	18390
	M 40–59	7273	7110	7089	6857	7112	7303	7494	8032	7396
	F 40–59	7348	7019	6856	6693	7032	7290	7536	7942	7544
	M 60+	4295	4710	4883	5118	5189	5225	5247	5225	3834
	F 60+	5995	6434	6615	6832	6837	6725	6613	6632	5501
	Total	57182	58983	60708	62417	64403	66756	69370	72168	55334

Migration pattern 2	M & F	0–14	13616	14687	15289	15558	16110	16991	18003	18777	12669
	M & F	15–39	18655	19023	19976	21359	22123	23222	24477	25560	18390
	M	40–59	7273	7110	7089	6857	7112	7303	7494	8032	7396
	F	40–59	7348	7019	6856	6693	7032	7290	7536	7942	7544
	M	60+	4295	4710	4883	5118	5189	5225	5247	5225	3834
	F	60+	5995	6434	6615	6832	6837	6725	6613	6632	5501
		Total	57182	58983	60708	62417	64403	66756	69370	72168	55334
Migration pattern 3	M & F	0–14	13616	14706	15359	15728	16437	17544	18849	19965	12669
	M & F	15–39	18655	19117	20253	21902	23004	24501	26212	27824	18390
	M	40–59	7273	7118	7112	6915	7227	7517	7850	8565	7396
	F	40–59	7348	7026	6877	6739	7124	7459	7824	8390	7544
	M	60+	4295	4714	4898	5149	5240	5302	5359	5384	3834
	F	60+	5995	6440	6631	6864	6891	6808	6733	6800	5501
		Total	57182	59121	61130	63297	65923	69131	72827	76928	55334
HIGH BIRTH RATE											
Migration pattern 1	M & F	0–14	13666	15159	16670	18153	19929	22075	25023	28754	12669
	M & F	15–39	18655	19023	19976	21410	22591	24589	27098	29815	18390
	M	40–59	7273	7110	7089	6857	7112	7303	7494	8032	7396
	F	40–59	7348	7019	6856	6693	7032	7290	7536	7942	7544
	M	60+	4295	4710	4883	5118	5189	5225	5247	5225	3834
	F	60+	5995	6434	6615	6832	6837	6725	6613	6632	5501
		Total	57232	59455	62089	65063	68690	73207	79011	86400	55334
Migration pattern 2	M & F	0–14	13666	15159	16670	18153	19929	22075	25023	28754	12669
	M & F	15–39	18655	19023	19976	21410	22591	24589	27098	29815	18390
	M	40–59	7273	7110	7089	6857	7112	7303	7494	8032	7396
	F	40–59	7348	7019	6856	6693	7032	7290	7536	7942	7544
	M	60+	4295	4710	4883	5118	5189	5225	5247	5225	3834
	F	60+	5995	6434	6615	6832	6837	6725	6613	6632	5501
		Total	57232	59455	62089	65063	68690	73207	79011	86400	55334
Migration pattern 3	M & F	0–14	13666	15178	16740	18323	20256	22628	25869	29942	12669
	M & F	15–39	18655	19117	20253	21953	23472	25868	28833	32079	18390
	M	40–59	7273	7118	7112	6915	7227	7517	7850	8565	7396
	F	40–59	7348	7026	6877	6739	7124	7459	7824	8390	7544
	M	60+	4295	4714	4898	5149	5240	5302	5359	5384	3834
	F	60+	5995	6440	6631	6864	6891	6808	6733	6800	5501
		Total	57232	59593	62511	65943	70210	75582	82468	91160	55334

SOURCE: NIESR estimates.

Table A3.5. *Central*

Hundreds

		1968	1973	1978	1983	1988	1993	1998	2003	1963
LOW BIRTH RATE										
Migration pattern 1	M & F 0–14	2959	3247	3435	3540	3597	3671	3777	3849	2732
	M & F 15–39	4209	4504	4913	5377	5675	6006	6330	6548	3924
	M 40–59	1533	1548	1601	1623	1780	1910	2033	2220	1540
	F 40–59	1534	1502	1512	1524	1663	1817	1973	2164	1549
	M 60+	933	1017	1058	1116	1147	1190	1266	1309	830
	F 60+	1295	1378	1415	1463	1485	1495	1507	1549	1201
	Total	12463	13196	13934	14643	15347	16089	16886	17639	11776
Migration pattern 2	M & F 0–14	2959	3240	3411	3486	3492	3494	3506	3470	2732
	M & F 15–39	4209	4474	4827	5203	5392	5600	5774	5823	3924
	M 40–59	1533	1546	1592	1605	1743	1841	1920	2050	1540
	F 40–59	1534	1501	1506	1511	1634	1764	1882	2022	1549
	M 60+	933	1014	1053	1106	1131	1165	1231	1259	830
	F 60+	1295	1377	1409	1452	1468	1468	1470	1496	1201
	Total	12463	13152	13798	14363	14860	15332	15783	16120	11776
Migration pattern 3	M & F 0–14	2959	3238	3404	3468	3457	3437	3418	3345	2732
	M & F 15–39	4209	4465	4798	5146	5303	5462	5592	5584	3924
	M 40–59	1533	1546	1589	1599	1731	1819	1883	1992	1540
	F 40–59	1534	1500	1504	1505	1624	1748	1851	1975	1549
	M 60+	933	1013	1052	1102	1125	1157	1219	1242	830
	F 60+	1295	1375	1408	1448	1463	1459	1456	1478	1201
	Total	12463	13137	13755	14268	14703	15082	15419	15616	11776
REGISTRARS GENERAL'S BIRTH RATE										
Migration pattern 1	M & F 0–14	2959	3247	3472	3686	3949	4286	4655	4961	2732
	M & F 15–39	4209	4504	4913	5377	5675	6043	6475	6897	3924
	M 40–59	1533	1548	1601	1623	1780	1910	2033	2220	1540
	F 40–59	1534	1502	1512	1524	1663	1817	1973	2164	1549
	M 60+	933	1017	1058	1116	1147	1190	1266	1309	830
	F 60+	1295	1378	1415	1463	1485	1495	1507	1549	1201
	Total	12463	13196	13971	14789	15699	16741	17909	19100	11776

Migration pattern 2	M & F	0–14	2959	3240	3448	3632	3844	4109	4384	4582	2732
	M & F	15–39	4209	4474	4827	5203	5392	5637	5919	6172	3924
	M	40–59	1533	1546	1592	1605	1743	1841	1920	2050	1540
	F	40–59	1534	1501	1506	1511	1634	1764	1882	2022	1549
	M	60+	933	1014	1053	1106	1131	1165	1231	1259	830
	F	60+	1295	1377	1409	1452	1468	1468	1470	1496	1201
		Total	12463	13152	13835	14509	15212	15984	16806	17581	11776
Migration pattern 3	M & F	0–14	2959	3238	3441	3614	3809	4052	4296	4457	2732
	M & F	15–39	4209	4465	4798	5146	5303	5499	5737	5933	3924
	M	40–59	1533	1546	1589	1599	1731	1819	1883	1992	1540
	F	40–59	1534	1500	1504	1505	1624	1748	1851	1975	1549
	M	60+	933	1013	1052	1102	1125	1157	1219	1242	830
	F	60+	1295	1375	1408	1448	1463	1459	1456	1478	1201
		Total	12463	13137	13792	14414	15055	15734	16442	17077	11776
HIGH BIRTH RATE											
Migration pattern 1	M & F	0–14	2970	3346	3764	4235	4759	5364	6146	7082	2732
	M & F	15–39	4209	4504	4913	5388	5774	6332	7030	7799	3924
	M	40–59	1533	1548	1601	1623	1780	1910	2033	2220	1540
	F	40–59	1534	1502	1512	1524	1663	1817	1973	2164	1549
	M	60+	933	1017	1058	1116	1147	1190	1266	1309	830
	F	60+	1295	1378	1415	1463	1485	1495	1507	1549	1201
		Total	12474	13295	14263	15349	16608	18108	19955	22123	11776
Migration pattern 2	M & F	0–14	2970	3339	3740	4181	4654	5187	5875	6703	2732
	M & F	15–39	4209	4474	4827	5214	5491	5926	6474	7074	3924
	M	40–59	1533	1546	1592	1605	1743	1841	1920	2050	1540
	F	40–59	1534	1501	1506	1511	1634	1764	1882	2022	1549
	M	60+	933	1014	1053	1106	1131	1165	1231	1259	830
	F	60+	1295	1377	1409	1452	1468	1468	1470	1496	1201
		Total	12474	13251	14127	15069	16121	17351	18852	20604	11776
Migration pattern 3	M & F	0–14	2970	3337	3733	4163	4619	5130	5787	6578	2732
	M & F	15–39	4209	4465	4798	5157	5402	5788	6292	6835	3924
	M	40–59	1533	1546	1589	1599	1731	1819	1883	1992	1540
	F	40–59	1534	1500	1504	1505	1624	1748	1851	1975	1549
	M	60+	933	1013	1052	1102	1125	1157	1219	1242	830
	F	60+	1295	1375	1408	1448	1463	1459	1456	1478	1201
		Total	12474	13236	14084	14974	15964	17101	18488	20100	11776

SOURCE: NIESR estimates.

Table A3.6. *East*

Hundreds

		1968	1973	1978	1983	1988	1993	1998	2003	1963
LOW BIRTH RATE										
Migration pattern 1	M & F 0–14	3348	3548	3644	3654	3596	3541	3510	3451	3175
	M & F 15–39	4560	4759	5044	5366	5562	5782	5948	5986	4400
	M 40–59	1677	1669	1697	1693	1785	1865	1942	2078	1680
	F 40–59	1690	1633	1618	1592	1693	1799	1904	2041	1698
	M 60+	1010	1080	1120	1179	1203	1231	1268	1300	959
	F 60+	1365	1447	1488	1550	1574	1564	1560	1576	1293
	Total	13650	14136	14611	15034	15413	15782	16132	16432	13205
Migration pattern 2	M & F 0–14	3348	3557	3674	3730	3747	3796	3899	3999	3175
	M & F 15–39	4560	4803	5170	5615	5971	6372	6749	7033	4400
	M 40–59	1677	1671	1709	1719	1837	1964	2106	2325	1680
	F 40–59	1690	1634	1628	1613	1735	1877	2037	2248	1698
	M 60+	1010	1080	1125	1195	1228	1266	1319	1373	959
	F 60+	1365	1447	1493	1567	1599	1601	1616	1653	1293
	Total	13650	14192	14799	15439	16117	16876	17726	18631	13205
Migration pattern 3	M & F 0–14	3348	3548	3639	3641	3575	3506	3454	3375	3175
	M & F 15–39	4560	4752	5027	5330	5506	5699	5836	5842	4400
	M 40–59	1677	1668	1697	1689	1778	1852	1919	2044	1680
	F 40–59	1690	1632	1617	1589	1686	1789	1887	2012	1698
	M 60+	1010	1080	1117	1179	1200	1226	1261	1290	959
	F 60+	1365	1447	1485	1550	1570	1558	1552	1565	1293
	Total	13650	14127	14582	14978	15315	15630	15909	16128	13205
REGISTRARS GENERAL'S BIRTH RATE										
Migration pattern 1	M & F 0–14	3348	3548	3687	3822	4001	4247	4516	4723	3175
	M & F 15–39	4560	4759	5044	5366	5562	5824	6114	6386	4400
	M 40–59	1677	1669	1697	1693	1785	1865	1942	2078	1680
	F 40–59	1690	1633	1618	1592	1693	1799	1904	2041	1698
	M 60+	1010	1080	1120	1179	1203	1231	1268	1300	959
	F 60+	1365	1447	1488	1550	1574	1564	1560	1576	1293
	Total	13650	14136	14654	15202	15818	16530	17304	18104	13205

Migration pattern 2	M & F	0–14	3348	3557	3717	3898	4152	4502	4905	5271	3175
	M & F	15–39	4560	4803	5170	5615	5971	6414	6915	7433	4400
	M	40–59	1677	1671	1709	1719	1837	1964	2106	2325	1680
	F	40–59	1690	1634	1628	1613	1735	1877	2037	2248	1698
	M	60+	1010	1080	1125	1195	1228	1266	1319	1373	959
	F	60+	1365	1447	1493	1567	1599	1601	1616	1653	1293
		Total	13650	14192	14842	15607	16522	17624	18898	20303	13205
Migration pattern 3	M & F	0–14	3348	3548	3682	3809	3980	4212	4460	4647	3175
	M & F	15–39	4560	4752	5027	5330	5506	5741	6002	6242	4400
	M	40–59	1677	1668	1697	1689	1778	1852	1919	2044	1680
	F	40–59	1690	1632	1617	1589	1686	1789	1887	2012	1698
	M	60+	1010	1080	1117	1179	1200	1226	1261	1290	959
	F	60+	1365	1447	1485	1550	1570	1558	1552	1565	1293
		Total	13650	14127	14625	15146	15720	16378	17081	17800	13205
HIGH BIRTH RATE											
Migration pattern 1	M & F	0–14	3359	3660	4019	4453	4932	5484	6222	7149	3175
	M & F	15–39	4560	4759	5044	5377	5673	6152	6748	7418	4400
	M	40–59	1677	1669	1697	1693	1785	1865	1942	2078	1680
	F	40–59	1690	1633	1618	1592	1693	1799	1904	2041	1698
	M	60+	1010	1080	1120	1179	1203	1231	1268	1300	959
	F	60+	1365	1447	1488	1550	1574	1564	1560	1576	1293
		Total	13661	14248	14986	15844	16860	18095	19644	21562	13205
Migration pattern 2	M & F	0–14	3359	3669	4049	4529	5083	5739	6611	7697	3175
	M & F	15–39	4560	4803	5170	5626	6082	6742	7549	8465	4400
	M	40–59	1677	1671	1709	1719	1837	1964	2106	2325	1680
	F	40–59	1690	1634	1628	1613	1735	1877	2037	2248	1698
	M	60+	1010	1080	1125	1195	1228	1266	1319	1373	959
	F	60+	1365	1447	1493	1567	1599	1601	1616	1653	1293
		Total	13661	14304	15174	16249	17564	19189	21238	23761	13205
Migration pattern 3	M & F	0–14	3359	3660	4014	4440	4911	5449	6166	7073	3175
	M & F	15–39	4560	4752	5027	5341	5617	6069	6636	7274	4400
	M	40–59	1677	1668	1697	1689	1778	1852	1919	2044	1680
	F	40–59	1690	1632	1617	1589	1686	1789	1887	2012	1698
	M	60+	1010	1080	1117	1179	1200	1226	1261	1290	959
	F	60+	1365	1447	1485	1550	1570	1558	1552	1565	1293
		Total	13661	14239	14957	15788	16762	17943	19421	21258	13205

SOURCE: NIESR estimates.

Table A3.7. *North and Central Wales*

Hundreds

			1968	1973	1978	1983	1988	1993	1998	2003	1963
LOW BIRTH RATE											
Migration pattern 1	M & F	0–14	1383	1452	1481	1439	1375	1314	1257	1190	1324
	M & F	15–39	1885	1918	1989	2070	2073	2119	2143	2123	1872
	M	40–59	724	686	665	659	701	722	744	759	761
	F	40–59	759	707	664	634	669	689	712	738	797
	M	60+	541	536	523	524	512	497	486	498	501
	F	60+	732	740	734	730	707	674	641	628	717
		Total	6024	6039	6056	6056	6037	6015	5983	5936	5972
Migration pattern 2	M & F	0–14	1383	1464	1526	1548	1591	1675	1811	1970	1324
	M & F	15–39	1885	1980	2170	2425	2653	2959	3280	3609	1872
	M	40–59	724	691	680	697	779	862	978	1109	761
	F	40–59	759	712	679	665	728	800	901	1031	797
	M	60+	541	540	534	545	546	547	559	602	501
	F	60+	732	744	746	750	742	729	720	737	717
		Total	6024	6131	6335	6630	7039	7572	8249	9058	5972
Migration pattern 3	M & F	0–14	1383	1450	1474	1425	1348	1269	1191	1097	1324
	M & F	15–39	1885	1912	1967	2026	2004	2017	2005	1944	1872
	M	40–59	724	685	661	654	692	706	717	717	761
	F	40–59	759	707	663	631	661	676	690	704	797
	M	60+	541	536	522	520	508	490	477	486	501
	F	60+	732	740	734	727	702	666	632	614	717
		Total	6024	6030	6021	5983	5915	5824	5712	5562	5972
REGISTRARS GENERAL'S BIRTH RATE											
Migration pattern 1	M & F	0–14	1383	1452	1499	1509	1546	1613	1684	1727	1324
	M & F	15–39	1885	1918	1989	2070	2073	2137	2212	2293	1872
	M	40–59	724	686	665	659	701	722	744	759	761
	F	40–59	759	707	664	634	669	689	712	738	797
	M	60+	541	536	523	524	512	497	486	498	501
	F	60+	732	740	734	730	707	674	641	628	717
		Total	6024	6039	6074	6126	6208	6332	6479	6643	5972

pattern 2	M & F	15–39	1885	1980	2170	2425	2653	2977	3349	3779	1872
	M	40–59	724	691	680	697	779	862	978	1109	761
	F	04–59	759	712	679	665	728	800	901	1031	797
	M	60+	541	540	534	545	546	547	559	602	501
	F	60+	732	744	746	750	742	729	720	737	717
		Total	6024	6131	6353	6700	7210	7889	8745	9765	5972
Migration pattern 3	M & F	0–14	1383	1450	1492	1495	1519	1568	1618	1634	1324
	M & F	15–39	1885	1912	1967	2026	2004	2035	2074	2114	1872
	M	40–59	724	685	661	654	692	706	717	717	761
	F	40–59	759	707	663	631	661	676	690	704	797
	M	60+	541	536	522	520	508	490	477	486	501
	F	60+	732	740	734	727	702	666	632	614	717
		Total	6024	6030	6039	6053	6086	6141	6208	6269	5972
HIGH BIRTH RATE											
Migration pattern 1	M & F	0–14	1388	1500	1640	1775	1938	2137	2406	2751	1324
	M & F	15–39	1885	1918	1989	2075	2121	2277	2481	2728	1872
	M	40–59	724	686	665	659	701	722	744	759	761
	F	40–59	759	707	664	634	669	689	712	738	797
	M	60+	541	536	523	524	512	497	486	498	501
	F	60+	732	740	734	730	707	674	641	628	717
		Total	6029	6087	6215	6397	6648	6996	7470	8102	5972
Migration pattern 2	M & F	0–14	1388	1512	1685	1884	2154	2498	2960	3531	1324
	M & F	15–39	1885	1980	2170	2430	2701	3117	3618	4214	1872
	M	40–59	724	691	680	697	779	862	978	1109	761
	F	40–59	759	712	679	665	728	800	901	1031	797
	M	60+	541	540	534	545	546	547	559	602	501
	F	60+	732	744	746	750	742	729	720	737	717
		Total	6029	6179	6494	6971	7650	8553	9736	11224	5972
Migration pattern 3	M & F	0–14	1388	1498	1633	1761	1911	2092	2340	2658	1324
	M & F	15–39	1885	1912	1967	2031	2052	2175	2343	2549	1872
	M	40–59	724	685	661	654	692	706	717	717	761
	F	40–59	759	707	663	631	661	676	690	704	797
	M	60+	541	536	522	520	508	490	477	486	501
	F	60+	732	740	734	727	702	666	632	614	717
		Total	6029	6078	6180	6324	6526	6805	7199	7728	5972

SOURCE: NIESR estimates.

Table A3.8. *West*

Hundreds

			1968	1973	1978	1983	1988	1993	1998	2003	1963
LOW BIRTH RATE											
Migration pattern 1	M & F	0–14	9859	10594	11055	11154	11081	11043	11069	11016	9243
	M & F	15–39	13832	14587	15573	16642	17195	17983	18672	19045	13229
	M	40–59	5107	5030	5046	5129	5594	5943	6283	6624	5206
	F	40–59	5139	4937	4900	4831	5215	5608	5957	6398	5258
	M	60+	3181	3410	3515	3668	3728	3760	3805	3990	2883
	F	60+	4328	4576	4685	4848	4872	4803	4791	4851	4054
	Total		41446	43134	44774	46272	47685	49140	50577	51924	39873
Migration pattern 2	M & F	0–14	9859	10608	11104	11275	11316	11438	11673	11864	9243
	M & F	15–39	13835	14652	15770	17031	17828	18896	19909	20662	13229
	M	40–59	5107	5035	5062	5171	5676	6098	6538	7004	5206
	F	40–59	5139	4941	4916	4864	5280	5727	6162	6717	5258
	M	60+	3181	3414	3526	3691	3765	3815	3885	4104	2883
	F	60+	4328	4580	4697	4872	4910	4863	4877	4971	4054
		Total	41446	43230	45075	46904	48775	50837	53044	55322	39873
Migration pattern 3	M & F	0–14	9859	10585	11016	11062	10902	10738	10607	10368	9243
	M & F	15–39	13832	14535	15423	16346	16714	17283	17724	17807	13229
	M	40–59	5107	5026	5031	5099	5530	5826	6090	6332	5206
	F	40–59	5139	4934	4890	4805	5165	5516	5801	6154	5258
	M	60+	3181	3407	3506	3652	3701	3717	3745	3903	2883
	F	60+	4328	4574	4676	4831	4842	4756	4725	4759	4054
		Total	41446	43061	44542	45795	46854	47836	48692	49323	39873
REGISTRARS GENERAL'S BIRTH RATE											
Migration pattern 1	M & F	0–14	9859	10594	11183	11651	12279	13128	14040	14771	9243
	M & F	15–39	13832	14587	15573	16642	17195	18109	19166	20232	13229
	M	40–59	5107	5030	5046	5129	5594	5943	6283	6624	5206
	F	40–59	5139	4937	4900	4831	5215	5608	5957	6398	5258
	M	60+	3181	3410	3515	3668	3728	3760	3805	3990	2883
	F	60+	4328	4576	4685	4848	4872	4803	4791	4851	4054
		Total	41446	43134	44902	46769	48883	51351	54042	56866	39873

pattern 2	M & F	15–39	13832	14652	15770	17031	17828	19022	20403	21849	13229
	M	40–59	5107	5035	5062	5171	5676	6098	6538	7004	5206
	F	40–59	5139	4941	4916	4864	5280	5727	6162	6717	5258
	M	60+	3181	3414	3526	3691	3765	3815	3885	4104	2883
	F	60+	4328	4580	4697	4872	4910	4863	4877	4971	4054
		Total	41446	43230	45203	47401	49973	53048	56509	60264	39873
Migration pattern 3	M & F	0–14	9859	10585	11144	11559	12100	12823	13578	14123	9243
	M & F	15–39	13832	14535	15423	16346	16714	17409	18218	18994	13229
	M	40–59	5107	5026	5031	5099	5530	5826	6090	6332	5206
	F	40–59	5139	4934	4890	4805	5165	5516	5801	6154	5258
	M	60+	3181	3407	3506	3652	3701	3717	3745	3903	2883
	F	60+	4328	4574	4676	4831	4842	4756	4725	4759	4054
		Total	41446	43061	44670	46292	48052	50047	52157	54265	39873
HIGH BIRTH RATE											
Migration pattern 1	M & F	0–14	9894	10928	12167	13511	15020	16780	19079	21932	9243
	M & F	15–39	13832	14587	15573	16677	17527	19084	21040	23277	13229
	M	40–59	5107	5030	5046	5129	5594	5943	6283	6624	5206
	F	40–59	5139	4937	4900	4831	5215	5608	5957	6398	5258
	M	60+	3181	3410	3515	3668	3728	3760	3805	3990	2883
	F	60+	4328	4576	4685	4848	4872	4803	4791	4851	4054
		Total	41481	43468	45886	48664	51956	55978	60955	67072	39873
Migration pattern 2	M & F	0–14	9894	10942	12216	13632	15255	17175	19683	22780	9243
	M & F	15–39	13832	14652	15770	17066	18160	19997	22277	24894	13229
	M	40–59	5107	5035	5062	5171	5676	6098	6538	7004	5206
	F	40–59	5139	4941	4916	4864	5280	5727	6162	6717	5258
	M	60+	3181	3414	3526	3691	3765	3815	3885	4104	2883
	F	60+	4328	4580	4697	4872	4910	4863	4877	4971	4054
		Total	41481	43564	46187	49296	53046	57675	63422	70470	39873
Migration pattern 3	M & F	0–14	9894	10919	12128	13419	14841	16475	18617	21284	9243
	M & F	15–39	13832	14535	15423	16381	17046	18384	20092	22039	13229
	M	40–59	5107	5026	5031	5099	5530	5826	6090	6332	5206
	F	40–59	5139	4934	4890	4805	5165	5516	5801	6154	5258
	M	60+	3181	3407	3506	3652	3701	3717	3745	3903	2883
	F	60+	4328	4574	4676	4831	4842	4756	4725	4759	4054
		Total	41481	43395	45654	48187	51125	54674	59070	64471	39873

SOURCE: NIESR estimates.

Table A3.9. *South West*

Hundreds

		1968	1973	1978	1983	1988	1993	1998	2003	1963
LOW BIRTH RATE										
Migration pattern 1	M & F 0–14	3205	3496	3727	3739	3704	3687	3733	3736	2993
	M & F 15–39	4589	4805	5136	5551	5766	6047	6293	6483	4310
	M 40–59	1675	1605	1593	1634	1829	1975	2103	2216	1793
	F 40–59	1843	1759	1669	1635	1777	1873	2000	2136	1956
	M 60+	1316	1328	1298	1282	1239	1222	1225	1291	1283
	F 60+	1899	1881	1874	1844	1773	1746	1684	1672	1854
	Total	14527	14874	15297	15685	16088	16550	17038	17534	14189
Migration pattern 2	M & F 0–14	3205	3506	3767	3835	3890	4000	4210	4406	2993
	M & F 15–39	4589	4856	5291	5857	6264	6770	7271	7762	4310
	M 40–59	1675	1609	1608	1666	1894	2097	2304	2517	1793
	F 40–59	1843	1764	1682	1662	1828	1968	2163	2388	1956
	M 60+	1316	1332	1306	1299	1268	1266	1289	1379	1283
	F 60+	1899	1884	1884	1862	1806	1792	1753	1768	1854
	Total	14527	14951	15538	16181	16950	17893	18990	20220	14189
Migration pattern 3	M & F 0–14	3205	3485	3686	3639	3508	3360	3234	3034	2993
	M & F 15–39	4589	4750	4970	5230	5244	5291	5268	5143	4310
	M 40–59	1675	1601	1578	1601	1761	1850	1894	1901	1793
	F 40–59	1843	1755	1657	1607	1722	1775	1831	1872	1956
	M 60+	1316	1325	1289	1263	1209	1177	1160	1195	1283
	F 60+	1899	1877	1866	1825	1742	1696	1613	1573	1854
	Total	14527	14793	15046	15165	15186	15149	15000	14718	14189
REGISTRARS GENERAL'S BIRTH RATE										
Migration pattern 1	M & F 0–14	3205	3496	3769	3900	4094	4369	4709	4967	2993
	M & F 15–39	4589	4805	5136	5551	5766	6088	6453	6871	4310
	M 40–59	1675	1605	1593	1634	1829	1975	2103	2216	1793
	F 40–59	1843	1759	1669	1635	1777	1873	2000	2136	1956
	M 60+	1316	1328	1298	1282	1239	1222	1225	1291	1283
	F 60+	1899	1881	1874	1844	1773	1746	1684	1672	1854
	Total	14527	14874	15339	15846	16478	17273	18174	19153	14189

pattern 2	M & F 15–39	4589	4856	5291	5857	6264	6811	7431	8150	4310
	M 40–59	1675	1609	1608	1666	1894	2097	2304	2517	1793
	F 40–59	1843	1764	1682	1662	1828	1968	2163	2388	1956
	M 60+	1316	1332	1306	1299	1268	1266	1289	1379	1283
	F 60+	1899	1884	1884	1862	1806	1792	1753	1768	1854
	Total	14527	14951	15580	16342	17340	18616	20126	21839	14189
Migration pattern 3	M & F 0–14	3205	3485	3728	3800	3898	4042	4210	4265	2993
	M & F 15–39	4589	4750	4970	5230	5244	5332	5428	5531	4310
	M 40–59	1675	1601	1578	1601	1761	1850	1894	1901	1793
	F 40–59	1843	1755	1657	1607	1722	1775	1831	1872	1956
	M 60+	1316	1325	1289	1263	1209	1177	1160	1195	1283
	F 60+	1899	1877	1866	1825	1742	1696	1613	1573	1854
	Total	14527	14793	15088	15326	15576	15872	16136	16337	14189
HIGH BIRTH RATE										
Migration pattern 1	M & F 0–14	3217	3608	4099	4514	4994	5563	6365	7324	2993
	M & F 15–39	4589	4805	5136	5563	5877	6415	7070	7869	4310
	M 40–59	1675	1605	1593	1634	1829	1975	2103	2216	1793
	F 40–59	1843	1759	1669	1635	1777	1873	2000	2136	1956
	M 60+	1316	1328	1298	1282	1239	1222	1225	1291	1283
	F 60+	1899	1881	1874	1844	1773	1746	1684	1672	1854
	Total	14539	14986	15669	16472	17489	18794	20447	22508	14189
Migration pattern 2	M & F 0–14	3217	3618	4139	4610	5180	5876	6842	7994	2993
	M & F 15–39	4589	4856	5291	5869	6375	7138	8048	9148	4310
	M 40–59	1675	1609	1608	1666	1894	2097	2304	2517	1793
	F 40–59	1843	1764	1682	1662	1828	1968	2163	2388	1956
	M 60+	1316	1332	1306	1299	1268	1266	1289	1379	1283
	F 60+	1899	1884	1884	1862	1806	1792	1753	1768	1854
	Total	14539	15063	15910	16968	18351	20137	22399	25194	14189
Migration pattern 3	M & F 0–14	3217	3597	4058	4414	4798	5236	5866	6622	2993
	M & F 15–39	4589	4750	4970	5242	5355	5659	6045	6529	4310
	M 40–59	1675	1601	1578	1601	1761	1850	1894	1901	1793
	F 40–59	1843	1755	1657	1607	1722	1775	1831	1872	1956
	M 60+	1316	1325	1289	1263	1209	1177	1160	1195	1283
	F 60+	1899	1877	1866	1825	1742	1696	1613	1573	1854
	Total	14539	14905	15418	15952	16587	17393	18409	19692	14189

SOURCE: NIESR estimates.

Table A3.10. *Midlands*

Hundreds

		1968	1973	1978	1983	1988	1993	1998	2003	1963
LOW BIRTH RATE										
Migration pattern 1	M & F 0–14	12490	13726	14352	14342	14147	14046	14109	14089	11419
	M & F 15–39	17756	18299	19416	20937	21853	23068	24138	24611	17243
	M 40–59	6602	6630	6794	6733	7176	7440	7683	8218	6480
	F 40–59	6445	6403	6450	6455	6892	7190	7503	8010	6390
	M 60+	3482	3949	4201	4579	4778	4937	5084	5203	3048
	F 60+	4786	5240	5518	5843	6031	6155	6234	6389	4353
	Total	51561	54247	56731	58889	60877	62836	64751	66520	48933
Migration pattern 2	M & F 0–14	12490	13718	14321	14265	13993	13790	13717	13538	11419
	M & F 15–39	17756	18256	19288	20685	21443	22474	23331	23561	17243
	M 40–59	6602	6626	6783	6706	7121	7341	7518	7971	6480
	F 40–59	6445	6400	6440	6433	6850	7110	7368	7802	6390
	M 60+	3482	3946	4193	4565	4755	4901	5030	5129	3048
	F 60+	4786	5239	5510	5828	6004	6116	6178	6311	4353
	Total	51561	54185	56535	58482	60166	61732	63142	64312	48933
Migration pattern 3	M & F 0–14	12490	13714	14306	14229	13923	13675	13539	13289	11419
	M & F 15–39	17756	18237	19231	20571	21256	22205	22967	23082	17243
	M 40–59	6602	6625	6778	6695	7097	7296	7442	7859	6480
	F 40–59	6445	6398	6436	6423	6832	7076	7308	7706	6390
	M 60+	3482	3945	4190	4558	4744	4885	5008	5096	3048
	F 60+	4786	5237	5507	5822	5994	6099	6154	6276	4353
	Total	51561	54156	56448	58298	59846	61236	62418	63308	48933
REGISTRARS GENERAL'S BIRTH RATE										
Migration pattern 1	M & F 0–14	12490	13726	14515	14971	15665	16687	17874	18855	11419
	M & F 15–39	17756	18299	19416	20937	21853	23230	24764	26114	17243
	M 40–59	6602	6630	6794	6733	7176	7440	7683	8218	6480
	F 40–59	6445	6403	6450	6455	6892	7190	7503	8010	6390
	M 60+	3482	3949	4201	4579	4778	4937	5084	5203	3048
	F 60+	4786	5240	5518	5843	6031	6155	6234	6389	4353
	Total	51561	54247	56894	59518	62395	65639	69142	72789	48933

pattern 2	M & F	15–39	17756	18256	19288	20685	21443	22636	23957	25064	17243
	M	40–59	6602	6626	6783	6706	7121	7341	7518	7971	6480
	F	40–59	6445	6400	6440	6433	6850	7110	7368	7802	6390
	M	60+	3482	3946	4193	4565	4755	4901	5030	5129	3048
	F	60+	4786	5239	5510	5828	6004	6116	6178	6311	4353
		Total	51561	54185	56698	59111	61684	64533	67533	70581	48933
Migration pattern 3	M & F	0–14	12490	13714	14469	14858	15441	16314	17304	18055	11419
	M & F	15–39	17756	18237	19231	20571	21256	22367	23593	24585	17243
	M	40–59	6602	6625	6778	6695	7097	7296	7442	7859	6480
	F	40–59	6445	6398	6436	6423	6832	7076	7308	7706	6390
	M	60+	3482	3945	4190	4558	4744	4885	5008	5096	3048
	F	60+	4786	5237	5507	5822	5994	6099	6154	6276	4353
		Total	51561	54156	56611	58927	61364	64037	66809	69577	48933
HIGH BIRTH RATE											
Migration pattern 1	M & F	0–14	12536	14162	15785	17347	19145	21314	24268	27962	11419
	M & F	15–39	17756	18299	19416	20983	22288	24487	27160	29995	17243
	M	40–59	6602	6630	6794	6733	7176	7440	7683	8218	6480
	F	40–59	6445	6403	6450	6455	6892	7190	7503	8010	6390
	M	60+	3482	3949	4201	4579	4778	4937	5084	5203	3048
	F	60+	4786	5240	5518	5843	6031	6155	6234	6389	4353
		Total	51607	54683	58164	61940	66310	71523	77932	85777	48933
Migration pattern 2	M & F	0–14	12536	14154	15754	17270	18991	21056	23876	27411	11419
	M & F	15–39	17756	18256	19288	20731	21878	23893	26353	28945	17243
	M	40–59	6602	6626	6783	6706	7121	7341	7518	7971	6480
	F	40–59	6445	6400	6440	6433	6850	7110	7368	7802	6390
	M	60+	3482	3946	4193	4565	4755	4901	5030	5129	3048
	F	60+	4786	5239	5510	5828	6004	6116	6178	6311	4353
		Total	51607	54621	57968	61533	65599	70417	76323	83569	48933
Migration pattern 3	M & F	0–14	12536	14150	15739	17234	18921	20941	23698	27162	11419
	M & F	15–39	17756	18237	19231	20617	21691	23624	25989	28466	17243
	M	40–59	6602	6625	6778	6695	7097	7296	7442	7859	6480
	F	40–59	6445	6398	6436	6423	6832	7076	7308	7706	6390
	M	60+	3482	3945	4190	4558	4744	4885	5008	5096	3048
	F	60+	4786	5237	5507	5822	5994	6099	6154	6276	4353
		Total	51607	54592	57881	61349	65279	69921	75599	82565	48933

SOURCE: NIESR estimates.

Table A3.11. *East Anglia*

Hundreds

		1968	1973	1978	1983	1988	1993	1998	2003	1963
LOW BIRTH RATE										
Migration pattern 1	M & F 0–14	2291	2466	2545	2536	2500	2483	2486	2472	2108
	M & F 15–39	3229	3351	3575	3778	3891	4094	4239	4286	3163
	M 40–59	1177	1172	1193	1246	1349	1396	1453	1495	1182
	F 40–59	1215	1164	1158	1136	1197	1251	1321	1427	1235
	M 60+	773	793	795	833	857	870	891	968	735
	F 60+	1067	1136	1113	1136	1160	1123	1119	1134	1027
	Total	9752	10082	10379	10665	10954	11217	11509	11782	9450
Migration pattern 2	M & F 0–14	2291	2481	2597	2666	2753	2906	3134	3380	2108
	M & F 15–39	3229	3423	3789	4196	4569	5074	5568	6024	3163
	M 40–59	1177	1178	1212	1289	1437	1562	1728	1903	1182
	F 40–59	1215	1169	1174	1172	1267	1379	1541	1771	1235
	M 60+	773	797	807	857	897	930	977	1089	735
	F 60+	1067	1140	1126	1161	1203	1187	1211	1264	1027
	Total	9752	10188	10705	11341	12126	13038	14159	15431	9450
Migration pattern 3	M & F 0–14	2291	2463	2524	2490	2407	2326	2248	2135	2108
	M & F 15–39	3229	3324	3500	3624	3643	3731	3748	3648	3163
	M 40–59	1177	1169	1186	1229	1317	1336	1354	1345	1182
	F 40–59	1215	1161	1152	1122	1172	1203	1240	1300	1235
	M 60+	773	789	791	825	842	850	860	923	735
	F 60+	1067	1132	1109	1127	1145	1098	1086	1087	1027
	Total	9752	10038	10262	10417	10526	10544	10536	10438	9450
REGISTRARS GENERAL'S BIRTH RATE										
Migration pattern 1	M & F 0–14	2291	2466	2574	2649	2774	2962	3171	3339	2108
	M & F 15–39	3229	3351	3575	3778	3891	4123	4352	4557	3163
	M 40–59	1177	1172	1193	1246	1349	1396	1453	1495	1182
	F 40–59	1215	1164	1158	1136	1197	1251	1321	1427	1235
	M 60+	773	793	795	833	857	870	891	968	735
	F 60+	1067	1136	1113	1136	1160	1123	1119	1134	1027
	Total	9752	10082	10408	10778	11228	11725	12307	12920	9450

Migration pattern 2	M & F 0–14	2291	2481	2626	2779	3027	3385	3819	4247	2108
	M & F 15–39	3229	3423	3789	4196	4569	5103	5681	6895	3163
	M 40–59	1177	1178	1212	1289	1437	1562	1728	1903	1182
	F 40–59	1215	1169	1174	1172	1267	1379	1541	1771	1235
	M 60+	773	797	807	857	897	930	977	1089	735
	F 60+	1067	1140	1126	1161	1203	1187	1211	1264	1027
	Total	9752	10188	10734	11454	12400	13546	14957	16569	9450
Migration pattern 3	M & F 0–14	2291	2463	2553	2603	2681	2805	2933	3002	2108
	M & F 15–39	3229	3324	3500	3624	3643	3760	3861	3919	3163
	M 40–59	1177	1169	1186	1229	1317	1336	1354	1345	1182
	F 40–59	1215	1161	1152	1122	1172	1203	1240	1300	1235
	M 60+	773	789	791	825	842	850	860	923	735
	F 60+	1067	1132	1109	1127	1145	1098	1086	1087	1027
	Total	9752	10038	10291	10530	10800	11052	11334	11576	9450
HIGH BIRTH RATE										
Migration pattern 1	M & F 0–14	2299	2544	2802	3077	3403	3800	4331	4989	2108
	M & F 15–39	3229	3351	3575	3786	3969	4349	4783	5257	3163
	M 40–59	1177	1172	1193	1246	1349	1396	1453	1495	1182
	F 40–59	1215	1164	1158	1136	1197	1251	1321	1427	1235
	M 60+	773	793	795	833	857	870	891	968	735
	F 60+	1067	1136	1113	1136	1160	1123	1119	1134	1027
	Total	9760	10160	10636	11214	11935	12789	13898	15270	9450
Migration pattern 2	M & F 0–14	2299	2559	2854	3207	3656	4223	4979	5897	2108
	M & F 15–39	3229	3423	3789	4204	4647	5329	6112	6995	3163
	M 40–59	1177	1178	1212	1289	1437	1562	1728	1903	1182
	F 40–59	1215	1169	1174	1172	1267	1379	1541	1771	1235
	M 60+	773	797	807	857	897	930	977	1089	735
	F 60+	1067	1140	1126	1161	1203	1187	1211	1264	1027
	Total	9760	10266	10962	11890	13107	14610	16548	18919	9450
Migration pattern 3	M & F 0–14	2299	2541	2781	3031	3310	3643	4093	4652	2108
	M & F 15–39	3229	3324	3500	3632	3721	3986	4292	4619	3163
	M 40–59	1177	1169	1186	1229	1317	1336	1354	1345	1182
	F 40–59	1215	1161	1152	1122	1172	1203	1240	1300	1235
	M 60+	773	789	791	825	842	850	860	923	735
	F 60+	1067	1132	1109	1127	1145	1098	1086	1087	1027
	Total	9760	10116	10519	10966	11507	12116	12925	13926	9450

SOURCE: NIESR estimates.

12

Table A3.12. *South East*

Hundreds

		1968	1973	1978	1983	1988	1993	1998	2003	1963
LOW BIRTH RATE										
Migration pattern 1	M & F 0–14	41544	46291	48521	48275	47877	48086	48821	49182	37103
	M & F 15–39	58422	60753	65289	71248	74868	79434	83653	85756	56855
	M 40–59	22402	22066	22242	22146	23871	25138	26275	28261	22442
	F 40–59	23558	22845	22512	22075	23268	24367	25493	27376	23902
	M 60+	13373	14538	15073	16015	16466	16619	16833	17344	12146
	F 60+	19905	20919	21430	22266	22492	22330	22111	22308	18757
	Total	179204	187412	195067	202025	208842	215974	223186	230227	171205
Migration pattern 2	M & F 0–14	41544	46247	48355	47873	47094	46770	46814	46359	37103
	M & F 15–39	58422	60533	64632	69955	72769	76392	79527	80369	56855
	M 40–59	22402	22049	22184	22009	23595	24628	25428	26993	22442
	F 40–59	23558	22829	22462	21961	23050	23968	24811	26312	23902
	M 60+	13373	14525	15035	15941	16346	16436	16569	16968	12146
	F 60+	19905	20907	21390	22189	22361	22132	21825	21907	18757
	Total	179204	187090	194058	199928	205215	210326	214974	218908	171205
Migration pattern 3	M & F 0–14	41544	46215	48229	47569	46501	45772	45291	44218	37103
	M & F 15–39	58422	60366	64137	68976	71174	74084	76398	76286	56855
	M 40–59	22402	22034	22138	21907	23386	24240	24788	26032	22442
	F 40–59	23558	22818	22424	21876	22886	23665	24294	25506	23902
	M 60+	13373	14515	15006	15886	16253	16296	16367	16681	12146
	F 60+	19905	20897	21361	22131	22268	21982	21610	21606	18757
	Total	179204	186845	193295	198345	202468	206039	208748	210329	171205
REGISTRARS GENERAL'S BIRTH RATE										
Migration pattern 1	M & F 0–14	41544	46289	49052	50331	52858	56764	61221	64889	37103
	M & F 15–39	58422	60753	65289	71246	74866	79962	85692	90694	56855
	M 40–59	22402	22066	22242	22146	23871	25138	26275	28261	22442
	F 40–59	23558	22845	22512	22075	23268	24367	25493	27376	23902
	M 60+	13373	14538	15073	16015	16466	16619	16833	17344	12146
	F 60+	19905	20919	21430	22266	22492	22330	22111	22308	18757
	Total	179204	187410	195598	204079	213821	225180	237625	250872	171205

[illegible]	M & F 0–14	[illegible]	[illegible]	[illegible]	[illegible]	[illegible]	[illegible]	[illegible]	[illegible]	37103
pattern 2	M & F 15–39	58422	60533	64632	69953	72767	76920	81566	85307	56855
	M 40–59	22402	22049	22184	22009	23595	24628	25428	26993	22442
	F 40–59	23558	22829	22462	21961	23050	23968	24811	26312	23902
	M 60+	13373	14525	15035	15941	16346	16436	16569	16968	12146
	F 60+	19905	20907	21390	22189	22361	22132	21825	21907	18757
	Total	179204	187088	194589	201982	210194	219532	229413	239553	171205
Migration	M & F 0–14	41544	46213	48760	49625	51482	54450	57691	59925	37103
pattern 3	M & F 15–39	58422	60366	64137	68974	71172	74612	78437	81224	56855
	M 40–59	22402	22034	22138	21907	23386	24240	24788	26032	22442
	F 40–59	23558	22818	22424	21876	22886	23665	24294	25506	23902
	M 60+	13373	14515	15006	15886	16253	16296	16367	16681	12146
	F 60+	19905	20897	21361	22131	22262	21982	21610	21606	18757
	Total	179204	186843	193826	200399	207441	215245	223187	230974	171205
HIGH BIRTH RATE										
Migration	M & F 0–14	41699	47738	53228	58121	64275	71971	82272	94894	37103
pattern 1	M & F 15–39	58422	60753	65289	71401	76308	84105	93566	103446	56855
	M 40–59	22402	22066	22242	22146	23871	25138	26275	28261	22442
	F 40–59	23558	22845	22512	22075	23268	24367	25493	27376	23902
	M 60+	13373	14538	15073	16015	16466	16619	16833	17344	12146
	F 60+	19905	20919	21430	22266	22492	22330	22111	22308	18757
	Total	179359	188859	199774	212024	226680	244530	266550	293629	171205
Migration	M & F 0–14	41699	47694	53062	57719	63492	70655	80265	92071	37103
pattern 2	M & F 15–39	58422	60533	64632	70108	74209	81063	89440	98059	56855
	M 40–59	22402	22049	22184	22009	23595	24628	25428	26993	22442
	F 40–59	23558	22829	22462	21961	23050	23968	24811	26312	23902
	M 60+	13373	14525	15035	15941	16346	16436	16569	16968	12146
	F 60+	19905	20907	21390	22189	22361	22132	21825	21907	18757
	Total	179359	188537	198765	209927	223053	238882	258338	282310	171205
Migration	M & F 0–14	41699	47662	52936	57415	62898	69657	78742	89930	37103
pattern 3	M & F 15–39	58422	60366	64137	69129	72614	78755	86311	93976	56855
	M 40–59	22402	22034	22138	21907	23386	24240	24788	26032	22442
	F 40–59	23558	22818	22424	21876	22886	23665	24294	25506	23902
	M 60+	13373	14515	15006	15886	16253	16296	16367	16681	12146
	F 60+	19905	20897	21361	22131	22262	21982	21610	21606	18757
	Total	179359	188292	198002	208344	220300	234595	252112	273731	171205

SOURCE: NIESR estimates.

APPENDIX 4

THE CALCULATION OF POPULATION PROJECTIONS

ALTERNATIVE NATIONAL PROJECTIONS

A projection for Great Britain, by male and female quinquennial age groups for every five years from 1963, based on the assumptions of the Registrars General, was supplied by the Government Actuary's Department. Alternative projections were required based on higher and lower marriage and fertility rates.

Because substantial changes in marriage rates were possible, and because the births to any age group are affected by variations in the proportion of that group who are married, simple age specific fertility rates for all women could not be used. It was necessary first to use fertility rates classified by age at marriage and duration of marriage in order to calculate the age specific fertility rates for all women for the year 2003. The age at marriage and duration of marriage fertility rates used were those for 1962/3, and so the age specific fertility rates immediately produced only reflected the change in marriage rates. These were adjusted to accord with the assumed changes in fertility. Subsequently the rates for each year were obtained by linear interpolation.

1. To estimate the population of women in 2003 classified by age and duration at marriage:

   (a) *Marriage rate*

   Let m_x^y = spinsters' marriage rate (calendar year) for ages x to $x+4$ in year y.

   From the assumptions in chapter 2:

   High birth rate, $m_x^{2003} = m_x^{1962} + 1{\cdot}33(m_x^{1962} - m_x^{1931})$

   Low birth rate, $m_x^{2003} = 0{\cdot}75 m_x^{1962}$

   The rates for other age groups were interpolated graphically, and the values for other years were obtained by linear interpolation.

   (b) *Proportion ever married*

   The equation $S_x^y = S_{x-1}^{y-1}[1 - \frac{1}{2}(m_{x-1}^{y-1} + m_x^y)(1 - \frac{1}{2}m_x^y)]$ (where S = the number of females unmarried at mid-year y to $y+1$ of age x to $x+4$) cannot be used until an initial value of S_{x-1}^{y-1} is available. The initial value chosen was for the cohort aged 11–15 in 1974 and this was taken, for convenience, to be 10,000. Therefore the expression $\left[1 - \frac{S_x^y}{10{,}000}\right]$ gives the proportion of this cohort who are now x years old and who have been married. Further, because a steady change in marriage rate was assumed in both projections, the proportion ever married of any other cohort at any year was found by interpolation or extrapolation as follows:

$$S_x^{y+\delta} = S_x^{1962} + \frac{y+\delta-1962}{y-1962}[S_x^y - S_x^{1962}].$$

An allowance for the effects of widowhood, remarriage and divorce was incorporated at a later stage, 3(a), in the calculations.

(c) *Numbers married*

The female population in the age groups 15–19, 20–24, . . ., 40–44 was next interpolated from the projection of the Registrars General for each mid-year from 1974 to 2000.

The number of women by age at marriage, and by duration of marriage in completed years, as at mid-year 2000 to mid-year 2001 was obtained from these figures as follows:

Let F_x^y = total female population aged x to $x+4$ at mid year y to $y+4$,

let ${}^dM_x^y$ = the female population ever married, who married at age x to $x+4$ with d years of marriage completed at mid-year y to mid-year $y+1$,

then $${}^{2000-y}M_x^{2000} = F_x^y \,.\, M_x^y \,.\, \frac{S_x^y}{10{,}000}.$$

Thus the population of women in 2000/1 was calculated with age at marriage and duration of marriage given by single years.

2. To develop age specific fertility rates for these women:

(a) *Total number of births*

The fertility rates by age at marriage, and duration of marriage in England and Wales in 1961–2 are given in Table 00 of Part II of the *Registrar General's Statistical Review, 1962.* These rates were used with the population figures for women previously calculated to get the number of births in 2000/1.

Let ${}^df_x^y$ = the fertility rate in year y for women married at age x to $x+4$ with d years of marriage completed,

and ${}^dB_x^y$ = the number of births to the same group of women,

then ${}^dB_x^{2000} = {}^dM_x^{2000} \,.\, {}^df_x^{1961}$.

For the calculations themselves it was necessary to transpose the figures for births and the female population ever married from a basis of age at marriage to age at birth. This was done graphically using the following link:

Let $\overline{{}^dM_x^y}$ = the female population ever married, aged x to $x+4$ with d years of marriage completed at year y,

then ${}^{d-\frac{1}{2}}M_x^y \simeq \overline{{}^{d-\frac{1}{2}}M_{x+d}^{y+1}}$.

Whereas ${}^dM_x^y$ refers to a group of women who married at age x to $x+4$, $\overline{{}^dM_x^y}$ refers to a group of women now aged x to $x+4$.

(b) *Age specific fertility rate* (*women ever married*)

The female population ever married was summed for all marriage durations at each age, as were the births. The ratio of births to female population ever married was then calculated for each age group to give the legitimate age specific fertility rates.

3. To obtain age specific fertility rates for all women for the years between 1963 and 2000:

(a) *Legitimate births*

Table A3 in part II of the *Registrar General's Statistical Review* gives the number of women single, married, and divorced. From this the ratio of women actually married to women ever married was calculated for each age group and applied to the projected female population ever married to give the female population actually married. Age specific rates calculated as in 2(b) were used with these corrected figures to get the total number of legitimate births.

(b) *Illegitimate births*

The difference between total female population and number of women actually married gives the number of women unmarried. This figure for each age group in 2000 was multiplied by the 1962 illegitimate age specific fertility rates to get the total number of illegitimate births to each age group.

(c) *Age specific fertility rates for all women*

The two totals of births for each age group were added together and the sum divided by the total female population in that age group to get the age specific fertility rates for all women.

These rates, while allowing for the assumed changes in marriage patterns, were still based on 1962 fertilities. They had, therefore, to be adjusted for the two assumptions:

high fertility rate $hf_x^{2000} = 1{\cdot}4f_x^{1962}$,

and low fertility rate $lf_x^{2000} = 0{\cdot}8f_x^{1962}$.

The rates for the years between 1963 and 2000 were then found by linear interpolation.

4. The calculation of the two alternative projections:

(a) *Survival rates*

Survival rates were calculated for each sex from the projection of the Registrars General as follows:

Let l_x^y = the proportion of the age group aged x to $x+4$ in year y who survive to year $y+5$,

then $l_x^y = \dfrac{P_{x+5}^{y+5}}{P_x^y}$, where P = total population of that sex.

These survival rates automatically include some allowance for the effects of immigration from abroad.

(b) *Number of births*

Starting in 1963, the number of births every five years was then calculated

taking $hB_x^y = F_x^y \,.\, hf_x^y$

and $lB_x^y = F_x^y \,.\, lf_x^y$

The births were then summed for all ages of mother, and a factor applied to allow jointly for infant mortality and the proportion of births which are female. This factor was based on recent experience and was not varied. If this factor is designated k,

$$k = \frac{F_0^{1963}}{\frac{1}{2}B^{1958}+B^{1959}+\ldots+B^{1962}+\frac{1}{2}B^{1963}}$$

then $$hF_x^{y+5} = k \sum_{x=15}^{45} hB_x^y.$$

Thus the population every five years up to 2003 was calculated using the survival rates already found.

(c) *Results*

On the high assumptions the total population of both sexes came to 85,597,000 and on the low assumptions to 65,382,000. The figures were rounded off to 85 and 65 million in view of the arbitrary nature of the assumptions and the many approximations made in the calculations.

(d) *Adjustments from 1963 to 1964*

The calculations described above were made in the summer of 1964, and were based on the population for mid-year 1963, but the base date for the whole study is 31 March 1964. When, therefore, the population estimates for mid-year 1964 became available at the end of 1964, the calculations were amended. At this stage it was only possible to increase all 1963 based projections by three-quarters of the national percentage increase from mid-1963 to mid-1964.

5. To calculate average completed family size:

In order to describe the high and low assumptions in a meaningful way, the average completed family size was required. This was first found on the basis of 1961 fertility and then adjusted for the higher and lower fertility assumptions. For each marriage duration from 0 to 26 the births and female population ever married were summed for all age groups; then the births at a given duration were divided by the female population ever married for that duration and the resulting fertility rates were summed. This value of the mean completed family size was then adjusted for the different fertility rate assumptions, being multiplied by 1·4 for the high one and by 0·8 for the low one.

REGIONAL PROJECTIONS

The three alternative national projections had to be divided between the twelve regions. In addition, three alternative patterns of internal migration had to be incorporated, giving a total of nine alternative projections for each region.

1. To develop three projections for each region assuming no internal migration:

The age and sex structure of each region in 1961 was first found by addition of the data given in the County Reports of the 1961 Census. Each age group was then expressed as a percentage of the equivalent age group at 1961 within the nearest equivalent Standard Region or group of Standard Regions. These percentages were then applied to the age and sex structures of the Standard Regions in 1963 given in the Registrars General's *Quarterly Returns* for 4th quarter, 1963. Where necessary the population so calculated was adjusted to give the correct all-ages total for each region, found by addition of the mid-1963 estimates. These estimates of the regional populations were then projected quinquennially to 2003, using the national survival rates that were calculated in the final stage of the national projections.

The group aged 0 to 4 cannot be found in this way. National ratios were therefore calculated of the males and of the females ages 0–4 to the females within the fertile ages 15–44 five years earlier. These ratios, which differ for each sex and for each of the three national alternatives, were then applied to the regional female populations.

The national survival rates used were derived from projections of the total population, which includes British Forces serving overseas. However, the study as a whole is concerned with construction within Britain only, and therefore the regional projections on which all estimates would be based had to be slightly reduced in certain male age groups to allow for Forces overseas. The mid-1963 estimates on which the regional projections were based were of home population which already excluded these Forces.

A comparison of home and total populations in 1963 showed differences in the age groups between 15 and 54. These differences were expressed as percentages of the total population in that age group and these percentages were then used to adjust the regional projections. The percentage of each age group serving abroad was assumed to be constant throughout the period to 2004.

If d_x is the difference between the total and home male populations aged x to $x+4$ expressed as a percentage of the total population in the age group, the correction factors required then become:

	1968	1973	1978	...	2003
15–19	$1-d_{15}$	$1-d_{15}$	$1-d_{15}$	...	$1-d_{15}$
20–24	$1-d_{20}+d_{15}$	$1-d_{20}$	$1-d_{20}$	...	$1-d_{20}$
25–29	$1-d_{25}+d_{20}$	$1-d_{25}+d_{15}$	$1-d_{25}$	...	$1-d_{25}$
30–34	$1-d_{30}+d_{25}$	$1-d_{30}+d_{20}$	$1-d_{30}+d_{15}$	...	$1-d_{30}$
35–39	$1-d_{35}+d_{30}$	$1-d_{35}+d_{25}$	$1-d_{35}+d_{20}$	...	$1-d_{35}$
40–44	$1-d_{40}+d_{35}$	$1-d_{40}+d_{30}$	$1-d_{40}+d_{25}$	...	$1-d_{40}$
45–49	$1-d_{45}+d_{40}$	$1-d_{45}+d_{35}$	$1-d_{45}+d_{30}$	...	$1-d_{45}$
50–54	$1-d_{50}+d_{45}$	$1-d_{50}+d_{40}$	$1-d_{50}+d_{35}$	...	$1-d_{50}$
55–59	$1+d_{50}$	$1+d_{45}$	$1+d_{40}$	...	$1+d_{15}$
60–64	1	$1+d_{50}$	$1+d_{45}$	...	$1+d_{20}$
65–69	1	1	$1+d_{50}$	...	$1+d_{25}$
.	.	.	.		.
.	.	.	.		.

The form of these correction factors may be explained as follows:

Let P^y_x = the total male population of age x to $x+4$ in year y,

and PR^y_x = a regional male population of age x to $x+4$ in year y.

Applying national survival rates to regional populations,

$$PR^{y+5}_{x+5} = PR^y_x \cdot \frac{P^{y+5}_{x+5}}{P^y_x}.$$

Therefore generally,

$$PR^{y+5n}_{x+5m} = PR^{y+5(n-1)}_{x+5(m-1)} \cdot \frac{P^{y+5n}_{x+5m}}{P^{y+5(n-1)}_{x+5(m-1)}} \qquad (1)$$

Substituting successively for $m, m-1, m-2,\ldots$ and for $n, n-1, n-2,\ldots$ and using the resulting equation in (1); if $m > n$,

$$PR^{y+5n}_{x+5m} = PR^y_{x+5(m-n)} \cdot \frac{P^{y+5n}_{x+5m}}{P^y_{x+5(m-n)}} \qquad (2)$$

To correct the natural male population P^{y+5n}_{x+5m} for those serving abroad it is multiplied by $[1-d_{x+5m}]$.

Let $\overline{PR}$ = the value of PR corrected for those serving abroad, then as

$$\overline{PR}^y_{x+5(m-n)} = PR^y_{x+5(m-n)} \text{ (first year figures)},$$

from (2),

$$\overline{PR}^{y+5n}_{x+5m} = PR^y_{x+5(m-n)} \cdot \frac{P^{y+5n}_{x+5m}}{P^y_{x+5(m-n)}} \cdot \frac{1-d_{x+5m}}{1-d_{x+5(m-n)}}.$$

Therefore the correction factor if $m > n$ is $[1-d_{x+5m}][1-d_{x+(5m-n)}]^{-1}$, which is approximately equal to $1-d_{x+5m}+d_{x+5(m-n)}$. It may be shown (without approximation) by a similar method that if $n \geqslant m$, the correction factor is $1-d_{x+5m}$.

In the matrix of correction factors given above, m is the row and n the column number.

These adjustments were made to each male group, and then the first stage of the calculations was completed, giving three alternative projections, all assuming no internal migration.

2. To add to each of these three populations three subsidiary populations attributable to internal migration:

It was first necessary to establish the recent pattern of net internal migration by subtracting the annual natural increase in each region from the annual increase in population. This was done for the seven years from mid-1956 to mid-1963, assuming that the net international migration into Britain was distributed between the regions in proportion to their population. Estimated population and natural increase figures were obtained from successive copies of the *Registrar General's Statistical Review of England and Wales*, Part II, table E.

With this background it was possible to decide on a level for the accumulated effect of internal migration over forty years in each region on each of the three assumptions discussed in chapter 3. In order to calculate the quinquennial flow of migrants necessary to achieve this level and to maintain the age and sex breakdown of each regional population, it was also necessary to assume a certain age and sex structure for the migrants. This is described in chapter 3.

In order to simplify the calculation of the migrant flow it was assumed that migration would always start from the current levels and would change by a constant amount in each quinquennium to give the required cumulative total after forty years. It was also assumed that the ratio of births to females aged 15–44 for migrants would not vary with the three alternative birth rate assumptions.

Taking a constant flow of 100,000 migrants per quinquennium, the first step was to calculate how many of these migrants in each age and sex group would survive the end of each successive quinquennium. This was done by using the national survival rates and ratios of births to women aged 15–44 already described.

Thus if PM_z^y = the surviving migrant population at year y, who moved during the quinquennium ending in year z,

then the accumulated migration after forty years = $\sum_{z=1968}^{z=2003} PM_z^{2003}$.

Equivalent calculations were made for each quinquennial date, assuming a steady flow of 100,000 migrants in each five years. A certain proportion of this flow could then be taken for each region, depending on the current and assumed future rate of migration.

Thus if A^{2003} = the assumed accumulated migration after forty years,

b = the recent migration per quinquennium in each region in hundred thousands,

k = the proportion by which the migration flows changes in each successive quinquennium,

then with b known, the value of k needed to give the assumed values for A could be calculated:

$$A^{2003} = b \,.\, PM_{1968}^{2003} + b(1+k) \,.\, PM_{1973}^{2003} + b(1+2k) \,.\, PM_{1978}^{2003} + \ldots + b(1+7k)PM_{2003}^{2003}$$

So

$$k = \left(\frac{A^{2003}}{b} - \sum_{z=1968}^{z=2003} PM_z^{2003}\right) \Big/ (PM_{1973}^{2003} + 2 \,.\, PM_{1978}^{2003} + \ldots + 7 \,.\, PM_{2003}^{2003}).$$

For each region b is a constant and there are three values of A^{2003}, one for each assumed migration pattern, each with a corresponding value of k. Once k has been found to satisfy the value assumed for A^{2003}, the accumulated migration at intervening dates is readily found:

$$A^y = b \sum_{z=1968}^{y} PM_z^y + bk\left[PM_{1973}^y + 2 \,.\, PM_{1978}^y + \ldots + \frac{y-1968}{5} \,.\, PM_{2003}^y\right].$$

The use of this method allows all the P terms to be calculated once only, with only A, b, and k varying, to give the 288 age and sex structures required for all the region, date and pattern alternatives.

As a final step these age and sex structures attributable to migration were added to the regional projections already produced on the assumption of no migration. The joint figures were updated from 1963 to 1964 in the same way as the national figures but using separate regional factors.

APPENDIX 5

THE SAMPLE OF LOCAL AUTHORITY AREAS

The starting point for this study was information on the volume, condition and potential use of the buildings and works in Britain. There appeared to be only two comprehensive sources of such information, the population Census (34), which provided information on housing, and the rating valuation returns (98), which provided information on most classes of buildings, although not on works. Unfortunately, neither source went very far towards supplying the information needed.

Some idea of the volume of buildings and works could be obtained by measurement of large-scale town plans, but field observations were still necessary to determine the number of storeys and the condition and potential use of each building. It was clear, therefore, that field studies of existing buildings would be essential, and since field work could only be carried out over a very small percentage of the area of Britain, it was important to find the most efficient way way of drawing the sample of areas for field study.

An attempt was made to find indicators of the physical volume and state of buildings in various parts of the country, so that a typical cross-section of areas could be drawn. Social differences between areas were expected to be related to the period and rate of growth, their past and present prosperity, the extent to which they served a hinterland, their size and their regional location. Many of the differences between areas are related to region and size, and published information relates the volume and state of buildings to these two factors only. It was decided, therefore, that the most reliable way of obtaining a cross-section of the existing buildings and works in Britain was to sample areas from every region and size of area in the country.

For this purpose Britain was divided into the twelve regions, and the local authority areas within them were divided by size into six urban classes and one rural class (table A5.1). The local authority areas and their mid-1961 populations were listed and one sample area was then allocated to represent each 500,000 persons. If this rule had been followed rigidly some of the size-region groups would not have been represented. Generally, therefore, a sample area was allocated where the population in the size-region group was over 100,000. Also, if a region would otherwise not have been represented, a sample area was allocated for the size-region group with the largest population. As a result 114 sample areas were allocated to represent a population of 51·3 million (table A5.2). Local authority areas within each size-region group were selected at random according to the number required to fill the allocation of a sample areas. Where the number of sample areas allocated was greater than the number of authorities, as it was for certain large cities, multiple sample areas were allocated to the cities in question. Thus Glasgow, Manchester and Birmingham were each allocated two sample areas. London, as covered by the former London

County Council, was allocated six sample areas taken as metropolitan boroughs.

Table A5.1. *Population of regions and administrative areas in Great Britain*

Millions

	Urban authorities [a]						Rural authorities [b]	Total
	1 million and over	½*mn* < 1*mn*	¼*mn* <½*mn*	50,000 <¼*mn*	10,000 <50,000	Less than 10,000		
Scotland	*(1)*	..	*(1)*	*(7)*	*(40)*	*(151)*	*(33)*	*(233)*
	1·1		0·5	0·7	1·0	0·6	1·5	5·4
North	..	..	*(1)*	*(9)*	*(47)*	*(17)*	*(49)*	*(123)*
			0·3	1·0	1·2	0·1	0·8	3·4
North West	..	*(2)*	..	*(29)*	*(82)*	*(42)*	*(28)*	*(183)*
		1·4		2·5	1·9	0·3	0·6	6·7
Pennines	..	*(1)*	*(3)*	*(14)*	*(73)*	*(24)*	*(36)*	*(151)*
		0·5	1·1	1·1	1·5	0·2	1·0	5·4
Central	..	..	*(1)*	*(2)*	*(11)*	*(12)*	*(18)*	*(44)*
			0·3	0·2	0·3	—	0·3	1·1
East	..	..	*(1)*	*(3)*	*(11)*	*(16)*	*(27)*	*(58)*
			0·3	0·2	0·2	0·1	0·4	1·2
North & Central Wales	..	..	..	..	*(9)*	*(40)*	*(33)*	*(82)*
					0·1	0·1	0·3	0·5
West	..	..	*(2)*	*(9)*	*(41)*	*(45)*	*(65)*	*(162)*
			0·7	0·8	1·0	0·2	1·2	3·9
South West	..	..	..	*(3)*	*(18)*	*(42)*	*(37)*	*(100)*
				0·3	0·3	0·2	0·5	1·3
Midlands	*(1)*	..	*(2)*	*(15)*	*(38)*	*(20)*	*(45)*	*(121)*
	1·1		0·6	1·1	1·0	0·1	0·8	4·7
East Anglia	..	..	..	*(3)*	*(4)*	*(18)*	*(26)*	*(51)*
				0·3	—	0·1	0·5	0·9
South East	*(1)*	..	*(1)*	*(81)*	*(112)*	*(59)*	*(109)*	*(363)*
	3·2	..	0·3	7·4	2·9	0·3	2·7	16·8
Total	*(3)*	*(3)*	*(12)*	*(175)*	*(486)*	*(486)*	*(506)*	*(1671)*
	5·4	1·9	4·1	15·6	11·4	2·3	10·6	51·3

SOURCES: *Registrar General's Annual Estimates of the Population of England and Wales and Local Authority Areas, 1961* (99); *Registrar General's Annual Estimates of the Population of Scotland, 1961* (100).

Note: Number of local authorities shown in italic figures in brackets.
[a] Burghs in Scotland.
[b] Landward areas in Scotland.

Table A5.2. *Sample of*

Size groups	Scotland	North	North West	Pennines	East	Central
Urban 1 million and over	Glasgow (2)					
$\frac{1}{2}mn < 1mn$			Liverpool Manchester (2)	Leeds		
$\frac{1}{4}mn < \frac{1}{2}mn$	Edinburgh	Newcastle upon Tyne		Nottingham Sheffield	Leicester	Kingston-upon-Hull
$50{,}000 < \frac{1}{4}mn$	Aberdeen Greenock	Darlington Middles-brough	Bebington Burnley Rochdale Royton-with-Roby Widnes	Doncaster York	North-ampton	Scunthorpe
10,000 < 50,000	Arbroath Kilmarnock	Consett	Bredbury & Romiley Hyde Litherland Lytham St. Annes	Darton Knottingley Pontefract	Corby	Spalding
Less than 10,000	Gourock Keith	Scalby	Longden-dale	Heckmond-wike		
Rural All sizes	Dumfries East Lothian Moray Perth	Chester-le-Street Wigton	Congleton	Clowne Nidderdale	Ashby-de-la-Zouche	East Elloe

local authority areas

North & Central Wales	West	South West	Midlands	East Anglia	South East
			Birmingham (2)		London (Bethnal Green, Chelsea, Finsbury, Greenwich, Hammersmith, Lambeth)
	Cardiff		Coventry		Croydon
	Gloucester Merthyr Tydfil	Plymouth	Dudley Walsall	Norwich	Carshalton Coulsdon and Purley Dagenham East Ham Eastbourne Esher Fareham Hastings High Wycombe Hornsey Orpington Oxford Poole Reigate Southampton
Conway	Penarth Salisbury	Exmouth	Kidder-minster Wednesbury		Banstead Chesham Dorking Newbury Rayleigh Wood Green
Neyland	Newcastle Emlyn	Ottery St Mary	Droitwich		Tring
New Radnor	Clutton Wellington	Sherborne	Cannock Evesham	Loddon	Alton Bedford Newport Pagnell Tenterden Winchester

APPENDIX 6

THE FIELD SURVEY OF HOUSING CONDITIONS

It was necessary to limit the field survey in order to accommodate it within the budget for the study. While over 3,500 dwellings were surveyed in thirty-four local authority areas spread over Great Britain, nearly a half were in the South East, where assistance from colleges was more readily forthcoming. The local authority areas which were surveyed were chosen as far as possible at random from table A5.2. For each area a 6-inch Ordnance Survey map was chosen at random, subject to the condition that at least half the area lay within the boundaries of the relevant local authority. Subsequently four 1 : 1250 Ordnance Survey plans were chosen at random from each 6-inch Ordnance Survey sheet, subject to the condition that the area lay within the urban fence of the relevant local authority.

The method of choosing the hereditaments and the nature of the data collected is described in the following schedule and instructions.

INSTRUCTIONS TO FIELD WORKERS

Method of choosing sample hereditaments

1. Survey every 20th separate hereditament along both sides of the road.
2. If a hereditament has *only* industrial, commercial, hotel, institution or other such use, note this fact on the questionnaire and proceed to the next sample hereditament, i.e. 20 hereditaments along.
3. If information for Sections A and B is not available (i.e. the occupant is not at home when the dwelling is surveyed) then one of the following procedures should be adopted:
   (*a*) if possible, call again at the dwelling at a later time,
   (*b*) if the dwelling appears identical with a neighbouring dwelling (i.e. semi-detached, part of a terrace), use this next dwelling as the sample. But the *next* 20th hereditament should be estimated from the first-choice sample.

Notes to the schedule

This is a schedule rather than a questionnaire. It is not framed as questions to ask the occupier of the dwelling, but is intended to indicate the type and form of information required.

Section A

Definition of a dwelling: in order to check that the housing unit being surveyed is a structurally separate dwelling, test these questions before completing the questionnaire.

1. Does it have its own front door opening from—
   (i) street
   (ii) common staircase or landing.

2. It is possible to move between rooms without making use of a common staircase or landing.
3. Does it provide (i) washing facilities
(ii) cooking facilities
(iii) toilet facilities
without crossing a common landing, passage or staircase.

The housing unit is to be counted as a separate dwelling if—
(*a*) the answers to all the questions are 'yes'.
or (*b*) the answers to questions 1, 2 and 3(i) and (ii) are 'yes' *and* the W.C.s are grouped either internally or externally (even if there is some sharing).

If (*a*) the answers to questions (1) and (2) are 'no',
or (*b*) the W.C.s and/or bathrooms and kitchen facilities are shared (except as in 1(*b*) above)
all the housing units sharing these facilities and/or the common access are to be considered collectively as forming one dwelling: all subsequent answers to Section A, B and C should refer to this dwelling (i.e. information should be given for *all* the household units).

Notes: In some cases it may be clear from an occupant's answers that the household unit is not a structurally separate dwelling but the occupant is unable to give information about the whole dwelling (i.e. all household units within the building). Complete the schedule as far as possible but mark it clearly to show that all the information is not available.

If the occupants of the household unit are provided with any dining facilities in public rooms within the building, the whole building should be classed as a boarding house and should not be included for the purpose of this survey.

Question 12 refers to the occupant's *use of* appliances based on these facilities (see section C question 9 for access to main services). Note that hot water system includes systems based on coal fires and geysers.

Section B

Definition of a building: a structure with one or more rooms within external or party walls. Each house in a semi-detached pair or a terrace or back-to-back group is to be regarded as a separate building. A block of flats in which separate apartments are linked by passages, balconies and staircases or lifts is to be regarded as a single building.

Notes: Question 1: where a flatted building is a converted house, note on the schedule that the building is flatted and also note the type of house, i.e. detached, semi-detached, etc.

Question 9 will probably only apply to rural areas. Mains services: water, sewerage, gas, electricity.

Section C

1. Age—give actual age where possible, otherwise as:

   (1) Pre-1875 (3) 1914–1939

   (2) 1875–1914 (4) Post-1939

   To determine age of dwelling:

   (1) date may be found on outside of building

   (2) ask the occupant

   (3) compare dwelling with another for which date of building is known.

2. Physical condition of building—

   (1) Good—excellent state of repair

   (2) Fair—structurally sound, in need of minor repairs

   (3) Fair/poor—structurally sound, in need of moderate repairs

   (4) Poor—some structural defects, in need of extensive repairs and decorations

   (5) Very poor—rebuilding to be considered.

   Note: structure—large cracks in wall, damp, movement of door or window frames, etc.

   repairs—missing tiles or slates, cracked chimney stacks, cracked or split window frames, broken gullies, etc.

3. Quality of building

   (1) Substandard

   (2) Low cost—local authority

   (3) Low cost—private owners

   (4) Medium cost—private owners

   (5) High cost—private owners.

4. Physical amenity of street

   (1) Good—attractive, well maintained

   (2) Fair—acceptable, in reasonable state of upkeep

   (3) Poor—unsightly, shabby.

Section D

Collect net and rateable values for all dwellings even if the schedule is not completed because the occupant was not at home.

The net and rateable values are to be found in the Valuation Rolls for the borough or district. These Rolls are kept in the Treasurer's Office which is usually situated in the Town Hall. A copy of the Valuation Rolls is always made available to the public so there should be no difficulty in obtaining this data. The time to be allowed for collecting the values should be 30–60 minutes for the dwellings surveyed on one 50-inch sheet, (i.e. about 30-dwellings).

SCHEDULE

Town	Sheet reference	Street Name Street Number

A. *Information on the separate dwelling*

1a. Does this dwelling occupy all the building on the plot?
 b. How many other flats are there in the building?
 c. How many commercial properties are there in the building?
 d. How many industrial properties are there in the building?
 e. How many other properties are there in the building?

2. Has this dwelling been converted? If so, how?

3. On which floors is this dwelling? (e.g. basement, ground, first floor etc.)

4. Please give number of bedrooms for this dwelling.

5. No. of living rooms (other than with cooker or sink).

6. Is the kitchen (room with cooker and sink) regularly used for family meals other than breakfast?

7. Is there a fixed bath?

8. Is it in (i) bathroom
 (ii) kitchen
 (iii) any other room?

9. Is there any other room (apart from kitchen or bathroom) with a basin?

10. How many W.C.s are within this dwelling?

11a. Is there exclusive use for the occupant of an external W.C.?
 b. Does the occupant share an external W.C.?

12a. Has the dwelling a cold water system?
 b. a hot water system?
 c. gas?
 d. electricity?

B. *Information about the building on the plot of which the separate dwelling is a part*

1. Is the building on this plot detached, semi-detached, terraced, flatted?

2. Has it a basement and/or semi-basement containing habitable rooms?

3. How many storeys has it? (above basement/semi-basement)

4. Is the roof of tiles, slates or other?

5. Are the walls of brick, concrete or other?

6. Has it a garage?

7. Is the garage of brick, concrete, timber, asbestos?

8. Is there space for a garage
   (i) beside the building?
   (ii) with access at rear of plot?

9. Is the building connected with mains services?

10. Is the road made up in front of the building?

C. *Notes: Section C*

1. Age of building on the plot

2. Physical condition of building on the plot

3. Quality of building on the plot

4. Physical amenity of the street

D. *Information to be obtained from the local rating office*

1. Gross value of the separate dwelling

2. Rateable value of the separate dwelling

APPENDIX 7

THE RATEABLE VALUES OF DOMESTIC PROPERTY

Gross values are a measure of the rent which a building would produce if it were let at current market prices. In determining the gross value, the valuation officers ignore the actual rent since this may have been determined under conditions prevailing at some earlier time, or may be subsidized. Instead, the gross value is fixed in relation to the market rent which could be obtained at that time in that area for a dwelling of the given size, facilities and amenities. Rateable value is obtained from the gross value by making a statutory deduction for maintenance and insurance, which is itself related to the gross value. Hence gross and rateable values are correlated and both provide an equally good measure of the amenity of the dwelling. As a result the distributions of rateable values for each rating area which are published by the Valuation Office (98) provide a potential index of the state of housing in each area.

THE DISTRIBUTION OF DOMESTIC RATEABLE VALUES

Rateable values of domestic property appear to be highest in the South East and lowest in Scotland and the North (figs. A7.1 and A7.2). It would appear from the regional distributions that the differences in rateable values are greater than would be expected from the probable differences in the quality of the housing. This is particularly true as between England and Scotland. Rents, the basis of value, are very low in Scotland as compared with England and the date of valuation is also different. However, even in different parts of England and Wales there are probably substantial differences in the rent levels for similar properties. Rateable values can only be used as a measure of the value of property, and hence as an indication of quality, if these differences in rating levels are first removed.

The previous analyses of rateable values have indicated that the rateable values for similar dwellings vary from one area to another broadly in relation to region and size of the town. A measure of such regional variation can be obtained by comparing the rateable values of similar dwellings in different areas. Local authority dwellings tend to be consistent from one area to another and are easier to specify than other types of dwelling. Postwar local authority dwellings were, therefore, used to provide a basis of comparison. Local authorities in the sample (appendix 5) were asked to give the rateable values and rents for a typical dwelling in each of twelve classes of houses and flats. Few authorities had built dwellings conforming to Parker Morris standards (38) and the analysis was based on dwellings built in accordance with the 1949 and 1951 *Housing Manuals* (101) (102) and their counterparts for Scotland. Just over seventy satisfactory returns were obtained (appendix 8).

Other things being equal, there appeared to be little difference between the

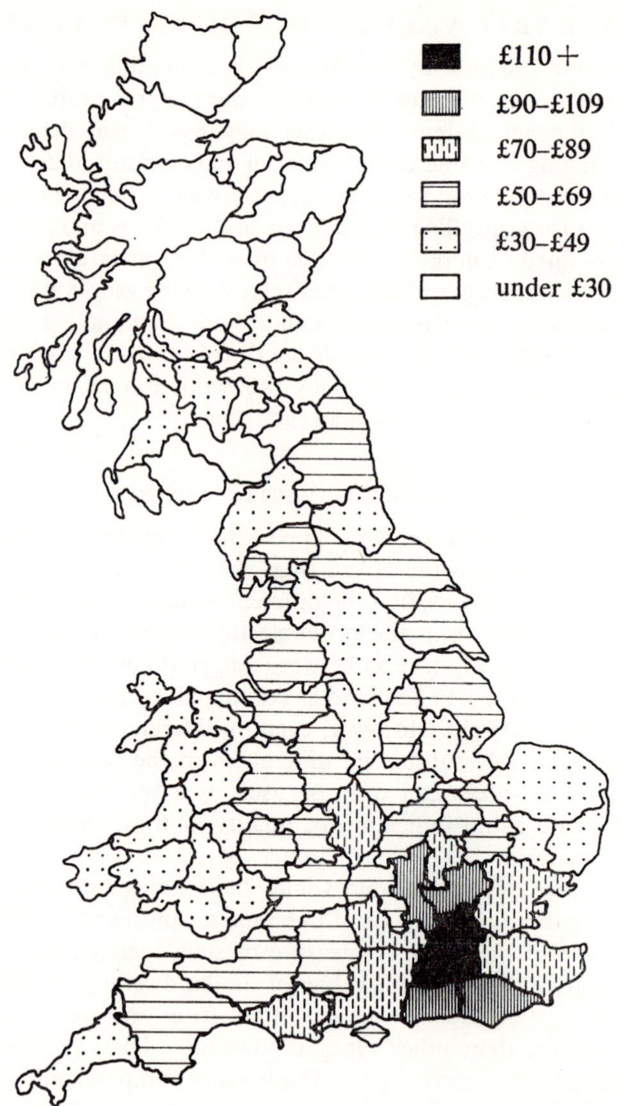

SOURCES: *Rates and Rateable Values in England and Wales, 1963–64* (98); NIESR estimates.

Fig. A7.1. Average domestic rateable values, administrative counties, 1963/4

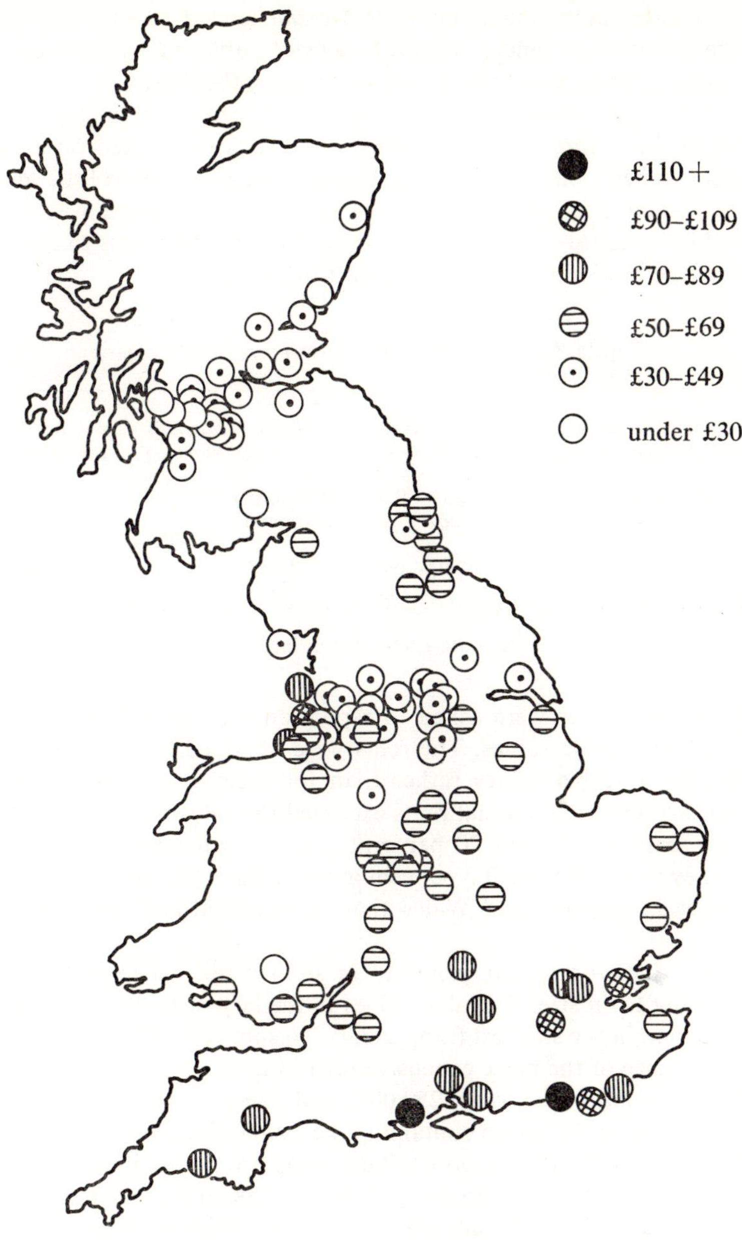

SOURCES: as fig. A7.1.

Fig. A7.2. Average domestic rateable values, county boroughs and large burghs, 1963/4

rateable value of dwellings built according to the 1949 or the 1951 *Housing Manuals*. Houses built under the 1949 *Manual* tended to be rated about £2 higher than those built under the 1951 *Manual* (table A7.1). Differences were very consistent. There was little difference between the flats.

The correlations between size and type were close and highly significant (table A7.1). Both three bedroom houses and flats were rated on average £9 more than two bedroom dwellings, but houses were rated only a little more than otherwise similar flats. While the range of dwellings studied was inevitably small, within it the rateable values bore consistent relationships to one another for most of the local authority areas in the sample.

Table A7.1. *Correlations between rateable values*

Houses (1951 *Housing Manual*)	= 5·14+0·89 (1949 *Housing Manual*)	$r = 0{\cdot}935$, $n = 92$
Flats (1951 *Housing Manual*)	= 2·20+0·97 (1949 *Housing Manual*)	$r = 0{\cdot}983$, $n = 51$
Houses (3 bedrooms)	= 13·10+0·93 (2 bedrooms)	$r = 0{\cdot}929$, $n = 62$
Flats (3 bedrooms)	= 2·08+1·11 (2 bedrooms)	$r = 0{\cdot}990$, $n = 42$
Houses (3 bedrooms)	= 12·93+0·82 (flats, 3 bedrooms)	$r = 0{\cdot}941$, $n = 40$

SOURCE: NIESR estimates.

The local authorities were asked to report on the normal rents charged as well as on the rateable values. The rents were obtained to provide a basis for evaluating the rateable values rather than for their own interest. Generally, apart from Scotland, the annual rents exceeded the rateable values. In England and Wales rents were about 20 per cent greater than rateable values, but in Scotland they were only about 5 per cent greater. Rateable values were generally much higher in England and Wales than in Scotland and rents were nearly double.

Rateable values for similar property in similar regions tended to increase with increasing town size. Rateable values in the largest town are about 50 per cent higher than in the smallest (table A7.2). To some extent these results reflect the predominance of the more expensive regions in the group of local authority areas with populations of over 250,000, and the predominance of the least expensive regions in the group containing the smaller local authority areas.

Of more interest for the purpose of this study are the regional differences in the rateable values of similar property. Expressed as an index, these range from 56 to 170 (table A7.3). As would be expected, the highest values are found in London, particularly in metropolitan London. The lowest values are recorded in the rural regions. The figures for Scotland cannot be compared with the other regions since the basis and year of valuation are different. Too much weight

Table A7.2. *The effect of town size on the rateable values of similar domestic property*

Town size	Indices of rateable values
250,000 persons and over	117
50,000 to 250,000 persons	105
10,000 to 50,000 persons	99
Less than 10,000 persons	79
All sizes	100

SOURCE: NIESR estimates.

should not be placed on the individual percentages since, for a few of the regions, these are based on indications from only two authorities. The results are particularly suspect for the East, the South West and, to a lesser extent, for North and Central Wales, where the difference between the rateable values quoted by the authorities reporting are particularly large, and where adjustments were made because the rateable values were out of line with the rents. Again, of course, the regional percentages reflect to some extent the size of the local authority areas within them. This is of no importance for the study and no attempt was made to carry out a joint analysis.

Table A7.3. *Regional differences in rateable values for a sample of property of a similar standard and size*

	Indices
Scotland	56
North	79
North West	96
Pennines	78
Central	96
East	63
North & Central Wales [a]	90
West	94
South West [a]	83
Midlands	89
East Anglia [a]	81
South East	
Metropolitan London	170
Rest of Greater London	139
Rest of South East	109

SOURCE: NIESR estimates.

[a] Only two authorities reported.

RATEABLE VALUES AS AN INDICATOR OF HOUSING STANDARDS

The average rateable values for a region reflect the size of dwellings as well as the standard. Allowance for the effect of the size distribution can be made by taking the required indicator of the regional level of rateable values as the weighted average of rateable values applicable to dwellings of different sizes, the proportions of different sizes being taken as weights. While the analysis of rateable values described earlier only provides information on two and three bedroom dwellings, these two sizes, except for Scotland, account for between 60 and 70 per cent of all dwellings. Therefore little error will be introduced by deducting the increment for a bedroom to obtain rateable values for the smaller dwellings, and adding to it for the larger dwellings. In fact, except for Scotland, 90 per cent of dwellings have between three and six habitable rooms. Adjusted regional, rateable value indicators were obtained on this basis (table A7.4). The effect of adjusting the indices to allow for the size distribution was small except for Scotland, because the sizes were distributed homogeneously.

Table A7.4. *Regional differences in rateable values for property of a similar standard adjusted for the average size of dwellings in the region*

	Indices
Scotland	48
North	75
North West	97
Pennines	77
Central	99
East	65
North & Central Wales	94
West	99
South West	85
Midlands	90
East Anglia	85
South East	
Metropolitan London	172
Rest of Greater London	140
Rest of South East	110

SOURCE: NIESR estimates.

Gross values of postwar, local authority, three bedroom houses were obtained in the form of the average for the highest and lowest value for such dwellings in each local authority area. These were analysed by region and compared with the previous indices (table A7.3). It will be seen that the agreement was close except for those regions where the sample of authorities was small (table A7.5). The corresponding indices were therefore averaged except in those cases where the original samples were very small and unreliable.

Table A7.5. *Comparison of indices of rating levels for local authority housing of standard size*

	Indices from table A7.3	Indices based on gross values	Average indices	Indices adjusted for regional size of dwelling
Scotland	56	..	56	48
North	79	83	81	77
North West	96	94	95	96
Pennines	78	81	80	79
Central	96	98	97	100
East	63	80	72	83
North & Central Wales	90	68	79	71
West	94	82	88	86
South West	83	85	84	86
Midlands	89	91	90	91
East Anglia	81	88	85	89
South East	126	123	125	126

SOURCE: NIESR estimates.

The corrected indices were then adjusted for the average size of property in the region on the basis of the ratios of the indices given in tables A7.3 and A7.4.

An analysis of the gross values of similar property within the regions showed a high degree of variability. The variability within the regional size-of-town

Table A7.6. *Indices of rateable value before and after standardization*

	Average rateable value	Rateable value standardized for regional rating differences	Rateable value standardized for regional rating differences and size of dwelling
Scotland	59	90	106
North	90	96	101
North West	102	92	92
Pennines	84	90	91
Central	111	99	96
East	87	94	91
North & Central Wales	74	94	91
West	100	106	101
South West	118	121	118
Midlands	106	102	101
East Anglia	95	96	92
South East	174	120	120
Great Britain	100	100	100

SOURCE: NIESR estimates.

groups was also very high. The differences in rating levels between local authority areas appear to be far too great for rateable values to be used as an index of standard unless they are first adjusted for local differences in rating levels.

A measure of the standard of domestic property was obtained by applying the two sets of indices of the level of rating in the various regions to the average rateable values for each region. The average rateable values were obtained for each rating district from the Valuation Office and built up regionally.

The largest changes in the indices of average rateable value as between actual values and values standardized to remove differences in rating levels are for the South East, Scotland, and North and Central Wales; differences for the other regions are less than 12 per cent (table A7.6). The changes for the South East and for Scotland were expected, since rents are abnormally high in the South East, especially in London, and abnormally low in Scotland. With some exceptions the standardized indices probably provide a reasonable indication of the relative standard of dwellings in the regions of Britain. Clearly, however, too much weight must not be put on small differences in the indices.

Part of the difference in average rateable values is, of course, a result of the size of the dwelling, but only in Scotland is the average size markedly different from other regions in Great Britain.

APPENDIX 8

LOCAL AUTHORITIES WHO COMPLETED A SCHEDULE ON RATEABLE VALUES

CITIES

* Birmingham
Coventry
Gloucester
* Hull
* Leeds
* Leicester
* Liverpool
Manchester
* New Sarum
Newcastle upon Tyne
* Norwich
* Nottingham
* Oxford
Plymouth
* Sheffield
Southampton
York

* Aberdeen
* Edinburgh
Glasgow

COUNTY COUNCILS

Moray
Perth

METROPOLITAN BOROUGHS

Bethnal Green
* Chelsea
Finsbury
* Greenwich
Hammersmith
Lambeth

COUNTY BOROUGHS

* Burnley
* Croydon
* Darlington
* Dudley
* East Ham
Eastbourne
* Middlesbrough
Northampton
* Poole
Rochdale
Wednesbury

BOROUGHS

* Bebington
* Conway
Dagenham
* High Wycombe
* Hornsey
* Kidderminster
* Reigate
Scunthorpe
* Widnes

URBAN DISTRICTS

Banstead
* Bredbury and Romiley
Carshalton
Chesham
Consett
Corby
* Coulsdon
* Darton
Dorking
Fareham
Neyland
Orpington
Ottery St Mary
Scalby
Tring

SCOTTISH BURGHS

* Arbroath
* Gourock
* Greenock
* Kilmarnock

RURAL DISTRICTS

Ashby-de-la-Zouche
Cannock
* Evesham
Loddon
Nidderdale
* Tenterden
Winchester

* Those who also completed a measured work schedule.

APPENDIX 9

SIZE OF DWELLINGS TO BE CONSTRUCTED, 1964–2004

Table A9.1. *Great Britain*

	Birth rate	Migration pattern	Habitable rooms 1–2	3	4	5	6	7+	All sizes	Total dwellings
			%	%	%	%	%	%	%	*000s*
1964 housing stock			6	14	27	34	12	7	100	*16808*
1964–84 construction	RG's	1, 2, 3	13	18	29	24	11	5	100	*5067* / *5068* / *5060*
	Low	1	13	19	29	23	11	5	100	*4966*
	High	1	11	17	28	26	12	6	100	*5507*
1984–2004 construction	RG's	1, 2, 3	7	12	31	30	12	8	100	*6319* / *6318* / *6306*
	Low	1	9	15	35	24	10	7	100	*5707*
	High	1	5	9	28	35	14	9	100	*8086*
2004 housing stock	RG's	1, 2, 3	6	13	29	34	12	6	100	*23364* / *23362* / *23353*
	Low	1	7	14	30	32	11	6	100	*22652*
	High	1	5	12	28	35	13	7	100	*25569*

SOURCE: NIESR estimates.

Note: Demolition programme A is assumed for this table: the following are the adjustments for the other demolition programmes—

Thousands

	Habitable rooms 1–2	3	4	5	6	7+	Total
1964–84 construction							
Demolition programme B	33	93	216	216	126	79	763
Demolition programme C	43	165	504	762	270	151	1895
1984–2004 construction							
Demolition programme B	115	308	546	518	325	201	2013
Demolition programme C	145	581	1284	1875	697	385	4967

Table A9.2. *Scotland*

	Birth rate	Migration pattern	Habitable rooms 1–2	3	4	5	6	7+	All sizes	Total dwellings
			%	%	%	%	%	%	%	*000s*
1964 housing stock			23	36	26	8	3	4	100	*1677*
1964–84 construction	RG's	1	0	0	16	51	27	6	100	*546*
		2	0	0	16	51	27	6	100	*546*
		3	0	0	18	51	25	6	100	*614*
	Low	1	0	0	16	52	26	6	100	*537*
	High	1	0	0	16	51	26	7	100	*588*
1984–2004 construction	RG's	1	32	23	18	14	6	7	100	*475*
		2	32	23	18	14	6	7	100	*475*
		3	21	19	24	22	8	6	100	*808*
	Low	1	37	28	21	5	3	6	100	*413*
	High	1	23	17	19	23	10	8	100	*647*
2004 housing stock	RG's	1	6	14	32	32	11	5	100	*1879*
		2	6	14	32	32	11	5	100	*1879*
		3	6	14	31	33	11	5	100	*2287*
	Low	1	7	15	32	31	10	5	100	*1810*
	High	1	6	13	30	34	11	6	100	*2091*

SOURCE: NIESR estimates.

Note: Demolition programme A is assumed for this table: the following are the adjustments for the other demolition programmes—

Thousands

	Habitable rooms 1–2	3	4	5	6	7+	Total
1964–84 construction							
Demolition programme B	0	0	18	22	4	6	50
Demolition programme C	0	0	48	49	5	6	108
1984–2004 construction							
Demolition programme B	33	66	34	17	11	16	177
Demolition programme C	35	153	109	44	13	16	370

Table A 9.3. *North*

	Birth rate	Migration pattern	Habitable rooms 1–2	3	4	5	6	7+	All sizes	Total dwellings
			%	%	%	%	%	%	%	*000s*
1964 housing stock			7	19	32	29	8	5	100	*1057*
1964–84 construction	RG's	1	5	11	21	36	22	5	100	*241*
		2	5	11	21	36	22	5	100	*241*
		3	5	11	23	36	20	5	100	*283*
	Low	1	5	11	21	36	22	5	100	*234*
	High	1	4	9	21	38	22	6	100	*268*
1984–2004 construction	RG's	1	9	19	34	22	9	7	100	*337*
		2	9	19	34	22	9	7	100	*337*
		3	8	17	33	26	10	6	100	*526*
	Low	1	12	23	40	14	6	5	100	*298*
	High	1	6	15	31	29	11	8	100	*449*
2004 housing stock	RG's	1	5	16	30	33	11	5	100	*1371*
		2	5	16	30	33	11	5	100	*1371*
		3	5	16	30	33	11	5	100	*1603*
	Low	1	6	17	31	31	10	5	100	*1326*
	High	1	5	15	29	34	11	6	100	*1510*

SOURCE: NIESR estimates.

Note: Demolition programme A is assumed for this table: the following are the adjustments for the other demolition programmes—

Thousands

	Habitable rooms 1–2	3	4	5	6	7+	Total
1964–84 construction							
Demolition programme B	4	19	22	6	3	3	57
Demolition programme C	4	22	44	37	9	7	123
1984–2004 construction							
Demolition programme B	9	49	57	15	9	7	146
Demolition programme C	10	58	114	94	24	17	317

Table A9.4. *North West*

	Birth rate	Migration pattern	Habitable rooms 1–2	3	4	5	6	7+	All sizes	Total dwellings
			%	%	%	%	%	%	%	*000s*
1964 housing stock			3	8	35	36	12	6	100	*2212*
1964–84 construction	RG's	1	22	18	26	24	6	4	100	*467*
		2	22	18	26	24	6	4	100	*467*
		3	21	17	27	24	6	5	100	*508*
	Low	1	23	18	27	23	5	4	100	*455*
	High	1	20	16	25	26	7	6	100	*520*
1984–2004 construction	RG's	1	3	6	42	34	8	7	100	*747*
		2	3	6	42	34	8	7	100	*747*
		3	3	8	39	34	9	7	100	*927*
	Low	1	4	8	47	29	6	6	100	*670*
	High	1	2	5	37	38	10	8	100	*968*
2004 housing stock	RG's	1	6	10	32	35	11	6	100	*2733*
		2	6	10	32	35	11	6	100	*2733*
		3	6	11	32	35	11	5	100	*2955*
	Low	1	7	11	33	33	11	5	100	*2644*
	High	1	6	9	31	36	12	6	100	*3007*

SOURCE: NIESR estimates.

Note: Demolition programme A is assumed for this table: the following are the adjustments for the other demolition programmes—

Thousands

	Habitable rooms 1–2	3	4	5	6	7+	Total
1964–84 construction							
Demolition programme B	3	7	42	40	7	6	105
Demolition programme C	4	17	85	102	35	16	259
1984–2004 construction							
Demolition programme B	7	18	109	103	17	16	270
Demolition programme C	10	43	220	261	91	41	666

Table A9.5. *Pennines*

	Birth rate	Migration pattern	Habitable rooms 1–2	3	4	5	6	7+	All sizes	Total dwellings
			%	%	%	%	%	%	%	*000s*
1964 housing stock			5	12	30	40	9	4	100	*1841*
1964–84 construction	RG's	1	16	17	21	22	16	8	100	*425*
		2	16	17	21	22	16	8	100	*425*
		3	15	17	21	23	16	8	100	*452*
	Low	1	16	17	21	21	16	9	100	*414*
	High	1	14	16	20	25	16	9	100	*469*
1984–2004 construction	RG's	1	5	11	34	34	11	5	100	*605*
		2	5	11	34	34	11	5	100	*605*
		3	5	12	33	34	11	5	100	*725*
	Low	1	7	14	38	28	9	4	100	*542*
	High	1	4	8	30	38	13	7	100	*789*
2004 housing stock	RG's	1	6	12	28	38	11	5	100	*2352*
		2	6	12	28	38	11	5	100	*2352*
		3	6	12	28	38	11	5	100	*2499*
	Low	1	7	13	29	36	10	5	100	*2277*
	High	1	5	11	27	39	12	6	100	*2580*

SOURCE: NIESR estimates.

Note: Demolition programme A is assumed for this table: the following are the adjustments for the other demolition programmes—

Thousands

	Habitable rooms 1–2	3	4	5	6	7+	Total
1964–84 construction							
Demolition programme B	4	14	27	30	8	3	86
Demolition programme C	6	22	68	98	19	10	223
1984–2004 construction							
Demolition programme B	11	36	71	77	21	7	223
Demolition programme C	15	57	175	252	49	25	573

Table A9.6. *Central*

	Birth rate	Migration pattern	Habitable rooms 1–2	3	4	5	6	7+	All sizes	Total dwellings
			%	%	%	%	%	%	%	*000s*
1964 housing stock			3	8	24	46	14	5	100	*396*
1964–84 construction	RG's	1	17	24	19	25	10	5	100	*135*
		2	17	25	19	25	10	4	100	*126*
		3	18	25	18	25	10	4	100	*123*
	Low	1	17	25	19	25	10	4	100	*133*
	High	1	15	23	19	27	11	5	100	*146*
1984–2004 construction	RG's	1	4	10	29	36	15	6	100	*197*
		2	3	9	29	36	16	7	100	*158*
		3	3	9	29	36	16	7	100	*145*
	Low	1	5	12	33	31	13	6	100	*182*
	High	1	2	7	27	40	16	8	100	*239*
2004 housing stock	RG's	1	6	13	24	40	12	5	100	*632*
		2	6	13	24	40	12	5	100	*584*
		3	6	13	24	40	12	5	100	*568*
	Low	1	7	13	25	38	12	5	100	*615*
	High	1	5	12	23	41	13	6	100	*686*

SOURCE: NIESR estimates.

Note: Demolition programme A is assumed for this table: the following are the adjustments for the other demolition programmes—

Thousands

	Habitable rooms 1–2	3	4	5	6	7+	Total
1964–84 construction							
Demolition programme B	—	1	4	8	3	1	17
Demolition programme C	—	2	10	23	6	3	44
1984–2004 construction							
Demolition programme B	—	2	9	22	7	3	43
Demolition programme C	1	6	25	60	15	7	114

Table A9.7. *East*

	Birth rate	Migration pattern	Habitable rooms 1–2	3	4	5	6	7+	All sizes	Total dwellings
			%	%	%	%	%	%	%	*000s*
1964 housing stock			3	9	29	40	12	7	100	*435*
1964–84 construction	RG's	1	17	25	21	23	9	5	100	*124*
		2	16	24	22	24	9	5	100	*137*
		3	17	26	21	22	9	5	100	*123*
	Low	1	17	26	21	22	9	5	100	*122*
	High	1	15	24	20	25	10	6	100	*135*
1984–2004 construction	RG's	1	3	8	34	32	14	9	100	*173*
		2	4	9	33	33	13	8	100	*229*
		3	3	8	34	32	14	9	100	*165*
	Low	1	5	11	37	27	12	8	100	*158*
	High	1	2	6	31	37	15	9	100	*219*
2004 housing stock	RG's	1	6	13	27	37	11	6	100	*596*
		2	6	13	27	37	11	6	100	*664*
		3	6	13	27	37	11	6	100	*586*
	Low	1	7	14	28	35	10	6	100	*578*
	High	1	5	12	26	38	12	7	100	*652*

SOURCE: NIESR estimates.

Note: Demolition programme A is assumed for this table: the following are the adjustments for the other demolition programmes—

Thousands

	Habitable rooms 1–2	3	4	5	6	7+	Total
1964–84 construction							
Demolition programme B	—	2	4	8	3	2	19
Demolition programme C	1	4	12	22	5	3	47
1984–2004 construction							
Demolition programme B	1	5	11	21	7	4	49
Demolition programme C	2	10	31	57	13	8	121

Table A9.8. *North and Central Wales*

	Birth rate	Migration pattern	Habitable rooms 1–2	3	4	5	6	7+	All sizes	Total dwellings
			%	%	%	%	%	%	%	*000s*
1964 housing stock			3	9	27	29	17	15	100	*207*
1964–84 construction	RG's	1	24	26	9	15	11	15	100	*40*
		2	17	22	18	20	11	12	100	*58*
		3	25	28	8	13	11	15	100	*38*
	Low	1	25	28	8	14	10	15	100	*39*
	High	1	22	25	9	18	11	15	100	*44*
1984–2004 construction	RG's	1	2	6	28	26	16	22	100	*75*
		2	3	10	30	30	14	13	100	*153*
		3	1	5	28	25	17	24	100	*65*
	Low	1	3	8	31	21	15	22	100	*68*
	High	1	1	5	27	31	17	19	100	*93*
2004 housing stock	RG's	1	6	12	24	28	16	14	100	*219*
		2	6	12	26	30	15	11	100	*316*
		3	7	12	23	28	16	14	100	*207*
	Low	1	7	13	24	27	15	14	100	*212*
	High	1	6	11	23	31	16	13	100	*241*

SOURCE: NIESR estimates.

Note: Demolition programme A is assumed for this table: the following are the adjustments for the other demolition programmes—

Thousands

	Habitable rooms 1–2	3	4	5	6	7+	Total
1964–84 construction							
Demolition programme B	0	1	1	1	1	1	5
Demolition programme C	—	1	4	5	3	2	15
1984–2004 construction							
Demolition programme B	—	1	3	3	3	3	13
Demolition programme C	—	3	10	14	7	4	38

Table A9.9 *West*

	Birth rate	Migration pattern	Habitable rooms 1–2	3	4	5	6	7+	All sizes	Total dwellings
			%	%	%	%	%	%	%	*000s*
1964 housing stock			3	8	22	38	20	9	100	*1251*
1964–84 construction	RG's	1	16	29	21	20	9	5	100	*456*
		2	15	28	21	21	9	6	100	*476*
		3	16	30	20	20	9	5	100	*441*
	Low	1	16	29	21	20	9	5	100	*448*
	High	1	14	26	21	23	10	6	100	*491*
1984–2004 construction	RG's	1	3	8	26	36	17	10	100	*564*
		2	3	9	27	35	16	10	100	*651*
		3	3	7	26	36	17	11	100	*497*
	Low	1	4	10	30	31	15	10	100	*517*
	High	1	2	6	25	39	17	11	100	*701*
2004 housing stock	RG's	1	6	14	23	34	16	7	100	*1882*
		2	6	14	23	34	16	7	100	*1988*
		3	6	14	23	34	16	7	100	*1800*
	Low	1	7	15	24	32	15	7	100	*1826*
	High	1	5	13	23	35	16	8	100	*2053*

SOURCE: NIESR estimates.

Note: Demolition programme A is assumed for this table: the following are the adjustments for the other demolition programmes—

Thousands

	Habitable rooms 1–2	3	4	5	6	7+	Total
1964–84 construction							
Demolition programme B	2	4	13	23	17	8	67
Demolition programme C	2	7	28	54	29	12	132
1984–2004 construction							
Demolition programme B	4	10	34	60	44	22	174
Demolition programme C	5	18	73	140	74	30	340

Table A9.10. *South West*

	Birth rate	Migration pattern	Habitable rooms 1–2	3	4	5	6	7+	All sizes	Total dwellings
			%	%	%	%	%	%	%	*000s*
1964 housing stock			3	10	26	32	16	13	100	*472*
1964–84 construction	RG's	1	20	28	16	19	8	9	100	*120*
		2	18	26	18	21	8	9	100	*135*
		3	23	30	13	17	7	10	100	*104*
	Low	1	21	28	16	18	8	9	100	*117*
	High	1	19	24	16	22	9	10	100	*132*
1984–2004 construction	RG's	1	3	10	28	32	13	14	100	*212*
		2	4	10	29	33	12	12	100	*281*
		3	2	8	27	31	13	19	100	*140*
	Low	1	4	12	31	28	11	14	100	*197*
	High	1	2	8	26	36	14	14	100	*257*
2004 housing stock	RG's	1	6	14	25	31	14	10	100	*627*
		2	6	14	25	31	14	10	100	*711*
		3	7	14	23	31	14	11	100	*539*
	Low	1	7	15	25	30	13	10	100	*609*
	High	1	6	12	24	33	14	11	100	*684*

SOURCE: NIESR estimates.

Note: Demolition programme A is assumed for this table: the following are the adjustments for the other demolition programmes—

Thousands

	Habitable rooms 1–2	3	4	5	6	7+	Total
1964–84 construction							
Demolition programme B	—	2	5	5	3	4	19
Demolition programme C	1	3	12	16	8	5	45
1984–2004 construction							
Demolition programme B	1	5	13	13	8	10	50
Demolition programme C	1	9	30	41	20	14	115

Table A9.11. *Midlands*

	Birth rate	Migration pattern	Habitable rooms 1–2	3	4	5	6	7+	All sizes	Total dwellings
			%	%	%	%	%	%	%	*000s*
1964 housing stock			3	10	27	43	12	5	100	*1512*
1964–84 construction	RG's	1	14	23	29	19	10	5	100	*605*
		2	14	24	29	18	10	5	100	*593*
		3	14	24	29	18	10	5	100	*587*
	Low	1	14	24	29	18	10	5	100	*595*
	High	1	13	21	28	21	11	6	100	*649*
1984–2004 construction	RG's	1	4	11	31	32	16	6	100	*645*
		2	4	11	31	31	16	7	100	*589*
		3	4	11	31	31	16	7	100	*563*
	Low	1	6	14	35	26	14	5	100	*585*
	High	1	3	8	28	36	17	8	100	*819*
2004 housing stock	RG's	1	6	14	28	36	11	5	100	*2390*
		2	6	14	28	36	11	5	100	*2321*
		3	6	14	28	36	11	5	100	*2290*
	Low	1	7	15	29	35	10	4	100	*2320*
	High	1	5	13	27	38	11	6	100	*2608*

SOURCE: NIESR estimates.

Note: Demolition programme A is assumed for this table: the following are the adjustments for the other demolition programmes—

Thousands

	Habitable rooms 1–2	3	4	5	6	7+	Total
1964–84 construction							
Demolition programme B	1	4	17	16	12	3	53
Demolition programme C	2	12	18	84	19	10	145
1984–2004 construction							
Demolition programme B	3	11	44	41	31	6	136
Demolition programme C	6	31	46	215	50	25	373

Table A9.12. *East Anglia*

	Birth rate	Migration pattern	Habitable rooms 1–2	3	4	5	6	7+	All sizes	Total dwellings
			%	%	%	%	%	%	%	*000s*
1964 housing stock			3	8	26	39	15	9	100	*318*
1964–84 construction	RG's	1	19	27	17	21	10	6	100	*97*
		2	16	25	20	23	10	6	100	*118*
		3	21	28	16	19	10	6	100	*90*
	Low	1	20	28	17	20	9	6	100	*96*
	High	1	17	25	17	23	11	7	100	*105*
1984–2004 construction	RG's	1	2	9	31	31	16	11	100	*134*
		2	3	10	31	33	14	9	100	*227*
		3	1	7	31	31	17	13	100	*99*
	Low	1	3	11	34	27	15	10	100	*123*
	High	1	1	7	28	36	17	11	100	*165*
2004 housing stock	RG's	1	6	14	24	35	13	8	100	*430*
		2	6	13	26	35	13	7	100	*544*
		3	6	14	24	35	13	8	100	*388*
	Low	1	7	14	25	34	13	7	100	*417*
	High	1	5	12	24	37	14	8	100	*469*

SOURCE: NIESR estimates.

Note: Demolition programme A is assumed for this table: the following are the adjustments for the other demolition programmes—

Thousands

	Habitable rooms 1–2	3	4	5	6	7+	Total
1964–84 construction							
Demolition programme B	—	—	2	4	2	1	9
Demolition programme C	—	1	6	14	4	2	27
1984–2004 construction							
Demolition programme B	—	1	5	10	5	2	23
Demolition programme C	1	3	16	33	11	6	70

Table A9.13. *South East*

	Birth rate	Migration pattern	Habitable rooms 1–2	3	4	5	6	7+	All sizes	Total dwellings
			%	%	%	%	%	%	%	*000s*
1964 housing stock			6	13	24	34	14	9	100	*5429*
1964–84 construction	RG's	1	11	18	43	17	7	4	100	*1811*
		2	11	19	43	16	7	4	100	*1746*
		3	11	19	43	16	7	4	100	*1697*
	Low	1	11	19	43	16	7	4	100	*1776*
	High	1	10	16	41	20	8	5	100	*1960*
1984–2004 construction	RG's	1	7	14	29	29	13	8	100	*2155*
		2	7	14	28	29	13	9	100	*1866*
		3	7	14	28	28	14	9	100	*1646*
	Low	1	9	17	33	23	11	7	100	*1954*
	High	1	4	11	26	35	15	9	100	*2740*
2004 housing stock	RG's	1	6	14	29	32	12	7	100	*8253*
		2	6	14	29	32	12	7	100	*7899*
		3	6	14	29	31	13	7	100	*7631*
	Low	1	7	15	30	30	12	6	100	*8018*
	High	1	5	13	28	33	13	8	100	*8988*

SOURCE: NIESR estimates.

Note: Demolition programme A is assumed for this table: the following are the adjustments for the other demolition programmes—

Thousands

	Habitable rooms 1–2	3	4	5	6	7+	Total
1964–84 construction							
Demolition programme B	18	40	61	53	63	41	276
Demolition programme C	23	74	169	258	128	75	727
1984–2004 construction							
Demolition programme B	46	104	156	136	162	105	709
Demolition programme C	59	190	435	664	330	192	1870

APPENDIX 10

REGIONAL COSTS

Table A10.1. *Total costs of new construction of dwellings with garages, 1964–2004*

£ millions

	Demolition programme A Birth rate assumption									Adjustments for demolition programme [a]	
	Low Migration pattern			RG's Migration pattern			High Migration pattern				
	1	2	3	1	2	3	1	2	3	B	C
Scotland											
1964–9	718	718	711	718	718	711	740	740	735	−19	−36
1969–74	513	513	555	521	521	563	559	559	603	67	139
1974–9	516	516	606	533	533	624	577	577	673	76	160
1979–84	530	530	668	541	541	685	608	608	760	100	206
1984–9	280	280	481	310	310	515	370	370	583	123	256
1989–94	332	332	603	387	387	668	522	522	815	151	324
1994–9	402	402	759	464	464	824	693	693	1073	187	401
1999–2004	485	485	915	610	610	1046	897	897	1365	250	553
1964–2004	3776	3776	5298	4084	4084	5636	4966	4966	6607	935	2003
North											
1964–9	296	296	296	297	297	297	307	307	307	0	0
1969–74	150	150	172	154	154	175	173	173	194	50	112
1974–9	138	138	181	147	147	189	169	169	214	56	128
1979–84	148	148	211	157	157	221	194	194	261	68	155
1984–9	189	189	276	204	204	295	233	233	328	81	186
1989–94	206	206	325	234	234	359	303	303	432	101	234
1994–9	234	234	389	263	263	419	382	382	548	126	289
1999–2004	257	257	446	320	320	511	466	466	671	160	375
1964–2004	1618	1618	2296	1776	1776	2466	2227	2227	2955	642	1479
North West											
1964–9	435	435	435	435	435	435	454	454	454	0	0
1969–74	347	347	370	355	355	376	396	396	417	111	276
1974–9	346	346	390	362	362	406	413	413	460	123	310
1979–84	355	355	425	377	377	448	462	462	537	150	379
1984–9	446	446	540	482	482	578	551	551	653	179	448
1989–94	536	536	667	601	601	738	753	753	892	220	575
1994–9	636	636	805	701	701	872	961	961	1144	274	713
1999–2004	763	763	966	899	899	1108	1225	1225	1446	355	928
1964–2004	3864	3864	4598	4212	4212	4961	5215	5215	6003	1412	3629
Pennines											
1964–9	464	464	464	464	464	464	479	479	479	0	0
1969–74	283	283	297	289	289	302	319	319	334	83	214
1974–9	269	269	296	281	281	309	321	321	348	92	243
1979–84	283	283	325	301	301	343	365	365	412	112	295
1984–9	360	360	417	389	389	447	442	442	503	134	353
1989–94	391	391	472	441	441	525	560	560	645	164	448
1994–9	452	452	555	501	501	606	700	700	811	204	560
1999–2004	530	530	655	635	635	761	884	884	1019	263	720
1964–2004	3032	3032	3481	3301	3301	3757	4070	4070	4551	1052	2833

Table A10.1—(*continued*)

	Demolition programme A Birth rate assumption									£ *millions* Adjustments for demolition programme [a]	
	Low Migration pattern			RG's Migration pattern			High Migration pattern				
	1	2	3	1	2	3	1	2	3	B	C
Central											
1964–9	116	116	116	116	116	116	119	119	119	0	0
1969–74	99	94	94	101	96	95	109	104	103	17	46
1974–9	98	89	86	102	93	89	113	103	100	20	52
1979–84	103	89	84	107	93	88	125	112	106	24	64
1984–9	132	111	105	139	119	112	153	130	124	28	76
1989–94	141	115	104	154	127	118	183	154	143	34	96
1994–9	166	131	121	179	141	131	228	189	178	45	122
1999–2004	175	132	115	199	155	140	259	213	197	57	154
1964–2004	1030	877	825	1097	940	889	1289	1124	1070	225	610
East											
1964–9	113	113	113	113	113	113	116	116	116	0	0
1969–74	82	87	82	84	89	84	93	98	91	18	45
1974–9	83	97	82	87	99	83	97	112	95	22	52
1979–84	91	110	86	94	115	93	109	132	109	26	63
1984–9	107	135	105	116	143	111	129	158	125	30	74
1989–94	117	153	112	129	168	125	159	196	151	40	99
1994–9	138	186	130	151	198	141	198	253	192	46	118
1999–2004	154	212	147	178	239	173	240	303	233	60	156
1964–2004	885	1093	857	952	1164	923	1141	1368	1112	242	607
North & Central Wales											
1964–9	55	55	55	54	54	54	56	56	56	0	0
1969–74	18	27	17	18	28	18	21	32	21	5	15
1974–9	20	40	18	23	42	19	27	46	23	6	18
1979–84	36	65	32	38	68	34	43	75	40	8	21
1984–9	47	89	44	49	91	45	56	99	50	10	25
1989–94	55	106	46	59	114	55	71	129	64	12	30
1994–9	65	138	60	72	144	63	92	168	85	13	41
1999–2004	83	166	70	92	177	81	118	209	105	18	55
1964–2004	379	686	342	405	718	369	484	814	444	72	205
West											
1964–9	593	593	593	593	593	593	605	605	605	0	0
1969–74	275	284	265	280	290	271	307	317	298	74	144
1974–9	260	281	244	272	293	254	307	328	288	83	160
1979–84	323	358	299	337	372	312	392	429	367	102	197
1984–9	401	446	366	427	471	390	469	517	430	121	231
1989–94	422	487	377	465	533	417	559	626	508	147	299
1994–9	488	568	426	527	608	466	691	778	625	185	361
1999–2004	538	636	461	620	721	544	824	931	742	237	484
1964–2004	3300	3653	3031	3521	3881	3247	4154	4531	3863	949	1876

Table A10.1—(*continued*)

	Demolition programme A Birth rate assumption									£ *millions* Adjustments for demolition programme [a]	
	Low Migration pattern			RG's Migration pattern			High Migration pattern				
	1	2	3	1	2	3	1	2	3	B	C
South West											
1964–9	167	167	167	166	166	166	171	171	171	0	0
1969–74	52	61	44	56	64	45	64	73	56	21	49
1974–9	68	85	49	71	88	53	81	100	63	24	56
1979–84	103	129	77	109	135	81	129	155	97	29	67
1984–9	143	179	103	149	187	112	163	203	123	35	80
1989–94	166	217	114	181	233	127	212	266	157	44	101
1994–9	188	252	121	202	267	133	256	324	183	51	125
1999–2004	220	298	139	248	327	166	316	401	226	69	167
1964–2004	1107	1388	814	1182	1467	883	1392	1693	1076	273	645
Midlands											
1964–9	769	769	769	769	769	769	785	785	785	0	0
1969–74	366	358	356	372	365	362	404	397	394	54	150
1974–9	359	345	340	371	357	353	412	399	393	61	171
1979–84	379	359	349	397	377	366	465	443	432	76	207
1984–9	455	427	414	485	456	442	540	509	497	88	247
1989–94	459	420	402	511	472	453	629	587	567	111	315
1994–9	499	446	425	549	496	472	747	692	666	135	392
1999–2004	545	488	457	648	586	559	896	830	800	176	505
1964–2004	3831	3612	3512	4102	3878	3776	4878	4642	4534	701	1987
East Anglia											
1964–9	111	111	111	111	111	111	112	112	112	0	0
1969–74	55	66	49	55	67	51	64	74	58	10	28
1974–9	55	79	48	57	81	51	65	89	58	11	32
1979–84	82	113	70	85	118	72	98	133	82	12	39
1984–9	96	145	79	102	151	84	111	162	94	15	46
1989–94	92	155	68	102	167	77	123	191	96	18	59
1994–9	112	196	82	122	206	90	156	246	124	21	75
1999–2004	126	226	89	144	245	106	187	298	147	30	97
1964–2004	729	1091	596	778	1146	642	916	1305	771	117	376
South East											
1964–9	2759	2759	2759	2759	2759	2759	2819	2819	2819	0	0
1969–74	1013	975	947	1037	1000	969	1153	1115	1086	315	829
1974–9	1083	1007	950	1132	1055	996	1287	1205	1146	353	930
1979–84	1330	1215	1127	1395	1279	1191	1658	1534	1440	432	1138
1984–9	1649	1487	1362	1761	1595	1468	1968	1796	1661	511	1392
1989–94	1624	1404	1237	1825	1598	1426	2251	2016	1837	637	1719
1994–9	1807	1519	1301	1984	1693	1475	2723	2415	2181	785	2162
1999–2004	2048	1701	1439	2424	2069	1804	3343	2965	2677	994	2730
1964–2004	13313	12067	11122	14317	13048	12088	17202	15865	14847	4027	10900

SOURCE: NIESR estimates.

[a] The adjustment factors for demolition programmes B and C for Scotland apply only to the Registrar General's birth rate assumptions; they can be used, however, to find approximate costs for the low and high birth rate assumptions.

Table A10.2. *Costs of garages for new dwellings, 1964–2004*

£ *millions*

	Demolition programme A Birth rate assumption									Adjustments for demolition programme [a]	
	Low Migration pattern			RG's Migration pattern			High Migration pattern				
	1	2	3	1	2	3	1	2	3	B	C
Scotland											
1964–9	47	47	47	48	48	47	49	49	49	−2	−3
1969–74	38	38	41	38	38	41	41	41	44	5	8
1974–9	37	37	44	38	38	45	41	41	49	5	11
1979–84	38	38	48	39	39	50	44	44	55	7	16
1984–9	23	23	39	24	24	41	29	29	45	10	20
1989–94	27	27	48	31	31	52	40	40	63	11	25
1994–9	33	33	61	37	37	65	54	54	83	14	29
1999–2004	40	40	74	49	49	83	70	70	106	18	37
1964–2004	283	283	402	304	304	424	368	368	494	68	143
North											
1964–9	20	20	20	21	21	21	21	21	21	0	0
1969–74	11	11	13	11	11	13	13	13	14	4	8
1974–9	10	10	13	11	11	14	12	12	16	4	10
1979–84	11	11	16	12	12	17	14	14	19	5	12
1984–9	14	14	21	15	15	22	17	17	24	6	14
1989–94	16	16	25	17	17	27	22	22	32	8	17
1994–9	18	18	30	20	20	31	28	28	41	9	20
1999–2004	20	20	34	24	24	38	35	35	50	12	25
1964–2004	120	120	172	131	131	183	162	162	217	48	106
North West											
1964–9	42	42	42	42	42	42	44	44	44	0	0
1969–74	25	25	27	26	26	27	29	29	30	8	19
1974–9	25	25	28	26	26	29	29	29	33	8	21
1979–84	26	26	31	27	27	33	33	33	38	10	25
1984–9	33	33	40	35	35	42	39	39	47	12	30
1989–94	39	39	49	43	43	54	54	54	64	15	37
1994–9	46	46	59	50	50	63	69	69	83	18	44
1999–2004	55	55	71	65	65	81	88	88	105	23	56
1964–2004	291	291	347	314	314	371	385	385	444	94	232
Pennines											
1964–9	37	37	37	37	37	37	38	38	38	0	0
1969–74	21	21	22	21	21	22	23	23	24	6	15
1974–9	19	19	22	20	20	23	23	23	25	7	18
1979–84	21	21	24	22	22	25	26	26	30	8	21
1984–9	27	27	31	29	29	33	32	32	37	10	25
1989–94	29	29	35	32	32	38	41	41	47	12	31
1994–9	33	33	41	37	37	44	51	51	59	14	37
1999–2004	39	39	49	46	46	56	64	64	74	18	47
1964–2004	226	226	261	244	244	278	298	298	334	75	194

Table A10.2.—(*continued*)

	Demolition programme A Birth rate assumption									£ millions Adjustments for demolition programme [a]	
	Low Migration pattern			RG's Migration pattern			High Migration pattern			B	C
	1	2	3	1	2	3	1	2	3		
Central											
1964–9	11	11	11	11	11	11	11	11	11	0	0
1969–74	7	7	7	8	7	7	8	8	8	1	3
1974–9	7	7	6	8	7	7	8	8	7	1	4
1979–84	8	6	6	8	7	6	9	8	8	2	4
1984–9	10	8	8	10	9	8	11	9	9	2	5
1989–94	11	8	8	11	9	9	14	11	10	2	6
1994–9	12	10	9	13	10	10	17	14	13	3	8
1999–2004	13	10	8	15	11	10	19	15	14	4	10
1964–2004	79	67	63	84	71	68	97	84	80	15	40
East											
1964–9	11	11	11	11	11	11	11	11	11	0	0
1969–74	6	6	6	6	6	6	7	7	6	1	3
1974–9	6	7	6	6	7	6	7	8	7	2	4
1979–84	7	8	6	7	8	7	8	10	8	2	5
1984–9	8	10	8	9	11	8	9	12	9	2	5
1989–94	9	12	8	9	12	9	12	14	11	3	7
1994–9	10	14	10	11	15	10	14	19	14	3	8
1999–2004	11	16	11	13	18	13	17	22	17	4	10
1964–2004	68	84	66	72	88	70	85	103	83	17	42
North & Central Wales											
1964–9	5	5	5	5	5	5	5	5	5	0	0
1969–74	1	2	1	1	2	1	1	2	1	0	1
1974–9	1	3	1	1	3	1	2	3	1	0	1
1979–84	2	4	2	2	5	2	3	5	3	1	1
1984–9	3	6	3	3	6	3	4	7	3	1	2
1989–94	4	7	3	4	8	4	4	9	4	1	2
1994–9	4	10	4	5	10	4	6	12	6	1	3
1999–2004	6	12	4	6	12	5	8	15	7	1	3
1964–2004	26	49	23	27	51	25	33	58	30	5	13
West											
1964–9	54	54	54	54	54	54	55	55	55	0	0
1969–74	20	20	19	20	21	19	22	23	21	5	10
1974–9	18	20	17	19	21	18	22	23	20	5	10
1979–84	23	26	21	24	27	22	28	30	26	7	13
1984–9	29	32	27	31	34	28	33	37	30	8	15
1989–94	30	35	27	33	38	29	39	45	36	10	19
1994–9	35	41	30	37	43	33	49	55	44	11	22
1999–2004	38	46	32	44	51	38	58	66	52	14	28
1964–2004	247	274	227	262	289	241	306	334	284	60	117

Table A10.2—(*continued*)

	Demolition programme A Birth rate assumption									£ *millions* Adjustments for demolition programme [a]	
	Low Migration pattern			RG's Migration pattern			High Migration pattern				
	1	2	3	1	2	3	1	2	3	B	C
South West											
1964–9	15	15	15	15	15	15	16	16	16	0	0
1969–74	3	4	3	4	4	3	4	5	4	1	3
1974–9	5	6	3	5	6	3	5	7	4	2	4
1979–84	7	9	5	7	10	5	9	10	6	2	4
1984–9	10	13	7	10	13	8	11	14	8	2	5
1989–94	12	16	8	13	17	9	15	19	11	3	6
1994–9	13	18	8	14	19	9	18	23	12	3	8
1999–2004	15	21	9	17	23	11	22	28	15	4	10
1964–2004	80	102	58	85	107	63	100	122	76	17	40
Midlands											
1964–9	67	67	67	67	67	67	68	68	68	0	0
1969–74	27	26	26	28	27	27	30	29	29	4	10
1974–9	27	25	25	27	26	26	30	29	29	4	12
1979–84	28	27	26	29	28	27	34	32	31	5	14
1984–9	34	32	31	36	34	32	39	37	36	6	17
1989–94	34	31	30	37	34	33	46	43	41	8	21
1994–9	37	33	31	40	36	34	54	50	48	9	24
1999–2004	40	36	33	47	42	40	65	60	57	11	31
1964–2004	294	277	269	311	294	286	366	348	339	47	129
East Anglia											
1964–9	10	10	10	10	10	10	10	10	10	0	0
1969–74	4	5	3	4	5	4	5	5	4	1	2
1974–9	4	6	3	4	6	4	5	6	4	1	2
1979–84	6	8	5	6	9	5	7	10	6	1	3
1984–9	7	11	6	8	11	6	8	12	7	1	3
1989–94	7	11	5	7	12	5	9	14	7	1	4
1994–9	8	15	6	9	15	6	11	18	9	1	5
1999–2004	9	17	6	10	18	7	13	22	10	2	6
1964–2004	55	83	44	58	86	47	68	97	57	8	25
South East											
1964–9	235	235	235	235	235	235	240	240	240	0	0
1969–74	75	72	70	76	74	71	85	82	80	21	54
1974–9	80	74	70	84	78	73	94	88	83	23	60
1979–84	100	92	85	105	96	89	122	113	106	28	74
1984–9	126	113	104	132	119	110	146	133	122	33	88
1989–94	123	106	93	136	118	105	166	148	134	41	108
1994–9	137	114	97	147	125	108	200	176	159	48	128
1999–2004	155	128	107	181	153	133	246	217	195	61	161
1964–2004	1031	934	861	1096	998	924	1299	1197	1119	255	673

SOURCE: NIESR estimates.

[a] The adjustment factors for demolition programme B and C for Scotland apply only to the Registrar General's birth rate assumptions; they can be used, however, to find approximate costs for the low and high birth rate assumptions.

Table A10.3. *Costs of upgrading housing areas, 1964–2004*

£ millions

	Demolition programme	Arrears of maintenance	Provision of services	Provision of garages	Upgrading the housing environment	Total upgrading costs
Scotland	A	351	131	369	85	936
	B	334	128	347	84	893
	C	319	125	323	83	850
North	A	207	51	186	42	486
	B	195	50	172	41	458
	C	184	48	156	40	428
North West	A	520	127	444	100	1191
	B	494	124	415	98	1131
	C	465	119	372	96	1052
Pennines	A	394	87	334	76	891
	B	373	85	312	74	844
	C	351	81	277	72	781
Central	A	78	24	76	17	195
	B	74	24	70	17	185
	C	68	24	62	17	171
East	A	86	24	77	18	205
	B	82	23	73	17	195
	C	77	23	66	17	183
North & Central Wales	A	39	14	37	8	98
	B	38	14	35	8	95
	C	36	16	33	8	93
West	A	297	67	251	56	671
	B	280	66	232	55	633
	C	267	65	213	54	599
South West	A	118	24	93	21	256
	B	112	24	88	21	245
	C	107	23	81	20	231
Midlands	A	313	78	282	65	738
	B	299	78	268	65	710
	C	278	76	243	63	660
East Anglia	A	56	19	56	13	144
	B	54	19	53	13	139
	C	51	19	49	12	131
South East	A	1421	265	1161	262	3109
	B	1342	259	1079	257	2937
	C	1244	258	945	250	2697
Great Britain	A	3880	911	3366	763	8920
	B	3677	894	3144	750	8465
	C	3447	877	2820	732	7876

SOURCE: NIESR estimates.

Table A10.4. *Costs of maintenance, 1964–2004*

£ millions

	Scotland	North	North West	Pennines	Central	East	N & C Wales	West	South West	Mid-lands	East Anglia	South East	Great Britain
Demolition programme A													
Low birth rate assumptions													
1964–9	466	227	564	416	92	101	56	332	131	359	79	1421	4244
1969–74	456	238	587	435	99	105	56	354	135	391	81	1544	4481
1974–9	432	247	599	451	104	108	56	366	136	413	83	1611	4606
1979–84	405	255	609	460	109	112	56	378	138	435	85	1688	4730
1984–9	400	261	620	472	115	116	55	389	141	456	87	1782	4894
1989–94	396	269	627	479	120	119	54	402	142	472	88	1863	5031
1994–9	380	274	628	486	126	121	51	415	142	487	90	1919	5119
1999–2004	360	275	632	489	132	123	49	419	142	507	90	1980	5198
1964–2004	3295	2046	4866	3688	897	905	433	3055	1107	3520	683	13808	38303
Registrars General's birth rate assumptions													
1964–9	466	227	564	416	92	101	56	332	131	359	79	1421	4244
1969–74	456	238	588	436	99	105	56	354	135	391	81	1545	4484
1974–9	434	245	600	452	104	109	56	366	136	414	83	1614	4613
1979–84	407	254	611	462	109	112	56	375	137	438	85	1676	4722
1984–9	403	263	624	475	114	117	56	388	139	454	87	1754	4874
1989–94	401	269	633	484	120	120	55	402	142	472	89	1842	5029
1994–9	382	275	639	489	126	121	53	412	145	495	91	1929	5157
1999–2004	367	279	641	496	132	123	50	424	144	514	92	2004	5266
1964–2004	3316	2050	4900	3710	896	908	438	3053	1109	3537	687	13785	38389
High birth rate assumptions													
1964–9	466	227	565	416	92	101	56	333	132	359	79	1424	4250
1969–74	464	240	591	438	99	105	56	356	136	393	82	1553	4513
1974–9	449	248	606	456	105	110	57	370	137	414	84	1631	4667
1979–84	419	258	622	470	111	114	57	382	139	435	87	1705	4799
1984–9	414	267	639	486	117	118	57	397	143	460	89	1798	4985
1989–94	417	276	656	501	124	122	56	416	146	488	92	1882	5176
1994–9	407	288	668	516	133	126	54	434	149	515	95	1984	5369
1999–2004	397	300	688	537	140	131	53	451	153	541	97	2108	5596
1964–2004	3433	2104	5035	3820	921	927	446	3139	1135	3605	705	14085	39355

Demolition programme B													
Low birth rate assumptions													
1964–9	474	227	565	422	92	102	57	333	132	360	80	1425	4269
1969–74	472	240	591	442	99	108	57	357	136	392	82	1534	4510
1974–9	448	247	605	455	105	111	57	370	137	411	84	1606	4636
1979–84	414	253	612	461	110	114	57	380	139	429	86	1669	4724
1984–9	407	258	619	470	115	117	57	390	140	451	88	1730	4842
1989–94	400	261	623	480	119	118	55	401	140	469	90	1817	4973
1994–9	383	264	622	479	124	119	53	407	141	480	91	1882	5045
1999–2004	335	264	601	474	126	117	48	398	136	478	88	1908	4973
1964–2004	3333	2014	4838	3683	890	906	441	3036	1101	3470	689	13571	37972
Registrars General's birth rate assumptions													
1964–9	474	227	565	422	93	102	56	333	132	360	80	1425	4269
1969–74	472	240	591	443	99	108	58	357	136	392	82	1535	4513
1974–9	449	247	606	456	105	111	57	371	138	412	84	1609	4645
1979–84	416	254	614	463	109	114	57	382	140	432	86	1676	4743
1984–9	410	260	617	473	114	118	57	392	141	454	88	1742	4866
1989–94	405	264	623	479	121	119	56	405	142	473	91	1816	4994
1994–9	390	269	625	482	125	121	53	414	143	487	92	1868	5069
1999–2004	345	264	609	474	126	120	50	408	140	502	90	1881	5009
1964–2004	3361	2025	4850	3692	892	913	444	3062	1112	3512	693	13552	38108
High birth rate assumptions													
1964–9	475	228	566	418	92	102	57	334	132	360	80	1427	4271
1969–74	475	241	594	435	100	108	58	359	137	394	82	1543	4526
1974–9	455	250	612	451	105	111	58	371	138	416	85	1607	4659
1979–84	424	256	625	466	110	115	58	384	139	439	88	1685	4789
1984–9	416	263	632	479	118	118	57	397	142	460	90	1785	4957
1989–94	411	273	646	491	125	122	56	409	145	484	92	1878	5132
1994–9	399	281	661	502	131	126	55	425	147	507	95	1940	5269
1999–2004	363	280	651	500	135	126	53	428	147	514	95	1972	5264
1964–2004	3418	2072	4987	3742	916	928	452	3107	1127	3574	707	13837	38867

Table A10.4—(*continued*)

£ millions

	Scotland	North	North West	Pennines	Central	East	N & C Wales	West	South West	Mid-lands	East Anglia	South East	Great Britain
Demolition programme C													
Low birth rate assumptions													
1964–9	477	228	566	424	93	103	57	334	133	361	81	1431	4288
1969–74	477	241	596	447	100	109	58	359	137	394	84	1550	4552
1974–9	455	249	615	458	105	112	58	369	139	414	85	1613	4672
1979–84	421	254	626	467	109	115	58	377	140	435	87	1687	4776
1984–9	417	257	631	473	115	117	57	387	140	458	89	1762	4903
1989–94	395	261	634	477	118	119	55	400	141	478	89	1800	4967
1994–9	349	256	623	468	119	120	52	398	141	485	87	1789	4887
1999–2004	283	244	581	441	118	115	47	380	133	479	83	1751	4655
1964–2004	3274	1990	4872	3655	877	910	442	3004	1104	3504	685	13383	37700
Registrars General's birth rate assumptions													
1964–9	477	228	566	424	93	103	57	334	133	361	81	1431	4288
1969–74	477	241	597	448	100	109	58	359	137	394	84	1550	4554
1974–9	456	250	616	458	105	113	58	370	139	415	85	1616	4681
1979–84	423	255	628	469	110	115	58	378	142	437	88	1694	4797
1984–9	419	259	636	477	115	118	57	390	144	461	90	1773	4939
1989–94	399	264	641	482	120	120	56	405	144	483	91	1820	5025
1994–9	356	260	634	476	121	118	53	405	143	493	92	1817	4968
1999–2004	292	251	597	452	121	113	48	389	136	491	88	1793	4771
1964–2004	3299	2008	4915	3686	885	909	445	3030	1118	3535	699	13494	38023
High birth rate assumptions													
1964–9	478	228	568	425	93	103	57	335	133	361	81	1433	4295
1969–74	480	243	593	445	101	108	58	361	138	397	84	1558	4566
1974–9	462	250	609	458	106	112	59	374	141	420	86	1632	4709
1979–84	431	257	625	471	112	117	59	385	143	444	88	1724	4856
1984–9	425	265	637	483	118	120	58	399	144	467	91	1817	5024
1989–94	399	271	648	493	124	123	56	413	147	488	94	1882	5138
1994–9	368	268	636	489	126	123	56	415	150	500	93	1911	5135
1999–2004	316	265	611	475	126	119	52	413	146	509	91	1928	5051
1964–2004	3359	2047	4927	3739	906	925	455	3095	1142	3586	708	13885	38774

SOURCE: NIESR estimates.

Note: Migration pattern 1 assumed throughout this table.

APPENDIX II

REGIONAL LAND REQUIREMENTS

Table A11. *Net land requirements, 1964–2004, for demolition programme A*

Thousand acres

	Low birth rate Migration pattern			RG's birth rate Migration pattern			High birth rate Migration pattern		
	1	2	3	1	2	3	1	2	3
Scotland									
1964–9	11·8	11·8	11·7	11·8	11·8	11·7	12·2	12·2	12·1
1969–74	7·6	7·6	8·4	7·8	7·8	8·5	8·5	8·5	9·3
1974–9	7·3	7·3	9·0	7·6	7·6	9·4	8·6	8·6	10·3
1979–84	7·0	7·0	9·6	7·2	7·2	9·9	8·6	8·6	11·5
1984–9	1·6	1·6	5·1	2·3	2·3	6·0	3·5	3·5	7·3
1989–94	1·8	1·8	6·6	3·0	3·0	8·0	5·7	5·7	10·9
1994–9	2·3	2·3	8·5	3·6	3·6	10·0	8·0	8·0	14·9
1999–2004	1·9	1·9	9·4	4·3	4·3	12·0	9·8	9·8	18·3
1964–2004	41·3	41·3	68·3	47·6	47·6	75·5	64·9	64·9	94·6
North									
1964–9	6·9	6·9	6·9	6·9	6·9	6·9	7·1	7·1	7·1
1969–74	2·7	2·7	3·1	2·8	2·8	3·2	3·2	3·2	3·6
1974–9	2·3	2·3	3·3	2·4	2·4	3·4	3·0	3·0	4·1
1979–84	2·0	2·0	3·5	2·4	2·4	3·8	3·5	3·5	5·0
1984–9	2·8	2·8	4·7	3·2	3·2	5·3	4·0	4·0	6·2
1989–94	2·7	2·7	5·5	3·5	3·5	6·5	5·3	5·3	8·3
1994–9	3·1	3·1	6·5	3·9	3·9	7·5	6·8	6·8	10·8
1999–2004	3·0	3·0	7·3	4·6	4·6	9·1	8·3	8·3	13·1
1964–2004	25·5	25·5	40·8	29·7	29·7	45·7	41·2	41·2	58·2
North West									
1964–9	4·6	4·6	4·6	4·6	4·6	4·6	4·9	4·9	4·9
1969–74	5·0	5·0	5·5	5·2	5·2	5·7	6·1	6·1	6·5
1974–9	4·7	4·7	5·6	5·1	5·1	5·9	6·3	6·3	7·3
1979–84	4·2	4·2	5·6	4·8	4·8	6·2	6·7	6·7	8·2
1984–9	5·3	5·3	7·2	6·3	6·3	8·3	8·1	8·1	10·2
1989–94	6·4	6·4	9·0	8·0	8·0	10·8	11·5	11·5	14·3
1994–9	7·6	7·6	11·0	9·2	9·2	12·7	15·0	15·0	18·8
1999–2004	8·8	8·8	12·9	11·9	11·9	16·1	19·1	19·1	23·7
1964–2004	46·6	46·6	61·4	55·1	55·1	70·3	77·7	77·7	93·9
Pennines									
1964–9	7·7	7·7	7·7	7·7	7·7	7·7	8·0	8·0	8·0
1969–74	4·8	4·8	5·0	4·8	4·8	5·2	5·5	5·5	5·9
1974–9	4·2	4·2	4·8	4·5	4·5	5·1	5·6	5·6	6·1
1979–84	4·0	4·0	4·9	4·4	4·4	5·4	6·1	6·1	7·2
1984–9	5·1	5·1	6·4	5·9	5·9	7·3	7·4	7·4	8·8
1989–94	5·3	5·2	7·0	6·7	6·7	8·5	9·5	9·5	11·4
1994–9	5·9	6·0	8·3	7·4	7·4	9·7	12·2	12·2	14·7
1999–2004	6·6	6·6	9·4	9·3	9·3	12·0	15·2	15·2	18·3
1964–2004	43·6	43·6	53·5	50·7	50·7	60·9	69·5	69·5	80·4

Table A11.—(*continued*)

Thousand acres

	Low birth rate Migration pattern			RG's birth rate Migration pattern			High birth rate Migration pattern		
	1	2	3	1	2	3	1	2	3
Central									
1964–9	1·3	1·3	1·4	1·4	1·3	1·4	1·4	1·4	1·4
1969–74	1·9	1·8	1·7	1·9	1·8	1·8	2·1	2·0	2·0
1974–9	1·8	1·6	1·6	1·8	1·7	1·6	2·2	1·9	1·8
1979–84	1·8	1·5	1·6	1·9	1·6	1·5	2·3	2·1	2·0
1984–9	2·3	1·9	1·7	2·5	2·1	2·0	2·9	2·3	2·3
1989–94	2·3	1·8	1·6	2·8	2·2	2·0	3·4	2·8	2·6
1994–9	2·8	2·1	1·9	3·1	2·3	2·1	4·3	3·5	3·2
1999–2004	2·8	1·9	1·6	3·4	2·5	2·2	4·9	3·9	3·5
1964–2004	17·0	13·9	13·1	18·8	15·5	14·6	23·5	19·9	18·8
East									
1964–9	1·1	1·1	1·1	1·1	1·1	1·1	1·1	1·1	1·1
1969–74	1·5	1·6	1·4	1·5	1·6	1·5	1·7	1·8	1·7
1974–9	1·5	1·7	1·4	1·6	1·8	1·5	1·8	2·1	1·7
1979–84	1·5	1·9	1·4	1·6	2·0	1·6	2·0	2·4	2·0
1984–9	1·7	2·4	1·6	1·9	2·5	1·8	2·3	2·9	2·2
1989–94	1·8	2·6	1·7	2·1	3·0	2·0	2·8	3·6	2·7
1994–9	2·1	3·2	1·9	2·5	3·5	2·3	3·6	4·9	3·5
1999–2004	2·2	3·5	2·1	2·8	4·1	2·7	4·4	5·8	4·2
1964–2004	13·4	18·0	12·6	15·1	19·6	14·5	19·7	24·6	19·1
North & Central Wales									
1964–9	0·1	0·1	0·1	0·1	0·1	0·1	0·1	0·1	0·1
1969–74	0·2	0·4	0·1	0·2	0·4	0·2	0·3	0·5	0·3
1974–9	0·2	0·6	0·1	0·3	0·6	0·2	0·3	0·8	0·3
1979–84	0·5	1·2	0·4	0·5	1·1	0·5	0·6	1·3	0·5
1984–9	0·7	1·5	0·6	0·7	1·6	0·6	0·8	1·8	0·7
1989–94	0·6	1·8	0·6	0·8	2·0	0·7	1·1	2·3	0·9
1994–9	0·8	2·3	0·7	1·0	2·5	0·8	1·5	3.1	1·3
1999–2004	1·0	2·8	0·7	1·3	3·1	1·0	1·9	3·9	1·6
1964–2004	4·1	10·7	3·3	4·9	11·4	4·1	6·6	13·8	5·7
West									
1964–9	7·7	7·7	7·7	7·8	7·7	7·8	7·9	7·9	7·9
1969–74	4·7	4·9	4·6	4·8	5·0	4·6	5·4	5·6	5·2
1974–9	4·3	4·7	4·0	4·5	5·0	4·2	5·3	5·8	4·9
1979–84	5·2	5·9	4·7	5·5	6·3	5·1	6·8	7·6	6·4
1984–9	6·4	7·3	5·7	7·1	8·0	6·4	8·2	9·2	7·4
1989–94	6·5	7·8	5·6	7·6	8·9	6·6	9·8	11·1	8·7
1994–9	7·4	9·0	6·2	8·5	10·2	7·2	12·1	13·9	10·8
1999–2004	7·9	9·8	6·3	9·8	11·8	8·2	14·3	16·5	12·6
1964–2004	50·1	57·1	44·8	55·6	62·9	50·1	69·8	77·6	63·9

Table A11.—(*continued*)

Thousand acres

	Low birth rate Migration pattern			RG's birth rate Migration pattern			High birth rate Migration pattern		
	1	2	3	1	2	3	1	2	3
South West									
1964–9	1·7	1·6	1·6	1·6	1·7	1·7	1·8	1·7	1·7
1969–74	0·7	0·9	0·5	0·7	0·9	0·5	1·0	1·1	0·8
1974–9	0·9	1·3	0·5	1·0	1·3	0·6	1·3	1·6	0·9
1979–84	1·5	2·0	1·0	1·7	2·1	1·0	2·1	2·7	1·5
1984–9	2·1	2·8	1·4	2·4	3·1	1·6	2·7	3·5	1·9
1989–94	2·4	3·4	1·4	2·8	3·9	1·7	3·5	4·6	2·4
1994–9	2·7	4·0	1·4	3·1	4·4	1·7	4·2	5·7	2·8
1999–2004	3·1	4·6	1·5	3·7	5·3	2·0	5·2	7·0	3·3
1964–2004	15·1	20·6	9·3	17·0	22·7	10·8	21·8	27·9	15·3
Midlands									
1964–9	12·0	12·0	12·0	11·9	11·9	11·9	12·2	12·2	12·2
1969–74	6·8	6·6	6·5	6·8	6·8	6·7	7·5	7·4	7·4
1974–9	6·4	6·2	6·1	6·7	6·4	6·3	7·7	7·4	7·4
1979–84	6·4	5·9	5·8	6·9	6·5	6·2	8·6	8·2	7·9
1984–9	7·6	7·0	6·7	8·5	7·8	7·6	9·9	9·2	8·9
1989–94	7·3	6·6	6·1	8·7	7·9	7·5	11·5	10·6	10·1
1994–9	7·8	6·7	6·2	9·2	8·0	7·5	13·8	12·6	12·0
1999–2004	8·1	6·8	6·3	10·5	9·2	8·7	16·3	14·9	14·2
1964–2004	62·4	57·8	55·7	69·2	64·5	62·4	87·5	82·5	80·1
East Anglia									
1964–9	0·6	0·7	0·6	0·7	0·7	0·7	0·7	0·7	0·7
1969–74	1·0	1·1	0·8	1·0	1·1	0·8	1·1	1·3	1·0
1974–9	0·9	1·5	0·8	0·9	1·5	0·9	1·1	1·6	1·0
1979–84	1·3	2·0	1·1	1·4	2·1	1·2	1·8	2·6	1·5
1984–9	1·6	2·6	1·2	1·7	2·8	1·3	2·0	3·0	1·5
1989–94	1·4	2·7	0·9	1·7	3·0	1·1	2·1	3·6	1·6
1994–9	1·8	3·4	1·0	1·9	3·7	1·3	2·7	4·7	2·1
1999–2004	1·8	3·9	1·0	2·3	4·4	1·5	3·3	5·7	2·3
1964–2004	10·4	17·9	7·4	11·6	19·3	8·8	14·8	23·2	11·7
South East									
1964–9	41·2	41·2	41·2	41·1	41·1	41·1	42·2	42·2	42·2
1969–74	16·4	15·6	15·1	16·8	16·1	15·6	19·2	18·5	17·9
1974–9	17·3	15·7	14·7	18·2	16·6	15·6	21·7	20·2	19·0
1979–84	20·6	18·4	16·7	22·1	19·9	18·2	27·9	25·5	23·7
1984–9	25·2	22·1	19·8	28·2	25·0	22·5	33·1	29·7	27·1
1989–94	23·5	19·4	16·2	28·4	24·1	20·8	37·5	33·0	29·6
1994–9	25·7	20·3	16·2	30·2	24·6	20·4	45·8	39·8	35·3
1999–2004	27·9	21·3	16·4	36·1	29·4	24·4	55·7	48·3	42·7
1964–2004	197·8	174·0	156·3	221·1	196·8	178·6	283·1	257·2	237·5

SOURCE: NIESR estimates.

APPENDIX 12

THE OUTPUT, PRODUCTIVITY AND PRICES OF CONSTRUCTION WORK

THE ORGANIZATION OF CONTRACTING

The assessment of the activities of the contracting industry is complicated by the division of work between firms and direct labour organizations. Both accept responsibility as principal contractors for the entire construction, but subcontract the work of some trades and other specialist work to specialist contractors, who may be the manufacturers of the components used, other building firms, or the public boards. In Scotland about half the work is still let on the basis of a separate contract between the client and each specialist contractor.

Direct labour organizations are the building departments of local authorities, the central government departments, public boards (gas, electricity, coal, railways, waterways and hospitals), and manufacturing and other firms outside the construction industry. Nearly a quarter of all operatives recorded are employed by public sector direct labour organizations. Half of the public sector direct labour operatives are employed by local authorities, and most of them are on maintenance work.

Information on output and the use of the labour force is not available on a uniform basis for the two types of organization, firms and direct labour. This is partly because direct labour organizations often do not function independently of their parent authority: a part of their administrative and overhead costs is often debited to other departments of that authority. As a result it is not possible to obtain a comprehensive picture of the operation of the contracting industry.

OUTPUT OF THE CONSTRUCTION INDUSTRY

Over the last fifteen years the real output of the construction industry appears to have increased on average by just over 3½ per cent a year. Substantial increases in output occurred during the periods 1952/3, 1955/6, annually from 1958/9 to 1961/2, and again during the period 1963/4. This last increase is in part a reflection of the extreme winter conditions during the first quarter of 1963 which reduced the increase that would otherwise have occurred in 1962/3. The periods during which output has increased the most have usually been periods following the end of government economic restrictions, although the increase in 1955/6 was achieved during a period of restriction. Nearly all the increase in real output has been obtained in the new work sector; the average rate of increase of which appears to have been about 5½ per cent per annum. As a result, whereas in 1950 the output of maintenance work nearly equalled new construction, by 1965 it was only just over a third (27 per cent of total output).

All figures relating to output and to manpower, and hence to productivity, must be accepted with some reservations. Construction work is very heterogeneous and, except for new housing, no acceptable single physical measure of output is available. Output is measured in terms of the value of work done, and accurate figures are difficult to obtain for a number of reasons. There are about 100,000 building firms and organizations, three-quarters of which are very small, many of only one or two partners working on their own. The units of building and civil engineering work are often very large. At any date of account the number of partly completed units will be large in relation to units which have been completed during the accounting period. It is difficult to measure accurately the value of the work performed on incomplete units. Because output is measured in value, the value figures need to be deflated to obtain estimates of real output. Price indices suitable for deflating are difficult to produce partly because there are no homogeneous units of output against which to measure price changes, partly because there are shifts in the composition of the work load, and partly because of the lack of reliable measures of labour input. For similar reasons it is difficult to measure price changes by using measures of productivity. Labour input is difficult to measure because of the number of organizations, the way direct labour is recorded and the movement of labour in and out of the poorly recorded self-employed sector. Measures of price change and productivity tend to depend on each other and are often related in a circular manner. Considerable care is necessary in interpreting results; they need to be tested against independent evidence.

There is no independent measure of the value of total output against which to check the figures of the Ministry of Public Building and Works. The deflated values of output of housing can, however, be compared with the output of dwellings, using a price index number.

BUILDING PRICE INDICES

The only published price index which relates exclusively to housing[1] is published by Carter in the weekly journal *Building*[2] on the basis of statistics supplied by the Ministry of Public Building and Works. The basis of this index follows a pattern common to other indices from this source. The method is to deduct, from the value of the work done, the wage bill calculated from employment, statutory costs and earnings figures, and a periodically revised percentage for overheads and profits. The residual is taken to be the cost of materials and this is deflated on the basis of the construction materials index of the Board of Trade. The resulting index is expressed as input of materials per man and taken to be an index of labour productivity. An index of wage costs is divided by this index to give an index of labour costs per unit of work. This in turn is combined with the index of material prices to give the construction price index. Adjustments

[1] The prices of public authority dwellings, published by the Ministry of Housing and Local Government, reflect rising housing standards as well as rising prices.

[2] Formerly *The Builder*.

are made to the percentage of profits from time to time as the returns from the Inland Revenue for construction companies become available. Clearly, however, the resulting measure of price changes depends to a large extent on the validity of accepting the residual as a measure of labour productivity.

Over the last seven years white-collar workers appear to have increased by about 4½ per cent a year on average, as compared with an increase in operatives of between 1 and 2 per cent.[1] The percentage of overheads should therefore be increasing, especially as the relative amount of plant is probably also increasing. Since many contracts are on the basis of a fixed price, an allowance has to be made in tendering for anticipated price increases during the period of the contract, and in so far as these do not occur, they swell the size of the residual. Moreover, when materials are used at a greater level of prefabrication, as is the tendency, this also increases the residual. Thus the measure of productivity, which is based on the residual, is likely to be overestimated, both because the residual is likely to be overestimated and because, as will be shown later, the labour force is likely to be underestimated. As a result, the measure of price change will itself tend to be an underestimate.

Clearly, if the indices published by the Ministry of Public Building and Works and in *Building* are used to deflate output values as a preliminary to estimating output per man, they will not produce a measure of productivity independent of the materials-input measure computed in the first phase of the calculation. These indices need to be checked against independent measures of price changes.

Many of the measures of changes in construction prices are not independent of the Ministry indices because they use either the same measure of material price changes or the same measure of productivity. The only indices which are constructed completely independently (103) are Venning's and the measured work index of the Building Research Station (104). The Venning index does not appear to have a statistical base but is derived from tender prices. The Building Research Station index is based on the movements of a weighted sum of measured work rates taken from building journals. These rates (there are over 200) are prepared by a firm of quantity surveyors on the basis of tenders passing through their office and quotations obtained from the trade. Their movements therefore depend on the speed and skill of the revision process, but they should be independent of the published price indices. It will be seen that, broadly, the three types of indices move together. The measured work index is more erratic and, over the last five years, shows a much greater rate of rise (fig. A12.1). There are negligible differences between the various indices prepared by the Ministry. The Ministry new work index shows a rise over the period 1950–65 of 162 per cent, the Venning index 180 per cent, and the Building Research Station measured work index 196 per cent. An index based on averaging their movements, the Building Research Station combined index, gives an increase of 180 per cent.

[1] This figure may be too low, since the number of self-employed operatives and subcontractors (labour only) has been increasing—this is considered later.

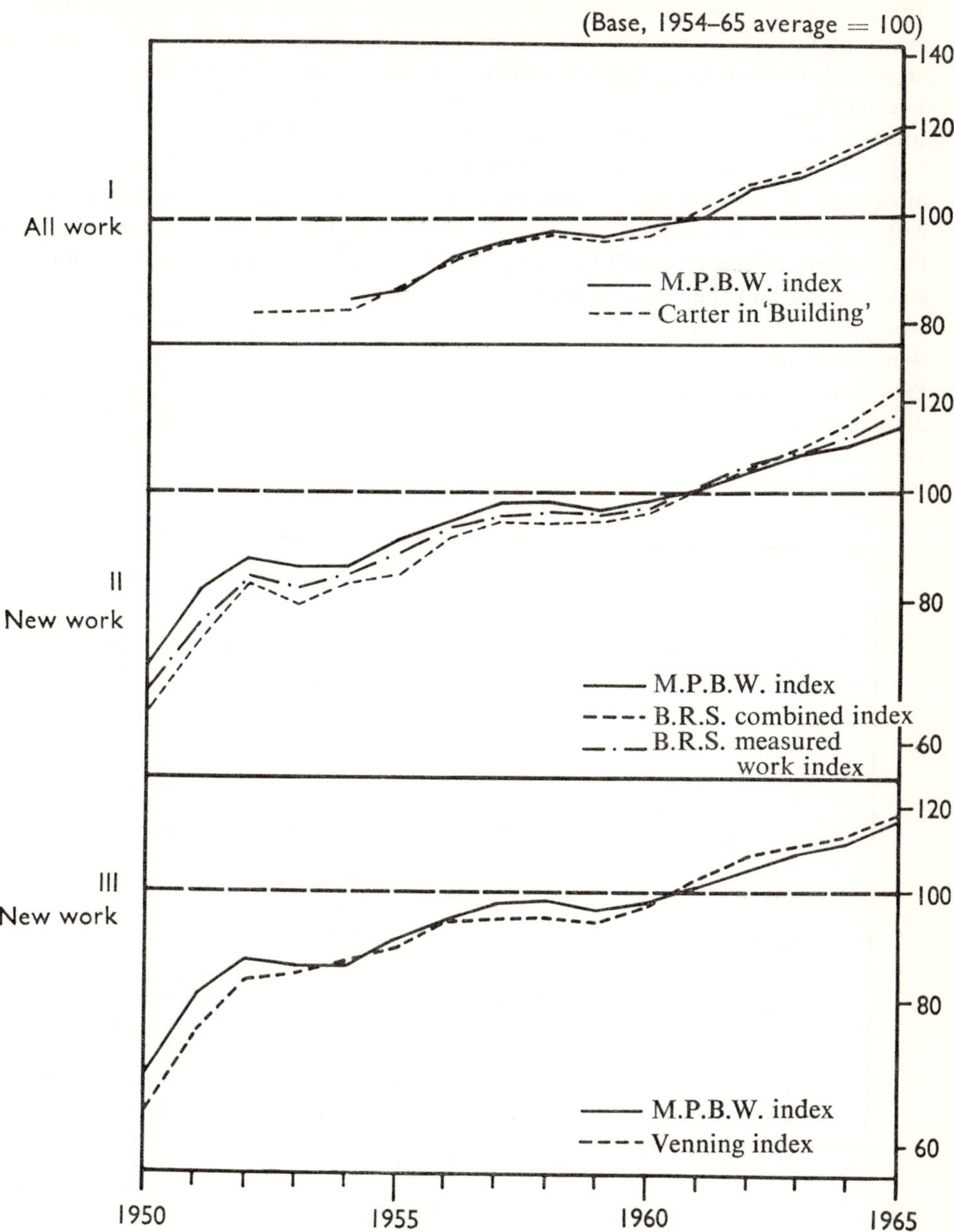

SOURCES: *Building;* unpublished figures supplied by the Ministry of Public Building and Works and the Building Research Station.

Fig. A12.1. A comparison of price indices

The differences, particularly over the last decade, are not very great; possibly the combined index provides the best estimate. Clearly, while the general trend in prices is not in doubt, little weight can be placed upon short-term movements. The fact that the Ministry index is the lowest gives some indication that the corresponding measure of productivity is probably too high.

Some idea of the reliability of the output figures can be obtained in the case of housing by comparing an index based on value of output at constant prices with one based on a physical measure of work done. This is formed by adjusting the annual number of dwellings completed for differences in the number under construction and the average number of rooms per dwelling. Close agreement would not be expected from such a crude measure. The expectation would be that the value index would rise faster than the physical index, since the latter makes no allowance for rises in standard. This is broadly so; subject to this, agreement is reasonably satisfactory (fig. A12.2). The output figures for other work cannot be tested.

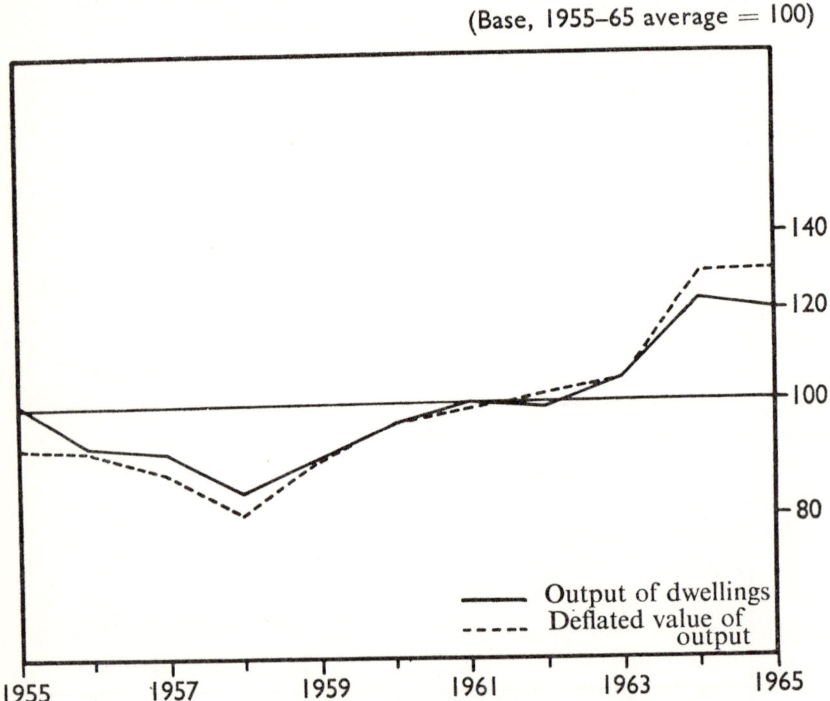

SOURCES: *Housing Statistics, Great Britain* (66); NIESR estimates.

Note: Annual housing totals have been adjusted for both number of rooms and work in progress. Value of housing output has been adjusted to 1964 constant prices using the B.R.S. combined index.

Fig. A12.2. Houses and output

INDICES OF LABOUR PRODUCTIVITY

It is not possible to produce any completely independent measures of labour productivity since the only source of output data is the Ministry of Public Building and Works. Estimates of changes in the labour force are available from two sources, but neither is completely reliable. The Ministry of Labour have frequently revised the basis of their figures, which probably indicate a larger percentage rise in the labour force than has occurred—more local authority direct labour operatives are now identified than formerly. In contrast, the figures of the Ministry of Public Building and Works tend to underestimate the increase in operatives—the National Federation of Building Trades Operatives believes that the Ministry figures considerably underestimate the growth of the operative labour force because a growing proportion of labour-only subcontractors is not recorded. It is difficult to obtain a measure of the secular trend of the labour force because of the combination of errors of estimate, and the growth and decline of the labour force with trade conditions. It would appear, however, that the force has grown in step with increases in the working population, and that, over the last five years, it has grown at a much faster rate.

The estimated rates of change in the productivity of building labour vary considerably with the estimates of the price changes and of the labour force on which they are based (fig. A12.3). The base of all the comparisons can only be the Ministry of Public Building and Works estimates of gross output per operative. An index based on the Ministry's estimates of price changes, and of the number of operatives adjusted to allow for working principals, gives an average rate of increase in productivity per man for new work, over the period 1958–65, of about 4·4 per cent per annum. If the Venning index of price change is used the figure is reduced to about 3·5 per cent, and if the Building Research Station measured work index is used the figure is about 2·7 per cent. If a price index based on the average movements of the three is used, the figure is 3·5 per cent. Using the index of average movement, and adding the Trades Union's estimate of unrecorded self-employed operatives to the Ministry estimates of operatives, gives a figure of about 2·3 per cent. It would appear that the true figure probably lies somewhere between 3 and 3·5 per cent.

A similar range of price indices is not available for repair and maintenance work, and the problem of self-employed operatives does not arise. It would appear that during the period 1958–65 the rate of increase in productivity per man was no more than 1 to 1·5 per cent per annum. Since 1960 it appears to have been even less. Too much weight must not be attached to these figures, since the rate measured depends largely on the rate assumed in estimating price changes.

BUILDING PRICES

Over the fifteen years from 1950 the price of construction labour rose by about 170 per cent (table A12.1), which is about average for industries in this country.

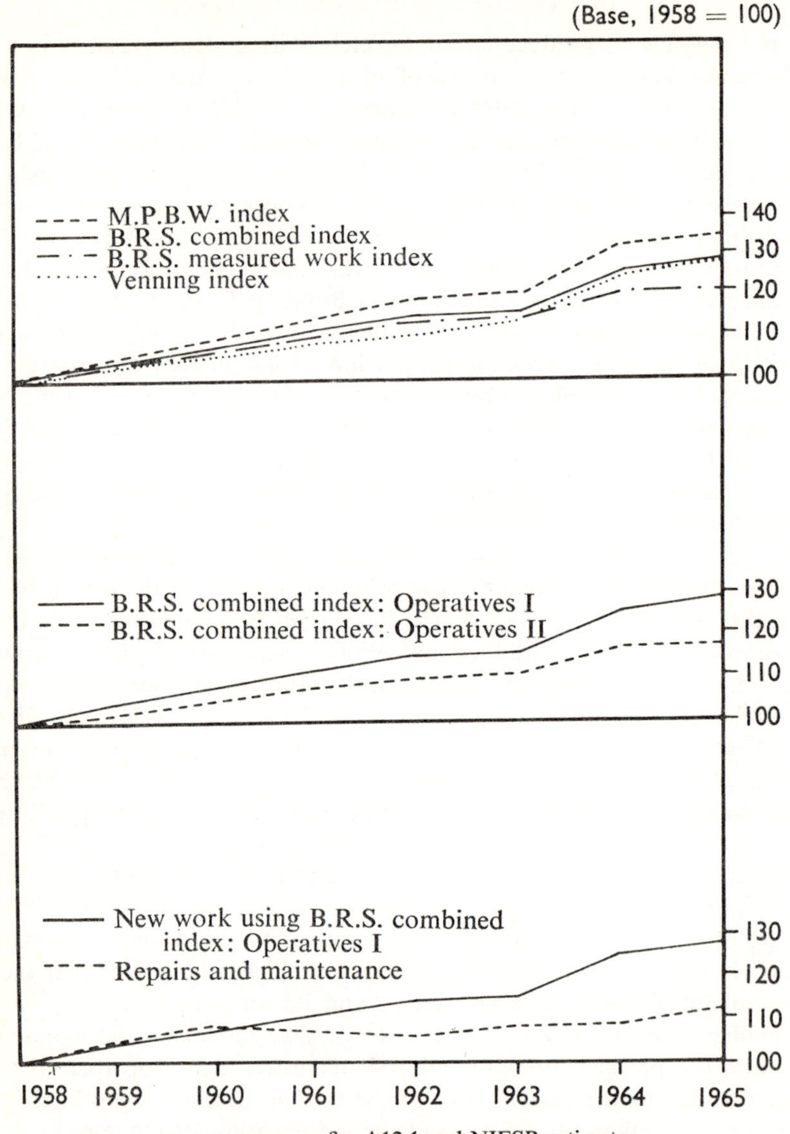

SOURCES: as fig. A12.1 and NIESR estimates.

Note: Figures for 'Operatives I' based on M.P.B.W. estimates adjusted for working principals; figures for 'Operatives II' as Operatives I adjusted also for the N.F.B.T.U.'s estimates of unrecorded self-employed.

Fig. A12.3. Productivity: gross output per operative

The final price of goods and services on the home market rose by about 70 per cent over this period, so that real wages increased by some 60 per cent. Since the level of productivity in new work also rose by about the same amount, the real cost of labour per unit of new output changed very little.

Table A12.1. *Earnings per hour in construction and other industries, males over 21*

Indices, 1954 = 100

	Earnings in construction	Earnings in all industries	Prices of final goods
April 1950	72	74	83
October 1955	107	108	104
October 1960	136	145	120
October 1965	195	198	141

SOURCES: *Monthly Digest of Statistics* (105); *National Income and Expenditure* (106).

The market prices of construction materials, in common with the prices of most other materials, have increased far less than the money prices of labour. The basic manufactured materials have shown the most marked rise in prices (table A12.2). Structural steel, bricks and asbestos cement have all about

Table A12.2. *Prices of construction materials, 1950–65*

Indices, 1954 = 100

	1950	1955	1960	1965
Heavy steel bars and sections	68	104	132	140
Bricks	77	103	115	138
Asbestos cement products	64	103	124	137
Cement	77	102	113	128
Softwood	66	109	105	118
Joinery	85	103	110	136
Cast stone and concrete products	84	101	103	118
Clay partition blocks	..	104	107	111
Thermal insulation materials	..	100	101	107
Plastic household mouldings	81	103	98	89
Polythene tubing	..	94	75	64
Construction materials	81	105	115	130
House building materials	80	105	114	131
Prices of final goods and services	83	104	120	141

SOURCE: *Board of Trade Journal* (107).

doubled in price over the fifteen years; the price of cement has risen a little less, and the increases for cast stone and for concrete products have been under 50 per cent. Softwood, a largely imported product, increased in price by nearly 50 per cent during the period 1950–5, but there has been little increase since then. This price increase seems to have been largely absorbed by the joinery trade up to 1955, but after that date the price of joinery has risen in line with other basic building materials. The newer products, cast stone and concrete, clay partition blocks and the plastic building materials, have shown the smallest price rises. In fact, since 1955, the prices of plastic household mouldings and polythene tubing have fallen substantially.

Overall, the prices of constructional materials have risen about 60 per cent over the period 1950–65. This increase is, in fact, a little less than the increase in the prices of final goods and services. The real price of materials has, therefore, fallen slightly but clearly not enough to have a significant effect on the relationship between materials and labour in the total price.

The net effect of a slight fall in the real prices of materials and little change in the real costs of a unit of labour is probably a slight fall in the real cost of new work (table A12.3). (On the basis of some price indices a slight rise would be indicated.) In contrast, the real costs of maintenance and conversion work have probably increased by about a quarter over the period.

Table A12.3. *Prices of materials, labour and output in construction*

Indices, 1954 = 100

	1950	1955	1960	1965
Construction materials index	81	105	115	130
Earnings in construction index	72	107	136	195
New construction index [a]	82	106	114	134
Final goods and services on the home market	83	104	120	141

SOURCES: *Board of Trade Journal* (107); *Monthly Digest of Statistics* (105); *National Income and Expenditure* (106); *Monthly Bulletin of Construction Statistics* (108).

[a] Ministry of Public Buildings and Works.

PRICE MOVEMENTS IN CONSTRUCTION AND OTHER SECTORS

While the prices for new construction appear to have risen a little less than those of final goods and services, they have risen a little faster than the prices of fixed assets generally and, since 1955, a little faster than manufactured products generally (table A12.4). The prices of iron and steel products have risen much more than those of new construction, but chemicals and textiles in particular have kept down price increases in manufactures as a whole.

Table A12.4. *Comparative price changes*

Indices, 1954 = 100

	1950	1955	1960	1965
New construction index [a]	82	106	114	134
Final goods and services	83	104	120	141
Fixed assets	81	105	116	131
All manufactured products	. .	103	113	128
Food manufacturing	. .	102	107	121
Chemicals	79	100	104	109
Iron and steel	71	104	126	137
Textiles	101	98	101	110
Clothing	91	100	107	115
Timber	. .	. .	108	122
Paper	76	105	108	119

SOURCES: As table A12.3.

[a] Ministry of Public Buildings and Works.

Comparisons of price changes and of productivity indicate that the performance of the construction industry has been just a little better than average for the economy as a whole. This is not unsatisfactory for an industry as long established as construction. The more striking increases in productivity are usually obtained by industries in the early stages of development when hand and batch production is being replaced by the mass production of standard products, and the advantages of scale are being obtained.

THE OUTPUT OF DESIGN WORK

The measurement of productivity in design work is difficult, as the amount of professional time required for such work varies considerably with the type of building, the amount of repetition, the type of service required and the amount of administrative and research work carried out by the design staff, as well as with the skill of the designers and the amount of non-professional assistance they receive. For example, the Royal Institute of British Architects has found that the highest levels of productivity, in terms of value of turnover to technical staff, are obtained in medium-size offices, in offices which do not require their design staff to carry out much administrative work, and in those which pay their designers the highest salaries and which generally have the most skilled staff (109).

While for building work the architect is usually the principal member of the design team, he needs the support, except in the case of the simplest buildings, of service and structural engineers, and of surveyors. The importance of the other groups is growing as the proportion of buildings with a sophisticated structure and extensive services increases, and as more attention needs to be paid to providing good value for money. The number of qualified structural engineers, surveyors and civil engineers has grown much faster than the number of architects in the last decade (table A12.5). Apparent rates of growth in the numbers of professional people are affected by changes in the regulations for registration and must be interpreted with caution—the figures for surveyors include all types of chartered surveyor – but it is notable that, whereas the increase in the number of registered architects has been much below the increase in the volume of new work, the increase in the numbers of other professions has been close to or above the increase in new work. It would appear that the proportion of new work designed by architects has fallen; while this is denied by the profession, it would seem more likely than the alternative—that the value of work passing through an architect's hands has increased by over 3 per cent a year during this period when architects were increasingly working in the field of planning. In comparison with other industrialized countries, Great Britain would appear to have a high ratio of architects to population.

Table A12.5. *Numbers of qualified professional workers and indices of real output*

Indices

	1950	1955	1960	1965
Architects	100	118	120	132
Civil engineers	100	122	141	213
Structural engineers	100	130	168	216
Surveyors	100 [a]	141	164	330
Town planners	100	119	139	173
New building	100	146	173	223
New civil engineering	100	128	199	254
All new work	100	142	178	229

SOURCE: NIESR estimates based on information obtained from the relevant professional associations.

[a] For 1951.

APPENDIX 13

HOUSING SUBSIDIES[1]

There have been several important changes in policy with regard to subsidies for local authority housing over the past decade. The most important are summarized below, together with a statement of present levels of subsidy under the 1967 Housing Subsidies Act.

The major changes have been related to the general needs subsidy, defined by the 1967 Act as a subsidy on dwellings provided by the local authority 'in exercise of its powers to provide housing accommodation'. This subsidy, which had increased in value over the first postwar decade to a level of £26 14*s.* per dwelling payable for sixty years, was abolished in 1956. In the past decade it has been slowly rehabilitated, but in a modified form.

Special subsidies—grants against specific forms of expenditure—whose range was gradually extended in an *ad hoc* manner over the postwar decade, have been largely maintained in their original form, with some changes of definition and some increases in value, mainly to compensate for the inflation of building costs and land prices rather than to change the direction of the policy.

HOUSING SUBSIDIES ACT 1956

1. Subsidy for general needs was reduced for a house to £10 per year and for a flat to £12 a year—less than for comparable dwellings built for slum clearance (see 2 below). Local authorities were relieved of the obligation to make a contribution out of the general rates. The subsidies for general needs were subsequently abolished by an Order.

2. Subsidies for dwellings built in connection with slum clearance, redevelopment and unsatisfactory temporary housing were as follows:

up to three storeys	£22 1*s.*
four storeys	£32
five storeys	£38
six storeys	£50

An additional £1 15*s.* was given for each storey in excess of six storeys.

An expensive site subsidy was also provided as follows:

Cost of site as developed:

£4,000 or less per acre	Nil
£4,000 to £5,000 per acre	£60
In excess of £5,000 per acre	£60 plus £34 for each £1,000 or part of £1,000 in excess of £5,000 per acre.

[1] The subsidies described are those which applied to England and Wales; in Scotland the subsidies were slightly different.

3. Subsidies for dwellings up to three storeys for town development, urgent industrial needs or new town development were increased to £24.
4. Subsidies were payable for sixty years.

HOUSING ACT 1961

1. A basic subsidy was provided of £28 a dwelling a year for town development, including new towns, and £24 for housing for urgent industrial needs. For other approved dwellings two rates of subsidy were laid down: broadly a subsidy of £24 a dwelling was to be paid to authorities whose total expenditure in the housing account exceeded twice the gross value of the dwellings covered by the account, while £8 per dwelling was to be paid to other authorities.
2. Additional subsidies for flats in high blocks were provided as follows:

up to three storeys	Nil
four storeys	£8
five storeys	£14
six storeys	£26

with an additional £1 15*s*. for each storey in excess of six storeys.
3. The subsidy on expensive sites remained unchanged.
4. Subsidies were payable for sixty years.

HOUSING SUBSIDIES ACT 1967

1. The latest form of general subsidy is on the total costs of new dwellings, including site development costs, and is not related to the individual dwelling. The amount is the difference between the cost of charges payable on a sixty-year loan at 4 per cent including interest and repayment of the principal, and the charges on such a loan at the average rate of interest paid by local authorities over the last year.
2. The extra subsidy given in the 1961 Housing Act for dwellings in blocks over six storeys was abolished.
3. The subsidy for town development remained unchanged.
4. For the purposes of subsidies on expensive sites, the definition of site costs was changed to exclude clearance costs. The subsidy was changed to £34 for every £1,000 per acre or part of a £1,000 over £4,000, and £40 per £1,000 for site costs over £50,000 per acre, subject to exclusion of subsidies for costs over £10,000 unless:

(i) the number of dwellings per acre was not less than 35
or (ii) the average number of persons per acre was not less than 70.

GRANTS FOR IMPROVEMENT

These represent an attempt to promote the improvement of old houses, thus extending their expected life. There are two forms of grant—the discretionary and the standard improvement grant. The discretionary grant dates from the 1949 Act which empowered local authorities to give grants for improvements by private persons of up to 50 per cent of the costs of improvement. Under the 1954 Act, a grant with financial limits of not less than £100 and not more than £800 was permissible provided the dwelling or dwellings had a prospective life of at least fifteen years. Under the 1958 Act the financial limit was reduced to £400, and amended again to £500 for three storey dwellings and above. The expected life of the improved dwellings was normally to be thirty years and never less than fifteen years.

Under the 1967 Act there is further provision for a subsidy to housing associations for the conversion or improvements required in the property they purchase. This is in the form of three-eighths of the charges, including repayment of the principal of a twenty-year loan to cover costs not exceeding £2,000 per dwelling.

Standard grants were introduced in 1959 for the installation of the five basic amenities: a fixed bath or shower in a separate bathroom; a washhand basin; hot water supply for bath or shower, washhand basin and sink; a W.C. inside or contiguous to the dwelling; facilities for food storage. The maximum grant was £155 or half the cost of providing the fixed amenities whichever is the less. This was modified in 1964 with the maximum grant increased to £350 and the addition of piped water to the list of eligible amenities. Costs of structural changes related to the improvement also became eligible for a grant.

The earlier Acts did little to encourage private landlords to improve their property, and in 1964 the local authorities were empowered to compel owners of private property to carry out standard improvements.

LIST OF REFERENCES

(1) Central Statistical Office, *Annual Abstract of Statistics, 1962*, H.M.S.O., London.

(2) *Registrar General's Quarterly Return for England and Wales*, 1st quarter 1967, H.M.S.O., London.

(3) Commonwealth Relations Office, *Overseas Migration Board Statistics: 1963*, Cmnd 2555, H.M.S.O., London, 1964.

(4) *Registrar General's Quarterly Return for England and Wales*, 1st quarter 1965, H.M.S.O., London.

(5) A. Holmans, 'Current Population Trends in Britain', *Scottish Journal of Political Economy*, Vol. XI, No. 1, February 1964.

(6) *Registrar General's Statistical Review of England and Wales, 1961*, Part III 'Commentary', table ix.

(7) B. R. Mitchell and P. Deane, *Abstract of British Historical Statistics*, Cambridge University Press, 1962.

(8) Central Statistical Office, *Economic Trends*, No. 139, May 1965, H.M.S.O., London.

(9) *Registrar General's Statistical Review of England and Wales, 1961*, Part II 'Population', table H; Part III 'Commentary', table xx.

(10) *Registrar General's Statistical Review of England and Wales, 1961*, Part III 'Commentary', appendix A, table 2.

(11) *Registrar General's Statistical Review of England and Wales, 1955* and *1963*, Part II 'Population', table EE.

(12) D. C. Paige, 'Births and Maternity Beds in England and Wales in 1970', *National Institute Economic Review*, No. 22, November 1962.

(13) *Registrar General's Statistical Review of England and Wales, 1962*, Part III 'Commentary', p. 6.

(14) *Registrar General's Statistical Review of England and Wales, 1962*, Part II 'Population', tables H and A3.

(15) *Registrar General's Statistical Review of England and Wales, 1962*, Part II 'Population', table EE.

(16) *Registrar General's Quarterly Return for England and Wales*, 4th quarter 1963, appendix B.

(17) D. V. Glass, 'Some Indicators of Differences between Urban and Rural Mortality in England and Wales and Scotland', *Population Studies*, Vol. XVII, No. 3. March 1964.

(18) *The South East Study, 1961–1981*, H.M.S.O., London, 1964, appendix 2, tables 7 and 9.

(19) *Registrar General's Quarterly Return for England and Wales*, 4th quarter 1966, appendices D and E.

(20) J. Saville, *Rural Depopulation in England and Wales, 1851–1951*, Routledge and Kegan Paul, London, 1957.

(21) M. F. W. Hemming, 'The Regional Problem', *National Institute Economic Review*, No. 25, August 1963.

(22) F. R. Oliver, 'Inter-regional Migration and Unemployment, 1951–61', *Journal of the Royal Statistical Society*, Series A, Vol. 127, Part I, 1964.

(23) *Central Scotland, a Programme for Development and Growth*, Cmnd 2188, H.M.S.O., Edinburgh, 1963.

(24) *Town and Country Planning*, Vol. 29, No. 6, June 1961.

(25) P. Sargant Florence, 'What is Regional Planning For?' *Town and Country Planning*, Vol. 32, No. 3, March 1964.

(26) M. P. Newton and J. R. Jeffrey, 'Internal Migration' *General Register Office Studies on Medical and Population Subjects*, No. 5, 1951, tables VI and VII.

(27) J. S. Siegel, M. Zitter and D. S. Akers, U.S. Department of Commerce, Bureau of the Census, *Projections of the Population of the United States by Age and Sex, 1964–85, with extension to 2010* (Series P–25, No. 286), Government Printing Office, Washington D.C., 1964 (13763).

(28) Centre for Urban Studies, *Estimates of Net Migration by Sex, Age and Marital Status, 1951–61, London and Home Counties* (unpublished evidence to the Milner Holland Committee on London housing).

(29) *The Population of California*, Commonwealth Club of California, San Francisco, 1946.

(30) G. H. Daniel, 'Labour Migration and Fertility', *Sociological Review*, Vol. XXXI, No. 1, July 1939, p. 370.

(31) L. Needleman, 'A Long-Term View of Housing', *National Institute Economic Review*, No. 18, November 1961.

(32) D. C. Paige (unpublished working tables prepared for W. Beckerman and Associates, *The British Economy in 1975*, Cambridge University Press, 1965).

(33) *Census 1951, England and Wales, Housing Report*, H.M.S.O., London, 1956;
—*Scotland, Housing Report*, H.M.S.O., Edinburgh, 1956.

(34) *Census 1961, England and Wales*, H.M.S.O., London, 1964;
—*Scotland*, H.M.S.O., Edinburgh, 1964, Housing tables.

(35) Ruth Glass (ed.), *The Social Background of a Plan: a study of Middlesborough*, Routledge and Kegan Paul, London, 1948, appendix B.4.

(36) Ruth Glass and F. G. Davidson, 'Household Structure and Housing Needs', *Population Studies*, Vol. IV, No. 4, 1951.

(37) *The Planning of a New Town*, London County Council, 1961.

(38) *Homes for Today and Tomorrow*, H.M.S.O., London, 1961, p. 35, (report of the Parker Morris Committee).

(39) P. G. Gray and R. Russell, *The Housing Situation in 1960* (Social Survey No. 319), Central Office of Information, London, 1962.

(40) M. Woolf, *The Housing Survey in England and Wales, 1964* (Social Survey No. 372), H.M.S.O., London, 1967.

(41) J. B. Cullingworth, Scottish Development Department, *Scottish Housing in 1965* (Social Survey No. 375), H.M.S.O., London, 1967.

(42) Ministry of Housing and Local Government, *Housing Return for England and Wales*, H.M.S.O., London, (quarterly).
Scottish Development Department, *Housing Return for Scotland*, H.M.S.O., Edinburgh (quarterly).

(43) Ministry of Housing and Local Government, *Housing Statistics, Great Britain*, No. 5, April 1967, H.M.S.O., London.

(44) Economic Commission for Europe, *A Statistical Survey of the Housing Situation in European Countries around 1960*, United Nations, New York, 1965.

(45) *Residential Use of Caravans* (Social Survey No. 299), Central Office of Information, London, 1959.

(46) A. Wilson, Ministry of Housing, *Caravans as Homes*, H.M.S.O., London, 1959.

(47) *Housing in England and Wales*, Cmnd 1290, H.M.S.O., London, 1961.

(48) *Report of the Commission of Inquiry into the Impact of Rates on Households*, Cmnd 2582, H.M.S.O., London, 1965.

(49) *Housing Statistics, Great Britain*, No. 1, 1966.

(50) *A Survey of Local Authority Housing Schemes in Great Britain*, Building Research Station, 1963 (unpublished).

(51) Co-operative Permanent Building Society, *Occasional Bulletin*, No. 51, October 1962.

(52) P. A. Stone, *Housing, Town Development and Land Costs*, Estates Gazette Ltd, London, 1963.

(53) P. A. Stone 'The Prices of Sites for Residential Building', *The Property Developer*, Estates Gazettes Ltd, London, 1964.

(54) *Growing Space Needs in the Urbanized Regions*, Conference of the International Federation for Housing and Planning, Stockholm, 1965.

(55) Ministry of Housing and Local Government, *The Density of Residential Areas*, H.M.S.O., London, 1952.

(56) P. A. Stone, 'Some Economic Aspects of Town Development', *Town and Country Planning Summer School*, 1965.

(57) Ministry of Housing and Local Government, *Housing Statistics, Great Britain*, No. 7, 1967.

(58) *Report of the Ministry of Housing and Local Government*, H.M.S.O., London (annual).

(59) C. N. Craig, 'Factors Affecting Economy in Multi-Storey Flat Design', *Journal of the Royal Institute of British Architects*, Vol. 63, No. 6, April 1956.

(60) W. J. Reiners, 'The Tender Prices of Local Authority Flats', *Journal of the Royal Institution of Chartered Surveyors*, Vol. 91, August 1958.

(61) Ministry of Housing and Local Government, *Flats and Houses, 1958*, H.M.S.O., London, 1958.

(62) Cost Research Panel, 'Factors Affecting the Relative Costs of Multi-storey Housing', *Journal of the Royal Institution of Chartered Surveyors*, Vol. 91, March 1958.

(63) W. J. Reiners, 'Cost Research', *Journal of the Royal Institution of Chartered Surveyors*, Vol. 90, September 1957.

(64) P. A. Stone and W. J. Reiners, 'Organization and Efficiency of the House-building Industry in England and Wales', *Journal of Industrial Economics*, Vol. 2, No. 2, April 1954.

(65) *House of Commons: Parliamentary Debates*, 21 December 1965, col. 392 (written answers to questions).

(66) Ministry of Housing and Local Government, *Housing Statistics, Great Britain*, H.M.S.O., London.

(67) W. V. Hole, 'Housing Standards and Social Trends', *Urban Studies*, Vol. 2, No. 2, 1965.

(68) J. C. Weston, 'International Comparisons of Housebuilding', *Journal of Industrial Economics*, Vol. 12, No. 1, November 1963.

(69) *Annual Bulletin of Housing and Building Statistics for Europe, 1963*, United Nations, New York, 1964.

(70) Ministry of Labour (now Department of Employment and Productivity), *Family Expenditure Survey*, H.M.S.O., London (annual).

(71) Economic Commission for Europe, *Financing of Housing in Europe*, United Nations, Geneva, 1958.

(72) P. A. Stone, 'The Prices of Building Sites in Britain', *Land Values* (ed. P. Hall), Sweet and Maxwell, London, 1965.

(73) M. A. Clapp, 'Cost Comparisons in Housing Maintenance', *Local Government Finance*, Vol. 67, October 1963.

(74) C. F. Carter, 'Productivity and Prices: quarterly analysis of trends', *The Builder* (now *Building*), 11 February 1966.

(75) H. J. Whitfield Lewis, 'Housing Centre Talk', *Architect and Building News*, Vol. 229/7, 16 February 1966.

(76) P. A. Stone, 'Building Standards and Costs' (unpublished paper given at the annual conference of the Royal Institute of British Architects, 1966).

(77) P. A. Stone, 'Decision Techniques for Town Development', *Operational Research Quarterly*, Vol. 15, 1964, p. 185.

(78) 'The Boom in Country Cottages', *Estates Gazette*, Vol. 196, 16 October 1965.

(79) *The National Plan*, Cmnd 2764, H.M.S.O., London, 1965.

(80) R. H. Best, *The Major Land Uses of Great Britain*, Wye College, London, 1959.

(81) Colin Clark, *United Kingdom Projected Level of Demand, Supply and Imports of Farm Products in 1965 and 1975*, U.S. Department of Agriculture, Washington D.C., 1962.

(82) G. P. Wibberley, *Pressures on Britain's Land Resources*, University of Nottingham, 1965.

(83) Dudley Stamp (ed.), *The Land of Britain: the report of the land utilization survey of Britain, 1938–42*, Geographical Publications Ltd, London, 1937–46.

(84) P. A. Stone, *Building Economy: Design, Production and Organization*, Pergamon Press, Oxford, 1966.

(85) Ministry of Housing and Local Government, *Housebuilding in the U.S.A.*, H.M.S.O., London, 1966.

(86) Economic Commission for Europe, *The Effect of Repetition on Building Operations and Processes on Site*, United Nations, New York, 1966.

(87) Economic Commission for Europe, *Cost, Repetition, Maintenance*, United Nations, Geneva, 1963.

(88) J. Carmichael, *Vacant Possession*, Institute of Economic Affairs, London, 1964.

(89) *Report of the Committee on Housing in Greater London*, Cmnd 2605, H.M.S.O., London, 1965.

(90) *Scotland's Older Houses: report of the sub-committee on unfit housing*, H.M.S.O., Edinburgh, 1967.

(91) Ministry of Housing and Local Government, *The Deeplish Study*, H.M.S.O., London, 1966.

(92) A. A. Nevitt, *Housing, Taxation and Subsidies*, Nelson, London, 1966.

(93) Co-operative Permanent Building Society, *Occasional Bulletin.*

(94) A. A. Nevitt, *Economic Problems of Housing*, Macmillan, London, 1967.

(95) *Housing Programme, 1965 to 1970*, Cmnd 2838, H.M.S.O., London, 1965.

(96) J. R. James, 'Population Movement and Growth' (unpublished paper given at the Annual Conference of the Royal Institute of British Architects, 1967).

(97) B. D. Cullen, 'Materials Usage in New Building', *Building*, Vol. CCXII, No. 5464, 27 January 1967.

(98) *Rates and Rateable Values in England and Wales, 1963–64*, H.M.S.O., London, 1963.

(99) *Registrar General's Annual Estimates of the Population of England and Wales and Local Authority Areas, 1961*, H.M.S.O., London.

(100) *Registrar General's Annual Estimates of the Population of Scotland, 1961*, H.M.S.O., Edinburgh.

(101) Ministry of Health, *Housing Manual, 1949*, H.M.S.O., London, 1949.

(102) Ministry of Local Government and Planning, *Housing for Special Purposes* (supplement to *Housing Manual, 1949*), H.M.S.O., London, 1951 (*Housing Manual, 1951*).

(103) M. C. Fleming, 'The Long-Term Measurement of Construction Costs in the United Kingdom', *Journal of the Royal Statistical Society*, Series A, Vol. 129, Part 4, 1966.

(104) P. A. Stone, 'The Economics of Building Designs', *Journal of the Royal Statistical Society*, Series A, Vol. 123, Part 3, 1960.

(105) Central Statistical Office, *Monthly Digest of Statistics*, H.M.S.O., London.

(106) Central Statistical Office, *National Income and Expenditure*, H.M.S.O., London.

(107) *Board of Trade Journal*, H.M.S.O., London (monthly).

(108) Ministry of Public Buildings and Works, *Monthly Bulletin of Construction Statistics*, H.M.S.O., London.

(109) *The Architect and his Office*, Royal Institute of British Architects, London, 1962.

INDEX

PUBLICATIONS OF THE NATIONAL INSTITUTE OF ECONOMIC AND SOCIAL RESEARCH

published by

THE CAMBRIDGE UNIVERSITY PRESS

Books published for the Institute by the Cambridge University Press are available through the ordinary booksellers. They appear in the three series below.

ECONOMIC & SOCIAL STUDIES

*I *Studies in the National Income, 1924–1938*
Edited by A. L. BOWLEY. Reprinted with corrections, 1944. pp. 256. 15*s*. net.

*II *The Burden of British Taxation*
By G. FINDLAY SHIRRAS and L. ROSTAS. 1942. pp. 140. 17*s*. 6*d*. net.

*III *Trade Regulations and Commercial Policy of the United Kingdom*
By THE RESEARCH STAFF OF THE NATIONAL INSTITUTE OF ECONOMIC AND SOCIAL RESEARCH. 1943. pp. 275. 17*s*. 6*d*. net.

*IV *National Health Insurance: A Critical Study*
By HERMANN LEVY. 1944. pp. 356. 21*s*. net.

*V *The Development of the Soviet Economic System: An Essay on the Experience of Planning in the U.S.S.R.*
By ALEXANDER BAYKOV. 1946. pp. 530. 45*s*. net.

*VI *Studies in Financial Organization*
By T. BALOGH. 1948. pp. 328. 40*s*. net.

*VII *Investment, Location, and Size of Plant: A Realistic Inquiry into the Structure of British and American Industries*
By P. SARGANT FLORENCE, assisted by W. BALDAMUS. 1948. pp. 230. 21*s*. net.

VIII *A Statistical Analysis of Advertising Expenditure and of the Revenue of the Press*
By NICHOLAS KALDOR and RODNEY SILVERMAN. 1948. pp. 200. 25*s*. net.

*IX *The Distribution of Consumer Goods*
By JAMES B. JEFFERYS, assisted by MARGARET MACCOLL and G. L. LEVETT. 1950. pp. 430. 50*s*. net.

*X *Lessons of the British War Economy*
Edited by D. N. CHESTER. 1951. pp. 260. 30*s*. net.

*XI *Colonial Social Accounting*
By PHYLLIS DEANE. 1953. pp. 360. 60*s*. net.

*XII *Migration and Economic Growth*
By BRINLEY THOMAS. 1954. pp. 384. 50*s*. net.

*XIII *Retail Trading in Britain, 1850–1950*
By JAMES B. JEFFERYS. 1954. pp. 490. 60*s*. net.

*XIV *British Economic Statistics*
By CHARLES CARTER and A. D. ROY. 1954. pp. 192. 30*s*. net.

XV *The Structure of British Industry: A Symposium*
Edited by DUNCAN BURN. 1958. Vol. I. pp. 403. 55*s*. net. Vol. II. pp. 499. 63*s*. net.

*XVI *Concentration in British Industry*
By RICHARD EVELY and I. M. D. LITTLE. 1960. pp. 357. 63*s*. net.

*XVII *Studies in Company Finance*
Edited by BRIAN TEW and R. F. HENDERSON. 1959. pp. 301. 40*s*. net.

XVIII *British Industrialists: Steel and Hosiery, 1850–1950*
By CHARLOTTE ERICKSON. 1959. pp. 276. 45*s*. net.

* At present out of print.

XIX *The Antitrust Laws of the U.S.A.: A Study of Competition Enforced by Law*
By A. D. NEALE. 1960. pp. 516. 55*s*. net.

XX *A Study of United Kingdom Imports*
By M. FG. SCOTT. 1963. pp. 270. 60*s*. net.

XXI *Industrial Growth and World Trade*
By ALFRED MAIZELS. 1963. pp. 563. 84*s*. net.

XXII *The Management of the British Economy, 1945–60*
By J. C. R. DOW. 1964. pp. 443. 60*s*. net.

XXIII *The British Economy in 1975*
By W. BECKERMAN and ASSOCIATES. 1965. pp. 631. 80*s*. net.

XXIV *Occupation and Pay in Great Britain, 1906–60*
By GUY ROUTH. 1965. pp. 182. 35*s*. net.

XXV *Exports and Economic Growth of Developing Countries*
By ALFRED MAIZELS, assisted by L. F. CAMPBELL-BOROSS and P. B. W. RAYMENT. 1968. pp. 445. 60*s*. net.

OCCASIONAL PAPERS

*I *The New Population Statistics*
By R. R. KUCZYNSKI. 1942. pp. 31. 1*s*. 6*d*. net.

*II *The Population of Bristol*
By H. A. SHANNON and E. GREBENIK. 1943. pp. 92. 17*s*. 6*d*. net.

*III *Standards of Local Expenditure*
By J. R. HICKS and U. K. HICKS. 1943. pp. 61. 4*s*. 6*d*. net.

*IV *War-time Pattern of Saving and Spending*
By CHARLES MADGE. 1943. pp. 139. 12*s*. 6*d*. net.

*V *Standardized Accountancy in Germany*
By H. W. SINGER. Reprinted 1944. pp. 68. 6*s*. net.

*VI *Ten Years of Controlled Trade in South-Eastern Europe*
By N. NOMTCHILOFF. 1944. pp. 90. 12*s*. 6*d*. net.

*VII *The Problem of Valuation for Rating*
By J. R. HICKS, U. K. HICKS and C. E. V. LESER. 1944. pp. 90. 10*s*. 6*d*. net.

*VIII *The Incidence of Local Rates in Great Britain*
By J. R. HICKS and U. K. HICKS. 1945. pp. 64. 12*s*. 6*d*. net.

*IX *Contributions to the Study of Oscillatory Time-Series*
By M. G. KENDALL. 1946. pp. 76. 12*s*. 6*d*. net.

*X *A System of National Book-keeping Illustrated by the Experience of the Netherlands Economy*
By J. B. D. DERKSEN. 1946. pp. 34. 15*s*. net.

*XI *Productivity, Prices and Distribution in Selected British Industries*
By L. ROSTAS. 1948. pp. 199. 30*s*. net.

XII *The Measurement of Colonial National Incomes: An Experiment*
By PHYLLIS DEANE. 1948. pp. 173. 25*s*. net.

*XIII *Comparative Productivity in British and American Industry*
By L. ROSTAS. 1948. pp. 263. 30*s*. net.

*XIV *The Cost of Industrial Movement*
By W. F. LUTTRELL. 1952. pp. 104. 21*s*. net.

XV *Costs in Alternative Locations: The Clothing Industry*
By D. C. HAGUE and P. K. NEWMAN. 1952. pp. 73. 21*s*. net.

*XVI *Social Accounts of Local Authorities*
By J. E. G. UTTING. 1953. pp. 81. 22*s*. 6*d*. net.

*XVII *British Post-war Migration*
By JULIUS ISAAC. 1954. pp. 294. 40*s*. net.

*XVIII *The Cost of the National Health Service in England and Wales*
By BRIAN ABEL-SMITH and RICHARD M. TITMUSS. 1956. pp. 176. 27*s*. 6*d*. net.

* At present out of print.

*XIX *Post-war Investment, Location and Size of Plant*
By P. SARGANT FLORENCE. 1962. pp. 51. 12*s*. 6*d*. net.

*XX *Investment and Growth Policies in British Industrial Firms*
By TIBOR BARNA. 1962. pp. 71. 12*s*. 6*d*. net.

XXI *Pricing and Employment in the Trade Cycle: A Study of British Manufacturing Industry, 1950–61*
By R. R. NEILD. 1963. pp. 73. 15*s*. net.

XXII *Health and Welfare Services in Britain in 1975*
By DEBORAH PAIGE and KIT JONES. 1966. pp. 142. 21*s*. net.

XXIII *Lancashire Textiles: A Case Study of Industrial Change*
By CAROLINE MILES. 1968. pp. 124. 21*s*. net.

* At present out of print.

STUDIES IN THE NATIONAL INCOME AND EXPENDITURE OF THE UNITED KINGDOM

Published under the joint auspices of the National Institute and the Department of Applied Economics, Cambridge.

1 *The Measurement of Consumers' Expenditure and Behaviour in the United Kingdom, 1920–1938*, Vol. I
By RICHARD STONE, assisted by D. A. ROWE and by W. J. CORLETT, RENEE HURSTFIELD, MURIEL POTTER. 1954. pp. 448. £10 net.

2 *The Measurement of Consumers' Expenditure and Behaviour in the United Kingdom, 1920–38*, Vol. II
By RICHARD STONE and D. A. ROWE. 1966. pp. 152. 90*s*. net.

3 *Consumers' Expenditure in the United Kingdom, 1900–1919*
By A. R. PREST, assisted by A. A. ADAMS. 1954. pp. 196. 55*s*. net.

4 *Domestic Capital Formation in the United Kingdom, 1920–1938*
By C. H. FEINSTEIN. 1965. pp. 284. 90*s*. net.

5 *Wages and Salaries in the United Kingdom, 1920–1938*
By AGATHA CHAPMAN, assisted by ROSE KNIGHT. 1953. pp. 254. 75*s*. net.

THE NATIONAL INSTITUTE OF ECONOMIC AND SOCIAL RESEARCH

publishes regularly

THE NATIONAL INSTITUTE ECONOMIC REVIEW

A quarterly Review of the economic situation and prospects.

Annual subscriptions £3. 10*s*., and single issues for the current year 20*s*. each, are available directly from N.I.E.S.R., 2 Dean Trench St., Smith Square, London, S.W.1.

Back numbers and reprints are distributed by

Wm. Dawson and Sons Ltd, Cannon House, Park Farm Road, Folkestone, Kent.

The Institute has also published

FACTORY LOCATION AND INDUSTRIAL MOVEMENT: a Study of Recent Experience in Britain, volumes I and II

By W. F. Luttrell

N.I.E.S.R. 1962. pp. 1080. £5. 5*s*. net the set.

TRANSLATED MONOGRAPHS: a new series on current economic problems and policies.

No. I *The IVth French Plan* by FRANÇOIS PERROUX, with the original foreword by Pierre Massé, Commissaire Général au Plan, and a new foreword to the English edition by Vera Lutz. Translated by Bruno Leblanc.
pp. 72. 10*s*. net.

These also are available directly from the Institute.